PIONEERS OF PSYCHOLOGY

FOURTH EDITION A HISTORY

Raymond E. Fancher
Alexandra Rutherford

W. W. NORTON & COMPANY, INC.
New York, London

W. W. Norton & Company has been independent since its founding in 1923, when William Warder Norton and Mary D. Herter Norton first published lectures delivered at the People's Institute, the adult education division of New York City's Cooper Union. The firm soon expanded its program beyond the Institute, publishing books by celebrated academics from America and abroad. By mid-century, the two major pillars of Norton's publishing program—trade books and college texts—were firmly established. In the 1950s, the Norton family transferred control of the company to its employees, and today—with a staff of four hundred and a comparable number of trade, college, and professional titles published each year—W. W. Norton & Company stands as the largest and oldest publishing house owned wholly by its employees.

Copyright © 2012 by Raymond E. Fancher and Alexandra Rutherford.
Copyright © 1996, 1990, 1979 by Raymond E. Fancher.

Editor: Ken Barton
Ancillaries Editors: Matthew Freeman and Callinda Taylor
Editorial Assistant: Mary Dudley
Project Editor: Christine D'Antonio
Copy Editor: Jackie Estrada
Photo Editor: Stephanie Romeo
Art Director: Hope Miller Goodell
Book Design: Guenet Abraham
Time Line Design: Joan Greenfield
Composition and Layout: TexTech
Manufacturing: Courier
Production Manager: Chris Granville

Library of Congress Cataloging-in-Publication Data

Fancher, Raymond E.
    Pioneers of psychology : a history / Raymond E. Fancher & Alexandra Rutherford. —
4th ed.
        p. cm.
    Includes bibliographical references and index.

    ISBN 978-0-393-93530-1 (pbk.)
    1. Psychology—History.   2. Psychologists—History.   I. Rutherford, Alexandra,
1971–   II. Title.
    BF95.F3 2012
    150.92'2—dc23

                                                        2011035757

W. W. Norton & Company, Inc.,
500 Fifth Avenue,
New York, N.Y. 10110
www.wwnorton.com

W. W. Norton & Company Ltd.,
Castle House, 75/76 Wells Street,
London W1T 3QT

2 3 4 5 6 7 8 9 0

For
Seth Wesley Fancher (in memoriam)
and
Joëlle Fancher Morton

For
Emily Jane Pickren
and
Graham Wesley Pickren

Brief Contents

1 René Descartes and the Foundations of Modern Psychology 15

2 Philosophers of Mind: *John Locke and Gottfried Leibniz* 51

3 Physiologists of Mind: *Brain Scientists from Gall to Penfield* 95

4 The Sensing and Perceiving Mind: *Theories of Perception from Kant through the Gestalt Psychologists* 139

5 Wilhelm Wundt and the Establishment of Experimental Psychology 189

6 Charles Darwin and the Theory of Evolution 231

7 The Measurement of Mind: *Francis Galton and the Psychology of Individual Differences* 269

8 William James and Psychology in America 305

9 Psychology as the Science of Behavior: *Ivan Pavlov, John B. Watson, and B. F. Skinner* 347

10 Social Influence and Social Psychology: *From Mesmer to Milgram* 401

11 Mind in Conflict: *The Psychoanalytic Psychology of Sigmund Freud* 455

12 Psychology Gets "Personality": *Gordon Allport, Abraham Maslow and the Broadening of Academic Psychology* 505

13 The Developing Mind: *Alfred Binet, Jean Piaget, and the Study of Human Intelligence* 563

14 Machines, Minds, and Cognitive Psychology 603

15 Origins of Applied Psychology: *From the Courtroom to the Clinic* 649

Contents

Preface to the Fourth Edition xv

Time Line xxiii

About the Authors xxxi

Introduction 3

1 René Descartes and the Foundations of Modern Psychology 15
   Descartes' Early Life and the Development of His Method 17
   The World: Descartes' Physics and Physiology 27
   Descartes' Philosophy of Mind 36
   Descartes' Influence 45
   Suggested Readings 49

2 Philosophers of Mind: *John Locke and Gottfried Leibniz* 51
   John Locke: Child of Revolution 53
   An Essay Concerning Human Understanding 62
   Locke's Influence 68
   Leibniz's Life and Career 71
   Serving the House of Hanover 76
   Leibniz's Philosophy of Mind 82
   Suggested Readings 93

3 Physiologists of Mind: *Brain Scientists from Gall to Penfield* 95
   Gall and Phrenology 97
   Flourens and the Discrediting of Phrenology 104
   Localization Theory Revived: The Brain's Language Areas 108
   Memory and the Equipotentiality Debate 118
   Stimulation of the Conscious Human Brain 122
   Suggested Readings 137

4 The Sensing and Perceiving Mind: *Theories of Perception from Kant through the Gestalt Psychologists* **139**

The Kantian Background 140

Helmholtz's Early Life 145

Helmholtz on Sensation and Perception 153

Fechner and Psychophysics 163

Gestalt Psychology 172

Later Developments in the Study of Sensation and Perception 177

Suggested Readings 186

5 Wilhelm Wundt and the Establishment of Experimental Psychology 189

Wundt's Early Life 192

Wundt at Leipzig 201

Titchener's Structuralism 215

Experimenting on the Higher Functions: Külpe and Ebbinghaus 221

Wundt's Reputation and Influence 225

Suggested Readings 229

6 Charles Darwin and the Theory of Evolution 231

Darwin's Early Life 233

The Voyage of the *Beagle* 237

The Theory of Evolution by Natural Selection 242

Darwin and Psychology 250

Darwin's Influence 259

Suggested Readings 266

7 The Measurement of Mind: *Francis Galton and the Psychology of Individual Differences* **269**

Galton's Early Life and Career 273

Darwinian Theory and *Hereditary Genius* 277

The Nature-Nurture Controversy 282

Eugenics 287

Galton's Influence and Continuing Controversies 295

Suggested Readings 302

8 William James and Psychology in America 305

James's Early Life 307

The Principles of Psychology 315

James's Later Career and the Philosophy of
Pragmatism 321

Three Eminent Students: Hall, Calkins, and
Thorndike 324

Suggested Readings 344

**9 Psychology as the Science of Behavior: *Ivan Pavlov,
John B. Watson, and B. F. Skinner* 347**

Pavlov's Early Life and Career 349

Conditioned Reflexes 353

Watson's Early Life and Career 360

Watson's Behavioristic Writings 364

Skinner and Operant Conditioning 379

Suggested Readings 393

**10 Social Influence and Social Psychology: *From Mesmer
to Milgram* 401**

Mesmer and "Animal Magnetism" 403

From "Mesmerism" to "Hypnotism" 408

The Nancy-Salpêtrière Controversy 415

Binet's Experiments on Suggestion 429

The Institutionalization of Social Psychology 431

Stanley Milgram and Obedience 440

Social Influence Today 447

Suggested Readings 452

**11 Mind in Conflict: *The Psychoanalytic Psychology of
Sigmund Freud* 455**

Freud's Early Life 459

The Interpretation of Dreams 466

Self-Analysis and the Theory of
Childhood Sexuality 472

Psychoanalytic Psychotherapy 478

Metapsychology and the Ego's Defense Mechanisms 482

The Psychology of Women 488
Final Controversies and Freud's Legacy 491
Freud and Psychology 494
Suggested Readings 502

12 **Psychology Gets "Personality":** *Gordon Allport, Abraham Maslow,*
and the Broadening of Academic Psychology **505**
Allport's Early Life and Career 509
Allport's Personality Psychology 517
Personality Psychology Comes of Age 520
Allport as Social Activist and Teacher 526
Abraham Maslow and Humanistic Psychology 530
Maslow's New York Postgraduate Education 537
Maslow's Theory of Human Motivation 545
Establishing a Humanistic Psychology 551
Suggested Readings 561

13 **The Developing Mind:** *Alfred Binet, Jean Piaget, and the*
Study of Human Intelligence **563**
Binet's Early Life and Career 567
The Binet Intelligence Scales 574
The Rise of Intelligence Testing 578
Piaget's Early Life and Career 585
Genetic Epistemology 589
Piagetian Influences 596
Suggested Readings 601

14 **Machines, Minds, and Cognitive Psychology 603**
Leibniz and the Mechanization of Logic 607
Charles Babbage and the Analytical Engine 611
Alan Turing's Machine and Test 617
Intelligent Machines 624
Minds Versus Machines 629
Ulric Neisser and Cognitive Psychology 635
Suggested Readings 646

15 **Origins of Applied Psychology:** *From the Courtroom to the Clinic* **649**

Hugo Münsterberg and Psychology in the Courtroom **651**

Lillian Gilbreth and the Psychology of Management **660**

Lightner Witmer and the Clinical Method **668**

Leta Stetter Hollingworth: Clinician, Feminist, Professionalizer **676**

Applied Psychology Today **686**

Suggested Readings **690**

Notes **A1**
Glossary **A25**
Credits **A61**
Index **A63**

A full package of ancillary resources for teachers is available at wwnorton.com/nr.

Preface to the Fourth Edition

From Raymond E. Fancher

The Preface to the first edition of *Pioneers of Psychology*, written more than thirty years ago, opened by saying:

> This book is about the lives and works of some of the people who shaped the modern science of psychology. It attempts to illustrate how several fundamental ideas and theories actually came into being by presenting them in the contexts of the lives and perspectives of the individuals who first grappled with them. By blending the biographical with the theoretical, and showing how the early psychologists were driven to make their particular discoveries as much by their own personalities and life histories as by their dispassionate scientific analyses, it aims to lend vitality and interest to important ideas that otherwise might seem less compelling.

These words still hold true for this fourth edition, although the cast denoted by the phrase "some of the people" has expanded with each succeeding edition. The present edition presents the single largest enlargement yet, bringing the book to a point where I believe it fairly represents the history of the broad discipline of psychology as a whole. In the expectation that this new edition will be found suitable for adoption as the primary text in history of psychology courses, several new features have been added. The textbook itself now includes an illustrated time line as its beginning and an extensive glossary of key names and terms at its end. Ancillary resources have also been prepared for teachers, including a 450-item multiple-choice testbank, PowerPoint slides for each of the chapters, and the collective artwork for the book—all available via the Norton website at wwnorton .com/nrl.

One major goal in this, as in the preceding two revised editions, is to make sure that its presentations are "up to date." Although it may be surprising to some, the study of the history of psychology has become a vibrant scholarly specialty area, and the sheer amount of reliable historical and biographical knowledge increases regularly. Formal organizations such as the Society for the History of Psychology (Division 26 of the American Psychological Association), Cheiron (The International Society for the History of Behavioral and Social Sciences), and the European Society for the History of the Human Sciences actively promote historical research, and provide collegial settings that welcome students and new researchers to the field. Specialized journals such as *History of Psychology*, *The Journal of the History of the Behavioral Sciences*, and *History of the Human Sciences* regularly publish new findings in the field. For the past three decades it has been my pleasure and privilege to be actively involved with these organizations and journals, making me keenly aware that there is always something new to be learned and said, even about subjects that are very old. The new edition attempts to take advantage of this emerging new knowledge to the greatest extent possible.

Further, a good portion of the emerging new knowledge relates to individuals and events from the middle years of the last century, the period in which I myself was educated, and which constituted "contemporary" psychology when I was writing the first edition. Now, however, many of those people and events are considered "historical" by the younger generations, clearly meriting inclusion among the pioneers of psychology. Accordingly, this new edition contains substantial new material on several mid-twentieth-century figures including Solomon Asch and Stanley Milgram in social psychology, Gordon Allport in personality, Abraham Maslow in humanistic psychology, and Ulric Neisser in cognitive psychology—among several others. I confess to experiencing mixed emotions while researching and writing about these individuals. On the one hand their new status as "historical" signified that I myself had become (within a blink of the eye, it seems) an elder figure—a sobering realization. In compensation, however, it was fascinating for me to gain closer acquaintance with the lives of some people whom I had known personally and who had positively influenced my own life and career. Prime among these was Gordon Allport, whose student I was fortunate to be during his final years of active teaching. Besides serving as a role model for me of the caring and socially committed teacher, he introduced me to the pleasures of historical research and first demonstrated to me the significance of psychology's history for an appreciation of its present. As a staunch advocate of the person-centered, case study approach to the understanding of individual lives, he also directly inspired the general style of all the editions of this book. I had less intensive but still significant personal contact with several other of the "new" pioneers covered in this book, and it was highly interesting to learn more about those mentors' own backgrounds and influences.

Another worthy group of new pioneers came increasingly to my attention over the years. Some reviewers of the first edition commented correctly on its almost exclusively male cast of characters. At the time it was relatively easy to justify this fact by noting that during most of the periods with which the book dealt, women had been systematically excluded from participation in psychological discourse. There simply was not very much to be said about them because they had not been allowed to say very much. Even when women were able to overcome these barriers and did participate, especially as the twentieth century progressed, their contributions had often been overlooked by historians. In the intervening years this situation has changed radically, however, as talented historians have uncovered and published extensive material documenting women's often important roles "behind the scenes" in early times, their persistent and often courageous struggles to gain education and equality during the late nineteenth and early twentieth centuries, and the increasingly prominent positions they have assumed ever since then. It was clear to me that a fourth edition should do a much better job at representing the contributions of psychology's female pioneers.

As I contemplated these prospective enhancements for a new edition, it also occurred to me that the revisions could benefit greatly from the perspectives of a younger coauthor who shared my enthusiasm for a personalistic approach to writing history, and with a complementary background of historical expertise. The first person to come to mind for such a role was Alexandra Rutherford, whom I knew first as one of those rare and delightful "students" from whom one learns far more than one teaches, and later as a friend and faculty colleague in York University's graduate program in the history and theory of psychology. Her awardwinning research on the history of behaviorism, applied psychology, and of the roles of women in psychology exemplified exactly the kind of recent work I thought the new edition should make use of. Accordingly I was overjoyed when she accepted my invitation to join me in this venture. My decision to extend that invitation has turned out to be one of the best I ever made, and it has been a complete pleasure to work with her in bringing forth this revised edition.

From Alexandra Rutherford

Ray Fancher's invitation to join him as co-author on the fourth edition of *Pioneers of Psychology* required practically no deliberation. I was "brought up" on *Pioneers* (so to speak) in my study of the history of psychology, and then assigned *Pioneers* as a required text when I began teaching the course as a faculty member. I had thus experienced firsthand the book's ability to make history come alive for students. Equally important, I had also witnessed the power of *Pioneers* to convey the most important intellectual developments in the history of psychology in a way that was both conceptually sophisticated *and* compelling as narrative. Thus, it was one of those decisions often referred to colloquially as a "no-brainer."

As anticipated, it has been both an honor and a delight to work with Ray Fancher on this substantially revised edition. I can clearly recall the day I sat in his office, having recently decided to devote myself to doctoral work in the history of psychology, and proposed B. F. Skinner as a dissertation topic.He was enthusiastic about the idea, and what ensued was a rich and colorful journey through multiple archives, interviews with many of Skinner's friends and followers, and memorable trips both to Skinner's house on Old Dee Road in Cambridge, Massachusetts, and to Twin Oaks in Louisa, Virginia, an intentional community originally inspired by Skinner's novel *Walden Two*. It has been over ten years since the completion of that dissertation, which inspired a book, and the process of writing both cemented my passion and commitment to making history come alive for others as it has, so vividly, for me. Participating in this revision of *Pioneers* was a natural extension of this passion.

I hope that this new edition continues the tradition of careful, informative scholarship combined with "vitality and interest" so well established in the first three editions, but also adds some exciting new features. In particular, this edition has been significantly expanded by two entirely new chapters on personality and applied psychology, areas that are of great interest to many psychology students. These chapters incorporate some of the most up-to-date scholarship by historians of psychology working in these areas. In fact, the entire text has been revised with an eye to adding recent scholarship that is constantly challenging, changing, and enhancing our knowledge of psychology's past. As Ray indicates above, this knowledge is not static; new material, new perspectives, and new interpretations are always being added to the historical record. It has been our aim to ensure that *Pioneers*, in its own evolution, reflects the dynamic nature of psychology's history.

Accordingly, one of the other new features of this revised edition that I have been particularly pleased to contribute to is the increased inclusion of female pioneers. Over the past several years my own scholarship has moved increasingly into the area of "women's history," a sub-field of history that coalesced in the 1970s under the influence of the women's movement. At this time, historians became interested in "re-placing" women in history. Clearly, since women have always represented half of humanity, they have always had a "place" in history. But why, feminist scholars asked, did recorded history not reflect this?

Some women's historians called for increased attention to topics that had, in the past, been invisible or overshadowed by the emphasis on military, economic, or political histories in which men were almost always the exclusive actors. Thus, histories of the family, of motherhood, of child rearing, and of women's labor, civic, and political leadership began to be written. The history of women in science became a burgeoning field and remains so to this day. Further, at this time psychologists also started to become interested in the history of women in their field. Who were psychology's early women, and what factors affected their participation in their chosen discipline? What contributions did they make? And since women had always been part of psychology (albeit in small numbers at the beginning), why did we know so little about them?

Although I was too young to be a part of the emergence of women's history in the 1970s, since that time there has been a steady increase in the scholarship on women in psychology's history, reflecting the dynamic nature of history to which we have alluded above. The majority of this scholarship has featured the histories of U.S. and Western European female pioneers, many of whom we include in this new edition. Women's early participation in psychology in other parts of the world has received less systematic attention, making it an exciting area ripe for historical scholarship. It is also worth noting that despite the truly remarkable growth of historical scholarship on women in psychology, works featuring the kind of detailed, rich, and extensive analysis of individual lives on which *Pioneers* draws are still more difficult to source for women pioneers. Two notable exceptions to this trend are Leta Stetter Hollingworth and Lillian Moller Gilbreth, and we have made use of this material to feature them as major—and fascinating—pioneers in this new edition.

Finally, as historians of psychology, we know the importance of having an archival record that is as comprehensive and inclusive as possible. If this record does not reflect the participation of all of the diverse contributors to our field, the histories that come to be written will provide a distorted and partial view of psychology's past. With this in mind, a number of years ago I became both personally and professionally interested in, and acquainted with, some of the women who had pioneered the psychology of women and gender as a distinct subfield within psychology in the early 1970s. Many of them were interested in telling their stories, so I began to conduct oral history interviews with them to ensure that their voices and experiences were included in the historical record. I was also genuinely interested in knowing more about their lives. This interest in "individual lives in context" is of course at the heart of the personological approach that guides this book. I trust that as the years pass and many of these women come to be considered "historical" for their substantive contributions to psychology, this material will become grist for future editions of this book, and others, that adopt our personological approach.

Acknowledgments

All of the editions of *Pioneers of Psychology* have benefitted enormously from the constructive advice and criticism of large numbers of people. We repeat our thanks here to those (some of whom have regrettably passed on) who helped so much with the first three editions: Neil Agnew, Howard Baker, Michael Blacha, Arthur Blumenthal, Adrian Brock, Darryl Bruce, Kurt Danziger, Maureen Dennis, Norman Endler, Stanley Finger, Catherine Gildiner, Melvin Gravitz, Christopher Green, Scott Greer, Norman Guttman, Walter Heinrichs, Robert Hoffman, John Hogan, Peter Kaiser, John Kennedy, Bruno Kohn, Alex Kozulin, Gregory McGuire, Paul McReynolds, John Meacham, Mark Micale, Hiroshi Ono, Roger Thomas, Ryan Tweney, Michael Wertheimer, Malcolm Westcott, George Windholz, and Theta Wolf. On the editorial side, Norton's Donald Lamm and Donald Fusting provided invaluable advice and encouragement throughout the preparation of all of the first three editions.

Our editor for this new edition, Ken Barton, went to extraordinary lengths in soliciting feedback on all or part of the proposed manuscript from more than eighty scholars whose reports were unfailingly thoughtful and constructive. We thank them all: Virgil H. Adams III, Elizabeth Anslow, Peter Assmann, David Barone, Colin Gordon Beer, Catherine Borshuk, Mary Brazier, S.M. Breugelmans, Charles L. Brewer, J. Corey Butler, Joanie Caska, Robin Cautin, Rosemary Cogan, Luis Cordón, Alex Cuc, Mary Ann Cutter, Everett Delahanty, George Diekhoff, Chris Dinwiddie, Robert Durham, Carlos Escoto, Rita Fike, Samuel Fillenbaum, Barbara Gentile, Steven Goldman, H. Alan Goodman, Arthur Gutman, Marshall Harth, Mark Hartlaub, Graham Higgs, Herman Huber, Tammy Jechura, Patricia Kahlbaugh, Suresh Karekar, Jane Karwoski, Allen Keniston, Gary

Kose, Russell Kosits, Dawn Kastanek Kriebel, Tera Letzring, Mark Mattson, John Mavromatis, Jean Mercer, Michelle Marks Merwin, Craig Nagoshi, Laurence J. Nolan, David Perkins, Clare Porac, Ruth Provost, Wendy Quinton, Darrell Rudmann, Micah Sadigh, Hank Schlinger, Lori Schmied, Duane Shuttlesworth, Elizabeth Siemanowski, Christina Sinisi, Tod Sloan, Karel Soudijn, Jean Strand, William Sturgill, Dennis Trickett, Stephen Truhon, Donald Vardiman, Dan Weber, Lawrence White, and Mark Yama.

Some of the respondents to Ken's inquiries did double duty, either in answering specific questions that we posed to them or otherwise engaging in follow up discussions with us after their initial reports. An extra-special note of thanks is due to each one of them: David Baker, Daniel Burston, Fran Cherry, Maarten Derksen, Jay Dowling, Ingrid Farreras, Benjamin Harris, Harry Heft, Robert Hoffman, John Hogan, Cheryl Logan, Edward Morris, Ian Nicholson, Ryan Tweney, and Andrew Winston. Although we were not equipped or able to take full advantage of all of the suggestions that were made, our book is immensely stronger for the input of all of these many individuals. Any errors, of course, remain our responsibility alone.

Ken Barton provided invaluable editorial guidance throughout the entire process of preparing this book, and during the production stages it was a pleasure to work with his professional and pleasant colleagues at Norton: Christine D'Antonio (Project Editor), Mary Dudley (Editorial Assistant), Callinda Taylor (Associate Editor, Supplements), Jackie Estrada (Copyeditor), Stephanie Romeo (Photo Editor), Hope Miller Goodell (Associate Design Director), and Chris Granville (Production Manager).

Finally, we acknowledge with great thanks the many contributions of Katherine Harper, our coauthor of the ancillary materials and a general support to us as we worked on all stages of the book.

June 7, 2011

Time Line

Key Pioneers

Key Events

René
Descartes
(1596–1650)

Blaise Pascal
(1623–1662)

John Locke
(1632–1704)

1619	Descartes has dream and inspiration for his method (Chapter 1)
1633	Descartes writes but suppresses publication of *Le Monde* (Chapter 1)
1637	Descartes publishes *Discourse on Method* (Chapter 1)
1639	Pascal begins building his mechanical calculator, the Pascaline (Chapter 14)

Gottfried
Wilhelm
Leibniz
(1646–1716)

1642	Descartes begins correspondence with Elizabeth of Bohemia, resulting in *Passions of the Soul* in 1649 (Chapter 1)
1671	Locke starts on his *Essay Concerning Human Understanding* after meeting with friends (Chapter 2)
1673	Leibniz exhibits his mechanical calculator in London (Chapter 2)
1690	Locke publishes *Essay Concerning Human Understanding* (Chapter 2)
1704	Leibniz writes but withholds publication of *New Essays on Human Understanding* (Chapter 2)

David Hume
(1711–1776)

Immanuel Kant
(1724–1804)

Franz Anton
Mesmer
(1734–1815)

Franz Josef
Gall
(1758–1828)

Charles Babbage
(1792–1871)

Pierre
Flourens
(1794–1867)

Charles
Robert
Darwin
(1809–1882)

Gustav
Theodor
Fechner
(1821–1894)

Hermann
Helmholtz
(1821–1894)

Francis Galton
(1822–1911)

1737	Hume publishes skeptical analysis of the notion of causality (Chapter 4)
1775	Mesmer introduces "animal magnetism" at Gassner's exorcism trial (Chapter 10)
1781	Kant writes about the innate intuitions of time and space perception (Chapter 4)
1784	Puységur discovers Mesmeric "perfect crisis" (Chapter 10)
1794–1796	Erasmus Darwin publishes speculative theory of evolution (Chapter 6)
1802	Paley publishes "argument from design" in opposition to evolution (Chapter 6)
1809	Lamarck publishes theory of evolution via inheritance of acquired characteristics (Chapter 6)

Paul Broca
(1824–1830)

1824   Flourens publishes ablation studies contradicting Gall and phrenology (Chapter 3)

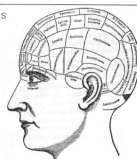

Jean-Martin Charcot
(1825–1893)

Wilhelm
Wundt
(1832–1920)

1831   Darwin departs on *Beagle* voyage (Chapter 6)

Gustave
Le Bon
(1841–1931)

William James
(1842–1910)

1843   Ada Lovelace publishes her "Notes" on Babbage's analytical engine (Chapter 14)

1843   Braid describes hypnotic effects in mainstream scientific journal (Chapter 10)

G. Stanley Hall
(1844–1924)

Ivan Petrovich
Pavlov
(1849–1936)

1850 Helmholtz measures the speed of the nervous impulse
(Chapter 4)

Hermann
Ebbinghaus
(1850–1909)

Sigmund
Freud
(1856–1939)

Alfred Binet
(1857–1911)

1859 Darwin publishes *On the Origin of Species* (Chapter 6)

1860 Fechner publishes *Elements of Psychophysics* (Chapter 5)

1860 Helmholtz publishes trichromatic theory of color vision
(Chapter 4)

1861 Broca reports the case of "Tan," confirming the localization
of speech in the brain's left frontal cortex (Chapter 3)

1861 Wundt conducts his "thought meter" experiment
(Chapter 5)

Oswald Külpe
(1862–1915)

Mary Whiton
Calkins
(1863–1930)

Hugo
Münsterberg
(1863–1916)

Edward
Bradford
Titchener
(1867–1927)

Lightner
Witmer
(1867–1956)

Edward Lee
Thorndike
(1874–1947)

Lillian Moller
Gilbreth
(1878–1972)

John B.
Watson
(1878–1958)

Max
Wertheimer
(1880–1943)

1869	Galton publishes *Hereditary Genius* (Chapter 7)
1870	James experiences crisis, resolved by believing in free will (Chapter 8)
1871	Darwin publishes *The Descent of Man* (Chapter 6)
1879	Wundt publishes first experimental psychology textbook, *The Principles of Physiological Psychology* (Chapter 5)
1882	Charcot introduces theory of *grand hypnotisme* (Chapter 10)
1884	Galton establishes Anthropometric Laboratory and prototype intelligence tests (Chapter 7)
1885	Ebbinghaus publishes *On Memory* (Chapter 5)

Leta Setter
Hollingworth
(1886–1939)

1888   Galton invents correlation coefficients (Chapter 7)

Floyd H.
Allport
(1890–1970)

Karl Spencer
Lashley
(1890–1959)

1890   James publishes *Principles of Psychology* (Chapter 8)

Wilder
Penfield
(1891–1976)

1892   Hall establishes American Psychological Association
(Chapter 8)

1895   Freud and Breuer publish *Studies on Hysteria* (Chapter 11)

1895   LeBon publishes *The Crowd* (Chapter 10)

Jean Piaget
(1896–1980)

1896   Witmer establishes first Psychological Clinic (Chapter 15)

Gordon W.
Allport
(1897–1967)

1898   Titchener publishes "Postulates of a Structural Psychology"
(Chapter 5)

1900   Freud publishes *The Interpretation of Dreams* (Chapter 11)

B. F. Skinner
(1904–1990)

1904   Pavlov introduces idea of conditioned reflexes in Nobel Prize
address (Chapter 9)

1905   Binet and Simon create first workable intelligence test for
children (Chapter 13)

Solomon Asch
(1907–1996)

Abraham
Maslow
(1908–1970)

1909 Freud visits
Clark University
(Chapter 11)

1910 Wertheimer has inspiration for phi phenomenon and Gestalt
psychology (Chapter 4)

Alan
Mathison
Turing
(1912–1954)

1913 Münsterberg publishes *Psychology and Industrial Efficiency*
(Chapter 15)

1913 Watson publishes "Psychology as the Behaviorist Views It"
(Chapter 9)

1914 Gilbreth publishes *The Psychology of Management*
(Chapter 15)

1916 Terman introduces the Stanford-Binet test for IQ
(Chapter 13)

1919 Floyd Allport completes first experimental social psychology
dissertation (Chapter 10)

1924 Gordon Allport teaches first university "Personality" course
(Chapter 12)

Ulric Neisser
(1928–2012)

1924 Mary Cover Jones publishes "A Laboratory Study of Fear:
The Case of Peter" (Chapter 9)

1929 Lashley publishes on cerebral equipotentiality and mass
action (Chapter 3)

1930 Freud publishes *Civilization and Its Discontents* (Chapter 11)

Stanley
Milgram
(1933–1984)

1934 Penfield establishes Montreal Neurological Institute and
begins stimulating cortexes of conscious epileptic patients
(Chapter 3)

1936	Piaget publishes *The Origins of Intelligence in Children* (Chapter 13)
1937	Gordon Allport publishes *Personality: A Psychological Interpretation* (Chapter 12)
1937	Newman, Freeman, and Holzinger publish first major study of separated twins (Chapter 7)
1937	Turing publishes account of his "Turing machine" (Chapter 14)
1938	Skinner publishes *The Behavior of Organisms* (Chapter 9)
1942	Hollingworth publishes *Children Above 180 IQ* (Chapter 15)
1943	Maslow presents "hierarchy of needs" in article "A Theory of Human Motivation" (Chapter 12)
1951	Asch publishes first results of his conformity research (Chapter 10)
1956	Milner publishes case of "HM" (Chapter 3)
1956	Newell and Simon develop *Logic Theorist* computer program (Chapter 14)
1958	Inhelder and Piaget publish *The Growth of Logical Thinking from Childhood to Adolescence* (Chapter 13)
1961	*Journal of Humanistic Psychology* is established (Chapter 12)
1963	Milgram publishes results of "shockbox" obedience research (Chapter 10)
1967	Neisser publishes *Cognitive Psychology* (Chapter 14)
1971	Skinner publishes *Beyond Freedom and Dignity* (Chapter 9)

About the Authors

Raymond E. Fancher is a Senior Scholar and Professor Emeritus at York University in Toronto. A founder of York's Ph.D. program in the History and Theory of Psychology, he has served as editor of the *Journal of the History of the Behavioral Sciences* and held top executive positions with the Society for the History of Psychology (Division 26 of the American Psychological Association) and Cheiron (The International Society for the History of Behavioral and Social Sciences). The author of nearly 100 publications on the history of Psychology, he is a recipient of the Lifetime Achievement Award from the Society for the History of Psychology.

Alexandra Rutherford is an associate professor of psychology in the History and Theory of Psychology Graduate Program at York University in Toronto. Her research interests include the history and contemporary status of feminist psychology and the relationships between psychology and American society from the mid-twentieth century to today. She is a fellow of four divisions of the American Psychological Association and is author of *Beyond the Box: B. F. Skinner's Technology of Behavior from Laboratory to Life, 1950s–1970s*. She divides her time between Toronto and New York City.

PIONEERS OF PSYCHOLOGY

Introduction

In 1908 *the German psychologist Hermann Ebbinghaus* wrote, somewhat cryptically, "Psychology has a long past but only a short history."[*] As we shall see later in this book, Ebbinghaus was famous for his invention of new techniques for the systematic and experimental study of memory. What he meant by his statement was that psychology *as he practiced it*—as an experimentally based scientific discipline worthy of having its own independent university departments—had begun only a few decades earlier in the mid-nineteenth century. Hence it had a short history. General psychological ideas and philosophical theories about the human mind and behavior dated far back into antiquity, however, and these constituted psychology's "long past."

Ebbinghaus's quotation implicitly raises some difficult questions that authors of history of psychology textbooks must confront. The first and most basic one is simply, where to start: How much of the "long past" should one cover before delving into the "history"? This question is complicated by the fact that psychology has had more than a century to develop since Ebbinghaus's statement, so its "history" is not nearly as short as it was in his time. And because old ideas

---

[*] Translated from Hermann Ebbinghaus, *Abriss der Psychologie*, 2nd ed. (Leipzig: Veit, 1908), 7.

3

have a tendency to recur in new guises and contexts, some elements of the long past that would have seemed incidental to Ebbinghaus have assumed new relevance in light of the later development of modern psychology.

Further, during that century of development psychology has metamorphosed from being a relatively minor academic discipline into one of the largest and most popular of all college and university subjects. Indeed psychology has proliferated into an extraordinarily diverse collection of loosely (sometimes *very* loosely) interrelated subdisciplines. Just consider the variety of psychology's branches that are routinely covered in undergraduate courses: physiological, abnormal, social, clinical, cognitive, sensory, personality, developmental, humanistic, differential, industrial/organizational, evolutionary, behavioral, psychology of gender—and many others. Each one of these branches has attracted a significant number of specialists and has by now accumulated a substantial historical record of its own. No single textbook can possibly do justice to the totality or complexity of these histories, so authors must confront a second difficult choice about exactly what to cover from psychology's twentieth-century history, and to what extent.

Besides considering these questions, authors must also decide what approach they want to adopt toward *historiography* (which is the technical term to denote the actual writing of history). Authors' historiographic decisions determine the principles of historical writing that guide their work. Here again the choices are many. Some historians choose to focus exclusively or primarily on the development of major *ideas*, to the relative neglect of the personal histories of the people who developed them; others may choose the reverse. Some approaches emphasize the crucial importance of the broad social and cultural contexts in which the major ideas arise. Some historians approach their subject from the standpoint of the present, explaining how we got where we are today and often emphasizing how our predecessors overcame a series of mistaken assumptions and thus "progressed" to the present state of increased knowledge and wisdom. Other historians object to this "presentist" orientation and approach their subject from a "historicist" viewpoint, attempting to re-create the past as it was actually experienced by our predecessors, without distortion by foreknowledge of how things later worked out. Each of these differing approaches has its own uses and virtues, as well as disadvantages.

This Book's Historiographic Approach

Our own historiographic approach had its origins many years ago when we became particularly interested in the work of three individuals: Sigmund Freud, Francis Galton, and B. F. Skinner. We quickly discovered that each of these men left behind not only the published works that had made him famous but also treasure troves of originally unpublished material: letters, notebooks and unfinished drafts, news clippings and photographs, informal reminiscences from friends and colleagues, and innumerable other items that provided the "back stories" and rich textures of our protagonists' professional lives. Like many historians and biographers before us, we got "hooked" on this kind of material. It revealed our eminent subjects not so much as Olympian figures who proclaimed their theories from exalted positions on high, but rather as flesh and blood human beings who grappled with real problems and uncertainties while doing their best to understand complicated psychological issues. Often enough, factors from their personal and private lives interacted with their scientific work, causing it to veer in one direction or another. We found that this background information was interesting in its own right, and further that it deepened our appreciation and understanding of the published scientific works that had attracted our attention in the first place.

Gradually we began incorporating some of this background material into our teaching about these figures and found that students responded well. Even highly abstract ideas and concepts became more memorable and meaningful when introduced in the contexts of the actual life experiences of the theorists who initiated them. In turn, the theorists themselves became transformed from dusty characters in psychology's past into lively participants in discussions and controversies that continue to the present day. This encouraged us to extend our approach from our original subjects to as many other psychological pioneers as we could, and the latest result of these efforts is this book.

In writing the book we have assumed that most of our readers will be psychology students interested in knowing how the main ideas and issues in modern psychology came into being, and along the way in deepening their understanding of them. Accordingly, the accurate presentation of major psychological ideas is a prime goal of our book. We attempt to do so, however, in the "personalistic" manner described above: helping those ideas "come to life" by presenting them, as much as possible, in the contexts of the life histories of those who promoted them. We show, for example, that for Gustav Fechner his "psychophysical law" was not a dry mathematical abstraction but rather proof of an underlying harmony between the physical and spiritual worlds, providing for him the resolution of an intense personal crisis. We also show how Francis Galton's conviction of the innate and hereditary nature of intelligence arose in part from his own personal sense of intellectual frustration and academic failure; and how the industrial psychologist Lillian Gilbreth developed her pioneering ideas about the nature and importance of efficiency in large part because of the demands she faced as the working mother of a dozen children. These and many other examples of the creative interaction between personal/biographical and intellectual/theoretical factors are more fully presented throughout the book.

Although our choices of which people to cover were determined largely by the relevance of their ideas to present-day psychology, our adoption of the personalistic approach helped us avoid many of the dangers of presentism by relating the pioneers' stories, as much as possible, from their own points of view. "Old" or "mistaken" ideas, when presented in the full context in which they originally occurred, are shown to have been reasonable and rational. René Descartes' conceptions of the nerves as hollow tubes through which "spirits" flowed or of light rays as traveling with infinite speed were later proven to be mistaken, for example, but in the context of the information that was available to him in his time they were completely reasonable ideas to propose. Moreover, they were *productive* mistakes that could be tested and later corrected. Our approach also enables us to show how various specific social and cultural factors actually influenced individuals in helping to determine their theories. Franz Mesmer's theory of "animal magnetism" as the force producing what we today call hypnotism may now seem outlandish, for instance, but late-eighteenth-century Paris was marked by innumerable enthusiasms and even "crazes" regarding the powers of invisible forces or "fluids" such as gravitation, electricity, or the heated air that caused balloons to rise. Magnetism was clearly another such force, and it was not implausible to speculate about its possible influence on human beings.

Our Selection of Pioneers

Although our personalistic approach brings many advantages, the fact that it requires more in-depth treatment of individual figures than is normally provided made our choices of when to start and whom to cover particularly challenging. Our decisions were based on three criteria. First and most obviously, each pioneer had to have been unquestionably important for the development of psychological thought. Second, we had to have enough biographical information available about the person to provide the basis for a compelling story about him or her. And finally, when considered collectively, the contributions of our selected pioneers had to constitute a representative sampling of the full range of psychological theorizing. Stated more concisely, we sought a collection of early pioneers from psychology's "long past" whose work laid the foundations for a science of psychology, followed by a group from its more recent "history" who collectively represent the broad range of topics covered by typical modern psychology departments

Many textbooks begin their account of the long past with the ancient Greeks, particularly Plato (429–347 B.C.E.) and his younger pupil Aristotle (384–322 B.C.E.). There is some logic to this, because some very important psychological ideas and issues indeed date back to them. Plato was an outstanding early proponent of the *nativist view* of the human mind, arguing that it contains within itself important forms, concepts and truths that are innate but that may require concrete experiences after birth to bring them out or instantiate them. His famous "Socratic dialogues" depict conversations in which a fictional Socrates uses skillful questioning not so much to "instruct" his student about certain externally determined truths, as to "draw out" true conclusions that were already implicit but unrecognized in the student's mind.

Aristotle, by contrast, was also trained as a physician and naturalist — occupations that naturally led him to emphasize the importance of *observation* of the external world. Accordingly, he promoted a more *empiricist view* of the mind than Plato's, stressing its capacities for *acquiring* knowledge based on its recording and remembering of the experiences that impinge upon it. Further, Aristotle wrote an extended treatise on the *psyche*, a term from his original Greek language that was subsequently translated into Latin as *anima* and then into English as "soul." It also became the root of our word "psychology," and Aristotle's writings include many observations relevant to it.

Despite their importance, the ancient Greeks were not an ideal starting point for the purposes of this textbook. This was partly because the sort of rich biographical information we try to use is not readily available for them. Furthermore, a gap of nearly two millennia occurred between their era and the time when their theories began to actually shape the modern discipline of psychology. Accordingly, we chose to begin our main account in the early 1600s with the story of René Descartes, who seemed an ideal starting point for a number of reasons. He was arguably the earliest seminal figure who left behind a substantial amount of the type of biographical information that lies at the heart of our book: letters, unpublished manuscripts, reminiscences by people who knew him, and the framework of an intellectual autobiography. He dealt actively and directly with the Aristotelian concept of the psyche and introduced elements of Platonic nativism into his theory of the mind, so his story provides a platform for introducing important aspects of ancient Greek thought. He also introduced and promoted several ideas and issues that became the foundations of modern psychology, starting with the conception of "body" and "mind" as two separate "substances" requiring two differing modes of analysis. For him the body was completely explainable in materialistic, mechanistic terms, while the highest rational and volitional faculties of the mind resisted such analysis. (The strange looking figure on this book's cover was used by Descartes to help illustrate these ideas and should become more meaningful to the reader after completing our first chapter.) The debate about whether body and mind (broadly conceived) are indeed separate, and the extent to which the higher rational and cognitive functions can be accounted for mechanistically and physiologically, have remained fundamental issues for all subsequent generations of psychology's pioneers up to the present day.

Our second chapter focuses on two late-seventeenth-century individuals who developed separate aspects of Descartes' thought in distinctively different ways. John Locke promoted an empiricist and "associationistic" point of view that has remained dominant among English speaking mental theorists ever since, while his contemporary Gottfried Leibniz argued that such explanations had to be complemented by an appreciative recognition of the innate properties of the human mind that are involved in the processing of empirical information. In doing so, Leibniz explicitly cast himself as a modern day representative of the nativist Plato, in contrast to the Aristotelian, empiricist Locke. More than coincidentally, the Leibnizian focus on an independent mind that imposes its own categories and properties on human experience took particular hold in Germany, helping to create a highly receptive climate there for the eventual emergence of a separate discipline devoted to the mind: namely psychology.

The next three chapters describe the gradual development of these ideas into that separate discipline. Chapter 3 relates how a series of individuals, beginning with Franz Joseph Gall and his colorful theory of phrenology, pioneered the study of the brain and its role in psychological functioning. Even with increasingly sophisticated methods of observation and analysis, the general question of whether the brain functions as a collection of separate "organs" or as a unified whole remains fundamental to modern neuroscience. Chapter 4 shows how the German philosopher Immanuel Kant built on Leibnizian ideas in specifying some of the particular ways that innate properties of the mind shape individuals' conscious experience of the world, thus stimulating the physiologists Hermann Helmholtz and Gustav Fechner, followed by the Gestalt psychologists, to undertake empirical investigations of the transformative and "creative" properties of human sensory and perceptual systems. Chapter 5 tells how Wilhelm Wundt seized on the work of Helmholtz and Fechner along with some related research of his own as evidence that many important aspects of psychological functioning could be studied in laboratory settings and thus become the basis of a new experimental and properly "scientific" discipline. He went on to establish the world's first graduate program and scientific journal explicitly devoted to the new field, earning a reputation as the "father" of modern experimental psychology. These developments brought Ebbinghaus's "long past" to an end.

The middle chapters describe how psychology became consolidated as an independent discipline in the late 1800s and early 1900s. Chapter 6 focuses on Charles Darwin and his evolutionary theory, which profoundly influenced the nascent discipline of psychology along with all of the more mature life sciences. Via its emphasis on the *adaptive* properties of inherited physical variables, Darwin's theory encouraged psychologists to place increasing emphasis on the functionality of psychological characteristics, and on the importance of inherited individual differences. Darwin's cousin, Francis Galton, featured in Chapter 7, applied these emphases to individual differences in *intellectual* characteristics as he promoted the notions of "hereditary genius" and "eugenics." Although highly controversial, Galton's efforts helped lay the foundations for modern differential psychology, behavior genetics and intelligence testing. Chapter 8 relates how William James and his students reflected a generally Darwinian outlook as they established academic psychology in the United States as a "pragmatic," "functional" and pluralistic discipline. This helped set the stage for the rise of *behaviorism* as a dominant approach, as described in Chapter 9 via the stories of Ivan Pavlov, John B. Watson, and B. F. Skinner. Each of these scientists promoted the possibilities of a nonmentalistic psychology with observable behavior replacing "the mind" as its basic subject. In the case of Watson and Skinner, behaviorism provided the basis for a series of practical prescriptions for human conduct, from how to raise children to how to design community life. Thus, behaviorism was not only a theoretical commitment but a practical guide for the prediction and control of behavior.

The major characters and themes covered in these first nine chapters follow a generally chronological order and can be seen as telling a consistently developing story. As the twentieth century progressed, however, psychology expanded almost explosively and its timeline of major pioneers became much more crowded. One humorist, writing in 1924 in *Harpers* magazine, actually referred to this explosion as an "*outbreak* of psychology."[*] During this outbreak many subdisciplines

---

[*] Stephen Leacock, "A Manual for the New Mentality," *Harpers* (March 1924), 471, emphasis added.

developed concurrently with one another, rather than sequentially. Accordingly, our final six chapters are organized topically rather than chronologically, as we portray the history of the most important of these subdisciplines.

Chapter 10 shows how early experiences with hypnotism and other social influence processes eventually gave rise to modern experimental social psychology, culminating in the important studies of conformity by Solomon Asch and of obedience by Stanley Milgram. Chapter 11 tells the story of Sigmund Freud and his psychoanalytic theory, which created an entire "intellectual climate" that profoundly influenced public opinion before being somewhat reluctantly taken seriously by academic psychologists. Freudian theory contributed to the development of abnormal psychology, and provided some of the impetus for a new subdiscipline of "personality." Chapter 12 documents the rise of that field and the subsequent development of humanistic psychology, mainly through the stories of Gordon Allport and Abraham Maslow but supplemented by shorter accounts of several neo-Freudian and Gestalt theorists. Chapter 13 traces the rise of modern intelligence testing and developmental psychology, centering on the work of Alfred Binet and Jean Piaget as inspired by their original observations of their own children. Chapter 14 uses an account of the creators of increasingly powerful calculating machines and computers with the potential for "artificial intelligence" as a springboard for discussion of the "cognitive revolution" of the 1960s and modern cognitive psychology. And finally, Chapter 15 takes up four representative pioneers in the rise of clinical, organizational, and other types of applied psychology. Although our treatment of these subdisciplines is not and could not be exhaustive, it is *representative*, and along the way we mention other "alternative" pioneers whose lives and works might usefully be pursued by students and their teachers.

Although the early chapters tell a roughly chronological story, and all of them contain occasional cross references to each other, each chapter is also designed to tell a comprehensible story by itself. Accordingly, the chapters can be read individually or in alternative sequences or combinations with minimal loss of information.

Two Subthemes

Finally, we should mention two subthemes that persist throughout our text. First, we include in nearly every chapter some aspect of the roles women have played in the development of modern psychology. Throughout psychology's long past and much of its short history, women's participation in the formal institutions of scholarship and research was completely or substantially limited. European universities, with very few exceptions, were generally closed to women until the end of the nineteenth century. Thus, in the early days women's intellectual influence was most often of an indirect or supporting nature and was made possible only by membership in an aristocratic or otherwise highly privileged social class. A woman's primary role during these times was often as a moderator or facilitator rather than an originator of psychology related discourse, because of her relative lack of specialized training compared to her male peers. Even so, recent historical research—which we draw upon in our text—has revealed that these roles were often very important, as when Elizabeth of Bohemia's pointed questions about the interactions of body with mind led Descartes to reformulate his theory of the passions, and when Elizabeth's niece Princess Sophie of Hanover persuaded Leibniz to write a comprehensible account of his theory of monads.

Women's exclusion from scientific training and activity actually accelerated with the founding of the major European academies of science in the seventeenth century. Although some women had participated actively and meritoriously in the *informal* scientific circles and intellectual salons that were the forerunners of these academies, they were explicitly excluded once the academies were formalized. For example, the Royal Society of London, established in 1662, did not admit women until 283 years later, in 1945! Even after psychology was established as an academic discipline in the late 1800s, the suitability of higher education for women was questioned by many laypeople, scientists, and professionals alike. Aspects of Darwinian and Freudian theory were often invoked to rationalize this position, as we describe in our text.

As psychology has matured, however, and the restrictions placed on women's participation have decreased, women have taken on increasingly prominent roles in the discipline. In the 1970s, a project was begun to recognize and to reinterpret women's contributions in psychology's history This project has resulted in an ever-growing body of historical work that continues to illuminate not only women's accomplishments, but the dynamics that have affected psychologists' theories about gender and race.* We make use of these important resources throughout this text.

Our second subtheme is to show consistently how early ideas, questions, and attitudes dating back to psychology's long past, and covered in our early chapters, tend to recur in new guises up to the present day. Although earlier pioneers may not have had access to the same kinds of resources and technologies that more contemporary psychologists have at their disposal, many of the original fundamental questions that intrigued them continue to stimulate today's researchers. The questions may now be phrased somewhat differently and investigated via different methods, but they nonetheless reflect enduring preoccupations with some of the most central concerns about human experience and life. What relative roles do innate factors and biology, versus environment and experience play in determining who we are? Can consciousness be explained solely in mechanistic and materialist terms, and if not, what alternative modes of explanation are appropriate? Is there an "unconscious," and if so what are its properties? How do evolutionary processes shape our psychological makeup and interpersonal behavior? What are the psychological similarities and differences between humans and animals? How do human beings interact with and influence one another? What are the key components of psychological health? What is the nature of intelligence? In describing and exploring these and other recurring questions, we show that important continuities exist between psychology's long past and its shorter history, and so in an important sense Ebbinghaus's distinction between the two is an arbitrary and artificial one.

We hope that you will enjoy reading about our pioneers' lives and contributions to this past and history as much as much as we did researching and writing about them.

---

*For an extensive web resource on women and feminism in psychology, see http://www.feministvoices.com/.

René Descartes and the Foundations of Modern Psychology

1

Descartes Early Life and the Development of His Method
Descartes' Method

The World: **Descartes' Physics and Physiology**
Physics
Mechanistic Physiology

Descartes Philosophy of Mind
An Important Intellectual Friendship
Mind-Body Interactionism

Descartes Influence

Summary

Key Pioneers

Key Terms

Discussion Questions and Topics

Suggested Readings

On November 10, 1619, most residents of the duchy of Bavaria celebrated the St. Martin's Eve holiday with drink and frivolity. A visiting French soldier named **René Descartes** (1596–1650; see Figure 1.1) did not join in the festivity, however, spending the day in his heated room engaged in almost obsessional meditation. Over and over, he mentally tested the surprising ideas that had recently occurred to him, scarcely daring to hope they might resolve a personal conflict that had tormented him for years. Finally, as a stormy night fell, the young man lay down exhausted on his bed and began to dream. At first, all was fever, panic, thunderstorms, and whirling phantoms. Caught in a whirlwind on a street near his old college, he could not walk normally,

15

FIG 1.1
René Descartes
(1596–1650), by Jan
Baptiste Weenix, 1643

although other people did so as they spoke of a missing person and a melon from a foreign land. He wished to enter the chapel and pray, but the wind blew him violently against its wall, then died down as he woke up.

After murmuring a prayer to exorcise the evil genius he thought was plaguing him, Descartes fell back asleep. He now dreamed—or was it real?—that a terrific lightning flash filled the room with sparks, and then his sleep and dreams became calm. He dreamed of a book of poetry with the line "What path in life shall I follow?" A stranger came and conversed about a poem beginning with the words "Yes and no." The man and book vanished, then the book reappeared newly decorated with engravings. As Descartes gradually woke up and reflected on his dreams, he interpreted them to mean his long crisis in fact was over. He concluded that his first dream meant his old way of life, which involved putting trust in authorities, had been mistaken. The terrifying wind represented an evil authority trying to drive him by force into the chapel, a place he ought better to visit under his own initiative. Lightning and sparks then marked the descent of the spirit of truth, which inspired the final dream with its theme of indecision ("Yes and no") and vocational choice ("What path in life shall I follow?"). The improved book at the end of the dream seemed a benediction on Descartes' new ideas: If he followed them on his own, without recourse to the authorities, great results might follow.

The literal accuracy of these interpretations need not concern us (though no less an authority than Sigmund Freud would later remark that they seemed reasonable to him). More important was the fact that *Descartes* believed them, and thus they marked a turning point in his life. Previously, he had been a shy, reclusive, and personally troubled young man drifting aimlessly through life. Now he became a man with a mission, embarking on a course that would make him the most influential philosopher of his time and the promoter of a theory of mind and body that set the stage for the modern science of psychology.

At the heart of Descartes' inspiration lay the idea for a new *method* of obtaining knowledge. Partly a reaction against the traditional authorities, a view Descartes shared with some other intellectual leaders of his time, the method also derived from Descartes' own remarkable and unique personality. To appreciate this method fully, we thus must begin with the story of Descartes' background, early life, and education.

Descartes' Early Life and the Development of His Method

Always an intensely private person, Descartes intentionally kept many of the details of his life a secret. He even tried to hide the date of his birth, lest he become the object of speculation by astrologers. Only because an indiscreet artist added the date "31 March 1596" to one of Descartes' portraits do we know that he was born that day near the small French town of La Haye. Just a few other sketchy details of his early life are known. His mother died shortly after his birth, and he grew up on his grandmother's estate near La Haye. His father, a wealthy lawyer, practiced mainly in Brittany, 150 miles away. Child-rearing duties fell mainly to his grandmother, an older brother and sister, and a nurse. In later life Descartes dealt with these people rather formally and distantly, suggesting that he had formed few close attachments within his family.

Still, young René's intellectual precocity impressed his father, who sent him at age 10 to the best and most progressive school in France, the College at La Flèche There the curriculum included not just the traditional academic subjects of literature, languages, philosophy, and theology, but also a certain amount of science and mathematics—though the science was still strongly tinged with theology, and the mathematics had not yet been integrated with science. With only slight exaggeration, Descartes could later argue that he had been taught everything there was to be taught from books by the time he completed his education at La Flèche.

Young Descartes learned an approach to science dominated by the Greek philosopher **Aristotle** (384–322 B.C.E.), whose writings had later been integrated into Christian thought by the so-called **scholastic philosophers** of the Middle Ages. The Aristotelian view of the universe placed the earth at the center, surrounded by a series of revolving, concentric, "crystalline spheres" carrying, in order, the moon, the sun, Mercury, Venus, Mars, Jupiter, Saturn, and the fixed stars. Beyond the sphere of the stars was the "unmoved mover"—equated with God—who set the spheres in motion about the earth and kept them in order. The Polish astronomer **Nicolaus Copernicus** (1473–1543) had published a book in 1543 hypothesizing that the sun rather than the earth was the center of the system, but his view was not taken seriously at La Flèche or any other school of the time.

Descartes was taught a biology dominated by the Aristotelian concept of the **soul**—called the *psyche* in Aristotle's original Greek and the *anima* in his many Latin translations. Although the term *psyche* had originally meant simply "breath" in ancient Greek, by Aristotle's time it had taken on additional meaning as the animating force within all living things, the essential ingredient differentiating the living from the nonliving. Souls were believed to come in varying degrees of complexity according to their possessors' places in the hierarchy of nature. All organisms, including the simplest plants, supposedly had **vegetative souls** which enabled them to nourish themselves and to reproduce. Animals were said to have additional **sensitive souls** (sometimes also called *animal souls*), which provided the more complex functions of locomotion, sensation, memory, and imagination. And alone among the living creatures, human beings presumably possessed **rational souls**, enabling them to reason consciously and take on the highest moral virtues. While the vegetative and sensitive souls supposedly perished with the death of an organism's body, the rational human soul was viewed as immortal and capable of existing without the body.

Aristotle and his scholastic followers had made some astute observations about the various organic functions they attributed to souls, but from the modern viewpoint their approach suffered from a major limitation. They regarded the functions of the soul as elemental explanatory factors, incapable of being explained themselves in terms of more basic units. Thus living organisms were believed to reproduce, to move, or to think *because* they had vegetative, animal, or rational souls—and the analysis went no further. Modern biologists and psychologists, of course, think of these functions as things to be explained rather than as units of explanation in themselves. As we shall see, Descartes became one of the major initiators of this reversal of strategy.

As a student, however. Descartes absorbed the doctrine of the soul along with everything else he was taught, becoming the best pupil in his school. According to legend, he even succeeded in convincing his teachers that he did his best thinking while meditating in bed, earning the extraordinary privilege of lying abed in the mornings while his fellow students were up and about their chores. A recent biographer of Descartes has seriously challenged this pleasant story, which originated not from Descartes himself but from an early follower overly eager to emphasize his hero's virtue and intellectual precocity.[1] It is known, however, that in later life Descartes did at least some of his serious thinking while in bed, jotting down notes on paper kept on his bedside table.[2]

In any case, when Descartes graduated from La Flèche at age 16, he was the top student from the top school in the country. Soon after, he migrated to Paris, where, as an independently wealthy young man with no adult supervision, he at first gambled and engaged in other mild debauchery. Then he briefly came under the wholesome influence of **Marin Mersenne** (1588–1648), a Franciscan monk and older alumnus of La Flèche with broad intellectual interests and wide acquaintance with the scholarly world. Mersenne took Descartes under his wing and provided intellectual as well as personal support. All too soon, however, Mersenne's clerical order transferred him from Paris. Devastated by the loss of his mentor, Descartes retreated from society altogether and secretly rented an apartment in the country suburb of St. Germain.

Descartes now experienced a deep emotional and intellectual crisis, brought on by his feeling that all of his hard-won academic knowledge was useless or uncertain. In a manner that many students may still sympathize with today, Descartes listed the deficiencies and inanities of all his academic subjects. The *classics* were occasionally interesting but also treacherous because "those who are too interested in things which occurred in past centuries are often remarkably ignorant of what is going on today." *Literature* was dangerous because it "makes us imagine a number of events as possible which are really impossible, and . . . those who regulate their behavior by the examples they find in books are apt to fall into the extravagances of the knights of romances." Great achievements in *poetry* or *theology* resulted from natural gifts or divine inspiration rather than study, so it was foolish to try to teach those subjects in school. *Mathematics* offered a pleasing certainty of result but seemed trivial because it had not yet been applied to the solution of practical problems. And worst of all was *philosophy*, which had been studied for centuries by the most highly reputed minds "without having produced anything which is not in dispute and consequently doubtful and uncertain." Descartes concluded, "When I noticed how many different opinions learned men may hold on the same subject, despite the fact that no more than one of them can ever be right, I resolved to consider almost as false any opinion which was merely plausible."[3]

Descartes summarized his troubled condition as follows:

> From my childhood I lived in a world of books, . . . taught that by their help I could gain a clear and assured understanding of everything useful in life. . . . But as soon as I had finished the course of studies which usually admits one to the ranks of the learned, . . . I found myself so saddled with doubts and errors that I seemed to have gained nothing in trying to educate myself unless it was to discover more and more fully how ignorant I was.[4]

For all his intellectual brilliance and accomplishment, Descartes felt that the attainment of *perfectly certain* knowledge was beyond him. The intellectual and emotional foundations cut from beneath him, he entered a crisis of profound doubt.

While at St. Germain, Descartes had an incidental but important experience when he visited the small town's most famous attraction, an intricate series of mechanical statues constructed by the queen's fountaineers in grottoes in the banks of the River Seine. When visitors stepped on plates hidden in the floor, water flowed through pipes and valves in the statues and caused them to move. As one approached a statue of the goddess Diana bathing, for example, she retreated modestly into the depths of the grotto; upon further approach, a statue of the god Neptune came forward waving his trident protectively. Though intended only as ingenious amusements, these statues would later serve Descartes as a model for how living bodies might be set into motion by mechanical means (see Figure 1.2).

Just how the statues struck Descartes on first viewing is impossible to know, just as it is impossible to assess the severity of his personal crisis at the time. The feelings Descartes expressed in his autobiography were obviously intense, but not terribly far out of the ordinary. Quite possibly the whole episode represented little more than a temporary "identity crisis" in an overschooled young man who needed to broaden his horizons. One commentator has noted, however, that tendencies to withdraw into isolation and private meditation while

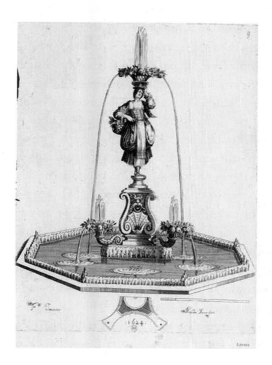

FIG 1.2
Engraving of a fountain at St. Germain-en-Laye, 1624

avoiding close emotional attachments, and to "depersonalize" oneself and others by seeing people as machine-like, characterize patients diagnosed today as suffering from schizophrenia. Because these symptoms are at least consistent with the little that is known about Descartes, it is possible that he may have suffered a schizophrenic-like breakdown at this period of his life.[5] Fortunately, one does not require an exact psychiatric diagnosis in order to appreciate the general relationship between Descartes' youthful personality and his later intellectual style. It suffices merely to note that he was a person who preferred solitude to society, his own ideas to those of others, and a skeptical as opposed to a credulous orientation to the world.

In any event, Descartes finally ended his self-imposed isolation and decided in 1618 to see whether the "real world" of practical experience could offer more satisfying knowledge than the academic ivory tower by becoming a soldier. Europe just then lay on the brink of the Thirty Years War, a conflict that would pit Catholic against Protestant armies in an outgrowth of the Lutheran Reformation. Although a Catholic, Descartes first enlisted in the Protestant army of Prince Maurice of Nassau, which was billeted relatively nearby in the Dutch city of Breda. The actual war had not yet begun, so Descartes experienced several months of boredom and quickly learned that soldiers possessed no more useful wisdom than scholars. "I found nothing there to satisfy me," he complained. "I noticed just about as much difference of opinion as I had previously remarked among scholars."[6]

A turning point occurred when Descartes encountered **Isaac Beeckman** (1588–1637), a physician and internationally known mathematician who happened to be visiting Breda. Surprised to find a soldier with an interest in mathematics, Beeckman befriended Descartes and, like Mersenne in Paris, became a mentor, revitalizing the young man's intellectual interests. At Beeckman's urging, Descartes wrote his first extended original scholarly work, an essay on music that he gratefully dedicated to his friend: "You alone have drawn me from my idleness," he wrote. "If I produce anything of merit, you will be entitled to claim it entirely for yourself." He also showed characteristic caution, however, by making Beeckman promise never to have the work published, or even to show it to others, who "would not overlook its imperfections, as I know you will."[7] Years later a prickly

Descartes would regret those words when Beeckman showed the work to others and suggested (correctly) that he had helped Descartes formulate some of his ideas. Infuriated, Descartes forgot his gratitude and retorted: "When you boast of such things in front of people who know me, it injures your own reputation. . . . Everyone knows that I am accustomed to instructing myself even with ants and worms, and one will think that is how I used you."[8]

This breach still lay far in the future, however, when Beeckman had to leave Breda in early 1619. Descartes now saw no strong reason why he should remain there either. With no personal commitment to Prince Maurice's cause, he decided to try life with the other side and set out to join the Catholic forces of Maximillian of Bavaria, some 350 miles to the south. Rather than going directly, however, he took a leisurely and meandering route through Poland and northern Germany. Early in this journey, Descartes reputedly had a crucial insight that led to his invention of **analytic geometry**.

According to one legend, the inspiration struck Descartes one morning during his habitual meditation in bed, as he watched a fly buzzing in the corner of his room.[9] He suddenly realized that the fly's position at any instant could be precisely defined by three numbers, representing the fly's perpendicular distances from the two walls and the ceiling. Generalizing from this, he recognized that *any* point in space could similarly be defined by its numerical distances from arbitrarily defined lines or planes. (These reference lines, since named *Cartesian coordinates* in honor of Descartes, include the *abscissa* and the *ordinate* so well known to generations of mathematics students.) Now, geometrical curves could potentially be defined by numbers, which reflected the paths traced by points as they moved with respect to the coordinates; in short, Descartes had devised a means of uniting and integrating the previously separate mathematical disciplines of geometry (involving shapes) and algebra (involving numbers). Soon this idea would have tremendous practical applications—helping astronomers to describe and calculate planetary orbits, for example. Because Descartes' major earlier complaint about mathematics concerned its lack of practical usefulness, he had special reason to feel pleased with this invention. If he had done nothing else in his life, he would have won a major place in the history of science for his analytic geometry.

Descartes' Method

In fact, Descartes' creative life was just beginning. By the fall of 1619 he reached Bavaria, and upon finding a comfortable and heated apartment, he decided to spend the winter there and postpone further soldiering until the spring. In his room he gave himself over to intense meditation, particularly on the question of how the nonmathematical disciplines might be granted the same certainty of results as analytic geometry. His doubting of all knowledge reached obsessional proportions once again, until at last he had two ideas that precipitated his climactic dreams on St. Martin's Eve.

First, the thought struck him: "Frequently there is less perfection in a work produced by several persons than in one produced by a single hand. Thus we notice that buildings conceived and completed by a single architect are usually more beautiful and better planned than those remodeled by several persons."[10] And most academic learning, acquired from an assortment of different teachers and books, was obviously a group product. How much better it might be if all knowledge could be the product of systematic experience and reflection by a single person! Here was a perfect rationale for Descartes to indulge his proclivity for solitary investigation, to dismiss the presumptuous "expertise" of the authorities, and to follow his own inclinations instead.

Descartes' second major insight pointed to a way of applying a geometry-like mode of reasoning to all fields of knowledge. In geometry, one begins with a small number of self-evident and certainly true *axioms*, such as the assertion that a straight line is the shortest distance between two points. Then one proceeds to link the axioms together by small but logically certain steps to arrive at complex and often surprising—but nonetheless certain—conclusions or theorems. Descartes' new "method" prescribed a similar step-by-step and systematic reasoning process for the other disciplines as well. Even more crucial for Descartes was a startling new idea about how to generate the self-evident starting points or "axioms" for nonmathematical fields. This "first rule" of the method was

> never to accept anything as true unless I recognized it to be certainly and evidently as such: that is, carefully to avoid all precipitation and prejudgment, and to include nothing in my

conclusions unless it presented itself so clearly and distinctly in my mind that there was no reason or occasion to doubt.[11]

In essence, Descartes here argued that the route to certainty was to *doubt everything* and then to take as axiomatic only that which proved to be indubitable. Yet even as he entertained this exciting possibility, he could not avoid being overcome by a final paroxysm of uncertainty. How could he know that his method would work? How could he know that if he gave himself up completely to systematic doubting he would ever come up with ideas whose truth was certain? He feverishly ruminated on these themes, until finally he had his dream.

The dream—or rather his optimistic interpretation of it—gave him confidence to proceed. Inspired by the thought that the ideas of individuals were generally superior to those of groups, he could now go his solitary way with a clear conscience. And his predilection for skepticism and doubt, previously a source of torment, could now be creatively employed in the search for positive truth. If Descartes had ever been emotionally ill, he was on the road to recovery, secure in his vocation as a solitary philosopher and scientist. Knowing at last what he wanted to do, Descartes gave up all thought of continuing as a soldier and began applying his method to a host of intellectual questions.

True to form, he worked in obscurity for nine years following his Bavarian experience, sometimes in Paris but often in other cities he visited throughout Europe. His major project for that period, an unfinished work entitled "Rules for the Direction of the Mind," attempted to show how his method could be applied to the analysis of the physical world. First, he argued, the most elementary and axiomatic units of a subject, which he called **simple natures**, had to be determined. A simple nature is an idea or impression that is at once *clear*, meaning that it is given immediately in experience, and *distinct*, meaning that it is incapable of further analysis or doubt. A primary source of error arises from accepting as simple natures ideas that are clear but not distinct—that is, that have been insufficiently doubted. The misleading image of a bent stick partly immersed in clear water exemplifies an idea that is clear but not distinct. Doubting the impression would lead to removing the stick from water and discovering it is really straight, its "bend" the result of light refraction in the water.

After Descartes systematically doubted the phenomena of the physical world, he hypothesized that just two properties are ultimate simple natures, incapable of further analysis or doubt: **extension** (the spatial dimensions occupied by a body) and motion. Besides being clear and distinct, these properties had the further virtue in Descartes' eyes of being analyzable in geometric-mathematical terms, particularly with the assistance of his new analytic geometry. Thus, he believed that all phenomena of the physical world should be ultimately explainable in terms of just these two properties. Light, heat, sound, and all other physical qualities presumably result from some sort of extended, material particles in motion. It also occurred to Descartes that living bodies could be thought of as mechanical contrivances, explainable according to the same principles.

Just as Descartes was developing these ideas, the great Italian scientist **Galileo Galilei** (1564–1642) published something very similar. In a 1623 work called *The Assayer*, Galileo distinguished between what he called the **primary** and **secondary qualities** of physical matter. The three primary qualities of shape, quantity, and motion presumably reside inherently in matter, whereas the secondary qualities arise only after the primary qualities impinge on the human senses. Thus, the sight, sound, smell, and feel of an object are secondary qualities, while the size, shape, and motion of its constituent particles are primary. The science of physics, for Galileo, entailed the analysis of the primary qualities of matter.

The obvious similarity between Descartes' and Galileo's ideas may have been more than coincidental. The two men probably knew about each other's work through Mersenne, who corresponded regularly with them and many other scientific figures of the time.* Descartes, despite his avowed mistrust of other people's work, might even have read *The Assayer* and been impressed by its consonance with his own thought. Or, perhaps the general idea of a physics based entirely on material particles in motion was simply "in the air" and was developed inde-

---

* Mersenne was one of a number of individuals who, while not original scientists themselves, nevertheless contributed greatly to the advancement of science because they were convivial and knowledgeable correspondents of scientists. In an age before scientific periodicals had been established for the easy dissemination of information, these sociable go-betweens helped scientists keep up with each other's work.

pendently by these two great figures. They were both working in the long period from the late sixteenth century through the early eighteenth century, later labeled by some historians and philosophers as a period of "scientific revolution." In any case, Descartes postulated a physical system much in tune with the ideas of his most able contemporaries, despite his penchant for isolation and solitary thought.

Still, Descartes published nothing and remained a largely anonymous figure until 1628. That year, however, he attended a public lecture on chemistry in Paris, finding the topic unacceptable because it used concepts that seemed to him only clear and plausible, but not distinct. Aroused to unusual boldness, Descartes spoke out in the public discussion following the lecture and in so doing impressed an influential cardinal in the audience. Upon learning that the shy philosopher had extended his ideas into physiology as well as physics, the cardinal implored him to publish.* Encouraged, Descartes decided to write a work synthesizing his physics and his physiology—or, as he called them, his "mechanics" and his "medicine."

But even with this new motivation, Descartes proceeded very slowly. The Parisian atmosphere became distracting, and he fled again to Holland. This time he stayed for twenty years, preserving his privacy by moving twenty-four times during that period and seldom leaving a forwarding address. He spent the first five years perfecting his physical analysis of the world and his mechanical analysis of the animal body. At last in 1633 he completed a lengthy manuscript in French entitled *Le Monde* (*The World*), subdivided into one part on physics called "Treatise of Light" and another on physiology, "Treatise of Man."

The World: Descartes' Physics and Physiology

Just as Descartes was about to entrust his new book to the printer, he received the staggering news that Galileo had been condemned by the Inquisition for supporting the Copernican theory of the universe.

---

* The chemist whose lecture inspired all this, a man named Chandoux, was less fortunate. Following his humiliation by Descartes he tried to use his scientific talents as a counterfeiter; unsuccessful with that endeavor as well, he was finally arrested and hanged for his crime.

Previously, the Catholic Church had tolerated publication of the theory as long as it was clearly labeled a hypothesis and not presented as established truth. But now the Church declared expressing the idea at all to be heretical, and Galileo had publicly recanted upon threat of torture. Descartes' "Treatise of Light" entertained the Copernican theory too, and while he was in no personal danger in Protestant Holland, he remained a Catholic and wanted his work and name to be acceptable in the Catholic universities of France. Thus, he withdrew his book from publication. Fortunately, he preserved the manuscript, which his followers managed to publish soon after his death.

Among the striking features of *The World*, as of Descartes' thought generally, was the way it integrated several previously separate branches of science. Ever since Bavaria, Descartes had sought to construct a "universal science" connecting all the arts and sciences within a single set of fundamental principles. This integrating quality made *The World* one of the first modern textbooks, not only of physics and physiology, but of psychology as well. Physical laws were applied to an understanding of physiology, which in turn was used to explain certain psychological phenomena. Few of Descartes' physiological ideas are accepted today exactly as he conceived them, and he did not carry his psychophysiological integration as far as many contemporary scientists do. But still, *The World* clearly set the style for the future emergence of psychology as a member of the family of sciences.

Physics

"Treatise of Light" presented Descartes' physical ideas, based on the analysis of material particles in motion. Following Aristotle, Descartes believed there could be no void or vacuum, so he saw the entire universe as completely filled with different kinds of material particles in different kinds of motion. When a particle moves, it leaves no empty space behind it, for that space is instantaneously filled by other particles—just as when a fish swims the space it leaves is instantaneously refilled with water.

Descartes hypothesized three basic types of particles in the universe, corresponding roughly to the classical elements of fire, air, and earth. He conceptualized the fire, or heat particles, as almost unimaginably tiny so that when aggregated they constituted "a virtually perfect fluid" capable of filling up space of any shape or size. Descartes argued that these particles had naturally sifted through all of the other larger particles in the universe, so as to congregate in particular intensity at its center and form the sun. Here was Descartes' version of the now-heretical Copernican theory.

Descartes thought of 'air" particles as somewhat larger, but still too small to be directly perceived. The most numerous of all the particles, these completely filled all the spaces between objects and, again like the water in a fish pond, instantaneously moved into the space just vacated by a moving object. All material objects—including the planets and comets as well as the earth and the things on it—were supposedly composed of accretions of "earth" particles, the third and heaviest variety in Descartes' hypothetical universe.

As its title suggests, much of this first treatise dealt with the various phenomena of light. Descartes argued that "air" particles naturally arrange themselves into *columns* between objects, forming the material basis of light rays. Thus, when we look at an object, innumerable light rays or columns of invisible air extend directly between it and our eye. Descartes further argued that the "earth" particles constituting the object are in constant vibratory motion, and these vibrations are inevitably transmitted to the columns of light rays extending to the eye. The vibrations of the rays in turn stimulate the material particles of the eye into sympathetic motion, providing the physical basis for the sensation of light in the perceiving individual.

In elaborating on this notion, Descartes used the analogy of a blind man sensing objects in the world with a stick. As he probes with his stick and encounters a solid object, pressure at the tip of the stick is transmitted along its length and perceived by the hand. The stick is thus analogous to a Cartesian light ray, transmitting the motion of a stimulus from one end (the perceived object) to another (the hand or eye). Descartes' theory implied that the speed of light is instantaneous, since both ends of the light rays (like both ends of the blind man's stick) were presumed to move together simultaneously, and he acknowledged that the theory would be discredited by any evidence of a finite speed for light. Such evidence did not appear until 1676, however, so the theory remained plausible for many years. And even though incorrect regarding the physical structure of light, Descartes' system still facilitated the analysis of many optical phenomena, such as the refracting or bending of straight rays in lenses and other devices.

Moreover, in conceptualizing the eye as a physical mechanism activated by the physical properties of light waves, Descartes introduced another idea of great and permanent influence: namely, that the structures of a living body could be thought of as physical systems operating according to physical laws. This mechanistic view of the body was more fully developed in the second, physiological part of *The World*, the "Treatise of Man."

Mechanistic Physiology

A few others before Descartes had examined animate bodies mechanistically. Galileo, for example, had analyzed the bones and joints of the body as if they were a system of levers, and the great British doctor **William Harvey** (1578-1657) had analyzed the heart as a physical pumping mechanism in his revolutionary demonstration that blood is not constantly created and dissipated anew, but instead circulates constantly throughout the body.

Thus Descartes' unique contribution lay not in the idea of physiological mechanism per se, but rather in the *scope* of the functions to which he applied the idea. He mechanistically analyzed ten physiological functions in his treatise: the digestion of food, the circulation of blood, the nourishment and growth of the body, respiration, sleeping and waking, sensation of the external world, imagination, memory, the appetites and passions, and the movements of the body. The result was to replace the traditional concepts of the vegetative and animal souls with mechanistic explanations. Descartes argued that the body's ten functions occur mechanically,

> no more nor less than do the movements of a clock or other automaton, from the arrangement of its counterweights and wheels. Wherefore it is not necessary on their account to conceive of any vegetative or sensitive soul or any other principle of movement and life than its blood and spirits, agitated by the heat of the fire which burns continually in its heart and which is of no other nature than all those fires that occur in inanimate bodies.[12]

Descartes conspicuously omitted just one traditional function of the soul from his mechanistic treatment—namely, *reason*. Though he replaced the vegetative and animal souls with new explanatory concepts, he could not bring himself to do the same for the rational soul. Instead, he dealt with the "highest" psychological processes in an altogether different way that we shall take up later. For now, however, we shall consider his revolutionary mechanistic treatment of several of the "lower" psychological functions, which he explained as consequences of the workings of the brain and nervous system. This work helped initiate a tradition of **neuropsychology** that continues to the present.

Descartes was particularly interested in the brain's internal cavities, or **ventricles**, filled with the clear yellowish liquid called **animal spirits** in his day and called **cerebrospinal fluid (CSF)** today. He speculated that these spirits were the smallest and finest particles in the blood, after being filtered from the grosser particles by passing through tiny arteries en route to the brain. He further adopted an idea proposed centuries earlier by the Greek physician **Galen** (ca. 130–200 C.E.) that the animal spirits might somehow flow through the body's network of nerves to activate specific muscle groups. Without benefit of a microscope, Descartes convinced himself (falsely, we now know) that the narrow nerve fibers were hollow. With liquid animal spirits and supposedly hollow nerves, animal bodies could be construed as mechanisms similar to the statues in St. Germain, set into motion by the flow of fluids through internal pipes. Descartes made this connection explicit when he wrote:

> In the same measure that spirits enter the cavities of the brain they also leave them and enter the pores (or conduits) in its substance, and from these conduits they proceed to the nerves. And depending on their entering . . . some nerves rather than others, they are able to change the shapes of the muscles into which these nerves are inserted and in this way to move all the members. Similarly you may have observed in the grottoes and fountains in the gardens of our kings that the force that makes the water leap from its source is able of itself to move diverse machines . . . according to the various arrangements of the tubes through which the water is conducted.[13]

Thus, Descartes conceived of the brain as a complicated system of tubes and valves for shunting animal spirits into specific nerves, thereby initiating specific actions. *Memory* and *learning* occurred when repeated actions in the brain caused certain "pores," under certain circumstances, to be particularly open and receptive to animal spirits.

Having hypothesized a mechanism for animal movement, Descartes next addressed the question of what starts the mechanism in the first place—that is, what regulates the opening or closing of the valves in the brain to start or stop the flow of animal spirits to the nerves? Again, St. Germain suggested a clue, for there the statues were activated by *external pressure on sensing devices*—the pressure of spectators' feet on special floor plates. Descartes imagined something similar in a living body. According to his physics, all sensory stimuli from the external world had to be material particles in motion, exerting pressures from their motion onto the various sense organs. Light, sound, and heat, for example, were vibrating columns of infinitesimal particles pushing themselves against the eye, ear, or skin. The movements thus initiated in the sense organs might in turn get transmitted via the nerves to the brain, causing selected valves to open and trigger specific actions.

Descartes even believed he saw a mechanism for the transmission of vibratory motions from sense organ to brain. While dissecting some of the larger nerves, he thought he saw extremely fine filaments running their length inside. Just as a fisherman's line transmits the swimming motion of a fish to the hand of the fisherman, these filaments could presumably transmit vibrations in the sense organs to the brain, as tugs and pulls that could open or close specific valves, releasing a flow of animal spirits to specific muscles.

Though Descartes did not use the exact term, he had here formulated the general idea of what we now call the **reflex**—a neurophysiological sequence in which a specific *stimulus* from the external world automatically elicits a specific *response* in the organism. Your doctor tests two of your reflexes by tapping your knee (stimulus) to produce an involuntary kick of your leg (response) and shining a light in your eye (stimulus) to produce a contraction of the pupil (response). The specific mechanism Descartes imagined for the reflex is now known to be incorrect; the nerves do not contain minute filaments for transmitting sensory messages, as he thought, and they are not hollow conduits for the flow of cerebrospinal fluid as motion initiators. (One historian has jokingly called Descartes' conception a "flush-toilet model" of the reflex, since the hypothetical mechanism he proposed

closely resembles that of a chain-operated water closet.[14]) But Descartes' general conception of the reflex has been enormously useful to
physiologists and psychologists, and we shall see in later chapters how
his successors developed more accurate theories for the mechanisms
underlying nervous transmission.

Descartes' theory enabled him to differentiate two kinds of reflexive responses. In one, the vital spirits presumably flowed immediately
down the same nerve whose fiber had been tugged, resulting in an
automatic and immediate response. In Figure 1.3, for example, we see
Descartes' scheme for explaining the reflexive response of withdraw-
ing one's foot from the heat of a fire. The particles of fire (A) move
quickly and with enough force to displace the skin (B), pulling a nervous fiber (cc) which tugs open the pore (de). Thus opened, the animal
spirits contained in the brain cavity (F) enter the pore and are carried
through the fiber, resulting in the withdrawal of the foot from the fire.

The second type of reflex accounted for *learned* reactions, in which
the response is not originally connected with its stimulus. Here Descartes postulated a sort of flexible shunting system in the brain,
whereby incoming tugs can activate the opening of nerves other than

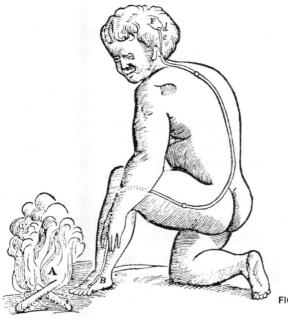

FIG 1.3
Reflex action

the one stimulated. Thus, the sound of a bell may initiate a response originally unconnected with it, such as participating in a fire drill. Descartes did not elaborate on exactly how the brain performs this mechanical shunting, but his general differentiation between innate and learned reflexes, with the latter presumably entailing more activity in the brain, has been an enduring and productive idea in modern psychology.

While innate and learned reflexes could explain the activation of an organism by stimulation from the external world, Descartes also recognized that people and animals do not always respond in the same ways to the same stimuli. *Internal* factors such as emotions also play a role in animal response, and Descartes proposed a mechanistic account of these differences in terms of variations in the animal spirits. He suggested that localized currents, eddies, or what he called "commotions" may develop in parts of the animal spirit reservoir, influencing the receptiveness of nearby nerves to flows of spirit toward the muscles. Through such variations, different emotional predispositions such as anger or fear might be created:

> When it is a question of forcefully avoiding some evil by over-coming it or driving it away—as anger inclines us to do—then the spirits must be more evenly agitated and stronger than they usually are. Whereas, when it is necessary to avoid harm with patience—as fear inclines us to do—then the spirits must be less abundant and weaker.[15]

In this way, Descartes explained the animate body's mechanical responses as occurring because of an *interaction* between the effects of external stimulation on the nervous system and the internal, "emotional" preparedness of the animal spirits to respond in particular ways.

Further mechanistic consequences of the animal spirits included the states of *sleeping* and *waking*. An alert waking state presumably arose when an ample supply of spirits in the brain cavities caused the brain tissue to expand somewhat, pulling the nerve fibers to a state of tautness and maximal sensitivity to the vibrations of external stimulation. Descartes saw the sleeping brain, by contrast, as relatively devoid of spirits, with flaccid tissues and slack nerve fibers incapable of transmitting most external vibrations. Only sporadically do random eddies in the depleted reservoir of spirits cause isolated parts of the brain to expand and stretch taut a few nerve fibers—much as a weak, intermittent wind occasionally pulls taut just a few of the ropes supporting sails on a ship. Thus, the sleeping organism is generally unresponsive to external stimulation, with just a few isolated and disconnected experiences, or *dreams*, created by the momentary tautness in the nerves.

Descartes believed his analyses demonstrated how all of the traditional functions of the vegetative and animal souls could be regarded mechanistically—which was to say that those Aristotelian concepts were outmoded and needed to be replaced. Indeed, in one of his most continuously controversial statements, he argued that animals could be understood *completely* in mechanistic terms, as automata. Their hydraulic mechanisms might be more complicated than those of man-made machines, containing more pipes more intricately interconnected with each other, but in principle they were the same. As Descartes summarized to a friend, "The soul of beasts is nothing but their blood."[16]

But Descartes would not go so far regarding human beings, in spite of the fact that their bodies resembled the bodies of animals in many ways and obviously operated like machines as well. The point of difference, Descartes believed, lay in human capacities for *consciousness* and *volition*. It seemed obvious to him that his own actions often occurred because he *wanted them to*, or because he freely chose them following rational deliberation. This supremely important, subjective side of human experience did not seem to lend itself to mechanistic analysis. Accordingly, Descartes attributed it to the presence of a soul or mind, which he thought interacted with the bodily machine in human beings. In sum, he got rid of the Aristotelian vegetative and animal souls, but retained the rational soul.

Much of Descartes' most important work after *The World* dealt with the features of this immaterial, rational mind and its interactions with the mechanistic body. As we shall see, these writings highlighted some of the most fundamental questions a scientific psychology can ask—questions that remain problematic to the present day.

Descartes' Philosophy of Mind

After suppressing publication of *The World*, Descartes started on new projects he hoped would be more acceptable to the Church. He spent four years writing detailed treatises on optics, meteorology, and geometry—all subjects he could discuss without raising the issue of a sun-centered universe. And he also prepared a brief autobiographical "Discourse on Method," describing how his method based on systematic doubt came into being and summarizing its major conclusions regarding the body and the soul.

In 1637, all of these works were finally published in a single volume bearing the lengthy title *Discourse on the Method of Rightly Conducting the Reason and Seeking the Truth in the Field of Science; plus Dioptric, Meteorology, and Geometry, Which are Some of the Results of That Method.* Characteristically shy, Descartes omitted his name from the title page and was annoyed when Mersenne wrote an introduction to the Paris edition that made its authorship clear. Nonetheless, he was eager to have his book widely read, and in lieu of royalties he accepted 200 copies, which he distributed to Europe's intellectual leaders. In an attempt to appeal to as large an audience as possible, he had written the work in vernacular French, rather than the Latin of most scholarly books of the time.*

The autobiographical *Discourse on Method*, with a succinct analysis of the rational human soul, quickly became a philosophical classic. Here Descartes described his earliest attempts at systematic doubt, following his Bavarian inspiration. He related that, at first, *everything* seemed to be doubtable, even the most clear and distinct sensory impressions and the simple natures of the physical world. For example, he could imagine that those impressions were merely illusory, that he *dreamed them* rather than really experienced them. But

---

* Galileo had also published much of his work in vernacular Italian. This self conscious appeal by Galileo and Descartes to readers who were not necessarily classically educated represented part of the general movement they led toward the "democratization" of science and away from the acceptance of ideas simply because of the authority or credentials of those proposing them. Galileo's works would have been (correctly) regarded as less of a threat to the authority of the Church had they been written in Latin.

as he continued to doubt, he at last came upon one idea that seemed absolutely certain and that he described in his *Discourse* in one of the most famous passages in modern philosophy:

> Finally, as the same percepts which we have when awake may come to us when asleep without their being true, I decided to suppose that nothing that had ever entered my mind was more real than the illusions of dreams. But I soon noticed that while I thus wished to think everything false, it was necessarily true that I who thought so was something. Since this truth, *I think, therefore I am, or exist*, was so firm and assured that all the most extravagant suppositions of the sceptics were unable to shake it, I judged that I could safely accept it as the first principle of the philosophy I was seeking.[17]

Almost paradoxically, the act of doubting provided Descartes with evidence of the certainty he desired. He could doubt the reality of his senses, or even the material existence of his body and the physical world, but he could not doubt the subjective reality of his own doubting mind. The experience of doubt itself was unquestionably real. Thus, one unquestionable reality was the activity of his own rational mind, or soul.

It followed logically—at least to Descartes—that the mind must stand in marked contrast to the body, as something altogether distinct:

> I concluded that I was a thing or substance whose whole essence or nature was only to think, and which, to exist, has no need of space nor of any material thing or body. Therefore it follows that this ego, this mind, this soul, by which I am what I am, is entirely distinct from the body and is easier to know than the latter, and that even if the body were not, the soul would not cease to be all that it is now.[18]

The body, like all physical things, consisted of extended particles in motion. The soul, whose essence was consciousness and thought, existed independently of spatial and material considerations as a separate kind of immaterial entity.

Reflecting further on the soul, Descartes concluded that it never appeared directly or immediately in consciousness, like a sensory experience. Although he was absolutely certain it existed, he never experienced its totality as a "thing" all at once. This train of thought stimulated him to search for other ideas that, while "real," also seemed incapable of being represented by a single sensory experience; notions such as "perfection," "unity," "infinity," and the geometrical axioms came to mind. Descartes concluded that such ideas, independent as they are of specific sensory experience (but capable of being suggested or alluded to by experience), must derive from the nature of the thinking soul itself. Accordingly, he called them the **innate ideas** of the soul.

Descartes' belief in innate ideas provided an anchor for much of the rest of his philosophy. The presumably innate idea of "perfection," combined with his certainty of the reality of his own mind, suggested to Descartes that there must exist a real God who embodies all aspects of perfection. Now certain of the existence of a perfect God as well as of his conscious soul, Descartes felt he could generally accept his sensorily based conclusions regarding the makeup of the physical world. That is, knowledge from the senses could be trusted—not because the knowledge was inherently certain itself, but because the integrity of the mind that perceived it, and the perfection of the God that created both matter and mind, were certain.

Thus Descartes' philosophy rated reason and the intellective functions of the conscious mind as more fundamental than, and potentially independent of, sensory experience. For this reason Descartes is commonly labeled a **rationalist**. And because his system posits innate ideas existing prior to concrete experience, he is also called a **nativist**. Opponents of these positions—arguing in various ways that the mind arises primarily out of concrete experience, or that there can exist no innate ideas independent of sensory experience—are referred to as **empiricists**. We shall meet several of them, as well as other sorts of nativists and rationalists, in later chapters.

Descartes is also called a **dualist**, because of his sharp division between the two substances of body and mind. Of course, philosophers and theologians long before Descartes had differentiated between the perishable body and the immortal rational soul, so his dualism per se was scarcely new. But he added something new by emphasizing that many important phenomena are the result of neither body nor mind acting alone, but rather of the many possible kinds of *interactions* between the two. Throughout the 1640s he was stimulated to

FIG 1.4
Princess Elizabeth
of Bohemia
(1618–1680)

elaborate further on this interactive dualism, in large part because of his friendship and correspondence with a remarkable royal figure, **Princess Elizabeth of Bohemia** (1618–1680; see Figure 1.4).

An Important Intellectual Friendship

Princess Elizabeth was the third child and eldest daughter in a large royal family that played an important role in intellectual history. As we shall see in the next chapter, Elizabeth's younger sister Princess Sophie (1630–1714), and Sophie's daughter Sophie Charlotte (1668–1705), would both be instrumental in furthering the career of the philosopher Gottfried Leibniz. The girls' mother was Elizabeth Stuart, the daughter of England's King James I, and their father was Elector Palatine Frederick V (an "Elector" was one of the eight German princes entitled to elect the Holy Roman Emperor, and the Palatinate was the region of present-day Germany surrounding Heidelberg). A year after Elizabeth's birth her father was named King of Bohemia, but in the political turmoil of the times he soon lost that throne along with most of his land in Germany. The family repaired to Holland where—at least by royal standards—they lived in relative poverty.

Still, the family had sufficient resources to provide the daughters with impressive tutoring in everything from etiquette to mathematics and philosophy to several foreign languages. Young Elizabeth became so proficient in classical languages that she was nicknamed *La Grecque* ("The Greek"). When she grew older, her family's financial situation apparently made her an unsuitable match for any aristocratic marriage, but this reportedly did not distress Elizabeth, as she had become far more interested in the life of the mind.[19] She read widely, and in 1642 she encountered and became immersed in some of Descartes' early writings. When the philosopher, also living in Holland at the time, learned about the princess's interest in his writings he arranged to have an audience with her. Thus began an important intellectual friendship, maintained by an extensive correspondence in which they discussed many philosophical as well as personal issues. Much of this correspondence has been published, and recent historical scholarship has established Elizabeth as a significant philosopher in her own right.[20]

For the history of psychology, Elizabeth's major contribution arose from some serious questions she raised about Descartes' proposed interactions between a material body and an immaterial soul. Although she greatly admired the basics of Descartes' philosophy, she pointedly asserted that she could not understand how, under the terms of his theory, an immaterial mind and a material body could actually interact with and mutually influence each other. She wondered precisely how a nonmaterial soul can possibly "determine the spirits of the body to produce voluntary actions," in the case of behavior that is freely willed and not merely reactive to external stimulus. "It would be easier," she added, "for me to concede matter and extension to the soul, than the capacity of moving a body, and of being moved, to an immaterial being."[21] This was then (and remains today) a very difficult issue, and Descartes grappled with it at length in his ensuing correspondence with Elizabeth. He then used this correspondence as the foundation for his important 1649 work, which he titled *Treatise on the Passions of the Soul.*

Mind-Body Interactionism

In this new work Descartes argued that a body without a soul would be an automaton, completely under the mechanistic control of external stimuli and its internal hydraulic or "emotional" condition—and completely without consciousness. Conversely, a soul or mind without a body would have consciousness, but only of the innate ideas; it would lack the sensory impressions and ideas of material things that occupy normal human consciousness most of the time. Thus, the body adds richness to the contents of the soul's consciousness, while the soul adds rationality and volition to the causes of behavior.

From our current perspective, some of Descartes' most peculiar theorizing concerned the *location* of these interactions between mind and body. From one point of view, the soul as an immaterial substance could not be said to be located anywhere in material space. But from another, it had to affect and be affected by the actions of the body, which *was* localized in space. Thus, Descartes was led to search for a place in the body where interactions with the soul were most likely—though recognizing that the soul was not completely confined to that location. He felt the most logical place was somewhere in the brain, the control center for the body's sensations and movements. Yet he worried because the brain was a physically divided organ with two symmetrical halves, whereas the soul seemed a unified, single entity. He expressed his dilemma as follows:

> I observe . . . the brain to be double, just as we have two eyes, two hands, two ears, and indeed, all the organs of our external senses double; yet since of any one thing at any one time we have only the single and simple thought, there must be some place where the two images which come from the two eyes, and where the two impressions which come from one single object by way of the double organs of the other senses, can unite before reaching the soul, and so prevent their representing to it two objects in place of one.[22]

From the purely mechanistic standpoint of the body, the double nature of the brain and senses posed no problem. As long as specific stimuli produced specific distinctive signals for the brain's mechanism to respond to, it made no difference whether those signals were single, double, or even resembled the objects that excited them at all. Only after consciousness entered the picture did the problem arise, for while the body received double representations of an object in the world, the soul consciously perceived only one. Further, Descartes believed that the conscious perception must accurately replicate the real world—that the single tree he saw in his head as he looked out the window, for example, corresponded accurately to a real, single tree in the external world. Thus, somewhere the two images from the two eyes must reunite and reassemble to form the unitary perception of a single tree in consciousness. Descartes thought it probable that this must happen in the only undivided structure he could find within the brain: the pineal gland, a small, roughly spherical organ lying near its center. Further, this gland extends into the largest ventricle, ideally situated to influence and be influenced by variations in the pool of animal spirits.

Figure 1.5 illustrates Descartes' conception of how visual images are transmitted to the soul. Light rays from an external object (the arrow) are refracted so that miniature, inverted images are projected onto the retinas of the two eyes. Vibrations thus initiated on the retinas stimulate nerve filaments, which open valves in the brain at their ends (the points 1, 2, and 3 mark the valves opened by stimulation from points A, B, and C on the arrow, respectively). At this point, an animal's processing of visual stimulation would end, as the resulting flow of animal spirits would produce mechanistic reflexes. In human beings, however, the process goes further, as signals from the double points 1, 2, and 3 are reinverted and reunited (presumably by further neural messages) on the single points a, b, and c on the pineal gland (marked P in the figure). The soul, interacting with the body at P, accordingly encounters and brings to consciousness a single and upright image of the arrow.

At this point the soul may cause the pineal gland to move about within the pool of animal spirits in such a way as to enhance, inhibit,

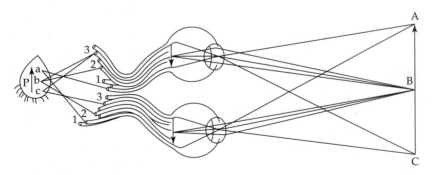

FIG 1.5 Descartes' conception of visual perception

or otherwise modify the flow of fluids toward particular valves—
depending on the soul's particular interpretation of the image. In
doing so the soul mediates behavior with reason, making the behavior conscious, and at least to some extent deliberate and freely willed.
(As Princess Elizabeth might have noted, however, the specific way
in which the soul can cause the pineal gland to move about deliberately remains a mystery.)

Further important consequences of the body-soul interaction hypothesized by Descartes are the **passions**, defined as the conscious experiences accompanying the body's emotions. When the emotion-causing
eddies and currents in the animal spirits flow past the strategically
located pineal gland and cause it to move slightly, the soul responds to
this information in two ways. First, as it senses the particular nature of
the gland's movement, it has conscious sensation of a passion—a feeling
such as love, hatred, fear wonder, or desire. Second, the soul may take
a conscious *attitude* toward that passion and attempt to influence it by
initiating voluntary movements in the pineal gland that enhance or
inhibit the emotional perturbations of animal spirit. If the soul experiences anger, for example, it can will to attack the offending person
and influence the pineal gland to splash even more spirits into the
nerves initiating attack responses. Alternatively. it can will to inhibit
the attack by moving the gland in order to block the flow of spirits into
those nerves.

While the soul may sometimes consciously will to oppose or modify the body's responses, Descartes emphasized that it is not always
successful. Indeed, he saw the soul's control over emotions as similar
to its control over external sensory impressions. For relatively mild
emotions, the soul can will to ignore or override their influences, just
as it can ignore or override mild background stimulation while in a
state of concentration. But with very intense emotions, the rational
influence of the soul may be insufficient; people often strike out in
anger or run away in panic even when rational consideration would
recommend otherwise. Descartes thought that, here, the strong commotions of animal spirits simply overpower the conscious soul's countervailing efforts.

Descartes asserted that such conflicts never occur within the soul
itself, but always involve the soul against the body. He chided those
who characterized the soul as anything other than a perfectly unified

and harmonious entity, in a passage that epitomized his interactive dualism:

> The error committed in representing the soul as displaying diverse personalities that ordinarily are at variance with one another arises from our failure to distinguish its function from those of the body, to which alone we must attribute whatever in us is observed to be repugnant to our reason. There is, therefore, no contest save that which takes place in the small gland which is the center of the brain, when it is impelled to one side by the soul, and to another by the animal spirits.[23]

For Descartes the soul was perfectly rational, consistent, and unified—but also limited in the power it could exert over the often unruly body. If the soul willed to augment the body's mechanical tendencies, all was well and harmonious. If it decided to oppose them, however, a struggle was played out in the pineal gland, in which neither side had the complete or consistent advantage; sometimes the soul prevailed, and sometimes it was overwhelmed by the strength of the body's demands. Thus Descartes saw competition between body and soul as the essence of the human condition.

In sum, Descartes presented a mixed message about the nature of human beings. On the one hand, he taught that people's bodies are like machines, capable of being studied by the methods of the physical sciences. But he also taught that the soul—the most valuable and unique of human attributes—lies beyond the reach of scientific method and can be approached only by rational reflection. And he approached the presumed interaction between these altogether different substances with a mixture of anatomical inference, psychological introspection, and logical analysis that strikes a modern reader—as it struck Princess Elizabeth—as strange.

Despite the archaic quality of some of his formulations, Descartes' interactive dualism has had a lasting appeal. Minds and bodies are still commonly thought of as different and often opposed entities today, in such expressions as "mind over matter," "strong bodies and sound minds," and the physician's "psychosomatic illness." And Descartes' basic contention that there is something scientifically different about subjective consciousness, placing it beyond the reach of ordinary "objective" investigation or explanation by mechanistic analysis, has exercised psychological theorists ever since. We shall see how some of his successors disagreed with him and how others deliberately tried to avoid the question altogether. But the general issue has remained alive, and at the heart of psychology's development as a science.

Descartes' Influence

The final decade of Descartes' life brought conflict, change, and tragic irony. He had followed his successful *Discourse on Method* with two more published philosophical works, the *Meditations on First Philosophy* (1641) and *Principles of Philosophy* (1644). To his disgust, however, these works aroused public controversy. After going out of his way to make his works acceptable to the Catholic Church, he found himself under attack by Protestant clergy in Holland, who succeeded for a time in getting his books banned from Dutch universities because they allegedly promoted free thinking and atheism. For Descartes, a man of sincere religious faith and tolerance, this was almost too much to bear. He drastically slowed down his rate of publication, sending only the *Passions of the Soul* to the printer, and confining the rest of his thought to unpublished manuscripts and long, discursive letters to a few trusted individuals, including Elizabeth and another royal figure who had become interested by his thought, Queen Christina (1626–1689) of Sweden.

Christina invited Descartes to come to Sweden and be philosopher-in-residence at her court. Even though she suggested he come in the warmer months of spring or summer, he inexplicably decided in the fall of 1649 to give up his blessed Dutch anonymity in favor of the fashionable life of a courtier. The venture spelled disaster from the beginning, as the philosopher was asked to spend part of his valuable time writing verses to accompany frivolous theatrical productions celebrating Christina's accomplishments. Most ironically of all, the queen demanded her philosophical lessons at five o'clock in the morning. Regularly forced to abandon his meditational bed before sunrise during the bitter Swedish winter, Descartes contracted pneumonia. On February 11, 1650, just four months after arriving in Sweden, he died at the age of 53.

Like many other philosophers of meditational bent, some of whom we shall meet later, Descartes never married. He fathered and provided for one illegitimate daughter, born to one of his servants, but she died in childhood. Thus, Descartes left no direct descendants. Few people, however, have ever left greater intellectual legacies. Besides his contributions to mathematics, philosophy, and the physical sciences, he provided many seminal ideas for a new science of psychology, which we shall investigate further in the following chapters.

In Chapter 3, for example, we shall see how Descartes' successors continued his analyses of the brain. The specific "hydraulic" mechanisms he proposed and the central organizing role he gave to the pineal gland both turned out to be wrong. But his general point—that the brain is the most important individual organ in the mediation of behavior—was certainly correct, and his mistaken specific hypotheses provided valuable starting points for future research. The filament-and-fluid method of neural transmission was another of Descartes' conceptions wrong in its specifics but immensely productive in general. In Chapter 4, we shall see how the nerves have continued to be recognized as the purveyors of sensory information from sense organ to brain; now, however, electrochemical mechanisms of transmission replace the ones proposed by Descartes. Further, his general idea of the reflex as a stimulus-response sequence mediated by the nervous system remains a basic psychological concept. Chapter 9 will show how the concepts of innate and acquired reflexes lay at the heart of the historically influential approach to psychology known as behaviorism.

In appreciating the importance of inner functions such as emotions and passions as complements to external stimulation in the causation of behavior, Descartes also anticipated the main tenets of modern "dynamic psychology." Chapter 11 will describe Sigmund Freud's psychoanalysis—a conception of human beings as creatures in conflict, constantly impelled in contradictory directions by their inner instincts for sex and aggression, their rational and moral precepts, and the constraints of external reality. Freud's model parallels Descartes' vision of the human body as a machine controlled by the combined and often conflicting influences of the animal spirits, the rational soul, and external stimulation.

Perhaps most seminal of all has been Descartes' general philosophy of mind, with its diverse aspects of nativism, rationalism, and interactive dualism. His successors have responded to various aspects of this philosophy in innumerably different ways, accepting and rejecting its various components in varying combinations. These debates laid the groundwork for the emergence of a scientific psychology of the mind by the latter part of the nineteenth century. One particularly important successor, the Englishman John Locke (1632–1704), admired Descartes' mechanistic physical analyses but reacted against his nativism and rationalism while establishing the most important tradition of empiricism in psychology. And the German Gottfried Wilhelm Leibniz (1646–1716) accepted much of Descartes' philosophy of mind but rejected his physics, while furthering a powerful countervailing tradition of nativism. Many further aspects of modern psychology have derived from these two great heirs to Descartes, whose lives and works are the subject of the next chapter.

Summary

This opening chapter introduced several of the most important issues central to the eventual emergence of a science of psychology through an account of the life and work of the important early modern philosopher, **René Descartes**. Descartes' comprehensive system of mental philosophy originated in his quest to discover how it was possible to know anything to be real or true. He developed a method of *doubting everything* and ultimately came to the conclusion that the one thing he could not doubt was the act of his own doubting. The action and existence of his own thinking mind, or soul, was indubitably real. This idea stimulated him to seek out other ideas that, while "real," were incapable of being represented by a single sensory experience. He came up with notions such as "perfection," "unity," "infinity," and the geometrical axioms. Descartes concluded that such **innate ideas**, independent as they are of specific sensory experience, must derive from the nature of the thinking soul itself. For the belief that we come to know through conscious and rational reflection, Descartes is considered a **rationalist**. Because his system posits the existence of innate ideas, he is also known as a **nativist**. This is in contrast to other **empiricist** philosophers who believe that ideas come primarily through experience.

Descartes then applied his method of doubting to the physical world and concluded that there existed two **simple natures** that constituted the most elementary units of this world and that cannot be doubted—**extension** and motion. He believed that all phenomena of the physical world should be ultimately explainable in terms of these two properties. Descartes was a pioneer in suggesting that the human body, as part of the physical world, could be *completely* explained in terms of its material components and mechanical processes. Descartes extended this mechanistic analysis to a large number of neurophysiological processes, introducing the notion of the **reflex** and accounting for many "psychological" processes, including sensation and perception, memory, and associative learning. At the same time, he insisted that the thinking and willing activities of the human **rational soul** *cannot* be subject to such explanation, stating that the body and the soul (or mind) are entirely different substances. He is thus known as a mind-body **dualist**. This issue regarding the extent to which the mind and mental processes can be subject to mechanistic explanations would retain its prominence throughout the history of scientific psychology, and variations of the debate continue today.

Key Pioneers

Aristotle, p. 18

Beeckman, Isaac, p. 22

Descartes, René, p. 15

Copernicus, Nicolaus, p. 18

Galen, p. 31

Galilei, Galileo, p. 26

Harvey, William, p. 30

Mersenne, Marin, p. 19

Princess Elizabeth of Bohemia, p. 39

Key Terms

analytic geometry, p. 23

animal spirits, p. 31

cerebrospinal fluid (CSF), p. 31

dualism, p. 38

empiricism, p. 38

extension, p. 26

innate ideas, p. 38

nativism, p. 38

neuropsychology, p. 31

passions, p. 43

primary qualities (Galileo), p. 26

rationalism, p. 38

reflex, p. 32

scholastic philosophers, p. 18

secondary qualities (Galileo), p. 26

simple natures, p. 25

soul, p. 18

   rational soul, p. 18

   sensitive soul, p. 18

   vegetative soul, p. 18

ventricles, p. 31

Discussion Questions and Topics

1 Although most of Descartes' *specific* formulations about the ways the human body and brain work have been discarded, why are his ideas relevant for understanding the history of scientific psychology?

2 Descartes believed that there are some concepts or ideas that can never be directly apprehended in experience, such as perfection or unity. Do you agree? How do we come to an understanding or knowledge of these concepts that we all share?

3 What are some of the implications of Descartes' mind-body problem for neuroscientists in the twenty-first century?

Suggested Readings

For fuller biographical information, see Jack R. Vrooman's *René Descartes: A Biography* (New York: Putnam's, 1970) and (for readers of French) the classic *La Vie de Monsieur Des-Cartes* by Descartes' younger contemporary Adrien Baillet, in Volume 13 of the complete edition of Descartes' *Oeuvres*, edited by Charles Adam and Paul Tannery (Paris: Cerf, 1897–1913). In *The Life of René Descartes* (Boston: Godine, 2002), a more recent biographer, Richard Watson, has challenged some of Baillet's details, charging that they show too much positive bias toward his hero. For a provocative discussion of Descartes' personality and its relation to his thought, see Julian Jaynes, "The Problem of Animate Motion in the Seventeenth Century," in *Historical Conceptions of Psychology*, edited by Mary Henle, Julian Jaynes, and John J. Sullivan (New York: Springer, 1973).

The best single introduction to Descartes' thought is unquestionably his own *Discourse on Method*, available in numerous editions; it is included along with several other of his important works in *Descartes: Philosophical Writings* (New York: Modern Library 1958). *Treatise of Man* has been translated, and published with a useful introduction and facsimile of the original French edition, by Thomas Steele Hall (Cambridge, MA: Harvard University Press, 1972). For details on Descartes' relationship and correspondence with Princess Elizabeth, see Andrea Nye, *The Princess and the Philosopher* (Lanham, MD: Rowman and Littlefield, 1999).

For useful explications of Descartes' works, see Norman Kemp Smith, *New Studies in the Philosophy of Descartes* (New York: Russell and Russell, 1963), and William R. Shea, *The Magic of Numbers and Motion: The Scientific Career of René Descartes* (Canton, MA: Watson Publishing International, 1991). Herbert Butterfield's *The Origins of Modern Science: 1300–1800* (London: Bell and Sons, 1957) describes the larger scientific context in which Descartes worked, and for a brief and highly accessible account of the "scientific revolution" and Descartes' role in it (which the author provocatively argues wasn't actually a revolution in any strict sense of the term), see Steven Shapin, *The Scientific Revolution* (Chicago: The University of Chicago Press, 1996).

Philosophers of Mind

John Locke and Gottfried Leibniz

2

John Locke: Child of Revolution
Shaftesbury and the Political Origins of Locke's Works

An Essay Concerning Human Understanding
The Nature of Human Knowledge

Locke's Influence

Leibniz's Life and Career
Discoveries in Paris

Serving the House of Hanover

Leibniz's Philosophy of Mind
The Monadology
New Essays on Human Understanding

Summary

Key Pioneers

Key Terms

Discussion Questions and Topics

Suggested Readings

In early 1697, the German philosopher **Gottfried Wilhelm Leibniz** (1646–1716) tried unsuccessfully to engage the Englishman **John Locke** (1632–1704) in correspondence. Leibniz had read and been impressed by Locke's recent book, *An Essay Concerning Human Understanding*, which discussed the nature of human knowledge from an empiricist's point of view—that is, as the result of concrete sensory experience But Leibniz had also felt the Englishman's empiricism went too far, overlooking the role of several important properties innate to the mind. He ventured to express these nativist reservations in a short paper, which he asked a mutual friend to transmit to Locke along with the assurance that "it is not possible to express in a letter the great character Monsieur Leibniz has of you."

Locke reacted coolly to Leibniz's comments, however, and did not condescend to reply. He told a friend, "Mr. L's great name had raised in me an expectation which the sight of his paper did not answer. This sort of fiddling makes me hardly avoid thinking that he is not the very great man as has been talked of him."[1] Upon learning that Locke had "not understood" his criticisms, Leibniz elaborated on them in a book-length manuscript titled *Nouveaux Essais sur l'Entendement Humain* (*New Essays on Human Understanding*), in which a fictional representative of Locke engages in Platonic-style dialogue with a mouthpiece for Leibniz himself. Unfortunately, Locke died just as Leibniz finished this work. Averse to disputing with dead authors, Leibniz put his manuscript aside and it remained unpublished until a half-century after his own death.

It was unfortunate that these two greatest philosophers of their time never entered into real dialogue, for Leibniz had some issues of genuine substance to argue, and Locke's replies would have been of great interest. Moreover, despite their theoretical differences, the two had much in common. Both had extremely wide interests, ranging from history and economics to science and religion. Both had rejected opportunities to pursue academic careers in favor of participation in the "real world" of politics and public affairs. Politics then being largely the domain of the wealthy aristocracy, both of these middle-class men had had to function as courtiers, working under the patronage of aristocratic sponsors who valued their services. And both had tried to integrate their political ideas with a larger and general philosophy of mind, derived in part from the earlier work of Descartes.

But here was the rub, for while each had been greatly influenced by the Frenchman, each had reacted for and against different aspects of his system. Locke had accepted many of Descartes' basic ideas regarding physics and physiology while emphatically rejecting the notion of a constantly active conscious soul, brought into the world with a ready-made supply of innate ideas. He endorsed Aristotle's suggestion that the mind resembles a blank slate at birth, capable only of recording impressions from the external world and subsequently recalling and reflecting upon them. Arguing that all human knowledge comes from experience and that the best models for obtaining truth were set by Galileo, Newton, and the new breed of scientists who arrived at conclusions by observation and experiment, Locke became the leading proponent of the empiricist reaction against Descartes.

Leibniz, by contrast, strongly objected to aspects of Descartes' physics. On logical grounds, he disputed that infinitely divisible material particles (Descartes' "simple natures") could ever be taken as the ultimate units of reality. He did agree with Descartes about the unquestionable reality of the conscious soul, however, and therefore concluded that the ultimate "substance" of the universe must be some consciousness-bearing, soul-like entity that precedes all apprehension of the physical world. Thus, he propounded a philosophy of mind emphasizing the nativist and rationalist tendencies of Descartes.

From Locke and Leibniz have sprung two major and often competing traditions in the history of psychology. The empiricist, Lockean tradition has been particularly influential in British and American psychologies, which have emphasized the role of experience in forming the mind and the functions of the mind in learning to predict and control events in the external, peripheral environment. The Leibnizean tradition, relatively stronger on the European continent, has placed greater emphasis on the controlling and central functions of an active and innately given mind. To see how these contrasting points of view developed, we turn now to the individual stories of their two great originators.

John Locke: Child of Revolution

The son of a minor attorney, John Locke was born in the English Somerset town of Wrington on August 29, 1632 (see Figure 2.1). He later said he had been born in the midst of a storm, for England then lay on the brink of revolution, and his family was involved. Like most people in their region, the Lockes favored the Puritan "roundheads," who shortly would battle for the rights of Parliament and dissenting religious groups against the Royalist "cavaliers," who endorsed the absolute and divine rights of the monarchy and the central religious authority of the established Church of England.

When civil war broke out in 1642, Locke's father fought briefly and somewhat ingloriously under Colonel Alexander Popham, the local Member of Parliament and one of his legal clients. Both men retired

FIG 2.1
John Locke (1632–1704)

from the military after some early losses, Popham to concentrate on parliamentary politics, and the elder Locke to become a county clerk for sewers. But after the war turned decisively in their side's favor in 1647, Popham was in a position to do his lawyer's son a favor. The famous Westminster School in London had come under parliamentary control, and Popham sponsored 15-year-old John Locke for admission.

Little is known of Locke's life until that time, except that he had grown up in a small, middle-class, provincial household. At Westminster, however, his experience broadened considerably under the influence of Richard Busby, the able Royalist headmaster who had been allowed to remain by his new parliamentary overseers in an act of tolerance that Busby reciprocated. Without hiding his own opinions—for example, he led the school in public prayer when King Charles I was executed nearby in 1649—Busby taught his pupils to think for themselves and to be wary of *anyone* who tried to influence them by mere propaganda. From Busby and some fellow pupils who were also Royalists, Locke learned the lasting lesson that there are two sides to most stories.

After five years at Westminster, Locke won a scholarship to Christ's Church College at Oxford University, which would remain his home for many years. There he befriended other conservatives, and after the failure of Oliver Cromwell's Commonwealth he greeted the 1660 restoration of the monarchy with King Charles II as enthusiastically as any hereditary aristocrat. At the same time, other moderating and liberalizing influences were also at work. Prime among these influences were the anti-authoritarian attitudes implicit in the work of several *scientists* he encountered, who stressed the concrete observation and experimentation with nature, rather than the traditional study of classical texts. Although Oxford's official curriculum still contained no science, a few members of the faculty practiced and taught the new observational approach to medicine. Thomas Willis, for example, studied brain anatomy in unprecedented detail and made several fundamental discoveries about the brain that we shall review in the next chapter. After earning a degree in classics, Locke studied seriously with Willis and some other progressive Oxford physicians and became a skillful doctor.

Another proponent of the new experimental science, **Robert Boyle** (1627–1691; see Figure 2 2), had settled privately at Oxford and built a home laboratory. There he conducted the famous experiments demonstrating what came to be known as *Boyle's law*, which states that the volume of a gas varies inversely with the pressure upon it. This work helped lay the foundations for modern chemistry. Sociable as well as scientifically ingenious, Boyle regularly invited others to his home for scientific discussion in gatherings that formed the nucleus for the future British Royal Society. Locke became one of the most active members and irritated one fellow participant who remembered him as "a man of turbulent spirit, clamorous and never contented." While most other members of the club "wrote and took notes from the mouth of their master," Locke "scorned to do it, so that while every man besides of the club were writing, he would be prating and troublesome."[2] Boyle himself enjoyed Locke's shows of independence and became a lifelong advisor, friend, and sharer of small jokes. He helped Locke to open a small scientific laboratory of his own in Oxford, and to solicit funds from fellow students to enlarge it. This led Locke to jest that they were thus engaging in "a new sort of chemistry; i.e., extracting money out of the scholars' pockets."[3]

Honble Robert Boyle

FIG 2.2
Robert Boyle
(1627–1691)

About this same time, Locke also encountered Descartes' works, which reinforced his growing belief that nothing should be taken on mere authority. He later recalled that Descartes' books first gave him "a relish of philosophical studies" and that "he rejoiced in reading of these because though he very often differed in opinion, . . . yet he found that what he had to say was very intelligible."[4]

In 1665, Locke's interests widened still further when he accepted a temporary post as secretary of a diplomatic mission to the German city of Cleves. There he got his first taste of practical politics and observed at first hand a higher degree of religious tolerance than prevailed in England. Locke's work pleased his superiors and led to another diplomatic offer, but he had not enjoyed all aspects of foreign living and felt reluctant to accept. Thus as the summer of 1666 began, John Locke had little sense of where his life was leading. Nearly 34 years old, he had tried and succeeded moderately well in classical scholarship, medicine, science, and diplomacy. Each had held its attractions, but none had really gripped him for a permanent vocation. And although he had inherited a modest independent income from his parents, it would not support him indefinitely. At this point, fate intervened as he had a fortuitous meeting with one of England's most important political leaders.

Shaftesbury and the Political Origins of Locke's Works

Sir Anthony Ashley Cooper (1621–1683; see Figure 2.3) had begun the Civil War a Royalist, but he changed sides to become one of Cromwell's major roundhead commanders in 1644. He then served in Cromwell's government, but when the Commonwealth failed he joined those advocating the restoration of the monarchy. As one of the parliamentary escorts who brought Charles II back from the continent as the new king in 1660, he impressed Charles and became a top advisor. In 1661 he was named Baron Ashley and appointed Chancellor of the Exchequer, a post he retained until he was elevated to Lord Chancellor and made the first Earl of Shaftesbury in 1672. When he met Locke in 1666, he was still called Lord Ashley (the title of address for a baron), and his political star was very much on the rise.

The meeting occurred because Ashley, in chronic ill health from a liver cyst, visited Oxford to drink medicinal waters drawn from a nearby spring. The doctor he had hired to bring him bottles of the water became ill and asked his colleague John Locke to fill in for him.

FIG 2.3
Sir Anthony
Ashley Cooper
(1621–1683)

A mix-up prevented the first day's delivery, so a deeply embarrassed Locke had to apologize to his eminent new client. Evidently he did so effectively, for Ashley wound up inviting him to stay for dinner.

Friendship developed, as Ashley found Locke to be a sensible, broadly educated gentleman as well as a knowledgeable physician, and Locke found in Ashley a mature political mentor whose diverse interests and tolerant views meshed perfectly with his own developing inclinations. Both men had sided at various times with each of the two great factions that divided England and had been repulsed by the violent extremes of each side. Both men favored toleration in religion and moderation in government. Ashley actively supported the religious rights of the numerous dissenting Protestant sects who sought protection from Parliament against persecution by the established Church of England and the aristocracy. And even as he now supported the new king, he advocated a constitutional as opposed to an absolute monarchy, and he strongly advocated parliamentary rights as a counterbalance to the king's power. Eventually, these views would bring Ashley into severe conflict with Charles. But they proved highly congenial to John Locke from the first, and when invited by his new friend to move to London as his personal physician, Locke happily accepted.

Locke quickly earned his keep when Ashley's cyst became dangerously inflamed and other doctors despaired of his life. After consulting the famous physician Thomas Sydenham, Locke took the radical step of inserting a silver drainage tube into the cyst through an abdominal incision. Ashley recovered wonderfully and soon after had Locke replace the silver tube with a gold one that he left in place for the remaining fifteen years of his life. Locke now became a trusted political as well as medical advisor, particularly so as Ashley became the leader of eight developers or "proprietors" of the wild "Carolina" territory in America (named after Charles, *Carolus* in Latin, and encompassing modern North and South Carolina). Ashley's importance is still reflected today in the names of the Ashley and Cooper Rivers that surround Charleston, SC, the first and most important city in the new region. Locke had a major hand in drafting the original "Fundamental Constitutions," or legal code for the Carolinas. This document was notable for its religious toleration and democratic principles, although both had limits. Freedom of worship was granted to all groups who believed in God except for Roman Catholics, whose influence was particularly feared in Restoration England. And the democratic right to vote was restricted to landowners of 50 acres or more. Property rights were paramount and strongly safeguarded, and among the "properties" explicitly defined and safeguarded were slaves, whose labor was essential to the Carolina economy from its earliest beginnings.[5]

Locke found London life stimulating in many other ways. Boyle had recently moved to town and helped found the Royal Society—quickly to become Britain's most important scientific organization—as an enlarged continuation of his Oxford groups. Locke became a Fellow of the Society in 1668 and thus kept abreast of the most important new scientific developments. He also developed the habit of meeting regularly with friends for the discussion of all sorts of political, religious, and philosophical issues. One informal but momentous gathering occurred in early 1671, when Locke met with a group of colleagues to discuss the vexed issue of "the principles of morality and revealed religion." With so many religious groups propounding different and sometimes mutually exclusive beliefs, the question arose as to how one might rationally choose among them. Locke recalled the meeting as follows:

> Five or six friends, meeting in my chamber and discoursing . . . , found themselves quickly at a stand by the difficulties that arose on every side. After we had awhile puzzled ourselves, without coming any nearer a resolution of those doubts which perplexed us, it came into my thoughts that we took a wrong course; and that before we set ourselves upon enquiries of that nature it was necessary to examine our own abilities, and see what objects our understandings were or were not fitted to deal with.[6]

Locke accordingly proposed a simple-seeming idea: to examine the nature of knowledge itself, and of the mind or "understanding" that obtains that knowledge, in order to discover exactly what it is possible to know—and just as important, not to know—with certainty. He optimistically thought he could resolve this preliminary issue in a page or two of analysis and then move on to the original religious and moral questions. In fact, it took nineteen years of intermittent work before he was satisfied, as his page or two expanded into his great book, the *Essay Concerning Human Understanding*.

In the meantime, political crises dominated much of Locke's attention, for in 1679 his patron confronted the most important and difficult battle of his life, regarding the succession to the monarchy. Charles II had no legitimate offspring, and under prevailing rules his younger brother James—a Catholic—would succeed. This troubled Shaftesbury and his allies because they feared that a Catholic king would owe primary allegiance to a non-English power, the pope. Thus, Shaftesbury successfully promoted an Exclusion Bill through Parliament, disqualifying Catholics from the succession. When Charles II refused to acquiesce, insisting on his brother's divine right to succeed him, a crisis ensued.

Shaftesbury now organized the first political party in England, the Whigs,* to champion the Protestant cause and limit the absolute, divine right claimed by Charles for the monarchy. Locke wrote several papers in support of the cause, including drafts for *Two Treatises of Government*—a work justifying the right of subjects to rebel against tyrannical authority—which laid the philosophical foundations of future American as well as British governments.

At first Locke prudently withheld publication of the *Treatises*, as matters went poorly for the Whigs. In 1681 Shaftesbury was seized by Charles's agents and imprisoned in the Tower of London. Although freed after a few months when a grand jury refused to indict him, he emerged a broken man. He fled to Holland and shortly died, leaving behind a party temporarily in retreat. Locke returned to Oxford, but upon discovering he was under unfriendly surveillance by the king's spies, he fled to Holland himself in 1684.

He remained there for five years, assuming the false name "Dr. van der Linden" and moving frequently to avoid being traced. While

---

* The name was originally coined by Shaftesbury's opponents from the Scottish "whiggamore," a term for cattle rustlers and horse thieves. In return, the Whigs labeled their foes the "Tories," another then-derogatory name for Irish-Catholic bandits who harassed the English in Ireland. The term *Whig* has largely lost its political meaning today, but of course Tory is still applied to the Conservative parties in Canada and the United Kingdom.

prudent, such secretiveness was also much in Locke's character. His major biographer has described him as "never a candid man," with an "almost Gothic fondness of mystery for the sake of mystery."[7] Even before coming to Holland, Locke had kept notes in secret codes and shorthand, and he sometimes used invisible ink in correspondence. A handsome bachelor, he had exchanged romantic letters with women he addressed only as "Scribelia" and "Philoclea" while calling himself "Atticus" and "Philander." And while it was obvious to all who knew him that he had fled to Holland because of its congenial political climate, he insisted publicly that it had been mainly for the beer.

Still, Locke overcame his secretiveness sufficiently to meet fellow English libertarians such as William Penn when they visited Holland, and to befriend several liberal Dutch scholars. And most important, he found leisure to work on his manuscripts for *Essay Concerning Human Understanding* and *Two Treatises of Government.* As he polished them in Holland, events occurred in England to clear the way for their eventual safe publication. Charles II died in 1685 and was in fact succeeded by his Catholic brother, James II. But after an abortive rebellion in 1685, the Whigs succeeded in overthrowing James three years later, replacing him with his own Protestant daughter Mary and her Dutch husband, William of Orange. Shortly after this so-called "Glorious Revolution,"* Locke returned to England openly and in triumph, as part of the new queen's personal party. Back home under the new regime, he at last felt safe to entrust his manuscripts to the printer. The first editions of his *Essay* and *Two Treatises* both appeared in 1690, followed by a stream of other works on philosophy, religion, education, and economics. For these works Locke became the most widely recognized and honored of English philosophers, rivaling in his own sphere the great Isaac Newton in science.

---

* Unsurprisingly, this term was coined by historians sympathetic to the Whig cause, and the term *Whig history* has come to be used by historians to refer to accounts that are primarily celebratory in nature, written by the victors, or that evaluate the past in terms of present standards that did not exist at the time of the events depicted. The limitations of Whig history are highlighted by the British historian Herbert Butterfield in his influential book *The Whig Interpretation of History* (New York: Norton, 1965).

Throughout this final phase of his, life Locke lived as a paying guest on the Essex estate of Sir Francis and **Lady Damaris Cudworth Masham** (1659–1708). Lady Masham, the daughter of a distinguished Cambridge philosopher named Ralph Cudworth, was an accomplished philosophical and theological scholar in her own right, and also the "Philoclea" of one of Locke's earlier romantic correspondences. The details of how they met and the extent of their actual romantic relationship are unknown, but while Locke had been in his Dutch exile Damaris Cudworth married Sir Francis Masham and the couple had a son. After Locke moved in, they all lived harmoniously under the same roof, as the aging philosopher took an interest in the growing boy and his education. In 1693 he published *Some Thoughts Concerning Education*, a short work advocating education based on experience and scientific observation, as opposed to the memorization of Greek and Latin. In the meantime, Lady Masham published some significant writings of her own on theology and corresponded with a number of important philosophers, including Gottfried Leibniz in Germany—although Locke seems to have taken little notice of these activities. When he died in 1704, he left a bequest of books and money to the Mashams' son and a text for his own gravestone that read, in part: "A scholar by training, he devoted his studies wholly to the pursuit of truth. Such you may learn from his writings, which will also tell you whatever else there is to be said about him more faithfully than the dubious eulogies of an epitaph."[8] In conformity with this advice, we turn now to the most important of Locke's writings.

An Essay Concerning Human Understanding

In introducing his *Essay*, Locke explicitly tied his own thought to the work of his great contemporary scientists. With perhaps a touch of false modesty he wrote: "Everyone must not hope to be a *Boyle* or a *Sydenham*; and in an age that produces such masters as the great *Huygenius* [the mathematician Christian Huygens] and the incomparable *Mr. Newton* . . . it is ambition enough to be employed as an under-labourer in clearing the ground a little, and removing some of the rubbish that lies in the way of knowledge."[9] Locke believed the recent discoveries of these men represented the pinnacle of human knowledge, and accordingly he adopted their observational and inductive methods as his ideal model for how the human mind operates best. At least in theory, the scientists had succeeded by making many concrete observations of the subjects they wished to understand, without initial presuppositions as to what to expect. Within such masses of observations, they detected recurrent patterns and regularities that formed the basis of their scientific laws.* Locke's *Essay* assumed a human mind that operates basically according to this inductive model, developing all of its knowledge from observations of things in the external world.

Locke thus saw the mind as essentially receptive and often passive, with the primary functions of sensing and perceiving. With a touch of sarcasm, he denied Descartes's conception of the mind as constantly active:

> I confess myself to have one of those dull souls, that doth not perceive itself always to contemplate ideas; nor can conceive it any more necessary for the soul always to think, than for the body always to move: the perception of ideas being (as I conceive) to the soul what motion is to the body: not its essence, but one of its operations.[10]

Locke further disagreed with Descartes by denying the reality of innate ideas. He argued that the ideas and principles most often claimed to be innate do *not* occur in inexperienced or enfeebled minds. Thus, the ideas of *infinity* and *perfection*, considered by Descartes to be beyond experience and therefore innate (see page 38), seemed to Locke to be the results of abstraction beyond the capabilities of the very young and the mentally disabled. The notion that the same thing cannot both be and not be—another idea widely held to be universal and part of the inborn wisdom of the mind—was according

---

* Philosophers and historians of science have noted that this model was never followed completely in practice, since it is impossible to make observations absolutely neutrally, without presuppositions about what to look for. We shall see shortly that a variant of this same argument was made against Locke's philosophy of mind by Leibniz.

to Locke manifestly not understood and accepted by young children and deranged adults. Because such "universals" were really not universal at all but existed only in reasonably well-functioning minds that had already had a certain amount of experience, they seemed the very opposite of innate.

Locke postulated a mind devoid of ideas at conception but passively receptive to sensation—a *tabula rasa* (blank slate) or "white paper void of all characters." And then, in one of the *Essay*'s most ringing passages, he asked:

> How comes this blank slate to be furnished? Whence comes it by that vast store which the busy and boundless fancy of man has painted on it with an almost endless variety? Whence has it all the materials of reason and knowledge? To this I answer, in one word, from *experience*; in that all our knowledge is founded, and from that it ultimately derives itself.[11]

Moving to the issue of what *kinds* of experiences the mind has, Locke said there were just two: sensations of objects in the external world, and reflections of the mind's own operations. Such experiences produce representations or ideas in the mind, which not only occupy consciousness immediately but also remain potentially recallable in the form of memories.

Locke argued that the inexperienced infant's earliest sensations and reflections give rise to a variety of **simple ideas**. Simple ideas from sensation are concepts such as redness, loudness, coldness, or saltiness; from reflection they are notions such as willing, perceiving, liking, or disliking. With further experience, simple ideas may be combined by the mind in varying combinations to produce **complex ideas**. For example, redness, roundness, and sweetness may combine in producing the idea of an apple; the ideas of apple and desiring may combine to produce part of the still more complex idea of hunger.

Although some complex ideas may represent things that do not exist in reality, Locke insisted that all of the simple *components* of such ideas must have been previously experienced concretely. For example, we can have the idea of a man with green hair without ever having seen such a person, but not without previous experience of men, hair, and greenness. Without a concrete experiential basis in simple ideas, even the most obviously "true" of complex ideas are impossible. The Irish scientist **William Molyneux** (1656–1696) suggested a famous illustration of this point in a letter Locke quoted in his *Essay*:

> Suppose a man born blind, and now adult, and taught by his touch to distinguish between a cube and a sphere of the same metal. . . . Suppose then the cube and sphere placed on a table, and the blind man made to see: *quaere* [query], whether by his sight, before he touched them, he could now distinguish and tell which is the globe, which the cube?

Such an experiment had never been performed, but Molyneux and Locke had no doubt the answer would be no: "Though the blind man has obtained the experience of how a globe, how a cube affects his touch, yet he has not yet obtained the experience that what affects his touch so and so must affect his sight so and so; or that a protuberant angle in the cube, that pressed his hand unequally, shall appear to his eye as it does in the cube."[12] That is, visual components cannot be part of the complex ideas of a cube or a sphere until they have first been experienced as simple ideas and then connected with the appropriate tactile ideas. (The general truth of this position has been dramatically demonstrated since Locke's time, as surgeons have been able to remove congenital cataracts and thus bestow sight on patients blind since birth. Such patients quite literally had to learn how to see—a prolonged and often difficult process.[13])

The Nature of Human Knowledge

After asserting these basic principles regarding the nature of ideas, Locke discussed what human minds can *know* about them. "Knowledge," he insisted, is "nothing but the perception of the connexion and agreement, or disagreement and repugnancy, of any of our ideas."[14] A very few such perceptions are immediate and irresistible, as when we recognize the difference (disagreement) between something black and something white, or between a circle and a triangle. Such knowledge—that black is not white or that a circle is not a triangle—Locke called **intuitive knowledge**. Less immediate but equally certain is **demonstrative knowledge**, arrived at by stepwise logical deductions, each of which is intuitively certain, but the total pattern of which is not. The conclusions arrived at in Euclidean geometry— for example, that the three internal angles of a triangle always add up to 180 degrees or that the sum of the squares of the sides of a right triangle exactly equals the square of the hypotenuse—exemplify demonstrative knowledge.

By far the largest part of human knowledge is neither intuitively nor demonstrably certain, however, but depends on the particular patterns of sensory experiences one happens to have with objects in the world. This **sensitive knowledge**, concerning the existence and nature of those objects and experiences, was problematical for Locke and can be accepted as "true" only subject to certain conditions. Like Galileo and Descartes, Locke posited a distinction between those **primary qualities** that actually inhere in perceived objects (akin to Descartes' "simple natures," as described in Chapter 1) and the **secondary qualities** imposed on objects by the senses. The primary qualities, Locke argued, are *solidity*, *extension*, *figure*, and *mobility*; material objects in the world truly "have" these qualities, which accordingly constitute the fundamental units for constructing a true picture of the world.

But the mind also perceives objects to have "secondary" qualities such as sounds, colors, temperatures, tastes, and odors—characteristics that derive as much from the sense organs as from the objects themselves. The sound of a bell and the taste of an apple, for example, reside just as much in the perceiving ear and tongue as in the objects themselves. Locke saw the ideas produced by secondary qualities as less certain and true than those of the primary qualities, and he illustrated this supposition with a concrete example: If you immerse one hand in cold water and the other in hot for a minute or so, then place both in tepid water, the tepid water "may produce the sensation of heat in one hand and cold in the other, whereas it is impossible that the same water, if those ideas were really in it, should at the same time be both hot and cold."[15]

Thus, our sensations of secondary qualities may deceive, and Locke accordingly saw the acquisition of "true" sensitive knowledge as requiring the explanation of secondary qualities in terms of the more basic primary ones, on which they ultimately depend. A bucket of water's "true" temperature lies not in inherent qualities of warmth or cold, but in the speed of vibration of its particles—which may appear fast to a hand whose own particles have been slowed down by previous insertion in cold water, but slow to the one previously speeded up by hot water. The sound of a bell can be reduced to the effect of its primary qualities—its vibrations or "motility"—in creating sound waves that produce complementary motion in the receptive organs of the ear. Such analyses, of course, were precisely the goals of the great physical scientists whose work Locke admired so much.

Locke saw further impediments to "true" sensitive knowledge in the inevitable fact that any one person's experience of the world is incomplete, and to some degree random. In the fourth edition of the *Essay* he introduced the term **association of ideas**, arguing that experience can cause ideas to become linked together in infinitely varying combinations. While some of these combinations have "a natural correspondence and connexion with one another," others, "not at all of kin," come to be connected "wholly owing to chance or custom."[16] The first category of "natural" associations includes the redness and roundness of apples and (especially) the lawfully interconnected phenomena discovered by scientific analysis. The second category includes all of one's "accidentally" linked ideas—for example, customs dictated by culture rather than nature, superstitions, and one's idiosyncratically connected experiences. Although only the first class of associations constitutes truly valid knowledge, both kinds can seem equally compelling. Thus, a child who has been repeatedly told that goblins inhabit the dark may come to believe in the association between darkness and goblins just as strongly as in that between the redness and roundness of apples.

Locke's *Essay* did not specify exactly *how* ideas come to be associated, although his examples suggest the importance of the factors of *contiguity* (the experiencing of two or more ideas either simultaneously or in rapid succession) and *similarity*. These themes would be substantially elaborated on by his philosophical successors. His own primary intention was simply to emphasize the provisional and uncertain nature of much of what passes for knowledge, because it is based on associations of ideas that occur by accident, rather than being truly grounded in nature.

Locke's Influence

The *Essay*'s essential message—that all knowledge comes from experience but that no one person's experience can be sufficient to create a complete and error-free knowledge of the world—accorded well with the new British political climate. Because no single person could claim absolute wisdom or exclusive access to truth, toleration was in order on religious questions, and wide participation was desirable in the affairs of government. Locke spelled out these implications in his second major book of 1690, *Two Treatises of Government.*

Here he modified and elaborated on the theory of the **social contract**, earlier introduced by his countryman **Thomas Hobbes** (1588–1679) to account for the origins and purposes of civil government. Hobbes saw human beings as innately aggressive, self-centered, and predatory. Left on their own in the state of nature, people's lives would inevitably be "solitary, poor, nasty, brutish and short." Thus expediency led our ancestors to join together in groups, with supreme authority invested in centralized powers to organize defenses against other groups and to curtail wanton aggression within their own groups. For Hobbes, survival itself required acquiescence to a centralized authority, and such acquiescence was obligatory regardless of the specific form one's particular authority took. Accordingly, Hobbes supported the absolute powers of the monarchy, or of any other established government.

Locke, too, saw rulers and their subjects as bound together by an implicit social contract, but he held a more positive view of humanity in its "state of nature." His *Essay* implied that humans have the capacity to gain increasing amounts of valid knowledge from their experience and to profit from the combined experiences of groups of people. (In science, organizations such as the Royal Society provided excellent examples of the collective benefits to be had from the sharing of experiences and information.) Thus, Locke saw the establishment of the social contract as a *rational* choice, bringing real advantage to individuals by investing protective and regulatory functions in a centralized authority. Under normal circumstances, reason and concern for the common good dictate that individuals obey that authority. But Locke argued that governments could and sometimes did exceed the reasonable limits of their authority. He saw the contract as going two ways, and when a government grossly violates its subjects' interests, those subjects have a "natural" right to be heard. And if the government's excesses persist, subjects have a right to rebel and establish a new authority. Here was justification for the "Glorious Revolution" in England, and here was the philosophy of government later to be adopted by America's founding fathers. The U.S. Constitution's system of participatory democracy, and its checks and balances among the executive, legislative, and judicial branches, were expressly designed to enshrine the values implicit in Locke's analysis.

Locke also profoundly influenced subsequent philosophy and psychology, inspiring a tradition in mental philosophy commonly called **British associationism**. Its most prominent early member, the Irish bishop **George Berkeley** (1685–1753), applied Locke's associationistic principles to the systematic analysis of visual depth perception. Berkeley argued that the ability to see things in three dimensions is not innate, but rather the result of learned associations between the visual impressions of objects at different distances and the concurrent sensations of muscular movements in the eyes and body as one moves toward or away from the objects. More controversially, Berkeley disputed Locke's distinction between primary and secondary qualities, arguing that *all* sensory ideas, including those of solidity, extension, figure, and mobility, were only "in the mind" and essentially mental creations rather than independently existing qualities.

Later, the Scotsman **David Hume** (1711–1776; see Figure 2.4) followed Aristotle in proposing two specific laws of association that determine how and when ideas get linked together by experience. The **law of association by contiguity** asserts that ideas experienced either simultaneously or in rapid succession (that is, contiguously in time) will tend to be linked together in the future; the **law of association by similarity** holds that ideas or experiences that resemble each other will also tend to be associated together. As we shall see in Chapter 4, Hume questioned the reality of any meaningful relationships among ideas apart from their associations by contiguity and similarity: He reduced even the cherished scientific notion of "causality" to the assumption— but not the absolute certainty—that patterns of association experienced in the past will continue indefinitely into the future.

Hume's contemporary **David Hartley** (1705–1757), a physician, attempted to integrate associationism with neurophysiology by arguing

FIG 2.4
David Hume
(1711–1776)

that specific "ideas" are occasioned by minute vibrations in specific locations of the brain and nerves. Nerve fibers presumably transmit vibrations from one location to another, thus constituting a physical basis for the association or linkage of specific ideas. In the nineteenth century, the father and son team of **James Mill** (1773–1836) and **John Stuart Mill** (1806–1873) claimed that virtually all important individual differences among people in character, conduct, and intellect arise according to associationistic principles; that is, people differ from each other mainly because of differences in their experiences and associations, rather than because of their innate endowments. Others have taken exception to the Mills' claim, and we shall later see several occasions where this "nature versus nurture" question has inspired important psychological developments.

Chapter 9 will show that many of these basic Lockean ideas came together, although stripped of their "mentalistic" terminology, in the important twentieth-century movement known as **behaviorism**. Behavioristic psychologists explained all learning as the acquisition and interconnection (association) of various neurologically mediated stimulus-response connections or reflexes and emphasized the extent to which individuals may be trained or "conditioned" by their experience.

But even as Locke inspired a large number of successors to accept and develop his basic empiricism and environmentalism, he also stimulated others to stress certain mental phenomena that his philosophy deemphasized, ignored, or denied. His contemporary Leibniz called attention to a number of these phenomena, thereby initiating a competing and equally influential school of thought for the subsequent development of psychology.

Leibniz's Life and Career

Gottfried Wilhelm Leibniz was born in Leipzig, Germany, on July 1, 1646. His father, a professor of moral philosophy at the city's famous university, taught Gottfried to read and love books, but unfortunately he died when his son was 6. Sent to school to continue his education, young Gottfried quickly astonished his teacher by translating a Latin text usually read only by university students. This precociousness created debate, for the teacher thought a young child should be kept away from books so unsuited to his age, while another family friend said it proved Gottfried should be granted access to his father's locked-up library. Fortunately, the latter advice prevailed, and by age 12 Leibniz had read most of the Latin classics and the works of the Church fathers, and had also made a good start at Greek. At 14 he was admitted to the University of Leipzig.

There he quickly completed the standard classical curriculum, and at 19 he wrote a dissertation on combinatorial logic and finished studies for a doctorate in law. Now his age worked against him, however, for the university awarded only twelve law doctorates each year, and if there were too many qualified candidates priority was determined by age. Leibniz was told to wait until the next year. Enraged, he left Leipzig for the smaller University of Altdorf, submitted his dissertation, and won his degree within six months. The impressed Altdorf authorities offered him a professorship, but Leibniz—perhaps understandably disgusted by academic politics—said he had "different things in view." In an age when paying positions for intellectuals outside universities or the Church were rare, he began his lifelong quest for work that would both support him financially and satisfy his voracious intellectual appetites.

At first he became secretary to a Nuremberg alchemical society, a position he later said he won by submitting a letter full of obscure alchemical terminology that even he did not understand but that still impressed the society's officers. While there Leibniz developed an enduring interest in the project of transmuting base metals into gold (a possibility then taken seriously by many leading scientists of the day, including Locke and Newton in England), but the job itself failed to satisfy and he soon decided to move on.

In the city of Mainz he met by chance Baron Johann Christian von Boineburg, an important statesman in the service of the Elector of Mainz (one of the eight major German princes entitled to elect the Holy Roman Emperor, hence his title). Much as Lord Ashley had taken to John Locke a few years earlier, Boineburg recognized Leibniz as a young man of great general promise and secured him a position as legal advisor to the Elector. Leibniz (see Figure 2.5) now began his lifelong career as a courtier, earning his keep by meeting the demands of his aristocratic patrons while also trying to find time for his own multitudinous interests. At first things went well, as Leibniz worked with the Elector's blessing on such varied projects as

FIG 2.5
Gottfried Wilhelm
Leibniz (1646–1716)

a new method for teaching law, a cataloging system for libraries, and a scheme for the systematic review of new scholarly books. He also conducted research on the history and culture of China, a subject that would remain a lifelong interest. Finally, in 1672 he was dispatched to Paris on a delicate diplomatic mission, for what became the most intellectually satisfying and exciting four years of his life.

Discoveries in Paris

Leibniz's diplomatic goal was to persuade France's King Louis XIV to invade Egypt, as a means of deflecting French bellicosity away from the German states. He had even devised a detailed invasion plan almost identical to the one actually followed by Napoleon more than a century later. But like many of Leibniz's other ideas, this one was ahead of its time, and Louis refused to rise to the bait. Leibniz's diplomacy failed at its immediate purpose.

Nevertheless, he found much else to do in the French capital, managing to complete enough official business to satisfy his patrons while pursuing a variety of private interests. An inveterate tinkerer, he invented a new kind of watch with two symmetrical balance wheels, a prototypical submarine, and a mathematical calculating machine far superior to anything previously developed and that will be described in Chapter 14. He took the calculator to London in 1673, where it greatly impressed the members of the Royal Society and helped him gain election as one of that organization's first non-British members. (Although John Locke was then in London and a fellow member, there is no evidence that they met personally then or at any other time.)

Back in Paris, Leibniz met and befriended many leading intellectuals, including the mathematician Christian Huygens (the "great Huygenius" to whom Locke modestly compared himself in the introduction to his *Essay*) and the Cartesian philosopher Nicolas de Malebranche. Through such contacts he gained access to Descartes' unpublished as well as published works, which he studied deeply and with great interest. He also greatly expanded his sophistication in mathematics and made two fundamental discoveries in that field before leaving Paris in 1576.

One discovery was **binary arithmetic**—the representation of all numbers with just ones and zeroes. As we shall see in Chapter 14, binary arithmetic has become the standard form of representation and calculation in modern electronic computers. In the seventeenth century, however, this application remained far in the future. Even the best of mechanical calculators, such as Leibniz's own, used a cog-and-gear technology much better served by the standard decimal than by the binary system. Thus, even for Leibniz, binary arithmetic remained a creation of purely intellectual and logical interest, with no practical application.

The usefulness of his second and greater mathematical discovery, the **infinitesimal calculus**, became apparent immediately. Leibniz did not and could not know that Isaac Newton had already developed this mathematical technique a few years earlier, for the secretive Englishman had not shared his idea with anyone else. Leibniz was not so shy, however, and thus became the first person to *publish* the calculus. Moreover, he used a notation system much more flexible and convenient than Newton's, and it has remained in standard use ever since. Nowadays the two men are usually granted shared credit for the great discovery.

Essentially, Leibniz's calculus represented an extension of Descartes' analytical geometry, which had represented algebraic equations geometrically and graphically as lines and curves drawn on systems of coordinates. Its applications were limited, however, to curves technically defined as *conic sections*—that is, those circles, ellipses, and parabolas that may be produced by slicing through cones at various angles. With the calculus, Leibniz (and Newton) provided a technique for subjecting many more kinds of curves and continuously varying quantities to precise calculation—a development that made it possible to mathematically analyze physical phenomena such as the orbits of planets, the motions of pendulums, and the vibrations of musical strings, and to calculate such values as the centers of gravity of three-dimensional objects and the moments of inertia of rotating flywheels.

Very briefly, the calculus works by conceptualizing any continuously varying quantity as an infinite series of imperceptibly changing "instants" or "infinitesimals." As a car constantly accelerates from zero to 60 miles per hour, for example, it passes through every intermediate speed but remains at each one for only an imperceptible instant. With each minutely fractional passage of time its speed increases minutely, and although we know there must be an instant when the speed is exactly 30 miles per hour, that exact instant must be infinitely brief. Earlier mathematics could not deal with such an instant, because speed equals the distance traveled divided by the time elapsed, and here the time involved is zero, a nonpermissible divisor. The calculus, however, enabled mathematicians to calculate the sums of infinite series of such infinitesimals (the *integral calculus*), as well as to extract the properties of individual infinitesimal instants from given curves (the *differential calculus*).

Quite apart from its enormous scientific and practical importance, the calculus embodied two general notions or attitudes that extended into all of Leibniz's subsequent philosophical and even psychological theorizing. First, the calculus dealt with variables undergoing *constant and continuous change*, and Leibniz would henceforth see the linked phenomena of continuity and change as essential features of the world in general. Second, Leibniz's calculus analyzed the physical world in terms of mathematical concepts that in a literal sense were mental "fictions." The calculus's individual infinitesimals could not themselves be concretely experienced in reality, yet they could figure as fundamental elements in mathematical equations that *did* mirror and predict concrete reality. As we shall soon see, Leibniz's philosophy reflected these ideas by positing a universe undergoing constant "organic" development in stages that imperceptibly merge one with the other, and by challenging the assertion of Locke and others that the fundamental elements of the world had to be the concrete and palpable "primary qualities" of particles of extended matter.

Leibniz's immensely productive sojourn in Paris came to an end after both of his major patrons—Boineburg and the Elector of Mainz—died within a few months of each other. Failing to find another position that would allow him to remain in the French capital, he reluctantly accepted a position as court councilor to the House of Hanover, rulers of a German state then less important than Mainz. He was to remain in this post for the rest of his life, but he started out in a characteristic fashion by taking several months to travel by a meandering route from Paris to his new German headquarters. He stopped in London for a return visit to the Royal Society, and then spent time in Amsterdam where he met two important people. One was the philosopher **Benedict Spinoza** (1632–1677), who promoted a view that has come to be known as **pantheism**—the notion that God is not an independent being that controls the universe but rather that God *is* the entire universe. The other was **Anton van Leeuwenhoek** (1632–1723), a lens grinder who developed the modern microscope. Amazed by the living microorganisms he saw in Leeuwenhoek's microscope, and impressed by Spinoza's pantheism, Leibniz had a vision of the entire cosmos as composed of hierarchies of living, organic units:

> In the smallest particle of matter there is a world of creatures, living beings, animals, entelechies, souls. Each portion of matter may be conceived as like a garden full of plants, and like a pond full of fishes. But each branch of every plant, each member of every animal, each drop of its liquid parts, is also some such garden or pond. Thus there is nothing fallow, nothing sterile, nothing dead in the universe; no chaos, no confusion save in appearance.[17]

Before he could fully develop such thoughts, however, Leibniz had to establish himself in Hanover.

Serving the House of Hanover

Once finally settled in Hanover, Leibniz plunged into official duties as court librarian to Johann Friedrich, the Duke of Brunswick-Lüneburg. Almost immediately he showed his versatility, becoming the family genealogist as well as a political and technological advisor. He got on well with his patron, but after only three years Johann Friedrich died and was succeeded by his younger brother Ernst August—who had fewer intellectual interests and was less sympathetic. Fortunately for Leibniz, however, the new Duke was married to **Sophie the Countess Palatine** (1630–1714; see Figure 2.6), the youngest sister of Descartes' intellectual confidante Elizabeth of Bohemia (see Chapter 1). Even as she mothered seven children (including a future king of England and a queen of Prussia) and carried out her duties as the supervisor of a busy household, Sophie shared her sister's intellectual curiosity and became a friend and influential supporter of Leibniz. Her daughter **Sophie Charlotte** (1668–1705; see Figure 2.7), a young

FIG 2.6
Sophie the Countess
Palatine (1630–1714)

girl when Leibniz arrived at Hanover, also grew up to become a sophisticated friend and self-described disciple of the philosopher. The two Sophies would become a major first audience for much of Leibniz's philosophizing, and like Descartes with Elizabeth, his letters to them provided the basis for much of his most important work.

Leibniz's career at Hanover was varied and sometimes tumultuous. During the early years he became obsessed with the idea of using windmill power to drain water from mines in the Harz Mountains. Promised a lifetime pension if he succeeded, Leibniz designed countless windmills, gear mechanisms, siphons, and pumps. Unfortunately, he overestimated the average winds for the region, and his designs did not work. As he desperately pressed ever newer and "improved" versions on the beleaguered mining engineers, he became both a nuisance and an object of ridicule. A book titled *Foolish Wisdom and Wise Folly* satirized Leibniz for designing impossible and fantastic contrivances, such as a coach capable of the unbelievable speed of 35 miles per hour! Finally, in 1685 Leibniz and his patrons struck a new bargain. He would get his pension, but for a historical rather than a technological project: He was to write an extended history of the House of Hanover's family, tracing it back to its earliest recorded

FIG 2.7
Sophie Charlotte
(1668–1705)

origins. For Leibniz, the job carried the important fringe benefit of justifying extensive travel to archives throughout Europe. For the male Hanoverians, it diverted their gifted but troublesome employee away from the mines.

Although this job provided Leibniz with a lifetime stipend, it also hung over him like a black cloud for the rest of his life. Never one to do things by halves, he accumulated huge masses of data and produced nine volumes of historical essays before he died. But these books only brought the family history up to the year 1024, and his employers grumbled constantly that he devoted his time primarily to projects he had not been commissioned to do while leaving the history centuries short of its goal. Their complaints bore at least a grain of truth, for Leibniz regularly undertook an almost unbelievable variety of ambitious projects, and he sometimes could not help but spread himself thin.

Some of these activities did directly serve his patrons' immediate interests. For example, he wrote briefs supporting Hanover's successful case to become the ninth German Elector state, on a par with Mainz in selecting the emperor. He also assisted in negotiations concerning succession to the British throne, when the shortage of

Protestant heirs in England made it possible that succession would eventually pass to Ernst August and Sophie's eldest son Georg Ludwig, a great-grandson of England's James I. In the civic arena, Leibniz promoted a public-health system and fire-fighting service, street lighting, and the establishment of a state bank. He also worked to introduce silk production into Germany, growing in his own garden the mulberry trees on which silkworms must feed.

But these represented only a fraction of Leibniz's activities. He interested himself in everything and corresponded with people about almost everything. He wrote at every possible moment, even when traveling about in his coach, and more than 15,000 of his letters still survive today. A staunch believer in the importance of information exchange, he promoted several new scientific societies and scholarly journals.

His interests extended well beyond the borders of Europe, as he revived his youthful interest in China and began corresponding intensively with some Jesuit missionaries to that country. He published much of this correspondence, along with an extended preface of his own, in a volume he called *Novissima Sinica* (*News from China*). Quite remarkably for a seventeenth-century writer, Leibniz was quite open-minded and non-ethnocentric, declaring that Chinese customs "should not be judged by ours."[18] He added that China and Europe had a good deal to teach each other—China being superior in the arts of civility and harmonious living together, and Europe in science and technology. He saw interesting and nonobvious connections between the two cultures, including the fact that Chinese hexagrams in the ancient *Book of Changes* were constructed of just two basic elements (the "yin" and the "yang"), which bore some striking relationships to the binary arithmetic he had invented. In general, he promoted openness and cultural sensitivity, and an awareness that non-European cultures could have valuable lessons to teach.[19] Late twentieth- and early twenty-first-century psychologists in North America and Europe may finally be coming to the same conclusion, as the growth of cultural psychology and interest in indigenous psychologies may indicate.[20]

During this period, Leibniz also worked independently in the fields of mathematics, physics, and logic, and with vast erudition in so many different fields, he tried to integrate all forms of knowledge together in a unified philosophical system. Yet for all these talents and ambitions, his life remained ironically unfulfilled. One biographer has summarized as follows:

> Leibniz's life was dominated by an unachievable ambition to excel in every sphere of intellectual and political activity. The wonder is not that he failed so often, but that he achieved as much as he did. His successes were due to a rare combination of sheer hard work, a receptivity to the ideas of others, and supreme confidence in the fertility of his own mind. . . . On the other hand, his desire to produce monuments to his genius, which would be both complete and all his own work, made it impossible for him to finish anything. Despite all his notes, letters and articles, he never wrote a systematic treatise on any of his special interests. His assistant Eckhart put it nicely when he said of the Hanover family history that, as with numbers in the calculus, Leibniz knew how to extend his historical journey to infinity.[21]

Most of Leibniz's contemporaries saw only fragmentary evidence regarding the range and depth of his thought, and later generations of scholars have had to sift through his enormous private correspondence and unpublished private papers to appreciate him fully. During his lifetime he was often ridiculed. With his enormous jet-black wig and overly ornate, old-fashioned clothes, he was described by one of his Hanoverian masters as "an archeological find" likely to be mistaken for a clown by those unfamiliar with him.[22] He became the model for the ridiculous philosopher Pangloss in Voltaire's satire *Candide*, who—in a misleading parody of Leibniz's actual philosophy—constantly asserts that this is "the best of all possible worlds" in the face of repeated catastrophes.

The final two decades of Leibniz's life were marked by great achievement as well as controversy and disappointment. In 1700 Sophie Charlotte—who had married King Frederick of Prussia and thus become a Queen—convinced her husband to establish a national scientific academy in Berlin, comparable to the Royal Society in London. Leibniz was named its first president, a post that he retained for ten years and that facilitated his contacts with scientific leaders both in Germany and abroad. It was during this period that he became seriously engaged with Locke's philosophy, and as we have noted, tried unsuccessfully to engage the Englishman in correspondence. He did exchange letters with Locke's hostess, Lady Damaris Masham, however, while also corresponding and conversing about philosophical questions with Sophie and Sophie Charlotte. These correspondences provided the basis for much of *Theodicy*, the only book Leibniz actually published in his lifetime, dealing with the question of how an omnipotent and presumably beneficent God could allow evil and catastrophe to occur. He also wrote, but did not publish, a statement of his general philosophy titled *Monadology*, and his extended response to Locke's *Essay*.

On a more negative note, during this period Leibniz became entangled in an unseemly priority dispute with Isaac Newton over who invented the calculus. On the basis of false evidence and questionable testimony from the pathologically secretive Newton, English mathematicians officially branded Leibniz a plagiarist. Leibniz, who had originally tried to be conciliatory, responded with some unseemly slanders of his own, and the result was an unfortunate and longstanding breach between English and continental mathematics.[*]

Ironically, Leibniz's fall from grace in England was followed in 1714 by the accession to the English throne of his patron, Georg Ludwig of Hanover, as King George I. Leibniz had participated in the negotiations leading to this event and hoped to follow the monarch to England as the official historian. The new king, only too aware that Leibniz's presence in England could produce diplomatic disaster, insisted that he remain home and finish the Hanover family history. Now approaching 70, Leibniz somewhat guiltily tried to acquiesce while carrying on with his philosophical writing. Soon, however, he became acutely ill with gout and colic, and he died on November 14, 1716. He was buried with proper ceremony, but both of the Sophies had predeceased him and no one of importance attended his funeral. Another half-century would pass before publication of his manuscripts and private

---

[*] The English were the long-term losers here, as their mathematicians continued for a century to use the relatively clumsy and inconvenient notation system for calculus devised by Newton, disdaining the clearer and more flexible one originated by Leibniz. As a consequence, mathematics developed much faster on the continent than in Britain.

papers began to reveal the true scope of his genius and the full dimensions of a philosophy of mind that set the stage for the emergence of scientific psychology in Germany.

Leibniz's Philosophy of Mind

Leibniz's reply to Locke, *Nouveaux Essais sur l'Entendement Humain* (*New Essays on Human Understanding*), contained his most incisive and influential discussions of psychological issues. Written in French because Leibniz lacked fluency in English and felt that his native German was not properly suited for philosophical discussion, the work was not published until a half-century after his death in 1765. To understand this important work fully, we must begin by reviewing some basic philosophical ideas regarding "**monads**" that Leibniz had developed previously.

The Monadology

Like Locke, Leibniz had been stimulated by the works of Descartes and moved to disagree with some aspects of the Frenchman's thought while accepting others. His *pattern* of acceptance and disagreement, however, differed markedly. As we have seen, Locke accepted Descartes' project for mechanistic analysis of the physical world and animal body while rejecting or ignoring most of his doctrine of the soul. Leibniz's major disagreement centered precisely on the mechanistic assumptions that Locke so enthusiastically adopted.

While Locke, following Galileo and Descartes, accepted extension and motion as the ultimate "primary qualities" of the universe, Leibniz argued that logically they could not be such. As his infinitesimal calculus illustrated, every extended material object is potentially divisible to infinity: No matter how small the pieces into which it is divided, each piece may be further subdivided still. Thus, as he put it, "We should never reach anything of which we could say, here is a real ultimate being." Motion, detectable only as changes in the relative positions of nonultimate physical bodies, logically could not be ultimate either. But while denying ultimate status to either matter or motion, Leibniz thought there must be forces or energies that produce the *impressions* of matter in motion: "Motion, that is change of place, is not something entirely real. . . . But the force or proximate cause of these changes is something more real."[23]

Thus Leibniz reasoned that the ultimate units of the world must be dynamic rather than static, containing within themselves energies and forces. And how may one conceptualize energies and forces? For Leibniz, the only answer seemed to be as a sort of "willing" or "striving," akin to the motives and drives that human beings perceive in themselves. Thus, the energies that drive the physical world have much in common with *spiritual* or *mental* qualities, attributed by Descartes to the soul rather than the body. Further, Leibniz accepted Descartes's *I think, therefore I am* argument, shown in the last chapter to assert the unquestionable and "superior" reality of the conscious soul. Accordingly, Leibniz adopted as his ultimate units of reality not material particles in motion, but rather an infinitude of energy-laden and soul-invested units that he called "monads"—a term derived from the Greek *monos*, meaning "unit."

Among the most important qualities of souls and hence of monads, apart from their motives and energies, is their capacity to *perceive*—to register impressions of the rest of the world. Leibniz saw the universe as composed of four kinds of monads, differing primarily in the clearness, distinctness, and completeness of their perceptions of the world. At the top of the hierarchy he posited a supreme monad, equated with God, from whose purposes and perceptions all other monads are created. Omniscient and omnipotent, this supreme soul knows and controls all else but is itself apprehensible only incompletely and to varying degrees by its creations, the three classes of "finite monads."

First and closest to God in the hierarchy are **rational monads**, corresponding to the conscious souls or minds of human beings. These exceed all other finite monads in the completeness, clearness, and distinctness of their consciousness. Indeed, Leibniz attributed to them a capacity not just for simple perception but for a still higher process he called **apperception**. In apperception, ideas are not simply "registered" in consciousness—they become subject to focused attention and rational analysis in terms of underlying principles and laws. Further, apperception is a "reflective" activity, during which the rational monad has an ongoing sense of its own "I-ness" or "self." As it thinks about something, it has a simultaneous sense of its own activity in so thinking. Thus while you read this page, as the agent of a rational monad you are aware not only of the specific words and their meanings but also of the fact that you are someone who is doing the reading and thinking.

Beneath the rational monads in Leibniz's system lie the **sentient monads**, which comprise the souls of living but nonhuman organisms. After a brief and uncertain period when Leibniz agreed with Descartes that animals cannot have conscious sensations, he changed his mind and concluded that their sentient monads do in fact have capacities for conscious pleasure, pain, and the voluntary focusing of attention. What they lack, which presumably remains the exclusive province of rational monads, is the ability to reason about their ideas, or to reflect upon their own mental activity.[24]

Finally, Leibniz postulated a large class of bare or **simple monads** that make up the "bodies" of all matter, whether organic or inorganic. The presumed "perceptions" of these lowest monads, while real, are indistinct and unconscious.

Leibniz saw the monads as organized hierarchically. Inorganic matter presumably consists simply of collections or aggregations of simple monads, acting under minimal organizing energies. When such an aggregation comes under the domination of a sentient monad, however, it constitutes a living organism—the activities of its parts coordinated and organized consistently with the purposes of that dominant monad. And as the vision of Leeuwenhoek's microorganisms within organisms suggested, these sentient organisms may themselves be hierarchically arranged. That is, aggregates of smaller sentient organisms may be dominated by "higher" sentient monads. Still further, some complex aggregations of sentient monads are dominated by individual rational monads in the constitution of individual human beings. And at the final level of the hierarchy, all of the simple, sentient, and rational monads of the universe fall under the perfect control and apperception of God, the supreme monad that created them.

As the supposed creations of a single perfect and supreme consciousness, all of the finite monads were said by Leibniz to possess a "preestablished harmony." That is, they do not mutually *influence* one another but rather pursue independent but parallel and harmonious courses. Thus, while the rational and sentient monads were described in the last paragraph as "dominant" over aggregates of simple monads, their dominance consists not in the physical power to control action but entirely in their higher levels of *awareness*. The view of the universe afforded to each rational monad is broader, clearer, and more distinct than that of the lower monads—but still only a part of the whole as apperceived by the supreme monad. Minds (or rational monads) and bodies (the aggregated sentient and simple monads "dominated" by the rational monads) thus do not truly interact with each other, as Descartes had it, but instead reflect differing aspects or perspectives on the same harmonious universe. In a famous metaphor, Leibniz likened the monads to a vast number of perfectly constructed clocks all set to the same time; each one runs independently of all the others but records exactly the same time. In contrast to Descartes' "interactive dualism," Leibniz's conception of the mind-body relationship is traditionally called **psychophysical parallelism**.

In sum, Leibniz posited a universe consisting of an infinity of energized, soul-like substances called monads, with varying capacities for the apperception or perception of subordinate levels of monads. Each monad has its own innate purposes and destiny but pursues them in preestablished harmony with all other monads because all are the creations of the single, perfect, and supreme monad. Thus Leibniz saw the universe as an organic entity, comprised of hierarchical levels of awareness and purpose.

Such metaphysical speculation about the ultimate nature of the cosmos had not concerned the more practically minded and commonsensical Locke, who simply followed the scientists in assuming a universe composed of material particles interacting in a comprehensible mechanistic way and drew the implications from that for how best to manage affairs in that real world. Unsurprisingly, Leibniz saw Locke's analyses as limited and incomplete, and expressed these reservations in his *New Essays*.

New Essays on Human Understanding

The *New Essays* open with a preface, which may be read by itself as a succinct summary of Leibniz's psychology, followed by a Socratic-style dialogue between "Philalethes," a fictional proponent of Locke's point of view, and "Theophilus," who speaks for Leibniz himself. Here Philalethes presents Locke's arguments in the same order and often exactly the same words as they appeared in his *Essay*, and Theophilus reacts to them.

The preface opens by describing Locke's system as basically derived from Aristotle, and Leibniz's own from Plato:

> There is the question whether the soul in itself is completely blank like a writing tablet on which nothing has as yet been written—a *tabula rasa* as Aristotle and the author of the *Essay* maintain, and whether everything which is inscribed there comes solely from the senses and experience; or whether the soul inherently contains the sources of various notions and doctrines, which external objects merely rouse up on suitable occasions, as I believe and as [does] Plato.[25]

To support his view, Leibniz cited the rules of arithmetic, the geometrical axioms, and the rules of logic, all of which he called "**necessary truths**." While we feel a perfect certainty as to their absolute correctness, such correctness is not proved by concrete experience but only *instanced* or *demonstrated* by it. Thus, as Leibniz put it, necessary truths "must have principles whose proof does not depend on instances nor, consequently, on the testimony of the senses, even though without the senses it would never occur to us to think of them."[26]

In elaborating on this, Leibniz likened the mind not to a neutral, blank slate, but to a veined block of marble whose internal lines of cleavage predispose it to be sculpted into some shapes more easily than others. Such shapes are "innate" in the marble, even though a sculptor's work is necessary to expose them and bring them to clarity. Leibniz declares, "This is how ideas and truths are innate in us—as *inclinations, dispositions, tendencies, or natural potentialities*, and not as actions." Locke, he complained, "seems to claim that there is nothing potential in us, in fact nothing of which we are not always actually aware."[27]

Leibniz's view here derived from his monadology. He supposed each human being to be constituted of countless energized and willfully striving simple and sentient monads, under the dominance of one rational monad that strives to apperceive the world as fully as possible and that contains the "necessary truths" implicitly within

itself. Thus inclinations, dispositions, and specific intellectual potentialities are part of human nature.

Leibniz conceded that *animals*, which lack a dominant rational
monad with inherent necessary truths, may in fact function in much
the way prescribed by Locke. The thought sequences of animals represent "only a shadow of reasoning." he wrote, and "are just like those of
simple empirics who maintain that what has happened once will happen again in a similar case, . . . although that does not enable them
to judge whether the same reasons are at work." Lacking the innate
necessary truths required for logical reasoning, animals cannot grasp
the underlying *reasons* for the empirical regularities they perceive.
Thus, Leibniz concluded, "what shows the existence of inner sources
of necessary truths is also what distinguishes man from beast."[28]

Leibniz saw these considerations as not so much *contradicting*
Locke as filling in details on points left implicit or unspoken by the
Englishman. Locke had seen two sources of ideas, in the sensations of
the external world and the reflections on the mind's own operations,
but had not elaborated much on the reflections. Leibniz argued that
many of the innate tendencies and dispositions he himself emphasized were implicit in Locke's notion of reflection. In discussing precisely the same mathematical and logical proofs in which Leibniz had
seen evidence for innate "necessary truths," Locke had seen evidence
of "intuitive and demonstrative knowledge," with a higher order of
certainty than "sensitive knowledge." Where might this added certainty come from, except from innate stores of knowledge implicit in
the processes of reflection?

Locke's point of view was summarized in the old Latin saying "*Nihil
est in intellectu quod non prius fuerit in sensu*"—"There is nothing in
the intellect that was not first in the senses." Leibniz simply added the
tag line "*nisi ipse intellectus*"—"except the intellect itself." That is,
Locke took for granted the mind's own activity in processing its sensations, subsuming a large number of important and interesting features
under the general term "reflection." Leibniz chose to emphasize and
elaborate on those features.

Another difference, however, proved more difficult to reconcile.
Locke had steadfastly insisted that the mind is *not* constantly active
and can sometimes be without thoughts, just as the body can sometimes be without movement. Leibniz just as steadfastly insisted that

the mind *is* constantly active, even during such states as dreamless sleep. Part of this conviction derived from the theory of monads as the constantly active and striving sources of the mind. Another part— momentous for the future history of psychology—lay in Leibniz's belief in *unconscious* mental activity.

Leibniz postulated a continuum of consciousness, ranging from the clear, distinct, and rational *apperceptions* through the more mechanical and indistinct *perceptions* and terminating in what he called **minute perceptions**. While real, these last never actually enter consciousness. Leibniz described them as follows:

> At every moment there is in us an infinity of perceptions, unaccompanied by awareness or reflection; that is, of alterations of the soul itself, of which we are unaware because these impressions are either too minute and too numerous, or else too unvarying, so that they are not sufficiently distinctive on their own.[29]

Some minute perceptions may rise to the level of full perceptions or apperceptions, as when we shift our attention to a previously unnoticed background noise. Others, however, are inherently too vague and indistinct to be consciously perceived at all. To illustrate these, Leibniz wrote:

> I like to use the example of the roaring noise of the sea which impresses itself upon us when we are standing on the shore. To hear this noise as we do, we must hear the parts which make up this whole, that is the noise of each wave, although each of these little noises makes itself known only when combined confusedly with all the others, and would not be noticed if the wave which made it were by itself.[30]

The minute perceptions held both metaphysical and psychological importance for Leibniz. Metaphysically, they enabled him to argue that all monads respond to and reflect all of the universe. Most perceptions remain minute, however, and out of consciousness; indeed for simple monads, all perceptions are unconscious. Rational and sentient monads bring constantly varying degrees of apperception or simple perception to a small portion of the universe, while the vastly larger part remains beyond full consciousness for them, too. Presumably, only the supreme monad can constantly apperceive the entire universe.

On the psychological level, Leibniz called the minute perceptions "more effective in their results than has been recognized" in creating several important phenomena. He argued that our sense of continuity as individual, distinctive *selves*, for example, is maintained by innumerable minute perceptions and unconscious memories of our previous states—some of which may occasionally be brought to consciousness, but most of which remain in the subliminal state. He saw unconscious perceptions as adding to experience "that *je ne sais quoi*, those flavours, those images of sensible qualities, vivid in the aggregate but confused as to the parts."[31] And in a brief but significant anticipation of his nineteenth-century successors, Leibniz saw unconscious perceptions as playing a telling role in human *motivation*: "It is these minute perceptions which determine our behaviour in many situations without our thinking of them, and which deceive the unsophisticated."[32] He added:

> [Minute perceptions resemble] so many little springs trying to unwind and so driving our machine along. . . . That is why we are never indifferent, even when we appear to be most so, as for instance whether to turn left or right at the end of a lane. For the choice that we make arises from these insensible stimuli, which, mingled with the actions of objects and our bodily interiors, make us find one direction of movement more comfortable than the other.[33]

Sigmund Freud and other successors would find more significant examples of unconsciously motivated behavior than this, but Leibniz was ahead of his time in calling attention to the possibility.

Elsewhere in the *New Essays*, Leibniz comments from his own perspective on Locke's most striking images and passages. Thus, he notes Locke's discussion of how tepid water may seem hot to one hand and cold to another, as a demonstration of the presumed uncertainty of secondary qualities. Leibniz adds, however, that similar contradictory perceptions may also occur with the supposed "primary" qualities of extension and number. When you cross your fingers and touch a marble or a pencil with the now-adjacent outside edges of your fingertips, for example, the single object will feel like two. Back in Britain, George Berkeley would shortly use a similar argument to deny the entire Lockean distinction between primary and secondary qualities.

On the "Molyneux problem"—the blind man suddenly granted the ability to see and confronted with a cube and a sphere—Leibniz agreed that in practice the outcome would probably be as Locke and Molyneux expected. He insisted, however, that the *ideas* underlying such geometrical distinctions must be to some degree independent of the specific sensory *images* that illustrate them. Thus, a blind person and a paralyzed person may both be taught geometry, the one in completely tactile terms and the other in completely visual terms. Yet while the specific images of the two differ completely, they learn the same underlying geometrical ideas and principles— showing once again that experience does not *create* the necessary truths, but merely brings them out or illustrates them. Following from this, Leibniz argued that *if* the hypothetical blind man could somehow be instructed that his new visual experience contained two stimuli, one a sphere and the other a cube, and if he could actually differentiate the one stimulus from the other, he would be able by rational principles to say which was which. Leibniz conceded, however, that such a situation could probably never happen in reality. A real person would probably be dazzled and confused by the strangeness of his visual sensations and be unable to make sense of them at all until correlating them with specific and familiar sensations of touch.

This analysis nicely epitomizes the differences of approach between Locke and Leibniz. For while the Englishman tried to analyze the *limits* of knowledge, and to establish rules for the solution of everyday practical problems, Leibniz focused more on the *potential* of the mind. Locke concerned himself with the understanding of events largely peripheral to the mind, with an analysis of the components of external reality. The mind itself interested him only secondarily, as the instrument necessary for understanding the external world and learning how to control it. But for Leibniz the mind itself, with its central organizing principles and innate necessary truths, was a primary object of interest in its own right.

Leibniz thus established a point of view equally as important and influential as Locke's. In Chapters 4 and 5, we shall see how Immanuel Kant and Wilhelm Wundt explicitly adopted a Leibnizean as opposed to a Lockean perspective while establishing the idea of psychology as an independent intellectual discipline. In Chapters 10 and 11 we shall hear echoes of Leibniz's ideas in the "dynamic" psychologies of several early investigators of hypnosis and of the psychoanalyst Sigmund Freud, with their emphases on internal and unconscious motivational factors. Chapter 13 will show how the Swiss psychologist Jean Piaget has analyzed the growth of intelligence in children as an organic, biologically based sequence of developmental stages in an active mind—a conception following directly in the tradition of Leibniz. And finally in Chapter 14 we shall return again to Leibniz himself and show the role he played in the history of the idea of "Artificial Intelligence"—the notion that *machines* might be constructed in a way to show the properties of rational thought.

Summary

John Locke and **Gottfried Wilhelm Leibniz** were mental philosophers who developed contrasting aspects of Descartes' system while becoming excellent exemplars of the empiricist, associationist tradition (Locke) and the rationalist, nativist tradition (Leibniz). Like Descartes, Locke grappled with how it is we acquire knowledge. Rejecting Descartes' notion of innate ideas, he concluded that *everything* we come to know arises through experience and that the human mind at birth may be likened to a blank slate, or *tabula rasa*. He argued that even **complex ideas** that do not appear to be available for direct experience are built up out of the association of **simple ideas** that *are* available to us in experience. Locke's successors later proposed that factors such as contiguity and similarity lead to the formation of these associations.

Leibniz accepted that *some* knowledge occurs as Locke described, but further, in the nativist mode of Descartes, he argued for the existence of certain innate predilections or tendencies in the mind that predispose it to organize knowledge in certain specific ways—according to the laws of logic, for example. For him, the metaphor for the mind at birth was not a completely blank slate, but rather a veined slab of marble that will respond to a sculptor's chiseling with predispositions to break only along certain fault lines. Leibniz further proposed that the human mind is dominated by a **rational monad** with innate capacities for consciousness, will, and the "apperception" of its own nature and activity. This conception presumes a more active mind than Locke's model, which presents the mind as passively receiving experiences from the outside world through the senses.

Both traditions have influenced the development of psychology. The empiricist, Lockean tradition has been particularly influential in British and American psychologies, which have emphasized the role of experience in forming the mind and theories of learning focused on experiences in the external environment. The Leibnizean tradition, which has been stronger in continental Europe, has placed greater emphasis on the controlling and central functions of an active and innately given mind.

Key Pioneers

Berkeley, George, p. 69
Boyle, Robert, p. 55
Cooper, Sir Anthony
   Ashley, p. 57
Hartley, David, p. 69
Hobbes, Thomas, p. 68
Hume, David, p. 69
Leeuwenhoek, Anton van, p. 76
Leibniz, Gottfried Wilhelm, p. 51

Locke, John, p. 51
Masham, Lady Damaris
   Cudworth, p. 62
Mill, James, p. 70
Mill, John Stuart, p. 70
Molyneux, William, p. 65
Sophie the Countess Palatine, p. 76
Sophie Charlotte, p. 76
Spinoza, Benedict, p. 75

Key Terms

apperception, p. 83
association of ideas, p. 67
behaviorism, p. 70
binary arithmetic, p. 73
British associationism, p. 69
complex ideas, p. 64
demonstrative knowledge, p. 65
infinitesimal calculus, p. 74
intuitive knowledge, p. 65
laws of association by contiguity or
   similarity, p. 69
minute perceptions, p. 88

monads, p. 82
   rational monads, p. 83
   sentient monads, p. 84
   simple monads, p. 84
necessary truths, p. 86
pantheism, p. 76
primary qualities (Locke), p. 66
psychophysical parallelism, p. 85
secondary qualities (Locke), p. 66
sensitive knowledge, p. 66
simple ideas, p. 64
social contract, p. 68

Discussion Questions and Topics

1 This chapter described some of the ideas in Locke's *Essays on Human Understanding* and Leibniz's response to Locke in his *New Essays on Human Understanding*. Compare and contrast the main ideas in these works as outlined in the chapter.

2 Do you agree with Locke that all knowledge comes through experience, or do you agree with Leibniz that people have innately given
tendencies or predispositions that emerge in their experience of the
world? Why?

3 Describe the "Molyneux problem" and the different outcomes suggested by the positions of Locke and Leibniz.

Suggested Readings

For full details on Locke's life see Maurice Cranston's *John Locke: A Biography* (London: Longmans, 1957). A good briefer account of his life and
work appears in Ricardo Cuintara's *Two Augustans: John Locke, Jonathan
Swift* (Madison, WI: University of Wisconsin Press, 1978). Locke's *An Essay
Concerning Human Understanding* appears in several inexpensive editions.

For Leibniz's full life, see E. J. Aiton, *Leibniz: A Biography* (Bristol, UK,
and Boston: Adam Hilger Ltd., 1985). An abridged edition of Leibniz's *New
Essays on Human Understanding*, preceded by a valuable Editors' Intro-
duction, has been translated and edited by Peter Remnant and Jonathan
Bennett (Cambridge, UK: Cambridge University Press, 1982). For a lucid
summary of Leibniz's general thought, see G. MacDonald Ross, *Leibniz*
(New York: Oxford University Press, 1984). Leibniz's specific influence on
psychology is further described in R. Fancher and H. Schmidt, "Gottfried
Wilhelm Leibniz: Underappreciated Pioneer of Psychology," in *Portraits of
Pioneers in Psychology*, Vol. 5, edited by G. Kimble and M. Wertheimer
(Washington, DC: APA Press, 2003).

Bertrand Russell presents useful and witty accounts of both Locke and
Leibniz in his classic *A History of Western Philosophy* (New York: Simon &
Schuster, 1945), although his biases lie clearly in favor of his countryman
Locke. A more sympathetic and detailed account of Leibniz's philosophical
disagreement with Locke is provided in Nicholas Jolley, *Leibniz and Locke: A
Study of the New Essays on Human Understanding* (Oxford, UK: Clarendon
Press, 1984).

Physiologists of Mind
Brain Scientists from Gall to Penfield

Gall and Phrenology

Flourens and the Discrediting of Phrenology

Localization Theory Revived: The Brain's Language Areas
Paul Broca and the Case of "Tan"
Sensory and Motor Areas
Wernicke's Theory of Aphasia

Memory and the Equipotentiality Debate

Stimulation of the Conscious Human Brain
Wilder Penfield and the Treatment of Epilepsy
Brenda Milner and the Multiplicity of Memory Systems
Cartesian Dualism Revisited
Recent Developments: Cognitive Neuroscience and Social Neuroscience

Summary

Key Pioneers

Key Terms

Discussion Questions and Topics

Suggested Readings

3

Today, we take it for granted that the bodily organ most responsible for our intelligence and higher mental abilities is the brain. An intelligent person is said to "have brains" or to be a "brain," while the opposite number is a "lamebrain." Indeed, the assumption seems so obvious that it may be surprising to learn that it has been universally accepted by scientists only for the past 200 years or so. Before that, scholars disagreed widely about the nature of the brain and its importance for the functions of the mind or soul.

Aristotle, the greatest scientist of ancient Greece, downplayed the importance of the brain because of some accurate but misleading observations. Although richly supplied with blood in life, the brain's vessels rapidly drain after death. Thus, the dissected brain struck Aristotle as unprepossessing in appearance, nearly uniform in its bloodless, grayish color and spongelike consistency. Moreover, he knew of soldiers whose brain surfaces had been exposed by battle wounds and who had reported no sensation whatsoever when their brains were touched. Aristotle found it hard to believe that such a "bloodless," "insensitive," and generally unimpressive-looking organ could be the seat of the highest human faculties. He assigned that role to the heart, seeing the brain as a relatively minor organ serving as a "condenser" for overheated vapors or "humors" that presumably rose to the top of the body. The cerebrospinal fluid in the ventricles, which Descartes later interpreted as "animal spirits," was for Aristotle the product of the brain's condensations.

While the brain also had some supporters, Aristotle's dismissive assessment of it continued to be echoed in various forms by other influential investigators for 2,000 years. We saw in Chapter 1 how in the seventeenth century Descartes localized some important functions in the brain but did not believe a perfect and unified entity like the rational soul could be housed in a divided structure like the brain. And while the pineal gland—his nominee for the most likely point of interaction between body and mind—was physically in the brain, it constituted but a very small part of the total structure.

Following Descartes, however, the brain attracted increasing attention. John Locke's teacher, the Oxford physician **Thomas Willis** (1621–1675), published the first accurate and detailed *Anatomy of the Brain* in 1664, illustrated with plates by the celebrated architect Christopher Wren. In relating anatomy to function, Willis emphasized the *substance* of the brain's various structures, rather than the ventricles and cerebrospinal fluid, as Descartes had. He observed that brain tissue was not undifferentiated, as Aristotle had thought, but rather consisted of two kinds of substances: (1) a pulpy **gray matter** occupying the outer surface, or "cortex," of the brain, the inner part of the spinal cord, and several discrete centers within the brain; and (2) a fibrous **white matter** in the other regions. Willis speculated that the white matter consisted of narrow canals whose function was to distribute "spirits" generated in the gray matter.* Willis also accurately described the blood vessels of the brain, firmly establishing that it was far from a bloodless organ in life.

Other doctors contemporary with Willis discovered that localized interruptions to the brain's blood supply could cause strokes, also called *apoplexy*—sudden attacks that left their victims without the power of speech, partly paralyzed, or with sensory disabilities of varying kinds. And by the early 1700s it was recognized that injuries to one side of the brain often produced paralyses or losses of feeling somewhere on the *opposite side* of the body.

But despite these gains in knowledge, the brain did not become an object of major scientific interest until the 1800s, when it became implicated in a sort of pseudoscientific craze that captured the imagination of the general public as much as of scientists. The German physician **Franz Josef Gall** (1758–1828; see Figure 3.1) played a major role in these developments, as he convincingly demonstrated the general importance of the brain for all of the higher human functions, while also originating the popular nineteenth-century movement known as *phrenology*. We turn to Gall's story for the origins of an important tradition in brain science that continues today.

Gall and Phrenology

Although some of Gall's ideas aroused instant suspicion and hostility among "establishment" scientists, he was also widely recognized as a brilliant anatomist—the greatest since Willis. Using new and delicate dissection techniques, he confirmed and elaborated on many of Willis's basic findings regarding gray and white matter. He showed that the two halves of the brain are interconnected by stalks of white

---

* Since the late nineteenth century, it has been recognized that the brain and spinal cord are composed of billions of cells called **neurons**, each with an electrochemically active cell body or nucleus interconnected to others by branchlike *dendrites* (which receive electrochemical stimulation from other neurons) and the long, fibrous *axon* (which transmits stimulation to other neurons). The axons tend to cluster together to form the brain's white matter, while the cell bodies and dendrites constitute the gray.

FIG 3.1
Franz Josef Gall
(1758–1828)

matter called **commissures** and that other, smaller tracts of white fibers cross over from each side of the brain to connect with the opposite sides of the spinal cord. This last finding helped explain how damage to one side of the brain could result in paralysis or other debility to the opposite side of the body.

Also the first great *comparative* anatomist of brains, Gall carefully examined the similarities and differences among brains of many animal species, children, the elderly, and brain-damaged people, as well as normal human adults. In a general but convincing way, these studies showed that higher mental functions correlated with the size and intactness of the brain in question, particularly its outer surface or cortex. We shall later see that the correlation is imperfect and can give rise to some misleading assumptions about intellectual differences *within* an adult human population. But Gall documented an undeniable tendency for animals with larger brains to manifest more complex, flexible, and intelligent behavior. More than any other single argument, this demonstration convinced scientists once and for all that the brain was in fact the center of higher mental activity.

These contributions should have earned Gall a secure and respected place in the history of science. Unfortunately for his reputation, however, he embedded these noncontroversial ideas within another doctrine his followers labeled **phrenology** (meaning "science of the mind," from the Greek root *phrenos*, for "mind"). Not content to stop at the assertion that the higher functions were localized *generally* within the brain, Gall held that discrete psychological "faculties" were housed within specific *parts* of the brain. Moreover, he believed that the bumps and indentations on the surface of an individual skull reflected the size of the underlying brain parts, and hence of the different faculties.

A curious mixture combining a few astute observations with some fanciful logic, phrenology never won the respect of the most orthodox scientists. And when Gall failed to win over the professionals, he appealed increasingly to the general public. Phrenology became very popular, earning Gall and a host of followers a good living; but its popularity only increased the disdain with which it was regarded by many establishment scientists. One prominent figure labeled phrenology a "sinkhole of human folly and prating coxcombry."[1]

Gall's controversial theory had an appropriately idiosyncratic origin in his childhood experience. According to his autobiography, he was irritated as a schoolboy by some fellow students who, while less intelligent than himself (or so he judged them), nevertheless got higher grades because they were better memorizers. As he thought about these exasperating rivals, he realized that they all had one prominent physical characteristic in common: namely, large and protuberant eyes.

At that time, people commonly associated particular facial characteristics with specific psychological qualities. The art of **physiognomy**—the reading of a person's character in his or her physical features—had been effectively promoted by the Swiss mystic and theologian **Johann Kaspar Lavater** (1741–1801) in the 1770s, and it remained a popular pastime throughout the 1800s.* But Gall's physiognomic observation

---

* In Chapter 6 we shall see how the youthful Charles Darwin was almost rejected for the post of naturalist aboard the ship H.M.S. *Beagle* in 1831 because the captain thought his nose inappropriately shaped for a seafarer. Later in the century the Italian criminologist Cesare Lombroso presented an influential physiognomic theory of the "criminal type," part of which still persists today in the myth that evildoers must have shifty eyes and irregular features.

took on a new and different significance when he recalled it as an adult, in the context of his emerging view of the brain.

Already convinced that the higher intellectual and psychological qualities were associated with large brains in a general way, he now speculated that perhaps specific parts of the brain were the seats of specific functions or faculties. If one of those parts of the brain happened to be unusually large and well developed, then the specific function it housed should be unusually strong. Thus, people with especially good "verbal memories," like his schoolboy rivals, might have particularly well-developed "organs of verbal memory" somewhere in their brains. And Gall believed he knew exactly where this was: in the region of the frontal lobes directly behind the eyes, where the pressure of the enlarged brain caused the eyes to protrude.

After tentatively localizing verbal memory in one part of the brain, Gall naturally began to look for other faculties in other locations. Of course, in an era before MRI scans and other modern techniques, he had no direct means of observing living people's brains and so had to make an important but questionable assumption. Just as the brain part responsible for verbal memory causes the eyes to protrude, he argued, so will the conformation of the rest of the brain cause observable irregularities in the skull that surrounds it. Through "craniometry"—the measurement of the physical dimensions of the skull—Gall hoped to draw conclusions about the shape of the brain beneath. Thus, he sought correspondence between particular bumps and depressions on the skull and the particular psychological characteristics of the people who had them.

Once embarked on this search, Gall quickly developed further hypotheses. One of his patients, a woman whose strong erotic inclinations earned her the title of "Gall's Passionate Widow," once conveniently collapsed into his arms in such a way that his hand supported the back of her neck. Gall could not help but notice that her neck and the base of her skull were unusually thick, leading him to suspect that her **cerebellum**—the structure at the base of her brain—was unusually well developed. Observations of other people with strong sexual drives convinced Gall that they, too, had well-developed necks and skull bases, and that led him to localize the personality characteristic of "amativeness" in the cerebellum.

Gall's further researches led him to befriend a gang of lower-class boys who did errands for him. After gaining their confidence, he found that the boys' attitudes toward petty theft varied greatly—some expressing an abhorrence of it, and others openly admitting to committing it, even bragging about it. Gall measured the boys' heads and found that the inveterate thieves had prominences just above and in front of their ears, while the honest boys were flat in that region. Thus, Gall hypothesized an "organ of acquisitiveness" in the brain beneath. He justified this hypothesis with further cases, including a man with an unusually large bulge in the region who had been repeatedly jailed for theft until he gained insight into his acquisitive nature. Gall reported that when the man realized he could not resist temptation, he decided to become a *tailor* so "he might then indulge his inclination with impunity."[2]

Gall did not justify his slander of tailors, but he made similar derogatory judgments about some other professions after identifying another region just above the ear as the organ of a faculty he called "destructiveness." After noting that this part of the skull was particularly well developed in carnivorous animals, he described two striking examples of men with large prominences there. One was an apothecary who changed his career plans to become an executioner, and the other was a student "so fond of torturing animals that he became a surgeon."[3]

Through similar observations of other people with outstanding characteristics, Gall localized the qualities of veneration, benevolence, and firmness in separate areas on the top of the brain, love of food and drink just below the organ of acquisitiveness, and a host of other qualities in other regions. While it is easy today to laugh at this phrenological theorizing we should observe that it did have a certain naive plausibility and was properly "scientific" in being derived from direct (if ultimately misleading) empirical observation. The major weaknesses of Gall's theory lay in three other factors.

First, Gall incorrectly assumed that the shape of one's skull accurately reflects the shape of the underlying brain. But while recognition of the incorrectness of this "fact" obviously invalidated the phrenologists' practical claims to be able to read character in head shapes, it did not discredit their more basic hypothesis of a relationship between *brain* shapes and character.

A second and more fundamental defect lay in Gall's choice of specific psychological qualities to localize within the brain—a collection of twenty-seven highly specific "faculties" for qualities such as "mirthfulness," "secretiveness," and "philoprogenitiveness" (parental love), in addition to the ones discussed so far. Gall's followers quickly added more, yielding complex configurations like that illustrated in Figure 3.2.[4] Thus, phrenologists saw these particular faculties as *basic* to human character, constituting the elemental building blocks out of which all significant personality variations are constructed. However, their arbitrary list included complex qualities that were themselves the result of many different interacting factors. The question of just what the basic dimensions of personality variation really are remains in some dispute to the present (see Chapter 12), but the faculty solution was unquestionably oversimplified. And as long as phrenology lacked an adequate classification of psychological characteristics, its attempts to localize those characteristics in the brain were doomed.

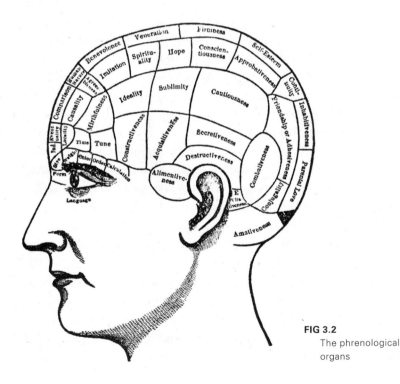

FIG 3.2
The phrenological organs

Phrenology's third and fatal defect lay in the feckless methods by which its hypotheses were often tested. Gall always maintained that his theory was grounded in observation, a claim literally true but unreflective of the selectivity and arbitrariness of many of the observations. Further, with twenty-seven or more interacting faculties to work with, it became almost ridiculously easy to explain away apparently discrepant observations. When confronted with a huge organ of acquisitiveness in a highly generous person, for example, Gall could claim that a large organ of benevolence (or some other convenient faculty) *counteracted* the acquisitive tendencies that would otherwise show clearly. Or he could claim that certain organs of the brain became selectively or temporarily impaired by disease, accounting for intermittent alterations in people's behavior. Between the presumably counterbalancing effects of several faculties and the "illnesses" that arbitrarily interfered with some faculties but not others, Gall explained away virtually any observation that ran counter to his theory.

And if *Gall* was cavalier in his interpretations of evidence, he attracted some followers who raised that tendency to an art form. When a cast of the right side of Napoleon's skull predicted qualities markedly at variance with the emperor's known personality, one phrenologist replied that his dominant side had been the left brain— a cast of which was conveniently missing. When Descartes' skull was examined and found deficient in the regions for reason and reflection, some phrenologists retorted that the philosopher's rationality had always been overrated.

Such tactics, and the promise of easy but "scientific" character analysis, helped phrenology retain a hold on the public imagination throughout much of the nineteenth century—in much the same way that astrology, biorhythm analysis, and ESP do today. Some practicing phrenologists undoubtedly actually helped some of the clients who flocked to them for readings, using their general knowledge of people (rather than any specific phrenological theories) to offer shrewd advice. But in contrast to the general public, most in the established scientific community regarded phrenology as a joke— as exemplified in one widely circulated story that Gall's own skull, when examined after his death, turned out to be twice as thick as the average.

FIG 3.3
Pierre Flourens
(1794–1867)

This attitude reflected not only the scientists' disdain for phrenology but also their respect for a series of experiments conducted in the early 1800s by the young French scientist **Pierre Flourens** (1794–1867; see Figure 3.3). Flourens's investigations, to which we turn now, ran counter to several of Gall's specific hypotheses and initiated a classic controversy about the nature of the brain that remains alive today.

Flourens and the Discrediting of Phrenology

In style and personality, as well as in the course of his career, Flourens contrasted dramatically with Gall. Whereas Gall was always an outsider, never accepted by orthodox scientists, Flourens epitomized the man of the establishment. Born near Montpellier in the south of France, he was graduated from that city's famous medical school at age 19. He had already published his first scientific article, and after moving to Paris he became the special protégé of **Georges Cuvier** (1769–1832), the most celebrated scientist in France, known appropriately as the "Dictator of Biology." Cuvier's endorsement guaranteed that Flourens's work would be greeted respectfully—although it was in fact good enough to stand out on its own.

Appalled by the cavalier observational strategies of the phrenologists, Flourens determined to study the functions of the brain strictly according to experiment—that is, where particular independent variables would be deliberately and systematically manipulated, and the resulting effects on dependent variables carefully observed. To do so, he used the technique of **ablation**, surgically removing specific small parts of an animal subject's brain and observing any consequent changes in the behavior or function of the animal after recovery from the surgery. He knew that brain tissue does not regenerate after removal. Thus, when he observed specific functions to be permanently missing or altered following an ablation, he hypothesized that the excised brain parts must normally be involved in the production of those functions.

Flourens did not actually invent the brain ablation experiment, but he refined it to a new degree. Showing great surgical skill, he removed more precisely defined areas from the small brains of his animal subjects than his predecessors had been able to do, with a higher survival rate. He always carefully nursed his animals back to as healthy a state as possible before drawing any conclusions, to avoid confusing the transient effects of surgical shock or postoperative complications with the permanent effects of his ablations.

Flourens tested Gall's hypotheses by ablating brain regions associated with particular phrenological faculties. Since he worked with animals, he could directly investigate only those few "faculties" presumably shared by animals and humans. Sexual responsiveness obviously qualified, so some of Flourens's earliest and most influential experiments involved ablations of the cerebellum—Gall's "organ of amativeness." His ablations produced alterations of behavior all right, but scarcely of the type that phrenological theory predicted:

> I removed the cerebellum in a young but vigorous dog by a series of deeper and deeper slices. The animal lost gradually the faculty of orderly and regular movement. Soon he could walk only by staggering in zigzags. He fell back when he wanted to advance; when he wanted to turn to the right he turned to

the left. As he made great efforts to move and could no longer moderate these efforts, he hurled himself impetuously forward, and did not fail to fall or roll over. If he found an object in his path, he was unable to avoid it, no matter what means he took; he hurled himself right and left; nevertheless he was perfectly well; when one irritated him he tried to bite; in fact, he bit any object one presented to him when he could reach it, but often he could no longer direct his movements with precision so as to reach the object. He had all his intellectual faculties, all his senses; he was only deprived of the faculty of coordinating and regularizing his movements.[5]

This classic description of a cerebellar lesion, originally published in 1824, has scarcely been improved on to the present (though such an experiment would not be allowed today for ethical reasons). Flourens clearly established the cerebellum's major role in the integration and "programming" of all the innumerable small muscular movements that make up any organized behavior. Even a simple act like walking requires the proper ordering of thousands of discrete movements, and the cerebellum helps achieve this ordering. Flourens observed that his experimental subjects often moved about as if drunk—and we now know that persistent and heavy alcohol use can in fact produce degenerative changes in the cerebellum, leading to the odd and clumsy walking style of many chronic alcoholics. In sum, Flourens proved that the cerebellum was indeed the center of a specific function— but unfortunately for Gall and phrenology that function bore little relation to "amativeness."

Flourens's ablation studies of the **cortex**—the brain's surface area implicated by Gall in most of the "higher" faculties—seemed at first even more damaging to phrenology. As Flourens ablated progressively larger sections of cortex from birds, they gradually lost the use of all of their senses and their capacity for voluntary action. One pigeon, with its entire cortex removed, was kept alive by force-feeding and other heroic ministrations but became completely insensitive to visual or auditory stimulation and never initiated a movement on its own. Only when prodded or physically disturbed would it move, to resume its customary resting position. In describing this bird's state, Flourens imagined it had lost all capacity for consciousness: "Picture to yourself an animal condemned to perpetual sleep, and deprived even of the faculty of dreaming during this sleep."[6] In his view, the animal had lost its *will* along with its cortex.

Flourens believed his findings demolished phrenology. Although he had demonstrated localization of a sort, with different functions attributed to the cerebellum and cortex, he believed these separate functions were evenly distributed *within* each organ. As increasingly larger sections of cortex were removed, for example, all of the various sensory and voluntary functions seemed to disappear *together*. Flourens argued that if the phrenologists were right and the cortex housed many different specific organs, then small ablations ought to have removed some organs while leaving others intact, producing more specific effects than he had in fact observed.

Actually, Flourens skated on thin ice here, since by his own description he had ablated progressively deeper "slices" of cortex. Any "slice," no matter how shallow, very likely interfered with many cortical regions at once, thus producing an apparently general effect. Gall, who contemptuously referred to all brain ablators as "mutilators," eagerly seized on this point: "[Flourens] mutilates all the organs at once, weakens them all, extirpates them all at the same time."[7] With hindsight, we know that Gall was correct and that Flourens did miss important effects of cortical localization.

More enduring, however, have been some of Flourens's other conclusions regarding the cortex's flexibility and plasticity. For example, he observed that sometimes (though not always) ablation-caused deficits improved over time, particularly if the animal was young and the ablations were relatively small. The fact that the lost brain tissue did not regenerate suggested that intact parts of the brain must somehow have been able to take over functions previously served by the ablated portions. The exact limits and conditions of such brain plasticity continue to be explored by scientists today.

Moreover, Flourens's investigations of the brain highlighted the state of integration and harmony that normally prevails among its separate parts. While he conceded a certain *"action propre"* ("specific action") for the cerebellum and cortex considered separately, he also emphasized the cooperation and communication between the two brain parts. Actions initiated by the "will" in the cortex had to be put together and integrated by the cerebellum, and the loss of coordination caused by damage to the cerebellum had to be dealt with by voluntary reactions in the cortex. In Flourens's terminology, the *actions propres* of the parts were subject to an overall *"action commune"* ("common action") of the brain acting as a whole. In a conception somewhat reminiscent of Descartes, Flourens saw the brain as the seat of an integrated and harmonious soul.

Flourens's views seemed much more scientifically respectable than phrenology and were generally accepted by the scientific establishment throughout the middle 1800s. In the 1860s, however, new findings came to light suggesting that even Flourens's meticulous experiments had failed to detect some important localized functions in the cortex and that he had in some ways overemphasized the unity of brain function.

Localization Theory Revived: The Brain's Language Areas

Even during the height of Flourens's influence, one particular phrenological localization continued to attract a degree of interest and support from a vocal minority of doctors: the placement of "verbal memory" in the brain regions directly behind the eyes. These doctors studied the mysterious speechlessness that sometimes followed strokes or other injuries to the brain.

Several such cases had been well documented, including that of the famous English author of *Gulliver's Travels*, Jonathan Swift (1667–1745). Following a stroke the year before he died, Swift became unable to speak with ordinary declarative language, even though he seemed to understand everything that was said to him, and he could sometimes utter highly emotional commands or exclamations. For instance, he once angrily shouted at a servant trying to break up a large piece of coal: "That is a stone, you blockhead!" Another time when upset with *himself,* he bitterly exclaimed, "I am a fool!" In circumstances calling for ordinary conversation, however, Swift remained completely mute.[8]

A similar case reported in 1843 involved a priest who suffered a stroke that left him without speech except for the ability to give forth "the most forceful oath of the tongue, which begins with an 'f,' and which our Dictionaries have never dared to print."[9] The emotion-laden exclamations by Swift and the priest demonstrated that the muscles necessary for the production of speech could still function normally, even though they had somehow lost the capacity for ordinary conversation.

Gall had known of cases like these and accounted for them as the result of injury or disease to the "organ of verbal memory," the region behind the eyes involved in his first phrenological hypothesis. He had produced one striking supporting case in his own practice, a soldier who had suffered a sword wound to the brain behind the left eye. Afterward, this soldier could no longer easily name things or people, resorting to vague catchall terms like "Mr. Such-a-one" in referring even to people he knew very well. Gall's description of this case was probably the first published observation of a specific correlation between speech deficit and injury to the left frontal lobe of the cortex.

Though largely ignored in the general devastation following Flourens's attack on phrenology, Gall's hypothesis was kept alive by his former student **Jean Baptiste Bouillaud** (1796–1881). Bouillaud eventually rejected much of phrenology, but he felt there was some truth to the notion of an area that controls language in the frontal region of the cortex, and he published what evidence he could find on the issue. This evidence was scanty, as no one had thought it important to perform autopsies on the brains of deceased patients who had suffered from speech losses. Nevertheless, Bouillaud spoke out at medical meetings and offered to pay 500 francs to anyone who could demonstrate a case of severe frontal lobe damage unaccompanied by speech disorder. Apparently, no one took him seriously enough to accept his challenge.

One doctor *had* to take Bouillaud seriously, however: his son-in-law, **Ernest Aubertin** (1825–1893). Moreover, Aubertin found one very interesting patient whose symptoms supported Bouillaud's theory. A soldier wounded by gunshot on the left front of his head had recovered completely except for a soft spot in his skull at the point of the wound. When the spot was gently pressed, he lost his otherwise normal power of speech. This case posed obvious opportunities for conscious or unconscious dissimulation by the patient, and it failed to impress skeptics. But Aubertin believed in the patient's sincerity and took up cudgels for his father-in-law's theory himself. When he presented his views at the Paris Anthropological Society in 1861, he precipitated one of the critical incidents in the history of brain science.

Paul Broca and the Case of "Tan"

Paul Broca (1824–1880; see Figure 3.4), a young chief of surgery at a major Parisian hospital, had founded the Paris Anthropological Society in 1859. Through his surgical work, Broca had become interested in variations among people's skeletal structures, particularly their skulls. He invented several instruments for measuring such variations and founded the Anthropological Society to bring together other people with similar interests (which in today's terminology would be considered part of *physical* as opposed to *cultural* anthropology). Several experts on head and brain anatomy joined, including Aubertin.

Most of these experts accepted Flourens's general argument about the brain and regarded Aubertin's contrary view with skepticism. On April 4, 1861, however, Aubertin made an announcement to the Society in the tradition of his father-in-law:

FIG 3.4
Paul Broca
(1824–1880)

I have studied for a long time a patient . . . who has lost his speech, who nevertheless understands all that is said to him, replying by signs in an intelligent manner to all questions put to him. This patient . . . is now at the Hospital for Incurables and will die, without doubt, in a short time. In view of the symptoms which he presents I have made a diagnosis of softening of the anterior [frontal] lobes. If at autopsy the anterior lobes are found intact, then I shall renounce the ideas which I have sustained.[10]

Just five days after this challenge, an event occurred that led to Aubertin's patient being largely forgotten, along with Aubertin himself. A patient with similar symptoms turned up on *Broca's* surgical ward, terminally ill with gangrene of the right leg. Twenty-one years earlier the man had lost his speech but had remained otherwise healthy and intelligent. He could understand what was said to him, point correctly to named objects, and answer numerical questions by holding up the appropriate numbers of fingers. Like Swift, he could use words only when angry, uttering the oath *"Sacre nom de Dieu!"* Otherwise, his only vocalization was the syllable *tan*, which he repeated rhythmically when he wished to speak, and which led to his being nicknamed "Tan" on the wards.

Ten years after Tan's speech loss, his right arm and leg gradually became paralyzed. Early in 1860 he began to go blind and took to his bed almost constantly—a solitary and pathetic creature. When an infection developed in his insensitive right leg, neither he nor the hospital staff noticed until it became gangrenous, and he was sent to Broca's surgical ward. Lacking modern antibiotics, Broca immediately saw the case as hopeless. He summoned Aubertin to ask if Tan fit the requirements for a test of his hypothesis; Aubertin replied that he did.

When Tan died a few days later, Broca promptly autopsied the brain and brought it to the Anthropological Society. An egg-sized portion of the left frontal hemisphere had clearly been damaged, with its center very close to Gall's 'organ of verbal memory." Though it could not be proved, it seemed likely that Tan's speech problem had begun with progressive brain deterioration starting at that center; his other symptoms developed as the degeneration spread.

One confirming case could not prove a theory, of course, and Broca reserved judgment until he found more. This task was more difficult than one might think, because he could not experimentally create frontal lesions in humans as Flourens had in animals, and cases of patients who had had both speech impairments and brain autopsies were rare. Thus, while Broca may have been lucky to steal Aubertin's thunder in producing the first demonstration case, he proved his real mettle as a scientist by collecting more supportive evidence. Over the next few years, he found autopsy information from several further cases of speech loss. While the extent of brain damage varied considerably among these cases, it almost always included the same region of the frontal lobe. A surprise finding, for Broca and everyone else, was that in right-handed patients the damage invariably occurred on the left side. The crucial region, shown in Figure 3.5, came to be known as **Broca's area**. After some debate, the speech debility resulting from damage to that area came to be called **aphasia**, after the term used by Plato to denote the state of being at a loss for words.

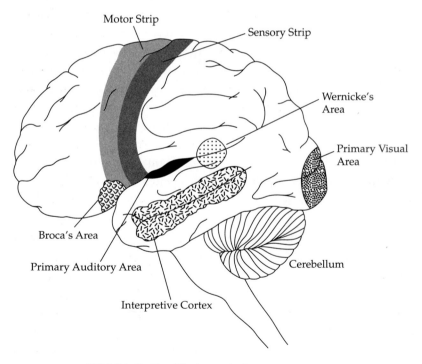

FIG 3.5 Left side of the human brain

With his investigations of aphasia, Broca became the first establishment figure seriously and effectively to challenge Flourens's conception of the undifferentiated cerebral cortex. His findings ushered in a new period of interest in the localized functions of the brain. In short order, individuals sometimes called the "new phrenologists" discovered many further important localizations. In a more dubious achievement, Broca also became known for promoting the ideas that differences in brain *size* correlated positively with differences in intelligence and that European males—with allegedly larger than average brain size than all women and the males of other racial backgrounds—were consequently innately superior to all other groups. Although both ideas were widely accepted for a time (mainly by other European males), neither has been confirmed by later and better research.

Sensory and Motor Areas

In 1870, two young German physiologists, **Gustav Fritsch** (1837–1927) and **Eduard Hitzig** (1838–1907), had the bright idea that the brain might not be the totally insensitive organ Aristotle had thought and in fact might respond to direct *electrical* stimulation. Recent discoveries about the electrochemical nature of the nervous impulse lent plausibility to this idea, and electricity in general was a fashionable and exciting scientific topic of the day, whose possible applications were being explored in many fields. Thus, Fritsch and Hitzig surgically exposed the cortex of a dog and applied mild electrical stimulation to various specific points with a penlike electrode.

Conducted with makeshift equipment on an unanesthetized animal in Hitzig's house, the experiment partly resembled a scene from a Gothic novel and would certainly not be approved by ethics committees today. But the results revolutionized brain science, for Fritsch and Hitzig discovered that stimulation to specific points in the region now known as the **motor strip** (see Figure 3.5) elicited specific movements on the opposite side of the body. Stimulation to one particular point on the right motor strip always produced a flexion of the left forepaw, for example, while a neighboring point's electrification caused extension of the left hind leg. Here was evidence for a previously unsuspected kind of localization in the brain, as well as a new experimental technique for studying it.

Many other scientists quickly followed Fritsch and Hitzig's lead, none more skillfully than a young Scottish neurologist named **David Ferrier** (1843–1928). Throughout the 1870s he demonstrated several other functionally distinct "centers" in the cortex, to accompany Broca's area and the motor strip. When he electrically stimulated the rear portion of the occipital (rear) lobe of a monkey's brain, for example, the animal's eyes moved rapidly and synchronously, as if looking at something. Ablation of the same region produced blindness but no deficiency in any other sense. Thus, the occipital cortex contained a **visual area** (see Figure 3.5). Ferrier also discovered an **auditory area** in the temporal (side) lobe and a strip immediately behind the motor strip that mediated *sensory* functions for the same body parts. Ablations from this **sensory strip** produced *losses of sensitivity* in specific parts of the body, while ablations from the bordering motor strip caused paralyses.

While these findings confirmed the reality of cortical localization, they also conclusively undermined the old phrenology, even in the popular view. Although Broca's area resembled Gall's organ of verbal memory in some ways, all of the other newly discovered localizations differed greatly from phrenological organs in that they mediated elementary sensory or motor functions, instead of complex and highly developed "faculties." One diehard phrenologist tried to claim that the leg movements produced by electrical stimulation of the "organ of self-esteem" were really rudimentary acts of *strutting*, but such desperate rationalizations generally received the contempt they deserved. Very quickly, an entirely new conception of brain function came into vogue, attempting to explain not only the newly discovered localizations but also the numerous "blank" areas on the cortical map—that is, areas whose stimulation or ablation produced no clearcut observable effects in animal subjects.

According to this conception, the brain receives sensory information at the various sensory centers, then stores it in the surrounding regions. Thus, visual memories are presumably stored in specific locations surrounding the visual area, auditory memories around the auditory area, and so on. (Animal subjects could not talk about their memories, of course, so stimulation or ablation of these memory regions had produced no clearly observable effects.) Further, all these localized memories were hypothesized to be potentially *interconnected* with one another by fibers of white matter. Brain parts particularly rich in white matter were called "association areas." The frontal lobes of human brains—very large compared to other species and also particularly rich in white matter—were speculated to contain the large association areas responsible for humans' superiority over other animals in thoughtfulness and intelligence.

Wernicke's Theory of Aphasia

In 1874, the young German neurologist **Carl Wernicke** (1848–1905; see Figure 3.6) used this new conception of the brain as the basis of an influential theory of aphasia. He started by noting that Broca's area lay directly in front of the part of the motor strip responsible for movement of the mouth, tongue, and face—precisely where one would expect to find memories of the movements involved in speech, according to the

FIG 3.6
Carl Wernicke
(1848–1905)

new conception. Thus, localized damage to Broca's area alone (that is, without extending onto the adjoining motor strip) should theoretically afflict the memories for spoken words but not the physical capacity for speaking. This could account for cases like Tan and Jonathan Swift.

Wernicke went on to describe a group of ten patients he had discovered with a very different sort of language disorder, which he called **sensory aphasia** to contrast with the **motor aphasia** previously investigated by Broca. These patients could speak perfectly fluently with correct syntax, but their *understanding* of spoken language was severely impaired, and their speech was marked by numerous peculiar words and mispronunciations that Wernicke called **paraphasias**. The speech of such patients sounded like something from the Theater of the Absurd, as in the following responses of a modern patient with sensory aphasia to the question of what brought him to the hospital:

> Boy, I'm sweating, I'm awful nervous, you know, once in a while I get caught up, I can't mention the tarripoi, a month ago, quite a little, I've done a lot well, I impose a lot, while on the other hand, you know what I mean, I have to run around, look it over, trebbin and all that sort of stuff.[11]

Wernicke showed that patients with sensory aphasia had suffered lesions to a part of the left temporal lobe close to the auditory area—precisely where the auditory memories for words should theoretically be stored. This finding made sense, because as long as the auditory regions themselves remain intact, such patients should hear what is said to them and recognize when they are being engaged in conversation, although without remembering what the heard words *mean*. If Broca's area also remains intact, such patients retain the *motor* memories of words necessary for fluent spoken responses, and they may try to reply out of social habit. But since they have not understood what was said to them, their responses seem bizarre to the listener. Wernicke observed that such patients are likely to be misdiagnosed as suffering from a psychotic mental illness if their brain injuries go undetected.

Wernicke explained his patients' mispronunciations, or paraphasias, as the result of the same lesions. Normally, he argued, people listen to themselves as they speak, constantly monitoring and correcting themselves as they go along. If they start to mispronounce a word, they rapidly stop, correct themselves, and begin again with scarcely a break in their sentence. Because sensory aphasics lack comprehension of their own as well as others' spoken words, however, they also lack this self-correcting ability and utter many paraphasias.

The brain region implicated in sensory aphasia has come to be known as **Wernicke's area** and is shown in Figure 3.5. Wernicke's terms, *motor aphasia* and *sensory aphasia*, are still commonly used, although the two conditions are also sometimes called **Broca's aphasia** and **Wernicke's aphasia**, respectively.

In a final impressive theoretical achievement, Wernicke successfully predicted the existence of still another kind of aphasic speech disorder, previously undescribed and undetected by doctors. He reasoned that an intact brain must contain association fibers connecting the sensory speech memories in Wernicke's area with the motor ones in Broca's area; these connections make possible the silent monitoring and correcting of one's own speech. If these association fibers become damaged while Broca's and Wernicke's areas remain intact, a condition Wernicke called **conduction aphasia** should occur—marked by paraphasias because of the loss of self-monitoring, but with comprehension and general fluency unimpaired. Such cases should be rare, as damage to the small connecting region would usually be accompanied by injury to the nearby Broca's or Wernicke's area, producing motor or sensory aphasia. Further, the predicted symptoms of conduction aphasia would be relatively mild, making it likely that many cases would be overlooked.

Once placed on the alert by Wernicke, neurologists everywhere went on the lookout for cases of conduction aphasia and soon found several. In addition to their paraphasias, these patients suffered from a striking inability to repeat aloud things that were said to them. Though not specifically predicted by Wernicke, this symptom too clearly accorded with his theory: Without connections between their auditory and motor word memories, the patients lacked a mechanism for modeling their own speech after something they had just heard.

This remarkable vindication of Wernicke's theory indicated that brain science had entered a new era of sophistication. Previously, work had been largely descriptive and atheoretical, directed simply toward the empirical localization of functions in the cortex. Most of these functions turned out to involve elementary sensory and motor reactions rather than complex faculties. Wernicke used that information to construct a theory of one complex function, language, as the result of an *interaction* among several simple sensory, motor, and associative factors. Following his lead, scientists no longer looked for high-level "faculties" localized in the brain but sought instead to demonstrate how complex psychological processes in general might be created out of the basic elements of sensations, movements, and their memory traces.

Memory and the Equipotentiality Debate

Even as Wernicke and others demonstrated the power of the new localization theories, a partially contrasting line of evidence regarding the brain's storage of memory came to prominence in the United States in the early 1900s. In 1902 a young American psychologist, named **Shepherd Ivory Franz** (1874–1933), published a study of the effects of cortical ablations on cats that had previously been trained to escape from a "puzzle box."[12] Such a study, of course, was much in the tradition of Flourens—except that instead of looking at the generalized effects of ablation as Flourens had, Franz was interested in the effects on a specific, learned response. His innovation was to combine ablation with animal training.

Of course, if the memories for the learned responses were localized in specific small regions of the cortex, only those ablations involving those particular regions should have affected the responses. Franz's study, however, found localization only of a highly general sort, in that lesions of the frontal cortex caused the responses to be lost, while lesions elsewhere did not. Even more significant, it seemed to Franz, was the fact that the frontally ablated animals were able to *relearn* the escape response quite easily and quickly. Obviously then, if the ablated regions had been somehow responsible for the original learning, altogether different brain parts were able to perform highly similar functions in the relearning. This finding led Franz to distrust the strong localization theory and to recall and respect Flourens's old dictum that the brain functions as a whole.

Franz spent much of his subsequent career in hospital settings and remained highly impressed by this plasticity and flexibility of the brain. He observed that human patients suffering lost functions from localized brain damage sometimes managed to reacquire those functions, either partially or completely. The recovery was likely to be greatest in young patients. Infants and children with extensive left-side damage, for example, regularly acquired language functions normally even though their Broca's and Wernicke's areas had been destroyed. Franz concluded, "Everything tended to show that there are not the definite and exact functions for parts of the cerebrum which were posited [by the most enthusiastic localizationists], but that there is rather a possibility of substitution."[13]

In 1915, Franz gained an ally and co-worker for further animal research in the person of **Karl Spencer Lashley** (1890–1958; see Figure 3.7). Although his Ph.D. was in genetics, Lashley had been attracted to psychology through his friendship and collaboration at Johns Hopkins University with John B. Watson (1878–1958), the charismatic founder of the behaviorist movement whose contributions are detailed in Chapter 9. Watson and the behaviorists ruled out any experimental methods involving introspection or reports of conscious states, but concentrated on the strictly observable and "objective" behaviors of their subjects. Animals such as tame white rats were favored subjects because they could be easily observed, their

FIG 3.7
Karl Lashley
(1890–1958)

environments could be controlled, and of course they could not mislead the experimenters with unverifiable subjective reports. Typical experiments studied the ability of animals to learn how to solve problems such as the running of mazes. These showed that hungry white rats could gradually learn to solve quite complicated mazes if rewarded with food whenever their trial-and-error explorations brought them to the ends of the mazes. The number of false turns or "errors" tended to decrease with each succeeding trial and provided objective indices of the animals' learning.

When Lashley met Franz, the two decided to pool their expertise in some experiments in which Lashley trained white rats on a maze and an inclined plane task and Franz performed selective ablations of their brains. As they expected, given Franz's earlier work, they found little evidence for localization, and they said so in a pair of papers in 1917. Subsequently Lashley on his own, now trained by Franz on ablation techniques, conducted a much more extensive and systematic series of studies in which large numbers of white rats were trained on a wide variety of mazes and other tasks, followed by systematically varying ablations. His highly detailed findings, recounted in the classic 1929 book *Brain Mechanisms and Intelligence* and summarized by the graph in Figure 3.8,[14] seemed the final nail in the coffin for localization-of-memory hypothesis. The graph shows the numbers of errors made by rats running mazes of three difficulty levels, following six degrees of ablation. On the whole, the specific locations of the ablations made little difference at all. Of much greater importance were absolute *sizes* of the ablations, and the *difficulty levels* of the mazes involved. In general, large ablations impeded performance on all mazes more than small ablations did, and the effect was much more marked on the difficult than on the easy mazes. Thus, memory seemed to pervade the entire cortex, and not to be selectively localized in it.

Just as Broca, Ferrier, and Wernicke had revived memories of Gall and the early localizationists, so Lashley now hearkened back to Flourens and the brain's *action commune*—though for Lashley it was memory rather than the will that seemed evenly distributed throughout the cortex. In summarizing his results, Lashley contributed two new terms Flourens would undoubtedly have approved of. First, he said that the brain is marked by **equipotentiality**, which he defined as "the apparent capacity of any intact part of a functional brain to carry

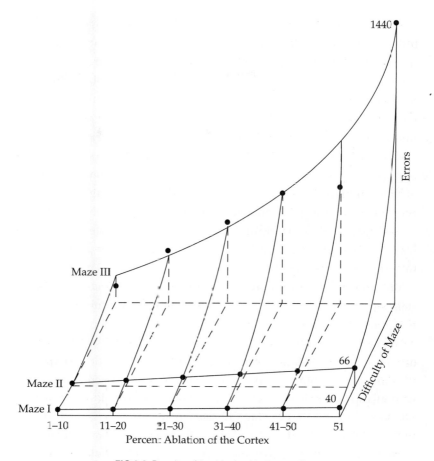

FIG 3.8 Results of Lashley's ablation studies

out . . . the [memory] functions which are lost by the destruction of [other parts]." But the brain's equipotentiality may sometimes be off-set by the **law of mass action**, "whereby the efficiency of performance of an entire complex function may be reduced in proportion to the extent of brain injury."[15]

In sum, Lashley's systematic experiments seemed to rule out any simple theory of memory localization in the brain, and toward the end of his life he wryly expressed his own frustration with the prob-lem: "I sometimes feel in reviewing the evidence on the localization of the memory trace, that the necessary conclusion is that learning just is not possible. It is difficult to conceive of a mechanism which can satisfy the conditions set for it."[16]

The exact mechanisms of memory remain something of a mystery today. Some of Lashley's successors have suggested that his original theory oversimplified the problem and that even elementary maze learning actually involves much more than the coupling of single sensory stimuli with single motor responses. In learning to run a maze, a rat must inevitably associate *many different stimuli* (involving touch, smell, and hearing as well as vision) with the various "correct" motor responses. Thus, even if localized stimulus-response connections really do underlie learning and memory, there should be many of them in many different parts of the brain for any single completed act of maze learning. Damage to just a small part of the brain would remove just a few of these and would have a small effect on overall learning; damage to larger areas would remove a larger portion of the total, and produce a larger decrement in performance.

The so-called **redundancy hypothesis** offers a related explanation, suggesting that each individual memory gets stored in *several* locations throughout the cortex, with the number increasing as the memory becomes better established and more widely associated with other memories. Ablation of an isolated brain area would be expected to remove some but not all of the traces of any particular memory. And in a speculative vein, some have pointed out that laser-generated *holograms* provide a possible physical model in which visual information is stored evenly throughout a photographic plate. Much work remains to be done to confirm these or any neurophysiological theory of memory, for here is one area in which the venerable localization of function debate remains very much alive. One certainty, however, is that any final solution will have to account for some very *non*-behavioristic experiments, involving the electrical stimulation of the conscious human brain. While many of their implications remain unclear, these studies represent one of the most intriguing and exciting phases of the localization-of-function controversy.

Stimulation of the Conscious Human Brain

Stimulation studies of the conscious human brain got off to a poor start in 1874, shortly after Fritsch and Hitzig first stimulated the conscious animal brain. A mentally retarded young woman with a cancerous lesion of the scalp and skull came under the care of the Cincinnati doctor **Roberts Bartholow** (1831–1904). Bartholow later reported that, because part of her brain was visible through the opening in her skull, he "supposed that fine needles could be introduced without material injury to the cerebral matter." Following Fritsch and Hitzig's lead, Bartholow connected his needles to a mild electrical supply and stimulated the exposed surface, producing involuntary muscular contractions on the opposite side of the body. When the needle was inserted deeper, the patient complained of an unpleasant tingling in her arm. Then, "in order to develop more decided reactions, the strength of the current was increased," with the following sad results:

> Her countenance exhibited great distress, and she began to cry. Very soon the left hand was extended as if taking hold of some object in front of her; the arm presently was agitated by clonic spasms; her eyes became fixed, with pupils widely dilated; her lips were blue, and she frothed at the mouth; her breathing became stertorous; she lost consciousness, and was violently convulsed on the left side. The convulsion lasted five minutes, and was succeeded by coma.

The patient's general condition worsened after the experiment, and she died before Bartholow could carry out a planned repetition. He examined her brain at autopsy and concluded that "although it is obvious that even fine needles cannot be introduced into the cerebral substance without doing mischief, yet the fatal result in this case must be attributed to the extension of [her original cancer]."[17] Despite Bartholow's attempt to minimize the harmfulness of his procedures, the grisly experiment created such an outcry that he shortly had to leave Cincinnati.

Wilder Penfield and the Treatment of Epilepsy

More than a half-century passed before the next stimulation experiments on conscious human subjects. These, by the Montreal-based neurosurgeon **Wilder Penfield** (1891–1976; see Figure 3.9), had much greater ethical justification and yielded much more valuable scientific results. Penfield began in the 1930s by seeking new surgical treatments

FIG 3.9
Wilder Penfield
(1891–1976)

for intractable cases of epilepsy, which he knew to be caused by abnormal activation of cerebral neurons beginning at a small "focus," and then spreading over larger and larger areas of the brain. When the abnormal activation spreads sufficiently far, patients lose consciousness and have convulsions. Shortly before the convulsions, patients frequently experience peculiar subjective warning signs called *auras*. These signs vary from patient to patient and include sensations such as a particular smell, a tingling or other feeling in some particular part of the body, an intense but inexplicable feeling of familiarity (déjà vu) or the unexplained arousal of an emotion such as rage, guilt, depression, or elation. One famous epileptic, the great novelist Fyodor Dostoyevsky, experienced two contrasting kinds of emotional auras. One was a feeling of irrational guilt, the conviction that he had committed some unknown but unspeakable crime; the other was "a feeling of happiness such as it is quite impossible to imagine in a normal state, . . . for a few seconds of such bliss, one would gladly give up ten years of one's life."[18]

Penfield had the idea that auras might result from early activation at the focus, before it spreads so far as to cause the convulsion and seizure per se. Further, he thought the specific *content* of an aura might depend on the *location* of the focus; an aura of tingling in the left arm, for instance, might be associated with a focus in the right sensory strip. This suggested a daring experimental treatment, to be tried only on the small proportion of epileptic patients whose seizures could not be controlled by ordinary medication.

Using a local anesthetic, Penfield surgically exposed the brains of his fully conscious, volunteer patients. He then gently stimulated different locations with an electrode, seeking specific spots whose stimulation would cause his patients to experience their auras. He often found such spots, and he concluded that they marked diseased brain tissue responsible for the epilepsy. He then surgically removed the suspect areas, unless they happened to lie near a language region whose ablation might produce aphasia. Most patients reported a subsequent lessening of their epilepsy that justified any side effects from the procedure.

Apart from its therapeutic value, Penfield's remarkable procedure provided invaluable information about localization of function in general. While searching for aura-producing spots, Penfield naturally stimulated many normal regions of the cortex and observed the effects on fully conscious, intelligent, and cooperative individuals. Some of these effects were predictable from earlier localization studies. Stimulation of the motor strip, for example, produced movements on the opposite side of the body—movements that surprised the patients themselves because they occurred involuntarily. When Penfield stimulated the sensory strip, his patients reported sensations such as tingling, quivering, or pressure in various parts of the body. Stimulation of the visual area produced flashes of light, color, and abstract patterns, while the auditory area yielded clicks, buzzes, chirps, rumbles, and other sounds.

There were also many surprises. When Penfield stimulated the regions *surrounding* the primary visual and auditory areas, for example, patients experienced full visual or auditory hallucinations replete with meaning, as opposed to the "contentless" flashes, clicks, and buzzes produced by the primary regions. For example, stimulation of one patient's secondary visual region (as Penfield called this surrounding area) led the patient to say, "Oh gee, gosh, robbers are coming at me with guns." He actually *saw* the robbers coming, from behind and to the left.[19] When Penfield stimulated another patient's secondary auditory region, one spot produced the sound of a mother calling a child, and another a Beethoven symphony. So real and surprising was the latter sensation that the patient accused Penfield of secretly turning on a radio.

Stimulation of the temporal lobe—the side area of the cortex above the ear—produced the most surprising effects of all. Apart from the relatively small auditory region and Wernicke's area, the temporal lobe had previously been a blank zone on the brain localizationists' map, unimplicated in any of the functions they knew about. But Penfield found what he called the **interpretive cortex** (see Figure 3.5), a temporal region whose stimulation produced two kinds of "psychical responses." First were **interpretive responses**, in which patients suddenly and inexplicably saw their immediate situations in new lights. Depending on the points of stimulation, interpretive responses included such feelings as déjà vu, the opposite sensation that everything was suddenly alien or absurd, senses of foreboding and fear, or sudden euphoria and exhilaration. These interpretive sensations duplicated some patients' epileptic auras (Dostoyevsky's, for example), which now became understandable for the first time as the results of focal discharges in the interpretive cortex. Moreover, Penfield had shown that highly specific emotional and orienting attitudes were localized in the brain, just as sensations and movements were.

Penfield's stimulation of other parts of the interpretive cortex produced **experiential responses**, described by his patients variously as hallucinatory "dreams" or "flashbacks" of real events from the past, usually with unremarkable content. For example, one patient reported: "Oh, a familiar memory—in an office somewhere. I could see the desks. I was there and someone was calling to me—a man leaning on a desk with a pencil in his hand." Other typical responses included "A scene from a play; they were talking and I could see it," and "A familiar memory—the place where I hang my coat up—where I go to work."[20] Unlike normal "memories," however, these scenes were vividly *experienced* subjectively, and not merely thought about.

Penfield's exciting findings actually raised more questions than they answered. They demonstrated new and unexpected localized functions of some sort, but the real nature of those functions remains in some doubt today. At first thought, for example, it may be tempting to argue that Penfield's "experiential responses" provided the long-sought evidence for the localization of memories. Their vivid detail suggests that even inconsequential experiences may become permanently recorded in specific brain cells, potentially available for exact recall. But Penfield himself hesitated to equate these responses with "memories."

First, he noted that patients described their experiential responses as being qualitatively different from normal memories—more on the order of vivid dreams than of ordinary thoughts or recollections. Thus, the normal functioning of memory must involve something different from the specific stimulation of neurons artificially produced by Penfield. He himself thought the electrical stimulations initiated a "scanning" of experiences recorded in the brain that is part but not all of the normal memory process. Penfield further cautioned that no one understood the exact effects of artificial electrical stimulation on the cerebral neurons. He personally suspected that electrical stimulation and abnormal epileptic discharges both tend to *inhibit* rather than to activate the normal functions of the neurons involved. Thus, interpretive and experiential responses may really be caused by the operation of unknown parts of the brain whose functions are normally *opposed* by the neurons of the interpretive cortex. When the cortical neurons are temporarily knocked out of commission by artificial electrical stimulation or epileptic discharge, the opposed functions are permitted to express themselves. Penfield further observed that experiential responses are much more like moving pictures than still pictures, indicating that cerebral neurons must somehow represent the "flow" of experience and not just stationary images of it. Much more must be involved than the simple storage of individual static "ideas" in single neural cells.

As if this were not enough, our understanding of memory and the brain's role in it became further complicated following another remarkable case study and related follow-up performed by one of Penfield's younger colleagues in the 1950s.

Brenda Milner and the Multiplicity of Memory Systems

Brenda Milner (b. 1918; see Figure 3.10) was a graduate student in psychology at Cambridge in England, whose studies were interrupted by World War II. She eventually immigrated to Montreal with her

FIG 3.10
Brenda Milner
(b. 1918)

husband, an engineer who had been invited to initiate a program of atomic energy research in Canada. Once established in Montreal, Milner used her proficiency in French to secure a teaching position at the newly formed Institut de Psychologie at the Université de Montréal. In 1947 **Donald O. Hebb** (1904–1985) arrived at Montreal's McGill University with the draft manuscript for his book *The Organization of Behavior* in hand. Published in 1949, this book related learning and other behavior to the hypothetical functioning of "neurological networks" in the brain that he called **cell assemblies**, and it became an instant classic. Milner attended weekly seminars where each chapter of the draft was discussed and debated, and she quickly decided to register in the Ph.D. program under Hebb. Recognizing Milner's promise as a student of brain and behavior, Hebb recommended that she do her dissertation research with the renowned Penfield at the nearby Montreal Neurological Institute. There, she became particularly interested in the effects of temporal lobe lesions and ablations and earned her Ph.D. with a dissertation on that subject in 1952.

In the course of their work together, Milner and Penfield became aware of the potential importance in brain functioning of the **hippocampus,**[*] a structure lying beneath the temporal lobe that was sometimes incidentally involved in deep lesions and ablations of that lobe. In particular, they observed and studied two cases in which hippocampal lesions had seemingly impaired memory for recent events, and they presented these cases in a paper given at a 1955 conference. Propitiously, as it turned out, a Yale University–based surgeon, William Scoville, read their abstract and telephoned Penfield about a patient he had just operated on who displayed a similar memory impairment. Penfield relayed the information to Milner, who traveled to Connecticut to take up the study of the fascinating case of "H.M.," perhaps the most famous case study in the history of the neuropsychology of memory.

H.M. had begun to experience minor, petit mal seizures at the age of 10 after an apparently minor fall, but they escalated into major grand mal seizures by the age of 16. These seizures occurred without warning and included tongue biting, urinary incontinence, convulsions, and loss of consciousness, followed by prolonged sleepiness. Despite extensive anticonvulsant therapy, the grand mal seizures continued to occur about once a week, and minor seizures struck him almost hourly. By the age of 27, H.M. had become completely incapacitated.

Because of the severity of his illness, and because EEG readings showed diffuse abnormalities in both hemispheres of the brain, H.M.'s neurosurgeon, William Scoville, decided to undertake a "frankly experimental operation,"[1] in which a probe was inserted into the brain and large sections of the hippocampus and surrounding tissue on both sides were ablated. Although substantially relieved of his seizures, H.M. immediately experienced profound memory deficits. In particular, he developed a severe form of amnesia in which he was unable to retain any *new* memories of events or experiences occurring subsequent to the operation. He could clearly remember his identity and details of his life up to about three years before his operation, but any new learning or

---

[*] The word *hippocampus* means "seahorse" in ancient Greek; it was adopted for this structure by early brain anatomists because its shape seemed to them to resemble that creature.

information remained with him only briefly and fleetingly. For example, if he read the newspaper, 15 minutes later he would be unable to recall doing so or remember any of the information he had read. Milner reported that she would have lunch with H.M. then ask him 30 minutes later what he had eaten. He was unable to name a single item of food or even remember that he had taken a meal.

Much like Broca after Tan, Scoville and Milner next undertook a comparative case study of ten patients, including H.M., who had undergone variations of the epilepsy surgery, differing only with respect to how much of the hippocampal region was destroyed. Patients like H.M. with the most extensive excisions of the hippocampus showed the most profound loss of recent memory. Some other patients, whose hippocampal regions were spared significant damage, showed completely intact memory. Scoville and Milner concluded that the ability to form recent memories somehow resided throughout this particular brain structure.[22]

Milner, assisted by her colleagues and students, continued to study H.M. for thirty years. Interestingly, despite this severe incapacitation, his personality and general intelligence remained largely unchanged. Even on the "digit span" test, in which he was asked to repeat back a series of numbers that had just been read to him, he performed normally. This finding led Milner to conclude that H.M.'s deficits did not involve short-term memory per se, since he was able to retain the numbers for a short time in a "working memory." What he could not do was to *transfer* the information from the working memory to long-term storage. Memory tasks on which there was a delay between learning and recall, especially if the delay was filled with a distractor task, were impossible for him. Milner proposed that this provided evidence for two separate memory processes, one a primary mental process with rapid decay, the other an overlapping secondary process through which long-term storage is achieved. She was also able to show that H.M.'s impairment did not hold for every type of task. For example, when H.M. was tested on a mirror-drawing task, in which he had to trace the outline of a star while looking only at its reflection in a mirror, his performance on the task improved substantially over successive trials, even though he could not remember, or declare, that he had ever performed the task before. That is, his *declarative memory* (i.e., his ability to remember and verbally describe) was impaired, but his *procedural memory* (to benefit from practice and repeat newly learned actions) was not. Milner's hypothesis that there exist distinct and multiple memory systems was a major new idea, and the investigation and detailed analysis of these systems on a psychological level became a major component in the emergence of cognitive psychology as a major discipline—as we shall see in Chapter 14.*

Cartesian Dualism Revisited

Toward the end of his life, Penfield published a surprising opinion on the extent to which our understanding of the neurological bases of cognitive functioning will help us explain the mind. He admitted that his own work had originally been inspired by the assumption that the mechanisms of the brain *account for* the phenomena of the mind. He assumed that once the brain was fully understood, all mental and psychological phenomena would be explained in consequence. But by 1975, he had doubts: Certain elements of experience—particularly the conscious *willing* or *deciding* to do something, or *believing* in something—had never been produced by electrical stimulation or any other mechanistic process. Penfield now doubted that they ever would be, and he wrote:

> Because it seems to me certain that it will always be quite impossible to explain the mind on the basis of neuronal action within the brain, and because it seems to me that the mind develops and matures independently throughout an individual's life as though it were a continuing element, . . . I am forced to choose the proposition that our being is to be explained on the basis of two fundamental elements.[23]

In other words, Penfield came to regard "brain" and "mind" as two independent though interacting entities, each with its own separate levels of explanation. He thus finally opted for a dualism not very

---

* In 2008, at the age of 82, H.M., whose real name was Henry Gustav Molaison, died of respiratory failure at his nursing home in Connecticut. With his prior consent, his brain has been preserved for future study. In life and in death, his legacy to our understanding of the human memory system has been immense.

different (except in detail) from Descartes'. Penfield admitted that he could not *prove* this opinion, and many contemporary brain scientists would contest it. As we shall see in Chapter 14, a similar debate has arisen regarding the *artificial intelligence* of sophisticated computer programs and the question of whether a machine that can simulate humanlike intelligent behavior perfectly can ever have the *subjective* experiences of consciousness, belief, and freedom of the will. Descartes' issue obviously remains very much alive, and it will continue to engage cognitive neuroscientists as well as philosophers well into the future.

Recent Developments: Cognitive Neuroscience and Social Neuroscience

Despite disagreement over whether the mind-brain relationship will ever be fully understood and what form that understanding will take, there is no question but that the *assumption* of a strong connection has been highly productive. This assumption stimulated the work of Penfield and Milner in the first place and continues to stimulate scientists to this day. Indeed, prominent psychologist and neuroscientist V. S. Ramachandran has called the efforts to understand how the brain gives rise to the mind, thus accomplishing an awareness of itself, the "holy grail" of neuroscience.

The search for the holy grail has been advanced with the invention and use of ever more powerful imaging technologies that permit increasingly detailed observation of the brain structures and even some of their activities that accompany specific mental processes. Many of these techniques fall under the general category of **tomography**, the imaging of objects as collections of sections or "slices" created by various kinds of penetrating waves. Among the more common types of tomograms are CT (computed tomography) or "CAT" scans, which are based on X-rays, and MRI (magnetic resonance imaging) scans, which use radio waves to produce images of magnetically aligned atoms within the object. When the object under observation is a physiological organ such as the brain, these techniques are often combined with positron emission tomography (PET) scans, which can detect the concentrations of radioactive "tracer" molecules that have been injected and which can reflect differing levels of ongoing metabolic activity in different parts of the brain. More recently, less invasive and time-consuming fMRI (functional MRI) procedures have been developed, which can provide images of blood oxygenation (an indirect index of blood flow) to reflect neural activity in particular brain regions.

Coincident with these technological developments, a shift was occurring in the field of academic psychology that is sometimes called the *cognitive revolution*. *Resurgence* is a more apt term than *revolution*, because cognitive functions—i.e., those relating to processes such as thinking, reasoning, memory, and perception—had traditionally been considered an important domain of psychology. During much of the early- to mid-twentieth century, however, the movement known as *behaviorism* (see Chapter 9) became dominant, particularly among English-speaking academic psychologists. The behaviorist orthodoxy declared that only directly and "objectively" observable behavior was appropriate subject matter for scientific psychology. Anything not directly and objectively observable, including subjective introspections, thoughts, reasoning, and so on, was ruled out of bounds. Details of these events will be provided in Chapters 9 and 14, but for now it suffices to note that throughout the latter half of the twentieth century psychologists increasingly returned to cognitive processes as major subjects for their investigations and analyses. As noted earlier, the work of Milner and her colleagues revealing part of the complex structure of memory stands as one example of this trend.

Perhaps inevitably, technological advances in brain imaging and revived interest in cognition came together, as cognitive psychologists and "neuroscientists" from diverse disciplines began using the new technologies to reveal what actually goes on in the different parts of the brain as various cognitive activities are performed. Here was localization research in the same traditions as described throughout this chapter, but with a previously undreamed of precision. In the late 1970s the pioneering cognitive psychologist George Miller and the younger neuroscientist Michael Gazzaniga coined the term **cognitive neuroscience** to denote the new interdisciplinary field. Both the field and its name "took off," with its signal accomplishments including PET studies of brain activity during varying states of *attention* and *memory* by the psychologist Michael Posner and neurologist Marcus Raichle in the 1980s. The psychologist Stephen Kosslyn used fMRI technology to show that the brain processes accompanying *mental* *imagery* are not unified or localized in a single region, but in fact occur in diverse regions, each responsible for different *aspects* of the imaging process. Too diverse and complex to be summarized here, the main accomplishments of the new field have been summarized by Gazzaniga and two colleagues in their book *Cognitive Neuroscience: The Biology of the Mind.*[24]

The excitement generated by these increasingly sophisticated methods for "seeing" inside the brain and uncovering the neurological correlates of human behavior has also extended into traditionally "soft" areas such as social psychology (whose history is outlined in Chapter 10). Researchers combining their interest in understanding how the brain processes social information with the new imaging technologies have coined the term **social neuroscience** to describe their endeavors. Their aim is to explore the neural mechanisms underlying social thought and behavior. At least two new journals have begun publishing studies in this area, *Social Neuroscience* and *Social Cognitive and Affective Neuroscience.* The journal *Social Neuroscience*, which began publication in 2006, states that its goal is to "to publish empirical articles that . . . further our understanding of the role of the central nervous system in the development and maintenance of social behaviors."[25] Studies reporting *behavioral* data in isolation, the journal editors note, will not be considered. Thus, although the American Psychological Association declared 2000–2010 to be the "Decade of Behavior," it seems as though the field's efforts to understand behavior will become increasingly tied to neuroscience as it moves further into the twenty-first century.

Summary

This chapter described the history of the debates over localization of function in the brain. **Franz Joseph Gall**, the founder of **phrenology**, proposed in the early 1800s that the brain is composed of many localized "organs," each one associated with a specific psychological "faculty" whose strength could be assessed by measuring the overlying bumps and indentations of the skull. Gall's theory was quickly challenged by **Pierre Flourens**, who through his careful surgical ablations of parts of the brain came to believe that separate functions were evenly distributed *within* each organ. Localization theory was revived, however, with the discovery of specific *language areas* by **Paul Broca** and **Carl Wernicke**, who relied on brain autopsies from patients who had demonstrated unusual expressive and receptive language impairments. Further evidence for localization of a different kind occurred when **Gustav Fritsch** and **Eduard Hitzig** used newly developed electrical probes to directly stimulate exposed areas of the brain's cortex and identified **motor and sensory strips** associated with specific movements or bodily sensations. **David Ferrier** subsequently used similar techniques to identify cortical regions responsible for vision and hearing.

In the early twentieth century attention shifted to the subject of learning and memory, and some wondered whether specific memories might be "stored" in specific regions of the brain. Some, such as **Shepherd Ivory Franz**, doubted this idea after observing the apparent plasticity of many patients' brains in their recoveries from major injuries and extirpations. When one area was damaged its function appeared, at least sometimes, to be taken over or compensated for by another. Franz collaborated with **Karl Lashley** on a series of studies investigating the impact of brain ablation on previously acquired maze learning in rats. The amount of learning loss turned out not to depend on the location of the ablations, but on the total amount of tissue removed, demonstrating what Lashley called the **law of mass action**, at least temporarily turning opinion away again from a strict localizationist position.

The next approach to studying brain function was research on the direct electrical stimulation of the conscious human brain, especially as perfected by **Wilder Penfield** in his work with epileptic patients in the 1930s. Depending on the specific area stimulated, Penfield found he could artificially produce a great variety of sensory, experiential, and interpretive impressions in the patient, some of which seemed like hallucinatory reliving of past memories. Penfield noted that these experiences differed from normal memories in various ways, however, and urged much further research before drawing conclusions about the cortical localization of memories. Penfield's younger colleague **Brenda Milner** advanced the case with the intensive study of H.M., an epileptic patient whose hippocampus had been ablated to provide relief from intractable seizures. H.M. showed a distinctive pattern of strengths and weakness that led Milner to postulate the existence of separate systems for declarative versus procedural memory, as well as separate storage areas for "working" as opposed to long-term memories.

Key Pioneers

Aubertin, Ernest, p. 109
Bartholow, Roberts, p. 123
Bouillaud, Jean Baptiste, p. 109
Broca, Paul, p. 110
Cuvier, Georges, p. 104
Ferrier, David, p. 114
Flourens, Pierre, p. 104
Franz, Shepherd Ivory, p. 118
Fritsch, Gustav, p. 113

Gall, Franz Josef. p. 97
Hebb, Donald O., p. 128
Hitzig, Eduard, p. 113
Lashley, Karl Spencer, p. 119
Lavater, Johann Kaspar, p. 99
Milner, Brenda, p. 127
Penfield, Wilder, p. 123
Wernicke, Carl, p. 115
Willis, Thomas, p. 96

Key Terms

ablation, p. 105
aphasia, p. 112
auditory area, p. 114
Broca's aphasia, p. 117
Broca's area, p. 112
cell assemblies, p. 128
cerebellum, p. 100
cognitive neuroscience, p. 133
commissures, p. 98
conduction aphasia, p. 117
cortex, p. 106
equipotentiality, p. 120
experiential responses, p. 126
gray matter, p. 96
hippocampus, p. 129
interpretive cortex, p. 126
interpretive responses, p. 126

law of mass action, p. 121
motor aphasia, p. 116
motor strip, p. 113
neurons, p. 97
paraphasias, p. 116
phrenology, p. 99
physiognomy, p. 99
redundancy hypothesis, p. 122
sensory aphasia, p. 116
sensory strip, p. 114
social neuroscience, p. 134
tomography, p. 132
visual area, p. 114
Wernicke's aphasia, p. 117
Wernicke's area, p. 117
white matter, 96

Discussion Questions and Topics

1 Although Gall's phrenological system appears somewhat farcical to us now, in what ways might his work be considered scientific, at least by the standards of his own time?

2 This chapter noted that Wilder Penfield came to regard "brain" and "mind" as two independent though interacting entities, each with its

own separate level of explanation. The implication of this position is that a thorough explanation of the functioning of the brain may not be equivalent to a complete understanding of the mind. Does this sound similar to positions taken by pioneers described in previous chapters of this book? Do you agree or disagree with Penfield? Why?

3 What role has technology played in our ability to research the structure and function of the brain? Give specific examples from the chapter in your response.

Suggested Readings

An encyclopedic, scholarly, and engaging survey of the history of brain science from antiquity through the near present is Stanley Finger's *Origins of Neuroscience: A History of Explorations into Brain Function* (New York: Oxford University Press, 1994). For general accounts of the history of the localization-of-function controversy, see David Krech's "Cortical Localization of Function" in *Psychology in the Making,* edited by Leo Postman (New York: Knopf, 1962), and Robert M. Young's *Mind, Brain and Adaptation in the Nineteenth Century* (Oxford, UK: Clarendon Press, 1970). For more specific aspects of the story see Owsei Temkin, "Gall and the Phrenological Movement," *Bulletin of the History of Medicine* 21 (1947): 275–321; Byron Stookey, "A Note on the Early History of Cerebral Localization," *Bulletin of the New York Academy of Medicine* 30 (1954): 559–576; Norman Geschwind, "Wernicke's Contribution to the Study of Aphasia," *Cortex* 3 (1967): 448–463; and Darryl Bruce, "Integrations of Lashley," in *Portraits of Pioneers in Psychology,* edited by G. A. Kimble et al. (New York: Erlbaum, 1991), 306–323.

Karl Lashley cogently summarized his own findings in his book *Brain Mechanisms and Intelligence* (Chicago: University of Chicago Press, 1929), as did Wilder Penfield in Wilder Penfield and Lamar Roberts, *Speech and Brain-Mechanisms* (Princeton, NJ: Princeton University Press, 1959). For a comprehensive survey of the historical evolution and contemporary status of the cognitive neuroscience of memory, including Milner's work with H.M., see Brenda Milner, Larry Squire, and Eric Kandel, "Cognitive Neuroscience and the Study of Memory," *Neuron* 20 (1998): 445–468. Suzanne Corkin, who worked with H.M. for many years at the Massachusetts Institute of Technology, has also written an informative summary and update of research findings (to 2002) on her famous patient and research participant titled "What's New with the Amnesic Patient H.M.?" in *Nature Reviews: Neuroscience* 3 (2002): 153–160. Penfield's late doubts about ever being able to account for the "mind" totally in terms of brain function are expressed in his *The Mystery of the Mind* (Princeton, NJ: Princeton University Press, 1975).

The Sensing and Perceiving Mind

Theories of Perception from Kant through the Gestalt Psychologists

4

The Kantian Background

Helmholtz's Early Life
The Triumph of Mechanism

Helmholtz on Sensation and Perception
Physical Properties of the Eye
Color Vision
Visual Perception
Helmholtz's Place in Psychology

Fechner and Psychophysics
The Invention of Psychophysics

Gestalt Psychology

Later Developments in the Study of Sensation and Perception
Helmholtz's Legacy
Stevens and the Power Law of Psychophysics
Further Developments in Gestalt Psychology
Conclusion: Sensation and Perception Today

Summary

Key Pioneers

Key Terms

Discussion Questions and Topics

Suggested Readings

In middle age, the German philosopher **Immanuel Kant** (1724–1804; see Figure 4.1) arose from what he called "my dogmatic slumbers." Trained in the Leibnizian tradition of German philosophy, he had previously written respected but unspectacular works on topics such as the existence of God and the difference between

FIG 4.1
Immanuel Kant
(1724–1804)

absolute and relative space. But now, stimulated by a challenge from one of John Locke's successors in the British associationist school, Kant embarked on a program of "critical philosophy" that subtly but crucially refashioned the German view of humanity and nature. Among its other consequences was a climate of opinion conducive to the scientific study of the mind and the development of a new and experimental psychology.

The Kantian Background

The Scottish philosopher David Hume had aroused the intellectually slumbering Kant by carrying Lockean empiricism and associationism to an extreme and questioning the logical status of the concept of *causality*—our intuitive belief that certain events have been directly "caused by" certain other preceding events. When one billiard ball strikes another, for example, we naturally interpret the motion of the second as having been directly caused by the impact of the first. Classical scientific theories assume that specific antecedent conditions cause specific and predictable consequences. These uses of the term *cause* imply a *necessary* sequential relationship between certain antecedent and consequent events and suggest that we immediately apprehend this necessity when we perceive the events and attribute causality to them.

Hume questioned this assumption. All we can ever really *know*, he argued, is that certain regular sequences of events have occurred in the past, leading us to expect their repetition in the future. The conviction that one billiard ball's motion has been caused by its impact with another really amounts to the recollection of associated impact-movement sequences from the past and the assumption that such cause-effect actions will continue in the future. "Causality" is nothing more than that. The presumed necessity of the connection between the events is never directly perceived, and causality thus has only a probabilistic instead of an absolute basis. As Hume summarized: "'Tis not, therefore, reason, which is the guide of life, but custom. That alone determines the mind, in all instances, to suppose the future conformable to the past."[1]

From a practical point of view, of course, these considerations make no difference. We fare best in the real world by anticipating lawful regularities in nature, whether their causation be real or merely assumed. But to a philosopher like Kant, concerned with the essential nature of human knowledge, the issue was crucial. If one could not actually "know" causality in nature, the logical underpinnings of science and the entire structure of knowledge seemed challenged.

Kant responded to this challenge with a simple but revolutionary variant of Leibniz's nativist argument. He argued that because causality cannot be proven to exist in the external world but nevertheless seems an inescapable part of our experience, it must represent an innate contribution of the mind. He postulated two separate domains of reality, one completely inside the human mind, the other completely outside. The external or **noumenal world** consists of "things-in-themselves"—objects in a "pure" state independent of human experience. Although presumed to exist and to interact with the human mind, the noumenal world can never be known directly, for once it encounters a human mind it becomes transformed by that mind into the inner or **phenomenal world**. The term *phenomenal* comes from the Greek *phainomenon*, meaning "appearance," and reflects Kant's argument that human beings never *directly* experience the pure reality of things-in-themselves, but rather a series of "appearances" or "phenomena" that are partly the *creations* of an active mind encountering the noumenal world. Thus for Kant the mind does not just passively reflect or record the external world but actively participates in the creation of each person's experience of that world.

In creating the phenomenal world, the Kantian mind inevitably follows certain rules of its own. It always localizes phenomena in *space* and *time*, for example—dimensions that Kant referred to as the **intuitions**. In addition, Kant argued that the mind automatically organizes phenomena in terms of twelve **categories**, defining their *quality, quantity, relationships*, and *mode*. Among the categories of relationship is the concept of *causality*. Thus, human beings inevitably experience the world as organized in time and space, and as operating according to causal laws—not because the noumenal world is necessarily or "really" that way, but because the mind can do nothing else but structure phenomenal experience that way.

Kant expounded on the implications of his critical philosophy in a series of books between 1781 and 1798, beginning with the *Critique of Pure Reason* and concluding with *Anthropology from a Pragmatic Point of View.*[2] The importance of these works for the future science of psychology lay not in his specific list of intuitions and categories but in his general insistence that the mind itself contributes importantly to our experience of external reality, in ways that are capable of systematic analysis and description. In the Kantian context, the inherent properties of mind assumed a crucial new importance, worthy of study in their own right.

Ironically, after staking a claim for the importance of the study of the mind's organizing properties, Kant went on to assert that such study would never be able to achieve the status of a true "science" like physics. He argued that mental phenomena, in contrast to the physical objects investigated by physical scientists, (1) have no spatial dimension, (2) are too transient to pin down for sustained observation, (3) cannot be experimentally manipulated, and (4) perhaps most important of all, cannot be mathematically described or analyzed. In other words, many of the categories and intuitions necessary for scientific thought seemed inapplicable to mental phenomena, and for this reason Kant thought psychology must always remain a "philosophical" rather than a "scientific" discipline.

Throughout the century after Kant, however, a number of unquestionably scientific investigators began serious study of human sensory processes and focused attention on many situations in which conscious experience is clearly different from, or a transformation of, the "objective" external stimuli giving rise to the experience. In the wake of Kant's philosophy, these transformations seemed interpretable as the effects of an active, creative agency, analogous to, if not identical with, the Kantian mind.

Among the simplest and most obvious of these situations were **optical illusions**, in which one's conscious impression of a visual stimulus differs demonstrably in some respect from its "objective" properties. In Figure 4.2, for example, a test with a ruler will show the two horizontal lines to be of exactly the same length. The simple imposition of seven converging lines, however, has made the top line *seem* markedly longer than the bottom one. The experienced difference in length, of course, lies not in the lines themselves but has been somehow contributed by the mind's perceptive process.

In a related vein, neurophysiologists in the early nineteenth century discovered the so-called **law of specific nerve energies**, asserting that each sensory nerve in the body conveys one and only one kind of sensation. First proposed by the Scottish scientist **Charles Bell** (1774–1842) in a privately published monograph of 1811, the law's implications were most fully explored and developed in the 1830s by the German physiologist **Johannes Müller** (1801–1858). The better reception and development of the law in Germany was no historical accident, for Kant's philosophy had created a particularly receptive intellectual climate there for appreciating the law's implications.

Essentially, the law of specific nerve energies contradicted the traditional concept of a sensory nerve as something like a hollow tube, capable of conveying light, sound, pressure, or any other kind of stimulation that happened to be introduced into it. Instead, the law held that each sensory nerve produces only one type of sensation—for

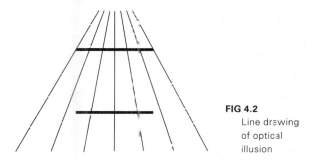

FIG 4.2
Line drawing
of optical
illusion

example, visual, auditory, or tactile—regardless of how it becomes stimulated.

A simple experiment will demonstrate the visual specificity of the *optic nerve,* which leads into the brain from the retina at the back of the eye. In normal vision, the optic nerve becomes stimulated by photochemical reactions of light on the retina and transmits signals to the brain that result in conscious visual sensations of light. If, however, you turn your eyes as far to the right as you can, close your eyes, and then press gently on the left side of your left eyeball, you will see a spot of colored light in the right side of your visual field. You have stimulated the retina and hence the optic nerve with *tactile* pressure rather than the normal light rays—but the effect is still a *visual* one. You have literally *seen* the pressure on your eyeball, because the stimulated optic nerve can convey no other sensations except visual ones. The same sort of specificity characterizes the other sensory nerves.

The law of specific nerve energies seemed especially interesting in the general context of Kantian philosophy, since now particular sensations could no longer be taken as infallible representations of external "reality." Seeing a particular pattern of light, for example, now only meant that the visual nerves had somehow been stimulated—and while the stimulation *might* have originated in light rays from a real external object, there could be no guarantee of the fact. The *immediate* source of sensory experience was revealed to be not the external world alone, but a sensory nervous system that has interacted with the external world and added its own contribution to the contents of consciousness.

Further, physical scientists had increasingly demonstrated the usefulness of conceptualizing the physical, "external" world as ultimately composed of various forces, waves, and energies, which, like Kant's things-in-themselves, are not directly apprehensible by the senses. Light, sound, or heat waves, for example, constantly impinge on the nervous system, but instead of being perceived as *waves* they somehow get transformed into the phenomenal experiences of color, sound, and warmth and cold. But while the ultimate qualities of the external world were not *directly* perceivable by the human senses, they became increasingly so *indirectly* thanks to new techniques of scientific measurement and analysis. Physicists devised apparatuses to give them precise, numerical values for the wavelengths and frequencies of light or sound waves, for example. Thus the nineteenth-century physicists' external world remained like Kant's noumenal world in being only indirectly knowable by the senses, but it increasingly differed from that world by being describable in mathematical and other scientific terminology.

Two nineteenth-century Germans helped psychology to gain recognition as a genuine science—Kant notwithstanding—by investigating and discovering lawful relationships between these newly specifiable aspects of the physical world and the ways they are consciously experienced by people. **Hermann Helmholtz** (1821–1894), a student of Johannes Müller working in what he explicitly saw as the tradition of Kant, carried the doctrine of specific nerve energies to far-reaching conclusions while becoming one of the greatest scientists of his time. **Gustav Theodor Fechner** (1801–1887) laid the groundwork for a mathematically based experimental psychology by studying how differences in the physical intensities of stimulation are perceived psychologically. Following in the same vein, in the early 1900s a group known as the **Gestalt psychologists** uncovered still other ways in which an active and creative mind molds important aspects of conscious perceptual experience.

Helmholtz's Early Life

Hermann Helmholtz (see Figure 4.3) was born on August 31, 1821 in the Prussian town of Potsdam near Berlin. His father, a high school teacher with strong interests in Kantian philosophy, encouraged Hermann's early enthusiasm for science. Physics became the boy's consuming passion from the moment he found some old textbooks in his father's library. He worked on optics diagrams beneath his school desk when he should have been studying Latin, spoiled the family linen with chemistry experiments, and in due course became the most promising young scientist in town.

At that time, however, a young person had to show more than promise in order to practice science seriously. Although the educated classes were beginning to appreciate the importance of science, job opportunities were scarce. The pursuit of "pure science" as a vocation remained the prerogative of the independently wealthy—whose numbers did not include the Helmholtz family. Fortunately, however, the Prussian

FIG 4.3
Hermann Helmholtz
(1821–1894)

government had instituted a program offering free medical training for poor but talented students at Berlin's Royal Friedrich-Wilhelm Institute, in exchange for eight years' service as army surgeons after graduation. While not as appealing to young Helmholtz as physics, medicine at least involved science; he applied at age 17 and was accepted. According to his letters home, he did little for the next year but study medicine, relieved only occasionally by playing piano, reading Goethe and Byron, and studying "sometimes for a change the integral calculus."

In the second year of the program, Helmholtz began to study physiology with Johannes Müller (see Figure 4.4), the eminent propounder of the law of specific nerve energies. He also became friends with a brilliant group of fellow students, including **Emil Du Bois-Reymond** (1818–1896), who would later establish the electrochemical nature of the nervous impulse; **Rudolf Virchow** (1821–1902), who would pioneer the field of cell pathology; and **Ernst Brücke** (1819–1892), who would become the favorite teacher of Sigmund Freud. Helmholtz shone even among this exceptional group, largely because of his unusual grasp of the concepts from physics that Müller frequently used in accounting for physiological processes. For example, Müller analyzed the eye as an optical device like a camera and the ear as a propagator of sound waves through solid and liquid media.

Even with his respect for physics, however, Müller still clung to an old physiological doctrine known as **vitalism**, according to which all living organisms are imbued with an ineffable "life force" that gives them their vitality and that is not analyzable by scientific methods. Müller did not deny that ordinary physical and chemical processes often take place in living organisms; his willingness to use physical principles in analyzing the eye and ear testified to that. But he also believed these processes are somehow harnessed and controlled in living organisms by the vital force. With death, the vital force presumably departs and physiochemical processes are allowed to run free, leading to the putrefaction and decay of the body, rather than to its maintenance. Belief in vitalism implied that there was a limit to the possible scientific understanding of physiological processes, because the life force itself presumably lay beyond scientific analysis.

Although respectful of their famous teacher, Helmholtz and his friends refused to accept this implicit limitation on science. To them, the gains from using physical principles in physiology had been so great that it seemed foolish to postulate *any* limits to the approach.

FIG 4.4
Johannes Müller
(1801–1858)

Accordingly, they rejected vitalism and adopted the doctrine of **mechanism**, declaring *all* physiological processes to be potentially understandable in terms of ordinary physical and chemical principles. The processes might be highly complex and beyond current comprehension, but ultimately they must be subject to the same universal physical laws as inanimate processes. Mechanism became an article of faith among the students, which they duly solemnized by composing and swearing to the following formal oath:

> No other forces than the common physical-chemical ones are active within the organism. In those cases which cannot at the time be explained by these forces, one has either to find the specific way or form of their action by means of the physical-mathematical method, or to assume new forces equal in dignity to the physical-chemical forces inherent in matter, reducible to the force of attraction and repulsion.[3]

The students' avowal of mechanism led them to differ from their teacher more in emphasis and attitude than in the actual methods of physiological research. No "ultimate experiment" could be done to choose between vitalism and mechanism, and Müller was quite happy to apply physical principles to physiology as far as they would go. He disagreed with his students only in his assumption that a limit to mechanism would be reached at *some* point, when the vital force entered the picture. Nevertheless, this difference subtly influenced the kinds of problems selected for investigation. Müller, for example, believed that the deepest mysteries of nerve functioning probably involved the life force and so remained impervious to scientific understanding. He believed that nervous impulses traversed nerve fibers with infinite or near-infinite speeds, probably because of their close involvement with the life force. Accordingly, he did not seriously contemplate research into possible physicochemical properties of the nervous impulse. Helmholtz and his mechanistic friends operated under no such constraint, and partly as a result they revolutionized physiology.

The Triumph of Mechanism

At 21, Helmholtz completed a dissertation on the microscopic nerve structure of invertebrates, received his medical degree, and faced his eight-year military obligation. As an army surgeon in his hometown of Potsdam, he found his medical duties tedious but scarcely all-consuming of his time, so he built a small physiological laboratory in his barracks, where he studied metabolic processes in frogs. Conceived and conducted within the mechanistic framework, his experiments demonstrated that the amount of muscular energy and heat generated by a frog was consistent with the amount of energy released by the oxidation of the food it consumed. That is, he showed that ordinary chemical reactions were *capable* of producing (though not necessarily that they *did* produce) all of the physical activity and heat generated by a living organism.

In 1847 young Helmholtz turned his attention to an idea implicit in this research—namely, the **conservation of energy**. According to this notion, all the kinds of forces in the universe—heat, light, gravity, magnetism, etc.—are potentially interchangeable forms of a single huge but quantitatively fixed reservoir of energy. Energy can be transformed from one state to another, but never created or destroyed by any physical process. The total amount of energy in the universe is constant and conserved.

Under this hypothesis, a machine is simply a device for transforming energy from a less useful to a more useful kind. A steam engine, for example, transforms the heat from a fire into the motion of steam molecules, whose energy is transformed into the motion of pistons, which in turn activates the usefully moving parts of the engine. The frog's muscles Helmholtz had studied were physiological machines that transformed the potential chemical energy stored in food and oxygen into movement and body heat.

Several scientists had promoted the conservation of energy hypothesis in the early 1840s, but Helmholtz approached the topic in a unique and particularly influential manner in his 1847 paper, "The Conservation of Force." In it he began by arguing that a perpetual-motion machine, if it could be successfully built, would necessarily violate the conservation-of-energy principle. Any machine with moving contiguous parts would inevitably generate heat by friction, for example, which would represent a loss of total energy in the system. Under the conservation principle, motion could never be "perpetual" but would have to be maintained by the constant input of new energy or fuel from without, to compensate for the energy lost as heat. Helmholtz proceeded to show that a successful, conservation-violating perpetual-motion machine had never been built and never *could be* given the accepted laws of gravity, heat, electricity, magnetism, and electromagnetism. This demonstrated that the conservation of energy must hold for each of those kinds of forces. After discussing these subjects from the domain of physics, Helmholtz concluded by noting that all *organic* processes studied up to this point had also seemed governed by the conservation of energy—thus implying that the range of this physical principle extended into physiology.

In recognition of this brilliant work, the Prussian government released Helmholtz from his military obligation and appointed him lecturer on anatomy at Berlin's Academy of Arts in 1848. The next year he was made professor of physiology at Königsberg, Kant's old university. Two major achievements marked Helmholtz's six-year tenure there. First, while preparing an optics lecture during his first year, he realized that a partially silvered mirror could be arranged in such a way as to allow an observer to look directly at the retina of a living subject's eye. This observation inspired him to invent the *ophthalmoscope*, an invaluable tool for eye examination quickly appreciated by eye doctors around the world, and still used today.

Helmholtz's second major project at Königsberg held greater direct importance for psychology. He became interested in the question of the speed of the nervous impulse, which Müller and other authorities had taken to be instantaneous or almost so, and thus immeasurably fast. During the 1840s, however, Helmholtz's mechanist friend Du Bois-Reymond had studied the chemical structure of nerve fibers and hypothesized that the nervous impulse might be an electrochemical wave traveling along the nerve at a slower rate than anyone had imagined. Helmholtz speculated it might even be slow enough for measurement in a laboratory.

To test this startling idea, Helmholtz devised an instrument capable of measuring smaller fractions of seconds than were detectable by existing timepieces. He used a simple laboratory galvanometer, an electricity-detecting device with a needle that deflected in proportion to the strength of current passing through it. Helmholtz knew that when current first came on, a short but measurable and consistent amount of time occurred before the needle reached its maximum deflection. If the current was switched on and off very quickly, before the maximum deflection had been reached, the proportion of full needle deflection achieved corresponded to the proportion of time necessary for full deflection.

With this galvanometric "stopwatch," Helmholtz ingeniously measured the speed of neural impulse in a severed frog's leg. He knew that mild electrical stimulation of the nerve in the leg would cause the foot to twitch and arranged his apparatus so a foot twitch could turn the electrical supply off. The electrical circuit also passed through the time-calibrated galvanometer. Thus, when Helmholtz turned on the current, the galvanometer needle began to move, but it stopped as soon as the foot twitch turned things off; its extent of deflection measured the fraction of a second the current had flowed.

Helmholtz compared these fractions of seconds when the originating current was applied to different locations on the nerve fiber and found that the farther the location from the foot, the longer the reaction took. Stimulation 4 inches from the foot began a reaction that took 0.003 second longer than one begun with stimulation just 1 inch away. Helmholtz concluded that this must have represented the time necessary for the nervous impulse to travel the extra 3 inches and calculated that the speed of the impulse must therefore have been about 83 feet per second—approximately 57 miles per hour. Although this was fast, it was certainly far from instantaneous or the speed of light.

Helmholtz next turned to *human* subjects, whom he trained to make a response such as pressing a button whenever a stimulus was applied to their legs. Subjects took slightly but measurably longer to respond when the toe was stimulated as opposed to when the thigh was stimulated. Assuming that a nervous impulse had to travel from the point of stimulation to the brain to initiate the response, Helmholtz estimated that its speed in the human leg was somewhere between 165 and 330 feet per second. High variability made these results less certain than those from the frog, but they at least confirmed that the speed of nervous impulse was finite and measurable. Helmholtz soon abandoned these studies of human **reaction times**, but we shall see in the next chapter how they were later expanded and developed by his followers in the earliest laboratories devoted explicitly to experimental psychology.

At first, however, most scientists failed to appreciate the significance of Helmholtz's experiments on the nervous impulse because of his opaque literary style. His friend Du Bois-Reymond chided: "Your work, I say with pride and grief, is understood and recognized by myself alone. You have, begging your pardon, expressed the subject so obscurely that your report could at best only be an introduction to the discovery of method." Helmholtz's father attended a lecture and found his son "so little able to escape from his scientific rigidity of expression, . . . that I am filled with respect for an audience that could understand and thank him for it."[4]

Further, some of the implications of Helmholtz's research were initially just too surprising to be easily believed. We generally experience mental processes subjectively as occurring instantaneously, and physiologists naturally assumed that any neurological events responsible for them must be nearly instantaneous too. Yet Helmholtz's experiments suggested that a whale receiving a wound to its tail could not become conscious of the injury until a full second had passed to allow an impulse to travel from tail to brain, and that another second would pass before a message triggering defensive reaction could be relayed from brain back to tail. Such long reaction times truly are characteristic of large animals, but many scientists in the 1850s found that hard to believe.

Despite their initial implausibility, Helmholtz's results gradually gained acceptance and immeasurably strengthened the general case for mechanism. His biographer noted: "The unexpectedly low rate of propagation in the nervous system was incompatible with the older view of an immaterial or imponderable [vitalistic] principle as the nervous agent, but quite in harmony with the [mechanistic] theory of motion of material particles in the nerve substance."[5] Such results showed mechanism to be more *productive* than vitalism, suggesting important experiments and ideas that vitalism discouraged. Had Helmholtz and Du Bois-Reymond not been mechanists, they would never have thought even to try their experiments. In the wake of their success, a "new physiology" came into vogue, with ambitions of accounting mechanistically even for those "higher" processes in the brain and nervous system that presumably underlay higher mental functioning.

Helmholtz on Sensation and Perception

Helmholtz would have won a place in the history of psychology for his experiments on nervous transmission alone, but he followed them with an even more monumental series of studies of vision and hearing that became a foundation for the modern psychology of sensation and perception. While at the universities of Königsberg, Bonn, and Heidelberg between 1853 and 1868, he not only conducted much original research in these fields but also personally replicated all the major experiments of other scientists to ensure their accuracy. In his *Handbook of Physiological Optics* (1856–1866) and the ponderously titled *The Theory of the Sensation of Tone as a Physiological Basis for the Theory of Music* (1863), he attempted to summarize all the available knowledge about the senses of vision and hearing. By most accounts he nearly succeeded, and both books remained in regular use for over a century.

Helmholtz approached both senses with a similar strategy, which we shall illustrate here by discussing his treatment of vision. He started by dividing his general subject into primarily *physical*, primarily *physiological*, and primarily *psychological* categories, while recognizing that they were all interrelated. The physical studies regarded the eye as an optical instrument, examining the processes by which light from the external world comes to be focused into an image on the retina. The physiological analyses concerned the problem of how an image on the retina conveys signals to the brain that result in conscious **sensations** of light. Psychological analysis followed the process a step further, asking how sensations of light become converted into meaningful **perceptions** of discrete objects and events.

His distinction between sensations and perceptions bears elaboration. Sensations are presumed to be the "raw elements" of conscious experience, requiring no learning or prior experience. In vision, they include the spatially organized patches of light with varying hues and brightnesses that fill one's visual field, quite independently of any "meaning." Perceptions, by contrast, are the meaningful *interpretations* given to sensations. As you look out a window, for example, your sensations might include patches of blue and white in the upper field of vision, with green, brown, and yellow areas below. Your perceptions of the same scene might be of a landscape, with sky and clouds above trees and fields. For Helmholtz, the conversion of an image on the retina of the eye into conscious sensations of light and color was a physiological process, mediated by neurological mechanisms between the eye and the brain. The further conversion of sensations into perceptions was a psychological process involving activities in the brain, but also dependent on the learning and experience of the individual. Because both processes transform input of one kind into conscious output of another, however, Helmholtz regarded both as examples of the sort of creative activities of the human mind that had been postulated by Kant.

We turn now to some of Helmholtz's specific points regarding the physical, physiological, and psychological aspects of the visual system.

Physical Properties of the Eye

Helmholtz showed how the physical components of the eye could be described as if it were a manufactured optical instrument such as a microscope or camera. As is shown in Figure 4.5, the eye has a curved and transparent surface called the *cornea*, in front of a transparent and elliptically shaped *lens*. Because of its curvature, the cornea-lens system refracts, or bends, incoming light rays such that a miniature and inverted image of the external object is projected onto the light-sensitive retina, analogous to the film in a camera, at the back of the eye.

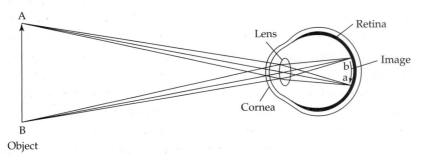

FIG 4.5 Physical features of the eye

In a camera, the images of nearby or distant objects may be brought to sharp focus by altering the distance between the lens and film. The eye achieves the same end, but by a different mechanism in the lens itself called *accommodation*: The lens assumes a relatively flat shape for sharply focusing distant objects on the retina, and it bulges in the middle to focus nearby objects.

Helmholtz also observed, however, that virtually all of the eye's physical features have "defects" or imperfections that would be considered unacceptable in a high-quality camera, telescope, or other manufactured instrument. The eye's field of maximum sharpness is very small, for example, consisting only of that part of the image that falls on a tiny section of the retina known as the *fovea*. The fovea's size can be appreciated by extending an arm fully and focusing on the nail of the forefinger; the image of the nail completely fills the fovea, whose size relative to the retina is thus the same as the size of the nail's image relative to the rest of the visual field. Visual acuity within the fovea is excellent, and a normal observer can distinguish images on it that are separated by less than 1 percent of its diameter. Acuity decreases rapidly for images falling outside the fovea, however, and images at the edge of the visual field are very imprecise indeed. A photograph providing an image like the ones recorded by the eye would be unsatisfactory, because everything but the very center would be blurred. We do not notice the situation, however, because of the eye's ability to "scan" a scene, shifting its focus quickly and flexibly from one part of the visual field to another.

Helmholtz observed many other "deficiencies" in the optical properties of the eye Colors are imperfectly reproduced on the retina, for example, because the fluid in the eyeball is not perfectly colorless and because the lens refracts the relatively longer rays of red light less than the shorter rays at the blue-violet end of the spectrum. An imperfect alignment of refractive surfaces known as **astigmatism** distorts images in all people's eyes, though to highly varying degrees. Perhaps the most dramatic defect of all is the **blind spot**, which occurs because a small part of the retina where the optic nerve leaves it contains no light-sensitive receptor cells. To demonstrate your own blind spot, draw two X's on a sheet of paper, side by side and two inches apart. Then hold the paper at arm's length, close your left eye, and focus on the left-hand X with your right eye. Now slowly draw the paper toward your eye; at some point the right-hand X will suddenly disappear as its image falls on your blind spot.

For Helmholtz, these "defects" had philosophical as well as practical significance, supporting what he regarded as a Kantian interpretation of experience. He argued that even at the level of the eye, the registered image of external "reality" on the retina is not a perfect reproduction of the external stimulus. A certain amount of change and distortion inevitably takes place because of the features of the eye. And at the next, *physiological* level of processing, as the image on the retina becomes converted into conscious visual sensations, the transformations and distortions increase further. Conscious visual sensations are *not* exact reproductions of the physical objects that give rise to them, or even of the images on the retina. Nothing better illustrates this point than Helmholtz's influential treatment of the subject of color vision.

Color Vision

A century and a half before Helmholtz's birth, Isaac Newton discovered that the "white" light from the sun is more complicated than it seems. He shined a narrow band of ordinary sunlight through a transparent crystal prism as represented at the left of Figure 4.6,

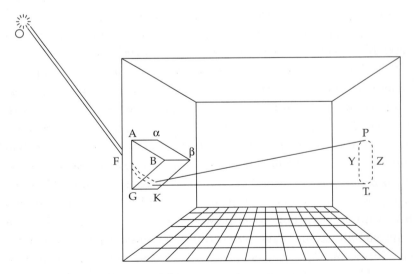

FIG 4.6 Newton's diagram of the solar spectrum
[From his *Optical Lectures*]

and observed the light to emerge on the right as the elongated, multicolored band known as the *solar spectrum*, with red at the bottom (T) followed by orange, yellow, green, and blue to violet at the top (P).

Newton explained his observation by hypothesizing that the different spectral colors represent light of different wavelengths and that the white light of the sun is composed of all of the wavelengths mixed together. When the mixture of sunlight passes through the prism, shorter waves get bent or "refracted" more than longer ones; thus, the emerging light is sorted out in the order of its wavelengths, with the relatively long red light having been bent relatively little, and the blue-violet light relatively much. At first thought, then, it might seem that our color sensation is simply a means of differentiating the various wavelengths of light we encounter: When we see orange, for example, we are encountering light whose waves are shorter than red but longer than yellow.

This idea turned out to be oversimplified, however, holding true only in certain circumstances. Experiments with **color mixing** revealed the true situation as more complex, showing that the visual sense sometimes responded to *mixtures* of wavelengths in exactly the same way it did to individual spectral colors. For example, if light from the red part and light from the yellow part of the spectrum are superimposed upon each other, the visual result is a sensation of orange indistinguishable from the orange of the spectrum. Thus, widely differing physical stimuli (in terms of the wavelengths of light striking the eye) can produce identical conscious sensations of color.

Several scientists studied the details of color mixing, with the most complete analysis being reported by the Scot **James Clerk Maxwell** (1831–1879) in 1855, just as Helmholtz was beginning his own studies of color vision. By then, many pairs of **complementary colors** had been identified—that is, pairs of spectral colors that, when mixed together, created a sensation of *white* light indistinguishable from sunlight. A certain red mixed with a certain blue-green always produced white, for example, as did a certain yellow when mixed with a certain blue-violet. Moreover, a particular combination of *three* spectral colors—a certain red, a green, and a blue-violet—not only produced white when mixed equally together but also could be mixed in various other combinations so as to produce *any other* color. These three, which seemed to be building blocks for all of the kinds of color sensation, came to be known as the **primary colors.**[*]

To explain these phenomena, Helmholtz theorized that the retina contains three different kinds of receptor cells, each one responding most strongly to light waves of one of the three primary colors and with diminishing strength to light waves increasingly different from it. Nerves attached to the receptors presumably transmit messages to the brain whenever their receptors are stimulated. Here was a refinement of Müller's specific energy theory, suggesting that individual nerves transmit sensory messages not only of a specific *kind* (visual, auditory, tactile, and so on) but also of a specific *quality* (red, green, or blue-violet). Helmholtz knew and acknowledged that the English scientist **Thomas Young** (1773–1829) had suggested a similar idea in 1802, so the name **Young-Helmholtz trichromatic theory** is commonly used for it.[†]

Helmholtz used his trichromatic theory to explain many facts of color vision and mixing. According to the theory, when spectral red, green, or blue-violet light strikes the retina, only one kind of receptor is strongly stimulated and results in a sensation of a "pure" primary color. Light of the nonprimary colors, or some combination of colors, results in the stimulation of some *combination* of the three receptor types and the sensation of a nonprimary color. Thus if the red and blue-violet receptors are simultaneously excited, the sensation of purple results; red and green together produce sensations of orange or yellow (depending on the proportions). When all three

---

[*] Children learn from experience with paintboxes that the primary colors are red, blue, and yellow, since those are the best paints to mix in making other colors. The discrepancy arises because paints contain *pigments* which selectively absorb as well as reflect light waves. The absorbing capacities of the pigments cause them to give different results when mixed, as compared to the simple mixture of projected colored lights on a screen.

[†] Actually, the basic idea had already been promoted as early as 1777, by an obscure and somewhat disreputable English pharmacist named G. Palmer. This illustrates that, to achieve scientific recognition, being first is not always enough; one must also successfully demonstrate and communicate the relevance and usefulness of the theory one proposes.

types of receptors are simultaneously and equally excited, sensations of *white* occur. Sunlight, consisting of all the wavelengths of light, naturally stimulates all three receptor types. Complementary colors do the same: In the combination of red and blue-green, for example, red light stimulates the red receptors and the blue-green light simultaneously stimulates both the green and the blue-violet receptors; in the combination of yellow and blue-violet, yellow simultaneously stimulates the red and green receptors, while blue-violet stimulates the third. In both cases, the combined excitation of all three receptor types produces a sensation of white.

Helmholtz thus explained the laws of color mixture as functions of the human visual apparatus itself, having relatively little to do with the "objective" physical properties of light waves. In evaluating the visual color sense as an accurate detector of physical "reality," Helmholtz observed: "The inaccuracies and imperfections of the eye as an optical instrument . . . now appear insignificant in comparison with the incongruities we have met with in the field of sensation. One might almost believe that Nature had here contradicted herself on purpose in order to destroy any dream of a pre-existing harmony between the outer and the inner world."[6] And since colors were now seen more as products of the human sensory system than as properties of physical reality, Helmholtz explicitly recognized their consistency with Kantian philosophy when he wrote: "That the character of our perceptions is conditioned just as much by our senses as by the external things is of the greatest importance. . . . What the physiology of the senses has demonstrated experimentally in more recent times, Kant earlier tried to do . . . for the ideas of the human mind in general."[7]

Visual Perception

When Helmholtz turned his attention from visual sensation to perception, he agreed less completely with Kant's point of view. In agreement, he recognized that as sensations are interpreted and given meaning by the perceptual process, they undergo further transformations worthy of a Kantian "mind." Sometimes, in fact, the mind imposes features on its perceptions that contradict the raw sensations that give rise to them, as in optical illusions. Thus, in Figure 4.2 at the beginning of the chapter, the two parallel lines are exactly the same length, even though you consciously perceive the top line as longer. Here, your mind makes a mistake in its interpretation of visual sensations.

Helmholtz's disagreement with Kant concerned the *origins* of many perceptual processes, including those involved in illusions. Kant's theory implied that spatial perception was mainly determined by the innate intuitions and categories. Helmholtz, while regarding the processes of sensation as innate, gave greater emphasis to the role of experience and learning in perception. Of course, no one denied that *some* perceptual processes are acquired by experience. Locke had already successfully argued that a person born blind and granted sight only later would still quite literally have to *learn* how to see—would have to have concrete experiences connecting specific ideas of objects to the new and initially bewildering visual sensations. The question separating empiricist from nativist—Helmholtz from Kant—was not whether *any* perceptual processes were acquired through experience, but *how many* and to *what extent.*

Helmholtz conceded that he could never conclusively disprove nativism, but he chose as a matter of strategy to regard all perception as acquired through experience (much as he had earlier adopted mechanism as a matter of strategy). He then demonstrated the usefulness of his strategy by showing that many observed facts about perception could be explained on the basis of experience and learning.

One classic series of experiments demonstrated how space perception could be altered by experience. Helmholtz fitted subjects with spectacles that systematically distorted the visual field in some way such as by shifting the images of objects several degrees to the right of their normal locations. When subjects were asked to look at an object, then close their eyes and reach out to touch it, their first responses were invariably to the right—toward the apparent rather than the real position. But if the subjects were given a few minutes to handle objects while looking at them through the glasses, something Helmholtz called **perceptual adaptation** occurred. At first the subjects had to instruct themselves consciously to place their hands to the left of the apparent objects they saw, but soon this action became natural, automatic, and unconscious. Now they could easily perform their original task and could touch remembered objects with their eyes closed. However, when the spectacles were removed, they began to make errors once again, but this time to the left instead of to the right. So complete and automatic had their adaptation become that it took them a minute or two to resume their normal spatial orientation.

Helmholtz theorized that perceptual adaptation and other perceptual phenomena might result from a process he called **unconscious inference**. Visual experience—such as the manipulation of objects while wearing distorting spectacles—might lead to the unconscious adoption of certain rules that operate like the major premises in logical syllogisms. For example, experience might teach that an object that fills a very small part of the visual field is farther away than a similar object filling a larger part. This would produce a rule or major premise that could operate as in the following syllogism:

> *Major premise*: The size of an object's image varies inversely with its distance from the eye.
> *Minor premise*: The size of the image of a ball currently in my visual field is getting smaller.
> *Conclusion*: The ball is moving away from me.

The difference between perception and syllogistic reasoning lies in the fact that perception occurs instantly and effortlessly, while the working out of a syllogism may be laborious and time consuming. Helmholtz accounted for this difference by assuming that the major premise of a perception has become so well learned as to be automatic and unconscious. As he put it: "Perceptual inferences are unconscious insofar as their major premise is not necessarily expressed in the form of a proposition; it is formed from a series of experiences whose individual members have entered consciousness only in the form of sense impressions which have long since disappeared from memory. Some fresh impression forms the minor premise, to which the rule impressed on us by previous observation is applied."[8]

Just as syllogisms may lead to false conclusions if based on false premises, so may unconscious inferences sometimes lead to faulty perceptions such as optical illusions. In Figure 4.2, for example, the perceptual error may be blamed on the incorrect premise that converging straight lines indicate depth. In three dimensions the premise is valid, because the retinal images of parallel lines do in fact appear to converge with increasing distance from the eye. In two dimensions, however, the convergence of lines gives the false impression that the top horizontal line is farther away than the bottom one. Because the retinal images of the two lines are equal but the top one is interpreted as being farther away, the top line is also perceived as being of greater real length. Since all of these inferences are unconscious, however, their result—the perceived difference in length—comes to consciousness directly and irresistibly, more like an intuition than a rational thought.

Helmholtz's Place in Psychology

Even as he studied sensation and perception, Helmholtz retained his original passion for physics and found spare time to write occasional articles on such topics as vortex motion in liquids and the motion of air waves in open-ended tubes. At last in 1871 he realized his childhood ambition by being appointed professor of physics at the University of Berlin. From then on, physiology and psychology became sidelights as he focused his research mainly on thermodynamics, meteorology, and electromagnetism. Indeed, he earned his greatest fame as a physicist and in 1882 was elevated by the emperor to the ranks of nobility; Hermann *von* Helmholtz became his legal name. Following his death in 1894, von Helmholtz was mourned at home and abroad as one of the world's greatest scientists.

Even as he won his greatest honors as a physicist, Helmholtz still earned a place as one of psychology's most important pioneers for two important achievements. First, he helped show how the neurological processes underlying mental functions, previously thought to be ineffable, could be subject to rigorous laboratory experimentation. And second, he helped develop a scientific conception of the Kantian "mind" with his integrated physical, physiological, and psychological studies of vision and hearing. No longer just a metaphysical entity, the sensing and perceiving mind was shown to operate by lawful and mechanistic principles as it created its phenomenal reality.

The next step in the evolution of scientific psychology was taken by Fechner, who demonstrated how some of the psychological aspects of sensation and perception could be *quantified* and could be demonstrated to be subject to mathematical regularities or laws.

Fechner and Psychophysics

Gustav Fechner (see Figure 4.7) demonstrated the transformative qualities of the human sensory system in ways that complemented Helmholtz's. Like Helmholtz, he held broad interests in physics as well as physiology and psychology, and he studied the relationship between external "physical reality" and one's conscious or phenomenal experience of that reality. Also like Helmholtz, he helped determine some of the apparent *laws* by which the human sensory system converts external physical stimulation into conscious sensation and perception. But while both men contributed to the same general problem, they did so in different styles and for different reasons, and they reacted in opposite ways to some of the major intellectual currents of their day.

Fechner was born into a family of Lutheran ministers on April 19, 1801, in the east German region of Lusatia. His father and grandfather were men of the cloth, and when his father died in 1806 young Gustav went to live with an uncle, another clergyman. His father, at

FIG 4.7
Gustav Fechner
(1801–1887)

least, seems to have appreciated science as well as religion, for he is reported to have startled his congregation by installing a lightning rod on his church's steeple, declaring that the laws of physics had to be honored just as those of God. The elder Fechner created another stir by preaching in the manner he insisted Jesus must also have done—without the then-customary minister's wig. Although Gustav's father may have died too soon to have had much direct influence on the molding of his character, these stories must have been known to him and must have encouraged his own sense of independence and moderate iconoclasm.

Gustav grew up with strong philosophical and broadly "religious" interests but felt no inclination to follow in his family's vocational tradition. At first medicine seemed appealing, so he entered the University of Leipzig's medical school at the early age of 16. But medicine proved to be his calling no more than the ministry had, and he never took up practice after completing medical studies in 1822. Indeed, even while a student he had begun publishing satirical attacks on the medical profession under the pen name of "Dr. Mises." One of these, "Proof That the Moon Is Made of Iodine," ridiculed a then current medical fad for that substance. Another portrayed a doctor who amputated the wrong leg of a patient and then proposed a new theory of medicine in which all treatments are best applied to the opposite side of the body from the one afflicted. Over the rest of his life, Fechner would publish several more times as Dr. Mises, retaining that pen name for much of his speculative, philosophical, or nonscientific writing.

After rejecting medicine, Fechner had to find another way to make a living, so he began translating French textbooks on physics and chemistry. This tedious and poorly paid work at least had educational benefits, enabling Fechner to thoroughly learn the physical sciences. He learned enough to undertake his own research on electricity, which became well enough recognized to gain him appointment as a lecturer on physics at the University of Leipzig in 1824. Over the next few years he enhanced his reputation by conducting original research on direct electrical current, and he was made a full professor of physics in 1833.

While becoming an accomplished physicist, Fechner also indulged his more speculative side by studying *"Naturphilosophie"* (literally,

"Nature-philosophy")—a semi-mystical, semi-scientific movement then popular in Germany. Part of the Romantic development of Kantian philosophy, this movement regarded the entire universe as an organic entity imbued with consciousness and other animate functions; at death, one's individual consciousness presumably merges with this "over-consciousness" of the whole universe. And throughout the phenomenal universe (that is, the universe as we know it in this life), the essential wholeness and organic unity of things is presumably revealed in the observable parallels and symmetries in nature.

Fechner recognized that some nature-philosophers carried their search for mystical regularities to ludicrous extremes, and as Dr. Mises he satirized them in an article titled "The Comparative Anatomy of Angels." In it he argued, tongue in cheek, that spheres are perfect shapes and angels are perfect beings, hence angels are spherical like planets—in fact, they *are* living planets. But even as he recognized certain excesses in nature-philosophy, Fechner also believed it offered an antidote to the rising tide of *materialism* that accompanied the increasing acceptance of the mechanistic, Newtonian worldview. While appreciating the potential scientific power of mechanistic analysis, Fechner also felt oppressed by its implications. Of a different temperament from Helmholtz and his cohorts, Fechner saw unbounded mechanism not as a means for liberating physiology, but as a philosophically deadening and depressing doctrine. (We shall see in later chapters that he was not alone in this reaction.)

Fechner was upset by the apparent "two-facedness" of nature: the fact that the immutable laws governing the physical, external side of the world seemed to contradict or be irrelevant to the impression of free will and volition that one actually experiences in consciousness. He became obsessed with the question "Does Nature or the world have a soul?"[9] As Dr. Mises, he wrote a series of works depicting two alternative conceptions of the universe, each suggesting a different answer to his question. The materialist conception, which he called the *Nachtansicht* (literally, "night view"), regarded the universe as essentially a dead mechanism, with life and consciousness occurring only as incidental and fully predetermined by-products of mechanistic laws. The contrasting *Tagesansicht* ("day view") had roots in Leibniz's monadology (see Chapter 2). It took consciousness itself as the fundamental characteristic of a "besouled" universe and regarded mechanistic laws as offering only a partial, "external" view of reality. As his choice of names implies, Fechner found the brighter day view more appealing than the gloomy night view, though he obviously harbored some doubts about its truth.

For several years, Fechner waged a mental battle between his night and day views, even as he successfully followed his career in physics. Then in 1839, apparently near the peak of his powers, he suffered a major breakdown. The exact circumstances are unclear, though a severe eye injury caused by looking too long at the sun while studying afterimages played some part. Emotional and philosophical factors undoubtedly aggravated the situation, as conflicts between the night and day views—and the Gustav Fechner and Dr. Mises aspects of his own personality—became increasingly acute. Whatever the exact causes, Fechner became almost a complete invalid, often unable to speak or even to eat. He had to resign his professorship, and retreated into a penurious isolation for several years.

He finally solved his eating problem by following a mystic's advice to subsist entirely on a diet of fruit, strongly spiced ham, and wine. He now began to engage in increasingly mystical speculation himself, and published under his own name the arcanely entitled *Nanna, or on the Soul-life of Plants* in 1848, followed by *Zend-Avesta, or on the Things of Heaven and the Beyond* in 1851. Understandably, these works did not enhance Fechner's scientific reputation.

But on October 22, 1850, while lying in bed meditating, Fechner had a sudden insight whose working out eventually brought him back into the scientific mainstream—and to a position as one of the fathers of modern experimental psychology. He was reflecting on the relationships between the material and the mental worlds—the same general problem that preoccupied Helmholtz. But while Helmholtz emphasized the *differences* between the two worlds—writing of the "inaccuracies and imperfections" of the eye as an optical instrument and of the "incongruities" imposed by the color-sensing apparatus—Fechner was suddenly impressed with a previously unappreciated and partly hidden example of *harmony* between the two worlds. Indeed, he joyfully took his insight to be a confirmation of the day view, as it signified the basic oneness of the physical and mental universes.

The particular subject that so roused Fechner involved the sensation of *stimulus intensities*. His subsequent experiments on this topic laid the groundwork for a new scientific discipline that he believed united the physical with the psychological and that he called, appropriately enough, **psychophysics**.

The Invention of Psychophysics

Some simple, everyday observations about hearing and vision help to introduce the subject of Fechner's psychophysics. With hearing, we take it for granted that a very slight sound will be drowned out by a lot of background noise but easily audible when the background is "so quiet you can hear a pin drop." And similarly with vision: A single lit match is much more noticeable in a darkened room than in a brightly lit one, and the stars are easily visible against the dark background of the night sky but are overwhelmed by the greater brightness of daylight.

These apparently obvious facts have some interesting implications. They indicate that conscious sensations of stimulus intensity do *not* perfectly reflect physical reality, because the same stimuli create different impressions of their magnitude under different circumstances. A dropped pin, a particular star, or a lighted match always emit sound or light waves of the same intensity, yet those waves are perceived differently depending on the background stimulation—sometimes being highly noticeable, sometimes dimly so, and sometimes completely unnoticeable. These are further examples of the general Kantian point of this chapter—namely, that the sensory system processes and transforms impressions from physical stimuli before bringing them to consciousness.

Helmholtz would probably have interpreted these reactions to stimulus intensity as further "distortions" or "incongruities" imposed by the senses, consistent with his general perspective. Fechner, however, took a different approach. He thought it should be possible to *measure* the perceived as well as the physical intensities of sensory stimuli and to determine the *mathematical relationships* between the two measures. His sudden intuition in October 1850 told him the relationships would turn out to be harmonious, and illustrative of the basic underlying unity of the psychological and physical worlds.

Of course, an immediate practical question arose: How might one hope to measure the subjective intensities of stimulation? The yardsticks, scales, and light meters used to measure physical intensities could not be placed inside people's heads to measure their subjective responses. Indeed, Kant had argued against the possibility of psychology's ever becoming a true science precisely because subjective mental phenomena seemed incapable of quantification or measurement.

Fechner saw an answer to this problem, as well as a strong hint as to what his final psychophysical relationships would look like, in some previously underappreciated work by his Leipzig friend and colleague, the physiologist **Ernst Heinrich Weber** (1795–1878). Several years before, Weber had investigated people's ability to discriminate accurately between different weights of similar appearance and reported: "In observing the disparity between things that are compared, we perceive not the difference between the things, but the *ratio* of this difference to the magnitude of the things compared."[10]

That is, Weber found that accurate discrimination depended on the relative rather than the absolute difference between the weights. The finest discriminations that could be made always involved judgments where the weights differed by approximately 3 percent. For example, a weight of 100 grams could be reliably detected as lighter than one of 103, but for 200 grams the second weight would have to be at least 206. The absolute difference had to be twice as large in the second case as it was in the first, when the weights themselves were twice as heavy as in the first. In sum, Weber determined that the **just noticeable difference** (commonly abbreviated as **jnd**) for weight discrimination—that is, the minimum amount of difference between two weights necessary to tell them apart—was always an amount approximately equal to 0.03 of the first of the two weights being compared.

Weber observed similar regularities for other kinds of sensory discriminations—though the specific fraction for the jnd differed with each sense. In comparing the length of lines, for example, the jnd value was always about 0.01; a line of 99 millimeters could be differentiated from one of 100, one of 198 from one of 200, and so on. For musical pitches, the jnd seemed to be about 0.006 of the vibrations per second. Weber suspected, though he did not prove, that a constant fraction could be determined for all of the other senses as well.

Weber's findings suggested a new way of looking at the phenomena discussed at the beginning of this section: The sound waves created by a dropped pin are noticeable only if the ratio of their intensity to that of the background noise exceeds the critical fraction for the jnd. Of course, that ratio will be higher, and more likely to exceed the critical fraction, when the intensity of background noise is lower.

This work gave Fechner a crucial clue as to how he might empirically demonstrate an intrinsic harmony between the physical and the psychological. If one accepted that the jnd was in fact a constant fraction within each of the senses, then the jnd itself could be taken as the unit of measurement for psychological intensities of stimulation. One could then take the smallest intensity of a stimulus that can be perceived at all—a value Fechner called the **absolute threshold**—as the zero point on a scale of psychological intensities. On a graph, successive jnd's above the threshold could be plotted against the measured increases in physical intensities necessary to produce them. Weber's findings suggested that the resulting graph should always show a striking mathematical regularity, as illustrated in the following hypothetical example.

Assume that the absolute threshold for a sense has been shown to be 8 units of physical intensity and that the jnd fraction has been determined to be 0.5. Thus when the subjective intensity of the stimulation (abbreviated S) is at the starting point, or 0, the corresponding intensity of physical stimulation (P) is 8. To get 1 jnd above the threshold, the physical intensity must increase by 0.5, or 4 units, thus becoming 12; to increase 1 jnd further requires an increase of half of 12, or 6, so the physical intensity now must be 18. Another jnd beyond that requires 9 further units of P for a total of 27, and so on, as represented in the graph in Figure 4.8.

The graph depicts a regular curve with a constantly increasing slope. Any of the sensory functions we have discussed so far would yield a graph of the same general shape (though with different individual values), because their characteristic feature is an ever-increasing number of units of P to produce each succeeding jnd. The rate of increase varies from sense to sense, according to its particular jnd fraction; but for every sense *some* increase is required, and thus its curve will show the gradually accelerating upswing demonstrated in our hypothetical figure. Note that if there were a perfect, one-to-one

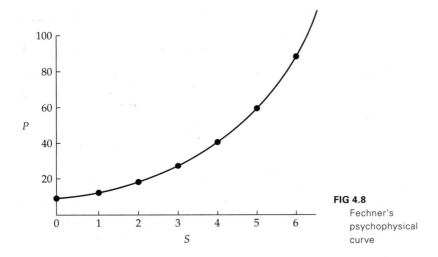

FIG 4.8
Fechner's
psychophysical
curve

relationship between *P* and *S*—that is, if every unit increase in physical stimulation produced an exactly corresponding unit increase in subjective intensity—the graph would not be a curve, but a straight line.

Fechner recognized that these observed relationships between physical and subjective stimulus intensities for many different senses could be expressed by the single, general mathematical formula $S = k \log P$.

That is, the subjective intensity of a stimulus (in jnd units) will always equal the *logarithm* of its physical intensity times some constant (*k*) which will vary for each sense, but which may be experimentally determined.* Fechner modestly referred to this equation as

---

* A number's logarithm is the power to which some base number must be raised to produce it. For example, the logarithms in base 10 for the numbers 10, 100, 1,000, and 10,000 are 1, 2, 3, and 4, respectively, since the former numbers represent 10 raised to the first, second, third and fourth powers, respectively. Note that each unit increase in the logarithms is associated with a progressively larger increase in the numbers they represent: When the logarithm goes from 1 to 2, the number increases by 90; from 2 to 3 by 900; and from 3 to 4 by 9,000. Thus, a graph representing the relationship between numbers and their logarithms assumes the same general shape as Figure 4.8.

"Weber's law" when he first published it, but it is now customarily called **Fechner's law** instead.

Nearly ten years passed between Fechner's crucial insight in 1850 and the publication of his law in his 1860 book *Elements of Psychophysics*. During that time he developed new methods for measuring jnd's for senses that had not been investigated by Weber and expanded on some implications of his own work. On the one hand, of course, the lack of perfect correspondence between subjective and physical stimulus intensities provided another example of the way human senses "distort" their representations of the physical world. But on the other hand, these distortions occurred in a regular, lawful way, expressible in a beautiful mathematical equation. To Fechner, this provided evidence of an underlying harmony between the "two faces" of nature—that is, between the psychological and the physical worlds.

Fechner's book and law aroused great interest, and some criticism. Critics pointed to studies showing that his law was accurate only approximately and tended to break down at the extremes of high or low sensory intensities They found that "absolute thresholds" differed somewhat from person to person, or even within the same person from time to time. Some objected theoretically to the use of the jnd as a unit of measurement, since it was not intuitively obvious that the first jnd above the threshold and, say, the twenty-first were identical to each other in the same way that the first and the twenty-first inches on a yardstick are.

But still, *Elements of Psychophysics* became generally accepted as representing a breakthrough for experimental psychology. Following Weber's lead, Fechner had demonstrated that a purely psychological phenomenon—subjective stimulus intensity—might at least approximately be quantified and mathematically related to other variables in apparently lawful ways. Because a field's susceptibility to mathematical expression was regarded as an index of its "scientific" status, Fechner's book gave an enormous boost to psychology's status as a potentially mathematical and experimental science. No longer would psychology be regarded as the merely metaphysical discipline described by Kant.

In sum, both Helmholtz and Fechner proved that it was possible to study at least some of the phenomena of the mind in the same general ways that the physical world was studied: in terms of general, mechanistic laws (Helmholtz) or mathematically specifiable ones (Fechner). Accordingly, they demonstrated the *promise* for a new discipline of experimental psychology—a promise that was soon fulfilled by a younger colleague of both Helmholtz and Fechner named Wilhelm Wundt. We shall detail these developments in the next chapter. In the meantime, we turn our attention to another important group of successors to Helmholtz and Fechner, who worked more directly in the fields of sensation and perception.

Gestalt Psychology

The Gestalt psychologists took their name from the German term *Gestalt*—roughly translatable into English as "form" or "shape"— which entered psychological vocabularies in 1890. That year the Austrian **Christian von Ehrenfels** (1859–1932) wrote of certain perceptual "form qualities"—*Gestaltqualitaten*—that could not be introspectively broken down into separate sensory elements, but instead resided in the overall configurations of objects or ideas. For example, the "squareness" of a square, or the melody of a musical piece, inhered not in the percepts' separate parts, but in their total configurations. A square may be constructed out of any group of four equal straight lines, as long as they are properly arranged; "squareness" resides not in the particular lines, but in their *relationships* to each other. Similarly, a melody retains its distinctive and recognizable quality regardless of the key in which it is played or the timbre of its specific notes. "Yankee Doodle" is still "Yankee Doodle" whether played in the highest register of the piccolo or the lowest of the tuba. The essence of its melody lies not in its specific notes, but in the relationships among its notes.

The implications of these Gestalt qualities were not fully explored until 1910, when a former student of Ehrenfels named **Max Wertheimer** (1880–1943; see Figure 4.9) had a sudden inspiration while waiting for a train to take him on summer vacation. He immediately abandoned his vacation to conduct research at the University of Frankfurt with the assistance of two younger colleagues, **Kurt Koffka** (1886–1941; see Figure 4.10) and **Wolfgang Köhler** (1887–1967; see Figure 4.11). The three of them subsequently founded the movement known as Gestalt psychology.

FIG 4.9
Max Wertheimer (1880–1943)

Wertheimer's inspiration was to study the optical illusion of **apparent movement**: the perception of continuous motion that occurs when observing a succession of slightly varying still images. This phenomenon had recently come to wide public attention through the invention of nickelodeons and early motion picture technology. Wertheimer's

FIG 4.10 Kurt Koffka (1886–194?)   **FIG 4.11** Wolfgang Köhler (1887–1967)

bright idea was that this interesting effect could be studied systematically in a laboratory, using very simple visual stimuli. With a tachistoscope—a device that projects images on a screen for measured fractions of a second—he and his colleagues flashed light alternately through two slits, one vertical and the other tilted by thirty degrees. When the interval between the flashes exceeded one-fifth of a second, observers saw the "true" state of affairs: two rapidly alternating but clearly separate lights. When the interval was less than one-hundredth of a second, both of the slits appeared to be illuminated constantly. But when the interval was intermediate between those values, and especially at about one-twentieth of a second, observers had an irresistible and distinct impression of a single slit of light "falling over" from the vertical to the inclined position, then rising back up again. Wertheimer named this apparent movement—a simplified version of a motion picture—the **phi phenomenon,**

Wertheimer went on to show that an observer, presented with randomly distributed examples of real movement and comparable apparent movement, could not distinguish one type from the other. Furthermore, both real and apparent movement could produce identical **negative afterimages**—a tendency to see stationary objects as moving in the direction opposite to that of a moving object that has been observed immediately before. Here was another perceptual situation like those previously described, in which widely differing physical stimuli can produce subjectively identical conscious experiences. When we observe actual movement, light images literally sweep across our retinas, falling upon all of the receptor cells lying in their path. With the phi phenomenon, only the retinal receptors lying at the beginning and at the end of the "sweep" become physically illuminated. Yet both of these differing physical states produce the same perception of continuous motion. These findings indicated that at least some of the processes responsible for the perception of movement take place at a neurological level higher than the retina. "Movement" is an attribute that may be imposed on stationary images by the higher brain processes.

After studying apparent movement, Wertheimer, Koffka, and Köhler concluded that human perceptual processes impose their own order and dynamic organization on the individual "elements" of physical sensation. Meaningful perception, they argued, entails far more than the simple addition of sensory elements, or even the unconscious inferring of logical relationships among those elements. The mind seems to organize the elements of experience into *wholes*, for example, whose significance completely transcends that of their summed individual parts. Ehrenfels's Gestalt qualities were prime examples: Squares, melodies, and phi phenomena alike are not only more than the sums of their sensory parts, but dynamic entities on their own whose parts are defined by their relationships to the whole. Wertheimer summarized: "There are wholes, the behavior of which is not determined by that of their individual elements, but where the part processes themselves are determined by the intrinsic nature of the whole. It is the hope of Gestalt theory to determine the nature of such wholes."[11] Thus, unlike many scientists who start by trying to isolate the simplest "elements" of their subject and then show how they combine to create wholes, the Gestalt psychologists started with the wholes themselves and then tried to describe the functions of the parts *within* those wholes.

Within this context the Gestalt psychologists pointed out that perception always occurs in a "field" divided into the figure and the ground, the *figure* being the whole percept immediately attended to in consciousness, and the *ground* the necessary backdrop against which the figure must define itself. Figure cannot exist without ground; thus, the printed words you are now reading cannot be perceived (as figure) except against the lighter background of the page. Figure and ground may never both be in consciousness simultaneously—for then both would be part of the figure—but under some conditions they may reverse. Figure 4.12 illustrates figure-ground reversal when you see it first as a white vase against a black ground, then as two black profiled faces against a white ground. You cannot see both the vase and the faces at exactly the same time, because that would constitute two figures with no ground. Thus the whole figures—or "Gestalts"—in your perceptual field constantly change, but each always appears as only a part of the entire field, standing out against the background.

Wertheimer, Koffka, and Köhler also emphasized that perceived Gestalts tend to *simplify* and *organize* the perceptual fields in

FIG 4.12
Example of
figure-ground
reversal

which they occur. Relatively complicated aggregates of stimuli inevitably become organized into simpler groups according to principles of contiguity and similarity. In the left-hand portion of Figure 4.13 for example, the circles' spacing (contiguity) leads most people to perceive "three groups of circles" rather than the more complex "seventeen scattered circles." On the right, the mind uses similarity cues to perceive "alternating rows of circles and dots" more readily than the more complicated "five columns of mixed circles and dots."

The same Gestalt principles seem to apply in other sense modalities besides vision. Perceived sounds, for example, must always be heard against a relatively neutral background. Auditory figure-ground reversals can easily occur, as when nervous airplane passengers "listen" for the ominous periods of silence that may punctuate the droning of a faulty engine. Complex temporal sequences of sounds may be organized into simpler contiguous groups, as in the perceived regularities of a drummer's beat, and they may be grouped by similarity, as when the violin part is clearly discerned against the background of the rest of the orchestra.

In general, then, the young Gestalt psychologists significantly expanded the list of known situations in which the human mind imposes an order of its own making on the objects of its perception. They extended and clarified the Kantian notion of a creative, transforming

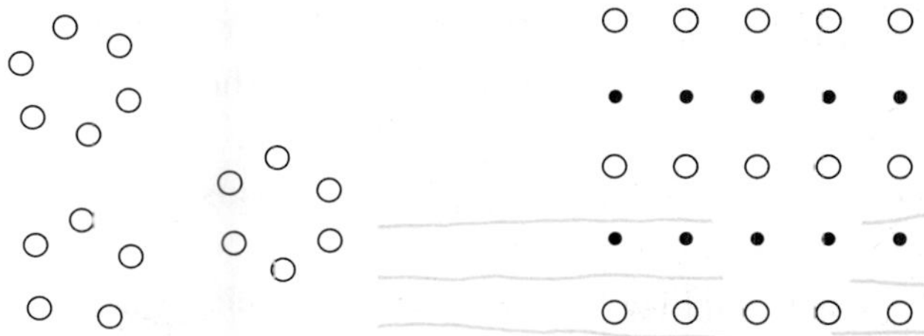

FIG 4.13
Gestalt principles of organization

mind to a greater and different extent than Helmholtz and Fechner had, and they supported their arguments with impressive empirical evidence.

Later Developments in the Study of Sensation and Perception

Helmholtz's Legacy

Many of Helmholtz's ideas and theories are still accepted today, much as he originally presented them. The trichromatic theory of color vision, for example, has been amply confirmed by modern research. The retina is now known to contain millions of tiny color receptor cells called *cones*, which come in three varieties, each one containing a photopigment that maximally absorbs light of one of the three spectral primary colors. The absence of one or more of these pigments or irregularities in their distribution cause the types of visual defects popularly known as "color blindness."

It is further accepted today, however, that color processing does not *end* with the cones on the retina. Indeed even during Helmholtz's lifetime his younger contemporary **Ewald Hering** (1834–1918) had emphasized the importance of **color afterimages**; for example, if you stare fixedly at a red stimulus and then shift your gaze to a neutrally colored background, you will see an afterimage of the same stimulus, only in the complementary color of blue-green. Such phenomena, Hering argued, suggest the existence of some sort of "opponent processes" in the visual system, causing it to respond in an either/or fashion. It is now recognized that receptor cells responding in just such a way and residing in the thalamus of the brain add a further level to the processing of visual signals, after they have left the retina. These findings do not invalidate the trichromatic theory, but they show that it does not tell the complete story of human color vision.

In general, Helmholtz's ideas on perception and unconscious inference have been modified more than those on sensation. No one denies that many aspects of perception are learned, but Helmholtz's relatively extreme empiricism has been challenged—perhaps most directly by the "visual cliff" experiments by Cornell University's **Eleanor Jack Gibson** (1910–2002) and her colleague Richard Walk in the 1950s. These experiments were prompted by her observations of baby goats, who are born with the ability to stand up and walk and who seem to show an innate ability to avoid tumbling over steep slopes. Gibson constructed a platform with a transparent glass floor set above a "cliff" and showed that extremely young animals, and human babies, systematically avoided walking or crawling on the parts of the platform with no visible surface directly below (see Figure 4.14). These studies suggested that depth perception occurs even in extremely young subjects who lack the sorts of experiences that Helmholtz believed were necessary for learning the "major premises" involved in unconscious inference.

Despite these elaborations and partial contradictions, Helmholtz's perceptual theories have had a continuous influence on the experiments psychologists perform. Perceptual adaptation is still studied,

FIG 4.14
A baby exploring
the visual cliff

often with distorting spectacles much like Helmholtz's originals. And even with the altered terminology and interpretations of some of the modern work, Helmholtz's basic ideas are still relevant, and he would feel very much at home in a modern perception laboratory. Much the same can be said about Fechner and his psychophysics.

Stevens and the Power Law of Psychophysics

A certain amount of technical discussion followed publication of Fechner's *Elements*, centering on the exact mathematical form of the psychophysical law. The Belgian physicist **Joseph Plateau** (1801–1883) suggested in 1872 that the relationship might more accurately be described as a *power function* rather than the logarithmic one proposed by Fechner, although he soon changed his mind and accepted Fechner's Law. Three quarters of a century later, the Harvard psychologist **S. Smith Stevens** (1906–1973) presented evidence to indicate that Plateau had been correct the first time. Stevens studied a large number of psychophysical situations and found a few—such as the reporting of the conscious impressions of how long an auditory stimulus had been turned on—in which the subjective judgments corresponded almost perfectly with the objective durations of the stimuli. And for a few other stimuli, subjective intensities increased at a faster rate than the objective intensities—the opposite of the Weber fractions. When a subject experiences increasing levels of electric shock to the finger, for example, small increases in voltage are relatively unnoticeable when the total current is weak, but strongly noticeable at higher intensities.

Stevens recognized that such cases were not covered by Fechner's law but that both they and the ones studied by Fechner could be covered by a still more general mathematical equation. This was the so-called **power law**, or **Stevens' law**, which asserts that S is a function of P raised to a particular power times a constant: $S = kP^n$. When the power represented by the exponent n is less than 1, this equation becomes generally equivalent to Fechner's law and accounts for the traditional cases. When the exponent is exactly 1, the graphed equation becomes a straight line and represents stimuli, such as the duration of a sound, that are subjectively judged very similar to their objective properties. Finally, if the exponent is greater than 1, the equation applies to stimuli such as electric shock, whose subjective intensities increase at a faster (exponential) rate than their physical intensities.

Like Fechner's law, Stevens' law must be recognized as an approximation, holding most accurately for the middle ranges of physical stimulation and subject to certain fluctuations across individuals and situations. But it still confirms the general robustness of Fechner's original inspiration: namely, that certain sensory judgments can be at least approximately quantified and shown to relate in a meaningful way to events in the physical environment.

Further Developments in Gestalt Psychology

In the late 1920s and the 1930s, the three Gestalt pioneers foresaw at least some of the horrors that were to come in Nazi Germany and fled to new posts in the United States. This was immensely to America's benefit, as all contributed importantly to its developing psychology. Koffka, from his new position at Smith College in Massachusetts, became a strong promoter of the general Gestalt point of view as a counterweight to the atomistic behaviorism that dominated most of American psychology at the time (see Chapter 9). His 1935 book, *Principles of Gestalt Psychology*, remains the most comprehensive and systematic statement of the Gestalt viewpoint.

Köhler and Wertheimer extended Gestalt principles from realms of sensation and perception to those of *thinking* and *learning*. From his observations of chimpanzee behavior while stationed in the Canary Islands during World War I, Köhler concluded that learning often involves *insight*: Rather than arising gradually from many trial-and-error efforts, as a behavioristic account would have it, new and adaptive responses often arise suddenly, following a completely new *organization* of the overall perceptual field. A stick in a chimp's cage, for example, became all at once perceived not just as an incidental object on the floor, but rather as a *tool* that could be used to drag within reach a banana from the ground outside the cage. Wertheimer, from his new position in New York City, analyzed creative human thinking in similar terms. This work was summarized in his posthumously published book, *Productive Thinking* (1945), in which he advocated the abandonment of rote, associationistic educational methods in favor of those that involved free exploration, and he encouraged flexibility and the generation of insights. During his final years in New York, Wertheimer also befriended and had a profound influence on the young American psychologist Abraham Maslow, whose subsequent pioneering of humanistic psychology shall be recounted in Chapter 12.

Köhler in the meantime had settled at Swarthmore College in Pennsylvania where, in the tradition of Helmholtz and Fechner, he attempted to integrate psychological findings with current developments in physics. He noted that in physics, the old Newtonian mode of explanation was proving inadequate, as many electrical, magnetic, and gravitational phenomena, in particular, could not be explained in terms of isolated material particles acting upon one another. Instead, entire *distributions* of forces, or *force fields*, had to be hypothesized. To take a simple example, the fate of a single charged particle could not be predicted in isolation, without reference to the entire electrical field in which it happened to be. Köhler summarized by asserting that the new physicist "begins with a given 'whole' and only then arrives at the parts by analysis, while the [traditional] procedures are founded on the principle of beginning with the parts and building up the wholes by analysis."[12] Here, of course, were clear echoes of the Gestaltists' previous implicit definition of the **perceptual field** as the overall environment in which figure/ground and other Gestalt effects occur, and of Wertheimer's earlier definition of Gestalt psychology as commencing with the whole before deducing the roles of its parts.

Köhler traced out these ideas and their implications in a series of popular lectures delivered shortly before his death in 1967 and published posthumously under the title *The Task of Gestalt Psychology* (1969). He emphasized, for example, that perceptual and physical force fields are alike in that each tends to organize itself over time into increasingly simpler configurations. Just as electrical charges tend to distribute themselves increasingly evenly, so complex stimulus arrays become simplified when grouped into Gestalts by similarity and contiguity, or when disjointed images fuse into continuous and smooth motion in the phi phenomenon. In a more speculative vein, Köhler noted that the organ of perception, the brain, is itself a physical system that distributes and processes electrical charges. Thus, the similarities between physical and perceptual fields are perhaps more than coincidental. He invoked the hypothesis of **psychophysical isomorphism**, which he and his colleagues had developed years earlier, and according to which "psychological facts and the underlying events in the brain resemble each other in all their structural characteristics."[13] This idea did not mean that perceptual and brain processes had to be *identical* with one another—but they would share the same structural and relational properties similarly to the ways a map resembles the terrain it depicts. Under this principle, the brain should be studied as an organized, whole system, not just a conglomeration of separate individual components.

This general idea was strongly promoted by the German neurologist **Kurt Goldstein** (1878–1965), who had been impressed by Gestalt principles and indeed in 1920 had been one of the founding editors of *Psychologische Forschung* (*Psychological Research*)—the original German language journal devoted to Gestalt psychology. He too emigrated to America, where as an expert on the treatment of brain injuries he promoted a "holistic-organismic" theory according to which the brain should be regarded as a whole, acting as a unified entity to promote the well-being or "self-actualization" of the entire organism. If one part of the brain is injured, the functions previously carried out by its particular neurons get taken over by other parts of the entire system—although often with less speed, efficiency, and adequacy. In thus bringing Gestalt principles to bear in their theories of brain functioning, Köhler and Goldstein carried on the anti-localizationist tradition begun by Pierre Flourens, as described in Chapter 3.

A younger Gestalt-trained psychologist, **Kurt Lewin** (1890–1947), came to America with his mentors and extended the notion of field in yet a different direction. Lewin argued that every individual person resides in a unique *psychological* field, or **life space**, which is the totality of his or her psychological situation at any given moment. The life space includes one's physical environment, *as it is perceived*, as well as the person's constantly changing motives and actions, or *locomotion* within the life space. All of these combine to create forces, or "vectors," within the field, which combine to determine the person's behavior.

A man of great versatility and broad interests, Lewin also became interested in the functioning of other kinds of psychologically relevant systems or networks. In an effort to promote greater awareness and sensitivity to the perception of others within interpersonal networks, he conducted sensitivity training groups, or "T groups," which were precursors to the "encounter groups" that became highly popular in the 1960s and 1970s. Of relevance to larger social units, he studied the comparative effects of democratic versus authoritarian leadership styles on the behavior of groups—one of the pioneering experimental studies in American social psychology to which we shall return in Chapter 10. In that chapter we shall also see that another major pioneer in American social psychology—Solomon Asch with his classic studies of suggestibility—had been a graduate student under Wertheimer before becoming Köhler's colleague at Swarthmore. And in Chapter 12 we shall see that the German Gestalt psychologists played a major role in shaping the views of Gordon Allport and Abraham Maslow as they established the foundations for the new subdisciplines of personality and humanistic psychology.

Conclusion: Sensation and Perception Today

Students at the outset of their introductory psychology course sometimes question why the topics of sensation and perception are presented so soon in the course, and so prominently. We trust that this chapter has answered that question, showing how increasing knowledge about the ways in which physical stimuli become converted into conscious experiences provided the first scientific evidence of a creative "mind," worthy of study in its own right. We shall see in Chapter 14 how further studies in this same vein have been rebranded as research on **information processing**—the complex sequence of activities by which stimuli are received, recognized, categorized, and recorded in memory—and lay at the heart of the new discipline of **cognitive psychology**, which came to prominence in the second half of the twentieth century.

Summary

The problem of how our experience of the external world is mediated through the sensory and perceptual processes of an active mind is an issue that provided one of the main starting points for an empirical *science* of psychology. In the late 1700s **Immanuel Kant** distinguished between the **noumenal world** and the **phenomenal world**. The first consists of "things-in-themselves" that exist independently of our experience of them, and the second of the world *as we know it*, after it has been processed and transformed by the senses and the innate categories of the mind. In suggesting that the mind *actively* transforms external reality, Kant provided an opening for the study of these active processes that was taken up by several subsequent scholars.

Hermann Helmholtz made several inroads into this problem. First, he devised a way to show that the speed of the nervous impulse, previously thought to be infinite, was measurably finite; this led to the discovery that reaction times are variable and can be studied scientifically. With his colleagues, Helmholtz further argued that the processes underlying nervous transmission were of the ordinary physical-chemical kind and did not involve an ineffable "life force." Thus, Helmholtz showed that something as seemingly instantaneous and mysterious as nervous transmission could be subject to mechanistic analysis and explanation. Turning his attention to the processes of sensation and perception, Helmholtz showed in great detail how the energies from the physical world, when conceived in their most elemental senses such as the frequencies and amplitudes of light, sound, and temperature waves, are analogous Kant's noumenal world. These energies are processed by our sensory and perceptual systems to produce conscious experiences of colors, sounds, objects, and so on that correspond to Kant's phenomenal world. Among Helmholtz's specific contributions was the trichromatic theory of color vision that is considered largely accurate to this day.

In founding the field he called **psychophysics, Gustav Theodor Fechner** became interested in the relationship between the *intensities* of physical stimuli as measured "objectively" versus the way they are experienced subjectively. Inventing the **just noticeable difference (jnd)** as the unit of subjectively experienced intensity, he showed that these jnd units related to objectively measured intensities in a regular logarithmic function that became known as **Fechner's law**. Here was another demonstration that a subjective, psychological quality could be subject to quantification and scientific analysis.

Later, the Gestalt psychologists **Max Wertheimer, Kurt Koffka**, and **Wolfgang Köhler** demonstrated further ways in which the mind actively orders and organizes its perceptions of the world. The phi phenomenon, figure-ground reversals, and the innate tendency to organize complex aggregates of stimuli into clusters or groups were all examples of this transformative and creative function of the mind.

It was through studies such as these that the sensing and perceiving mind became recognized as something more than a passive recorder of sensory stimuli, and in fact as an active and creative entity in its own right, and susceptible to scientific observation and analysis.

Key Pioneers

Bell, Charles, p. 143
Brücke, Ernst, p. 146
Du Bois-Reymond, Emil, p 146
Ehrenfels. Christian von, p. 172
Fechner, Gustav Theodor, p. 175
Gibson, Eleanor Jack, p. 178
Goldstein, Kurt, p. 182
Helmholtz, Hermann, p. 145
Hering, Ewald, p 177
Kant, Immanuel, p. 139
Koffka, Kurt, p. 172

Köhler, Wolfgang, p. 172
Lewin, Kurt, p. 182
Maxwell, James Clerk, p. 157
Müller, Johannes, p. 143
Plateau, Joseph, p. 179
Stevens, S. Smith, p. 179
Virchow, Rudolf, p. 146
Weber, Ernst Heinrich, p. 168
Wertheimer, Max, p. 172
Young, Thomas, p. 158

Key Terms

absolute threshold, p. 169
apparent movement, p. 173
astigmatism, p. 155
blind spot, p. 155
categories, p.142
cognitive psychology, p. 183
color afterimages, p. 177
color mixing, p. 157
complementary colors, p. 157
conservation of energy, p. 149
Fechner's law, p. 171
Gestalt psychologists, p. 145
information processing, p. 183
intuitions, p. 142
just noticeable difference (jnd),
    p. 167
law of specific nerve energies,
    p. 143
life space, p. 182

mechanism, p. 148
negative afterimages, p. 174
noumenal world, p. 141
optical illusions, p. 143
perceptions, p. 153
perceptual adaptation, p. 160
perceptual field, p. 181
phenomenal world, p. 141
phi phenomenon, p. 174
power law (Stevens' law), p. 179
primary colors, p. 158
psychophysical isomorphism, p. 181
psychophysics, p. 167
reaction times, p. 151
sensations, p. 153
unconscious inference, p. 161
vitalism, p. 147
Young-Helmholtz trichromatic
    theory, p. 158

Discussion Questions and Topics

1 Fechner was faced with the problem of how to "get inside the heads" of people to measure their subjective experience of physical sensory stimuli (e.g., heat, brightness, loudness, etc.). Can you think of any other subjective experiences that are of great interest to psychologists? What methods have they devised to measure them?

2 What is the distinction between vitalism and mechanism, and why was the "triumph of mechanism" important for the eventual emergence of scientific psychology?

3 Describe how Kurt Goldstein and Kurt Lewin were influenced by Gestalt principles.

Suggested Readings

For discussion of Kant's influence on the development of psychology, see Chapter 15, "The Kantian Background," in D. B. Klein's *A History of Scientific Psychology* (New York: Basic Books, 1970). The classic description of the development of the law of specific nerve energies appears in Chapters 2 and 5 of Edwin G. Boring, *A History of Experimental Psychology* (New York: Appleton-Century-Crofts, 1957).

A good sampling of Helmholtz's work—including his paper on conservation of energy, a brief autobiographical sketch, and popularized accounts of his theories of vision and hearing—has been collected and edited by Russell Kahl in *Selected Writings of Hermann von Helmholtz* (Middletown, CT: Wesleyan University Press, 1971). The standard biography of Helmholtz is Leo Koenigsberger's *Hermann von Helmholtz*, translated by Frances A. Welby (New York: Dover, 1965).

For a lucid account of the origins of psychophysics, see David J. Murray, *A History of Western Psychology*, 2nd edition (New York: Prentice Hall, 1988), 176–185. Murray also presents a detailed description of the technical debates that followed the publication of Fechner's *Elements*, in "A Perspective for Viewing the History of Psychophysics," *Behavioral and Brain Sciences* 16 (1993): 115–186. William R. Woodward's article, "Fechner's Panpsychism: A Scientific Solution to the Mind-Body Problem," in the *Journal of the History of the Behavioral Sciences* 8 (1972): 367–386, usefully discusses the relationship between Fechner's philosophical and scientific concerns. For a full-length intellectual biography, see Michael Heidelberger's *Nature from Within: Gustav Theodor Fechner and His Psychophysical Worldview* (Pittsburgh: University of Pittsburgh Press, 2004).

An engaging and accessible brief introduction to Gestalt psychology is provided in Wolfgang Köhler's *The Task of Gestalt Psychology* (Princeton, NJ: Princeton University Press, 1969). For a more extended account, see Köhler's *Gestalt Psychology* (New York: Liveright, 1947). Max Wertheimer's life and career have been chronicled by D. Brett King and Michael Wertheimer in *Max Wertheimer & Gestalt Theory* (New Brunswick, NJ: Transaction Publishers, 2005).

Wilhelm Wundt and the Establishment of Experimental Psychology

5

Wundt's Early Life
Early Research
Experimental Psychology and *Völkerpsychologie*
Principles of Physiological Psychology

Wundt at Leipzig
Research at Leipzig
Voluntaristic Psychology
Völkerpsychologie and Its Implications

Titchener's Structuralism
The Experimentalists

Experimenting on the Higher Functions: Külpe and Ebbinghaus
Ebbinghaus's Studies of Memory

Wundt's Reputation and Influence

Summary

Key Pioneers

Key Terms

Discussion Questions and Topics

Suggested Readings

In 1861, a young German physiologist named **Wilhelm Wundt** (1832–1920) rigged his pendulum clock into a "thought meter" for a simple but clever home experiment. He wanted to test the common-sense assumption that when two different stimuli strike our senses at the same time—as when we hear a person speak and simultaneously watch his lips move—we become *consciously aware* of both stimuli at the same instant.

Figure 5.1 illustrates Wundt's apparatus.[1] The clock's pendulum, marked B in the diagram, swung above the calibrated scale M. A knitting needle (S) was attached to the shaft of the pendulum so that it would strike a bell (g) at precisely the instant the pendulum reached an extremity of its swing (position b). Thus, the bell sounded at exactly the instant the pendulum was at position b.

When Wundt tested his own reactions, however, he discovered an anomaly. As he looked at the swinging pendulum and judged the position it *seemed* to occupy at the instant he heard the bell, he found it was never exactly at position b but always somewhere on the swing *away* from that spot. He calculated that the time necessary for the pendulum to swing this extra distance was between one-tenth and one-eighth of a second. He concluded that he had *not* consciously experienced the auditory and visual stimuli simultaneously, even though they had actually occurred together. Instead, separate acts of *attention* had apparently been required, first to register the bell in consciousness, then to note the position of the pendulum. Each act of consciousness had presumably taken up a tenth to an eighth of a second.

This result carried important implications for Wundt. As Hermann Helmholtz's assistant at the University of Heidelberg, Wundt knew all about his superior's pioneering studies (reviewed in the

FIG 5.1
Wundt's
"thought-meter"

previous chapter) measuring the speed of the nervous impulse. Those studies, however, had been restricted to the speed of neural events on the *periphery* of the nervous system—that is, impulses in the sensory and motor nerves, transmitting messages to or from the brain. Wundt's new study demonstrated how the reaction-time experiment could be refined to measure the exact duration of a *central* process, presumably mediated by neurological activity within the brain itself, and responsible for the psychological reaction of attention.

Wundt further recognized that he had now joined Hermann Helmholtz and Gustav Fechner (whose *Elements of Psychophysics* had just been published) in subjecting a clearly psychological process to experimental study. He was struck by the fact that suddenly *several* experimental approaches to mental phenomena had been developed, contrary to Kant's influential opinion that such was impossible. In fact, Wundt concluded that there now were sufficient grounds for establishing a whole new field of *experimental psychology*, which might be explicitly pursued in the universities along with more traditional subjects.

Wundt proposed this possibility in the introduction to his 1862 book, *Contributions to the Theory of Sensory Perception*, and then worked on and off for many years to make it a reality. Finally, in 1879, he established an official "institute" at the University of Leipzig, where graduate students could come for the express purpose of earning Ph.D. degrees in experimental psychology. He attracted students from around the world, many of whom returned to their home countries to establish experimental psychology programs there. By 1900, more than a hundred psychological laboratories had been established worldwide, and psychology was widely recognized as an important and independent academic subject. Today, less than 150 years after Wundt started things, psychology is one of the most frequently studied subjects in Western universities. For having started these institutional developments, Wundt is often regarded as the "father" of modern academic and experimental psychology.

Of course, progeny do not always turn out exactly as their parents might wish, and such was also the case with Wundt's intellectual offspring. The strong-minded founder held very clear notions of what psychology should and should not be, and despite his advocacy of experimental methods he also retained a strong sense of their limitations. Many important psychological problems, he believed, could only be approached with non-experimental techniques. Not all of Wundt's students and immediate successors agreed with him, and some promptly pushed the fledgling science further and in different directions than he thought appropriate. As these trends gained popularity, Wundt developed a reputation for being an old-fashioned father, one who got things started but then lacked the vision or modernity to carry his ideas to fulfillment. One historian of psychology in 1964 went so far as to characterize Wundt's psychology as "an interruption in the development of a natural science of man."[2]

More recent historians, however, have rehabilitated Wundt's reputation. Many of his views turn out to have been misinterpreted or misrepresented by his successors, and at least some of his cautions about experimentalism now seem better founded than they once did. Thus, as we turn now to the story of Wundt's life, and of his "founding" of experimental psychology, we take up issues that have more than antiquarian interest.

Wundt's Early Life

Wilhelm Maximilian Wundt (see Figure 5.2) was born near Mannheim, Germany, on August 16, 1832, in a small village where his father was an Evangelical pastor. The family had solid academic connections, for his father's father had been a professor of history at the University of Heidelberg, and two of his mother's brothers were physicians and professors of physiology. One of these, Wilhelm's "Uncle Friedrich" (Philipp Friedrich Arnold), would play a particularly important role in his later life.

As an infant Wilhelm contracted malaria. His worried parents, who had already lost two children in infancy, moved to less lucrative but climatically healthier parishes in farming villages near Heidelberg. They sent their only other surviving child, 8-year-old Ludwig, to live with an aunt and attend school in Heidelberg. As a result, Wilhelm grew up essentially as an only child, in small rural communities.

Wundt's earliest memory was of falling down a staircase, his head striking painfully on every step. A similar depressive tone pervaded most of his other childhood reminiscences. A clumsy and unathletic youth saddled with the further social stigma of being a pastor's son,

FIG 5.2
Wilhelm Wundt
(1832–1920)

he was ostracized and frequently manhandled by the rough-and-ready country boys who were his only peers. In his loneliness he became a chronic daydreamer, and while he liked to imagine himself as a prolific author of scholarly tomes on comparative religion, the habit severely interfered with his schoolwork. Once his father visited his school and became so incensed at Wilhelm's inattentiveness that he slapped the boy publicly.

One moderately happy interlude began at age 8, when his father's assistant pastor also became Wilhelm's private tutor. Wilhelm idolized this kindly young man, who taught Latin quite proficiently, mathematics less so. Independent reading in his father's library aroused lifelong interests in literature and history. Wilhelm continued to daydream, however, and the habit brought disaster once again when he had to go to *Gymnasium*, or high school, at age 12. In this 'school of suffering" he was constantly humiliated by students and teachers alike, and he completely failed his first year.

Wundt's despairing parents sent him to Heidelberg to live with his aunt and brother Ludwig, now a university student. In this cosmopolitan university town, he found not only a studious older brother to emulate but also some new schoolmates with interests similar to his own. Under these improved circumstances he at last curbed his daydreaming and graduated at 19 with a respectable academic record.

He had not done well enough to win a university scholarship, however, and he had no occupational goal except to avoid the ministry. His family had just enough money to finance four years of university study, but they worried that it might be wasted on him. At this point his uncle Friedrich Arnold, a physician and professor of anatomy and physiology at the University of Tübingen, emerged as a role model. Wundt enrolled in medical school at Tübingen, and after a slow start the first year suddenly became inspired as never before by his uncle's course on brain anatomy.

The next year Arnold became professor of anatomy at Heidelberg, and Wundt followed his uncle back home to complete his training. Still inspired and now working prodigiously, he enjoyed genuine academic success for the first time in his life. He finished first in his class in several subjects and after three years passed his final medical examinations summa cum laude. Even more important, he had begun to experience the pleasures of conducting his own experimental research.

Early Research

Wundt's first independent experiment at Heidelberg was supervised by Robert Bunsen, the eminent chemist whose name is still memorialized today in the laboratory "Bunsen burner" he invented. Wundt studied the influence of salt deprivation on the composition of his own urine and in 1853 reported the results in his first scientific publication. The next year he studied the effect of the vagus nerve on respiration. Working at home with the loyal assistance of his mother, he severed the vagus nerves on experimental animals, observed the effects, and submitted a report to the Heidelberg faculty. This effort won a gold medal from the university and publication in Johannes Müller's prestigious journal of anatomy and physiology. Wundt evidently found real-life authorship to be just as rewarding as it had seemed in his childhood daydreams, for these student papers marked the beginning of an extraordinarily prolific publishing record that eventually totaled almost 60,000 printed pages.

After taking his degree, Wundt briefly practiced medicine as an assistant pathologist, but then went to Berlin to study physiology with Johannes Müller and Emil Du Bois-Reymond. Finding he enjoyed research and academics more than medical practice, he returned to Heidelberg and became accredited by the University as a *Privatdozent*, or lecturer. This lowest rung on the academic ladder carried no salary but authorized him to offer courses privately while he sought to enhance his reputation by research. Wundt's first course, taught in his home on experimental physiology, attracted only four students and was prematurely terminated when Wundt contracted mild tuberculosis. He used his convalescence period to write his first book, a not terribly original treatise on the physiology of muscular movement, published in 1858.

That same year, thanks largely to Uncle Friedrich's recruiting, the young but already famous Hermann Helmholtz came to Heidelberg to establish an Institute of Physiology. Wundt became Helmholtz's assistant—a salaried but low-paying position that carried responsibility for much of the actual teaching of physiology at the university. (Like some eminent professor/scientists today, Helmholtz stayed in the laboratory and out of the classrooms as much as possible.) Wundt held this post for six years, although he buried himself in private research as much as possible and kept rather aloof from both Helmholtz and his fellow assistants.

Wundt later suggested that he and Helmholtz never became close because of the similarity of their research interests. While one might expect similarity of interest to *attract* an aspiring young scientist to an eminent elder, Wundt was no ordinary young scientist. Over the years he had somehow developed a fierce drive for independence and dominance, a desire to be a leader rather than a follower in his chosen field. Thus, while he was unquestionably influenced by Helmholtz in his choice of subjects to investigate, he kept much to himself in the actual conduct of his research.

While working as Helmholtz's assistant, Wundt independently studied and wrote on vision and the perception of space—both topics close to the heart of his employer. In one paper he postulated a process of "unconscious inference" in the conversion of visual sensations into perceptions—and completely failed to mention that Helmholtz had already used exactly that term in accounting for optical illusions! It was a mark of Helmholtz's tolerance, as well as of his respect for his assistant's industry and ability, that he later wrote Wundt favorable recommendations for several university positions.

Wundt's crucial "thought meter" experiment also occurred during this time, and we have seen that it, too, had clear connections with Helmholtz's prior work on nervous velocity. Wundt knew that his study also had roots predating Helmholtz's work, for certain aspects of the reaction-time problem had long concerned astronomers. In 1796, the English Astronomer-Royal Nevil Maskelyne had discovered that his own "transit readings" for stars—that is, the precise times he noted when stars under observation crossed grid lines in his telescope—regularly differed by more than half a second from those of his assistant, Kinnebrook. As often happens when employee differs with employer, Kinnebrook was fired. But twenty years later, the German astronomer **Friedrich Wilhelm Bessel** (1784–1846) showed that all astronomical observers differed from one another in their transit readings, and in generally consistent ways; that is, some observers tended to mark the transits consistently earlier or later than others. With knowledge of one another's "**personal equations**," as these consistent individual differences came to be called, astronomers could render their readings equivalent to one another.

Helmholtz's research on the nervous impulse suggested that part of the differences among astronomers' personal equations could be explained by individual differences in the lengths of their sensory and motor nerves, or in the speed with which those nerves transmitted impulses. Wundt reasoned that the differences might also be partly the result of differences in the speeds of *central* processing in their brains. By demonstrating with his thought-meter experiment that a measurable amount of time was required for one such central process—the shifting of attention from one stimulus to another—Wundt added to the plausibility of his hypothesis and contributed to the venerable debate about personal equations.

But while Wundt's study connected with earlier work in physiology and astronomy, it also carried implications for a future science of psychology. In detecting and following up these implications, Wundt at last established his own originality and began to make the name he sought for himself.

Experimental Psychology and *Völkerpsychologie*

As we have seen, Wundt's thought-meter experiment highlighted the importance of central as opposed to peripheral processes—of events in the very core of the nervous system, occurring between the reception of stimuli by the sensory nerves and the activation of responses by the motor nerves. Stimuli were not simply received by the senses and responded to instantaneously and mechanically by motor nerves, but were registered in consciousness by an attentional process whose independent reality was proven by the extra time required for it to occur. Wundt believed this finding supported the general philosophical tradition of Leibniz as opposed to Locke, requiring a psychology that accounts for the receptive and creative properties of the mind itself, above and beyond the influence of external stimuli in creating "ideas."

Wundt also believed that times for other central processes besides attention could be studied by refinements of the reaction-time experiments, in a systematic program of **mental chronometry**. The details remained to be worked out, but here was a possible experimental program that could join Fechnerian psychophysics and Helmholtzian studies of sensation and perception to form the basis of a new science of experimental psychology. As we have noted, Wundt expressed this idea publicly in the preface to his 1862 book, *Contributions to the Theory of Sensory Perception*, a work whose main body reprinted his recent articles on vision, unconscious inference, and reaction time. The idea for a new and separate discipline of experimental psychology traditionally dates from then.

But even as he proposed a new discipline of experimental psychology, Wundt also firmly believed that experimentation could never be the *only* method for psychology as a whole. He thought experimental methods would have to be confined to the study of individual consciousness—that they could not be readily applied to mental processes that were essentially *collective* or *social* in nature. Preeminent among the collective human processes was *language*, and because language seemed crucial to all of the "higher" mental functions including thinking and reasoning, Wundt saw those functions as immune to experimental investigation. Accordingly, he proposed a second and complementary branch of psychology that would use comparative and historical methods rather than experiments, and that he chose to call *Völkerpsychologie*.

Wundt borrowed this name from a new journal, the *Zeitschrift fur Völkerpsychologie und Sprachwissenschaft*. *Zeitschrift* translates easily as "journal" and *Sprachwissenschaft* as "linguistics," but *Völkerpsychologie* has no clear English equivalent. German *Volk* refers to "people, nation, tribe, or race," and so the term has sometimes been translated as "ethnic psychology," "folk psychology," or even "social psychology," but none of these is totally accurate. Basically, Wundt meant to signify a type of nonexperimental psychology that deals with the *communal* and *cultural* products of human nature: religions, mythologies, customs, and, above all, languages and their derivative higher processes.

After formulating the two branches of psychology, Wundt lost little time in actively pursuing both. In the summer of 1862 he offered a new course of lectures on the experimental side, for students in physiology and medicine, titled "Psychology from the Standpoint of Natural Science." At the same time he started writing *Lectures on the Human and Animal Mind*, a two-volume work published in 1863 and 1864, covering issues such as the origin of speech and the sensual, aesthetic, intellectual, and religious feelings. Although Wundt would later call this book a "youthful indiscretion," it started him on the path to his mature *Völkerpsychologie*.

But even with these accomplishments, Wundt had to struggle to earn a decent living. In 1863 he resigned as Helmholtz's assistant, under conditions that remain uncertain. One rumor had it that Helmholtz found Wundt lacking in mathematics and physics and dismissed him. Wundt denied this, claiming that his duties did not involve mathematics or physics, and scoffing at the idea that Helmholtz required "assistance" in those fields in any case. But for whatever reason, Wundt lost his only steady source of income with his resignation. The university granted him a new title of assistant professor, but it carried no salary and left him even more dependent on privately paying students at his lecture courses.

Wundt's three published books to this point were all on highly specialized topics and had sold poorly. He decided that at least temporarily he must write to make money, and so he wrote three more popular books in three years: a textbook on human physiology, a handbook of medical physics, and a philosophical analysis of the physical basis of causality. These books did sell reasonably well, and the last had the great advantage of helping to establish Wundt's credentials in philosophy—a field in which he had taken only one undergraduate course as a student.

Wundt continued his private courses on psychology, and the subject returned to the forefront of his consciousness in early 1867 with an invitation to write on "Recent Advances in the Field of Physiological Psychology" for a new interdisciplinary journal. In response he wrote a 33-page review of recent work on visual space perception and mental chronometry, and he promised a further work in which he would elaborate on the connections between physiology and psychology.[3] This article aroused more attention than anything he had previously written and convinced many that a new scientific psychology was truly on the horizon. Among those so convinced was a young American named **William James** (1842–1910), who read it and wrote:

> It seems to me that perhaps the time has come for psychology to begin to be a science—some measurements have already been made in the region lying between the physical changes in the nerves and the appearance of consciousness (in the shape of sense perceptions), and more may come of it. . . . Helmholtz and a man named Wundt at Heidelberg are working on it.[4]

As we shall see in Chapter 8, James went on to become the major promoter of the new experimental psychology in the United States.

But even this enhanced international recognition did little to help Wundt's position at Heidelberg. When Helmholtz left for Berlin in 1871, Wundt was passed over as his replacement in favor of a rival five years younger than he. The defeat stung badly, for the intensely ambitious Wundt had already gone overboard in his zeal to succeed. He had engaged in some unseemly priority disputes with other scientists and had labeled himself as "Professor" on the title pages of his books while omitting the important modifier "Assistant." Nevertheless, he had also worked enormously hard, producing seven books and scores of articles in several fields. He had also been politically active, serving a term as elected representative to the Baden legislative assembly and acting as president of the Heidelberg Workers' Educational Association. Yet for all his effort and real accomplishment, he approached the age of 40 still holding a minor and poorly paid academic position.

Principles of Physiological Psychology

Wundt's fortunes improved markedly after 1874, when he fulfilled the promise in his 1867 paper and completed the two volumes of *Principles of Physiological Psychology*. In this landmark book Wundt not only defined a "new domain of science," whose task was to conjoin the two previously separate disciplines of physiology and psychology, but also provided detailed examples of how the task could be accomplished. In providing the first genuine textbook for the new field, Wundt emphatically established himself as its leader.

In defining the new field, Wundt observed that physiology investigates living organisms "by our external senses," while psychology examines things "from within" and tries to explain those processes that "inner observation discloses." Physiological psychology was to be the discipline in which "psychological introspection goes hand in hand with the methods of experimental physiology," to study processes simultaneously accessible to *both* kinds of observation.[5] Wundt saw two major examples of such processes: sensation, in which externally observable stimuli give rise to describable psychological states, and voluntary movement, in which psychological impulses give rise to externally observable muscular reactions. Most of his book was devoted to detailed descriptions of studies that conformed to this definition. Because this "physiological psychology" used experimental techniques along with introspection, Wundt suggested it could also be called "experimental psychology," the name he had used before 1867.

Enthusiastic reviewers observed that *Principles of Physiological Psychology* "corresponds exactly to the need for a specialized scientific treatment of the actual relations between body and consciousness"[6] and that it "fills a lacuna, and circumscribes in a very convenient way all those phenomena of human life which can be studied both by introspection and by objective investigation."[7] Thus, even though Wundt himself had not done a great deal of actual research in the new experimental psychology, as its definer and documenter he became the person most closely identified with it.

Wundt now found himself in unwonted but highly pleasing professional demand. In 1874 he won a full professorship in philosophy at the University of Zurich, despite the fact that he had taken only one philosophy course in his own education. A year later he accepted an equivalent position at Leipzig—one of the largest and most prestigious of German universities and home of the aging but still active Gustav Fechner and E. H. Weber. Here, in due course, Wundt created the first full-fledged *program* in experimental psychology.

Wundt at Leipzig

For all the promise of his new position, Wundt could not get physiological psychology off to a fast start at Leipzig. He had accepted the job on condition that the university provide storage space for the large collection of apparatus he had assembled, and which for the past ten years he had used for demonstrations to augment his lectures on experimental psychology. Disappointingly, the university proved unable to provide the space during his first year, and his first courses were on language, anthropology, and logic rather than on experimental psychology.[*]

Another difficult situation marred Wundt's early years at Leipzig, although in a very different way, when he became embroiled in a disagreeable controversy with **Johann Zöllner** (1834–1882), a Leipzig colleague who had previously been an enthusiastic supporter. An astrophysicist by training, Zöllner had also done research on optical illusions, was a close friend of the psychophysicist Fechner, and had warmly welcomed Wundt as the leader of the new experimental psychology.

Zöllner became estranged from Wundt after an 1877 visit to Leipzig by the American "spiritualist" and "medium" Henry Slade. Slade had already confessed to fraud in America but still found ready audiences for his séances in Europe. At the time, many people believed in the reality

---

[*] History of psychology textbooks sometimes mistakenly report that Wundt and William James shared priority for establishing the first psychological demonstration laboratories in 1875, James at Harvard and Wundt in his new position at Leipzig. Actually Wundt was prevented from doing experimental demonstrations in 1875 because of the unavailability of his equipment—but he had already begun the practice a decade earlier in his Heidelberg courses. Thus, Wundt actually preceded James by several years but ironically was unable to continue his practice the very year James began his.

of paranormal or occult powers and were willing to pay those who purported to have them; then as now, a few trained scientists were among the believers. Slade held séances for several leading Leipzig scientists, including Fechner, Zöllner, and Wundt. At these events Slade caused tables to tip, produced knots in a taut piece of string, and purported to receive messages "from a departed spirit," which he wrote down in broken German on a slate board. Fechner was impressed but noncommittal about the performance, while Zöllner became enthusiastically convinced of Slade's genuineness. Wundt viewed the proceedings skeptically, however, and published an article entitled "Spiritualism as a Scientific Question" that can still be read today as a model challenge to many claims for the paranormal.[8]

Wundt pointed out that the effects he observed occurred only when Slade had the opportunity to cheat. Everyone had to sit in a tight circle around a table, and Slade permitted no one to observe from outside. Slade's hands, and the slate on which he received "spirit messages," were frequently out of sight beneath the table. Most of these messages had nonsensical content and came in English or poor German even though the presumed "senders" and all the sitters except Slade were German. Wundt added that scientists, despite their reputations for brilliance, are probably very *poor* judges of the reality of psychic phenomena; being themselves devoted to the disinterested pursuit of truth, they do not expect deceit in others and are ill equipped to detect it. Thus, magicians or conjurers would make much better judges than scientists, because they would know what kinds of tricks to look for. Wundt concluded that he himself lacked the competence to judge definitively, but he strongly suspected Slade had produced his effects by "jugglery."

Wundt's article greatly offended Zöllner, who also seems to have been becoming mentally unbalanced at this time. This former ally wrote a sarcastic and defamatory reply, claiming that Wundt should be jailed for five years for lying and calling him a "suckling child" who had directly copied skeptical and materialistic opinions from his "lord and master" Helmholtz and "the Berlin vivisectionist" Du Bois-Reymond. Wundt, perhaps realizing that Zöllner was no longer fully in control of himself, refrained from replying. He reprinted his article a few years later, however, and added an introduction stating that belief in the paranormal, while unfounded, perhaps filled a useful social purpose "like beer and tobacco." As a form of superstition, it was likely to recur from time to time in "epidemics" and "like pain and illness, to disappear from earth only with humanity."[9]

Despite his early problems, Wundt gradually established himself very well in Leipzig. In 1876 he got his storage space and resumed teaching experimental psychology, and by 1879 he had several students clamoring to do research under his supervision. Late that year, two German students named Max Friedrich and Ernst Tischer joined with the visiting American G. Stanley Hall (whom we shall meet again in Chapter 8) to work on a reaction-time study that Friedrich later presented as his Ph.D. dissertation. Thus, 1879 is traditionally given as the date of the first working research laboratory explicitly devoted to experimental psychology, and Max Friedrich is credited with earning the first Ph.D. in experimental psychology.

From this modest start, the discipline grew rapidly. In 1881 Wundt founded the journal *Philosophische Studien* (*Philosophical Studies*) to publish the new laboratory's research.[*] Two years later, after threatening to move to Breslau, Wundt was rewarded with a quadrupling of his laboratory space and a 40 percent salary increase at Leipzig. The university now officially designated his laboratory and program as the *Institute* for Experimental Psychology, lending them enhanced prestige and prominence in the university catalog. So popular was the Institute that it had to be physically enlarged again in 1888, 1892, and 1897.

Wundt's institutional and organizational accomplishments were aptly summarized by one of his earliest American students in 1888:

> Professor Wundt, by the publication of his *Physiologische Psychologie* in 1874 and the establishment of a psychological laboratory at Leipzic [sic] in 1879, has made himself the representative of the efforts to introduce experimental methods

---

[*] Wundt had considered calling the journal *Psychological Studies*, but he abandoned the idea because a journal with a similar name already existed, and dealt with the scientifically unrespectable subjects of spiritism and parapsychology. Further, he genuinely believed that psychology was a subdiscipline of philosophy and wished to emphasize that fact in the title of his new journal.

into psychology. Weber, Lotze, Fechner and Helmholtz . . . had cleared the way, but their books and researches remained to a certain extent isolated attempts, until Wundt directed toward one centre the divergent lines, and persuaded men of science on the one hand and students of philosophy on the other to accept the new science.[10]

For these organizational accomplishments alone, Wundt could have earned the title of father of experimental psychology. But he also played a major role as designer, supervisor, and sometimes subject in the multitudinous experiments that were conducted in his laboratory. He habitually *assigned* research topics to his students, only rarely allowing those who struck him as unusually mature to propose their own studies. He took a keen interest in every project and was extremely helpful to students as they prepared for their oral examinations; some reported that he seemed as nervous as they and that he coached them to let them know what kinds of questions to expect from their nonpsychological examiners. Moreover, the results of many of his students' experiments helped shape Wundt's voluminous mature theoretical writings about psychology. Thus, we shall first consider some of the important experiments conducted at Leipzig and then take up Wundt's more general theories.

Research at Leipzig

Early experimental research at Leipzig fell into three general areas: psychophysics, studies of the time sense, and mental chronometry. The psychophysical studies tested Fechner's general law on previously uninvestigated sensory stimuli, such as the loudness or pitch of sound and the brightness of light. Although not outstandingly original in conception, these studies often required ingeniously constructed apparatus and helped fill out the psychophysical program by confirming the general (although not perfect) accuracy of Fechner's law in a variety of new situations.

Studies of the time sense investigated the amount of time by which stimuli had to be separated in order to be recognized as distinct. Visual stimuli, for example, had to be separated by at least one-tenth of a second, or else they would fuse together into a single continuous impression—a fact soon to be taken advantage of by the inventors of motion picture cameras (and as we saw in Chapter 4, character-ized by the Gestalt psychologists as the *phi phenomenon*). For sound and touch, the smallest detectable intervals were much shorter. And when stimuli for two different senses were presented (for example, a sound and a touch), separations ranging from one-twentieth to one-sixth of a second were necessary before subjects could accurately say which one occurred first. Like the psychophysical studies, these lacked theoretical momentousness, but they added valuable facts to the growing store of detailed information about the senses.

The studies of mental chronometry lay closest to Wundt's heart, for these not only provided new factual observations, but also bore directly on his own innovative psychological theory. Most of these studies used the **subtractive method**, a technique originally devel-oped in 1868 by the Dutch physiologist **F. C. Donders** (1818–1889). Donders had started by measuring simple reaction time, in which a subject responded to a single visual stimulus as quickly as possible. He then complicated the experimental task by randomly presenting two kinds of visual stimuli but instructing the subject to respond to only one of them. Reaction times became somewhat longer than for the simple situation, presumably because the subject required extra time to differentiate one stimulus from the other. Donders subtracted the average simple reaction time from the average for the complex task and concluded that the difference—about a tenth of a second—had been the time required for a mental act of "discrimination."

Max Friedrich elaborated on Donders's study for his thesis research, and many other subtractive studies followed. The most systematic and extensive of these were done by Wundt's American student **James McKeen Cattell** (1860–1944; see Figure 5.3), and we shall describe them in some detail as illustrative of Leipzig research.

Like many other successful pioneers in experimental psychology, Cattell showed great ingenuity in designing apparatus. He invented the instrument shown in Figure 5.4a[11] to present various kinds of visual stimuli in reaction-time studies. The stimulus for any trial would ini-tially be hidden behind the sliding black metal screen, suspended at the top of the apparatus by an electromagnet. To start a trial, the experi-menter would turn off the magnet, causing the screen to drop and to reveal the stimulus. At precisely the instant the stimulus was uncov-ered, the falling screen would trigger a switch starting a chronoscope,

FIG 5.3
James McKeen Cattell
(1860–1944)

or timing device. The subject would then make a response to turn off the chronoscope, whose reading accurately reflected the full reaction time.

Most reaction-time experiments before Cattell's required the subject to respond by pressing a simple finger-key, but Cattell also invented keys activated by movement of the lips (Figure 5.4b), or by sound vibrations from the subject's voice. As a result, he could measure the reaction times for *verbal* responses as well as for ordinary finger presses. In sum, he devised ways to measure reaction times more accurately, and in a wider and more interesting variety of situations, than had ever been done before.

Using just himself and one fellow student as subjects, Cattell measured thousands of reaction times under varying conditions. In the simplest situation, in which the revealed stimulus was always a blank white patch and the response a press of the finger-key, reaction times averaged about fifteen-hundredths of one second. In the first complication, two kinds of stimuli were randomly presented—for example, a red patch and a blue one—and the subject was told to respond

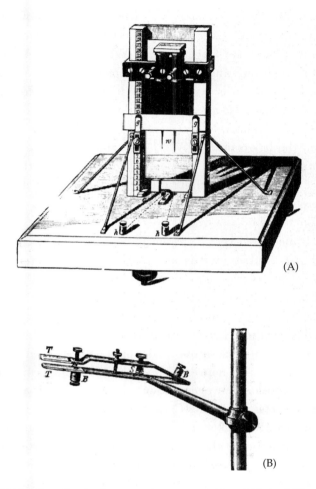

FIG 5.4 Cattell's stimulus-presenting apparatus (A) and "lip key" (B)

to only one of them. As in Donders's study, reaction times increased by about one-tenth of a second—the time presumably required for "discrimination" or "perception." When the subject had to perform a separate response to each stimulus—say, press a right-hand key for red and a left-hand one for blue—average reaction times increased by another tenth of a second. Wundt believed that the subject had to make a voluntary decision to move either the right or left hand, and he referred to this increment as the "will time." Cattell preferred the more neutral term "motor time."

Some of Cattell's most interesting findings occurred when he presented *verbal* stimuli, such as letters or words, and required spoken responses rather than finger presses. When letters and colors were presented as stimuli and named in response, average reaction times were three-hundredths to four-hundredths of a second longer for the letters. The times also varied surprisingly from letter to letter, however, with the relatively common "E" requiring considerably longer than the less common "W." When short *words* were presented as stimuli, reaction times were only negligibly longer than for individual letters. This important finding led Cattell to conclude, "We do not therefore perceive separately the letters of which a word is composed, but the word as a whole."[12]

Cattell measured verbal "association times" by presenting verbal stimuli and requiring words associated with them as responses. For example, subjects reacted to German words with their English translations, or to the names of cities with the countries in which they are located, or to famous authors' names with the languages in which they wrote. These diverse association tasks required reaction times ranging between 0.35 second and 1.0 second—a good deal longer than the simple and nonverbal reactions. The range indicates considerable variation, however, not only across tasks but also between the two subjects. Sometimes Cattell and at other times his colleague was significantly quicker on a particular type of task. In speculating on the implications of these differences, Cattell suggested that some people may have *generally* quicker association times than others. If so, he believed the quick reactors not only would think faster but also would literally experience more ideas in the same objective period of time and thus "live so much the longer in the same number of years."[13] Here was a suggestion that differences in people's average reaction times might reflect differences in their *intelligence*—a notion that Cattell and others would later pursue, and that we shall return to in Chapter 7.

Shortly after Cattell's thesis, another student performed a further reaction-time experiment that greatly interested Wundt. In 1888, **Ludwig Lange** (1863–1936) compared simple reaction times when the subject's attention was focused on the expected *stimulus*, with reaction times obtained when attention was on the *response* to be made. That is, in one case the subject paid particular attention to what he was about to see, and in the other to what he was about to do. Reaction times in the first case were about one-tenth of a second longer than those in the second.

In interpreting these results, Wundt adopted Leibniz's distinction between the processes of simple perception and apperception, described in Chapter 2. In perception, he argued, one simply responds to a stimulus automatically, mechanically, and "thoughtlessly." In apperception, one's full attention is focused on the stimulus, and it is consciously recognized, interpreted, and "thought about." As an example, compare the reaction to a street sign reading "Main Street" by a local native with that of a stranger trying to locate an unfamiliar address. To the native, the sign is a familiar landmark on a well-known path, and on encountering it he turns right on his way home without giving it a thought. He has *perceived* the stimulus and responded to it, but without deliberation. To the stranger, however, the Main Street sign is something he has been carefully looking for, because his directions have told him to turn right there to get to his destination. Thus, the sign fully enters and occupies his attention—in Wundt's language is *apperceived*—at least for a brief period of time.

Wundt believed that Lange's subject merely perceived the stimulus in the condition in which he was concentrating on the response; although fast, this "thoughtless" reaction was also relatively error-prone and liable to be triggered by inappropriate stimuli. By contrast, the subject concentrating on the stimulus apperceived it, requiring an extra fraction of a second for its full registration in consciousness.

Apperception became a major concept in Wundt's psychology, both experimental and theoretical. His students conducted experiments to measure the span of apperception—that is, to determine the number of separate stimuli that can be fully grasped in consciousness at once. Arrays of random numbers, letters, or words were flashed on a screen for one-tenth of a second (the time presumably necessary for a single act of apperception), and subjects were asked to recall as many of them as they could. The number of correctly recalled stimuli almost always lay between four and six, regardless of the level of complexity of the stimuli. Thus, if a four-by-four array of random *letters* was flashed, subjects typically apperceived four to six of them; if the array comprised sixteen random *words* of six letters each, subjects recalled four to six of *them*, for a total of twenty-four to thirty-six individual letters. This result reinforced Cattell's earlier finding that familiar words could be reacted to as quickly as individual letters and his contention that such words are responded to as wholes rather than as collections of individual letters. In these cases, subjects did not "see" all of the individual letters of the words, but apperceived the complete words as independent entities. Of course, if unfamiliar words were flashed, apperception was reduced to the level of individual letters. Thus, while typical English-speaking subjects would easily apperceive familiar words such as *taller* with little more than a glance, they would have trouble with its equally long Polish equivalent, *wyzszy*, being able to remember it only as a collection of six individual letters.

Voluntaristic Psychology

The concept of apperception took a central place in Wundt's theoretical writings on psychology, in which he likened it to the events occurring in the very center of the visual field. In normal vision, a large number of individual stimuli may be present in the field, but only the very few whose images have fallen on the tiny fovea in the retina are sharply focused. Because the eye is extremely mobile, however, it constantly shifts its sharpest focus from object to object. As you read this page, for example, your eye movements constantly bring new words into sharp focus as previous ones fade into the periphery. Wundt argued the same sort of thing happens with consciousness in general. At any given moment, a maximum of six ideas are apperceived in direct attention, while many others may be perceived peripherally and indistinctly. Like visual focus, attention can shift rapidly from one small group of ideas to another.

Wundt further believed that perceived and apperceived ideas are subject to different rules of organization and combination. Perceived ideas organize themselves mechanically and automatically, along lines laid down by past experience: the associations a person has experienced in the past. Apperceived ideas, however, may be combined and organized in many ways, including some that have never been experienced before. In Wundt's terminology, a **creative synthesis** takes place at the center of attention.

Consider a simple example: a person's conscious response to a card on which the digit 1 has been printed immediately above the digit 2. If the stimulus is merely perceived, it will elicit the idea most strongly associated with it in the past—perhaps the number "3" since the stimulus resembles an elementary arithmetic problem. This straightforward reaction has been fully determined by past experience. But later, if apperceptive attention becomes focused on the stimulus, a host of new and "creative" responses may occur: the idea of "minus 1," perhaps, or "12," "21," notions of a secret code or cipher, or anything else depending on the imagination of the subject.

Theoretically, if one knew a person's complete history in advance, one could predict that person's reactions to perceived stimuli with complete accuracy. But Wundt believed reactions to apperceived stimuli are *not* predictable, subject as they are to unobservable and "inner" influences such as motives, innate predilections, emotions and feelings, and the ineffable effects of the will itself. Accordingly, he argued that an entirely different order of causality determines apperceptive as opposed to merely perceptive processes, a **psychic causality** whose rules are not reducible to the purely mechanistic processes of physical causality. In a sense, Wundt rejected the complete mechanism of the Helmholtz school in favor of Descartes' old contention that at least some central mental processes closely connected with consciousness and "will" require an altogether different kind of analysis.

Wundt did not deny the power and usefulness of mechanistic physiology for explaining events on the periphery of conscious experience—but he insisted that something further was needed for the complete explanation of that experience itself. Believing that this something—responsible for apperception, creative synthesis, and psychic causality—closely involved the conscious experiences of "will" and "voluntary effort," Wundt often referred to his entire approach as a **voluntaristic psychology**.

Wundt further believed that mental processes determined by psychic as opposed to physical causality must logically be largely insusceptible to laboratory experimentation. Here was another strong argument for the development of a nonexperimental *Völkerpsychologie* to deal with such issues, and he accordingly devoted the final years of his career to that project.

Völkerpsychologie and Its Implications

Higher and central mental processes such as apperception and thinking had been experimentally demonstrated to exist by mental chronometry, and a few of their features, such as the span of apperception, had been measured in the laboratory. But Wundt believed that their most essential features would always resist experimental analysis and would have to be studied naturalistically by comparative and historical rather than experimental methods. Wundt himself tried to do this between 1900 and 1920, publishing his results in the ten large volumes of his *Völkerpsychologie*. He dealt here with the *collective* products of human culture: myth, religion, custom, and—the heart of his analysis—language.

Several theorists before Wundt had equated *thought* with language, arguing that even silent thinking was a sort of low-level talking to oneself. Wundt believed otherwise, however, and cited several common situations in which people's words apparently do *not* accurately or uniquely represent their thoughts. Sometimes, for example, we suddenly realize that our speech is not expressing our thoughts properly and exclaim something like, "That's not what I meant to say; let me start over again." Other times we listen to someone else speak and recognize a point of disagreement before we can put it into words; we interject a "What?" or "No!" or "Wait a minute!" long before we can actually *describe* what it is that disturbs us. Or again, we can often repeat the gist of ideas or messages in words totally different from those of their original speaker. The fact that we often have to work to put our thoughts into words, and that the same thoughts can be represented by different patterns of words, suggested to Wundt that words and thoughts cannot be exactly the same thing.

Accordingly, Wundt concluded that the most basic unit of thought is not the word or other linguistic element, but rather a "general impression" or "general idea" (*Gesamtvorstellung*) that is independent of words. The process of speaking begins with an apperception of the general idea, followed by its analysis into linguistic structures that represent it more or less adequately. In listening, we first apperceive the language and then connect it with some appropriate general idea.

In analyzing language itself, Wundt argued that the fundamental linguistic unit is not the word but the *sentence*, the overall structure that somehow "contains" a complete thought or general idea. When we use language, our attention is focused not only on the specific words as they are uttered but also on the role of each word in an over- all sentence structure. As we speak, we somehow know that each of our words has a specific role in the larger structure of our sentence— as subject, object, verb, or the like. And conversely, as we listen, we automatically assign each word to a vacant place in our awaiting thought structure. Wundt thus described the sentence as a structure that is at once "simultaneous" and "sequential":

> It is simultaneous because at each moment it is present in con- sciousness as a totality even though individual subordinate elements may occasionally disappear from it. It is sequential because the configuration changes from moment to moment in its cognitive condition as individual constituents move into the focus of attention and out again one after the other.[14]

As this brief discussion shows, Wundt's *Völkerpsychologie* made use of, and was consistent with, concepts derived from his experimental psychology. Apperception of words, sentences, and general impres- sions all presumably followed the rules of speed and capacity that had been demonstrated in the laboratory. But a full understanding of thought and language also involved the comparative study of many languages to determine what they had in common and thus what was presumably universal in human speech. And it involved the intro- spection and analysis of ongoing naturalistic speech processes— processes Wundt believed were too complicated to be manipulated experimentally in the laboratory.

In this way, Wundt actually practiced the two-sided approach to psychology he had prescribed early in his career. Among the first to apply the emerging mechanistic, deterministic, and experimental approaches of the "new psychology" to central psychological processes, he is justly remembered as the father of experimental psychology. But he also believed these approaches were useful mainly in studying the relatively simple and peripheral aspects of psychological functioning: sensation, muscular activation, and the times required for mental pro- cesses to occur. For studying the complex and central functions—those at the farthest remove from easily observable sensory and motor inter- actions with the physical world—Wundt relied on nonexperimental techniques and posited a nonmechanistic psychic causality.

Not all of Wundt's students and immediate successors agreed completely with this conception of psychology, and two particularly lively debates arose during the later part of his career. Both of these debates centered partly on the role of **introspection**—the observation and reporting of one's own subjective "inner experience"—in psychological experiments.

Because Wundt saw psychology as the science of conscious experience, he saw introspection as the most direct source of much psychological data. On the basis of introspection, he concluded that the contents of consciousness could be usefully described as composed of varying combinations of specifiable *sensations* and *feelings*, which in turn could be classified according to basic dimensions. Thus, he believed that sensations could be categorized as to their *modes* (that is, whether visual, auditory, tactile, and so on), their *qualities* (for example, their colors and shapes if visual, their pitches and timbres if auditory), their *intensities*, and their *durations*. Wundt classified feelings according to the three basic dimensions of *pleasantness-unpleasantness*, *tension-relaxation*, and *activity-passivity*.

But while accepting introspective analysis of consciousness as a useful descriptive tool, Wundt firmly expressed two kinds of reservations about it. First, he warned that the introspectively revealed dimensions of consciousness ought not be taken overly seriously as "elements" of consciousness analogous to the chemical elements—that is, as ultimate units capable of combining to form complex psychological states in the same way chemical elements combine to create physical compounds. He noted that chemical elements such as hydrogen, oxygen, and carbon can actually exist and be seen in their pure states, while the dimensions of sensation and feeling *only* exist in combination with each other and are in fact really abstractions rather than concrete conscious experiences. One of Wundt's most influential students, **Edward Bradford Titchener** (1867–1927), came to disagree with this view, and to propound an experimental psychology whose major goal was the atomistic analysis of the elements of consciousness. Titchener's atomism in turn aroused considerable opposition, most strikingly from the Gestalt psychologists.

Wundt's second reservation about introspective psychology derived from the essentially private and unverifiable nature of subjective reports and the fact that memory often plays tricks with the recollection of psychological states. Accordingly, he set strict limits on the use of introspection in experiments—restricting it to simple and immediately recallable experimental situations or to the generation of hypotheses that could be tested by nonintrospective experiments. To Wundt, the higher mental processes seemed much too complicated to be accurately recalled and introspected—part of the reason they could never be studied experimentally. In contradiction to Wundt's belief, his former student **Oswald Külpe** (1862–1915) supervised a series of experiments at the University of Würzburg in which several of the higher processes were in fact approached introspectively. And in Berlin, **Hermann Ebbinghaus** (1850–1909) devised a nonintrospective but still experimental approach to studying memory—one of the higher processes that Wundt had ruled out of bounds to experimental methods of any kind.

Both of these debates led to developments that endure in modern psychology, and we turn now to each of them in more detail.

Titchener's Structuralism

An Englishman who had absorbed the predilections of his native associationist tradition before studying with Wundt, Edward Titchener (see Figure 5.5) completed his Ph.D. in 1892 and then moved to Cornell University in New York State to establish a laboratory in the general Wundtian mold. There he ruled with an iron hand, lectured in academic robes (which he reputedly said gave him the right to be dogmatic) and quickly built the largest psychology Ph.D. program in the United States. He also staunchly advocated an introspective approach to psychology he called **structuralism**. He selected this name because he believed experimental psychologists' first task should be to discover the *structure* of the phenomena they dealt with, before concerning themselves with *functions*—following the example of biologists who supposedly had to know the anatomy of organs before being able to understand their physiology. As Titchener put it, the experimental psychologist's first task is "to discover, first of all, what is there [in the mind] and in what quantity, not what it is there for."[15] (Titchener's "structuralism" bears no relationship to the movements of the same name associated with recent figures important to cognitive psychology, such as Jean Piaget, Noam Chomsky, and Claude Lévi-Strauss.)

Titchener represented himself as a loyal student of Wundt, and in the absence of translations of most of the German's work, structuralism came to be accepted in English-speaking countries as synonymous with Wundtian psychology. In fact, however, Titchener had adopted only part of Wundt's psychology and rejected much that was essential to it. He agreed with his teacher that introspection must be used carefully and only under precisely controlled conditions. But he did not share Wundt's distrust of the chemical-element analogy and indeed argued that the *primary goal* of experimental psychology was the introspective analysis of conscious experience into its elements of sensation and feeling.

Titchener himself had strong visualizing tendencies, holding very concrete images even for abstract terms. He literally *saw* the concept of "meaning," for example, as "the blue-grey tip of a kind of scoop which has a bit of yellow above it . . . and which is just digging into a dank mass of . . . plastic material."[16] Predisposed as he was toward such vivid imagery, it is perhaps unsurprising that he believed all

FIG 5.5
Edward Bradford Titchener
(1867–1927)

conscious experience could be reduced to introspectively accessible sensory images—if only one knew how to introspect properly.

Accordingly, introspection for Titchener was no casual inner pondering, but rather a rigorous procedure that one had to be carefully trained to perform. Introspectors had to reduce all of their mental contents into their most basic elements, while assiduously avoiding what Titchener called the **stimulus error**—the imposition of "meaning" or "interpretation" on their subject. In the language we introduced in Chapter 4, all perceptions would have to be reduced to the concrete sensations that underlie them. Titchener's own mental image of "meaning" would not qualify as a proper introspective report because it contained such meaning-laden terms as "scoop" and "digging." To qualify, the image would have to be further reduced to its pure sensory elements: to minutely described patches of light with different colors, shapes, intensities, and durations. Titchener's introspection attempted to cut through the learned categories and concepts that define everyday experience and to arrive at the pristine building blocks of consciousness from which everything presumably begins. From such painstaking introspections, Titchener concluded that there exist more than 43,000 distinguishable elements of sensory experience, more than 30,000 being visual and 11,000 auditory. He found just 4 specifiable elements involved in taste, and 3 in the sensations of the alimentary tract.

True to his premise, Titchener believed he had found an elemental sensory base for virtually everything he analyzed introspectively, even including Wundt's key processes of apperception and attention. Attention, he argued, was simply a matter of the *clarity* of the imaginal process—one of the elemental sensory attributes. He interpreted the vague sense of concentration and effort that accompanies attention as nothing more than sensations from the minute frowns, movements, and muscle contractions that occur simultaneously with a thought. To Wundt, such analyses distorted the essential nature of central psychological processes, which he saw as much more than the sum of their constituent elements. Indeed, Titchener's goal of avoiding the stimulus error, and of stripping experience of its "meaning," ran counter to Wundt's general approach to psychology. Needless to say, it also ran counter to the anti-elementistic approach that was concurrently being developed by the Gestalt psychologists (see Chapter 4), and in another way to the "psychoanalytic" approach of

Sigmund Freud. Freud, as we shall see in Chapter 11, used an intro-spective method of "free association" precisely for the purpose of *uncovering* the symbolic meanings of ideas, rather than removing the meaning from them. Titchener himself did not rule out these com-peting approaches as valueless in principle. But he did think of them as examples of functional or applied psychology, as opposed to experi-mental, scientific psychology. And since the structural foundations had yet to be firmly established, he felt that these applied attempts were destined to be premature.

In due course Titchnerian structuralism, along with other introspection-based psychologies, came under severe attack from the behaviorist movement (see Chapter 9) and was largely abandoned. At his peak Titchener was highly influential, however, and under his direction Cornell became one of the leading American producers of Ph.D. degrees in psychology. Titchener alone graduated 56 doctoral students between 1894 and 1927.[17] Interestingly, as a land grant institu-tion Cornell was one of the few American universities of the time that would grant Ph.D. degrees to women. Even more unusual was Cornell's policy of giving women students access to fellowships. Nearly half of Titchener's students were women, and he appears to have been quite open to the notion—not widely accepted at that time—that women could become accomplished scientists. In fact, **Margaret Floy Wash-burn** (1871–1939), the first American woman to be awarded the Ph.D. degree in psychology, was one of Titchener's students and the first stu-dent he recommended to the Ph.D. program (see also Chapter 8). She became well known for her work on conscious processes such as learn-ing and attention in animals, publishing a widely used comparative psychology text in 1908 called *The Animal Mind*. But even though in many ways Titchener supported his female students, from today's per-spective his overall record was—to say the least—mixed. Perhaps most notoriously, he established a "Society of Experimentalists" that explic-itly discriminated against women, solely on the basis of their gender.

The Experimentalists

In the late 1890s, Titchener and a number of other experimental psy-chologists became disillusioned with the composition and emphasis of the American Psychological Association, feeling that philosophical and various applied topics were dominating at the expense of a truly experimental science of the mind.[18] Titchener accordingly decided to establish a small, invitation-only group of experimentalists who would meet once a year to discuss research in progress, engage in experimental demonstrations, and have freewheeling discussion, or *conversazione*, that would serve to socialize younger researchers in the field. Smoking and frank language were to be encouraged, and because Titchener did not regard these as appropriately "feminine" activities, women would not be admitted, whatever their scientific credentials. Although there is some evidence that a handful of the male psychologists Titchener invited to the group at least questioned this policy, none directly challenged it.[19]

One woman who did openly and vociferously challenge Titchener's membership policy was the eminent **Christine Ladd-Franklin** (1847–1930; see Figure 5.6), twenty years Titchener's senior and a highly respected mathematician and vision researcher who had earned her Ph.D. in 1882 as a special student at Johns Hopkins University in Baltimore, Maryland. There, under the direction of **Charles Sanders Peirce** (1839–1914), she became interested in symbolic logic and turned her attention to a longstanding problem called the transformation of the syllogism. Her solution of this problem led philosopher Josiah Royce of Harvard to note that it was remarkable that the crowning achievement in a field worked over since the days of Aristotle should be attributed to an American woman. After graduation, she worked on a mathematical question underlying a theory of binocular vision and became interested in theories of color vision. In the early 1890s she studied with Helmholtz and others in Germany, and in 1892 she delivered a paper outlining a novel theory of color vision at the International Congress of Psychology in London. She spent much of the rest of her career elaborating and defending this theory, which hypothesized that the red-green receptors in the human visual system had evolved at a later stage than the blue-yellow ones (see Chapter 4).

Based solely on her scientific credentials, Ladd-Franklin was clearly qualified to join the Experimentalists, and at first she may have considered it just an oversight that she had not been invited. In 1912, however, she came face to face with Titchener's stubborn

FIG 5.6
Christine
Ladd-Franklin
(1847–1930)

refusal to acknowledge the sexism underlying his policy. After writing to express her desire to present a paper at the upcoming meeting of Titchener's group at Clark University, she received a negative response that both surprised and incensed her. Her reply to Titchener emphasized the irrationality as well as the sexism underlying his position. Titchener, however, stood firm. Two years later, when the meeting was held on Ladd-Franklin's home turf, at Columbia University, she was allowed to attend one session but was unsuccessful in convincing Titchener to reverse his general policy. Despite Ladd-Franklin's repeated admonitions that the policy was medieval and unscientific, it was not changed until two years after Titchener's death in 1927. Even so, only four women—Margaret Floy Washburn, June Etta Downey, Eleanor Gibson, and Dorothea Jameson—had been elected to membership by the 1970s. In assessing the impact of Titchener's sexist practice, one historian of psychology has argued that the exclusion of women from this elite group was an effective act of social ostracism that took "a heavy toll on women's participation and advancement in experimental psychology."[20]

Experimenting on the Higher Functions: Külpe and Ebbinghaus

A different kind of challenge than Titchener's to Wundtian psychology was posed by Oswald Külpe (see Figure 5.7), who took his Ph.D. with Wundt in 1887 and then remained as his chief assistant and right-hand man for seven years. In 1894, however, Külpe established his own psychological laboratory at the University of Würzburg and soon began supervising students in introspective studies of which Wundt did not approve. Most of them involved setting relatively complex mental tasks for subjects to perform and then asking them to recall what they had consciously experienced as they solved the tasks. Subjects reported two kinds of experiences that Külpe thought important but that Wundt found arguable.

First were **imageless thoughts**. After associating to stimulus words, or judging the relative heaviness of different weights, Würzburg introspectors recalled that they had experienced certain transitory states

FIG 5.7
Oswald Külpe
(1862–1915)

that were not definable in terms of sensations or feelings. They said they had been aware of their own processes of associating or judging but that these experiences had seemed impalpable and devoid of specifically definable content. Wundt refused to accept these findings, on grounds that the experimental conditions had not been sufficiently controlled and because he believed the mental processes involved were too complex to be reliably introspected and recalled.

Studies of **directed association**, conducted by Külpe's Scottish student **Henry J. Watt** (1879–1925) and his junior colleague **Narziss Ach** (1871–1946), posed an even more direct challenge to Wundt's experimental psychology. Watt asked his subjects to associate to stimulus words in a highly specific rather than "free" manner—by naming the first superordinate or subordinate concepts to come to mind. Thus, to the stimulus word *bird*, associations such as "animal," "creature," and "living thing" would be appropriate superordinate concepts, while "canary," "robin," and "hawk" would be acceptable subordinate replies. Ach's experiment presented subjects with pairs of numbers, after first suggesting they be added, subtracted, multiplied, or divided. Thus, a card with a 4 over a 3 elicited responses of 7, 1, 12, or 1.33, depending on his instructions.

Under all of these conditions, subjects gave correct replies easily and with negligible differences in reaction time. And when they introspectively recalled their experiences, they said that the instructions, after having once been heard and registered in consciousness, played no further conscious role in the process of associating. The subjects instructed to subtract responded "one" to the stimulus above just as quickly, automatically, and "thoughtlessly" as they replied "seven" when asked to add. It seemed that the instructions, or in Watt's language the *task* set by the experimenter, predetermined the subjects' associational patterns in different ways before the experiment began. Ach wrote that the instructions established different **determining tendencies** or **mental sets** that did not consciously enter into the subjects' associational processes but that predetermined them in particular directions before the experiments began.

In one way these results accorded well with Wundt's voluntaristic psychology, for the task, determining tendency, and set were precisely the kind of central, directive, and motivational variables he had proposed to enter into the process of apperception. But Külpe, who had been suspicious of many mental chronometry experiments even before he left Leipzig, saw the Würzburg results as undermining the logic of Wundt's subtractive procedure. Külpe argued that subjects in the more complicated situations did not perform mere aggregates of simple reactions (perception plus apperception plus discrimination plus association, and so on) but instead operated under "sets" completely different from those of subjects in simpler situations. Thus, Külpe thought the logic of the subtractive procedure grossly oversimplified the true process of thinking and reacting. Although Wundt protested, Külpe's argument proved generally persuasive. The Würzburg experiments on directed association are still considered to be classic demonstrations of the predetermining influence of *motives* on association and thought.

Ebbinghaus's Studies of Memory

A different and even more influential challenge to Wundt's conception of experimental psychology came from his younger compatriot Hermann Ebbinghaus (see Figure 5.8). After earning history and philosophy degrees at the University of Bonn, Ebbinghaus fought in the Franco-Prussian War and then spent seven years in travel and independent study, earning his keep by tutoring. Sometime in the late 1870s he chanced upon a secondhand copy of Fechner's *Elements of Psychophysics* in a London bookshop. The book impressed him greatly, and he decided to see whether he could apply the same sort of experimental mathematical treatment that Fechner had given sensation to the new subject of *memory*. Wundt had just published his *Physiological Psychology* declaring that higher processes such as memory could not be studied experimentally, but Ebbinghaus evidently took this as a challenge rather than a deterrent and proceeded completely on his own to conduct one of the classic research programs in experimental psychology.

Serving as his own subject, Ebbinghaus investigated the amount of time he required to study material before being able to remember it perfectly. The major problem was to find appropriate material to memorize. He knew from experience that stimuli differed greatly in their ease of memorization, and he believed that most of this variability occurred because of differing prior associations. Because of previous experience, a person finds some stimuli but not others to

FIG 5.8
Hermann
Ebbinghaus
(1850–1909)

be particularly familiar, meaningful, and memorable. Ebbinghaus sought for his experiments a large number of stimuli to be memorized that he could feel confident were equally unfamiliar at the outset.

As a result, he created **nonsense syllables** by systematically going through the alphabet and constructing more than 2,000 consonant-vowel-consonant combinations such as *taz*, *bok*, and *lef* that could serve as originally neutral or meaningless stimuli to be memorized in his experiments. He randomly assembled these nonsense syllables into lists, usually between twelve and sixteen syllables in length, and set about memorizing them under fixed conditions. Typically he read aloud through a list at a fixed rate of speed, over and over again until he thought he had memorized it perfectly. Then he would test himself, and if he made any mistakes in the syllables or their order he would go back to reading the list again. For each list, he recorded the amount of learning time he had required before the first perfect recollection. On the average, he perfectly memorized a single sixteen-syllable list in just over 20 minutes.

Having once memorized his lists, Ebbinghaus tested himself on their *retention* under varying conditions. He always had to restudy a list to get it right again but for a shorter period of time than at first. After an interval of 24 hours, for example, he typically relearned lists of sixteen syllables in 14 minutes each—a reduction in learning time of one-third compared to the previous day. Ebbinghaus used this fractional "savings" in learning time as a quantitative measure of his memory strength.

When Ebbinghaus calculated his average savings for various periods of time between the original and the second memorizations, he was not surprised to find that savings decreased as the interval increased. More surprisingly and delightfully, however, the rate of decrease was not constant but fell on a regular **forgetting curve**, in which memory declined rapidly immediately after the initial learning but then almost leveled off. For example, when he retested himself on one typical series of lists, the savings were 58 percent after 20 minutes, 44 percent after an hour, 36 percent after 8 hours, 34 percent after one day, 25 percent after a week, and 21 percent after a month. Ebbinghaus did not fail to mention that the shape of this forgetting curve approximated a mathematical function similar to that in Fechner's psychophysical law (except that Fechner's curve *increased* at a progressively slower rate, while his own *decreased*). In sum, he demonstrated that memory could be studied experimentally and yield mathematically regular results. Wundt's limitation on experimental psychology, it seemed, had been too extreme.

Ebbinghaus's memory research has remained for over a century one of the most cited and most highly respected studies in all of experimental psychology. Wundt could (and did) argue that nonsense syllables stripped of all meaningfulness were parodies of *normal* mental stimuli and claimed that Ebbinghaus had only studied an artificial sort of memory. But even though Wundt had a point, it was largely overlooked by later generations of experimental psychologists who seized upon Ebbinghaus's methods as a model for their research on human verbal learning.

Wundt's Reputation and Influence

Wundt remained fully intellectually engaged until the very end of his long life. He retired from teaching in 1917 at age 85 but continued to write his *Völkerpsychologie*. He completed his autobiography on August 23, 1920, just eight days before his death. He left behind 60,000 pages of published works and most of the thousands of students he had taught during his prodigious career.

In general, however, historians have been unkind to Wundt, particularly in English-speaking countries. This attitude developed partly because of his mistaken association with the ultra-introspectionist, structuralist school of Titchener, which turned out to be particularly out of tune with the incipient American movement toward practicality, "objectivity," and, eventually, behaviorism. In addition, Wundt's personal and stylistic qualities were uncongenial to William James, the influential leader of academic psychology in the United States, whom we shall learn more about in Chapter 8. When these intellectual and attitudinal differences became exacerbated by the all-too-physical antagonisms of World War I, the ardent German patriot Wundt became easily dismissed in England and America. Unread and largely untranslated, he came to be caricatured as the founder of an ineffective experimental psychology, a dogmatic tyrant who suppressed everyone else's point of view, and an indefatigable author of boring tomes.

More recently, however, some English-speaking historians have taken the trouble to find out what Wundt really said and have found much of current relevance. Psychology's present preoccupation with central cognitive processes represents a clear return to "Wundtian" interests. Although experimental techniques and terminologies have changed since Wundt's day, he would still feel at home with modern cognitive psychologists who study such phenomena as information processing, selective attention, and perceptual masking, or with clinical psychologists who study schizophrenia as a disease interfering with attention and the apperceptive processes or psycholinguists who comparatively analyze languages according to the "transformational grammar" theory of Noam Chomsky. Further, increasing numbers of psychologists today join Wundt in questioning whether the purely "objective" and "detached" techniques of the laboratory experiment can ever do full justice to the complexity of human experience. In sum, there seems good reason to believe that the father of experimental psychology will be better remembered by his later than by his earlier intellectual descendants.

Summary

Wilhelm Wundt, often considered the "founder" of modern experimental psychology, developed an approach to studying basic mental processes that built on the German tradition of Fechnerian psychophysics and Helmholtz's studies of sensation and perception. He established a program of **mental chronometry** for measuring the time it took to perform basic attentional tasks, established the first large-scale laboratory explicitly for experimental psychology, and founded the first journal exclusively devoted to experimental psychology research. Despite his championing of experimental psychology, however, he also argued that *higher* mental processes such as apperception and language, as well as the products of culture such as religion, myth, and custom, could *not* be studied experimentally. For these, he proposed a non-experimental, "voluntaristic" approach he called *Völkerpsychologie*, which would use comparative, qualitative, and historical methods instead.

One of Wundt's students, **James McKeen Cattell**, worked extensively on reaction-time studies, devising elaborate instruments to measure a variety of reaction times under highly varying conditions. Another of his students, the Englishman **Edward Bradford Titchener**, imported a somewhat deviant brand of Wundtian psychology he called **structuralism** to the United States, advancing this position during his tenure at Cornell University. Titchener's primary goal was the discovery and enumeration of the elementary structures of consciousness—sensations and feelings—through a rigidly defined introspective method. For many years Titchenerian structuralism was taken by English-speaking psychologists to be a literal translation of Wundt's position. Actually, however, it ignored many of the most important aspects of Wundt's **voluntaristic psychology**, including such crucial concepts as apperception, **creative synthesis**, and **psychic causality**.

Oswald Külpe, another of Wundt's students, challenged his teacher's assumption by applying experimental introspective methods to certain "higher" mental processes such as **imageless thought** and **directed association** at a laboratory he established in Würzburg. A different kind of challenge was provided by **Hermann Ebbinghaus**, who conducted an experimental analysis of the higher process of memory after inventing the technique of using **nonsense syllables**. Thus, disagreements between Wundt and his challengers on the appropriate scope of the experimental approach represented a continuation of the debate started by Descartes regarding the limits of scientific analysis in psychology.

Key Pioneers

Ach, Narziss, p. 222

Bessel, Friedrich Wilhelm, p. 196

Cattell, James McKeen, p. 205

Donders, F. C., p. 205

Ebbinghaus, Hermann, p. 215

James, William, p. 199

Külpe, Oswald, p. 215

Ladd-Franklin, Christine, p. 219

Lange, Ludwig, p. 208

Peirce, Charles Sanders, p. 219

Titchener, Edward Bradford, p. 214

Washburn, Margaret Floy, p. 218

Watt, Henry J., p. 222

Wundt, Wilhelm, p. 189

Zöllner, Johann, p. 201

Key Terms

creative synthesis, p. 210

determining tendencies, p. 222

directed association, p. 222

forgetting curve, p. 225

imageless thoughts, p. 221

introspection, p. 214

mental chronometry, p. 197

mental sets, p. 222

nonsense syllables, p. 224

personal equations, p. 196

psychic causality, p. 211

stimulus error, p. 217

structuralism, p. 215

subtractive method, p. 205

Völkerpsychologie, p. 197

voluntaristic psychology, p. 211

Discussion Questions and Topics

1 The kinds of studies undertaken by Wundt and the students in his laboratory under the name of the new *experimental* psychology differ in many ways from how we now design and conduct psychological experiments. What are some of the features of the contemporary psychological experiment? Were any of these features present in Wundt's laboratory studies?

2 Discuss the various factors—both intellectual and contextual—that may have prevented Wundt's entire system (including his *Völkerpsychologie*) from being fully or accurately represented—until recently—in psychology's history.

3 For what reasons is it justifiable to portray Wundt as the founder of experimental psychology? What reasons can you think of that complicate this designation in Wundt's case?

Suggested Readings

Arthur Blumenthal initiated the modern revival of interest in Wundt with his book *Language and Psychology: Historical Aspects of Psycholinguistics* (New York: Wiley, 1970) and his paper "A Reappraisal of Wilhelm Wundt," *American Psychologist* 30 (1975): 1081–1088. The centennial of Wundt's Leipzig laboratory in 1979 inspired two excellent collections of invited articles, containing extensive biographical as well as analytical material; these are *Wundt Studies: A Centennial Collection*, edited by Wolfgang G. Bringmann and Ryan D. Tweney (Toronto: Hogrefe, 1980), and *Wilhelm Wundt and the Making of a Scientific Psychology*, edited by Robert W. Rieber (New York: Plenum, 1980). Of particular biographical interest are Solomon Diamond's "Wundt before Leipzig," in the Rieber volume and two articles by Wolfgang Bringmann et al. in the Bringmann and Tweney collection: "Wilhelm Maximilian Wundt, 1832–1874: The Formative Years" and "The Establishment of Wundt's Laboratory: An Archival and Documentary Study." For an interesting firsthand account of Wundt's Leipzig laboratory by his student Cattell, see *An Education in Psychology: James McKeen Cattell's Journal and Letters from Germany and England, 1880–1888*, edited by Michael M. Sokal (Cambridge, MA: MIT Press, 1981).

Kurt Danziger has written several important interpretive articles on Wundt and his contemporaries, including "The Positivist Repudiation of Wundt," *Journal of the History of the Behavioral Sciences* 15 (1979): 205–230; "The History of Introspection Reconsidered," *Journal of the History of the Behavioral Sciences* 16 (1980): 241–262; and "Origins and Basic Principles of Wundt's Völkerpsychologie," *British Journal of Social Psychology* 22 (1983): 303–313.

Charles Darwin and the Theory of Evolution

6

Darwin's Early Life

The Voyage of the *Beagle*
Geological Discoveries
Biological Discoveries
The Return Home

The Theory of Evolution by Natural Selection
The Origin of Species

Darwin and Psychology
The Descent of Man
Race and Gender
The Expression of the Emotions
"A Biographical Sketch of an Infant"

Darwin's Influence
Social Darwinism
Comparative Psychology and Individual Differences
Recent Developments: Emotions, Sociobiology, and
Evolutionary Psychology

Summary

Key Pioneers

Key Terms

Discussion Questions and Topics

Suggested Readings

In early September 1831, the young Cambridge graduate **Charles Robert Darwin** (1809–1882; see Figure 6.1) went to London for the most important interview of his life. Unexpectedly recommended for the post of naturalist aboard the survey ship H.M.S. *Beagle*, Darwin had already had some difficulty convincing his father it would be a good thing to do. Now he faced a crucial meeting with Captain Robert

FIG 6.1
Charles Darwin
(1809–1882)

FitzRoy, the ship's formidable commander, to determine if he would be finally accepted for the job.

A direct although illegitimate descendant of King Charles II, Fitz-Roy was already a veteran surveyor and ship's captain at age 26. He now planned a multiyear voyage to survey the coasts of South America, and then proceed around the world. He wished to engage a congenial gentleman who would not only make geological, mineralogical, and biological observations but also share his table and cabin and be his personal companion on the voyage. The post carried no pay, and some experienced naturalists had already declined it before the inexperienced but wealthy Darwin had been suggested.

At first the interview went badly, partly because of political differences between the liberal Darwin and the aristocratic, archconservative captain—but mainly because of the shape of Darwin's nose! FitzRoy subscribed to the theory of "physiognomy"—which held that a person's facial features reflect his or her character—and Darwin's nose had a shape supposedly associated with a lack of energy and determination.* And indeed Darwin's modest academic record did little to

---

* As noted in Chapter 3, the theory of physiognomy—originally promoted by the Swiss mystic Johann Lavater—was a precursor of phrenology.

contradict that diagnosis. As the interview proceeded, however, Darwin's great geniality and charm gradually won the captain over and encouraged him to take a chance. Darwin spent the next five years on one of the most scientifically consequential voyages of modern times.

Departing raw and untrained, Darwin returned home from the *Beagle* as an accomplished and respected geologist and collector of biological specimens. Even more important, he had made some crucial observations that started him toward developing the **theory of evolution by natural selection**, a revolutionary biological theory with vast implications for psychology. This chapter tells Darwin's story, and that of his momentous theory.

Darwin's Early Life

Charles Darwin was born on February 12, 1809 (the same day as Abraham Lincoln), in the English town of Shrewsbury, the fifth and next-to-last child in a wealthy and distinguished family. His father, Robert Darwin, ranked among the most highly paid of all English physicians outside London; his mother, born Susannah Wedgwood, came from the famous chinaware-producing family. His grandfather **Erasmus Darwin** (1731–1802) had been one of the most famous intellectual figures of his day: a doctor, inventor, poet, and general man of science. He had even formulated an early theory of evolution, expressing it colorfully although without the range of supporting evidence necessary for it to be taken seriously by most scientists of his time.

Educated first at home and then at the nearby Shrewsbury School, young Charles proved an indifferent scholar in the then-standard classical curriculum. He recalled, "Nothing could have been worse for the development of my mind. . . . The school as a means of education to me was simply a blank." He failed to impress his schoolmasters and once led his exasperated father to declare, "You care for nothing but shooting, dogs, and rat-catching, and you will be a disgrace to yourself and all your family."[1]

But despite his father's immortally unprophetic lament, young Darwin already possessed two qualities that eventually stood him in good stead. First was a strong curiosity and love of nature that drove him to spend countless hours observing, collecting, classifying, and experimenting in the natural world. He maintained extensive collections of plants, shells, and minerals, and his explosive experiments in a home chemistry laboratory earned him the nickname "Gas." Although unrewarded in school, these activities provided excellent training for a scientist.

Second, Charles Darwin showed from youth onward a warm and sympathetic personality that made him almost universally liked. This quality later commended him to Captain FitzRoy and won him the post on the *Beagle*. Moreover, his sympathy extended to animals as well as people, predisposing him in a peculiar way to appreciate the functional, adaptive value of many animal behaviors that seemed incomprehensible or repugnant to others—a key insight in his evolutionary theory.

Nevertheless, Charles's academic situation improved only slightly at age 16, when his father finally released him from classical study and sent him to medical school at the University of Edinburgh. There he learned the art of taxidermy and presented his first scientific papers—reports on local marine life to the student scientific society. But medicine itself proved unappealing. One professor "made his lectures on human anatomy as dull as he was himself, and the subject disgusted me"; another teacher's early-morning classes were "something fearful to remember." And worst of all, Darwin witnessed two live operations performed without anesthesia, one on a child: "I rushed away before they were completed. Nor did I ever attend again, for hardly any inducement would have been strong enough to do so; this being long before the blessed days of chloroform."[2]

Darwin's father understood, for he himself hated the sight of blood and maintained that he practiced medicine only out of economic necessity. He thus proposed yet another change: that Charles move to Cambridge University and prepare to become an Anglican clergyman. Attracted by the prospect of becoming a country parson and pursuing natural history as an amateur, Charles accepted the plan.

At Cambridge, Darwin joined "a sporting set, that sometimes drank too much, with jolly singing and playing at cards afterwards."[3] His dining society—officially called the Gourmet Club but appropriately nicknamed the Glutton Club—was notorious for its "devouring raids on birds and beasts which were before unknown to human palate." It "came to an untimely end by endeavouring to eat an old brown owl." The Cambridge academic curriculum emphasized mathematics as well as classics, and although Darwin enjoyed geometry, he was described by a fellow Glutton Clubber as having "a special quarrel" with the binomial theorem.[4] Darwin never bothered to compete for honors, but "went out in the poll" with an ordinary or pass degree in 1831. He mastered enough geometry, classics, and natural theology to graduate tenth out of the 178 non-honors students in his class.

Although respectable, Darwin's formal academic career at Cambridge contained little to foretell that his alma mater would one day name a new college after him. He stood out only in extracurricular activity, with his passion for nature study. "No pursuit at Cambridge . . . gave me so much pleasure as collecting beetles," he recalled, and he offered the following "proof of my zeal":

> One day, on tearing off some old bark, I saw two rare beetles and seized one in each hand; then I saw a third and new kind, which I could not bear to lose, so that I popped the one which I held in my right hand into my mouth. Alas it ejected some intensely acrid fluid, which burnt my tongue so that I was forced to spit the beetle out, which was lost, as well as the third one.[5]

Darwin's enthusiasm for natural history and his genial personality attracted the attention of Cambridge's more scientifically minded faculty, particularly **John Stevens Henslow** (1796–1861; see Figure 6.2) and **Adam Sedgwick** (1785–1873), professors respectively of botany and geology. Both were ordained Anglican clergymen who earned no salary for their professorships and offered no formal courses in their fields, for the university still considered the sciences to be distinctly minor subjects. They did, however, give occasional lectures and sponsor extracurricular excursions into the countryside for the small number of scientifically interested students. Darwin participated enthusiastically in these, and became known as "the man who walks with Henslow." Although Henslow and Sedgwick were knowledgeable in their fields and reasonably good teachers, both men's scientific views were colored by High Church conservatism. Darwin could not avoid noticing that they were particularly antagonistic to speakers who occasionally came to Cambridge espousing evolutionary ideas; indeed, they used their not inconsiderable influence to destroy the reputation and career of anyone daring to promote such a radical doctrine.

FIG 6.2
John Stevens Henslow
(1796–1861)

Nevertheless, Darwin profited greatly from the teaching and friendship of these men, which proved fateful immediately after his graduation in 1831. He accompanied Sedgwick on a summer geological tour of north Wales, which kindled a real interest in a science he had found rather dull at Edinburgh. And on returning home to Shrewsbury, another surprise awaited in the form of a letter from Henslow, who had just been offered the naturalist's post on Captain FitzRoy's *Beagle* but had declined because of family commitments. He told Darwin:

> I have stated that I consider you to be the best qualified person I know who is likely to undertake such a situation—I state this not on the supposition of your being a finished Naturalist, but as amply qualified for collecting, observing, and noting anything worthy to be noted in Natural History. . . . The Voyage is to last 2 years and if you take plenty of Books with you, any thing you please may be done. . . . In short I suppose there never was a finer chance for a man of zeal and spirit.[6]

Darwin's father, who would have to pay his son's expenses on this venture, at first called it a "wild scheme" that would interfere with a clerical career. Charles wrote Henslow regretfully declining the offer and went off to console himself on a shooting expedition with his uncle, Josiah Wedgwood. Fortunately, however, Robert Darwin had also said that if Charles could find "any man of common sense, who advises you to go," he would reconsider his objections. And Uncle Josiah—universally regarded as a man of eminent common sense—thought the offer a wonderful opportunity. Instead of hunting, uncle and nephew together confronted the elder Darwin, who relented with good grace. To mollify his father, the often extravagant Charles told him "that I should be deuced clever to spend more than my allowance whilst aboard the *Beagle*." Robert answered with a resigned smile, 'But they all tell me you are very clever."[7]

That brings us to Darwin's fateful interview with FitzRoy, in which his amiable manner triumphed over the weak shape of his nose and won him the position. Learning the news, a Glutton Club crony wrote a congratulatory letter saying: "Woe unto the Beetles of South America, woe unto all tropical butterflies."[8] Although Darwin in fact would collect thousands of insect specimens on this two-year voyage that expanded to five, these specimens would hardly be the most important of the journey's consequences.

The Voyage of the *Beagle*

Darwin's voyage on the Beagle began unpropitiously in December 1831, as fierce gales in the Bay of Biscay left the former landlubber constantly and miserably seasick. "Nobody who has only been to sea for 24 hours has a right to say that sea-sickness is even uncomfortable," he lamented. "I found nothing but lying in my hammock did me any good."[9] But when the seas calmed slightly, Darwin found he could read and work. He devised a specimen-catching bag to drag behind the ship, capturing thousands of marine creatures that he studied and classified. He read voluminously on geology, geography, and biology, and kept a detailed journal of his observations and thoughts. With his good humor he soon became a favorite of the crew, who affectionately called him "Philosopher." FitzRoy wrote of him: "I never saw a 'shore-going fellow' come into the ways of a ship so soon and so thoroughly."[10]

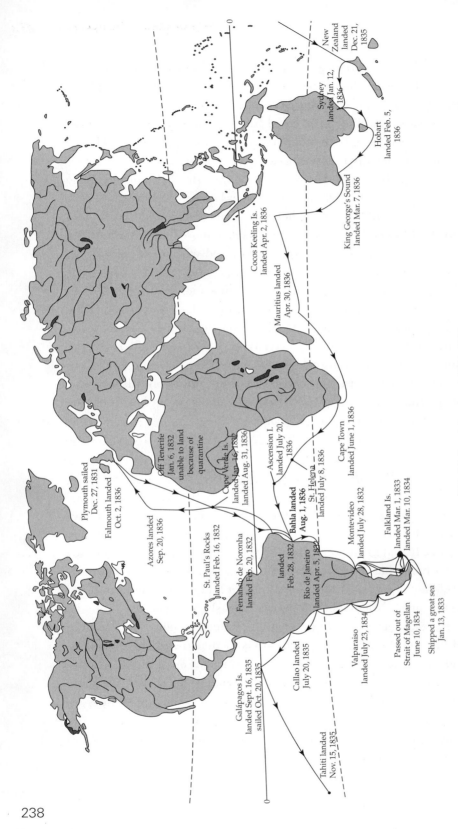

Plymouth sailed
Dec. 27, 1831

Falmouth landed
Oct. 2, 1836

Azores landed
Sep. 20, 1836

St. Paul's Rocks
landed Feb. 16, 1832

Fernando de Noronha
landed Feb. 20, 1832

Off Tenerife
Jan. 6, 1832
unable to land
because of
quarantine

Cape Verde Is.
landed Jan. 16, 1832
landed Aug. 31, 1836

Ascension I.
landed July 20,
1836

**Bahia landed
Aug. 1, 1836**

St. Helena
landed July 8, 1836

Cape Town
landed June 1, 1836

landed
Feb. 28, 1832

Rio de Janeiro
landed Apr. 5, 1832

Montevideo
landed July 28, 1832

Falkland Is.
landed Mar. 1, 1833
landed Mar. 10, 1834

Galapagos Is.
landed Sept. 16, 1835
sailed Oct. 20, 1835

Callao landed
July 20, 1835

Valparaiso
landed July 23, 1834

Passed out of
Strait of Magellan
June 10, 1834

Shipped a great sea
Jan. 13, 1833

Tahiti landed
Nov. 15, 1835

Cocos Keeling Is.
landed Apr. 2, 1836

Mauritius landed
Apr. 30, 1836

King George's Sound
landed Mar. 7, 1836

New
Zealand
landed
Dec. 21,
1835

Sydney
landed Jan. 12,
1836

Hobart
landed Feb. 5,
1836

FIG 6.3 Darwin's voyage, 1831–1836

This was a good thing, as the projected two-year voyage stretched to five. After two years only the east coast of South America had been surveyed, and the Beagle spent another two years on the west coast before finally starting the long westward voyage home via the Galápagos Islands, Tahiti, New Zealand, Australia, and the Cape of Good Hope. Figure 6.3 maps the entire voyage.

Geological Discoveries

During his first months at sea, Darwin spent much time studying the recently published first volume of *Principles of Geology*, by the English geologist **Charles Lyell** (1797–1875). This book promoted a controversial theory called **uniformitarianism**, which held that the earth's major features have resulted from gradual processes occurring over vast stretches of time and which continue in the present much as they have in the past (hence the "uniform" nature of geological development). Lyell disputed the then-predominant alternative theory of **catastrophism**, according to which geological features arose because of a few relatively sudden and massive cataclysms or catastrophes on the earth's surface. Part of catastrophism's appeal lay in its compatibility with a literal interpretation of the Bible, with Noah's flood representing the most important geological cataclysm. Catastrophism also accorded well with the then widely accepted estimate of the earth's age as only about 6,000 years, as calculated by the Irish archbishop **James Ussher** (1581–1656) after adding up the ages of the Old Testament patriarchs after Adam and Eve, as given in the Bible. Uniformitarianism required an immensely longer period of time for gradual processes to have built mountains and worked their other cumulative effects.

Before Darwin's departure, Henslow and Sedgwick had encouraged him to read and *think about* Lyell's book, but not to *believe* it. But as he read and thought, and then observed the geological features of the exotic places he visited, he became increasingly impressed. For example, he found seashells embedded in rock high in the Andes, then witnessed an earthquake in Chile that left coastal features a few feet higher above sea level than they had been before. Although terrible for those caught in it, this earthquake hardly constituted a catastrophe of the order required by the older geological theory. But similar events occurring over vast periods of time—as prescribed by uniformitarianism—could easily have produced a gradual raising of land from sea level in the distant past to a current mountainous height.

After examining the geology of several oceanic islands and atolls, Darwin became convinced that these, too, could be accounted for by gradual uniform processes, such as lava flows from undersea volcanoes, coral growth, and the slow rising and subsidence of the ocean floor. He wrote of all this to Henslow, who passed his letters on to Lyell and other geologists. Although Darwin did not know it at the time, these missives won him a reputation in England as a gifted geological observer and helped turn the tide of informed scientific opinion in favor of uniformitarianism. Even more important, Darwin began in his own mind to accept a very ancient age for the earth—a necessary precondition for his later theory of evolution.

Biological Discoveries

The inveterate collector also found and shipped home thousands of biological specimens. FitzRoy wrote of "our smiles at the apparent rubbish Darwin frequently brought on board,"[11] but many of the specimens won immediate scientific recognition back home. Among them were the fossilized remains of several large extinct creatures found embedded in the stratified cliffs of Argentina. The *megatherium*, for example, had the skeletal structure of a modern sloth, but the size of an elephant. Bones from a giant armadillo, a wild llama the size of a camel, and a strange, rhinoceros-sized but hornless creature called the *toxodon* also fascinated the English naturalists.

Such fossils bore on the uniformitarianism-catastrophism debate, when the question naturally arose as to how and when they came to be embedded in rock. Aboard the *Beagle*, the devoutly religious FitzRoy offered a catastrophist explanation: The extinct species represented animals that had not made it onto Noah's ark and therefore succumbed in the deluge. Darwin privately doubted this but for the time being kept a discreet silence on the issue.

Darwin also collected and described thousands of *living* plant and animal species, many previously unknown to scientists. While reflecting on his biological findings, he adopted two general lines of thought. First, he habitually asked himself about the possible *functions* of all animal characteristics. When he saw an octopus change color to match its background, the camouflage value of such a reaction seemed obvious. And even when a marine iguana in the Galápagos behaved in a repetitive and seemingly "stupid" way, Darwin still could imagine a function:

> I threw one several times as far as I could into a deep pool left by the retiring tide; but it invariably returned in a direct line to the spot where I stood. . . . As often as I threw it in, it returned. . . . Perhaps this singular piece of apparent stupidity may be accounted for by the circumstance, that this reptile has no natural enemy whatever on shore, whereas at sea it must often fall a prey to the numerous sharks. Hence, probably, urged by a fixed and hereditary instinct that the shore is its place of safety, whatever the emergency may be, it there takes refuge.[12]

While an ordinary observer would simply have remarked on the oddity or stupidity of such behavior, Darwin sought to understand its possible *usefulness*. This sensitivity to the functional adaptiveness of all biological phenomena later helped lead him to his theory of evolution.

A second important line of thought began almost casually, when Darwin began noting the *geographical distributions* of species. He saw that many entirely different animals existed on either side of the Andes, for example, even though climate and other conditions were generally similar. His most surprising observations of this kind came in the Galápagos Islands, 600 miles off Ecuador in the Pacific Ocean. These geologically recent volcanic islands supported many animals who closely resembled species found on the South American continent and whose predecessors had presumably originated there. But despite the resemblances, the Galápagos creatures had developed distinctive characteristics of their own, some of which even varied discernibly from island to island within the chain. For instance, giant tortoises (whose Spanish name *galápagos* had given the islands their name) showed slight but characteristic differences in the shapes of their shells that enabled an experienced observer to know on which island they had been born. And several populations of common brown finches differed only in the shape and size of their bills: On some islands they were long, pointed, and well suited for digging out insect prey, while elsewhere they were short but powerful and capable of cracking open hard nuts and seeds. These casual observations later assumed great importance when Darwin began thinking about the possible origins of different animal species.

The Return Home

After leaving the Galápagos in October 1835, nearly a year's sailing still lay ahead for the *Beagle*—to Tahiti, New Zealand, Australia, and South Africa. These places held little charm for Darwin, however, who now only wanted to return home to his family and to enter English scientific life. His eagerness increased when family and friends wrote to tell him that his name was already becoming well known in scientific circles. His shipped specimens had been well received, and Henslow had excerpted geological passages from his letters in a pamphlet published by the Cambridge Philosophical Society—Darwin's first scientific publication.

At last on October 2, 1836, the *Beagle* docked at Falmouth, England, and Darwin took the first coach to Shrewsbury. Arriving in the middle of the night, he stayed at an inn before strolling home to surprise his family before breakfast the next morning. A delighted Robert Darwin exclaimed to his daughters, "Why, the shape of his head is quite altered."[13] In fact, Charles Darwin *was* a matured and transformed person, now ready to begin some momentous theorizing about the significance of his *Beagle* observations.

The Theory of Evolution by Natural Selection

Darwin won election to the London Geological Society in 1836, and to the still more prestigious Royal Society in 1839. That year he also married his cousin Emma Wedgwood and published his first book, the edited journal from his voyage. Despite its deceptively ponderous title—*Journal of Researches into the Geology and Natural History of the Various Countries Visited during the Voyages of the H.M.S. Beagle, under the Command of Captain FitzRoy, R.N., from 1832 to 1836*—this lively book became an immediate bestseller and established Darwin as a leading popular naturalist and travel writer.

Even more significant events occurred privately, for in 1837 Darwin had begun reflecting on the implications of his *Beagle* observations and recording his thoughts in a series of notebooks.[14] In them he deliberately and specifically addressed one of the most puzzling and controversial questions in all of biology, sometimes called "the mystery of mysteries": namely, how the millions of different species that inhabit the earth originally came into being.

The traditional answer had each species being created at a single time, as a complete, distinctive, and unchangeable entity. This view was cogently summarized by one of Darwin's leading contemporaries as follows:

> I assume that each organism which the Creator educed was stamped with an indelible specific character, which made it what it was, and distinguished it from everything else, however near or like. I assume that such a character has been, and is, indelible and immutable; that the characters which distinguish species from species now, were as definite at the first instant of their creation as now, and are as distinct now as they were then.[15]

Upholders of this traditional view claimed support from the first chapter of Genesis, which declares that on the fifth day of creation God created "every living creature that moveth." On more scientific grounds, they cited the so-called **argument from design**, originally promulgated by the philosopher/theologian **William Paley** (1743–1805). According to Paley, the marvelously complicated organs of various species—the delicate but strong hinge muscle of a bivalve shellfish, for example, or the mammalian eye—are so perfectly constructed and adapted that they must have been *designed* as finished products by some powerful and knowledgeable creator. Paley saw "an invisible hand, . . . the hand of God," in these adaptive wonders and said that to study the structure of an eye was "a cure for atheism."[16]

Of course, Darwin knew that a rival theory of gradual evolution of species had already been promoted by his grandfather Erasmus Darwin.* He also knew that in 1809—the year of his own birth—the

---

* For a time Erasmus Darwin had even had the half-joking Latin motto *E conchis omnia* ("Everything from shells") painted on the side of his traveling carriage, but he removed it after some of his patients and neighbors found it sacrilegious.

French zoologist **Jean-Baptiste Lamarck** (1744–1829) had proposed that species evolve and change owing to the inheritance of bodily changes produced by the voluntary exercise or disuse of particular organs. Presumably the giraffe, for example, had begun as a short-necked animal that browsed off tree foliage above its head, thus exercising its neck muscles; the slightly strengthened and stretched muscles of each generation were subsequently inherited by its successor, until eventually the modern giraffe evolved.

Although Lamarck and Erasmus Darwin helped bring the *idea* of evolved species to scientific awareness, neither view was widely accepted. The elder Darwin had proposed no plausible *mechanism* by which evolution might occur, and the mechanism proposed by Lamarck—the voluntary use or disuse of particular muscles and organs—could not account for evolution of nonvoluntary characteristics such as protective coloration. Further, the notion of evolution contradicted the literal account of separate creation of all species in Genesis, then strongly upheld by the Church of England. As we have noted, those bold enough to argue publicly for evolution were dealt with harshly by establishment scientist/clergymen such as Henslow and Sedgwick. Thus, when Charles Darwin returned from his voyage, the general notion of evolution was stirring in the intellectual atmosphere but was still considered unrespectable and had not yet been proposed in a form that could be taken seriously as an alternative to the argument from design.

In the months following his return, however, Darwin concluded that the idea of the evolution or "transmutation" of species had to be taken seriously. The staggering number of different species in nature, often varying from each other only slightly and subtly, seemed more compatible with a longstanding and ongoing species-generation process than with a separate creation of each. Further, he had personally observed extinct fossil species that resembled modern species in all but size, and Galàpagos finches whose slight but distinct differences in bill structure suggested that gradual changes and developments over generations were in fact possible.

Darwin also knew that breeders had been able to produce strikingly different *varieties* or *breeds* of domestic animals by careful selection of parental stock over many generations; for example, bulldogs, sheepdogs, and dachshunds had all been created by the careful and selective breeding of originally similar canine stock. No domestic breed had ever become a genuinely separate *species*, however, capable of interbreeding only with its like. Purebred dogs can all interbreed or "mongrelize" with other breeds, producing fertile offspring who lack the distinctive characteristics of the pure parent breeds. By contrast, genuine species in a state of nature maintain their distinctive qualities automatically, by breeding successfully only like with like.

In the autumn of 1838, Darwin suddenly thought of a plausible mechanism for the gradual evolution of countless stable species in a state of nature. He later recalled that he had been reading, "for amusement," the rather gloomy economic theories of **Thomas Malthus** (1766–1834). Malthus believed that most human beings are destined to live in poverty because their capacity to increase population greatly exceeds their capacity to increase food production. When a small population settles in a fertile region, good times may persist for a while. Malthus argued that eventually, however, population growth would inevitably outstrip food production, leading to a general state of scarcity and poverty. And then disease, famine, and the other effects of poverty will act as a *check* on future population growth, so a stable population living at a bare subsistence level becomes established as the "normal" outcome of human social and economic existence.

This idea of a naturally occurring check on population growth seized Darwin's imagination. In *any* species, he reasoned, countless individuals will be conceived over many generations, but only a proportion of them will survive the rigors of their environment to propagate their kind. Those who survive will disproportionately tend to be the ones *best adapted* to overcoming the dangers of their own particular environments. And if their adaptive characteristics are *inheritable*, their offspring will also tend to have them and to survive and propagate in greater numbers than their less advantaged fellows. Here was a mechanism for the evolution of species!

Consider the Galápagos finches, all of whose progenitors presumably arrived from South America with slightly varying but generally medium-sized bills. Assume that one group arrived at an island rich in nuts and seeds but lacking in crevice-hiding insects. Here, a slight survival advantage accrued to individual birds with relatively strong and stout beaks for breaking open and eating the seeds. These birds must have survived and propagated at a slightly higher rate than their slim-billed relatives, producing a second generation with slightly stouter bills than the first, on the average. After many generations of the same process, a stable population of broad-billed birds would have evolved. A second group of progenitor finches, arriving in an island environment poorer in seeds and nuts but richer in concealed insects, presumably underwent the opposite process. In this case the advantage would have lain with slender bills for digging out prey, and a population so equipped would gradually have evolved.

Darwin therefore hypothesized that different environments inevitably and constantly impose a **natural selection** on their inhabitants, disproportionately favoring certain kinds of individuals to survive and propagate their kind. Just as the original breeders of basset hounds selected only animals with floppy ears and other desirable basset characteristics to be their breeding stock, so "nature," or the environment, constantly selects the individuals best suited to survive and propagate. The selective effects of nature go on inexorably and for countlessly more generations than the efforts of any domestic animal breeder, leading to the creation of stable species rather than to ephemeral breeds or varieties.

Thus Darwin saw "nature"—that is, the presence or absence of food, competitors, predators, and the other ever-varying exigencies of the environment—as not only imposing checks on the unrestricted increase of any species' population but also selecting which individuals, with which inheritable characteristics, will tend to survive and propagate. Acting over vast ages of time (and here the new uniformitarian geology suggested a time span at least in the millions rather than the thousands of years), changes and variations in the natural environment must have produced countless localized changes in selection pressures, leading to the gradual evolution of countless different species. Thus natural selection provided the "engine" or mechanism theoretically necessary to support an evolutionary process.

The Origin of Species

Darwin knew his new theory would not gain easy acceptance, for it challenged a long-held view of the origin of animal species and also carried disturbing implications for the role of *human beings* in nature. The literal Bible story placed humanity in a category separate from animals—formed on the sixth and final day of creation, in God's own image, and granted dominion over the rest of the earth's inhabitants. But Darwin recognized that human beings, with their evident anatomical similarities to many animals, would logically have to be included in any consistent evolutionary system. Animals and humans "partake from our origin in one common ancestor, so we may be all netted together," he wrote in an early notebook.[17]

Recognizing his theory's disturbing implications, Darwin tried to an unusual degree to seriously consider every possible objection to it. He adopted a personal "golden rule" that whenever he encountered a fact or argument apparently contrary to his theory, he would "make a memorandum of it without fail and at once; for I had found by experience that such facts and thoughts were far more apt to escape from the memory than favourable ones."[18] He realized, for example, that the "perfect" mammalian eye cited in the argument from design posed difficulties for the theory of evolution. Only after reading Helmholtz's discussion of the eye's optical *imperfections* (see Chapter 4) did he feel fully comfortable about describing the eye as an evolved (and evolving) organ rather than as a finished product of deliberate design.

For years Darwin proceeded cautiously, collecting more and more evidence regarding his theory while keeping it mainly to himself. In 1842 and 1844 he wrote out summaries of the theory but never published them. He told just a handful of trusted friends, including the geologist Lyell and the botanist **Joseph Hooker** (1817–1911), about his belief in evolution, and even then very cautiously; "it is like confessing a murder," he confided to Hooker.[19] Only in 1856—eighteen years after his original inspiration—did Darwin feel he had enough evidence to publish his theory. He now finally began a work entitled *Natural Selection*, which he expected to reach 3,000 pages.

In the spring of 1858, however, Darwin was rudely interrupted by a letter and manuscript from the naturalist **Alfred Russel Wallace** (1823–1913; see Figure 6.4). While recovering from malaria in the East Indies, Wallace had thought of a new theory of evolution, written it up in a short paper, and sent it to Darwin, whom he knew by reputation as one of the most congenial as well as generally knowledgeable naturalists in Britain. A shocked Darwin now read a brief outline of essentially his own theory, independently conceived by

FIG 6.4
Alfred Russel Wallace
(1823–1913)

Wallace. At a loss how to respond, he sent the manuscript to Lyell and Hooker—who had long been warning him to publish his theory before someone else beat him to the punch.

His friends arranged an honorable compromise: Excerpts from Darwin's unpublished summary of 1844 and Wallace's new paper would both be read, in the absence of both authors, at the next meeting of the Linnean Society (a prestigious organization devoted to the study and classification of plants and animals). In this way priority for the public presentation of the theory of evolution by natural selection was jointly shared by Darwin and Wallace in July 1858. Ironically, however, the session attracted little attention, and the Linnean Society's official report for 1858 declared that the year had *not* produced "any of those striking discoveries which at once revolutionize, so to speak, the department of science on which they bear."[20]

That statement shows that Darwin had been correct in assuming his theory would not receive serious attention until buttressed by a tremendous amount of supporting evidence. But now that his secret was out, he wanted to get a substantial exposition of natural selection quickly into the public eye—less substantial than the projected three thousand pages of *Natural Selection*, perhaps, but long enough to illustrate the theory's power Thus he spent a year feverishly writing *On the Origin of Species by Means of Natural Selection, or the Preservation of Favoured Races in the Struggle for Life*, a 490-page "abstract" of the theory, which was published at the end of 1859. Arguably the most important book of the century, this detailed, systematic, and plausible presentation of an evolutionary theory demanded to be taken seriously, and in fact it created the sensation Darwin had expected and feared.

Although *Origin of Species* dealt almost exclusively with plants and animals, debate immediately raged over its implied question of whether human beings are a separate and special creation of God or are "descended from the apes." The noncombative Darwin shrank from polemics himself but attracted one particularly outspoken advocate in **Thomas Henry Huxley** (1825–1895). This expert on primate anatomy wrote to Darwin immediately after reading and being convinced by *Origin of Species*, pledging willingness "to go to the stake" in support of the theory. Huxley added, "I am sharpening up my claws and beak in readiness" against "the curs which will bark and yelp."[21]

Appropriately nicknamed "Darwin's Bulldog," Huxley defended natural selection most spectacularly in an 1860 debate with Samuel Wilberforce, the bishop of Oxford, at a public meeting of the British Association for the Advancement of Science. Although lacking scientific training, the smooth-talking Wilberforce had been primed on some of the strongest apparent scientific arguments against evolution. Unwisely, however, he resorted to sarcasm in debate and asked Huxley whether it was through his grandfather or his grandmother that he claimed descent from a monkey. Hearing this, Huxley reportedly whispered, "The Lord hath delivered him into mine hands," then expertly countered Wilberforce's scientific objections before turning to him to say:

> If the question is put to me, "would I rather have a miserable ape for a grandfather, or a man highly endowed by nature and possessed of great means of influence, and yet who employs these faculties and that influence for the mere purpose of introducing ridicule into a grave scientific discussion"—I unhesitatingly affirm my preference for the ape.[22]

To rebuke a bishop in public was highly unusual, to say the least, and Huxley's retort created a sensation. But most observers, particularly the undergraduates in attendance, felt Huxley had been justified, and, more important, had carried the day for Darwin and evolution.

The following year, two new scientific discoveries further advanced the case for evolution. First, fossil remains of the extinct *archeopteryx*, the most ancient of birds, were found in Bavaria. Although feathered, this creature had "fingers" on its wings, and vertebrae and tail like a reptile's. Darwin had speculated that birds might have evolved from reptiles in the distant past, and here was a transitional form fully consistent with that unlikely seeming idea. And also in 1861, an African explorer recovered the skulls and stuffed bodies of gorillas, a form of great ape previously unknown to Western science. Anatomically similar to human beings, the gorilla had several features previously argued by anti-evolutionists to be exclusively human and thus proof of humanity's biological uniqueness. Although neither of these finds alone could "prove" the case for the evolution and interrelatedness of species, they offered dramatic evidence of the plausibility of that view. Further evidence rapidly accumulated, and within a very few years the *Origin*'s general case was accepted by the overwhelming majority of knowledgeable scientists.

Darwin and Psychology

Although Darwin largely ignored his theory's implications for human beings in *Origin of Species*, he did include one short and prophetic paragraph near the end of the book suggesting that human mental qualities would eventually be understood as the results of evolution: "In the distant future I see open fields for far more important researches. Psychology will be based on a new foundation, that of the necessary acquirement of each mental power and capacity by gradation. Light will be thrown on the origin of man and his history."[23]

For the next decade, Darwin left the public working out of this idea to others, including his cousin **Francis Galton** (1822–1911), whom you will learn more about in the next chapter. Privately, however, he never ceased to think about human issues, and finally in the 1870s he published three seminal works about them: *The Descent of Man, and*

Selection in Relation to Sex (1871), *The Expression of the Emotions in Man and Animals* (1872), and "A Biographical Sketch of an Infant" (1877).

The Descent of Man

In *The Descent of Man* Darwin finally argued explicitly and publicly that human beings have descended from animal ancestors. He opened his argument by noting the structural similarities between humans and the higher animals with respect to bones, muscles, blood vessels, internal viscera, nerves, and that "most important of all the organs," the brain: "Every chief fissure and fold in the brain of man has its analogy in that of the orang."[24] In addition, humans share many diseases with animals, possess certain "rudimentary organs" (such as projecting points on the ear) that assume considerable importance in other animals, and pass through stages of embryological development in which they closely resemble other animals. All of these features plausibly located *Homo sapiens* within the domain of physically evolving species.

Next, Darwin tried to show "that there is no fundamental difference between man and the higher mammals in their *mental* faculties."[25] He cited cases of animals showing "higher" qualities such as courage (in defending themselves, their young, or their human masters) and kindness (sometimes taking in and caring for orphaned members of other groups and species). He argued that dogs manifestly experience many of the same emotions as humans, including jealousy (when a rival pet receives its master's attention), pride (when carrying the master's basket, with head held high), shame (when reprimanded), and even a rudimentary sense of humor (when playfully and repeatedly running off with a ball or stick, just before the master can get it). Animals obviously demonstrate memory, attention, and curiosity, and since dogs seem often to dream when they sleep—twitching, quietly yelping, and breathing irregularly exactly as if imagining themselves in some exciting situation—they must have the capacity for imagination. Darwin further argued that animals show the rudiments of *reason*—the only faculty of the soul that Descartes had reserved exclusively for human beings: They profit and learn from experience, communicate with each other by sound and

gesture, and appreciate "beauty" through distinctive mating preferences for various body markings and adornments. After considering
many of these examples, Darwin concluded categorically: "The difference in mind between man and the higher animals, great as it is,
certainly is one of degree and not of kind."[26]

Race and Gender

Also in *Descent of Man*, Darwin touched on the two topics of race and
gender. On both subjects he was relatively circumspect, but his comments nonetheless sowed the seeds for considerable controversy.

The Victorian era in Britain was notable for extreme differences in
attitudes and beliefs about race and the causes of ethnic differences.
At one extreme were the **polygenists**, who argued that non-European "savage" peoples represented a distinctly different *species* of
being. The **monogenists**, on the other hand, believed in the common
ancestry and relatedness of all human groups, although they also
entertained widely varying theories to try to explain the observed
differences among them. Some attributed those differences primarily to environmental and cultural variables, for instance, while others
believed that the African groups were descended from the biblical
Noah's son Ham, whose offspring had been cursed by God and condemned to be enslaved by the progeny of Noah's other sons.

In *Descent*, Darwin came down firmly in the monogenist camp.
"All the races agree in so many unimportant details of structure
and in so many mental peculiarities," he wrote, "that these can be
accounted for only by inheritance from a common progenitor."[27]
Darwin further had no doubt that environmental and educational
variables were extremely important in producing human individual
differences and that the institution of slavery, in particular, had had
horrible effects on its victims. As a young student at Edinburgh he
had been skillfully trained in taxidermy by a freed slave named John
Edmondstone, who had prospered in his freedom and whom Darwin
admired both for his pleasantness and his intelligence.[28] On his *Beagle* voyage Darwin had been appalled at the relations between masters and slaves on Brazilian plantations and had concluded that the
slaves' character was generally superior to that of their white masters,
the "polished savages" who oppressed and denigrated them.[29]

But even as he accepted the biological unity of all human beings, Darwin also believed that the widely varying environmental conditions to which differing groups were exposed would inevitably create differing selection pressures among them. Such pressures might help account for the evolution, over time, of slightly differing races or, as Darwin said they may be more accurately called, "sub-species."[30] Differences in skin color, for example, were natural adaptations to differing exposures to direct sunlight. An elaboration of this theory held that the struggle for survival in harsh northern climates promoted the development of inventiveness and creativity and accounted for a presumed intellectual superiority of the so-called Nordic races. This view overlooked the facts that equatorial climates produce harsh challenges of their own and that other ethnic groups besides European "Nordics" managed to survive and thrive in cold conditions. This idea was more strongly supported by some of his contemporaries and followers than by Darwin himself, although he never explicitly refuted it. Two prominent historians have concluded that Darwin's personal, ambiguous position regarding evolution and race is less significant than the fact that his theory "was stripped of nuance and appropriated [by others] to serve a scientific racism that aimed to prove comparative differences in mental abilities."[31] As we shall see in later chapters, this area has been a problematic one ever since.

The full title of Darwin's book was *The Descent of Man, and Selection in Relation to Sex,* and the second part of that title alludes to a second controversial subject: the issue of differences between males and females. Darwin's book hypothesized a variant of natural selection that he called **sexual selection**—that is, the gradual selection and evolution of characteristics that are specifically favorable for *reproductive* success. To pass on their genetic material (their *genes*, we would say today, although that term was unknown in Darwin's time), individuals must not only survive physically but also mate and procreate. Darwin argued that within a particular species, females and males come to prefer certain qualities in their mates and to select their partners on that basis—thus creating a pressure for a particular type of "beauty" to evolve. Classic examples are provided by birds, whose male members have evolved spectacular colors and ornamentation while the females remain drab (an adaptive characteristic for them, rendering them inconspicuous to predators while tending their nests).

Darwin believed that sexual selection had also influenced human evolution, resulting in some characteristic *mental* as well as physical differences between the sexes:

> Woman seems to differ from man in mental disposition, chiefly in her greater tenderness and less selfishness. . . . Owing to her maternal instincts [she] displays these qualities towards her infants in an eminent degree; therefore it is likely that she would often extend them towards her fellow creatures. Man is the rival of other men; he delights in competition, and this leads to ambition which passes too easily into selfishness. . . . With women the powers of intuition, of rapid perception, and perhaps of imitation, are more strongly marked than in man.[32]

Despite his apparent evenhandedness in attributing some positive mental qualities to women, Darwin was unequivocal on the issue of *intellectual* power: "The chief distinction in the intellectual powers of the two sexes is shown by man's attaining to a higher eminence . . . than can woman—whether requiring deep thought, reason, or imagination, or merely the use of the senses and hands."[33] Like most of his Victorian male contemporaries, he simply assumed a general masculine intellectual superiority. His general notion that men and women have evolved so as to manifest separate psychological characteristics that—in the Victorian stereotypes—"complement" each other has come to be known and criticized as the **complementarity hypothesis**.[34]

On a related issue, Darwin argued that across all species including human beings, males have been more modified by evolution than females and consequently tend to show more variability among themselves. According to this **variation hypothesis**, as it has come to be known, if you measure the heights of populations of adult males and females, the *range* of heights between the tallest and the shortest male individuals will be greater than that for the females. Darwin stated that the cause of this greater male variation was unknown, and he himself did not explicitly apply the idea to intellectual differences between men and women. But others subsequently did, asserting that a large population of men will contain more extreme cases of prodigiously high intellectual ability (counterbalanced by more cases of extreme stupidity) than a comparably sized group of women, who will be more closely clustered about an average figure. Here was a potential "explanation," of course, for the great preponderance of males among the eminent figures in history, as well as a rationalization for restricting education for the presumably highly "gifted" to boys and young men.

The Expression of the Emotions

Darwin started to write a chapter on emotions in *Descent of Man*, but when it ballooned in size he deferred the subject for a book all its own, *The Expression of the Emotions in Man and Animals*. In it he argued that human emotional expressions are inherited and evolved characteristics, best understood as the direct or indirect consequences of reactions that had adaptive or survival value.

The functional origins and purposes of many emotional expressions seemed straightforward. The wide staring eyes of surprise, for example, presumably originated as a mechanism for seeing the surprising object more fully and clearly. The bared teeth of rage naturally followed the adoption of a fighting and biting posture, while the curled lip of a sneer may have originated in a wrinkling of the nose after smelling something unpleasant.

Some other, less obviously "adaptive" emotional expressions presumably arose because they were *antitheses* of directly serviceable reactions. A dog expressing affection or playfulness, for example, assumes an attitude directly opposite to its angry or aggressive posture: Instead of walking upright with hair and tail erect and teeth bared, the affectionate animal crouches, flexes and wiggles its forward body, lowers and wags its tail, and relaxes its lips. While all of the angry expressions are directly interpretable as preparations for attack, the affectionate ones are only indirectly intelligible as the opposites of aggression.

Darwin thought that still other emotional expressions occur as side effects from the general activation of the nervous system that accompanies emotional arousal. In states of fright, flight, and anger, for example, a general arousal of the body into an active, excited state has adaptive value. Darwin believed that sometimes this excess excitation "spills over" into the body and produces trembling, grimacing, or flexion and contortion as a side effect.

In summary, Darwin concluded that these three general principles—direct serviceability of the expression, antithesis, and direct activation of the nervous system—could account for all emotional expression in animals and human beings alike.

One major purpose of *The Expression of the Emotions* was to show that many human reactions with no current survival or utilitarian value did have it back in the evolutionary past. For example, Darwin explained the act of *blushing*—widely regarded in Victorian times as a uniquely human characteristic bestowed by the creator along with an innate conscience and sense of morality—as the consequence of several interacting but perfectly intelligible "animal" reactions. These reactions included flushing and the engorgement with blood of body parts that become the subject of conscious attention, combined with the self-consciousness that is made possible by language.

In general, *Descent of Man* had argued that animals possess the rudiments of human mentality. *The Expression of the Emotions* made the complementary case that human beings possess many remnants of "animality." Not always guided by conscious and rational thought, people often betray unconscious and instinctive signs of their long animal ancestry. Other theorists, including Sigmund Freud, would soon expand on the implications of that point.

Finally, Darwin noted that human emotional expressions tend to be similar throughout all known human groups. Smiles and laughter, weeping and shrieks of rage, contortions of pain, cringings of fear—all of these emotional manifestations are universally recognized. Darwin argued that this similarity of expression points to the common descent of all human groups from the same earlier, pre-human ancestor. "It seems to me improbable," he wrote, "that so much similarity, or rather identity of structure, could have been acquired by independent means. . . . It is far more probable that the many points of close similarity in the various races are due to inheritance from a single parent-form."[35]

"A Biographical Sketch of an Infant"

Five years after *The Expression of the Emotions*, Darwin made his final specific contribution to psychology. After reading an article describing the acquisition of language by a young child, Darwin recalled that he had kept a detailed log on the development of his own firstborn infant, thirty-seven years earlier. He now reexamined those notes, and wrote them up in an article entitled "A Biographical Sketch of an Infant," published in the journal *Mind* in 1877. Only 10 pages long, this modest work still stands as a landmark in the history of child psychology—among the very first in the genre of "baby biography."

Darwin's notes on his son William, or "Doddy," began during the first week of life with the observation that numerous reflexes such as sneezing, yawning, stretching, sucking, and screaming were "well performed by my infant, . . . the perfection of these reflex movements show[ing] that the extreme imperfection of the voluntary ones is not due to the state of the muscles or the coordinating centres, but to that of the seat of the will."[36] In his first successful voluntary movements, William moved his hands to his mouth at about the age of 40 days. Over the next several months he acquired several more complex intentional movements, the first ones involving the hands and arms, later ones the legs and trunk.

William's earliest obvious emotional expression was of startle or fear, after hearing a loud sudden sound during the first few weeks of life. Anger first appeared at 10 weeks, when William frowned after being given unwarmed milk. By 4 months the baby could be worked into a "violent passion" by small causes such as dropping a lemon he was playing with.

Clear evidence of "association of ideas, reason, etc." first occurred at 5 months when William became angry after being dressed in his outdoor hat and coat but not being taken immediately outdoors. At 7 months he showed that he recognized his nurse's name when he heard it, but he did not spontaneously utter a meaningful word of his own until 12 months, when he used "mum" to indicate food. The baby acquired other words rapidly thereafter, and sometimes creatively combined them—as when he coined "black-shu-mum" ("shu" was his version of sugar) for licorice. Evidence of a "moral sense" began only at 13 months, with signs of discomfort at being chided for not kissing his father. At 27 months, however, "he gave his last bit of gingerbread to his little sister, and then cried out with high self-approbation 'Oh kind Doddy, kind Doddy.'"[37]

In a small way, Darwin's paper dealt with the grand themes he had developed in his other works: the roles of instinctive reflexes, habits, emotions, and other sensibilities in an increasingly effective adaptation to the world. In general, he saw his son's development as the gradual strengthening, complication, and fusion of originally simple and separate tendencies. Language, for example, arose only after a period of emotional and associative development had enabled the child first to connect names with people or things important to him (for example, his nurse). Only after hearing and understanding words for some time did William begin to invent and utter meaningful words himself. Darwin observed that this sequence—understanding words and interpreting them as signals before making them up and using them—"is what might have been expected, as we know that the lower animals easily learn to understand spoken words."[38]

Darwin was suggesting that an *individual's* development proceeds along roughly the same lines as the previous evolution of the *species* to which it belongs. In acquiring language, Doddy rapidly traversed the same stages it had presumably taken his pre-human ancestors countless generations to reach through natural selection. Darwin had earlier noted something similar in the development of the human embryo, which passes through stages in which it resembles increasingly higher life forms. This rapid "recapitulation" in an individual of stages and patterns consistent with earlier and less highly evolved species suggested to Darwin that each individual somehow retains rudiments of the long evolutionary past—and was one more element in his general argument for evolution.[*]

---

[*] This idea that "ontogeny recapitulates phylogeny"—that an individual's earliest development copies the antecedent evolution of its species—was later popularized and raised to the level of a literal dogma by Darwin's German follower Ernst Haeckel. In modified form it also became central to the psychology of the American G. Stanley Hall, whom we shall meet in Chapter 8. For Darwin himself, however, the idea remained a suggestive generalization rather than a literal truth—a view generally substantiated by further research.

Darwin's Influence

In 1842, while he was just beginning to think about how to publish his theory of natural selection, Darwin had moved to a lovely country house 16 miles from London, in Downe, Kent. There he found a privacy and freedom from the distractions of the big city that he cherished for the rest of his life. He raised a large and thriving family, invested his substantial inheritance shrewdly enough to become an independently rich man, and after 1859 turned out a steady stream of important books. In addition to the works already discussed, he produced major studies of orchids (1862), vines and climbing plants (1865), plants and animals under domestication (1868), the power of movement in plants (1880), and the effect of worms in producing vegetable mold (1881). Although these were specialized topics, each of them helped build the case for evolution and consolidated Darwin's reputation as the foremost naturalist of his age.

But while his family, his fortune, and his reputation and influence all grew steadily, Darwin suffered chronically from a mysterious digestive malady of uncertain diagnosis. The once-intrepid world traveler became something of a recluse, never again venturing out of Britain, and seldom even going to London for scientific gatherings. He did maintain a vast correspondence, however, and when physically able served as a congenial host to the many friends and admirers who came to see him at home.

Despite the original outcry that had greeted Darwin's theory in 1859, the British religious establishment rapidly accommodated to it. And when Darwin (see Figure 6.5) died in April 1882—at the age of 73 and from a heart ailment rather than his mysterious intestinal malady—the Church consented to his being buried in Westminster Abbey, next to Isaac Newton. There the pair still rests today—the two greatest and most influential scientists that England has produced.

Social Darwinism

Shortly after Darwin's death, a movement called **social Darwinism** came much into vogue. Despite its name, this movement owed as much to the prolific philosopher **Herbert Spencer** (1820–1903) as to Darwin

FIG 6.5
Charles Darwin in
his older years

himself and contained some ideas that Darwin did not endorse. Spencer had been a supporter of Lamarck's theory of evolution even before Darwin's *Origin of Species* and had written about the general importance of an evolutionary viewpoint for psychology in an 1855 text, *Principles of Psychology*. After Darwin published his theory of natural selection, Spencer contributed the catchphrase *survival of the fittest* to summarize its effective principle—a term that Darwin somewhat reluctantly adopted and that quickly caught on in the public mind. Further, Spencer's own ideas—which had previously not attracted great attention—took on a new plausibility and popularity because of their association with Darwin's theory.

In an ambitious program Spencer called "synthetic philosophy," he attempted to subsume the diverse disciplines of biology, psychology, sociology, and anthropology under a basically evolutionary view. He argued that individual organisms, species, political systems, and entire societies are alike in that all tend to evolve from relatively simple and homogeneous entities into complex and heterogeneous ones. He believed such evolution to constitute highly desirable "progress," with its presumed vehicle being unbridled *competition* among the individual units, in which only the fittest survive and perpetuate their kind. Accordingly progress of all kinds should be maximized by societies and governments that allow free competition to reign in all spheres of activity. This idea accorded particularly well with the capitalistic spirit of a United States, where Spencer's doctrine of social Darwinism became tremendously popular and was seen as justification for a system of unregulated free enterprise. Virtually any business practice, however predatory, could be rationalized as beneficial because it presumably contributed toward the survival of the "fittest" and the subsequent evolution of society.

Darwin himself held reservations about Spencer and his synthetic philosophy, writing that "his fundamental generalisations . . . partake more of the nature of definitions than of laws of nature."[39] Had he lived to see them, Darwin undoubtedly would have deplored the excesses of unbridled capitalism committed in the name of social Darwinism. Indeed, these excesses soon enough became evident to almost everyone and led to the demise of social Darwinism everywhere, even in America.

Comparative Psychology and Individual Differences

Within the developing discipline of psychology, Darwin had a much more permanent and positive influence. Given the evolutionary interrelatedness of all species posited by his theory, human psychological functions could no longer be viewed as isolated or unconnected with their animal counterparts. Thus, in Darwin's wake the study of animal behavior assumed a new importance. Shortly before his death, he granted full access to his voluminous notes on animal behavior to a younger friend, **George J. Romanes** (1848–1894). Romanes added to these notes with research of his own and published two groundbreaking books: *Animal Intelligence* (1882) and *Mental Evolution in Animals* (1883) Romanes described his work as constituting a **comparative psychology**—a name chosen by analogy to the established discipline of comparative anatomy. Romanes argued that the study of the similarities and differences among various animals' psychological functions could shed light on their human counterparts in the same way that previous study of their physical structures had. Although Romanes's work was subsequently criticized for being too anecdotal and for too often attributing humanlike states of consciousness to lower animals, the specialty of comparative psychology has remained an important branch of the general field.

Within human psychology, Darwin's theory demanded that the brain, the mind, and behavior in general could no longer be looked at as static "givens" merely to be described and analyzed. All of them had to be understood both as "functional" entities aiding the adaptation of the individual to the environment and as potentially transmutable phenomena that may be modified or replaced with future evolution. Within the field of visual sensation, for example, Christine Ladd-Franklin (whom we met in Chapter 5) introduced a Darwinian perspective by hypothesizing that the differing "components" of color vision arose at differing points of evolutionary development: black-white first, then blue-yellow, and finally red-green.

Further, since evolution proceeds by the natural selection of inheritable variations within breeding populations, the entire issue of variation and *individual differences* among people assumed great importance; such variation and differences presumably constitute the basis for the future evolution of humanity. Thus, after Darwin, human psychology inevitably became more "functional" and "differential"—that is, more concerned with the uses and adaptive significance of psychological phenomena and more focused on questions of variability and differences among people, as opposed to their generality or similarity. We shall see in the next chapter how Darwin's cousin, Francis Galton, laid many of the more specific foundations for the new functional and differential psychology.

Recent Developments: Emotions, Sociobiology, and Evolutionary Psychology

Darwinian evolutionary theory has continued in recent times to exert profound influence on many aspects of psychologically related research. Within the field of emotion research, for example, recent work by American psychologist Paul Ekman has empirically validated Darwin's contention in *The Expression of the Emotions* that there are indeed "emotional universals"—that is, remarkable cross-cultural agreement on the facial expressions that indicate fear, anger, disgust, sadness, and enjoyment. Different aspects of expression, however, appear to be culture-specific, and large individual differences exist in the details of the facial expressions associated with these emotions.

Like any scientific theory, evolution by natural selection has inevitably encountered certain problematic issues regarding its details, which scientists continue to debate. For example, biologists have recently been divided over the question of whether evolution always proceeds gradually by minutely small steps, as Darwin believed, or whether genetic mutation can produce rather sudden and dramatic "jumps" in the evolutionary succession.

The explanation of *altruistic behavior* has posed another debatable issue for evolutionary theorists. Individuals who jeopardize their own well-being for the sake of others—sometimes even sacrificing their lives—would logically seem to be at a selective disadvantage when compared to completely self-centered individuals. So the question arises as to why altruism, an apparently "maladaptive" characteristic, does not disappear as a result of natural selection. One suggested answer to this question sets the unit of evolution as the *group*, rather than the individual; that is, groups of interbreeding individuals with many altruistic members might be expected to survive and prosper better than groups without them. A different approach, stimulated partly by increasing knowledge about the structure of DNA, hypothesizes that the basic evolutionary unit is the individual *gene*. Because altruistic acts are most often performed in the service of individuals who are genetically similar to the actor, the net effect of such acts would be to favor the survival and propagation of genes like one's own. This approach, applied to a wide range of social behaviors, came to wide public prominence with the publication of E. O. Wilson's *Sociobiology: The New Synthesis* in 1975 and Richard Dawkins's bestseller *The Selfish Gene* in 1976. This basic approach, attempting to account for social behavioral traits as the result of individual but interacting genes tending to replicate themselves throughout successive generations, came to be known as **sociobiology**.

Sociobiology aroused considerable controversy, partly because it was seen by some as implying an excessive *biological determinism* of many social behaviors, and a corresponding neglect of cultural and social factors. Within the biological community, work has continued on the group-selection hypothesis, which remains a plausible alternative or complement to gene selection for many characteristics. And among psychologists, a field known as **evolutionary psychology** has developed whose practitioners go beyond sociobiology and freely use all aspects of modern evolutionary theory to devise empirically testable hypotheses about human behavior. In developing their hypotheses, evolutionary psychologists have emphasized the argument that the environment most humans live in now differs strongly from the environment of our ancestors. Therefore, one must consider how human behavioral and psychological traits might have been adaptive in the past, and not just whether they are adaptive now. Further, many evolutionary psychologists suggest that the "mind" is not a single unified entity but rather a diverse collection of independently evolved "modules" acquired by the brain, each one an adaptation to a particular set of evolutionary pressures. The capacity for language, the tendency to avoid incest, and phobic reactions to snakes and spiders are examples of such modules. Given their independence of each other, and changes in the environments that originally produced them, these modules may sometimes conflict with one another or lose their adaptive values. Evolutionary psychologists have also acknowledged that a broad and flexible intelligence is among the most important of human evolved adaptations and that the particular behavior generated by a module may be influenced by cultural and educational factors. The general case for this extremely broad field was made in the 1992 book *The Adapted Mind: Evolutionary Psychology and the Generation of Culture*, edited by Jerome Barkow, Leda Cosmides, and John Tooby. Stephen Pinker's bestselling *How the Mind Works* brought the approach to wide public attention in 1997.[40]

Sociobiologists, evolutionary psychologists, and evolutionary scientists in general continue to debate and study many specific questions. Despite their disagreement and uncertainty about many specific details, however, they overwhelmingly agree that Darwin's general conclusion that evolution by natural selection did occur, and is responsible for the vast proliferation of life forms on earth, is correct. Certain self-styled "creation scientists" still try to exploit the technical debates and uncertainties among evolutionary theorists while promoting a literalist interpretation of creation much like that prevailing before 1859. That view remains unconvincing, however, because like its predecessor it leaves many more important problems unsolved than Darwinian theory does. The evolutionary perspective remains an essential and vibrant aspect of modern psychological research and theorizing.

Summary

Charles Darwin's theory of evolution by natural selection has had far-reaching impact not only in many scientific disciplines but on the way we think about ourselves as human beings, our relationships with each other, and our society. Darwin's systematic observations of a number of features of the natural world during his voyage on the *Beagle*, combined with his previous exposure to theories by his grandfather **Erasmus Darwin**, French zoologist **Jean-Baptiste Lamarck**, English geologist **Charles Lyell**, and theoretical economist **Thomas Malthus**, led to his proposal of a mechanism whereby evolution could occur—namely, **natural selection**. He suggested that the environment constantly selects the individuals best suited to that environment to survive and thus propagate. Over generations, changes and variations in the natural environment have produced countless localized changes in selection pressures, leading to the gradual evolution of thousands of species. Darwin further argued in *The Descent of Man* that human beings have descended from animal ancestors and noted in *The Expression of the Emotions* that some of our human emotions betray our evolutionary "animal" past.

Several aspects of Darwin's theory of evolution by natural selection influenced the form and content of scientific psychology. The theory's general emphasis on adaptation and function proved congenial especially to early psychologists in the United States, whose work quickly took on a functionalist cast. The importance of individual variation as the "raw material" for evolution provided the foundation for individual differences psychology, and Darwin's contention that animals and humans are related on a continuum provided a rationale for comparative psychology. Further, his detailed observations of the development of his own infant son constituted one of the earliest "baby biographies," later to become a staple in developmental psychology. Finally, Darwin's theory itself has spawned the whole field of evolutionary psychology, in which using his ideas to explain current behaviors, attitudes, and characteristics has become a cottage industry.

Key Pioneers

Darwin, Charles Robert, p. 231

Darwin, Erasmus, p. 233

Galton, Francis, p. 250

Henslow, John Stevens, p. 235

Hooker, Joseph, p. 247

Huxley, Thomas Henry, p. 249

Lamarck, Jean-Baptiste, p. 244

Lyell, Charles, p. 239

Malthus, Thomas, p. 245

Paley, William, p. 243

Romanes, George J., p. 267

Sedgwick, Adam, p. 235

Spencer, Herbert, p. 259

Ussher, James, p. 239

Wallace, Alfred Russel, p. 247

Key Terms

argument from design, p. 243

catastrophism, p. 239

comparative psychology, p. 261

complementarity hypothesis, p. 254

evolutionary psychology, p. 264

monogenesis, p. 252

natural selection, p. 246

polygenesis, p. 252

sexual selection, p. 253

social Darwinism, p. 259

sociobiology, p. 263

theory of evolution by natural selection, p. 233

uniformitarianism, p. 239

variation hypothesis, p. 254

Discussion Questions and Topics

1 Describe some of the observations that Darwin made during his voyage on the *Beagle* that contributed to the formulation of his theory of evolution by natural selection.

2 Why would Darwin's theory have been controversial in its time? In what ways does it remain controversial for some people today?

3 After *Origin of Species*, Darwin wrote a number of other books and articles that had relevance for psychology. We discuss a few of these in this chapter. Describe how these works influenced psychology, in Darwin's time and today.

Suggested Readings

Charles Darwin's published journal for the *Beagle* voyage and *The Origin of Species* are both highly recommended and are available in several paperbound editions. A good, representative collection of excerpts from his major writings is found in Mark Ridley, ed., *The Darwin Reader* (New York: Norton, 1987). For Darwin's own account of his life, see *The Autobiography of Charles Darwin, 1809–1882*, edited by his granddaughter Nora Barlow (New York: Norton, 1969)

For a biography with details not only about Darwin's life but also about the intellectual and social environment in which he created his theory, see Adrian Desmond and James Moore, *Darwin* (New York: Norton, 1993). And for the most complete biography, see the two volumes by Janet Browne: *Charles Darwin: Voyaging* (New York: Knopf, 1995) and *Charles Darwin: The Power of Place* (New York: Knopf, 2002).

Howard E. Gruber's *Darwin on Man: A Psychological Study of Scientific Creativity* (London: Wildwood House, 1974) provides an excellent discussion of Darwin's psychological ideas. In 2009 the *American Psychologist*, the flagship journal of the American Psychological Association, published a special issue with nine articles on "Charles Darwin and Psychology" to commemorate the 200th anniversary of Darwin's birth (vol. 64, no. 2).

The Measurement of Mind

Francis Galton and the Psychology of Individual Differences

Galton's Early Life and Career

Darwinian Theory and *Hereditary Genius*
The Normal Distribution
Pedigrees of Genius
Studies of Adoptive Versus Biological Relatives

The Nature-Nurture Controversy

Eugenics
Intelligence Tests
Statistical Correlation and Regression
Other Contributions

Galton's Influence and Continuing Controversies
Twin Studies and the Nature-Nurture Issue

Summary

Key Pioneers

Key Terms

Discussion Questions and Topics

Suggested Readings

7

London's International Health Exhibition of 1884 featured a curious exhibit called an **Anthropometric Laboratory** (see Figure 7.1), which attracted many spectators. Enclosed behind a wall of trelliswork that afforded onlookers a partial view inside, the laboratory contained several strange-looking contrivances laid out on a long bench. As spectators watched, a volunteer subject would enter the laboratory and manipulate the device at one end of the bench while consulting with an attendant. After a minute or two, the attendant wrote something down on two small cards, and the subject

FIG 7.1 The Anthropometric Laboratory

moved on to the second contrivance. The procedure continued at each stop along the bench, after which the attendant filed one of the cards away and gave the other to the subject to keep. Subjects invariably left studying their cards with keen interest, and by the Exhibition's end more than 9,000 spectators had been sufficiently intrigued by what they saw behind the trellis to pay a fee of three pence and become subjects themselves.

For their time and money, subjects received both the gratification of contributing to science and some comparative information about themselves. Each of the devices measured or tested them in some way, and the cards recorded the subjects' personal scores as well as the averages obtained by people who had gone before. Scores reflected the subjects' head size and other physical measurements, as well as their performance on several tests of reaction time and sensory acuity.

Surprisingly, from a present-day perspective, these tests were thought of by their inventor as *mental* tests, measuring aspects of *intelligence*. Today we take it for granted that intelligence involves "higher" mental processes such as thinking, reasoning, and logic, and we may find it hard to see how physical variables such as reaction time or sensory acuity could possibly be thought of as measuring intelligence. Yet the tests' inventor did have a plausible, if ultimately misguided, rationale for them.

He reasoned that people with the highest intellectual abilities must have the most powerful and efficient nervous systems and brains. He thought that the power of a person's brain would probably be related to its size, so his first and simplest test of presumed natural intelligence was to measure head size (which presumably reflected the size of the brain within). He further thought people's neurological efficiency must be related to the *speed* with which they can respond to things, and so included a test of reaction time.

He defended his tests of sensory acuity by arguing: "The only information that reaches us concerning outward events appears to pass through the avenue of our senses; and the more perceptible our senses are of difference, the larger the field on which our judgement and intelligence can act." He further shared two incorrect but widely held prejudices that suggested to him a rough correlation between sensory acuity and intelligence. First, he believed that mentally retarded people were deficient sensorily as well as intellectually: "They hardly distinguish between heat and cold," he wrote, "and their sense of pain is so obtuse that some of the more idiotic seem hardly to know what it is." Second, like many other Victorian males, he assumed that women were generally less intelligent than men, and he argued that they have less acute senses as well. Otherwise how could one account for the fact that women seldom held jobs requiring fine sensory discrimination, such as piano tuning, wool sorting, or wine tasting? Ungallantly, he added: "Ladies rarely distinguish the merits of wine at the dinner-table, and though custom allows them to preside at the breakfast-table, men think of them on the whole to be far from successful makers of tea and coffee."[1] Accordingly, he felt justified in trying to assess "intelligence" by measuring subjects' relative abilities to bisect a line, discriminate weights and colors, and hear high-pitched sounds.

Note that these earliest "intelligence tests" involved measures and phenomena that had been very important in the recent rise of experimental psychology—only with a new twist. Fechner's psychophysics had explored the limits of sensory discrimination, and Wundtian mental chronometry experiments had carefully measured reaction times. But these earlier studies had aimed at establishing *general* psychological principles, applicable equally to all people, while evading or dismissing issues of **individual differences** in acuity or reaction time. The Anthropometric Laboratory's founder, by contrast, operated within the new Darwinian framework that emphasized variability and adaptation. For him, individual differences in acuity or reaction time were not "errors" or "irregularities" to be smoothed over or avoided, but the very machinery of evolution and therefore the object of prime interest.

His Darwinian orientation came naturally, for **Francis Galton** (1822–1911; Figure 7.2) was a younger cousin and friend of Charles Darwin. At age 22, Galton had inherited a substantial fortune that enabled him to devote his entire life to his personal interests. Typical of many upper-class Victorian men, Galton often demonstrated a smugness and insensitivity to the position of women and others less privileged than himself. In other respects, however, he was extraordinarily atypical. An energetic, humorous, and above all *curious* individual, he had been a noted explorer, geographer, meteorologist, and biological researcher before turning his lively attention to the measurement of intelligence and other psychological attributes.

FIG 7.2
Sir Francis Galton
(1822–1911)

Many of Galton's psychological ideas—like his theory of intelligence testing—turned out to be incorrect or overly simplified. Some of them played a role, after his death, in social movements and policies that were controversial at best and that extended to the atrocities of Nazi Germany. But these negatives should not mask the fact that Francis Galton numbers among modern psychology's great pioneers. His theories also provided several positive foundations on which others could build. He pioneered the very *idea* that tests could be used to measure psychological differences among people. He also offered provocative theories about the origins of those psychological differences and prescribed controversial social policies intended to foster positive psychological qualities in the general population. He elevated the scientific study of individual differences to the level of a major psychological specialty with important social implications. Many of the general issues he raised well over a century ago still preoccupy psychologists today. We turn now to their origins, in the context of Galton's life story.

Galton's Early Life and Career

Francis Galton was born in Birmingham, England, on February 16, 1822, his wealthy banker father a descendant of founders of the Quaker religion and his mother a Darwin—the younger half-sister of Charles Darwin's father. Francis received his earliest education at home from an older sister and under her doting care seemed a child prodigy as he read and wrote before the age of 3, mastered the rudiments of Latin and arithmetic by 5, and quoted knowledgeably from the *Iliad* and the *Odyssey* by 6. At 5, he said his life's wish was to win honors at the university, a goal denied earlier generations of Galtons because as Quakers they could not take the Anglican vows then required at Oxford and Cambridge. Raised as an Anglican, Francis would not be so barred.

But despite his promising start, Galton was no happier or more successful than Charles Darwin had been when sent to traditional schools that emphasized discipline, rote learning, and the classics. His schoolboy diaries recounted floggings, canings, punitive assignments, fights with local boys, and general hell-raising—but contained hardly a single reference to a scholarly or intellectual idea. He did well only at mathematics, a subject considered less important than classics.

At 16, Galton, like Darwin, was removed from school (to his great satisfaction) and enrolled as a medical pupil at Birmingham General Hospital. Also like his half-cousin, he experienced the horrors of operations without anesthesia and confronted disease and death daily. But unlike Darwin, he lacked confidence that his father would support him in yet another change of plans, so he gritted his teeth and adapted to the situation. He recalled in his autobiography: "The cries of the poor fellows who were operated on were . . . terrible, but only at first. It seemed after a while as though the cries were somehow disconnected with the operation, upon which the whole attention became fixed."[2] A tendency to "objectify" other people—seeing them as cases to be studied or examples to be counted, as opposed to fellow beings to be sympathized with—remained with Galton for the rest of his life, and undoubtedly contributed to some of the weaknesses as well as the strengths of his later psychological theorizing.

Medical training also provided Galton ample opportunity to indulge his exceptionally lively curiosity. Required to prepare medicines and pills in the pharmacy, he could not resist trying out small quantities of his creations on himself. Samples of poppy-seed and herbal licorice proved quite delightful, while a decoction of quassia wood chips proved to be "an experiment that I recommend to the notice of students who may wish to taste the *ne plus ultra* of bitterness." He started taking small doses of all the medicines listed in the pharmacopoeia, beginning with the letter A. He found this "an interesting experience, but it had obvious drawbacks. . . . I got nearly to the end of the letter C, when I was stopped by the effects of Croton oil. I had foolishly believed that two drops of it could have no notable effects as a purgative and emetic, but indeed they had, and I can recall them now [as he wrote his autobiography 60 years later]."[3]

At 18, Galton interrupted medical training to attend Cambridge University, where he hoped to fulfill his childhood wish by winning high honors in mathematics. There he became caught up in Cambridge's intensely competitive examination system, the culminating event of which was the Mathematical Tripos Examination, held each January for that year's graduating class. Survivors of this weeklong ordeal, which entailed 44 hours of writing in an unheated room at the coldest time of year, were precisely ranked from first to last, with the top 35 or 40 finishers earning the title of "wranglers." Keen interest always focused on who would take the top or senior wranglership, with university personnel often laying wagers on the outcome as if it were an athletic contest.

Galton, a better mathematician than a classicist, entered Cambridge with hopes of emerging as a high wrangler. He became keenly interested in the university's examination procedures and noted approvingly that the tripos grading system sharply differentiated the top scorers from the rest of the class. In one class ahead of his own, for example, the first and second wranglers had been "very far superior to the rest, for the second wrangler was 1000 marks ahead of the 3rd wrangler, and the getting of 500 marks only entitles a man to be a Wrangler."[4] This observation helped convince Galton that the very best people in a given field tend to be almost in a class by themselves, and it later contributed to his belief in the normal, or bell-shaped, distribution of human ability (with many people clustered around the average, and diminishing numbers toward the extremes).

On his own early, non-honors examinations, Galton obsessively compared his performance with that of his fellows. At first he did well enough to keep up hopes of an eventual wranglership, but at the end of his second year he had a second-class finish in a university-wide examination. A severe emotional breakdown followed, in which "a mill seemed to be working inside my head. I could not banish obsessing ideas; at times I could hardly read a book, and found it painful even to look at a printed page."[5] Recovery came slowly, and only after Galton had abandoned all thought of competing for honors. He graduated from Cambridge in 1844 with an ordinary or "poll" degree like Darwin's, and then resumed medical study in London. His spirit seemed broken, however, and when his father died in 1845 and left him a substantial fortune, Galton abandoned formal study forever.

For the next several years Galton joined the idle rich. He hunted and gambled, tried the dangerous and not-quite-respectable sport of ballooning, and traveled extensively from Scandinavia in the north to Egypt and the Sudan in the southeast. Such aimless activity failed to satisfy him, however, and finally in April 1849 he consulted a London phrenologist for a reading—based on the shape of his head—of his "natural" abilities, aptitudes, and inclinations. The shrewd phrenologist, undoubtedly relying on more than just the shape of Galton's head, reported that brains constituted like his innately lacked "much spontaneous activity in relation to scholastic affairs" but were ideally suited for more vigorous activity. "It is only when rough work has to be done that all the energies and capacities of minds such as this are brought to light," he advised.[6]

This judgment probably comforted Galton, who could now attribute his mediocre academic record to lack of innate scholarly ability rather than lack of effort or moral fiber. And the assurance that he had natural strengths in more practical fields stimulated Galton positively: Reflecting that he already enjoyed travel and had the financial resources to do so in a really major way, he decided to become an African explorer.

After consulting with the Royal Geographical Society, Galton left England on April 5, 1850, and returned exactly two years later after exploring previously unmapped territory in the part of southwest Africa now called Namibia. He found he had a talent for precise measurement on this expedition, using heliostat, sextant, and other surveying instruments to take readings for a highly detailed and accurate map of the country. He indulged his penchant for measurement rather more unorthodoxly after encountering some African women whose figures (he confided to his brother) "would drive the females of our native land desperate. . . . I sat at a distance with my sextant, and . . . surveyed them in every way and subsequently measured the distance of the spot where they stood—worked out and tabulated the results at my leisure."[7] Galton encountered one native African group whose habits and character he praised, and he recognized wide differences among individuals, but many of his descriptions of native Africans were decidedly Eurocentric and, from today's perspective, racist. Although he was scarcely the only Victorian explorer to express such views, they were by no means universal and they reflected a tendency from the start to emphasize innate as opposed to acquired or learned differences in character.[8]

For his detailed map and geographical measurements of the country, Galton won the Royal Geographical Society's gold medal for 1853. That same year he published *Tropical South Africa*, an entertaining book about his expedition that first put him in the public eye. His cousin Charles Darwin, whom he had not seen in several years, wrote a note of congratulations: "I last night finished reading your volume with such lively interest that I cannot resist the temptation of expressing my admiration. . . . What labours and dangers you have gone through!" Darwin who at this time had formulated but not yet published his epochal theory of evolution, added a typically modest personal note: "I live in a village called Downe . . . and employ myself in zoology; but the objects of my study are very small fry, and to a man like you accustomed to rhinoceroses and lions, would appear infinitely insignificant."[9] The cousins remained in friendly contact thereafter, but Galton would have to await *The Origin of Species* in 1859 before learning the exact nature of Darwin's "infinitely insignificant" studies.

Galton's successful expedition gained him entry into the governing councils of the Geographical Society, and for ten years he busied himself productively with geography, travel, and meteorology. He helped plan many of the epic African expeditions to locate the source of the Nile, including those of Burton, Speke, Grant, and Livingstone. He developed new and improved instruments for geographical measurement and in 1855 wrote a handbook for travelers in the wild, *The Art of Travel*. This classic guide subsequently went through eight editions and offered practical advice on such diverse subjects as pitching a tent in the sand, preventing one's asses from braying all night, and avoiding the rush of an enraged animal.

In the early 1860s Galton turned to another subject of great interest to travelers, and everyone else besides: the weather. He had the bright idea to collect simultaneous weather information from many different places and represent it on the world's first *weather maps*. From his early maps, he discovered the alternating patterns of high- and low-pressure systems now known to determine weather changes. For this meteorological accomplishment alone, Galton earned an honorable place among Victorian scientists. But beginning in the early 1860s, he turned his attention in yet another direction—with momentous consequences for the sciences of biology, genetics, statistics, and psychology. The stimulus for this shift was his cousin's *Origin of Species*.

Darwinian Theory and *Hereditary Genius*

As surprised as the rest of the world by Darwin's great work, after reading it Galton immediately wrote his cousin to say: "Pray, let me add a word of congratulations on the completion of your wonderful volume. . . . I have laid it down in the full enjoyment of a feeling that one rarely experiences after boyhood days, of having been initiated into an entirely new province of knowledge which, nevertheless, connects itself with other things in a thousand ways."[10] For some time, however, Galton was also troubled by the book. His previously orthodox religious faith and literal belief in the Bible were shattered, and for several years he experienced symptoms of an emotional breakdown. But gradually, some implications of Darwinian theory combined with his own predilections to create a guiding vision that Galton pursued for the rest of his long life.[11]

Although Darwin had not discussed human beings in *The Origin of Species*, Galton quickly grasped its implication that humans must be constantly evolving like other species. Moreover, he believed the most distinctive human variations, and those most likely to form the basis of future evolution and development, were *intellectual* and *psychological* in nature—although presumably mediated by small inheritable differences in the structure of the brain and nervous system.

Galton's personal experience had already led him to believe that individual differences in intelligence must be primarily innate. He himself had had high academic aspirations and had come from a wealthy family and good environment, yet despite these advantages he had been unable to win the honors he wanted at Cambridge. More successful students thus must have exceeded him in innate "natural ability."

Galton had also observed that intellectual eminence tends imperfectly but markedly to run in families. His own family had now produced two scientific superstars in Erasmus and Charles Darwin, along with many other figures of lesser but still substantial distinction. Other notable families such as the Bachs in music, the Brontës in literature, and the Pitts in politics easily came to mind. After reading Darwin's book, Galton decided to exercise his penchant for measuring and counting and to approach this issue statistically. He examined biographical dictionaries similar to the *Who's Who* volumes of more recent times and calculated that people who achieved sufficient eminence to be listed in them represented a proportion of about one in 4,000 from the normal population. Galton next examined the family trees of samples of these eminent individuals, and found that about 10 percent had at least one close relative also sufficiently eminent to be listed in a biographical dictionary. Even accounting for the fact that each person has many relatives, this percentage represented a far greater number of eminent relatives than would be expected by chance. Here was concrete empirical evidence of the statistical tendency for eminence to run in families.

Galton recognized that such evidence alone could not logically prove that the ability necessary for eminence is *inherited*, because members of a family tend to share similar environments as well as similar heredity. One could argue that these were the more effective causes—and indeed this general heredity-environment question remains strongly alive today. But Galton was predisposed from the outset to emphasize the hereditarian side of the story, and when he presented his detailed statistical findings of eminent families in the 1869 book *Hereditary Genius*, he boldly stated: "I propose to show in this book that a man's natural abilities are derived from inheritance, under exactly the same limitations as are the form and physical features of the whole organic world."[12]

Galton's book went on to offer three new arguments in support of this contention, based on the normal distribution of intellectual qualities, the specific patterns of eminent relatives Galton most frequently observed, and the comparison of adoptive versus biological relatives.

The Normal Distribution

In the first part of his case, Galton argued that measures of intellectual ability tend to fall into statistical distributions similar to those of inheritable physical traits. The great Belgian statistician **Adolphe Quetelet** (1796–1874) had earlier shown that measurements such as height or weight, when collected from large populations, invariably fall into bell-shaped, **normal distributions**, like the one illustrated in Figure 7.3. In such distributions, many more measurements fall in the middle ranges than at the extremes, and successive scores tend to be more widely separated from one another at the extremes.

The greater dispersal of measurements in the tail of a normal distribution reminded Galton of Cambridge tripos examination results, in which top wranglers had scored *far* higher than anyone else. To confirm this observation he obtained the distributions of raw examination scores for the top 100 candidates in two successive Cambridge tripos exams and showed that the 200 raw scores ranged from a high

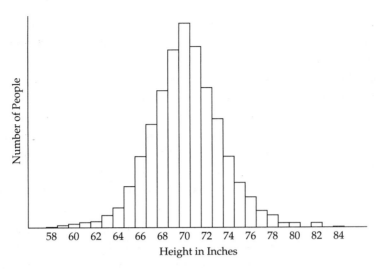

FIG 7.3 An example of a normal distribution: Height measurement for 300 adult men

of 7634 to a low of 237; the highest score exceeded the second highest by more than 2000, while more than half of the population fell in the range from 500 to 1500 total points. Thus the scores in fact approximated an upper tail of a normal distribution (with most of those who would have been in the lower tail presumably not even taking the honors exam). Mathematical ability—at least as measured by the Cambridge examinations—seemed to fall in a distribution closely resembling the known distributions of inheritable physical variables such as height or weight.

Of course, resemblance does not prove identity, and in fact it is now well known that normal distributions characterize innumerable variables that are not hereditary. Galton's study had still been worth doing, because had the distribution not turned out to be normal, it would have counted against his hypothesis. But once again his observations were merely *consistent with* his thesis, without offering positive proof of it.

Pedigrees of Genius

Galton's second new line of argument—derived from a close analysis of the family trees of eminent people—had a similar limitation. He examined the family trees of twelve groups of eminent people (Judges of England, statesmen, great military commanders, writers, scientists, poets, musicians, divines, painters, top classical scholars, champion oarsmen, and champion wrestlers) and found two general patterns throughout.

First, the eminent relatives of eminent people tended to be close rather than distant: first-degree relations (sibling or parent-child) appeared four times more frequently than second-degree relations (grandparents, grandchildren, nephews-nieces, or uncles-aunts), who were in turn four times more likely than third-degree relations (great-grandparents, cousins, etc.). Even third-degree relations, however, occurred more frequently than would have been expected by chance. This pattern again duplicated that for inherited physical variables: Fathers and sons tend to resemble each other in height more than grandfathers and grandsons do, and they in turn are more similar than average cousins.

Second, Galton found an imperfect but clear tendency for relatives to excel in the same fields. Thus the eminent relatives of eminent writers were most often writers too, although they also showed eminence in other occupations with greater than chance frequency. Such would be expected, Galton argued, if the requisite "natural ability" for each particular field were some complex combination of physical, mental, and emotional characteristics, each one separately and partially inherited. Each offspring of an eminent parent would then inherit *some proportion* of the requisite qualities for eminence in that same field, but not necessarily the full complement.

Note again, however, that one might expect exactly the same patterns of results if the major familial advantages predisposing to eminence were environmental rather than hereditary. Close relatives share environments to a greater degree than distant relatives do, and any specific environmental factors conducive to success in particular fields should expectably be found in some families more than others.

Studies of Adoptive Versus Biological Relatives

In *Hereditary Genius* Galton acknowledged but minimized the possibility that environmental advantages within eminent families could have helped produce his results, insisting that "social advantages are incompetent to give eminent status to a man of moderate ability."[13] He probably had himself partly in mind as he wrote that, recalling his own disappointing academic career in spite of his socially advantaged background. He went on to suggest a research design that, if properly implemented, promised to offer concrete evidence for his contention. This approach involved the comparative study of adoptive relations of eminent people.

Galton observed that Roman Catholic popes had once commonly "adopted" young boys to be brought up in their own privileged households as their "nephews." Such boys thus shared the environmental but not the genetic advantages of their patrons, and Galton wondered whether they went on to attain eminence to the same degree as the biological children of eminent fathers. He suspected they did not:

> I do not profess to have worked out the kinships of the Italians with any special care, but I have seen amply enough of them, to justify me in saying that . . . the very common combination of an able son and an able parent, is not matched, in the case of high Romish ecclesiastics, by an eminent nephew and an eminent uncle.[14]

On this rather impressionistic basis, Galton concluded that social and environmental advantages count for much less than heredity in producing eminence.

Galton's *idea* of comparing similarities between adoptive versus biological relatives was a good one that has been used productively by many later generations of genetic researchers. But Galton's particular use of the idea left something to be desired. Not only did he fail to lavish the same statistical care on this analysis that he did elsewhere, but he also confined his study to a small and unusual sample of questionable general representativeness.

In general then, Galton's three lines of evidence in *Hereditary Genius* were consistent with his hereditarian thesis, but they did not prove it conclusively. Nevertheless, he succeeded in presenting the thesis clearly and graphically, and henceforth it would have to be taken seriously by hereditarians and environmentalists alike.

The Nature-Nurture Controversy

Unsurprisingly, Galton received mixed reviews for *Hereditary Genius*. On the positive side, Charles Darwin liked the book and wrote privately to say, "I do not think I have ever in my life read anything

FIG 7.4
Alphonse de Candolle
(1806–1893)

more interesting and original." Publicly, in his subsequent *Descent of Man*, Darwin wrote: "We now know, through the admirable labours of Mr. Galton, that genius which implies a wonderfully complex combination of high faculties, tends to be inherited."[15]

The eminent Swiss botanist **Alphonse de Candolle** (1806–1893; see Figure 7.4) responded more critically. Like Galton, de Candolle came from an old and distinguished scientific family and in fact had been listed along with his father and grandfather among the eminent relatives in *Hereditary Genius*. Unlike Galton, however, he was highly impressed with the importance of environmental and cultural factors in perpetuating successful families like his own.

To test his view, de Candolle collected biographical information on more than three hundred eminent European scientists, which he analyzed statistically in his 1873 book, *History of the Sciences and Scientists over Two Centuries*. In it he conceded that heredity plays a certain role in creating scientific excellence, but he also showed clearly that eminent scientists came disproportionately from small to moderate-sized countries with moderate climates, democratic governments, tolerant religious establishments, and thriving commercial interests. Here was concrete evidence for the power of environment, and de Candolle explicitly contrasted his findings with Galton's: "My accounts of the men of science have been gathered in a different manner from those of Mr. Galton. I employed more complete biographical documents . . . and thus flatter myself to have penetrated farther into the heart of the question."[16]

A piqued Galton wrote de Candolle complaining of "the injustice you have done to me" but also confessed to being impressed by the depth and originality of the research. "I feel the great service you have done in writing it," he generously concluded, "and shall do what I can to make it known, as it ought to be, in England." De Candolle responded with a conciliatory statement of his own: "If there escaped from me, in the 482 pages of my book, one phrase, one word making it possible to doubt my respect for your impartiality, your character, and your talent for investigation, it could only have been in error and contrary to my intentions." He added that they basically disagreed not about facts, but their interpretation: "I have had the advantage of coming after you, and while it was not difficult for me to confirm with new facts the influence of heredity, . . . I never lost sight of the other causes, and the remainder of my researches convinced me that they are generally more important than heredity."[17]

De Candolle's book and letters stimulated Galton to carry out his own further study of scientists, to try to sort out the effects of heredity and environment in their backgrounds. He devised an extensive questionnaire asking for detailed personal information and distributed it to 192 Fellows of the Royal Society who had gained distinction for their scientific work. This marked the first time the now-ubiquitous **self-questionnaire method** had systematically been used to investigate a major psychological issue. The questionnaire items ranged from the social, religious, and political backgrounds of the respondents and their parents to their hair color and the size of their hats. Respondents rated themselves and their relatives on psychological qualities such as "energy of mind," "retentiveness of memory," and "studiousness of disposition." They described their educational experiences, with special emphasis on factors that had led them to science. And they answered the three questions that Galton regarded as the heart of his questionnaire: "Can you trace the origin of your interest in science in general and in your particular branch of it? How far do your scientific tastes appear to have been innate? Were they largely determined by events after you reached manhood, and by what events?"

Galton received completed forms from 104 of his 192 subjects, a majority of whom declared their taste for science as innate. Typical replies: "As far back as I can remember, I loved nature and desired to learn her secrets," and "I was always observing and inquiring, and this disposition was never checked or ridiculed."[18] These responses, naive and unsubstantiated though they might seem to a skeptical environmentalist's eye, nevertheless satisfied Galton that most of the scientists had been *born* with the requisite tastes and aptitudes for their craft. Hence he concluded that the predominant causes must have been hereditary.

But some other responses led Galton to make one important concession to de Candolle. Many scientists cited experiences or influences that presumably *strengthened* or *reinforced* their scientific inclinations: Darwin's opportunity to travel on the *Beagle*, for example, or Huxley's youthful apprenticeship to a doctor. Further, a disproportionate share of the eminent scientists were Scottish, and the Scots much more frequently than the others cited their formal education as a positive factor. This finding seemed evidence for an environmental cause, as Scottish public education was notably broader and less focused on classics than its English counterpart. As a result, Galton moderated his hereditarianism slightly, maintaining that inherited tastes and aptitudes were necessary but not sufficient causes of scientific talent, requiring at least a modicum of support from the environment before being fulfilled.

In writing up this study, Galton contributed incidentally but importantly to the language of science. He had long been looking for a pair of convenient terms to denote the separate effects of heredity and environment and in one early article had written of them as "race" versus "nurture." While analyzing his questionnaire data, however, Galton apparently recalled a short section of de Candolle's book that criticized many popular uses of the word *nature,* and argued that one of its few legitimate usages was as an opposite of *art* or *artifice*. Soon thereafter Galton adopted the euphonious catchphrase "nature and nurture," which he called "a convenient jingle of words, for it separates under two distinct heads the innumerable elements of which personality is composed. Nature is all that a man brings with himself into the world; nurture is every influence that affects him after his birth."[19] The phrase caught on, and ever since 1874 biologists and psychologists have used it to differentiate innate developmental factors from environmental ones.

Galton himself used the phrase in the subtitle of his 1874 book describing the questionnaire study results: *English Men of Science: Their Nature and Nurture.* In the book he acknowledged that both nature and nurture had influenced the lives and careers of his subjects, while maintaining that the former had been relatively more important than the latter.

Galton also recognized that nature and nurture can often *interact* with each other in complicated ways, however, and he sought some means of sorting them out for separate appraisal. To this end he shortly devised the **twin study method**—a research technique that remains at the heart of behavior genetics today and that he introduced in an 1875 article titled "The History of Twins, as a Criterion of the Relative Powers of Nature and Nurture."

The essence of this method lay in the fact that there are, biologically speaking, two different kinds of twins. Some twin pairs develop from the separate fertilization of two ova by two sperm, while others are produced when a single fertilized ovum splits in half and the two halves develop into separate embryos. The first type, today called **fraternal (or dizygotic) twins**, bear the same genetic similarity to each other as ordinary brothers and sisters, with an average of 50 percent of their genes in common. The other—**identical (or monozygotic) twins**—are genetically identical to each other. Galton—who himself had a pair of identical twins as nephews and a fraternal pair as an aunt and uncle—decided to conduct a broader survey of different twin pairs.

He solicited detailed case histories from all the twin pairs he could locate, without initial regard for their type. More than a hundred different pairs responded, and he found that a significant number of their reports fell into two general categories. Some, including his nephews, had gone through life showing marked similarity to each other psychologically as well as physically, in spite of having experienced quite different life circumstances. Other pairs, however, grew up to be markedly different from each other, even when they had been deliberately treated alike by their parents. Galton lacked direct evidence regarding the biological type of these twins but reasoned that these two categories were exactly to be expected if character and physique had been strongly determined by heredity and less so by environment. Genetically identical monozygotic twins *should* develop similarly regardless of differences in their nurture, while fraternal twins should differ as ordinary siblings do, even when treated alike. Thus, Galton concluded that his first category must have been composed of primarily monozygotic twins, and his second category of dizygotic types. He confidently asserted, "There is no escape from the conclusion that nature prevails enormously over nurture when the differences in nurture do not exceed what is commonly to be found among persons of the same rank in society and in the same country."[20]

Galton did not address the possibility that genetically identical twins who start out *looking* alike may consequently be *treated* alike, so their similarities might logically have been produced by nurture as much as nature. Nor did he note that any differences that do occur between identical twins *cannot* be attributed to heredity, since they are identical in that respect. And because some differences inevitably arose even between the most highly similar pairs, here was positive proof of an environmental effect of some kind. Thus, Galton's twin study introduced an ingenious but still inconclusive approach to the complex issue of nature versus nurture. As we shall soon see, more elaborate and sophisticated replications of the technique have been performed by later generations of scientists, with highly interesting results. But even so, environmentalists and hereditarians continue to differ about the proper way to interpret twin studies, and the nature-nurture controversy remains almost as unsettled today as when Galton and de Candolle debated it over a century ago.

Eugenics

Almost from the outset of his interest in Darwinian theory, Galton had been possessed by a utopian vision, whose ultimate practicability depended on the correctness of his hypothesis concerning hereditary ability. He clearly if crudely expressed its central idea in the opening paragraph of *Hereditary Genius*:

> As it is easy . . . to obtain by careful selection a permanent breed of dogs or horses gifted with peculiar powers of running, or of doing anything else, so would it be quite practicable to produce a highly-gifted race of men by judicious marriages during several consecutive generations.[21]

A few years later, Galton coined the name **eugenics** for this project of improving the human race through selective breeding.

As we have seen, Galton easily convinced himself (if not everyone else) that human ability is in fact strongly inheritable. This belief suggested to him that eugenics should be a workable reality. For the second half of his long life, eugenics became Galton's consuming passion—quite literally a substitute for the orthodox religious faith he had abandoned after reading Darwin's challenge to the literal interpretation of the Bible. Almost everything he did related in some way to this central vision, and with great imagination and versatility he developed dozens of ideas, many of which had implications beyond their original eugenic purposes. Two of the most important for the history of psychology were **intelligence tests** and the concept of **statistical correlation**.

Intelligence Tests

To create a eugenic society, Galton believed it necessary to encourage the most highly able young men and women to intermarry and have children at a greater rate than parents of lesser abilities. But how was one to identify these eugenic parents? Ideally, Galton thought they should be men and women like those he had studied in *Hereditary Genius*, whose concrete accomplishments and contributions to society had marked them for eminence. But those kinds of accomplishments usually occurred in middle age or later, and Galton sought a means of identifying potentially eminent people at a younger age, while still within their childbearing prime.

As early as 1865, Galton envisioned the development of competitive eugenic examinations to be administered by the state to all young men and women of prime marriageable age. He half-humorously described a future awards ceremony "in which the Senior Trustee of the Endowment Fund would address ten deeply-blushing young men" to congratulate them on having taken the highest places on an examination measuring "those qualities of talent, character, and bodily vigour which are proved, on the whole, to do most honour and best service to our race." Ten young women would also have been selected in a parallel examination measuring "grace, beauty, health, good temper, accomplished housewifery and disengaged affections, in addition to noble qualities of heart and brain." Should these young paragons agree to marry each other, the queen herself would give away the brides at a state wedding, and—of paramount importance—the government would provide ample funds for the care and education of the "extraordinarily talented issue" that would undoubtedly flow from the marriages.[22] In this fanciful scene, we find the first published statement of the idea (although not yet the name) of intelligence tests.

Of course, it was one thing to *imagine* the existence of valid examinations of hereditary ability and something else again to develop them in reality. Galton devoted intermittent attention to the problem for many years, until at last in 1884 he established his Anthropometric Laboratory for London's International Health Exhibition. As we saw at the beginning of this chapter, there he tried to measure people's hereditary intelligence by means of a series of simple tests of head size, reaction time, and sensory acuity.

In due course, Galton's specific tests were found not to work. High scores failed to correlate with meaningful, real-life intellectual accomplishment. The first successful intelligence tests had to await the development of altogether different procedures by the French psychologist Alfred Binet, based on assumptions very different from Galton's. That story shall be told in Chapter 13. For now, it is sufficient to note that Galton originated the *idea* of intelligence testing in a eugenic context and made it seem an important scientific project worth being taken up by others. From his day onward, the whole issue of intelligence testing has been inextricably connected with genetics, eugenics, and the nature-nurture controversy.

Statistical Correlation and Regression

Galton's concern with heredity and eugenics led to another important innovation—this one of a statistical nature—when he sought to express the relative strengths of various hereditary relationships with mathematical precision. Heredity obviously involves variables that *tend* to be associated with one another, although to less than perfect degrees. Tall fathers tend to have tall sons, for example, but only rarely are their heights exactly the same. Between grandfathers and grandsons, the average resemblance is even less, although it is still greater than chance. Galton sought an exact means of expressing and comparing these cases of partial or imperfect association between variables.

His solution emerged gradually over many years, and began, characteristically, with his measuring, counting, and obtaining some large empirical databases to work with. He planted peas of varying sizes and compared the sizes of offspring with those of their parents. In his Anthropometric Laboratory, he solicited families to come in and be measured on height, weight, and several other physical traits, in addition to the tests described earlier.

After poring over these sorts of data for countless hours, Galton developed the habit of casting them in the form of **scatter plots** like the one shown in Figure 7.5, which records the heights of 314 adult children and their parents.[23] Before preparing this particular plot, Galton had multiplied all females' heights by 1.08 to render their average equal to males'; he then calculated a "mid-parent's" height for each child as the mean of the father's and corrected mother's

Children's Heights (Mean = 68.0″)

Parents' Heights (Mean = 68.1″)	63″	64″	65″	66″	67″	68″	69″	70″	71″	72″	73″
72″							1	2	2	2	1
71″				2	4	5	5	4	3	1	
70″	1	2	3	5	8	9	9	8	5	3	
69″	2	3	6	10	12	12	2	10	6	3	
68″	3	7	11	13	14	13	10	7	3	1	
67″	3	6	8	11	11	8	6	3	1		
66″	2	3	4	6	4	3	2				
65″											
Mean Height of parents in Each Column	67.2	67.3	67.4	67.6	67.9	68.2	68.4	68.8	69.1	69.3	

FIG 7.5 One of Galton's scatter plots

heights. Each cell of Galton's scatter plot records the number of cases for that particular combination: the 1 in the upper right-hand cell indicates there was one child between 72 and 73 inches tall with a "mid-parent" between 71 and 72 inches; the 3 diagonally adjacent signifies three children between 71 and 72 inches with mid-parents between 70 and 71 inches; and so on.

From scatter plots such as this, Galton discerned a pattern he called **regression toward the mean**—a forbidding-sounding expression meaning simply that extreme scores on one variable tend to be associated with scores closer to the mean on the other. Consider the eleven pairs of scores represented in the far left-hand column of Figure 7.5. The children all fall between 63 and 64 inches, so their mean height may be estimated as 63.5 inches; this value is 4.5 inches shorter than the average (68.0 inches) for all 314 children. The figure at the bottom of that column shows that the mid-parents of those eleven children had a mean height of 67.2 inches (calculated by averaging two cases of 65.5 inches, three of 6.5 inches, and so on up the column); this value is only 0.9 inch shorter than the overall parents' mean of 68.1. Thus, those parents' heights deviated from the overall mean in the same direction as their children's (both groups were shorter than average), but not as far; the parents' scores showed "regression" toward the population mean.

The pattern repeats throughout. For instance, the third column from the right lists thirty-four children between 70 and 71 inches whose average of 70.5 is 2.5 inches taller than the overall population mean. Their mid-parents' mean height of 68.8 inches, however, exceeds the overall parents' average by only 0.7.

Galton recognized a further mathematical quality of scatter-plotted data: If the means of each of the columns are represented by X's across a graph, they tend to array themselves into an approximately straight line he called a **regression line**. Figure 7.6 shows the regression line plotted from the data on children's and mid-parents' heights in Figure 7.5.

In a great insight, Galton saw that the *steepness* of any regression line will vary directly with the strength of the relationship between the two variables. This becomes clear after considering two "ideal" cases: a perfect relation between the variables, and a completely random relationship between them. The left-hand graph in Figure 7.7 shows the regression line for a hypothetical perfect relationship, which would occur if every child's height turned out to be exactly the same as his or her mid-parent's;

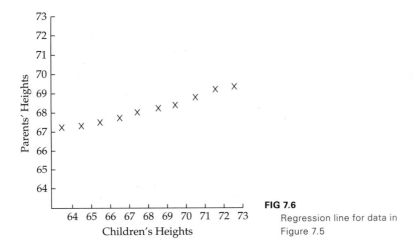

FIG 7.6

Regression line for data in
Figure 7.5

the line would form a perfect diagonal, with a mathematical slope of 1.0. But if children's heights bore absolutely no relation to parental stature, then all groups of children—short, average, and tall—would have mid-parents whose average height was close to the mean for the overall parents' group. The regression line in this case would be perfectly horizontal like the right-hand side of Figure 7.7, with a mathematical slope of 0.0.

Galton saw that for positively but imperfectly related variables—such as he expected regularly to find when investigating real-life hereditary relationships—the regression line's slope would always lie somewhere between these values of 0.0 and 1.0 (as it does in Figure 7.6). Moreover, he recognized in 1888 that if all scores were transformed into standardized statistical units (such as the "standard deviations" or "probable errors" that will be familiar to students of elementary statistics) before their regression lines were drawn, the mathematical slopes of their lines could be directly and uniformly interpreted as **coefficients of correlation**. These are numerically precise indices of the strength of the relationships: If the value lies close to 1—say, 0.8 or 0.9—it indicates a very strong correlation; a value near 0.5 signifies a moderate degree of association, and one close to zero shows a weak correlation.

Galton presented these ideas in a short 1888 paper titled "Co-relations and Their Measurement, Chiefly from Anthropometric Data."[24] The brilliant young mathematician **Karl Pearson** (1857–1936) subsequently took up these ideas and refined them, developing a convenient formula for computing "product moment" correlation coefficients

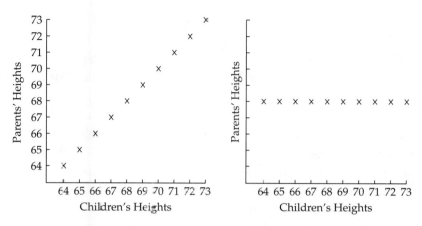

FIG 7 7 Two "ideal" regression lines

and extending their range to cover *negative* relationships (in which high scores on one variable are associated with low scores on the other). **Pearson's r**, as this statistic has come to be called, has become one of the most widely used of all statistical tools in psychological, biological, and sociological research. Its application extends far beyond the biological and hereditary relationships originally investigated by Galton to literally any situation in which one wonders about the degree of association between two measurable variables. Many modern investigators regard Galton's pioneering discussions of regression and correlation as his greatest gift to science.

Ironically, one of these extended applications of correlation ultimately demonstrated the failure of Galton's own approach to intelligence testing, described in the preceding section. When Pearson's r's were calculated between Galton's test scores and real-life measures of intellectual ability such as college grades, they turned out to be very low. Reaction time and class standing correlated at 0.02 in one study, for example, indicating the former was virtually useless in predicting the latter.[25] Alternative types of tests, producing higher correlations, had to be developed before intelligence testing could be taken seriously as a practical reality.

Other Contributions

Over the course of his long life, the versatile and inventive Galton conducted scores of other inquiries that related directly or indirectly to his consuming eugenic passion. Some of these, too, had important consequences.

Galton was among the first serious investigators of fingerprints, which he hoped would prove to have an inherited basis. He developed the method of classifying prints (into "loops," "arches," and "whorls") that was first adopted by Scotland Yard and that remains in standard use by police agencies today.

Closer to psychology, Galton also devised questionnaires to study individual differences in **mental imagery**, asking subjects to imagine various scenes and then to describe their images in detail as to brightness and color, distinctness, apparent location, and the like. He found wide individual differences, with some subjects literally "seeing" their images with almost the same distinctness as a real scene and others reporting only abstract "thoughts" that had no visual properties at all. Galton's questionnaire became a standard instrument for studying mental imagery for many years. His major finding—that normal people vary widely in the frequency, intensity, and vividness with which they imagine things—has been widely replicated.

Another important study focused on associations, something obviously created by experience and representing one of Galton's few explicit concessions to the nurture side of the nature-nurture controversy. Galton invented the **word-association experiment**, writing down seventy-five different stimulus words on paper slips, then drawing the slips in random order and recording the first two or three thoughts that came to his mind after each stimulus. He went through his list four times and discovered that many of his associations recurred repeatedly and often dated from events in childhood. He did not find the rich variety of associations he had expected, and commented, "The roadways of our minds are worn into very deep ruts." The task in general seemed "repugnant and laborious," as many of his associations proved to be anxiety arousing or embarrassing. He declined to publish his associations verbatim, noting simply that "they lay bare the foundations of a man's thought with curious distinctness, and exhibit his mental anatomy with more vividness and truth than he would probably care to publish to the world."[26] Although Galton himself never carried these ideas further, the journal in which they appeared in 1879 was read by the young Viennese doctor Sigmund Freud; it is likely Galton's study was one of many sources of Freud's later development of the technique he called *free association*, which we shall describe further in Chapter 11.

Many of Galton's other studies were [...]
reflected his curiosity and inventivenes[...]
"composite portraiture," in which facial [...]
bers or members of the same groups [...]
insane, or tuberculosis patients) were su[...]
in an attempt to identify and accentua[...]
mon. He constructed "beauty maps" [...]
to which the best-looking inhabitan[...]
ment) came from London, the least [...]
ducted a statistical study of the efficacy of prayer, [...]
effects of influenza on imagination, tried (unsuccessfully) to do arithmetic by using only the sense of smell, and experimented systematically with different techniques of tea making. He pursued all of these
endeavors with the same enthusiasm and energy he had shown as a
young man.

Galton's always-lively writings won him a considerable reputation—
and in 1909 a knighthood. At age 87 he found the idea of being a knight
on horseback highly amusing and joked: "A precious bad *knight* I should
make now. Even seven years ago it required some engineering to get me
on the back of an Egyptian donkey! and I have worsened steadily since."[27]
But still the honor pleased him. Indeed, the elderly Galton looked back
on just one major life disappointment. Despite the fact that he had married according to the best eugenic principles, to an able woman from a
family nearly as distinguished as his own, they had been unable to have
children: an ironic caprice of fate that his eugenic science could not have
predicted. His consolation would have to be the prospering of his intellectual as opposed to his biological descendants.

Galton's Influence and Continuing Controversies

Few individuals have influenced as many different disciplines as
Galton did—from geography, meteorology, and biology through statistics, criminology, behavior genetics, and psychology. He remains
one of the most important figures in the history of psychology. Twin
studies, questionnaire studies, correlational studies, and investigations of imagery and association remain the lifeblood of much

nological research, to say nothing of the vast industry with intelligence testing.

Besides being influential, Galton and his ideas have also continued highly controversial. We continue to speak of the nature-nurture controversy" even though almost everyone agrees that both factors are significant, and there continues to be debate about the relative contributions of each. Also, unfortunately, *race* has often become a confounding, acrimonious issue in the controversy. Galton himself contributed to this, as his writings sometimes expressed a casual racism that, while more characteristic of the Victorian age than of our own, was nonetheless significant.[28] While recognizing wide individual differences in abilities within all ethnic populations, he believed there were significant *average* differences among the populations, with white Europeans topping the list. Several years after his death, some of Galton's eugenic ideas were adopted and perverted by self-proclaimed "race hygienists" in Nazi Germany and were used to promote the holocaust.

Twin Studies and the Nature–Nurture Issue

On the scientific front, a major Galton-inspired controversy has continued to be prominent as psychologists have debated the relative contributions of nature and nurture to intelligence, as measured by IQ tests. By the 1920s behavior geneticists recognized that a virtually perfect indication of the "heritability"* of any trait, including IQ, can potentially be obtained from the study of **separated identical twins**, provided two important conditions are met. The first condition is that the twins must be demonstrably monozygotic, sharing identical genetic makeups. The second and much more problematic condition is that they must have been truly and genuinely *separated* in earliest childhood and placed *randomly* in a representative selection of foster homes. If—and only if—these conditions are fully met and the twins' IQs (or any other variables one is interested in studying) are measured in adulthood, the correlation between their IQs will provide an exact measure of the heritability of that trait.

---

* "Heritability" denotes the proportion of *variance* within a given population that is attributable to hereditary as opposed to environmental factors.

The problem, of course, is that in reality the condition of complete separation and random foster home placement is virtually never met. Adoption agencies always make strong efforts to keep siblings, and especially twins, as close together as possible, and in most cases if they must be separated they are placed in different branches of the same families. Further, the agencies make every effort to ensure that adoptees are not placed in impoverished or obviously pathological homes. Thus, in the vast majority of cases that have been available for study, the twins have been only partially "separated," and the range of environments in which they have been raised has been more restricted than in the general population.

The first major study of "separated" twins was published in 1937 by the team of **Horatio Newman** (1875–1957), a biologist; **Frank N. Freeman** (1880–1961), a psychologist; and **Karl Holzinger** (1893–1954), a statistician.[29] After a strenuous search they identified and studied nineteen pairs of identical twins who had been reared in separate households, although with varying degrees of contact with each other. The correlation of these twin pairs' IQs turned out to be .67—strongly positive, but far from absolute. Because the twins' degree of separation and random placement were less than perfect, their environments were not perfectly independent, and the correlation undoubtedly inflated the heritability estimate to some degree.

The study's main interest and charm, however, lay not in its bare cumulative result but in its detailed case studies, complete with photographs, of all nineteen pairs. Consider "Ed" and "Fred," for example, who "discovered" each other after a friend of Fred's spotted Ed in a distant city from his home and mistook him for his friend. Acting on this hint, and with distant childhood memories of having a twin brother, the two got together and subsequently volunteered to be part of the study. They had been born in a New England town and adopted by different local families of similar social status but who did not socialize with each other. For a short time they attended the same school before both families moved away to different states. On rediscovering each other in early adulthood, they found that they had led very similar academic and occupational careers, and when tested they had very similar IQs. Another striking case was that of "Reece" and "James," who were adopted by separate branches of their biological parents' families, one of which lived in an impoverished and isolated

FIG 7.8
James (left) and Reece at
26 years of age

mountain community and did not communicate with the other, a sol-idly middle-class, small-town family. James, the mountaineer boy, grew up to have a poor academic record, had little occupational suc-cess, and had scrapes with the law. Reece fared much better in all regards and as a young adult had an IQ some 20 points higher than that of his identical twin (see Figure 7.8).

Investigation of the nineteen case histories demonstrated that those twin pairs who had been placed in the most obviously dis-similar environments—for example, Reece and James—showed the largest differences in their adult IQs. Here was clear evidence for an environmental effect of some sort, complementing or modifying the equally clear evidence for a genetic effect. The authors summarized their results by saying:

> If, at the inception of this research project over ten years ago, the authors entertained any hope of reaching a definitive solution of the general nature-nurture problem . . . in terms of a simple formula, they were destined to be rather disillusioned. . . . We feel in sympathy [with the] dictum that what heredity can do environment can also do.[30]

Other studies of separated twins since Newman, Freeman, and Holzinger's have used larger numbers of cases and more sophisticated test measures, but with generally similar results: raw IQ correlations in the .60s and .70s but with few cases of complete twin separation and a positive association between the degree of separation and dif-ference in the twins' IQs.[31] For a brief time in the 1960s an exception to these results seemed to be provided in publications by the eminent British psychologist **Sir Cyril Burt** (1883–1971), who deliberately represented himself as Galton's intellectual successor. Burt claimed to have identified a sample of separated twins who had been placed completely randomly into a full socioeconomic range of adoptive families—something no other investigators had been able to do. He further reported intelligence test correlations of about .80—indicating a *much* stronger effect of nature than of nurture. For a short time these results were considered definitive by many psychologists, and nature seemed to have the upper hand. It was soon noted, however, that Burt never provided any details about his cases, or even about the specific tests supposedly used, and after his death no raw data were found among his papers. His study seems to have been essentially fictitious, either the result of deliberate fraud or of wishful thinking by an aging Galtonian.[32]

In more recent times a large study of separated twins has been ongoing at the University of Minnesota. The authors report IQ correlations in the .70s but acknowledge that extremely few of their subjects had been reared in impoverished or illiterate families and that their results "should not be extrapolated to the extremes of environmental disadvantage still encountered in society." They conclude: "In the current environments of the broad middle class, two–thirds of the observed variance in IQ can be traced to genetic variation."[33] Here is a nearly exact echo of Francis Galton's assertion in 1875, following his own much more informal study of twins, that nature prevails over nurture "when the differences in nurture do not exceed what is commonly to be found among persons of the same rank in society and in the same country."

The point, which both Galton and the Minnesota scientists made implicitly, is that when environment and nurture are equalized or optimized within a population, the observed variation of characteristics within that population will be largely determined by nature. When the environments are very *un*equal, however (as is the case in so much of the real world), the relative contribution of nurture is much greater. A corollary of this point is that all estimates of "heritability," no matter how precisely measured, refer not to individuals but to specific *populations* of individuals. In Galton's case, when he compared himself to others in the socially privileged group of Cambridge undergraduates who competed for honors and found he was not among the very best, he could only blame his own relative lack of innate "natural ability." But of course when compared to the total group of young people in England at the time, or indeed in the entire world, the social and cultural advantages that enabled him even to be a participant in such a rarefied competition have to be seen as supremely important factors.

It is vital to keep these points in mind when assessing the disputes that continue to the present. Two of the most controversial and widely discussed books of the 1990s, Richard Herrnstein and Charles Murray's *The Bell Curve* and Arthur Jensen's *The g Factor: The Science of Mental Ability*,[34] adopt two of Galton's assertions as their fundamental premises: namely, that variations in intelligence are primarily innate and hereditary and that they occur in normal distributions (the "bell curve" of Herrnstein and Murray's title). This is not the place to detail the books' extensive arguments, or the critical responses they received. But clearly the nature-nurture controversy with respect to differences in human intelligence remains very much alive today and is still discussed in many of the exact terms introduced by Galton more than a century ago.

In the next chapter we shall return to the historical narrative and show how Galton's general ideas joined with those of Darwin in giving psychology a new "functional" and "differential" emphasis, especially as the new science developed in America.

Summary

Francis Galton introduced several important concepts regarding the nature and measurement of intelligence that became central to the scientific and applied efforts of later psychologists. Believing that individual differences in intelligence must be primarily innate, he hypothesized that intelligence would be reflected in the strength and size of the nervous system. Accordingly, he devised a series of anthropometric tests measuring such things as head size, reaction time, and sensory acuity that he felt would reveal individual variations in intelligence. Although this underlying theory proved incorrect, these measures were the first serious attempt to develop what we today call intelligence tests.

After reading his cousin Darwin's *Origin of Species*, Galton concluded that humans must be constantly evolving like other species and that variability was the substrate upon which natural selection must work. He believed that the human variations most likely to form the basis of future evolution and development were *intellectual* and *psychological*, and he set out to demonstrate that these qualities were heritable. He supported this contention by citing the **normal distribution** of intellectual qualities in the population, the tendency for intellectual eminence to run in families, and the comparison of adoptive versus biological relatives. He also pioneered the **twin study method** to assess the relative impact of genetics and environmental factors. All of these techniques, in more refined forms, became foundations for the field of behavior genetics. Although Galton recognized the existence of environmental factors and popularized the term *nature and nurture* to denote the interactions between heredity and environment, he consistently underplayed the importance of nonhereditary influences. Convinced of the supreme importance of heredity, he envisaged a program of **eugenics** in which the most gifted young people would be identified by intelligence tests and encouraged to intermarry and have many children. From Galton's time to today, the whole issue of intelligence testing has been inextricably linked with genetics, eugenics, and the nature-nurture controversy, sometimes with quite deleterious consequences. And although Galton himself emphasized positive eugenics (the identification and promotion of good qualities), some who came after him emphasized the negative side: seeking to eliminate presumably hereditary negative traits. This idea led, in some places, to the involuntary sterilization of the mentally deficient, and in Hitler's Germany to the enormities of the holocaust.

The versatile Galton also made notable contributions to statistical reasoning, including the notions of **scatter plots, regression toward the mean, regression lines,** and **coefficients of correlation** to visually and mathematically convey the relationship between variables in a population, or across two populations (such as children's heights and parents' heights). These innovations enabled Galton's follower **Karl Pearson** to develop a formula for computing correlation coefficients that extended their range to cover negative relationships. This statistic, the well-known **Pearson's** *r*, has become one of the most widely used of all statistical tools in psychological, biological, and sociological research.

Key Pioneers

Burt, Sir Cyril, p. 299
de Candolle, Alphonse, p. 283
Freeman, Frank N., p. 297
Galton, Francis, p. 272

Holzinger, Karl, p. 297
Newman, Horatio, p. 297
Pearson, Karl, p. 292
Quetelet, Adolphe, p. 279

Key Terms

Anthropometric Laboratory, p. 269
coefficients of correlation, p. 292
eugenics, p. 288
fraternal (or dizygotic) twins, p. 286
identical (or monozygotic) twins,
    p. 286
individual differences, p. 272
intelligence tests, p. 288
mental imagery, p. 294
normal distribution, p. 279

Pearson's *r*, p. 293
regression line, p. 291
regression toward the mean, p. 291
scatter plots, p. 290
self-questionnaire method, p. 284
separated identical twins, p. 296
statistical correlation, p. 288
twin study method, p. 286
word-association experiment,
    p. 294

Discussion Questions and Topics

1 As this chapter has highlighted, beliefs about the respective influence of heredity versus environment on intelligence have stimulated much research. Even though most scientists would concede that both nature *and* nurture are influential, it is clear that important social consequences arise out of each position. Describe the social implications of the extreme hereditarian view and the extreme environmentalist view of human intelligence.

2 Galton made several contributions unrelated to intelligence testing that were taken up in psychology. Describe these contributions and their significance.

3 Describe some of the ways in which Galton's personal experiences and life situation influenced his views on intelligence.

Suggested Readings

Reprinted editions have been issued of Francis Galton's *Hereditary Genius* (Gloucester, MA: Peter Smith, 1972) and *English Men of Science* (London: Frank Cass, 1974). Many of his important shorter works, including his studies of twins, anthropometric tests, association, and mental imagery, are reprinted in his *Inquiries into Human Faculty and Its Development* (New York: Dutton, 1907). Galton's highly readable autobiography is titled *Memories of My Life* (London: Methuen, 1908) for more on his life and work see D. W. Forrest, *Francis Galton: The Life and Work of a Victorian Genius* (London: Elek, 1974), and Nicholas W. Gillham, *A Life of Sir Francis Galton: From African Exploration to the Birth of Eugenics* (New York: Oxford University Press, 2001). Further discussion of Galton and his influence is included in Raymond E. Fancher, *The Intelligence Men: Makers of the IQ Controversy* (New York: Norton, 1985).

William James and Psychology in America

8

James's Early Life
James the Teacher

The Principles of Psychology
The Stream of Consciousness
Habit
Emotion
Will

James's Later Career and Philosophy of Pragmatism

Three Eminent Students: Hall, Calkins, and Thorndike
G. Stanley Hall
Mary Whiton Calkins
Edward Lee Thorndike

Summary

Key Pioneers

Key Terms

Discussion Questions and Topics

Suggested Readings

The well-attended Third International Congress of Psychology, held in Munich in 1896, signified that psychology had fully arrived on the world scene as a respectable scientific and academic discipline. Strangely, however, the two men who had been most responsible for the new science's growth—and who had been informally proclaimed the "psychological popes" of the old and the new worlds—both stayed away from the conference.[1] The old-world "pope" was Wilhelm Wundt, whose pioneering labors we reviewed in Chapter 5; his missing American counterpart was the Harvard professor **William James** (1842–1910; see Figure 8.1). James had

FIG 8.1
William James
(1842–1910)

taught the first American university courses on the new scientific psychology and in 1890 had vibrantly summarized the field in an acclaimed textbook, *The Principles of Psychology*. Less of a program builder but more of a popular communicator than Wundt, James helped create an intellectual climate in America highly receptive to the new science. Thanks largely to the efforts of Wundt and James in their home countries, Germany and the United States led the world in the numbers of psychologists and psychological laboratories they had produced.

Ironically, the two psychological popes did not highly esteem each other's work. Wundt found little new or original in James, except for a style that he judged overly personal and informal. "It is literature, it is beautiful, but it is not psychology," he grumbled about James's *Principles*.[2] Part of his dissatisfaction doubtlessly arose from James's treatment of his own work, for after praising the innovative features of Wundtian experimental psychology, the American had added acidly that it "could hardly have arisen in a country whose natives could be *bored*. . . . There is little of the grand style about these new prism, pendulum, and chronograph-philosophers. They mean business, not chivalry."[3]

In a private letter to a friend, James wrote even more acerbically:

> Wundt aims at being a sort of Napoleon of the intellectual world. Unfortunately he will never have a Waterloo, for he is a Napoleon without genius and with no central idea which, if defeated. brings down the whole fabric in ruin. When his critics make mincemeat of some one of his views by their criticism, he is meanwhile writing a book on an entirely different subject. Cut him up like a worm, and each fragment crawls; there is no vital center in his mental medulla oblongata, so that you can't kill him all at once.[4]

Just possibly, a touch of envy here colored James's outburst about Wundt's great literary productivity. Himself a slow writer, he had labored for twelve years on *Principles of Psychology*.

Obviously, a vast difference in personality style separated the mercurial James from the professorial Wundt, and much of their antagonism arose from this difference. But the difference in personality also correlated with a difference in the substance of the psychology each promoted. And for all of their individuality, Wundt and James were also each broadly representative of the different intellectual climates of their respective countries. The psychology that James fostered, and that flourished in America after him, had a character quite different from its continental counterpart. More personal and focused on the individual, and more practical than theoretical in its goals, American psychology still retains much of this distinctive character today.

In this chapter, we shall examine the development of modern American psychology by focusing first on the life and pivotal work of William James, and then turning to three of his most important students and successors.

James's Early Life

William James was born on January 11, 1842, in New York City, the eldest child in a family very wealthy by virtue of his grandfather's shrewd investment in the building of the Erie Canal. During his boyhood and adolescence, he and his family moved incessantly throughout America and Europe, as his unconventional father sought but never found the ideal place for bringing up his five children.

The father, Henry James Sr. (1811–1882), had led a materially privileged but spiritually troubled life. After attending Princeton Theological Seminary for two years, he had felt oppressed by the stern Presbyterian doctrines of predetermination taught there and dropped out. Despite his substantial inherited fortune, he had worried acutely about his lack of a meaningful vocation, especially during the years following his marriage to Mary Walsh in 1840. His life reached a dramatic crisis—one that would later be echoed by his eldest son—in 1844. The father vividly remembered his own crisis as follows:

> One day, . . . having eaten a comfortable dinner, I remained sitting at the table after the family had disappeared, idly gazing at the embers in the grate, thinking of nothing, and feeling only the exhilaration incident to a good digestion, when suddenly— in a lightning flash, as it were—"fear came upon me, and trembling, which made all my bones to shake." To all appearances it was a perfectly insane and abject terror, without ostensible cause, and only to be accounted for to my perplexed imagination, by some damned shape squatting invisible to me within the precincts of the room, and raying out from his fetid personality influences fatal to life. The thing had not lasted ten seconds before I felt myself a wreck; that is, reduced from a state of vigorous, joyful manhood to one of the most helpless infancy.[5]

Doctors could do nothing to help, and for two years Henry James Sr. remained prone to anxiety attacks and a constant sense that the foundations had been pulled from beneath his existence. Then he learned that the Swedish mystical philosopher Emanuel Swedenborg (1688–1772) had written about conditions like his, calling them "vastations." The elder James now read everything he could find by or about Swedenborg, and somehow this pursuit brought him the assurance he needed to recover from his breakdown. Moreover, he at last found his vocation and spent the rest of his life trying to communicate Swedenborgian philosophy to others in rather obscure lectures and books.[*]

---

[*] His opaque literary style hindered sales of his books and became something of an open joke among family and friends. Following publication of his book *The Secret of Swedenborg*, a friend quipped that he had not only found the secret, but also kept it.

Now Henry Sr. developed another consuming interest: the education of his children. William had been followed in turn by Henry Jr. (the future great novelist), Garth Wilkinson, Robertson, and Alice. Determined that they should have the best possible education, the father could never quite decide what that was. Consequently, he led them on an educational odyssey from private school to private tutor, from one continent to another and back again. Nothing ever worked out quite as he hoped. Throughout these numerous transitions, only the stimulating intellectual atmosphere of the James home remained an educational constant. Everyone was encouraged to engage in active discussion, to express opinions freely, and to defend them against lively familial opposition. Guests observed with amusement that the children, in the heat of dinner-table discussion, would sometimes leave their seats to gesticulate on the floor or to invoke humorous curses on their father, such as that "his mashed potatoes might always have lumps in them."[6]

Perhaps unsurprisingly, this vagabond and intellectually roistering lifestyle produced mixed effects. All five children became cosmopolitan and proficient in several languages, and the two oldest boys went on to become famous intellectual figures. The two younger sons seem to have felt intimidated and overshadowed by their seniors, however, and despite early promise they grew up unhappily susceptible to neurotic illness and alcoholism. Alice, the youngest child and only daughter, suffered worst of all Although extremely gifted, she was denied educational opportunity because she was female. And partly because so many of her contemporary males were killed in the Civil War, she was unable to do what her Victorian father thought women ought to do: marry and raise a family of her own. She grew up to become a chronic invalid, plagued by bouts of hysterical prostration and disturbing inclinations toward "knocking off the head of the benignant pater."[7] She produced a fascinating diary before her early death from cancer at age 43 and was unquestionably a prime victim of the restrictive gender attitudes of her time.

Even the ultimately famous oldest sons had problems. Henry Jr., born just fifteen months after William, was old enough to be a companion but young enough to feel perpetually overshadowed. Unable to match the venturesome antics and aggressive wit of his brother, he retreated into a world of books and literature. William himself, the oldest and thus the prime subject of his father's educational experiments, was always "out front" and under constantly vacillating paternal pressure. He wound up having just as much difficulty as his father in finding a vocation.

As a teenager, William showed considerable talent and inclination for drawing and art—a profession Henry Sr. did not find suitable. The father exerted both direct and indirect pressure to deflect this interest, moving the family away from William's art teacher and hinting that he might even commit suicide if his son persisted in an artistic direction. Finally in 1861, William was sent to Harvard to study chemistry—another field in which he had shown some interest and aptitude. But while Henry Sr. saw science as preferable to art as a career for his son, he also worried that it would lead William to adopt materialism and lose sight of the spiritual values he himself found so important. Unsurprisingly, William absorbed much of his father's ambivalence and indecision.

Once at Harvard's Lawrence Scientific School, William quickly shifted his interest from chemistry to physiology, a science just then making great strides under the mechanistic doctrines of the likes of Müller, Helmholtz, and Du Bois-Reymond. Soon afterward, the James family fortune showed its first signs of being finite, and William was forced to consider ways of eventually earning a living. Thus in 1864 he turned to applied physiological study and enrolled in Harvard's Medical School.

A year later he interrupted medical study to go on a specimen-hunting expedition to the Amazon led by **Louis Agassiz** (1807–1873), the eminent Harvard biologist and America's most outspoken critic of Darwin's recently published *Origin of Species*. James responded to the southward sea journey with seasickness to rival Darwin's on the *Beagle*. He wrote his family, "No one has a right to write about the 'nature of Evil,' or to have any opinion about evil, who has not been at sea."[8] His job in Brazil—the collecting and crating of jellyfish—failed to cheer him up before he was stricken with smallpox. He soon concluded he was not cut out to be a field biologist, and he returned home to resume medical study.

Now he suffered from a residual eye weakness from smallpox that made it difficult to read and from a lower back condition that made it painful to stand. Worse still, he felt oppressed by his family, who had moved to Cambridge and insisted he live with them. Privately he contemplated suicide, but in April 1867 he succeeded in convincing his father that he should go to Germany—both for its mineral spring baths for his back and for the opportunity to perfect his familiarity with scientific German.

James stayed in Germany for a year and a half, while his eyes improved more than his back and enabled him to meet at least his second goal. He read omnivorously in the German physiological literature, attended lectures by Du Bois-Reymond, and became even more impressed by the explanatory power of the new mechanistic physiology. He also read a 33-page article by a then little-known Heidelberg physiologist named Wilhelm Wundt, on "Recent Advances in the Field of Physiological Psychology." As noted in Chapter 5, this reading led him to report enthusiastically to a friend:

> It seems to me that perhaps the time has come for psychology to begin to be a science—some measurements have already been made in the region lying between the physical changes in the nerves and the appearance of consciousness. . . . I am going to study what is already known, and perhaps may be able to do some work at it. Helmholtz and a man named Wundt at Heidelberg are working at it, and I hope I live through this winter to go to them in the summer.[9]

James's frail back precluded travel to Heidelberg, so both his first meeting with Wundt and his personal antagonism toward him were postponed for several years. He returned home and went through the motions of completing his medical degree, outwardly full of enthusiasm but inwardly in despair. The new German mechanistic physiology had powerfully impressed him intellectually, but it oppressed him spiritually with its deterministic philosophical implications. The death of a favorite cousin depressed him further, and in the spring of 1870 he suffered a sudden crisis that he later recalled as follows:

> Whilst in a state of philosophical pessimism and general depression about my prospects, I went one evening into a dressing-room in the twilight to procure some article that was there; when suddenly there fell upon me without any warning, just as if it came out of the darkness, a horrible fear of my own existence.

> Simultaneously there arose in my mind the image of an epileptic patient whom I had seen in the asylum, a black-haired youth with greenish skin, who used to sit all day on one of the benches, . . . moving nothing but his black eyes and looking absolutely non-human. This image and my fear entered into a species of combination with each other. That shape am I, I felt, potentially. Nothing that I possess can defend me against that fate, if the hour for it should strike for me as it struck for him. There was such a horror of him, and such a perception of my own merely momentary discrepancy from him, that it was as if something hitherto solid within my breast gave way entirely, and I became a mass of quivering fear. After this the universe was changed for me altogether.[10]

This crisis remarkably resembled Henry James Sr.'s "vastation" of twenty-six years earlier. Like his father, William had been chronically worried about finding a vocation, and oppressed by a deterministic doctrine. And like his father's, his life too was instantaneously transformed by a sudden awareness of "that pit of insecurity beneath the surface of life" that left him feeling utterly prostrated and unable to work.

And again like his father, William James worked a gradual recovery and found a new purpose in life, partly through the chance exposure to some philosophical writings. On April 29, 1870, he read an essay on free will—precisely the agency that seemed to be denied by mechanistic physiology—by the French philosopher **Charles Renouvier** (1815–1903). The next day he confided in his diary:

> I think that yesterday was a crisis in my life. I . . . see no reason why [Renouvier's] definition of free will—"the sustaining of a thought *because I choose to* when I might have other thoughts"—need be the definition of an illusion. At any rate, I will assume for the present—until next year—that it is no illusion. My first act of free will shall be to believe in free will. . . . Hitherto, when I have felt like taking a free initiative, like daring to act originally, . . . suicide seemed the most manly form to put my daring into; now, I will go a step further with my will, not only act with it, but believe as well; believe in my individual reality and creative power.[11]

While James's decision to believe in free will occurred suddenly, a more gradual element in his recovery derived from his reading the British philosopher/psychologist **Alexander Bain** (1818–1903) on the subject of *habit*. In his 1859 book *The Emotions and the Will*, Bain had stressed the importance of *voluntary repetition* of morally desirable actions if they are to become habitual and automatic. Only after many repetitions, he argued, do permanent neural connections become established between the sensory impressions created by a given situation and a particular desirable response to it. Thus, desirable actions such as getting out of bed early in the morning may be difficult to perform at first, but after they have been assiduously repeated many times they become permanently impressed into the nervous system, and automatic. Bain emphasized the moral danger of allowing exceptions to occur while a habit is being formed, as "every gain on the wrong side undoes the effect of many conquests on the right."[12]

Combining the advice of Renouvier and Bain, William James tried to will himself to think more optimistic and less oppressive thoughts. And with repetition, the initially difficult reactions gradually became habitual. His trial adoption of a belief in free will lasted not just to the end of the year, but to the end of his life. In a curious way, his adoption of this most unmechanistic of beliefs freed him of his intellectual inhibitions and enabled him to regard the implications of the new mechanistic physiology and psychology even more seriously than before.

Gradually, he found he could entertain mechanistic ideas and take them seriously *scientifically*, without fully accepting them *personally*. In personal life it was useful to think and behave as if he had free will, while as a scientist it was useful to accept mechanistic determinism. Both views were essentially articles of faith, incapable of absolute proof or disproof. In the absence of any absolute criterion for judging their "truth," James decided to evaluate ideas according to their *utility* within specified and limited contexts. Thus, since free will seemed a useful concept in personal life, he would accept it as "true" there; determinism, useful scientifically, could be equally "true" when he functioned as a scientist. The evaluation of ideas relativistically, according to their varying usefulness in varying situations, eventually became a hallmark of James's general philosophy, which he later called **pragmatism**.

In the immediate aftermath of his crisis, however, James was still far from advancing a coherent philosophy. Although he had completed his medical training and had read widely in the new physiological and psychological sciences, he had never held a real job or completed a major independent project. Nearing 30 years of age, he still lived with his parents and remained dependent on them.

At last in 1872 he received a crucial vocational opportunity when Harvard's president, Charles Eliot, a Cambridge neighbor, invited him to teach half of a newly instituted physiology course. After much deliberation he accepted and did well enough to be asked to take over the entire course. He was on his way to becoming one of Harvard's most outstanding and legendary teachers.

James the Teacher

Once James got used to teaching, he effectively conveyed his personal involvement in ideas with infectious zest and treated his students as intellectual equals engaged in a common quest for knowledge. Unlike many of his authoritarian colleagues, James regularly walked to and from class with his students, constantly engaged in animated conversation. Noting his casual and informal manner, one visitor to his class thought him more like a sportsman than a professor.

A student recalled James's intense absorption in his subject as he lectured: "James would rise with a peculiar suddenness and make bold and rapid strokes for a diagram on the blackboard—I can remember his abstracted air as he wrestled with some idea, standing by his chair with one foot upon it, elbow on knee, hand to chin." Another student remembered a seminar held in James's own home, when he had trouble keeping his small portable blackboard within the full class's vision: "Entirely bent on what he was doing, his efforts ended at last in his standing the blackboard on the floor while he lay down at full length, holding it with one hand, drawing with the other, and continuing the flow of his commentary."[13]

Genuinely interested in his students' reactions to his classes, James solicited their written course evaluations many years before that became a common practice in university classrooms. Perhaps his most celebrated teaching episode involved the soon-to-be famous writer Gertrude Stein, one of his best students while a Radcliffe undergraduate. After looking at James's final exam questions, she wrote, "Dear Professor James, I am sorry but really I do not feel like an examination paper in philosophy today" and left the exam room. James responded, "Dear Miss Stein, I understand perfectly how you feel; I often feel like that myself" and awarded her the highest mark in the class.[14] (Stein's ploy is not recommended for students less secure in their professor's esteem than she obviously was.)

Preeminently, James succeeded as a teacher because of his personalized and lively approach to subject matter. No ivory tower professor, he constantly sought to extract from his subjects something useful for living. Having found philosophical and psychological ideas useful in resolving his own problems, he tried to make such ideas seem personally relevant to his students.

James regularly changed the subject matter of his courses as his own interests changed, teaching himself first and then transmitting the new information to his students. Initially hired to teach physiology and anatomy, he soon altered his course's title to "The Relations between Physiology and Psychology." Between 1878 and 1890, as he worked on *The Principles of Psychology*, he dropped traditional physiology altogether to focus exclusively on psychology. And as he became increasingly involved with philosophy after 1890, psychology in turn gradually disappeared from his course offerings. But while James's tenure as a "psychologist" was temporary and brief, it was extraordinarily influential. In his lectures, articles, and textbooks—particularly *The Principles of Psychology*—he made the new science come alive. Wundt had brought psychology to the university for specialists; James made it a living subject for anyone who chose to read or listen to him.

The Principles of Psychology

In 1878, just as James began to teach courses exclusively devoted to psychology, he contracted with the publisher Henry Holt to write a comprehensive textbook of the field. Already familiar with most of the German, French, and English literature on the subject, he confidently promised to finish it in two years. But by 1880 he had scarcely begun, and the project began to seem a dark cloud destined to hover over him indefinitely. Over the next several years he managed to write several journal and magazine articles on psychological subjects, and as the 1880s ended he realized he could shape these into chapters of his textbook. At last, in January 1890, he sent Holt the first 350 pages of manuscript, with assurance that the remaining 1,400 pages would soon follow. He thought Holt might wish to begin setting it in type immediately and seemed surprised when the publisher decided to wait for the rest before proceeding! But this time James was true to his word and actually completed the long manuscript within the next few months.

By now thoroughly sick of the project—which he characterized to his publisher as "the enormous *rat* which . . . ten years gestation has brought forth"—James showed that he could treat himself and his own work with the same acerbity he had directed at Wundt:

> No one could be more disgusted than I at the sight of the book. No subject is worth being treated of in 1000 pages! Had I ten years more, I could rewrite it in 500; but as it stands it is this or nothing—a loathsome, distended, tumefied, bloated, dropsical mass, testifying to nothing but two facts: 1st, that there is no such thing as a *science* of psychology, and 2nd, that W. J. is an incapable.[15]

Two aspects of this self-critique were partly correct: the book *was* huge, and it did reveal psychology as unsystematic and incomplete ("like physics before Galileo," James remarked in a letter to a friend). But it also revealed James as a master of English prose rather than "an incapable," and once published it quickly became the leading psychology text in English. The book succeeded for the same reasons his teaching succeeded: it stressed the personal utility and relevance of psychological ideas and used an unself-conscious frankness and naturalness in discussing them.

James's great text resists easy summarization. In twenty-eight chapters and nearly 1,400 pages, it touched on all of the major topics of the day's psychology, including brain function, habit, the stream of thought, the self, attention, association, memory, sensation, imagination, perception, instinct, the emotions, will, and hypnotism. We will here consider just a few of these subjects, to give the flavor of James's style.

The Stream of Consciousness

James's most famous psychological metaphor occurs in a chapter devoted to the **stream of thought** in which he argues that the contents of human consciousness are better likened to a *stream* than a collection of discrete elements or ideas. The Greek philosopher Heraclitus had observed that one can never enter twice into the same stream, for its fluid contents change constantly even while its banks and course remain much the same. Analogously, thought James, one can never have exactly the same sensation, idea, or other experience twice. Every new experience is inevitably molded and framed by all the old experiences that have gone before, and because this background constantly changes and enlarges, no two experiences can ever be precisely alike.

Further, James believed thought and a stream share the quality of *continuousness*. Even when gaps occur in consciousness, as from anesthesia, epileptic fits, or sleep, a subjective sense of continuity is maintained. The remembered experiences immediately before and after the periods of unconsciousness—"the broken edges of sentient life," as James put it—seem to "meet and merge over the gap, much as the feelings of space of the opposite margins of the 'blind spot' meet and merge over that objective interruption to the sensitiveness of the eye. Such consciousness as this, whatever it be for the onlooking psychologist, is for itself unbroken. It feels unbroken."[16]

James warned that thought's streamlike quality makes it foolish to analyze it introspectively in terms of static "elements," such as particular sensations or feelings. Real thought can never be "frozen" and studied analytically without doing damage to its essential nature:

> Let anyone try to cut a thought across the middle and get a look at its section, and he will see how difficult the introspective observation . . . is. The rush of the thought is always so headlong that it almost always brings us up at the conclusion before we can arrest it. Introspective analysis is in fact like seizing a spinning top to catch its motion, or trying to turn up the gas quickly enough to see how the darkness looks.[17]

James privately referred to psychologists such as Titchener (see Chapter 5), who persisted in trying to break consciousness down into static elements, as "barbarians." For James, psychology entailed the study of dynamic and constantly changing conscious processes.

Habit

In another famous chapter on the subject of "Habit," James stressed the enormously important influence of habitual responses for the maintenance of society:

> Habit is . . . the enormous fly-wheel of society, its most precious conservative agent. It alone is what keeps us all within the bounds of ordinance, and saves the children from the envious uprisings of the poor. It alone prevents the hardest and most repulsive walks of life from being deserted by those brought up to tread therein. . . . It dooms us all to fight out the battle of life upon the lines of nurture or our early choice, and to make the best of a pursuit that disagrees, because there is no other for which we are fitted, and it is too late to begin again. It keeps different social strata from mixing. Already at the age of twenty-five you see the professional mannerism settling down on the young commercial traveller, on the young minister, on the young counsellor-at-law. You see the little lines of cleavage running through the character . . . from which the man can by-and-by no more escape than his coat-sleeve can suddenly fall into a new set of folds.[18]

After emphasizing the power and inevitability of human habits, James characteristically proceeded to draw a lesson. Echoing the ideas of Alexander Bain that had so influenced his own life, he noted that the laws of habit formation are impartial, capable of producing either morally good or bad actions. And once a good or bad habit has begun to be established, it is difficult to reverse the course:

> Every smallest stroke of virtue or vice leaves its never so little scar. The drunken Rip Van Winkle, in Jefferson's play, excuses himself for every fresh dereliction by saying, "I won't count this time!" Well! *he* may not count it, and a kind Heaven may not count it; but it is being counted up none the less. Down among his nerve-cells and fibres the molecules are counting it, registering and storing it up to be used against him when the next temptation comes.[19]

James believed his university student audience still had just enough youthful flexibility left to counteract old bad habits and foster new good ones. Thus, he urged them to decide on some desirable behavior, and then practice it deliberately and repeatedly: "Never suffer an exception to occur till the new habit is securely rooted in your life. . . . Seize the first possible opportunity to act on every resolution you make. . . . Keep the faculty of effort alive in you by a little gratuitous exercise every day." A student who does so need have no anxiety about the upshot of his education: "If he keep faithfully busy each hour of the working-day, he may safely leave the final result to itself. He can with perfect certainty count on waking up some fine morning to find himself one of the competent ones of his generation."[20] Of course, this advice represented exactly the prescription James himself had followed in dealing with his personal crisis of 1870, when he willed himself to think undeterministic, free, and cheerful thoughts.

Emotion

Another chapter devoted to "Emotion" also derived directly from James's crisis and its resolution and introduced one of his rare original theoretical contributions to psychology. According to James, an emotion is actually the *consequence* rather than the cause of the bodily changes associated with its expression—a reversal of the common-sense view:

> Common sense says we lose our fortune, are sorry, and weep; we meet a bear, are frightened, and run; we are insulted by a rival, are angry, and strike. The hypothesis here to be defended says this order of sequence is incorrect, that the one mental state is not immediately induced by the other, that the bodily manifestations must first be interposed between, and that the more rational statement is that we feel sorry because we cry, angry because we strike, afraid because we tremble, and not that we cry, strike, or tremble because we are sorry, angry, or fearful, as the case may be.[21]

The Danish physiologist Carl Lange (1834–1900) published a similar view at just about the same time as James. To honor both men, the idea that emotions represent the perception of bodily reactions has traditionally been called the **James-Lange theory of emotion**.

As usual, James tried to derive practical lessons from his theorizing, including a technique for dealing with emotional distress:

> Whistling to keep up courage is no mere figure of speech. On the other hand, sit all day in a moping posture, sigh, and reply to everything with a dismal voice, and your melancholy lingers. There is no more valuable precept in moral education than this, as all who have experience know: if we wish to conquer undesirable emotional tendencies in ourselves we must assiduously, and in the first instance cold-bloodedly, go through the *outward movements* of those contrary dispositions which we prefer to cultivate. The reward of persistency will infallibly come, in the fading out of sullenness or depression, and the advent of real cheerfulness and kindliness in their stead.[22]

James himself had done precisely this to overcome depression during his youthful crisis. After repeatedly willing himself to *think* that he was free and cheerful, he began actually to feel that way. He had also followed this prescription after his parents' deaths in 1882, willing himself to act more cheerfully than he really felt until his grief gradually passed. The James-Lange theory is now recognized to have limitations, but for all its stiff-upper-lip oversimplicity, it can still usefully account for many aspects of emotional experience.

Will

James's personal experience shone clearly through one further chapter on the subject of "Will." In it he dealt openly with the question that had troubled him during his crisis: whether free will exists. He started by defining an act of will as one accompanied by some subjective sense of mental or attentional effort: "The most essential achievement of the will, . . . when it is most 'voluntary,' is to ATTEND to a difficult object and hold it fast before the mind. . . . Effort of attention is thus the essential phenomenon of will."[23] Then he asked whether the subjective sense of effortful attention is a completely mechanistically determined consequence of the thought process, or whether it introduces certain *non*mechanistic and *non*predictable influences of its own. Scientific psychology assumes the former to be true, while personal, subjective experience suggests the latter.

James believed that a true science has to postulate complete determinism, because under indeterminism, "science simply stops." Modern psychology's most impressive gains had occurred via the assumptions of mechanism and determinism. As long as he was writing as a psychologist and a scientist, James would accept the tenets of determinism and push them as far as possible. "Psychology will be Psychology, and Science Science, as much as ever (as much and no more) in this world, whether free will be true in it or not. . . . We can therefore leave the free-will altogether out of our [scientific] account." He hastened to add, however, that science "must be constantly reminded that her purposes are not the only purposes, and that the order of uniform causation which she has use for, and is therefore right in postulating, may be enveloped in a wider order, on which she has no claims at all."[24] Science and psychology did not and could not contain all the answers for James. Thus, when he was not functioning as a psychologist, but as moral philosopher or simply as a feeling, willing, and socially responsive human being, he could and would adopt a belief in free will.

Such was the essence of James's psychology: neither a finished system nor a provider of absolutely certain conclusions, but a collection of vivid and informed personal reflections on all of the major areas of the emerging new science. Students who read James not only learned the major facts in the new psychology but also were challenged to think about them in useful and creative ways.

James's Later Career and the Philosophy of Pragmatism

After 1890, James felt increasingly frustrated by the limitations and uncertainties of the science he had so brilliantly elucidated. He complained to a colleague that psychology was "a nasty little subject; . . . all one cares to know lies outside." His son recalled how he occasionally chafed at being personally identified as a "psychologist":

In June, 1903, when he became aware that Harvard was intending to confer an honorary degree upon him, he went about for days before Commencement in a half-serious state of dread, lest, at the fatal moment, he should hear President Eliot's voice naming him "Psychologist, psychical researcher, willer to believe, religious experiencer." He could not say whether the impossible last epithets would be less to his taste than "psychologist."[25]

James exaggerated his feelings in a typically colorful way, for he still carried on considerable psychological activity. He twice accepted the presidency of the American Psychological Association (in 1894 and 1904) and continued to write on psychology. In 1892 he abridged his textbook into a single volume titled *Psychology: Briefer Course.* Informally called "Jimmy" as opposed to its longer predecessor "James," it too met great success. In 1899 James applied his psychological ideas to pedagogy in *Talks to Teachers,* and three years later he explored the relationships between abnormal psychology and religious experience in *Varieties of Religious Experience.* He remained sufficiently interested in psychology to travel to Clark University in 1909, just before his death and at considerable expense to his health, "to see what Freud was like" when the founder of psychoanalysis made his only visit to America. (James had been the first American to call favorable attention to Freud and Breuer's early work on hysteria, in 1894. At Clark he was still impressed, but with reservations. Freud's ideas "can't fail to throw light on human nature," he wrote to a friend, "but I confess that he made on me personally the impression of a man obsessed with fixed ideas.")[26]

But still, psychology did become less prominent among James's activities after 1890. In 1892 he brought the German psychologist and former Wundt student **Hugo Münsterberg**[*] (1863–1916) to Harvard to assume major responsibility for scientific psychology, while he turned his own primary attention to other subjects.

One of them was psychic research, a topic much in the news of the time as several self-proclaimed "mediums" claimed the ability to communicate with departed spirits. Unlike the skeptical Wundt, who disdained such phenomena as unworthy of serious attention (see pp. 201–204), James became a leader in an organization devoted to the scientific investigation of "spiritistic" phenomena: the American

---

[*] See Chapter 15 for details about Münsterberg at Harvard.

Society for Psychical Research. James openly hoped to find convincing positive evidence for paranormal phenomena, but time and again his hard data proved inconclusive or worse. Once a hidden observer detected that Eusapia Faladino, a famous medium in whom James had invested particularly high hopes, produced her "psychic manifestations" through contortionist-like movements of her foot. Her séance came to an ignominious end when the observer seized her foot, inspiring one of James's friends to compose a poem:

> *Eeny, meeny, miney mo,*
> *Catch Eusapia by the toe,*
> *If she hollers, then you know,*
> *James's theory is not so.*[27]

James took the jibe in good spirit, and shortly before his death confessed that although he had devoted twenty-five years to psychical research,

> I am theoretically no "further" than I was at the beginning; and I confess that at times I have been tempted to believe that the Creator has eternally intended this department of nature to remain *baffling*, to prompt out hopes and curiosities and suspicions all in equal measure, so that, although ghosts and clairvoyances, and raps and messages from spirits, are always seeming to exist and can never be fully explained away, they also can never be susceptible of full corroboration.[28]

During the final decades of his life, James devoted his greatest attention to philosophy. As a young man he had joined with some Cambridge friends in a "Metaphysical Club" to discuss philosophical questions. There **Charles Sanders Peirce** (1839–1914) promoted a view he called *pragmatism*, according to which scientific ideas and knowledge can never be absolutely certain, but only subject to varying degrees of "pragmatic belief." That is, ideas *worked* with varying degrees of effectiveness in adapting to the world. Peirce and the other Metaphysical Club members enthusiastically adopted the new Darwinian worldview, according to which no adaptation to the world should be considered perfect or permanent but always subject to evolution or replacement by a better competitor. Peirce extrapolated this perspective to ideas and knowledge: Just as a biological trait that is adaptive in one environment may prove ineffective or danger-ous in another, or just as a once-successful species may be surpassed and overrun by a new and better-adapted one, so may ideas gain or lose their value depending on their particular "environments" and "competitors."

Of course, this attitude meshed nicely with James's personal convic-tions following his crisis; his decision to believe in free will was prag-matically adaptive and "correct" because it worked. Later, he had implicitly applied the pragmatic criterion to psychological theories in *Principles of Psychology*. Never interested in facts for their own sake, or theories in isolation from their context, he always stressed their usefulness (or lack thereof) in specific contexts.

Toward the end of his life, James expanded on the philosophical implications of this approach in numerous articles and books, includ-ing *Will to Believe and Other Essays* (1897), *Pragmatism* (1907), and *A Pluralistic Universe* and *The Meaning of Truth* (both 1909). Although he adopted Peirce's term "pragmatism" to define his phi-losophy, he extended its approach to include emotional, ethical, and religious ideas as well as scientific theories. Peirce disagreed with this elaboration of his philosophy and tried vainly to rename his own view "pragmaticism" to differentiate it from James's. This disagreement led one of James's biographers to declare, "The movement known as pragmatism is largely the result of James's misunderstanding of Peirce."[29] But whatever their origin, James's philosophical writings became very popular, and following his death from heart disease in 1910 no less a philosopher than Bertrand Russell described him as "one of the most eminent, and probably the most widely known, of contemporary philosophers."[30]

Three Eminent Students: Hall, Calkins, and Thorndike

Despite James's relatively brief and ambivalent tenure as a full-time psychologist, and the unsystematic and incomplete nature of his psy-chological work, he also had a huge impact on American psychology. His influence differed markedly from that of his fellow "pope" Wundt, however, for rather than building a school or a specific theoretical orientation to psychology, he created a general atmosphere about the subject that made it seem something interesting and worthwhile to pursue. Instead of training "followers" to carry forth with a "Jamesean" psychology, he inspired many students to develop their own individual approaches. Indeed, because he treated so many subjects as interesting but open and did not presume to offer more than "pragmatic" solutions to the problems he posed, his writings seem less obsolete than those of his contemporaries and can still be read for pleasure and stimulation today.

Thus, it is fitting to illustrate James's influence with sketches of three of his most important students, who all went on to contribute significantly to the development of American psychology in their own distinctive ways. **G. Stanley Hall** (1844–1924) encountered James at the very beginning of his teaching career. Nearly James's own age, and with an already established agenda of his own, Hall was not so much "taught" by James as assisted by him in the launching of his career. Hall went on to become something James was not—a major "founder" and institution builder for the new science in America. **Mary Whiton Calkins** (1863–1930), by contrast, met James just after *Principles of Psychology* had been published and got her real introduction to psychology from that work. As one of the first women to seek a career in psychology, Calkins faced appalling discrimination; James provided moral as well as intellectual support as she went on to become a president of the American Psychological Association. **Edward Lee Thorndike** (1874–1949) went to study with James after being inspired by *Principles*. James encouraged Thorndike to start a study of animal learning that subsequently became his Ph.D. thesis at Columbia, and one of the most cited papers in the history of American psychology. After James's death, Thorndike replaced him as the best-known psychologist in the country.

G. Stanley Hall

G. (for Granville) Stanley Hall (see Figure 8.2) was born near Ashfield, Massachusetts, the son of an educated farmer who had also taught school briefly and had served a term in the Massachusetts state legislature. His deeply religious mother had also been a schoolteacher and was pleased when Hall entered Union Theological Seminary in

FIG 8.2
G. Stanley Hall
(1844–1924)

New York after graduating from Williams College in 1867. She was less pleased when her son found the secular stimulation of the big city, and the controversial Darwinian theory then so much in the air, more appealing than theology. Hall recalled that after he preached his trial sermon to faculty and students at the seminary, the president did not offer a customary critique and commentary but instead knelt and prayed for the salvation of Hall's soul. Realizing his prospects must lie elsewhere, Hall borrowed money for three years of independent study in Germany, where he concentrated on philosophy but also studied physiology with the great mechanist, Du Bois-Reymond.

Running out of funds before he could take a degree, Hall returned to the United States in 1871. After losing one position because of his avowed Darwinian sympathies, he finally won a junior appointment teaching philosophy and religion at Antioch College in Yellow Springs, Ohio. While there he read Wundt's newly published *Principles of Physiological Psychology* and decided that the new experimental science of the mind was for him. He left Antioch in 1876 intending to go to Wundt in Leipzig, but en route he stopped off at

Harvard and was fortuitously offered an instructorship in English. He accepted, and although he found his duties arduous he also met William James. Just two years older than Hall and at the beginning of his own teaching career, James encouraged Hall to do an experiment on the role of muscular cues in the perception of space, which could serve as a Harvard Ph.D. dissertation. Hall did so, and although awarded nominally in Philosophy his degree actually represented the first American Ph.D. based on research in experimental psychology.

In 1878, James's first Ph.D. student carried out his plan to study in Leipzig and arrived just as Wundt's institute was getting established. Thus, Hall became Wundt's first American student, although a postgraduate one. He stayed just long enough to serve as a subject in some of the early Ph.D. research at Leipzig and to win Wundt's recommendation for any future openings in the new psychology in America.

Upon returning home in 1880, however, Hall found that no permanent jobs were available. He went back to Cambridge and was invited by Harvard's president to deliver a series of Saturday morning lectures on the subject of education. This opportunity proved crucial to Hall in two ways. First, it turned his serious attention for the first time to problems of developmental psychology and pedagogy—topics that would dominate the rest of his professional life. Second, the popular success of his lectures attracted the attention of Daniel Coit Gilman, president of the new Johns Hopkins University in Baltimore.

Established in 1876, Hopkins was the first in a series of new American universities modeled deliberately after the German system and intended primarily to be graduate institutions specializing in research training for the Ph.D. With positive recommendations from both Wundt and James, Hall won the new university's first professorship of psychology and pedagogy in 1884. Hopkins also provided a research laboratory for Hall to direct, the first such in the United States. In 1887 Hall raised funds to establish the *American Journal of Psychology*, the first English-language periodical explicitly devoted to the new experimental psychology.

Following these administrative successes, Hall in 1888 was appointed the first president of Clark University in Worcester, Massachusetts—another institution originally devoted exclusively to graduate study. He remained there for the rest of his life, despite some difficult times that arose partly because of Clark's limited financial resources but also because of Hall's rather high-handed administrative style. He continued to teach psychology and pedagogy, and throughout the 1890s his institution produced more than half of all the new American Ph.D.'s in psychology. The entrepreneurial Hall also founded the journal *Pedagogical Seminary* in 1891, a periodical still published today as the *Journal of Genetic Psychology*. He had also taken the lead in organizing a national professional society for psychologists, the American Psychological Association, and was elected its first president. Starting with just thirty-one members in 1892, the APA has grown almost exponentially ever since. With well over 100,000 members, the organization's annual conventions can be accommodated only in the largest and most hotel-rich of North American cities.

As American psychology's most important "founder"—of laboratories, departments, journals, and professional societies—Hall resembled Wundt more than James. But in his research he lay more clearly in the functional and practical American tradition that had been pioneered by James. His most innovative work arose out of his combined interests in psychology, pedagogy, and evolutionary theory. In the early 1880s he began a large series of questionnaire studies of kindergarten-aged children, designed to find out what they knew and thought about a great variety of things, including their bodies, games and stories, animals, the sun and stars, and religion. Hall published his findings in an 1893 work whose title—*The Contents of Children's Minds on Entering School*—suggests its partly practical goal of informing teachers of what to expect in dealing with their young charges.

Subsequently, Hall and his students issued questionnaires to older children, and in 1904 he summarized these results in his most famous book: *Adolescence: Its Psychology and Its Relation to Physiology, Anthropology, Sociology, Sex, Crime, Religion and Education*. This book brought the previously unusual word "adolescence" into popular use, and fully documented for the first time the emotional turbulence associated with that phase of the life cycle. The book also reflected Hall's interest in developmental issues and his conviction that children must be regarded as constantly growing and changing individuals, with different kinds of knowledge, emotions, and intellectual characteristics at varying stages of the life cycle.

Hall proposed a Darwinian and "recapitulationist" theory of child development, according to which each individual's intellectual, emotional, and general psychological development parallels the stages traversed by our pre-human ancestors. This idea had been hinted at in Darwin's essay on his infant son and was more explicitly espoused by the German biologist Haeckel (see pp. 256–258). Hall carried the idea further still, arguing that a child's progress from crawling on all fours to walking upright, and through successive stages of social, playful, and artistic activity, essentially repeats the evolutionary sequence leading to modern humanity. This strict recapitulationist view is not generally accepted today, but Hall's work nonetheless marks the beginning of a general interest in developmental psychology. Clark University remains a major center for that field.

Hall's work on adolescence inevitably involved him with many of the same issues of emotional turbulence and sexuality concurrently being investigated in a different way by the Viennese psychoanalyst Sigmund Freud. Among the first to recognize Freud's importance, Hall invited him to speak at Clark University's twentieth anniversary celebrations in 1909. The event—Freud's only visit to America—proved a great success and effectively introduced his ideas to the New World. His lectures were published afterward in Hall's *American Journal of Psychology* and have remained ever since one of the most popular and effective short introductions to psychoanalytic theory.[31] The fuller story of Freud's American visit will be described in Chapter 11.

Unfortunately, the imperious Hall was often difficult to get along with and wound up alienating Freud along with many others. Sometimes he even turned against his mentors, as when he published a review of James's *Principles of Psychology* that sarcastically called the James-Lange theory the "sorry because we cry theory" and one of the chief "impediments" to psychology's future progress. In 1912 Hall published a critical account of Wundt's life and work, alleging among other things that the young Wundt had been fired as Helmholtz's assistant because of mathematical incompetence. Wundt labeled Hall's work "a biography of me which is invented from the beginning to the end."[32]

America's first historian of psychology, **E. G. Boring** (1886–1968), wrote of Hall and James: "Each appreciated the other's qualities, but they were on different tracks. . . . Hall was a comet, caught for the moment by James's influence, but presently shooting off into space never to return."[33] Yet for all the bitter distance Hall placed between himself and his teachers, he also genuinely promoted their new psychologies. Thanks to the institutions, journals, and organizations that Hall founded, the ideas of Wundt, James, Freud, and countless others found a much larger, more receptive, and better-educated audience in America than would have been the case otherwise.

A final note on one other aspect of Hall's legacy is in order. Four years before Hall died in 1924, he supervised his last Ph.D. student: **Francis Cecil Sumner** (1895–1954). Sumner was the first African–American to receive a Ph.D. in psychology, receiving his degree on June 14, 1920, three days after the successful defense of his dissertation, titled *Psychoanalysis of Freud and Adler*. Following graduation, and after a short tenure at West Virginia Collegiate Institute, Sumner became head of the Department of Psychology at Howard University in Washington, DC, a post he held from 1928 until 1954. There, he wrote on a variety of subjects, but he was especially interested in the psychology of religion. He attended the First International Congress for Religious Psychology at the University of Vienna in 1931, where he presented a paper on mental hygiene and religion, establishing connections with many leading European psychologists. He taught courses on the subject during the 1940s and prepared a massive manuscript titled *The Structure of Religion: A History of European Psychology of Religion*.

Also at Howard, Sumner supervised the most famous African American couple in psychology's history to date—**Mamie Phipps Clark** (1917–1983) and **Kenneth B. Clark** (1914–2005)—who conducted the famous doll studies that were cited in a brief submitted to the Supreme Court case of 1954, *Brown v. Board of Education of Topeka*. This was the first Supreme Court case in United States history to use social science data in its deliberations, ultimately rendering a decision that made it illegal to segregate public schools on the basis of race. Unfortunately, Sumner would not live to see this historic decision; he died of a heart attack while shoveling snow at his home in Washington, DC, in January of 1954.[34]

Mary Whiton Calkins

A later and more consistently friendly student of James was Mary Whiton Calkins (see Figure 8.3). The eldest child of a Presbyterian minister, Calkins was born in Hartford, Connecticut, grew up in Buffalo, New

York, and moved with her family to Newton, Massachusetts, at age 17. Her mother had earlier suffered a physical and mental collapse, leaving her daughter with much of the responsibility for raising a younger sister and three brothers. Calkins also assumed increasing responsibility for the care of her mother, remaining unmarried and in the parental home for the rest of her life.

Still, she grew up in an intellectually stimulating early environment. Her parents had lived in Germany before her birth and deliberately spoke only German to each other as their daughter was learning to talk; Calkins thus became fluent in German as well as English. Unusually supportive of education for daughters as well as sons, her father sent 17-year-old Calkins to study at Smith College in Northampton, Massachusetts, shortly after the family's move to Newton. Founded in 1875 as one of America's first women's colleges, Smith provided young Calkins with excellent training in English and classics.

After graduation Calkins planned to offer private Greek tutoring in Newton but was unexpectedly offered a position in the Greek department of nearby Wellesley College—another new women's college founded the same year as Smith. Unlike Smith, however, Wellesley hired only women for its faculty. The pool of highly trained candidates being small, Wellesley often recruited promising but relatively

FIG 8.3
Mary Whiton Calkins
(1363–1930)

untrained scholars like Calkins and supported their further study even while they themselves were teaching undergraduates.

Then, after just one year of teaching Greek, Calkins found herself under consideration for the job of introducing experimental psychology into Wellesley's curriculum. Her only real qualification was an interest in the subject, for she had taken and enjoyed just one psychology course at Smith, and that had been in the philosophical, speculative tradition. No better qualified candidate appeared, so in 1890 Calkins was offered an instructorship in psychology, contingent on her completing a year of advanced study in that field.

But where? Nearby Harvard and Clark Universities offered graduate training in psychology, but they admitted only men. Indeed, the number of graduate schools in the entire world willing to admit women could be counted on one's fingers, and they were inconveniently located. She finally contacted Josiah Royce, Harvard's professor of mental philosophy, about the possibility of studying with him at the "Harvard Annex"—an officially unsanctioned program of private courses offered by a few of the Harvard faculty. She impressed Royce, who recommended instead that she attend the regular Harvard seminars offered by himself and William James, who did not teach at the Annex. After interviewing Calkins, James enthusiastically concurred.

At first, Harvard's president, Charles Eliot, refused to support this plan, arguing that the two sexes ought to be educated separately. Royce told Calkins, "I regard this official view as one of the mysteries which no one may hope to penetrate who is not himself accustomed to the executive point of outlook." James added, "It is flagitious[*] that you should be kept out.—Enough to make dynamiters of you and all women." Both professors continued to press Eliot, aided by a long petition from Calkins's father noting that what was being asked for was "post-graduate and professional instruction for one who is already a member of a college faculty," so her acceptance would not open the floodgates to other women. Eliot finally relented, and

---

[*] This excellent but now little-used word means "shamefully wicked, vile, and scandalous."

in October 1890 the Harvard Corporation reluctantly allowed Royce and James to admit Calkins to their seminars with the stipulation that "by accepting this privilege Miss Calkins does not become a student of the University entitled to registration."[55]

Thus Calkins began to study with James. And when the other members of the seminar dropped out (for unexplained reasons), Calkins found herself and her teacher "quite literally at either side of a library fire. *The Principles of Psychology* was warm from the press, and my absorbed study of those brilliant, erudite, and provocative volumes, as interpreted by their writer, was my introduction to psychology."[56] She immediately proved to be a pupil who could teach her teacher, for during the first year she wrote a paper on "Association" suggesting an elaboration and modification of James's published treatment of that topic. Saying the paper gave him "exquisite delight," James encouraged her to revise and publish it—which she duly did for her first professional publication in 1892. When he soon after revised his chapter on association for his *Briefer Course*, James referred approvingly to this paper.

In the meantime, Calkins had also been receiving unofficial but expert advice on how to equip a psychological laboratory from **Edmund C. Sanford** (1859–1924), a young Johns Hopkins Ph.D. whom Hall had brought with him to Clark the year before. Although another ten years would pass before Clark University officially admitted a female student, Sanford agreed to help Calkins plan a laboratory for Wellesley. As he was then preparing the laboratory manual that for years remained the standard in its field, Sanford was arguably the best-qualified person in the world for that job. And like James, he found a valued collaborator as well as pupil in Calkins, as they worked together on an experimental study of dreams ultimately published in Hall's *American Journal of Psychology*.

After this productive year of study, Calkins returned to Wellesley to teach psychology from her small but well-equipped laboratory. Immediately, however, she felt she needed further graduate study. After considering several possibilities, she applied to carry on at Harvard with James's newly arrived protegé, Hugo Münsterberg. Münsterberg enthusiastically supported her application, and the Harvard Corporation grudgingly conceded her permission "to attend the instruction of professor Münsterberg in his laboratory as a guest, but not as a registered student of the University."[37]

Once again Calkins justified her teacher's confidence, as she originated the **paired-associates technique** while conducting an important experimental study of associative learning. She presented subjects with stimuli consisting of numerals paired with colors. After varying numbers of presentations, she showed the colors alone and tested for recall of their paired numerals. She showed that numerals associated with vivid colors were remembered somewhat better than those with neutral colors, but that the single most important determinant of remembering was simply the frequency of exposure to each pair. This study—far more original and extensive than most Ph.D. theses of the time—appeared in print as a monographic supplement to *Psychological Review* in 1896.

The year before, Calkins had requested and been given an unofficial Ph.D. examination. James described her performance as "much the most brilliant examination for the Ph.D. that we have had at Harvard," and he jibed at his junior colleague who had had the best previous examination: "Now Santayana, go hang yourself." Münsterberg petitioned the Harvard Corporation to reconsider and admit Calkins to official degree candidacy, calling her superior to all the male students and "surely one of the strongest professors of psychology in the country."[38] The Corporation peremptorily refused.

Thus, Calkins returned to Wellesley in 1895 having completed more than the substance of a Harvard Ph.D., but without the title. And so she would remain for the rest of her life. In 1902 she was offered a *Radcliffe* Ph.D.—Radcliffe College having been founded in 1894 as Harvard's coordinate institution for women. But Calkins declined on the grounds that Radcliffe was exclusively an undergraduate school that had not even existed during much of the time she studied in Cambridge and that the degree would not reflect the fact that she had actually worked at Harvard. Rather than acquiesce in deception, she would entirely forgo the degree she had earned.[39]

The degreeless Calkins went on to a predictably distinguished professional career at Wellesley. In addition to writing a well-received *Introduction to Psychology* in 1901, she developed and advocated throughout the early 1900s an influential psychology of the self. Calkins saw the self as an active, guiding, and purposive agency present in all acts of consciousness, and essential to any complete introspective report. She regarded the conscious self to be the basic subject matter of psychology and defended this position against behaviorist and Gestalt formulations. Although couched in the terms and procedures of an introspective experimental psychology that are no longer common today, Calkins's **self psychology** anticipated in some ways the influential personality theory later developed by the Harvard psychologist Gordon W. Allport (described more fully in Chapter 12). In 1905 Calkins was officially recognized by her colleagues in being elected president of the APA—the first woman to be so honored.

Afterward, she followed the model of her teacher James by gradually giving up psychology in favor of philosophy. In this field, too, she distinguished herself and in 1918 became the first woman elected president of the American Philosophical Association.

In 1903, Calkins and two other women were identified by a poll of their peers as ranking among the fifty most important American psychologists, worthy of having their names starred in the biographical dictionary *American Men of Science*. In making their outstanding careers, all of these women had had to overcome innumerable discriminatory obstacles because of their gender (partially reflected in the exclusionary title of the dictionary, which was not changed to *American Men and Women of Science* until the 1960s).

Like Calkins, the other two starred women had experienced great difficulty in getting graduate training. As a brilliant young mathematician, Christine Ladd-Franklin (see Chapter 5) had grudgingly been allowed to attend graduate classes at Johns Hopkins between 1878 and 1882, but not to register officially or earn a Ph.D. Only in 1926 did Hopkins relent and officially award her the degree she had truly earned forty-four years earlier. In the meantime, she had worked in Helmholtz's laboratory and become an acknowledged expert on color vision. As noted in Chapter 6, in 1892 she published an important paper proposing that differing color-receptor systems arose in differing stages of evolutionary development. **Margaret Floy Washburn** (1871–1939) audited James McKeen Cattell's graduate courses at Columbia and won his full respect and support, but university authorities denied her official credit. On Cattell's advice she transferred to Cornell, one of the few universities that did accept women as official graduate students, even offering them lucrative fellowships. In 1894 she became the first woman actually to obtain a Ph.D. in psychology, under the nominal supervision of the newly arrived E. B. Titchener. As noted in Chapter 5, Titchener's openness to women as Ph.D. students did *not* lead to his accepting them as members of his exclusive Society of Experimental Psychologists once they had graduated. Nonetheless, he forwarded a copy of Washburn's thesis, which examined the influence of visual imagery on judgments of tactile distance and direction, to Wundt for publication in his psychology journal, *Philosophische Studien.* This was a great honor, as Wundt generally declined to publish any but his own students' work. Washburn eventually achieved a professional record equaled by few male members of Titchener's Society, writing the country's leading comparative psychology textbook, *The Animal Mind* (1908), editing several major psychological journals, and in 1921 being the second woman elected president of the APA.

The pioneering efforts of Calkins, Ladd-Franklin, and Washburn helped somewhat to clear the path to graduate training for the next generation of women. By 1917, thirty-nine women had qualified for membership in the APA (usually by completing Ph.D.'s), and made up more than 10 percent of the total. But even with excellent credentials, women were still excluded from good jobs at the major universities. Washburn spent her teaching career at Vassar—like Calkins's Wellesley, an excellent women's college, but lacking a graduate program in which students could be supervised in truly advanced research. Most women psychologists had to make do with lower-status and lower-paying jobs than Washburn's, often in teacher training schools. Those who did not remain single suffered further discrimination still, as married women were barred from faculty positions and indeed many other kinds of professional employment at this time.

Edward Lee Thorndike

The last in our trio of James's students, Edward Lee Thorndike (see Figure 8.4), was the son of a Methodist minister. He grew up in a succession of New England towns and at 17 entered Wesleyan University in Middletown, Connecticut. There he edited the college newspaper and won his class tennis championship while compiling a brilliant

FIG 8.4
Edward Lee
Thorndike
(1874–1949)

academic record. He disliked his only psychology course, taught from a traditional, philosophically oriented textbook. But in preparing for an optional prize examination (which he subsequently won), he had to read parts of James's recently published *Principles of Psychology*. He liked this so much that he bought both volumes for his personal library—the only books outside of literature he purchased voluntarily during his entire Wesleyan career.

Thorndike next went to Harvard for graduate study in English and French literature, but during his first semester he also took one of James's psychology courses. It so fascinated him that he took two more the second semester and changed his field of concentration to psychology. Deciding to become a teacher of psychology, he sought the quickest possible route to a Ph.D. In the meantime, the English biologist and comparative psychologist C. Lloyd Morgan had visited Harvard and described some experiments he had done on the ability of chickens to distinguish among different-colored corn kernels. Although James and Harvard had no tradition in animal psychology, Thorndike evidently decided that a study of learning in chickens would provide a relatively quick Ph.D. dissertation. James, who little understood exactly what he was getting into, accepted Thorndike's proposal. Thorndike recalled:

> I kept these animals and conducted the experiments in my room until the landlady's protests were imperative. James tried to get the few square feet required for me in the laboratory. . . . He was refused and with his habitual kindness and devotion to underdogs and eccentric aspects of science, harbored my chickens in the cellar of his own home for the rest of the year.[40]

To the delight of James's children, Thorndike constructed a series of pens inside a larger enclosure that contained his chicken flock. Then he placed individual chickens in the pens and observed how and how quickly they learned to find the exit to the pen and rejoin the flock. At first, a chicken would typically peep loudly and run around agitatedly, in obvious distress, until finally finding the exit. With successive trials, however, both the signs of distress and the time required to find the exit diminished markedly.

At this point, Thorndike began to think of leaving Harvard. For all of James's charisma and helpfulness, he had not built a strong *program* in psychology. Münsterberg had left Harvard after a three-year stint in 1895, and although he came back in 1897, his continuing presence could not yet be counted on. James's own main interests were shifting to philosophy, so he taught relatively few courses in psychology. Several other graduate students Thorndike knew had come to Cambridge and been inspired by James, but then went elsewhere to complete their actual Ph.D.'s.

In 1897, prompted further by a distressing personal situation, Thorndike too followed this route. He had proposed marriage to a young woman from a nearby town and had been rejected. Wishing to leave the scene of his emotional distress, Thorndike applied successfully (and with James's blessing) for a graduate fellowship under James McKeen Cattell at Columbia University.

Thorndike moved into a New York apartment along with "the most-educated hens in the world" and briefly led his neighbors to believe he was "an animal trainer, sort of a P. T. Barnum lion-trainer, etc."[41] But Cattell soon proved more successful than James at finding laboratory space for the animals at the university, and after adding cats to his collection, Thorndike was set to perform his soon-to-become famous research in a proper institutional setting.

Shifting his main emphasis from the chickens to the cats, he constructed some fifteen makeshift "puzzle boxes" that an enclosed animal could escape from only by making some specific response: pulling a string, pushing a button or lever, and so on. In more difficult boxes, the cats had to make two responses in sequence in order to escape—for example, first pull a loop and then slide a latch. In his experiments proper, he placed hungry cats in the boxes and observed their behavior as they tried to get out and obtain food (see Figure 8.5).

Like Thorndike's chickens, the cats originally responded with a great deal of random-seeming, "trial-and-error" behavior until accidentally making the correct response. On successive attempts, the trial-and-error behavior gradually decreased and the animals escaped ever more quickly and smoothly.

In discussing these results in his doctoral dissertation, Thorndike suggested that various specific stimuli and responses became connected or dissociated from each other according to what he called the **law of effect**. This law asserts that when particular stimulus–response sequences are followed by pleasure, those responses tend to

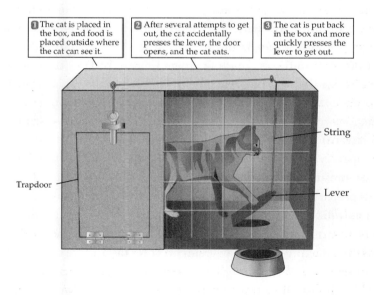

1 The cat is placed in the box, and food is placed outside where the cat can see it.

2 After several attempts to get out, the cat accidentally presses the lever, the door opens, and the cat eats.

3 The cat is put back in the box and more quickly presses the lever to get out.

String

Trapdoor

Lever

FIG 8.5 Thorndike's puzzle box

be strengthened, or "stamped in" the subject's repertoire; responses followed by annoyance or pain tend to be "stamped out." When a cat first encountered the stimulus of being inside a particular puzzle box, it made many responses that kept it inside. This situation presumably produced "annoyance" and reduced the likelihood of those unsuccessful responses being repeated. The successful response, once finally made, presumably led to immediate pleasure with escape, and so became stamped in and rendered more likely to be repeated in the future.

Within sixteen months of arriving at Columbia, Thorndike had completed his study, presented it to the APA and the New York Academy of Sciences, written it up as a successful doctoral dissertation, and published it as a monographic supplement to the *Psychological Review*. He had not only finished quickly but also made a lasting contribution to the literature on animal intelligence and learning. And to cap the year off, the young woman he had left behind in Massachusetts found that absence had made her heart grow fonder, and she accepted Thorndike's proposal of marriage.

After a year's teaching at the Women's College of Western Reserve University in Cleveland, Thorndike returned to New York for a position at Columbia's Teachers College, where he remained for the rest of his academic career. Promptly upon his return, he collaborated on an important study with his friend **Robert Sessions Woodworth** (1869–1962), a fellow James student at Harvard who had also come to Columbia to finish his Ph.D. under Cattell. In 1899 they began to investigate the so-called **transfer of training**—the effect of instruction and exercise in one mental function on performance in a different one. According to the then-popular "doctrine of formal disciplines," such transfer did occur, providing a rationale for instructing students extensively in subjects like classics: The "discipline" acquired in such study presumably transferred to all other areas of mental function, thus preparing students for almost anything.

Thorndike and Woodworth tested this notion by first training subjects in various tasks such as estimating weights or geometrical areas, and then looking for improvement on other tasks more or less similar to those on which training had occurred. Transfer turned out to be very slight, as the authors reported in a major *Psychological Review* paper of 1901.[42] These results seemed consistent with Thorndike's theory of learning from his dissertation: namely, that learning consists of the stamping in or out of highly *specific* stimulus-response connections. Thorndike and Woodworth's research helped undermine the doctrine of formal disciplines in education, in favor of more specifically task-oriented educational practices.

For the rest of his long career Thorndike remained concerned with human subjects rather than animals, and his work invariably had an applied, functional orientation. Consistent with his early work, he maintained that "intelligence" was not a single quality but rather a combination of many specific skills and aptitudes. Accordingly, he developed intelligence tests that measured skill on separate functions such as arithmetic, vocabulary, and direction following, rather than "general intelligence." He also believed these components of intelligence to be largely hereditary and strongly agreed with the eugenic policies of Francis Galton (for more on intelligence testing see Chapter 13). Interested in how children could better be taught to spell and read, Thorndike made extensive counts of the frequencies with which 20,000 different English words were used in various kinds of writing, and he constructed dictionaries based on the principle that words should always be defined by using terms simpler and more common than themselves.

All of this work led Thorndike to become identified as a leader of the loosely defined movement in American psychology known as **functionalism**. In contrast to Titchenerian "structuralism," which sought only to define and describe the contents of conscious experience, functionalism focused attention on the utility and purpose of behavior. Of course, this orientation had been anticipated by the utilitarian approach of William James. Other leading functionalists of Thorndike's generation included Woodworth at Columbia and **James Rowland Angell** (1869–1949), **Harvey Carr** (1873–1954), and **John Dewey** (1859–1952) at the University of Chicago.

Thorndike also wrote several textbooks on educational and general psychology, including a 1905 introductory text that carried a warm and generous introduction by William James. His texts enjoyed such success that in 1924 his author's royalties amounted to five times his professor's salary. For his varied accomplishments, Thorndike was elected APA president in 1912, and in 1917 he became one of the first psychologists admitted to the National Academy of Sciences. A poll of psychologists in 1921 ranked Thorndike first among those recommended for starred listing in *American Men of Science*. Thus, he came to occupy a position at the head of American psychology comparable to that of James a generation earlier.

Of course, Thorndike was not James, and his lasting influence and reputation have been somewhat less. Thorndike's books lack the literary flair of his old teacher's, and do not remain in print. His theories of learning, education, and hereditary intelligence came to be regarded as oversimplified, and the structuralism-functionalism debate lost urgency as the new movement of "behaviorism" swept the American psychological field in the 1920s. Indeed, Thorndike's name is probably best remembered among psychologists today for his very first publications about trial-and-error learning in cats and the law of effect. These provided a starting point for some of the American behaviorists, whose work we shall discuss in the next chapter.

Summary

Arguably the most important founder of academic experimental psychology in America, **William James** opened a demonstration laboratory at Harvard in 1875, and in 1890, after years of laborious effort and much soul-searching, published his immensely successful textbook *Principles of Psychology*. In laying out the subject matter, methods, and aims of the new psychology as he conceived of them, he included chapters on a diverse array of psychological topics. He articulated the notion of the stream of consciousness—the idea that thought has a fluid, dynamic, continuous quality that cannot be studied by breaking it down into its separate elements. He put forth what has become known as the **James-Lange theory of emotion**, which states that emotions are the consequence, not the cause, of changes in our physiology. He also wrote famously about the will, asserting that a true science of psychology *had* to be predicated upon complete determinism, although *outside* science a belief in free will could hold sway. He also noted that a science of psychology would itself have certain limits, and in many ways the rest of his career reflected his interest in topics that lay outside psychology thus defined (such as philosophy and spiritism).

James nonetheless influenced a number of students who stayed in psychology and became leaders of the new discipline. **G. Stanley Hall**, the first person in the United States to earn a Ph.D. with a dissertation in experimental psychology, made important contributions in the areas of pedagogy, child development, and evolutionary theory, while also becoming a leading institution builder: He was the founding president of the American Psychological Association, he created and edited several journals including the *American Journal of Psychology,* and he established America's largest graduate program in the new psychology at Clark University.

As a woman in the early 1900s, **Mary Whiton Calkins** had to overcome many obstacles before studying under William James at Harvard but quickly became a prize student. She developed an influential **self psychology** and pioneered the **paired-associates technique** to study learning and memory. She set up the experimental psychology laboratory at Wellesley College but, like her mentor, increasingly turned to philosophical questions as her career progressed.

Edward Lee Thorndike began his graduate work with James at Harvard and set up a small laboratory to study learning in chickens in James's basement. After transferring with James's approval to the better facilities of Columbia University, he constructed his famous puzzle boxes in which he demonstrated that trial-and-error behavior led to learning that could be explained by the **law of effect**. Post-Ph.D., he turned his attention to human subjects and studied **transfer of training** with Robert Sessions Woodworth. Most of Thorndike's research had an applied, functional cast that was becoming characteristic of a distinctly American approach to psychology known as **functionalism**.

Key Pioneers

Agassiz, Louis, p. 310

Angell, James Rowland, p. 341

Bain, Alexander, p. 313

Boring, E. G., p. 329

Calkins, Mary Whiton, p. 325

Carr, Harvey, p. 341

Clark, Kenneth B., p. 330

Clark, Mamie Phipps, p. 330

Dewey, John, p. 341

Hall, G. Stanley, p. 325

James, William, p. 305

Lange, Carl, p. 319

Münsterberg, Hugo, p. 322

Peirce, Charles Sanders, p. 323

Renouvier, Charles, p. 312

Sanford, Edmund C., p. 333

Sumner, Francis Cecil, p. 330

Thorndike, Edward Lee, p. 325

Washburn, Margaret Floy, p. 335

Woodworth, Robert Sessions, p. 340

Key Terms

functionalism, p. 341
James-Lange theory of emotion,
    p. 319
law of effect, p. 339
paired-associates technique, p. 334

pragmatism, p. 313
self psychology, p. 335
stream of thought, p. 317
transfer of training, p. 340

Discussion Questions and Topics

1 At the beginning of the chapter, it was noted that James's and Wundt's approaches to psychology were in many ways mirrored in their own personalities but were also broadly representative of the different intellectual climates of their respective countries. In what ways was the psychology that flourished in America different from its continental counterpart? Do such regional or national differences persist in shaping psychology?

2 Describe the position known as functionalism and give some examples of research that could be thought of as functionalist in character.

3 Justify the statement, "William James was the founder of American experimental psychology." Conversely, describe the aspects of his thought and career that do not accord with this designation.

Suggested Readings

For more on James's life, see Gay Wilson Allen, *William James: A Biography* (New York: Collier Books, 1967), and Howard M. Feinstein, *Becoming William James* (Ithaca, NY: Cornell University Press, 1984). Biographical information is interspersed with delightful examples of James's correspondence in Henry James, ed., *The Letters of William James*, 2 vols. (Boston: Atlantic Monthly Press, 1920). A "group biography" of the entire remarkable James clan is R. W. B. Lewis's *The Jameses: A Family Narrative* (New York: Anchor Books, 1991). James's relationship to other American psychologists is well discussed in Daniel W. Bjork, *The Compromised Scientist: William James in the Development of American Psychology* (New York: Columbia University Press, 1983). James's own *Principles of Psychology, Psychology: Briefer Course*, and *The Varieties of Religious Experience* all remain in print in various editions, and are still well worth reading today.

For biographies of Hall and Thorndike see, respectively, Dorothy Ross, *G. Stanley Hall: The Psychologist as Prophet* (Chicago: University of Chicago

Press, 1972), and Geraldine Joncich, *The Sane Positivist: A Biography of Edward L. Thorndike* (Middletown, CT: Wesleyan University Press, 1968). The stories of Calkins and her fellow female pioneers are well told in Elizabeth Scarborough and Laurel Furumoto, *Untold Lives: The First Generation of American Women Psychologists* (New York: Columbia University Press, 1987). For details of Calkins's self psychology, readers are referred to Phyllis Wentworth's article, "The Moral of Her Story: Exploring the Philosophical and Religious Commitments in Mary Whiton Calkins' Self-Psychology," *History of Psychology* 2 (1999): 119–131.

Psychology as the Science of Behavior

Ivan Pavlov, John B. Watson, and
B. F. Skinner

9

Pavlov's Early Life and Career
Pavlov's Laboratory
The Physiology of Digestion

Conditioned Reflexes
Generalization, Differentiation, and Experimental Neuroses
Pavlov's Theory of the Brain
Pavlov's Influence

Watson's Early Life and Career
The Founding of Behaviorism

Watson's Behavioristic Writings
Conditioned Emotional Reactions
Advertising and Behaviorism
The Little Albert Study Revisited
Psychological Care of the Infant and Child
Watson's Legacy

Skinner and Operant Conditioning
Operant Conditioning
Behavior Shaping and Programmed Instruction
Philosophical Implications of Operant Conditioning
Skinner's Influence

Summary

Key Pioneers

Key Terms

Discussion Questions and Topics

Suggested Readings

Around the turn of the twentieth century, the eminent Russian physiologist **Ivan Petrovich Pavlov** (1849–1936) felt troubled. He had just completed a monumental set of studies on the

347

physiology of digestion that would shortly win him a Nobel Prize, and he was seeking new scientific challenges. Some incidental observations he had made while studying digestion suggested one possibility, but Pavlov questioned its scientific propriety.

His idea was to study a type of salivary reaction he called "psychic secretions." His earlier research had dealt with innate and reflexive salivary responses in dogs, such as those that occurred automatically and involuntarily whenever food or a mild acid solution was placed in their mouths. But Pavlov had also noted that after dogs became accustomed to laboratory routine, their mouths watered while merely being placed in the apparatus in which their salivation was tested. These "psychic" salivary secretions were obviously *learned*, and the result of experience rather than innate reflexes.

Pavlov had already developed apparatus and procedures that could enable him to study these psychic secretions with the same precision he had achieved for innate salivary reflexes. But he worried about the scientific company he might have to keep in such a venture. Psychic secretions seemed obviously within the domain of psychology, and Pavlov disdained the unreliable and introspection-based procedures used by most of his contemporary academic psychologists. It is "open to question," he wrote, "whether psychology is a natural science, or whether it can be regarded as a science at all."[1] Pavlov thought of himself as a rigorous, completely scientific *physiologist*, and he feared being associated with the soft-minded psychologists.

Pavlov finally resolved his dilemma after recalling *Reflexes of the Brain*, a book written in 1863 by his compatriot **Ivan M. Sechenov** (1829–1905). Sechenov had tried to account for all behavior—including such higher functions as thinking, willing, and judging—in terms of an expanded reflex concept. The higher functions theoretically occurred when acquired reflexes localized in the brain became interposed between the sensory and motor components of innate reflexes. Descartes had long before proposed a similar idea in *Treatise of Man* (see Chapter 1), but Sechenov stated the case in up-to-date physiological language that provided the hint Pavlov needed. Pavlov now decided that his dogs' psychic secretions could be redefined in the pristine physiological terminology of the reflex, thereby completely avoiding all embarrassing reference to subjective psychological states.

In Pavlov's new terminology, psychic secretions were renamed as **conditioned** (or **conditional**) **reflexes**, while innate digestive responses were called **unconditioned reflexes**. The relations between the two kinds of reflexes could be studied in the laboratory and interpreted in terms of brain physiology. Pavlov formally banned psychological terminology from his laboratory and threatened to fire anyone who discussed experiments in mentalistic terms. He spent the rest of his long life studying conditioned reflexes, secure in his belief he was not a psychologist but a physiologist.

Inevitably, however, other people who did consider themselves psychologists took an interest in Pavlov's work. Prime among them was the American **John Broadus Watson** (1878–1958), who, like Pavlov, grew suspicious of the unverifiable and "unscientific" nature of introspective psychology. In 1913 Watson electrified many American psychologists by asserting that their proper subject was not the traditional mind and its subjective consciousness, but rather objective, observable *behavior*. Citing Pavlov's conditioned reflex as a model for objective and nonmentalistic theorizing, he went on to create the influential school known as **behaviorism**. This chapter tells the story of behaviorism, focusing first on the lives and works of Pavlov and Watson, then concluding with **B. F. Skinner** (1904–1990), the Harvard psychologist who became the movement's most eloquent and effective spokesman in the latter part of the twentieth century.

Pavlov's Early Life and Career

Ivan Pavlov (see Figure 9.1) was born on September 27, 1849, in the ancient Russian town of Ryazan. Although his father was the local priest and his mother the daughter of a priest, both parents had to earn their subsistence by working the fields all day as peasants. At age 10 Ivan suffered a serious fall that required a long convalescence in the care of his godfather, the abbot of a nearby monastery. The busy abbot encouraged Ivan to read, but he insisted that whenever the enthusiastic boy tried to talk about his reading that he first write down his observations and comments. This strategy not only bought the abbot some time free from interruption but also started young Pavlov on a lifelong habit of systematic observation and reporting.

This habit proved useful in school and helped Pavlov to benefit from the liberal educational reforms recently instituted by Czar

FIG 9.1 Ivan Petrovich Pavlov (1849–1936) with co-workers in his laboratory at the Military Medical Academy, 1911

Alexander II. As a poor but gifted student who had done well in school, he won a government-supported scholarship to the University of St. Petersburg. Pavlov's choice of major subject there followed his fortuitous reading of a popularized book on physiology that contained a diagram of the digestive tract. "How does such a complicated system work?" the fascinated Pavlov asked himself, and he enrolled in the natural science program.[2] Thus began a scientific quest that would culminate in a Nobel Prize.

At the university Pavlov absorbed the new mechanistic physiology that was then the rage and became an exceptionally meticulous researcher and organizer, much sought out as an assistant by the faculty and advanced students. He used assistantships to support himself through graduate medical training, being named director of one internal medicine laboratory while still a student. Indeed, he helped many doctoral students get *their* degrees even before he completed his own in 1883.

Even though Pavlov had excellent credentials after graduation, good jobs in research were scarce. He had to make do, and support a wife as well, on a series of subordinate and ill-paying positions until he was past 40. In 1890, however, he finally won appointment as a professor at St. Petersburg's Military-Medical Academy, where at last he was free to create and staff his own laboratory and to pursue his long-standing ambition: experimental study of the physiology of digestion.

Pavlov's Laboratory

Pavlov habitually showed two different faces to the world, depending on whether he was outside or inside his laboratory. Outside, he was sentimental, impractical, and absent-minded—often arousing the wonder and amusement of his friends. He became engaged while still a student, lavishing much of his meager income on extravagant luxuries such as candy, flowers, and theater tickets for his fiancée. Only once did he buy her a practical gift: a new pair of shoes to take on a trip. When she arrived at her destination she found only one shoe in her trunk, accompanied by a letter from Pavlov: "Don't look for your other shoe. I took it as a remembrance of you and have put it on my desk."[3] Following marriage, Pavlov often forgot to pick up his pay, and once when he did remember he immediately loaned it all to an irresponsible acquaintance who could not pay it back. On a visit to America in 1923, he carried all of his money in a conspicuous pocketbook, which was stolen as he boarded a train in New York's Grand Central Station.

But if sentimentality, impracticality, and financial negligence characterized Pavlov's personal life, those traits never showed in his laboratory. In pursuing his research he overlooked no detail. While he uncomplainingly lived frugally at home, he fought ferociously to ensure that his laboratory was well equipped and his experimental animals well fed. Punctual in his arrival at the lab and perfectionistic in his experimental technique, he expected the same from his workers. During the Russian Revolution, he once disciplined a worker who showed up late because of having to dodge bullets and street skirmishes on the way to the laboratory.

The most remarkable aspect of Pavlov's laboratory was its organization. Whatever his deficiencies in organizing his private life, he ran a large and efficient scientific enterprise that any administrator might envy. Experiments were performed and replicated systematically by the hundreds, according to a simple but ingenious scheme. New workers in the lab were never assigned to new or independent projects but were required instead to replicate experiments that had already been done. In a single stroke, the new people learned firsthand about work in progress and provided Pavlov with a check on the reliability of previous results. If the replications succeeded, those results were confirmed and the new worker was ready to move on to something new; if they failed, another replication by a third party would be ordered to resolve the discrepancy.

When he was an old and famous man, Pavlov wrote the following advice in an article for Soviet youth:

> This is the message I would like to give the youth of my country. First of all, be systematic. I repeat, be systematic. Train yourself to be strictly systematic in the acquisition of knowledge. First study the rudiments of science before attempting to reach its heights. Never pass to the next stage until you have thoroughly mastered the one on hand.[4]

Someone who only knew Pavlov nonprofessionally might understandably have been incredulous to hear such advice from someone like him. Those who worked in his laboratory, however, knew that he accurately described the secret of his own success.

The Physiology of Digestion

Pavlov spent the first decade in his new laboratory attacking the problem that had originally attracted him to science: the complicated workings of the digestive system. Digestion had long resisted direct physiological study, because the organs involved were both well concealed and highly susceptible to surgical trauma. When surgically exposed, the digestive organs of experimental animals ceased to function normally; thus, observations of them were of limited scientific value. Pavlov's great contribution was to observe *normal* digestive functions in experimental animals by imitating an almost incredible "natural experiment" that had occurred earlier in the century.

In 1822, a young French-Canadian trapper named Alexis St. Martin suffered a terrible gunshot wound to his stomach. His doctor, William Beaumont (1785–1853), thought the wound would be fatal but patched him up as best he could. Surprisingly, however, St. Martin gradually recovered and returned to normal—except for the remarkable fact that the hole in the wall of his stomach never fully closed, but remained as a "window" on whatever happened within. Beaumont seized his opportunity and persuaded St. Martin to serve as a subject for studies of digestion. Beaumont directly observed the stomach as it digested food, inserting instruments to collect, measure, and analyze the substances it secreted. Until Pavlov, Beaumont's observations of St. Martin provided the best available knowledge about normal digestive processes.

Pavlov decided to replicate Beaumont's observations, only on a more selective and controlled basis, by surgically creating openings, or *fistulas*, in different parts of the digestive tracts of dogs. Others had tried this before and failed, but Pavlov succeeded for two major reasons. First, he was an unusually skillful surgeon who disliked the sight of blood and who therefore minimized the surgical trauma experienced by his subjects. Second, he was among the first to appreciate the importance of aseptic surgery. At a time when human patients still died in multitudes from infections contracted in unsanitary surgical wards, Pavlov went to extreme lengths to assure the antiseptic cleanliness of his animal operations. Even though the digestive tract was a particularly dangerous source of infection, most of Pavlov's animals completely recovered from their operations, while most of his predecessors' animals had died.

Pavlov created fistulas in many different parts of the digestive tract and then conducted hundreds of experiments in his systematic way. After feeding his animals different substances, for example, he collected, measured, and chemically analyzed the resulting secretions from the different parts of the digestive system. These studies won Pavlov the Nobel Prize for physiology in 1904 and are still cited today in modern textbooks on the physiology of digestion.

Among the gastric responses Pavlov studied was *salivation*, and he learned very early that a splash of dilute acid on a dog's tongue immediately produced a copious secretion. And then, of course, he incidentally noticed the "psychic secretions" of animals who had become accustomed to the laboratory routine: They would begin to salivate even before the acid was splashed on their tongues, as they went through the preliminary procedures of being placed in their experimental apparatus. Thus began his study of conditioned reflexes.

Conditioned Reflexes

Pavlov publicly introduced his idea of conditioned reflexes in his Nobel Prize address of 1904; he then devoted the remaining thirty-two years of his life to their study. Conducted with the assistance of nearly 150 collaborators and subordinates, his studies involved the systematic manipulation of the four basic components of a conditioned reflex, which he named in his new, non-psychological terminology: the **unconditioned stimulus** (US), the **unconditioned response** (UR), the **conditioned stimulus** (CS), and the **conditioned response** (CS).

An unconditioned stimulus and unconditioned response together constitute an *unconditioned reflex*, the innate and automatic reaction that must exist prior to any conditioning or learning. Descartes had described one unconditioned reflex, although he did not call it that, when he wrote of the heat from a fire (an unconditioned stimulus) producing the automatic withdrawal of a foot that has been brought too near (the unconditioned response). Pavlov's earlier research had focused on unconditioned gastric reflexes, such as the salivation (unconditioned response) automatically produced when dilute acid was splashed in the mouth (the unconditioned stimulus).

Pavlov noted that a typical conditioned stimulus starts out by being "neutral" and eliciting no strong response at all, but it subsequently *acquires* the property of eliciting a response after being paired with an unconditioned stimulus a number of times. For his dogs, the sight of their keeper at mealtime or the experience of being placed in their experimental apparatus became a conditioned stimulus regularly followed by the unconditioned stimuli of food or acid in the mouth. Soon, these originally neutral stimuli aroused salivation all by themselves, in new stimulus-response connections that Pavlov called conditioned reflexes.

Although conceptually very simple, conditioned reflexes lent themselves perfectly to the sort of systematic research program that Pavlov was so good at supervising. To start, he and his associates could systematically vary the types of stimuli, the numbers of pairings, and the conditions under which they occurred and then observe the strengths of the resulting conditioned reflexes. The following example illustrates one of the earliest but most fundamental experiments.

The sounding of a tone served as the conditioned stimulus, followed immediately by the unconditioned stimulus of dilute acid on the tongue. The experimenters varied the number of pairings of these two stimuli before presenting the tone without the acid, to see how many were necessary for conditioning to occur. Dogs received 1, 10, 20, 30, 40, or 50 pairings before the test, with their response magnitudes measured by the number of drops of saliva secreted, and latencies by the number of seconds between the presentation of the tone and the first observable salivation:

Number of Pairings	Response Magnitude	Response Latency
1	0	—
10	6	18
20	20	9
30	60	2
40	62	1
50	59	2

As you can see, the conditioned reflexes became progressively stronger, with response magnitudes regularly increasing and latencies decreasing, over the first thirty or so pairings; after that, the conditioned reflex's strength leveled off.

Other early experiments that varied the time interval between the conditioned and unconditioned stimuli showed that the strongest and quickest conditioning occurred when the interval was short. If the conditioned stimulus *followed* the unconditioned stimulus, however—even by a very short interval—no conditioned reflexes were produced at all. Another series of basic studies demonstrated **higher-order conditioning,** in which a strong conditioned salivary reflex was first established to one stimulus, such as the sound of a bell, which then served as the unconditioned stimulus in a further series of pairings with *another* conditioned stimulus, such as a flash of light. For instance, the bell was first paired with a mild acidic solution, then the light was paired with the bell, and the animals became conditioned to salivate to the light.

Generalization, Differentiation, and Experimental Neuroses

Another important series of experiments showed that conditioned reflexes could be elicited by stimuli similar but not identical to the original conditioned stimulus—a phenomenon Pavlov called **generalization.** When a tone of one pitch served as the conditioned stimulus during training and the test was made with a slightly higher or lower tone, a conditioned reflex still occurred, but with somewhat diminished magnitude. The greater the dissimilarity between the conditioned and test stimuli, the weaker the generalized response.

If the dissimilar stimulus was then presented repeatedly, but never "reinforced" by a succeeding unconditioned stimulus, a further kind of learning occurred that Pavlov called **differentiation**. For example, a dog was first conditioned to salivate to an image of a circle flashed on a screen. Then, the circular stimulus was randomly alternated with an oblong, elliptical figure of about the same size; each presentation of the circle was followed by a splash of acid on the tongue, while the ellipse was never so reinforced. At first, generalization occurred and the dog salivated copiously to the ellipse; but after repeated trials the response to the ellipse decreased in strength and finally disappeared altogether. A differentiation had occurred.

Some of the Pavlov laboratory's most surprising experiments tested the limits of his animals' ability to differentiate. In the circle-ellipse differentiation, for example, they started with a very oblong ellipse. When the dog stopped salivating to that, they shifted to another that was slightly less oblong and more circle-like. After the animal successfully differentiated that from the circle, they tried one that was more circular still, and so on, progressively reducing the difference between the stimuli. When the nonreinforced stimulus became almost circular, with its height to width in a 9 to 8 ratio, a sudden and dramatic change came over the dog's behavior. Previously placid and tractable, the animal now made frantic efforts to escape from its apparatus, and it *remained* agitated and hard to handle long afterward. In fact, animals forced to confront this ambiguous stimulus for very long remained disturbed for weeks or months after the experiment. When retested on some of the easier differentiations that had been easily mastered before the crucial trial, the dogs failed. Likening this behavior to stress-induced breakdowns in human beings, Pavlov called these reactions **experimental neuroses**.

From experiments like this, Pavlov theorized that experimental neuroses were likely to occur whenever animals were confronted by unavoidable *conflicts* between two strong but incompatible conditioned-response tendencies, such as to salivate or to suppress salivation at the sight of the ambiguous ellipse. And from this basic idea, he deduced a new theory of brain functioning.

Pavlov's Theory of the Brain

As a self-identified physiologist, Pavlov tried to account for his conditioning results in terms of a physiological theory. Following Sechenov, he argued that unconditioned reflexes are mediated by connections between sensory and motor nerves in the spinal cord and the lower brain centers. Conditioned reflexes presumably occurred when neural pathways in the *cortex* became part of the circuitry, connecting stimuli with responses in new combinations. Crude evidence for the cortical localization of conditioned reflexes came from animals whose cortexes were surgically ablated after they had acquired some conditioned reflexes. Although these animals could be kept alive for several years with full retention of their *un*conditioned reflexes, they permanently lost all of their old conditioned reflexes and never acquired any new ones.

Consistent with the recent discoveries of cortical localization described in Chapter 3, Pavlov reasoned that different conditioned stimuli must excite different specific locations on the cortex, with the locations for similar stimuli lying closer together than those for dissimilar stimuli. He further speculated that two distinctly different kinds of processes must occur in these locations to produce conditioning—*excitation* presumably leads to the acquisition or generalization of conditioned responses, while *inhibition* causes an already acquired response tendency to be suppressed.

Pavlov suggested that excitatory processes arise in a cortical area when the stimulus represented there is reinforced by the presentation of an unconditioned stimulus. Inhibitory processes arise when such reinforcement fails to occur. Moreover, he argued that excitation and inhibition must *irradiate* or spread out in a wavelike fashion over surrounding locations, with their strength dissipating as they get farther away from their center. Cerebral irradiation had never been actually observed (and still has not been), but Pavlov noted that such a process could theoretically account for the phenomena of generalization, differentiation, and experimental neurosis.

In generalization, the presentation of a similar alternative stimulus presumably arouses a wave of excitation in a cortical center *close to* that for the original conditioned stimulus. As the irradiation spreads, it soon reaches and excites the location of the original stimulus, which has acquired (by conditioning) connections to the salivary response apparatus. Thus, a salivary response is initiated, although it is somewhat diminished in strength because the excitation at the conditioned stimulus's location has been partly dissipated through irradiation.

In differentiation training, the cortical centers representing nonreinforced stimuli presumably begin to send out waves of inhibition instead of excitation. Stimuli immediately surrounding these centers correspondingly *lose* the ability to arouse generalized conditioned reflexes. If *many* surrounding stimuli are systematically nonreinforced, the entire cortex surrounding the center for the true conditioned stimulus becomes a field for inhibition rather than excitation. As one textbook observes: "When a differentiation is firmly established, only a small region of the brain corresponding to the conditional stimulus will produce a response. Inhibition lies over the rest of the brain like winter over the empty plains of central Russia, limiting all activity to the lonely stockades."[5]

The winter snow metaphor is somewhat misleading, however, because it suggests that inhibition-irradiated areas of the cortex are inert. To the contrary, Pavlov thought of them as fields of great potential energy, which under the conditions of experimental neurosis can violently influence behavior. Pavlov hypothesized that experimental neurosis occurs whenever a stimulus that cannot be avoided arouses very strong excitation and inhibition at the same time. That is, its cortical location lies exactly on a "boundary" between powerful excitatory and inhibitory fields. When this location is strongly stimulated, the boundary may literally "rupture," so that the entire cortical region becomes inundated with an indiscriminate mixture of both excitation and inhibition. These two forces, previously confined within boundaries and producing the precise and regular effects of generalization or differentiation, now intermix wildly and produce the disorganized behavior of experimental neuroses.

While studying experimental neuroses in dogs, Pavlov made a further observation that stimulated a new major interest for the final years of his life. He noted striking individual differences in the specific symptoms of his subjects. Those animals that had been naturally active in temperament before the experiments became excessively so in their neuroses—snapping, chewing, howling, and clawing indiscriminately. Animals with more placid prior dispositions tended to develop more "depressive" types of symptoms, such as excessive lethargy and apathy. Pavlov hypothesized that the naturally active animals had brains with more excitatory than inhibitory energy innately within them, while for the "depressive" animals the proportions were reversed. Thus each animal's particular type of neurosis depended on the excitatory or inhibitory predilections of its brain.

In 1929, the 80-year-old Pavlov began seriously to contemplate the implications of this theory for *human* psychopathology. He attempted to account for the varieties of psychiatric illness in terms of an excess or deficiency of excitation and inhibition, the weakening of cortical neurons, and other variables he had found to be related to experimental neuroses in dogs. He devised physical therapies for these presumed deficiencies, intended to rest or exercise the brain cells at fault or to restore them to health by the application of chemicals such as bromides. In doing so he established a strong tradition of organically based psychiatric treatment in the Soviet Union.

Pavlov's Influence

Pavlov worked vigorously and full time on his new psychiatric projects until February 21, 1936, when he fell ill after a full day's work. As his symptoms rapidly worsened into pneumonia, Pavlov characteristically made systematic observations of his mental state. On the afternoon of February 27 he told his doctor: "My brain is not working well; obsessive feelings and involuntary movements appear; mortification may be setting in."[6] An hour after making this final scientific observation, the 86-year-old Pavlov died.

By the time of his death, Pavlov was a Soviet national hero, with even a new town named after him. Pavlov's influence had also spread to the United States, where his nonmentalistic approach appealed strongly to a group of young scientists who called themselves *behaviorists*. But unlike Pavlov, who steadfastly insisted he was not a psychologist but a physiologist, the behaviorists changed their definition of psychology so as to accommodate their nonmentalistic orientation. Less concerned than Pavlov about the cortical and neurological underpinnings of conditioning, the behaviorists used techniques like his to establish *behavioral* laws regarding stimuli and responses that could stand independent of physiology. For them, psychology became transformed from the science of consciousness or the mind to the science of behavior. We turn now to the story of the major founder of American behaviorism.

Watson's Early Life and Career

John Broadus Watson (see Figure 9.2) was born on January 9, 1878, near Greenville, South Carolina, the son of a wayward father and a deeply pious mother. Named after John Broadus, a local fundamentalist minister, and constantly steered in a religious direction by his mother, young Watson nonetheless developed a fierce rebellious streak that became a permanent part of his character. His youthful pugnacity earned him the nickname "Swats," and as a teenager he got arrested for fighting and for firing a gun inside city limits. He recalled that at school "I was lazy, somewhat insubordinate, and . . . never made above a passing grade."[7]

Still, Watson at 16 was admitted as a subfreshman to Greenville's Furman University, where his mother hoped he would prepare for a career as a clergyman. He almost did, succeeding in his courses and applying to Princeton Theological Seminary. He would have gone there were it not for a peculiar but characteristic episode during his senior year. His philosophy and psychology professor, Gordon Moore, had warned that any student handing in a paper with the pages back-

FIG 9.2
John Broadus Watson
(1878–1956)

ward would automatically flunk. Watson had been an honor student all year, but, as he put it, "by some strange streak of luck, I handed in my final paper . . . backwards." Moore kept his word, and Watson had to return for an extra year at Furman instead of enrolling in seminary. As partial recompense, he graduated from Furman in 1899 with a master's rather than a bachelor's degree.

During that extra year, Watson's mother died, so he no longer faced family pressure to become a minister. He now made an "adolescent resolve" to upstage his professor by earning a Ph.D. (which Moore did not hold) and one day inducing the older man to come to *him* for training. Moore genuinely appreciated Watson's raw ability and helped him get admitted to the still-undivided philosophy-psychology department at the recently founded University of Chicago in 1900. (A dozen years later, Moore actually did apply to study with Watson but sadly had to abandon the plan because of failing eyesight.[8])

Watson went to Chicago expecting to work with the department's eminent chairman, and leader of American "functionalist" psychology, John Dewey (see Chapter 8). Ever the maverick, he found Dewey's approach uncongenial: "I never knew what he was talking about then, and unfortunately for me, I still don't know," Watson recalled in his autobiography. Equally unappealing were the introspective methods required for much of the traditional psychological research conducted in the department: "I hated to serve as a subject. I didn't like the stuffy, artificial instructions given to subjects. I was always uncomfortable and acted unnaturally."[9] A fellow student remembered that Watson never learned to give consistent introspective reports that agreed with other people's.[10]

But if the philosophical and introspective aspects of psychology came hard, Watson found an emerging area of *animal study* at Chicago in which he truly excelled. As a country boy comfortable with animals, Watson felt at home in this field. He was particularly attracted by the work of department members **Jacques Loeb** (1859–1924), the staunchly mechanistic biologist who had introduced the concept of "tropism" to account for plant and animal movement, and **Henry H. Donaldson** (1857–1938), a neurologist who studied the nervous system of white rats. Donaldson proved supportive practically as well as intellectually, hiring the financially pressed graduate student to tend his colony of experimental rats. As Watson became intimately familiar with the behavior of these tame creatures, he realized they would make suitable subjects for his own doctoral thesis research. Under the joint supervision of Donaldson and psychologist James Angell, he demonstrated that the increasing complexity in the behavior of developing young rats was strongly correlated with the increasing growth of myelin sheaths around the neural fibers in their brains. In 1903, Donaldson loaned Watson $350 to publish his thesis under the rather unbehavioristic-sounding title *Animal Education: The Psychical Development of the White Rat.*

Despite his difficulties with traditional psychology, Watson the animal psychologist had become a departmental star—the youngest Ph.D. yet turned out by the university, with the second-best final examination in his department's history. Still, Watson was plagued by an inferiority complex. His supervisors reminded him that a previous doctoral student, Helen Bradford Thompson, had graduated Summa Cum Laude (a step above Watson's own Magna Cum Laude) and had turned in a superior performance at her examination. Watson later noted, "I wondered then if anybody could ever equal her record. That jealousy existed for years."[11] Watson also had to hold several jobs to support himself, and overwork contributed to an emotional breakdown. He could not sleep without a light on and suffered anxiety attacks that dissipated only after taking 10-mile walks. He later hinted that sexual concerns may have been involved, when he reported that his breakdown "in a way prepared me to accept a large part of Freud."[12]

Watson's breakdown coincided with complications in his personal life, following his rejection by one young woman he had fallen in love with and his subsequent engagement to a 19-year-old student named Mary Ickes. Mary's brother Harold—a rising figure in Chicago politics who would later become President Franklin Roosevelt's Secretary of the Interior—saw Watson as unreliable and he strenuously opposed the match with his sister. Thus, Watson and Mary married secretly in December of 1903 but lived apart and did not publicly declare their status until the fall of 1904.[13]

Professionally, Watson's life began to improve. As an expert in the newly emerging area of animal psychology, he found himself in demand and received several job offers. He elected to stay at Chicago as an instructor, and four years later he was about to become promoted to assistant professor when he was offered an associate professorship by Johns Hopkins University. at the comfortable salary of $2,500 per year. When he hesitated in hopes Chicago would match the associate professorship, Hopkins increased its offer to a full professorship at $3,500. Although Watson liked Chicago, it was more than he could refuse. He set off for Baltimore at age 29 to assume a major position at one of America's major universities.

The Founding of Behaviorism

At Hopkins, Watson's professional advancement continued. A year after he arrived, his department chairman, James Mark Baldwin, was arrested in a bordello and resigned in the ensuing scandal. As the department's only remaining full professor, Watson inherited its leadership as well as the editorship of an important journal, the *Psychological Review*. From his position of power Watson immediately began pressing the university president to separate psychology from philosophy and to forge new ties between psychology and biology.

For a while, he maintained an uneasy alliance with traditional academic psychology and taught courses along the lines of James and Wundt while conducting his own research on animals. But he increasingly bridled when people asked what his research had to do with "real" psychology—which they took to be the study of conscious experience. "I was interested in my own work and felt it was important," he complained, "yet I could not trace any connection between it and psychology as my questioner understood psychology."[14] With characteristic boldness, Watson decided no longer to accommodate himself to the traditional definition of psychology but instead to redefine psychology so it afforded his specialty a dominant position. In fact, several other psychologists were doing work similar to Watson's, within a behaviorist rather than an introspectionist framework. Their position needed an articulate spokesperson, and Watson, as it turned out, filled the bill.

He started to promote behaviorism in 1913, with the article "Psychology as the Behaviorist Views It," which he conveniently published in *Psychological Review*. The opening paragraph clearly defined the alternative "behavioristic" psychology he envisioned:

> Psychology as the behaviorist views it is a purely objective experimental branch of natural science. Its theoretical goal is the prediction and control of behavior. Introspection forms no essential part of its methods, nor is the scientific value of its data dependent upon the readiness with which they lend themselves to interpretation in terms of consciousness. The behaviorist, in his attempts to get a unitary scheme of animal response, recognizes no dividing line between man and brute. The behavior of man, with all of its refinement and complexity, forms only a part of the behaviorist's total scheme of investigation.[15]

Watson here declared independence from traditional psychology in three ways. First, he asserted that a properly behavioristic psychology must be completely objective and rule out *all* subjective data or interpretations in terms of conscious experience. While traditional psychology used objective observations to complement or supplement introspective data, for Watson they became the sole basis of psychology.

Second, Watson declared that psychology's goal was not to *describe and explain* conscious states, as the traditionalists would have it, but rather to *predict and control* overt behavior. Behavioristic psychology was to be highly practical, much more concerned with concrete effectiveness than with theoretical understanding.

And finally, Watson denied the traditional psychological distinction between humans and other animals. Drawing on Darwin's demonstration of the common ancestry of all animal species, Watson argued that psychological similarities among species are just as important as differences. Studies of the behavior of apes, rats, pigeons, and even flatworms should interest psychologists because of the continuity of life forms.

Watson's Behavioristic Writings

After declaring the general principles of a behavioristic psychology, Watson faced the problem of actually putting them into practice. His first attempt, a 1914 textbook titled *Behavior: An Introduction to Comparative Psychology*, reprinted "Psychology as the Behaviorist

Views It" as its first chapter and went on to summarize the field of animal psychology. The book was well received as a comprehensive account of that field, and enhanced Watson's reputation as he successfully ran for president of the American Psychological Association. But despite the radical prescriptions of its opening chapter, the book had little to say about *human* psychology and as a whole did not seem revolutionary.

Although Watson had condemned introspection, he had not yet been able to replace it, and he candidly admitted as much in the opening of his presidential speech to the American Psychological Association in 1915:

> Since the publication two years ago of my somewhat impolite papers against current methods in psychology I have felt it incumbent upon me before making further unpleasant remarks to suggest some method which we might begin to use in place of introspection. I have found, as you easily might have predicted, that it is one thing to condemn a long-established method, but quite another thing to suggest anything in its place.[16]

But now Watson saw the beginnings of an answer, since his younger colleague Karl Lashley had introduced him to recent Russian writings on the conditioned reflex.* He thus learned about Pavlov's conditioned salivary reflexes and about the related work of Pavlov's compatriot **Vladimir M. Bechterev** (1857–1927). Bechterev had extended Pavlov's technique to study muscular responses such as the withdrawal of a paw when electric shock was administered as the unconditioned stimulus. He had also tried conditioning *human* subjects, an idea that Lashley and Watson pushed further. Lashley devised a removable tube that could be fitted inside the cheek of human subjects and used to measure their salivations, and Watson constructed an apparatus that administered mild shock to a human subject's finger or toe and measured the strength of the subsequent withdrawal reflex. After pairing neutral conditioned stimuli with shock, he had been able to obtain and measure conditioned withdrawal responses.

---

* Lashley went on in his career to become a leading neuropsychologist and to conduct the studies on cerebral localization of memory reviewed in Chapter 3.

Watson believed the main significance of these studies lay not in the bare fact that people and dogs could both be conditioned to salivate to, or withdraw their toes from, inherently neutral stimuli, but in their implications for further and broader conditioning experiments. Pavlov, as a physiologist, had been more interested in the brain than in the behavior of his subjects, and for drawing his speculative physiological inferences one type of response—salivation—had been as good as any other. Watson, however, sought a general principle to account for many different kinds of behavior and seized on the conditioned reflex as a *model* for a wide variety of responses. In particular, he suggested in his presidential address that human *emotions* might profitably be thought of as glandular and muscular reflexes that, like salivation, readily become conditioned. If so, then Pavlovian-style conditioning offered a properly behavioristic, nonintrospective avenue for studying one of the most important and complicated subjects in human psychology.

Conditioned Emotional Reactions

In 1917, shortly after Watson's APA address, his plan to extend behavioristic methods into human psychology had to be temporarily shelved when the United States entered World War I. He joined the service as a major in the Signal Corps, where his job was to help select and train aviators. Predictably enough, he chafed at the authoritarian military atmosphere, and let his contempt for his superiors show. They, in turn, recommended "that he be not allowed to serve his country in his scientific capacity, but be sent to the line." Only the war's quick end in 1918 spared him from assignment to a highly dangerous intelligence mission.[17]

Safely returned to Johns Hopkins and civilian life, Watson took up where he had left off and in 1919 published *Psychology from the Standpoint of a Behaviorist*. While his first book had limited itself to comparative and animal psychology, this one aimed at being a *general* text concentrating on *human* behavior—covering such subjects as thought, language, child development, and emotion. As promised, research on conditioned reflexes played a large part in the book, especially its treatment of emotions.

Watson began by asking which human emotional responses are innate and "unconditioned," and his answer described his observations of human infants who presumably had not yet had time to acquire any conditioned responses. (Infants made excellent behavioristic subjects because they could not talk and contaminate the experiments with subjective or introspective reports.) He had presented a great variety of stimuli to infants to see what sorts of reactions they elicited, and he had concluded that there were just three kinds of unconditioned emotional responses, each one produced by a surprisingly small number of stimuli.

First, Watson observed an apparently innate **fear response**, defined behavioristically as "a sudden catching of the breath, clutching randomly with the hands, . . . sudden closing of the eyelids, puckering of the lips, then crying."[18] Only two kinds of stimuli seemed able to produce this reaction in very young infants: a sudden and unexpected loud sound, and a sudden loss of support, as when the infant was suddenly dropped (and then caught without any physical harm being done). Infants did not react in this or any other dramatic way when confronted with darkness or other stimuli commonly regarded as fearful by older people. (This must have led Watson to conclude that his own fear and inability to sleep in the dark during his emotional breakdown in Chicago had been an acquired rather than an innate emotional reaction.)

Second, Watson observed an emotional reaction in infants he called **rage**, in which "the body stiffens and fairly well-coordinated slashing or striking movements of the hands and arms result; the feet and legs are drawn up and down; the breath is held until the child's face is flushed." Just one kind of stimulus—the physical hindering of movement—produced this reaction in a newborn: "Almost any child from birth can be thrown into a rage if its arms are held tightly to its sides; sometimes even if the elbow joint is clasped tightly between the fingers the response appears; at times just the placing of the head between cotton pads will produce it."[19]

Finally, Watson saw evidence for a third unconditioned emotion in infants that he provisionally called **love**:

> The original situation which calls out the observable love response seems to be the stroking or manipulation of some erogenous zone, tickling, shaking, gentle rocking, patting and turning on the stomach across the attendant's knee. The response

varies. If the infant is crying, crying ceases, a smile may appear, attempts at gurgling, cooing, and finally, in older children, the extension of the arms, which we should class as the forerunner of the embrace of adults.[20]

Watson believed that these three responses, and the restricted range of stimuli that produced them, made up the entire complement of innate human emotional reactions. He saw everything else, including such supposedly "natural" reactions as fear of the dark and love for one's mother, as the results of Pavlovian-style conditioning: "When an emotionally exciting object stimulates the subject simultaneously with one not emotionally stimulating, the latter may in time (often after one such joint stimulation) arouse the same emotional reaction as the former."[21] All the complications and complexities of adult emotional experience were presumably nothing more than conditioned responses built on three relatively simple unconditioned emotional reflexes.

When he wrote his textbook in 1919, Watson had no real empirical support for this theory. It seemed plausible, but he had never observed the actual creation of a conditioned emotional reaction. In 1920 he attempted to remedy this deficiency in research conducted with his graduate student **Rosalie Rayner** (1899–1935). Published under the title "Conditioned Emotional Reactions," the Watson-Rayner study of "Little Albert" remains today one of the most famous and controversial in psychological literature (see Figure 9.3). They conditioned "Albert B.," the 11-month-old son of a wet nurse in the hospital adjacent to their infant laboratory, to fear a white rat—a stimulus that initially evoked his interest and pleasure rather than fear. For their unconditioned stimulus, they loudly struck a steel bar with a hammer just behind Albert's head. They described the first trials as follows:

1. White rat suddenly taken from the basket and presented to Albert. He began to reach for the rat with left hand. Just as his hand touched the animal the bar was struck immediately behind his head. The infant jumped violently and fell forward, burying his face in the mattress. He did not cry, however.
2. Just as the right hand touched the rat the bar was again struck. Again the infant jumped violently, fell forward and began to whimper. In order not to disturb the child too seriously no further tests were given for one week.[22]

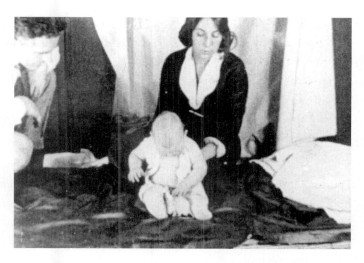

FIG 9.3 John B. Watson and Rosalie Rayner with Little Albert

When Albert first saw the rat the next week, he kept his distance from the animal but did not cry. Then, on five separate occasions, the experimenters deliberately moved the rat close to Albert and clanged the bar behind his head. After this, the rat alone produced what they interpreted as a full-fledged fear response: "The instant the rat was shown the baby began to cry. Almost instantly he turned sharply to the left, fell over on his left side, raised himself on all fours and began to crawl away so rapidly that he was caught with difficulty before reaching the edge of the table."[23]

Five days later Albert still responded to the rat with whimpering and withdrawal. Watson and Rayner tested for generalization of the conditioned response by presenting other furry stimuli: a rabbit, a dog, a seal coat, cotton wool, and a Santa Claus mask. Each produced a noticeable but weakened avoidance reaction. Then Watson put his own hair—which was showing streaks of white—near the child, and got a poetically just response: "Albert was completely negative. Two other observers did the same thing. He began immediately to play with their hair."[24]

Later, Watson and Rayner decided for some unstated reason to "freshen" Albert's generalized response to the rabbit and dog, and clanged the bar after presentation of each of those stimuli. The white rat was similarly freshened, and then Albert was presented with all three stimuli in a room different from that in which the conditioning had occurred. Albert actively feared them all in this new setting. After a further month with no trials at all, Albert was retested with the Santa mask, the fur coat, the rat, the rabbit, and the dog. All still produced fear responses.*

And that was the last Watson and Rayner saw of Little Albert! Irresponsibly—from the standpoint of today's research ethics—they let him leave the hospital without trying to decondition the fear reactions they had produced. They only added a section to their paper describing what they *would have* done:

> Had the opportunity been at hand we should have tried out several methods, some of which we may mention. 1) Constantly confronting the child with those stimuli which called out the responses in hopes that habituation would come in. . . . 2) By trying to "recondition" by showing objects calling out fear responses (visual) and simultaneously stimulating the erogenous zones (tactual). We should first try the lips, then the nipples and as a final resort the sex organs. 3) By trying to "recondition" by feeding the subject candy or other food just as the animal is shown. . . . 4) By building up "constructive" activities around the object by imitation and by putting the hand through motions of manipulation.[25]

Watson and Rayner further stated that the fear responses "in the home environment are likely to persist indefinitely, unless an accidental method for removing them is hit upon." And in a concluding section of their article, they ridiculed the Freudian psychoanalyst who might one day try to treat Albert's phobia:

> The Freudians twenty years from now, . . . when they come to analyze Albert's fear of a seal skin coat . . . will probably tease from him a recital of a dream which upon their analysis will show that Albert at three years of age attempted to play with the pubic hair of the mother and was scolded violently for it. If the analyst has sufficiently prepared Albert to accept such a dream . . . he may be fully convinced that the dream was a true revealer of the factors which brought about the fear.[26]

---

* For an analysis of the mythical status of the Little Albert study in psychology, see Benjamin Harris's article "Whatever Happened to Little Albert," *American Psychologist* 34 (1979): 151–160.

These words must have come as cold comfort to Albert's mother, if she saw them at all. It is likely she did not. In a piece of retrospective detective work undertaken almost 90 years later, a team of psychologist/sleuths attempted to uncover Little Albert's real identity. Their conclusion, based on a seven-year scavenger hunt involving extensive archival and genealogical research and biometric analysis of photographic evidence, was that Little Albert's real identity was probably Douglas Merritte, son of Arvilla Merritte of Baltimore. If these psychologist-sleuths are correct, Arvilla would likely have been too preoccupied to read the published account of her son's conditioning experiences; Douglas developed hydrocephalus in 1922, probably as a result of meningitis. Three years later, at the age of 6, Douglas, immortalized as "Little Albert," was dead.[27]

Watson and Rayner, as we noted, had no contact with Little Albert after he left the hospital. They were soon embroiled in controversy in their personal lives. They fell in love, had an affair, and were discovered by Mary Watson. Encouraged by Harold Ickes, who still despised his brother-in-law and had once even hired a private detective to uncover damaging information about him, Mary divorced him.[28] Although such an event would make little news today, both the Rayners and the Ickeses were socially prominent families, and Baltimore newspapers gave the story full play. Johns Hopkins had just become coeducational, and its administration, particularly sensitive to scandal at that time, forced Watson's resignation. He happily married Rayner but suddenly found himself in need of a new job. A new and entirely different phase of his career was about to begin.

Advertising and Behaviorism

Watson moved to New York, where he soon received job offers from the New School of Social Research and the J. Walter Thompson advertising agency—the latter at a salary of $25,000 per year, four times his previous professor's pay. This eased his sense of loss when he chose advertising over academia, and he plunged into his new career with typical vigor. He started by getting practical experience in the field—conducting door-to-door surveys in the rural South to determine the market for rubber boots peddling Yuban coffee in Pittsburgh, and working part time as a clerk in Macy's department store in New York to study consumer attitudes. Then, back in the main office, he helped plan many innovative and successful advertising campaigns. He got Queen Marie of Roumania to endorse the beauty-enhancing qualities of Pond's cold cream, in one of the first uses of celebrity testimonials in advertising. He hired pediatricians to vouch for the infection-fighting properties of Johnson and Johnson's baby powder, and pretty models to suggest that it was fine for women to smoke as long as they brushed their teeth with Pebeco toothpaste.[29] As Watson later put it, "I began to learn that it can be just as thrilling to watch the growth of a sales curve of a new product as to watch the learning curve of animals or man."[30] By 1924 he was a vice president of the agency.

He still kept a hand in psychology, however, lecturing part-time at the New School for Social Research and in 1924 publishing those lectures under the title *Behaviorism*. Here Watson used his new communication skills to produce his most engaging and flamboyantly written book; it sold well and was acclaimed by a *New York Times* review as marking "a new epoch in the intellectual history of man."[31] While that evaluation may have been exaggerated, the book did present the behaviorist viewpoint with completeness, flair, and colorful examples.

For example, Watson's discussion of conditioned emotions was not only illustrated by the case of Albert but further enlivened by descriptions of children's behavior when their parents fight or make love in their presence. In accounting for personality disturbances as the potentially reversible results of maladaptive conditioning, Watson described a hypothetical dog who might be conditioned to sleep in an ashcan, foul its own bed, salivate constantly, and fear small animals— before being deconditioned of all these behaviors and turned into a blue-ribbon winner at the dog show.

He also turned his behaviorist's eye toward one of the most popular and controversial concepts of psychoanalysis, unconscious thought. In a chapter titled "Do We Always Think in Words?" Watson suggested that unconscious thought indeed exists, but not as the mysterious metaphysical entity he accused the psychoanalysts of fostering. He started by defining conscious thought as a series of vocal or subvocal verbal responses—that is, conscious thinkers literally talk to themselves. Each verbal response presumably serves as a stimulus capable of calling up one or more new responses, so thinking proceeds in a chainlike fashion. All of the newly elicited responses need not be verbal, however; they can also be visceral or kinesthetic, and can include emotional reactions. These nonverbal reactions can serve as links in the chain of thought and call up their own verbal or nonverbal responses. Thus, they function as important and sometimes emotion-laden parts of the thought process, but since they are nonverbal they are not experienced as "conscious" by the thinker.

In *Behaviorism*, Watson also strongly presented a case for **radical environmentalism** the view that environmental factors have overwhelmingly greater importance than heredity or constitution in determining behavior. Of course, his theory of emotions had suggested that the great variety of human emotional responses derives from the conditioning of just three, relatively simple innate reflexes. He now suggested it was much the same for all other aspects of human personality—that innate factors are so quickly modified and developed by conditioning and experience as to become virtually negligible in accounting for individual differences in human adults. "We draw the conclusion," he wrote, "that there is no such thing as an inheritance of *capacity, talent, temperament, mental constitution,* and *characteristics.* These things . . . depend on training that goes on mainly in the cradle. . . . A certain type of structure, plus early training—*slanting*—accounts for adult performance." He continued, in one of his most famous passages, to emphasize the degree of *control* caretakers could potentially exert over the development of children, if only they systematically applied the principles of conditioning:

> Give me a dozen healthy infants, well-formed, and my own specified world to bring them up in and I'll guarantee to take any one at random and train him to become any type of specialist I might select—doctor, lawyer, merchant-chief and yes, even beggar-man and thief, regardless of his talents, penchants, tendencies, abilities, vocations, and race of his ancestors.[32]

If Watson heard the ground rumble beneath his feet as he wrote that passage, it was perhaps the ghost of Francis Galton rolling over in his grave.

The Little Albert Study Revisited

During the brief period when Watson had officially left academia but still had a hand in academic psychology, he had one last opportunity to *scientifically* test the tenets of his radical environmentalism, this time in the service of *removing* rather than *creating* emotional reactions. In 1924, Columbia University Teachers College in New York City received a large grant from the Laura Spelman Rockefeller Memorial (LSRM) for research on child development and parent education. Watson, with his established reputation for practical, applied work, was hired as a research consultant on the grant. One of his first tasks was to oversee the work of an LSRM fellow, **Mary Cover Jones** (1896–1987), a graduate of Vassar College who had been a classmate and friend of Watson's wife, Rosalie Rayner.[33] In fact, Jones had become acquainted with Watson several years earlier when she attended one of his public lectures in New York City. As a result of Watson's lecture, Jones not only cemented her desire to pursue psychology instead of pediatrics but also became intrigued by the notion that if a fear could be *created* through conditioning, then perhaps it could also be *removed*.

Jones, supervised by Watson, had an opportunity to test her idea when she was appointed associate in psychological research at the Institute of Educational Research during her graduate training. As part of this appointment, Jones worked at the Heckscher Foundation, a home for children who had been abandoned by, or temporarily separated from, their parents. To facilitate her research, Jones (and her young family) moved into Heckscher House, where she encountered the 3-year-old boy whom she would subsequently dub "Albert, grown a little bit older."[34] Jones noted that the child, given the pseudonym Peter, had a strong fear of rabbits. Her attempts to rid Peter of his fear would be singled out by later behavior therapists as one of the first demonstrations of **systematic desensitization.**

Building on Watson and Rayner's recommendations from the abruptly terminated Little Albert study, Jones tested the idea that Peter's fear could be eliminated by presenting a pleasant stimulus (candy) at the same time as the rabbit, which was introduced at a distance that did not evoke a fear response. The rabbit was then brought closer and closer to Peter, always in the presence of the pleasing stimulus, until he was able to tolerate the rabbit and even hold it in his lap and play with it for several minutes at a time. She called this procedure *direct conditioning*. Other children who were not afraid of the rabbit were also brought in as positive role models throughout the process. Jones noted in a subsequent publication that of several fear removal methods tried on a sample of infants, only the methods of direct conditioning and social imitation (which were combined in the Little Peter study) achieved "unqualified success"[35] in eliminating infants' fear responses. Watson was heavily involved in the study; Jones later noted that Watson "faithfully followed Peter's progress, reverses, and final freedom from his fear . . [and] paid us a professional visit on most Saturday afternoons throughout the conduct of the therapeutic sessions."[36] In this capacity, Watson saw the Little Albert study to its logical conclusion, although obviously not with Little Albert himself. Although Watson would no longer work in the laboratory, it must have been gratifying for him to witness Jones's demonstration of the power of the environment to make an infant *less* fearful.

Psychological Care of Infant and Child

During the 1920s, Watson's psychological writings became geared increasingly to the general public and appeared more often in popular magazines than in scholarly journals. Many bore catchy titles, such as "The Weakness of Women," "What about Your Child?" and "Feed Me on Facts," and dealt with practical issues in childrearing. Assisted by his wife, Watson published *Psychological Care of Infant and Child* in 1928, a how-to book on childrearing that achieved considerable popular success.

Consistent with Watson's radical environmentalism, this book urged parents to take direct and frankly manipulative control of their children's environments, quite contrarily to the permissive "progressive education" advocated by Watson's old teacher and nemesis, John Dewey. Dewey, said Watson, espoused a "doctrine of mystery" according to which "there are hidden springs of activity, hidden possibilities of unfolding within the child which must be waited for until they appear and then be fostered and tended." Watson argued that, in reality, "there is nothing from within to develop."[37] Parents need only to control their children's environments properly, so that the most adaptive conditioned reflexes will develop.

The book elaborated on Watson's theory of emotions and offered practical suggestions about how to avoid the creation of inappropriate conditioned emotional reactions. The home should be set up to minimize the occurrence of banging doors and other random loud sounds that would frighten the child and establish inappropriate fear reactions. Clothing should always be loose enough to allow free movement and prevent unnecessary rage. And above all, Watson recommended that children should *never* be stimulated into "love" responses when they ought to be developing self-reliant behavior. Nothing drew his scorn more than the coddling of children, which he saw as the rewarding of ineffective behavior with hugs, kisses, or other signs of solicitude. "When I hear a mother say 'Bless its little heart' when it falls down, stubs its toe, or suffers some other ill," he grumbled, "I usually have to walk a block or two to let off steam." Instead, parents should treat children "as though they were young adults." "Never hug and kiss them, never let them sit on your lap. If you must, kiss them once on the forehead when they say good night. Shake hands with them in the morning. Give them a pat on the head if they have made an extraordinarily good job of a difficult task."[38]

Few child-care experts today would endorse this Spartan approach (which was not universally accepted even in 1928), and virtually all would say that a substantial degree of physical affection is necessary. But Watson also explicitly recognized that there is no single ideal way to raise children and that behavior deemed desirable may vary widely from time to time and from culture to culture. And the book's general point—that parents can exert much more purposeful control over the upbringing of their children than was commonly supposed—probably helped many parents a great deal.

Watson's Legacy

Despite the success of Watson's popular writings, such work was never more than a sideline for him as he became increasingly absorbed in the advertising business. And when he revised *Behaviorism* in 1930, it marked the end of his professional psychological career. He still continued to practice his behavioristic principles, however, both in advertising and together with his wife in the raising of two sons, born in 1922 and 1924. The boys were assiduously trained to be practical, self-reliant, fearless, and "masculine," with expressions of affection or emotional tenderness strictly curbed.

The outcome of Watson's home childrearing experiment must be interpreted cautiously, because tragedy intervened when Rosalie

Watson died prematurely in 1935, leaving her young sons motherless. Both boys were subsequently sent to boarding school, and the deeply shaken Watson had only sporadic contact with them afterward. After some initial difficulty adjusting to school, both sons went on to successful academic and occupational careers—one becoming a psychiatrist and the other an industrial psychologist and vice president of a major food company. But both were also plagued by severe depression as adults; one attempted suicide before being helped by psychoanalytic therapy, and the other—the psychiatrist—actually did take his own life in 1963. The surviving son, while recognizing his father's virtues, has placed much of the blame on his childrearing practices:

> I have some unhappy thoughts about . . . the effects of behavioristic principles on my being raised into an adult. . . . In many ways I adored my father as an individual and as a character. He was bright; he was charming; he was masculine, witty, and reflective. But he was also conversely unresponsive, emotionally uncommunicative, unable to express and cope with any feelings of emotion of his own, and determined unwittingly to deprive, I think, my brother and me of any kind of emotional foundation. . . . He was very rigid in carrying out his fundamental philosophies as a behaviorist.[39]

Of course, many other factors, including the premature death of their mother, could have contributed to the sons' difficulties. But Watson's view of emotional development, like many other aspects of his theory, was unquestionably simplistic. He habitually made his points by exaggeration and overstatement, so his ideas have subsequently had to be toned down.

For example, most would now agree that children are not so easily conditioned into becoming paragons of adjustment and virtue; that emotional development involves far more than conditioning on just three basic reactions; that language and thought are more than simple chains of verbal, visceral, and kinesthetic reflexes; and that radical environmentalism underestimates the effects of constitution and heredity. Pavlovian conditioning, while still recognized as an important form of learning, has proved insufficient to account for the more active ways organisms learn to manipulate and control their environments.

But still, Watson's ideas contained an element of good sense that continues to impress many psychologists. Some still define their science as the study of behavior, and most still insist that their basic data must be observable and "objective," at least to a degree. Prediction and control of behavior remain the major goals of many psychologists, and the study of learning and conditioning in animals as well as human beings is still an important psychological sub-area. Pavlovian conditioning theories have been retained, although complemented by other models of the learning process. In his autobiography, written long after he had left psychology, Watson assessed his contribution by saying, "I still believe as firmly as ever in the general behavioristic position I took in 1912. I think it has influenced psychology."[40] He was not being immodest.

In fact, the rise of neobehaviorism as the dominant theoretical position in North American academic psychology departments from the 1920s through the 1950s was perhaps the most immediate and visible form of Watson's influence. Psychologists such as **Edward Chace Tolman** (1886–1959) and **Clark Hull** (1884–1952) followed Watson's lead in terms of viewing conscious experience as outside the purview of direct psychological investigation. However, under the influence of a philosophy known as **logical positivism**, they attempted to derive and test theories about behavior that translated nonobservable constructs (such as motivation) into observable ones.

Tolman is perhaps best known for his experimental work with rats in mazes, in which he demonstrated the concept of **latent learning**. In one of these experiments, Tolman and his graduate student placed one group of rats in a maze and let them wander around freely. A second group of rats were also allowed to wander freely, but each successful navigation of the maze was rewarded with food. A third group of rats were allowed to wander freely with no reward, but a reward was introduced on the eleventh day of the experiment. If latent learning had taken place, as Tolman hypothesized (which put him in opposition with other neobehaviorists such as Hull who adhered to a more associationistic view), the rats in the last condition should have shown a drastic decrease in navigational errors as soon as the reward was introduced, in effect giving them incentive to demonstrate their latent learning of the maze. This is indeed what occurred. During the first ten days, the rats in the eleventh-day reward condition showed error rates similar to the rats allowed to wander freely with no reward. Rats in the second (reward) condition gradually reduced their errors over the course of the ten days. When the reward was introduced to the rats in the last condition, they quickly exceeded their compatriots in group 2 in terms of accuracy of maze running. Tolman used experiments such as these to support his theory of **purposive behaviorism**—that is, that all behavior is purposive or goal directed.

Hull's theoretical position, sometimes called **mechanistic behaviorism**, involved establishing complex mathematical laws in which learning was accounted for in terms of the specifiable relationships among a host of operationally defined variables, such as habit strength, drive strength, and stimulus intensity. A typical Hullian equation might define the probability that an organism will produce a response r to a stimulus s (written as sEr, which was itself defined in terms of the relationship between habit strength and drive strength) as the function of nine different constructs, each of which would be operationally defined with its own mathematical equation. Although his theoretical apparatus became extremely complicated and abstract, Hull was nonetheless interested, as were most behaviorists, in the practical applications of psychology, and he directed research on many human and social problems at the Institute of Human Relations at Yale from 1929 until his death in 1952.[41]

Another among those significantly influenced by Watson, but who came to adopt quite a different position from those of the neobehaviorists, was a struggling young writer named B. F. Skinner. Skinner first encountered behaviorism at a particularly low point in his literary career and decided that his future lay in psychology rather than literature. Skinner went on to become the most important behaviorist of his day and one of the most acclaimed psychologists of the twentieth century. We conclude this chapter with his story.

Skinner and Operant Conditioning

Burrhus Frederic Skinner was born on March 20, 1904, in the small railroading town of Susquehanna, Pennsylvania. His father, a self-taught lawyer who had never attended college and who passed his bar examination after one year at law school, was a persuasive speaker and author of a well-regarded textbook on workmen's compensation law. Skinner described his mother as "bright and beautiful"—a Susquehanna native like her husband who had been popular, a good singer, and the second-ranked student in her high school class. Concerning her strict notions of propriety, Skinner wrote: "I was taught to fear God, the police, and what people will think. As a result, I usually do what I have to do with no great struggle."[42]

As a boy in Susquehanna, Skinner showed musical, mechanical, and literary aptitudes. He enjoyed opera on the family Victrola, played the piano and saxophone, and earned pocket money throughout high school by playing in a dance band. His mechanical creations included a Rube Goldberg contraption reminding him to keep his room neat: "A special hook in the closet of my room was connected by a string-and-pulley system to a sign hanging above the door to the room. When my pajamas were in place on the hook, the sign was held high above the door and out of the way. When the pajamas were off the hook, the sign hung squarely in the middle of the door frame. It read 'Hang up your pajamas.'"[43]

Skinner published his first literary work at age ten, a poem titled "That Pessimistic Fellow," in the *Lone Scout* magazine. Unpublished works written during high school included a morality play featuring the characters Greed, Gluttony, Jealousy, and Youth and a melodramatic novel about a young naturalist's love affair with the daughter of a dying trapper. Skinner did well academically, and in 1922 he became the first in his family to attend college, entering Hamilton College in Clinton, New York as a freshman.

At Hamilton, Skinner took some biology courses and one philosophy course taught by a former student of Wundt's, but no psychology. He majored in English and wrote regularly for the college newspaper, literary magazine, and humor magazine—adopting the pen name of Sir Burrhus de Beerus for the last. An inveterate practical joker, he helped spread a false rumor that Charlie Chaplin was going to speak on campus. After a large crowd gathered for the event and was sorely disappointed, Skinner wrote an editorial in the school newspaper declaring, "No man with the slightest regard for his Alma Mater could have done such a thing."[44] As a senior, Skinner publicly parodied the speech teacher, subverted the traditional oratory competition by submitting a farcical speech, and decorated the hall for class day exercises with less than complimentary caricatures of the faculty.

But he also showed a more serious side and worked hard to improve his writing skills. The summer before his senior year he attended a writer's workshop whose faculty included the poet Robert Frost. Frost delighted and encouraged Skinner by telling him, "You are worth twice anyone else I have seen in prose this year."[45]

After graduation Skinner moved into his parents' home in Scranton, Pennsylvania, built a study in the attic, and tried to settle in and write professionally. There he underwent what he later called his "Dark Year," as he experienced loneliness, depression, and, worst of all, a profound case of writer's block. He read great literature but found little to say about it. He tried to write about writing but that seemed empty. As he later put it, "The truth was, I had no reason to write anything. I had nothing to say, and nothing about my life was making any change in that condition."[46] He considered consulting a psychiatrist, but he finally found some distraction along with remuneration when his father set him up with a job abstracting several thousand legal decisions for Pennsylvania's Anthracite Board of Conciliation.

Gradually, Skinner consoled himself with the thought that even the best of literature could tell only a part of the truth about human nature. He pondered a critic's comment about one of the novelist William Thackeray's characters, to the effect that "Thackeray didn't know it, but she drank," and decided that good writers often accurately describe *how* people behave but offer little insight as to *why* they do so. At this crucial point in his life, he encountered behaviorism.

Skinner read a book in which the philosopher Bertrand Russell, one of his favorite writers, discussed John B. Watson's recently published *Behaviorism* critically but seriously. "I do not fundamentally agree with Watson's view," wrote Russell, "but I think it contains much more truth than most people suppose, and I regard it as desirable to develop the behaviourist method to the fullest possible extent."[47] Intrigued, Skinner read Watson as well as the recently translated Pavlov, liked what he read, and began to suspect that behavioristic analyses might just be able to account for many of those "whys" of behavior that were missing in literature.

A symbolic turning point occurred when Skinner read an article by H. G. Wells about Pavlov and the famous British writer George

Bernard Shaw. The irascible and colorful Shaw had greatly disliked Pavlov's writings and had sarcastically described the Russian as a scoundrel and vivisectionist with the habit of boiling babies alive just to see what would happen. Wells expressed admiration for both men and posed a hypothetical question: Pavlov and Shaw are drowning on opposite sides of a pier and you have but one life belt to throw in the water; to which side would you throw it? Skinner instantly knew that his own choice would be for Pavlov, and he further resolved to go to graduate school and become a behavioristic psychologist. He applied and was accepted at Harvard, for the fall of 1928.

Although hardly a hotbed of behaviorism, Harvard's psychology department was nevertheless tolerant and stimulating. Skinner found a few fellow graduate students who shared his interests, and faculty who allowed him to go his own way. During the eight years between 1928 and 1936—first as a graduate student, then as a postdoctoral fellow, and finally as a junior fellow in Harvard's prestigious Society of Fellows—Skinner laid the groundwork for a whole new kind of behavioristic analysis.

Operant Conditioning

Skinner's accomplishment followed his invention of an ingeniously simple piece of apparatus now commonly called the **Skinner box**, which became for him what the salivary reflex apparatus had been for Pavlov and which made possible the study of a different kind of learned behavior he called **operant conditioning** (see Figure 9.4). Skinner has told the story of how he came to invent this box (although he preferred to call it an operant chamber) in a delightfully tongue-in-cheek article, "A Case History in Scientific Method."

According to this account, four "unformalized principles of scientific practice" led to success. First, his box was the result of a long series of partly completed experiments that had been abandoned in midcourse; thus, his first principle: "When you run into something interesting, drop everything else and study it." Second, the box was highly automated and required little work by the experimenter once an animal subject was placed inside; hence "Some ways of doing research are easier than others." Further, some of his most interesting results occurred accidentally or when the apparatus malfunctioned,

FIG 9.4

B. F. Skinner (1904–1990)
conditioning a rat in an
operant chamber

illustrating principles three and four: "Apparatus sometimes breaks down," and "Some people are lucky."[48]

Besides following these unformalized principles, Skinner was also inspired by a major guiding idea. He had admired the precision Pavlov brought to the study of conditioned reflexes, and he appreciated Watson's attempts to extend the concept of conditioned reflexes into explanations of emotions. But still, something seemed lacking: "I could not . . . move without a jolt from salivary reflexes to the important business of the organism in everyday life."[49] Learning in everyday life involves more than the passive acquisition of reflexive reactions to stimuli that are presented to the organism from the outside; normal organisms also learn to actively manipulate, control, and "operate upon" their environments. Thorndike's chickens and cats had demonstrated this type of learning when they escaped confinement in his famous experiment of 1898 (see Chapter 8). Skinner devised his box to enable him to study actively acquired learning even more systematically.

His box, illustrated in Figure 9.5,[50] was essentially a cage for a white rat with a lever-bar mounted on one wall near a food tray and connected to a mechanism that dropped a food pellet into the tray when the bar was pressed. Each press of the bar also caused a pen mechanism touching a constantly moving roll of paper to rise by a small fixed amount, so that a permanent, **cumulative record** of all of the rat's bar presses could be kept. Figure 9.6 illustrates one typical cumulative record, for an animal that made its first response after being in the box about 14 minutes and its second at about 25 minutes, and that then began to respond at an increasingly rapid rate. Such cumulative records resembled mathematical curves whose steepness reflected the rates of responding. When rates were low there were few pen elevations and the record remained flat, as in the left-hand portion of Figure 9.6; higher rates produced curves with steeper slopes, as on the right.

Figure 9.6 typifies the cumulative records Skinner obtained with hungry but untrained rats when first placed in the box. At first, bar-pressing responses occurred infrequently and "accidentally," as the animal explored its new environment. After the first few presses were reinforced with food, however, the rate increased dramatically and continued high as long as the rat remained hungry.

In further experiments, Skinner varied the **contingencies of reinforcement**—that is, the specific conditions under which the responses were reinforced or not with food pellets. One experiment occurred by chance (illustrating Skinner's third and fourth unformalized principles), when the food dispenser jammed after an animal had already been regularly reinforced and established in a steady response

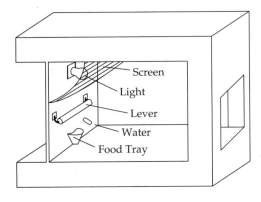

FIG 9.5
Diagram of a typical
Skinner box

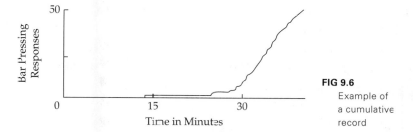

FIG 9.6
Example of
a cumulative
record

rate. The ensuing cumulative record showed an **extinction curve** like that illustrated in Figure 9.7. At first, the animal responded at a very high rate, partly because it was no longer pausing between responses to eat and partly because of an "emotional" or "frustrated" activation of the response. After a few minutes, however, the rate slowed down except for a series of progressively diminishing, wavelike "bursts" of response. Finally, the curve flattened out almost completely, indicating that the response was almost never repeated—that is, that it had been "extinguished." Except for the wavelike bursts, the overall shape of the cumulative record approximated a regular, negatively accelerating mathematical curve.

Other experiments varied the contingencies of reinforcement by providing food pellets only intermittently, according to four main types of **reinforcement schedules**. On a **fixed-interval reinforcement schedule**, for example, reinforcement came only on the first response following a predetermined period of time, regardless of how many responses had been made in the interim. After an acquisition period in which cumulative records generally resembled those for regular reinforcement, the records assumed a characteristic and highly regular scallop

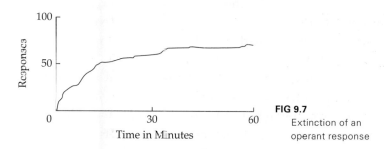

FIG 9.7
Extinction of an
operant response

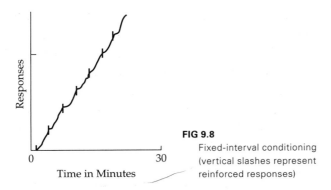

FIG 9.8
Fixed-interval conditioning
(vertical slashes represent
reinforced responses)

shape, illustrated in Figure 9.8 for a 3-minute interval schedule. After each reinforced response (designated by a vertical slash), the response rate decreased for a minute or two and then increased sharply as the end of the interval approached. Such a response pattern maximized the total reinforcement for the animal by assuring a response would occur immediately after the end of each interval; it also minimized the effort expended, as responses were seldom "wasted" during the nonreinforced periods immediately following each reinforcement.

On a **fixed-ratio reinforcement schedule**, reinforcement always followed a preset *number* of responses—after every fourth response, every tenth, or any other number Skinner decided on. Although it took longer for response rates to stabilize under these conditions, eventually they leveled off at about the same steady slope as for regular reinforcement. Skinner found he could speed things up by increasing his ratios gradually, starting off by reinforcing every second response, then every fourth, and so on—doubling the ratio each time the response rate stabilized. In one experiment, a rat so conditioned pressed industriously at the bar when only every 192nd response was reinforced. Obviously, under the proper conditions organisms could be induced to work harder and harder for progressively diminishing rewards—a principle perhaps already familiar to unscrupulous employers in human society.

Skinner also experimented with **variable-interval** and **variable-ratio reinforcement schedules**, in which the times or numbers of responses between reinforcements were varied randomly. These schedules resembled the irregular pattern of payoffs dispensed by slot machines in gambling casinos. As casino owners well know, such schedules can produce very high rates of response that are remarkably resistant to extinction. After being placed on such schedules, Skinner's animals responded for much longer after reinforcement was cut off altogether than they would have if the original schedule had been regular. It was as if the irregular reinforcement nurtured a constant hope that the "next" response would be rewarded. Rat and casino player alike became hooked and responded well past the point of diminishing returns.

Skinner saw the rat's bar-pressing behavior as conveniently representing a whole range of learned behaviors by animals and humans in the real world that, in his words, "operate on the environment" to produce various ends. When he published these results in his first book, *The Behavior of Organisms* (1938), he established operant conditioning as a kind of learning distinctly different from the Pavlovian conditioned reflex, but equally as important. He referred to the general Pavlovian type of learning as **respondent conditioning**, and contrasted it with operant conditioning on several dimensions. Respondent conditioning creates completely new connections between stimuli and responses, for example, while operant conditioning strengthens or weakens response tendencies that already exist in the organism's behavioral repertoire. In respondent conditioning the response is *elicited* by the conditioned stimulus, whereas in operant conditioning it must be *emitted* by the subject before conditioning can take place. In respondent conditioning both conditioned and unconditioned stimuli may be precisely defined, while in operant conditioning one can never say with any certainty which stimuli give rise to the response. And the *strength* of respondent conditioning is typically measured in terms of response magnitude or latency, while that of operant conditioning is measured by response rate. In sum, Skinner had demonstrated a controlled and properly behavioristic method for studying a whole new range of learned responses.

Behavior Shaping and Programmed Instruction

After laying the foundations for the study of operant conditioning at Harvard, Skinner taught at the University of Minnesota and the University of Indiana for twelve years before returning permanently to

Harvard in 1948. Over the years he attracted a growing number of followers who sought to apply the techniques and findings of operant conditioning to a wide variety of experimental and practical situations, and who eventually created a separate division of the American Psychological Association devoted to "The Experimental Analysis of Behavior" (today's Division 25). Skinner himself became increasingly concerned with the practical applications and philosophical implications of operant conditioning.

In the 1940s, for example, he extended operant-conditioning techniques to behaviors considerably more complex than bar pressing. He hypothesized that complex behaviors could be thought of as *chains* of simple ones, and he developed methods for building up complex sequences of simple responses in animals. First, he needed a **reinforcer** that could be easily administered to animal subjects without interfering with the flow of their behavior. Thus he started out by using *respondent* conditioning to pair the sound of clicks from a toy clicker with a strong **primary reinforcer** such as food. After a while, the clicks by themselves became effective **secondary reinforcers**, as demonstrated by the fact that animals would maintain high rates of responding in a Skinner box when reinforced only by clicks unaccompanied by food.

Skinner now used this secondary reinforcer to progressively "shape up" increasingly complicated or difficult chains of responses. When he wanted to train a pigeon to peck a certain small spot on the wall, for example, he began by clicking each time it made a partial turn in the spot's direction. Once the animal was constantly oriented in the right direction, Skinner withheld reinforcement until the pigeon extended its head toward the spot. When this response was established, reinforcement was withheld until a peck occurred. And after this highly specific response was emitted and reinforced the first time, repetitions followed much more quickly. Using such patient shaping procedures, Skinner trained pigeons to perform some spectacular feats, such as rolling a ball back and forth to each other across a table in a rudimentary game of Ping-Pong.

Skinner saw no reason that the same basic techniques he used to teach pigeons to play Ping-Pong could not serve as models for *human* education. Inspired by a visit to his daughter's fourth-grade class in 1953, he launched the development of **programmed instruction**—

an educational technique in which complicated subjects such as mathematics are broken down into simple, stepwise components that may be presented to students in order of increasing difficulty. The beginning student answers an easy question about the simplest component, and immediately learns whether the response was right or wrong. If right, that knowledge presumably serves as a secondary reinforcer, so the correct response is strengthened. In a carefully designed program, this correct response should also provide the basis for responding correctly to the next, slightly more difficult question—and so on. When incorrect answers occur they are followed by reviews and supplementary instructions providing the small amount of new information necessary for success on the next try. Thus, Skinner argued that students may gradually be "shaped" into becoming proficient mathematicians, just as his pigeons were shaped into becoming Ping-Pong players.

Today, operant teaching programs have actually been developed for many subjects, at difficulty levels from preschool through graduate school. And while they may not have become an educational panacea capable of replacing the traditional student-teacher relationship, they have nevertheless proved to be valuable additions to the teacher's resources.

Philosophical Implications of Operant Conditioning

As a former man-of-letters, Skinner constantly thought about the philosophical as well as the practical implications of his theory. He concluded very early that if **negative reinforcements** are considered along with positive ones—that is, the environmental consequences an organism will work to avoid or to escape from, as well as those it will work to obtain—then virtually *all* behavior must be controlled by the contingencies of reinforcement. Therefore, the notion of behavioral freedom or free will must be an illusion. Skinner argued that when we *believe* we are acting freely, we are merely free of negative reinforcement or its threat and are fully determined instead by the pursuit of things that have reinforced us positively in the past. When we feel that other people are behaving "freely," we are simply unaware of their complete reinforcement histories and of the contingencies that have shaped their behavior.

Skinner dramatized these ideas in his 1948 utopian novel, *Walden Two*, which described an ideal society in which negative reinforcement has been completely abandoned as a means of social control. Children are reared only to seek the **positive reinforcement** that has been made consequent upon their showing socialized and civilized behavior. Inevitably—so the novel claims—they grow up to be cooperative, intelligent, sociable, and happy. The society's justification and rationale are summarized in the following dialogue between Frazier, the novel's hero, and a skeptical visitor named Castle:

> "Mr. Castle, when a science of behavior has once been achieved, there's no alternative to a planned society. We can't leave mankind to an accidental or biased control. But by using the principle of positive reinforcement—carefully avoiding force or the threat of force—we can preserve a personal sense of freedom. . . ."
>
> "But you haven't denied that you are in complete control," said Castle. "You are still the long-range dictator."
>
> "As you will," said Frazier, . . . "When once you have grasped the principle of positive reinforcement, you can enjoy a sense of unlimited power. It's enough to satisfy the thirstiest tyrant."
>
> "There you are, then," said Castle. "That's my case."
>
> "But it's a limited sort of despotism," Frazier went on. "And I don't think anyone should worry about it. The despot must wield his power for the good of others. If he takes any step which reduces the sum total of human happiness, his power is reduced by a like amount. What better check against a malevolent despotism could you ask for?"[51]

Unsurprisingly enough, *Walden Two* aroused considerable controversy, and many readers condemned its happy but controlled society as totalitarian. Others responded more positively to Skinner's vision, and a few even tried to create real communities based on his principles in the 1970s. Although these utopian attempts could not provide systematic tests of the underlying principles of Skinner's system, the few communities that remain are nonetheless interesting real-life examples of behavioral experimentation in pursuit of the "good life."[52]

Skinner often reported that epistemology (the branch of philosophy that investigates the nature and origin of knowledge) was his first love.[53] The most thoroughgoing statement of his epistemology can be found in his 1957 book *Verbal Behavior*, which contained many ideas he had previously expressed in an unpublished draft he entitled *Sketch for an Epistemology*. To understand *Verbal Behavior* and Skinner's views on language and epistemology more generally, one must adopt the behaviorist position that a theory of knowing is a theory of behaving and that language is one form of behavior. As one behaviorist philosopher has written, in a behavioral epistemology, knowledge is conceptualized "in terms of the behavior of the knower."[54] Therefore, how we come to know can be analyzed and indeed explained by the science of behavior itself. According to Skinner, the only way we acquire knowledge is through the experience of contingencies of reinforcement in the environment. We do not generate internal copies of objects or experiences in the world in order to perceive and know them; rather, we act as if we know them when these acts have been reinforced by the physical or social environment. Furthermore, the only way we demonstrate this knowledge is through behavior, which is often—especially in response to private events—verbal behavior. In Skinner's words, "The simplest and most satisfactory view is that thought is simply *behavior*—verbal or nonverbal, covert or overt."[55] Hence, for Skinner, generating an analysis of verbal behavior was akin to generating a theory of knowledge.

In 1959, **Noam Chomsky** (b. 1928), then a young linguist at the Massachusetts Institute of Psychology, took critical aim at Skinner's position, publishing a vitriolic critique of *Verbal Behavior*.[56] Chomsky, who had himself published a book on language in 1957 called *Syntactic Structures*, not only objected to the specifics of Skinner's theory of language, but was also opposed to the entire behaviorist agenda. His critique was lengthy, thorough, and intense, but one of his main arguments was that behaviorist theories were inadequate to account for the multiple theoretical levels in which **grammatical structure** is represented. Chomsky himself posited both *surface* and *deep structure*, invoking the phrase "Colorless green ideas sleep furiously" to indicate that a sentence that is meaningless on a deep or semantic level nonetheless has an intact and immediately recognizable surface or syntactic structure that all speakers can immediately recognize. He further argued that only human infants can acquire language because only they, and no other species, have the innate knowledge of its fundamental structure. Chomsky also took behaviorists to task for invoking mentalistic constructs but cloaking them in behaviorist terms, thus violating their own philosophical position. Although Skinner reportedly never read Chomsky's critique in its entirety (realizing from the outset that they held fundamentally different and likely irreconcilable positions), its publication has often been invoked as the turning point at which behaviorism began to lose its disciplinary dominance in favor of cognitivism (see also Chapter 14).

In the meantime, Skinner continued to speak out provocatively about the desirability of social control based on positive reinforcement. His bestselling 1971 book, *Beyond Freedom and Dignity*, argued that the assumption of "autonomous man," upon which so many of Western society's institutions are based, is false and has many deleterious consequences. According to this assumption, we "credit" people more for doing good deeds "of their own free will" than for doing them because they have to. But the only real difference, argued Skinner, is that in the first case we do not know the contingencies that produced the behavior, and in the second we do. And the dark and obverse side of this position is that if people are to be "credited" for unexplained good behavior, then they must be *blamed and punished* for their "freely" produced bad behavior. The *assumption* that people are free requires that punishment or its threat be constantly used to control behavior. Skinner summarized: "Under punitive contingencies a person appears to be free to behave well and to deserve credit when he does so. Nonpunitive contingencies generate the same good behavior, but a person cannot be said to be free, and the contingencies deserve credit when he behaves well."[57]

But since the autonomy of autonomous man is only apparent, the winning of personal "credit" seemed to Skinner very small recompense for the constant exposure to punishment. Further, his experiments had suggested that positive reinforcement is more effective than punishment in producing lasting conditioning effects. He therefore argued that we should abandon our illusory belief in behavioral freedom, forthrightly accept the inevitability of control, and deliberately start to design real environments like Walden Two in which behavior is shaped toward socially desirable ends by exclusive means of positive reinforcement.

Skinner's theory did not directly bear on the classic political question of exactly *who* should design the environments and seize the control, but he argued that once the power of operant conditioning becomes well known, someone will surely do so. And since he believed psychologists are likely to have attitudes just as enlightened (or more so) as other groups, he urged them not to be shy about participating in the project.

These assertions about the ubiquity of environmental control, and the desirability of openly seizing it, made Skinner at once the most famous and the most controversial of American psychologists. He was listed in *The 100 Most Important People in the World* and was shown in a 1975 survey to be the best-known scientist in the United States. But recognition did not always imply approval, and Skinner frightened or enraged some people with his pronouncements. He himself was made aware of his darker reputation one evening after attending a particularly pleasing concert. The musicians were young and their music delightful—precisely the sort of event Skinner envisioned as part of the good life in a Walden Two—and while he was leaving he praised the young conductor who had done so well. His companion, who knew the conductor, remarked, "You know, he thinks you are a terrible person. Teaching machines, . . . a fascist."[58]

Unpleasant and unfounded rumors also circulated about Skinner's personal and family life. When his younger daughter was an infant, he designed a temperature-controlled, glass-enclosed crib for her which he first playfully called an "Heir Conditioner" and later patented and marketed (not terribly successfully) as the "Aircrib" (see Figure 9.9). This device's sole purpose was to provide a comfortable and safe environment for infants, and it compared favorably on both scores to traditional cribs or playpens. Yet inaccurate stories began to circulate that Skinner had raised his children like rats "in a box," and that they had suffered grievously as a result. Perhaps conflating Skinner's children with Watson's, some rumors had it that they became mentally ill or committed suicide. In fact, one of Skinner's daughters became a successful professor of educational psychology, and the

FIG 9.9
Skinner's daughter
Deborah in her aircrib

other became an artist whose work has been exhibited at London's Royal Academy.

Unpleasant and unfair publicity was perhaps the inevitable price for Skinner's raising and taking a stand on difficult questions. A more principled and knowledgeable reaction was also expressed against some aspects of Skinner's ideas and behaviorism in general, which we shall refer to in later chapters. But in recompense for all of the attacks, legitimate or otherwise, Skinner had the satisfaction of knowing that many psychologists, educators, and other workers regularly applied his ideas in their everyday research and practice.

Skinner's Influence

Although behaviorism in general, and Skinnerian behaviorism specifically, no longer features prominently in most academic psychology departments, the community of researchers and practitioners who use Skinner's approach – now known as **behavior analysis—** remains vibrant. Multiple journals are devoted to publishing a wide range of scholarly work in the Skinnerian tradition, including the *Journal of Experimental Analysis of Behavior*, the *Journal of Applied Behavior Analysis*, *The Behavior Analyst*, and *Behavior and Social Issues*. The Association for Behavior Analysis International is the Skinnerian community's main scholarly and professional organization, comprising over 5,500 members and multiple international affiliates, from Brazil to India to New Zealand. The Association hosts a lively annual conference in a major American city featuring presentations on the experimental, applied, and philosophical branches of Skinner's system. Skinner's ideas have been applied fruitfully to the treatment of developmental disabilities, especially autism, in which applied behavior analysis is widely accepted as one of the most effective treatment approaches. In education, an area close to Skinner's heart, behavioral principles are used to help children with attention deficit disorder and learning disabilities do better in the classroom, and a number of popular online reading programs, such as *Headsprout*, have been developed using the principles of programmed instruction. Finally, in the field of animal training, Skinnerian shaping techniques are used extensively, not only to train Fido to sit and heel but to train a wide variety of animals for work in the entertainment industry. Clearly, applications of Skinner's principles have extended far beyond the academy, and he would undoubtedly have been pleased with this influence.

Summary

In the early twentieth century several important figures changed their definition of psychology from the study of the conscious mind to the study of observable *behavior*. The Russian physiologist **Ivan Pavlov** helped initiate this transition with his thoroughgoing insistence that explanations of reflexive behavior must be expressed in terms of objective physiological and behavioral indices. Building on his earlier work on the physiology of digestion and the reflexive responses of salivation in dogs, Pavlov conducted meticulous

although the joke makes sense only in English because *hell* in Mesmer's native German means not the underworld but "bright" or "clear"). Mesmer claimed to have restored the girl's sight by magnetism, until her parents prematurely removed her from his care and she became blind again. Her parents, supported by orthodox physicians, called Mesmer a charlatan and charged him with improper conduct. Mesmer retorted that the parents were upset only because Maria-Theresia's celebrity value decreased when she gained normal vision. Today we cannot know the real facts about this case, although quite possibly she suffered from a psychogenic blindness that Mesmer really did alleviate temporarily. Whatever the truth, he found it expedient to flee Vienna for Paris.

In its unstable state on the eve of the French Revolution, Parisian society was just then particularly prone to fads or "crazes." And if anything was suited to become a craze it was animal magnetism, effectively promoted by the colorful Mesmer. Even though he spoke a heavily accented French that few fully understood and charged enormous fees that not many could afford, he soon attracted more clients than he could handle individually. Thus he devised his famous **baquet** (the French word for "tub") as a means of mass-producing magnetic cures.

The use of a tub may seem quaint today, but in the 1780s it made plausible scientific sense to store an invisible magnetic "fluid" in some sort of receptacle. The so-called Leyden jar, which presumably stored charges of electrical fluid and which was in fact an effective early battery, served as one model for Mesmer. And lighter-than-air balloons—which were just then another craze, thrilling the French public with their flights—also worked their wonders by containing and storing an invisible but powerful fluid substance. Thus, when Mesmer placed magnetized iron filings and water in the bottom of a covered wooden tub, he and his contemporaries could sincerely believe that it became filled with an invisible but therapeutic magnetic fluid.

Mesmer inserted metal handles into his baquet, and placed it in the middle of a dimly lit treatment room. Patients entered in groups and sat around the baquet grasping the handles while Mesmer, in an adjoining room, played ethereal music on his glass harmonica to help set the mood (see Figure 10.2). After a suitable state of anticipation had been established in the patients—most of whom already had a good idea of what to expect before they came—Mesmer emerged dressed in a flowing, lilac-colored robe and began pointing his finger or an iron rod at the afflicted parts of the patients' bodies. Invari-

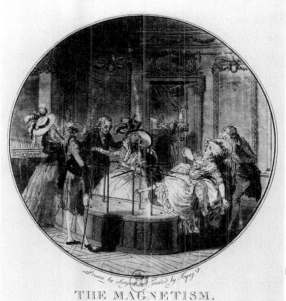

THE MAGNETISM.

FIG 10.2
A scene around
Mesmer's baquet.

ably one or two patients passed into a crisis state and served as models for the others. Soon the room was full of convulsing, crisis-ridden
patients, the most violent of whom were carried by Mesmer and his
assistants to a clearly marked *chambre de crises* ("crisis room") for
individual attention. Not all patients experienced a complete crisis, but even some of these partial responders found their symptoms
improved after the séance was over.

By treating people in groups, Mesmer increased not only his profits
but also the strength of response of many patients, because of a phenomenon social psychologists have since called **social contagion** or
social facilitation—concepts we shall return to later in the chapter.
Mesmer's early responders effectively showed the others what they
were supposed to do, and as more and more members of the group
entered crisis the pressure to go along with the crowd increased in
the holdouts. As a net result, more people entered crisis, and entered it
more strongly, than would have been the case had they been magnetized individually by Mesmer.

Despite—or perhaps because of—his popular and commercial success, Mesmer eventually came under scrutiny by more mainstream
medical and scientific authorities. Finally, in 1784, the king himself
appointed a blue-ribbon scientific commission to investigate him,
chaired by none other than the American ambassador and inventor

of the glass harmonica, Benjamin Franklin. Other eminent commissioners included the great chemist Antoine Lavoisier and the physician Joseph Guillotin (who shortly promoted the use of the "humane" execution device that now bears his name, and to which Lavoisier and many others would lose their heads during the French Revolution). When the commissioners submitted themselves to magnetic induction, they proved insusceptible, but they discovered that "good" subjects fell into crisis when presented with something they merely *believed* was magnetized but really was not. The commissioners reported that they "unanimously concluded, on the question of the existence and the utility of animal magnetism, that there is no proof of its existence, that this fluid without existence is consequently without utility."[4] They did not deny that patients were sometimes affected, but this they attributed to the influence of suggestion or "imagination" rather than a physical force. And while that concession may seem significant today, at the time it was generally interpreted to mean that the effects had been simulated, a sham. Essentially, the commission branded animal magnetism as bogus science, and discouraged legitimate scientists and doctors from taking it seriously. For many years, then, the subject lay in the hands of amateurs.

From "Mesmerism" to "Hypnotism"

While at the zenith of his fashionability, Mesmer had founded a series of mystical, quasi-religious, and expensive schools called "Societies of Harmony," where wealthy students were taught how to magnetize patients. And although Mesmer himself disappeared into relative obscurity after 1784, his nonprofessional but enthusiastic students kept the practice of magnetism alive. One of them, **Amand Marie Jacques de Chastenet**, the **Marquis de Puységur** (1751–1825), made some particularly important discoveries that propelled the field into a new phase.

Puységur and Artificial Somnambulism

Uncomfortable with the convulsive and often violent nature of the "crisis" state patients typically entered, Puységur one day must have implicitly conveyed this attitude while magnetizing one of his male servants. Instead of becoming crisis ridden, the young man entered a peaceful, sleeplike trance. Unlike a truly sleeping person, however, he continued to respond to Puységur's voice, answering questions and even performing complicated activities when told to. Upon command, for example, he pretended to shoot a gun for a prize and danced happily to imagined music. He "awoke" with no recollection of these events, although on being remagnetized and resuming the trance, he promptly remembered them. Puységur found he could reproduce this state in many other patients and bypass the crisis altogether, simply by suggesting it clearly in the course of induction. He first referred to the new state as a **perfect crisis** and later called it **artificial somnambulism** (because of its apparent similarity to sleepwalking).

In artificially somnambulistic subjects, Puységur and his colleagues soon discovered most of the common hypnotic effects as they are known today. They confirmed that a drastically enhanced **suggestibility** characterized the state; all they had to do was assert that something was so, and subjects would behave as if it were in fact true. Paralyses and pains appeared and moved about in the subjects' bodies upon suggestion; parts of the body could be anesthetized so subjects easily tolerated normally painful stimuli without signs of distress; and a wide variety of authentic-seeming emotional expressions could be produced upon command.

Like Puységur's servant, many other subjects also "forgot" the trance experiences upon awakening but remembered them when remagnetized—an effect called **post-hypnotic amnesia** today. Puységur also demonstrated what we now call **post-hypnotic suggestion**, in which subjects in trance are told they will perform a certain act after awakening—for example, scratch their left ear when the hypnotist coughs—but will forget that they had been instructed to. Many subjects comply with such suggestions and when asked why, fabricate some plausible but incorrect explanation—for example, they might say that they had a sudden itch.

Many of Puységur's observations of hypnotic effects have stood the test of time, but he also held two beliefs that have not been justified by further research even though they remain part of the popular mythology about hypnotism. First, he believed that somnambulistic subjects could do things they would find completely impossible normally. In fact, hypnotized subjects will sometimes do things they *think* are impossible in the waking state, such as make their bodies so rigid that they can remain suspended in air with only one support beneath the head and another under the heels. In reality, most people can easily do this when "normal," as long as they remain confident and do not panic. Hypnosis may sometimes make people more relaxed and confident about their ability to do something, thus indirectly improving their performance. But it cannot miraculously add to a person's normal abilities or strengths.

Puységur also believed that subjects could not be magnetized against their will, or made to do things in a trance contrary to their moral scruples. In fact, this is only sometimes true. Modern stage hypnotists often hypnotize "defiant" subjects—people who loudly proclaim they can never be hypnotized and challenge the hypnotist to try—simply by issuing firm commands that they shall *not* fall asleep when told to. Such people sometimes fall immediately into a trance state and respond positively to further suggestions. Whether they have been hypnotized "against their will" depends on how one defines "will." On the question of violating moral scruples, defendants in some criminal trials have pleaded innocent on grounds they acted under the influence of hypnotists. Although such persons may have had deep underlying aggressive tendencies, at least some juries have been convinced they would never have committed their crimes without the hypnotic influence. In these cases the actual perpetrators of the crimes received lighter sentences than the hypnotic masterminds. In sum, magnetists/hypnotists can induce some very striking behaviors in their subjects, but to no greater extent than effective leaders in other "normal" situations. Successful football coaches, for example, can inspire their teams to play "beyond themselves" and to ignore pain while doing so. Effective political leaders can inspire their followers to make sacrifices or to do things they would otherwise not do—sometimes for the better and sometimes the worse.

Faria and Hypnotic Susceptibility

Another amateur, the abbé **José Custódio di Faria** (1746–1819), made important early contributions to the understanding of hypnosis. A Portuguese priest who eventually settled in Paris, Faria addressed the question of why all people did not respond equally well to the magnetists' induction procedures. Even Mesmer had recognized wide individual differences in his patients' responses, and from a theorist who placed most of his emphasis on the power presumably inherent in the magnetist, this concession represented something of an embarrassment. Why should only a portion of the population respond to a force of theoretically universal influence? Faria, while convinced of the genuineness of mesmeric effects, was skeptical about the magnetic theory, and in his own attempt to explain the phenomena he shifted his emphasis from the powers of the magnetizer to the susceptibilities and predispositions of the *subjects*.[5]

To make his points, Faria first demonstrated that trance states could be induced without using magnetic paraphernalia or terminology. Sometimes he asked seated subjects to fixate their gaze on his hand as he slowly moved it toward their face, while commanding them to sleep. Other times he simply had them close their eyes and concentrate on his voice as he authoritatively instructed them, "Sleep." About one person in five responded to these procedures by falling into a deep trance state identical to Puységur's artificial somnambulism, but that Faria named **lucid sleep**. To remove them from the state, Faria simply instructed them to wake up. These are essentially the procedures still followed by most hypnotists today.

Faria further showed that virtually anyone, even a child, could successfully induce lucid sleep in appropriately predisposed subjects. Thus, the "secret" of mesmeric phenomena lay not in the magnetic or other mysterious powers of the operator, but in the predispositions and susceptibilities of the subjects. Faria referred to trance-predisposed subjects as *époptes* (a term he coined from a Greek root meaning "the led" or "the overseen"), and he argued that their susceptibility arose from a thinness of the blood—a physiological explanation. The physiology was incorrect, but in switching the emphasis from the hypnotizer to the hypnotized, and in attempting to pinpoint the differentiating characteristics of hypnotizable subjects, Faria began a major research tradition that continues today.

Unfortunately, Faria's very real contributions received scant attention from his contemporaries, partly because of his nonprofessional status. Further, he was humiliated when an actor simulated lucid sleep at a public demonstration and Faria failed to detect the deception. Thus, after Faria's death in 1819 his ideas passed into obscurity, and hypnotic practice remained in the hands of scientifically unrespectable "mesmerists" who continued to speak of their activities in terms of magnetism and other occult fluids supposedly concentrated in their own persons. When Faria's ideas were finally rediscovered, and many mesmeric phenomena were at last given a semblance of respectability, a full generation had passed and the scene had switched from France to Great Britain.

The Founding of "Hypnotism"

Traveling mesmerists commonly produced artificial anesthesias in their public performances. Subjects would be told that parts of their bodies had lost feeling, and then when normally painful stimuli were applied they would show no distress. These performances lacked full credibility because most of the subjects were hired assistants to the mesmerists, but the demonstrations eventually aroused the serious attention of a few legitimate physicians and surgeons. Chemical anesthetics were unknown until the mid-1800s, so surgical patients of the time inevitably experienced excruciating pain and had to be strapped to the operating table for restraint. Surgeons made their reputations by speed rather than delicacy, and prolonged operations were impossible. Although conservative medical opinion held that pain was *necessary* for a successful operation, a few pioneering doctors sought some means of lessening the misery of surgery.

John Elliotson (1791–1868), a physician at London's University College Hospital, was accustomed to the ridicule of his colleagues for embracing new ideas. Among the first to use the newly invented stethoscope for listening to the sounds of the heart, he had been told by a superior, "You will learn nothing by it, and, if you do, you cannot treat the disease any better." The instrument itself—now perhaps the most universally used of all medical tools—was castigated as "hocus pocus," a useless "piece of wood," and "just the thing for Elliotson to rave about." This was mere rehearsal for what happened in 1837 after Elliotson observed a stage mesmerist, was intrigued by what he saw, and made plans to investigate the anesthetic properties of mesmerism in his hospital. On learning of these plans, the university council passed a resolution banning any practice of mesmerism or animal magnetism within the Hospital.[6] Elliotson resigned his position in protest and never got the opportunity to test mesmeric anesthesia on patients. He did use mesmerism for other medical purposes, however, and in 1843 he founded a new journal, the *Zoist*, to carry articles on "cerebral physiology and mesmerism, and their applications for human welfare."[7] His journal lasted only a few years and never attracted much attention from the medical establishment. But still, it marked the start of a formal information exchange for scientists interested in mesmerism.

Meanwhile, a few other physicians had actually begun to test mesmerism as an anesthetic. In 1842 the English surgeon W. S. Ward performed a leg amputation and reported to the Royal Medical Society that his mesmerized patient experienced no pain. One eminent physiologist typified the Society's response when he charged that the patient had been some sort of imposter. Another authority contended that even if Ward's account was true, which he doubted, "still the fact is unworthy of consideration, because pain is a wise provision of nature, and patients ought to suffer pain while their surgeons are operating; they are all the better for it and recover better." The Society's best response, according to this expert would be to expunge all record of Ward's report from the minutes, as if it had never occurred at all.[8]

The more extensive experiments of **James Esdaile** (1808–1859), a Scottish physician practicing in India, proved only slightly more difficult to dismiss. Esdaile trained his assistants to magnetize patients before their operations and became the first person to use mesmeric anesthesia on a large scale and tabulate his results. He performed more than 300 such operations in the late 1840s, many of them for the removal of scrotal tumors. Among his mesmerized patients, the mortality rate for this dangerous operation dropped from its normal 50 percent to 5 percent. Unfortunately, however, these impressive results were widely dismissed on the racist grounds that highly suspect "native" patients had been used, magnetized by equally suspect "native" assistants. The patients actually *liked* to be operated on, it was said, and merely acted to help Esdaile.[9]

Thus, mesmerism ranks historically as one of the first successful anesthetics to be systematically used in Western surgery. And despite its initial dismissal by the establishment, it was gaining ground and would probably have been generally accepted were it not for the independent discovery of effective chemical anesthetics. In 1844, the American dentist Horace Wells extracted teeth painlessly from patients put to sleep by nitrous oxide. Within three years the blessings of ether and chloroform were discovered by doctors. These chemical anesthetics seemed much more understandable to mechanistically trained doctors than mesmerism, and they had the further real advantage of being more reliable and universally applicable. Thus, after a brief flurry of excitement, the idea of mesmeric anesthesia faded into the background, and this apparently promising avenue to scientific respectability became closed off.

The Scottish physician **James Braid** (1795–1860) finally steered mesmerism close to the British scientific mainstream. After skeptically observing a stage mesmerist perform, Braid had been surprised and impressed when the mesmerist allowed him and a medical colleague to examine the entranced subject. The subject's insensitivity to pain seemed genuine, and his pupils remained dilated after his eyelids were forced open. Braid concluded that mesmerism was something real and that he would study it on his own.

He made few new or original discoveries when he did so, but he confirmed the results of earlier fringe figures, particularly Puységur and Faria. In carefully controlled experiments, he demonstrated the full range of mesmeric effects and highlighted the susceptibility of the subject as opposed to the power of the operator. Also following Faria, he saw the trance state as akin to the state of sleep and sought a new name for the condition to reflect that similarity. Quite possibly, Braid knew that some French writers in the early 1800s had already occasionally used terms such as *hypnotique, hypnotisme,* and *hypnotiste,* based on the Greek root *hypnos,* for "sleep," to describe certain aspects of the mesmeric situation.[10] In any case, Braid in 1843 conjoined *hypnos* with the Greek *neuro* ("nervous") in proposing **neurohypnology**, or just **neurypnology** ("nervous sleep"), as a new name for mesmerism. Later he altered this to *hypnotism,* which has been the standard term in English ever since.

Unlike the iconoclast Elliotson, Braid maintained ties to the medical establishment and published his studies in standard scientific form and in standard journals. Although he discovered little that was new, he took mesmerism out of the disreputable medical netherworld in which it had traditionally been practiced and brought it, as "hypnotism," into the scientist's laboratory. Braid thus helped pave the way for the scientific rehabilitation of hypnosis, which occurred most fully in France during the final quarter of the nineteenth century.

This happened in the context of a lively controversy about the nature of hypnosis between two competing "schools," one centered in the provincial city of Nancy and the other in the capital, Paris.

The Nancy-Salpêtrière Controversy

The so-called Nancy school of hypnosis developed around the unlikely figure of a modest country doctor named **Ambroise Auguste Liébeault** (1823–1904). As a medical student he had been fascinated by an old book on animal magnetism he chanced upon. After establishing a successful orthodox practice just outside Nancy, he decided to experiment with hypnotic therapies by offering his patients an unusual bargain: They could be treated hypnotically for free or by standard methods for the standard fees. At first only a few dared try the still-disreputable hypnosis, but the technique's success and popularity soon grew great enough to endanger the doctor's livelihood. "Good Father Liébeault," as he came to be known, finally had to adopt a voluntary system in which he charged no fixed fees but gratefully accepted whatever his numerous hypnotic patients offered to pay. He used a simple, straightforward treatment method, telling each patient to stare deeply into his eyes while he repeatedly gave instructions to sleep. As soon as the patient fell into a light sleeplike state, Liébeault asserted that the symptoms would soon disappear. Often they did, showing once again the extent to which physical complaints can be manipulated by psychological and suggestive factors.

Liébeault published an obscurely written and poorly selling book about his techniques and would probably have died with no more than a local reputation had he not attracted the attention of **Hippolyte Bernheim** (1840–1919), a younger doctor from the city of Nancy. An internist originally specializing in typhoid fever and heart disease, Bernheim heard improbable-sounding stories about the success of Good Father Liébeault's approach and visited the hypnotic clinic to see it for himself in 1882. Instead of finding the farce he expected, Bernheim was impressed and returned repeatedly to learn the older doctor's methods for himself. Soon he abandoned orthodox internal medicine to become a full-time hypnotherapist, treating hundreds of patients and carefully analyzing their varying responses to hypnosis.

Following Faria and Braid's dictum that the most important hypnotic factors lay in the subject rather than the hypnotist, Bernheim compared the characteristics of strong versus weak responders to hypnosis and concluded that his more successful cases tended to come from the lower as opposed to the upper social classes. He speculated that lower-class patients may have been more conditioned toward strict obedience than their wealthier counterparts, which may have predisposed them to greater hypnotic susceptibility. In his 1886 book, *De la Suggestion et de ses Applications à la Thérapeutique* (literally, "On Suggestion and Its Therapeutic Applications," but translated into English as *Suggestive Therapeutics*), Bernheim argued that human beings vary on a general trait of *suggestibility*, defined as "the aptitude to transform an idea into an act."[11] Strongly hypnotizable individuals presumably ranked high on this general tendency. Bernheim further argued that suggestible patients could be successfully treated by straightforward persuasion techniques as well as by hypnosis. If only patients could be made to *believe* they would be cured, often they really would. Considerably more effective at writing and communicating than Liébeault, Bernheim elaborated these ideas in several books and articles that came to be identified as the main statements of the Nancy school. Essentially, they argued that hypnotic susceptibility is a trait closely related to a characteristic of general suggestibility, which varies widely from one person to another within the normal population.

The Salpêtrière School

As Bernheim was formulating this view in Nancy, a radically different theory of the hypnotizable personality was being promoted in Paris by **Jean-Martin Charcot** (1825–1893), the powerful director of Paris's enormous Salpêtrière Hospital and one of the most eminent figures in European medicine. This "Napoleon of the Neuroses" had observed similarities between hypnosis and the illness called **hysteria**, and declared that hypnotizability and hysteria were aspects of the same underlying abnormal neurological condition. Thus he disputed the Nancy contention that hypnotic susceptibility was a normal characteristic. Adherents of the Nancy and Salpêtrière positions vigorously debated with one another for several years, in a well-publicized controversy that returned hypnotism to the forefront of French public consciousness.

The son of a carriage builder, Charcot had chosen medicine over art as a career after considerable deliberation. As a relatively impoverished medical student, he had been required to spend time working in Paris's vast Salpêtrière Hospital, a "city within a city" housing several thousand indigent and ill women in more than forty buildings on its 125-acre site. Although not considered a plum or fashionable assignment, the Salpêtrière struck young Charcot as a potential treasure trove of cases for neurological research. He resolved to make his fortune first, and then return to the Salpêtrière as senior physician.

As a young man he became the private physician and traveling companion of a wealthy banker and then used his contacts to establish a flourishing private practice. Like Mesmer, he married a wealthy widow who furthered his entrée into Parisian society. And with his financial security assured, Charcot made good his earlier vow and returned to the Salpêtrière as senior physician in 1862.

He quickly expanded the research and teaching facilities of the hospital and conducted or directed much important research on epilepsy, multiple sclerosis, poliomyelitis, and other neurological diseases. A master showman, he gave brilliant clinical lectures in which he imitated the symptoms of various neurological diseases, engaged patients in dramatic dialogue, and had them wear hats with long feathers whose different vibrations illustrated different kinds of tremors. By the 1880s his lectures had become major cultural events, attracting large audiences of writers, philosophers, and even famous actors as well as doctors The French government officially recognized Charcot's achievements in 1882 by creating a new post especially for him, as professor of neuropathology at the Salpêtrière.

An autocratic and imperious personality, Charcot commanded the rigorous devotion of many disciples who worked with him in close daily collaboration. Unsurprisingly, a few subordinates chafed under his discipline and sarcastically referred to his circle as "*la charcoterie*" (a play on the French word *charcuterie*, for a pork butcher's shop).[12] One disenchanted colleague, who knew Charcot well enough to be familiar with his medical history, sent him anonymous letters forecasting his imminent demise from a heart condition.

But whatever their personal reactions might have been, almost everyone admired Charcot's clinical brilliance. Recalling his artistic inclinations, Charcot described himself as a "*visuel*," a person who *saw* things rather than thought them and who imposed order on his clinical observations of individual patients only after long periods of careful watching. Sigmund Freud, who as a young doctor spent the winter of 1885–1886 studying with Charcot, recalled that his teacher "used to look again and again at the things he did not understand, to deepen his impression of them day by day, till suddenly an understanding of them dawned on him. . . . [N]ew diagnostic pictures emerged, characterized by the constant combination of certain groups of symptoms."[13]

Charcot's diagnoses were based on an assumption that many neurological diseases occurred either in a relatively rare pure and complete form, which he referred to as the *type* for each particular illness, or, more commonly, in a partial or incomplete *forme fruste* (literally, "blurred form"). His strategy was to minutely observe groups of patients with a particular disease until he could single out a small number of individuals as representing its type. Then he would study these "pure" cases intensively, in the belief they could reveal the essence of the problem.

Epileptic seizures provided a model for this approach, subclassified into "grand mal" (the *type*) and "petit mal" (*formes frustes*) forms. A grand mal epileptic seizure entailed three sequential stages: first, an aura, a characteristic sensation or feeling that signals the onset of an attack; second, a "tonic phase" in which the large muscles of the body go rigid and the patient loses consciousness and falls (hence the ancient designation of epilepsy as "the falling sickness"); and third, a "clonic phase" in which the body convulses spasmodically. This, presumably, was the "pure" form of epilepsy, in contrast to petit mal seizures in which patients merely experienced inexplicable "spells" or brief fainting sensations.

Beginning in the 1870s, Charcot turned his attention to a group of patients traditionally housed in the same Salpêtrière wards as epileptics but experiencing a more bewildering variety of symptoms. These patients, suffering from what was called *hysteria*, sometimes experienced "fits" of violent emotion, paralysis, anesthesia, convulsion, and memory loss that partially mimicked epileptic seizures or other neurological symptoms. Hysterics showed no obvious organic lesions, however, and their symptoms had several other features uncharacteristic of ordinary neurological disease. For example, some hysterical paralyses and anesthesias occurred only in sharply delineated body areas such as the part of the hand and wrist normally covered by a glove. Anatomically, this made no sense because the nerves of the hand and arm fall in no such pattern; afflictions resulting from ordinary nerve damage would not have such sharp boundaries. In general, hysterics suffered from symptoms that *resembled* ordinary neuropathology but did not quite follow the accepted and understood rules of neurology.

The term *hysteria* dated from the ancient Greeks, who first described and named the condition. They believed it to be an exclusively feminine disease, caused by the physical "wandering" of the uterus (the Greek word for which was *hystera*) from the abdomen to other parts of the body where it caused symptoms to occur. As therapy, they often prescribed a foul-smelling substance to be rubbed on the afflicted area and a sweet-smelling one for the abdomen, to entice the uterus back to its proper place. Sometimes this treatment seemed to help. The great Greco-Roman physician Galen recognized that the uterus itself could not wander and refined the theory by suggesting that that organ instead gave off pathogenic fluids or vapors that collected in the symptom sites. He prescribed smelling salts to disperse and dilute the pathological vapors, and sometimes this treatment was followed by improvement as well.

When Charcot began to study hysteria seventeen centuries later, most medical thinking about hysteria had not radically improved. The prevailing medical opinion dismissed hysteria as simple malingering; symptoms that violated the accepted rules of neuroanatomy strained the credulity of many mechanistically oriented doctors, who felt patients were merely simulating their illnesses. Those physicians who did take the condition seriously still overwhelmingly believed hysteria to be exclusively feminine and caused by some sort of abnormality of the female reproductive system.

Charcot challenged both of these common views. He thought hysterical symptoms caused too much genuine distress to be merely faked. Further, he had examined several *men* outside the Salpêtrière who showed similar symptoms. Because hysteria could occur in men (although apparently less often than in women), it clearly could not be a disease of the female reproductive system. To get to the heart of the problem, Charcot closely observed substantial numbers of hysterical patients and eventually identified a small number who he thought represented the *type* for the condition—who suffered, in his language, from **grande hystérie**, or "major hysteria."

Intensive examination of these few patients convinced Charcot and his assistants that when major hysterical attacks occurred, they—like grand mal seizures—came in a regular, multistage progression. An "epileptoid stage," with symptoms similar to the onset of a grand mal epileptic seizure, came first. It was followed, in order, by a "large movement stage" in which the patient performed seemingly automatic and sometimes violent acts; then a "hallucinatory stage" in which imaginary sensations and feelings seemed subjectively real to the patient; and a final "delirious stage." The majority of hysterical patients who failed to display this spectacular and perfectly regular sequence of symptoms were said to have **petite hystérie**, or "minor hysteria." Charcot's patients with *grande hystérie* were regularly featured at his public lectures and became genuine celebrities who reveled in their role. Charcot speculated that the root cause of hysteria lay in a hereditary, progressive, and generalized degeneracy of the nervous system that interferes with the ability to integrate and interconnect memories and ideas in the normal way. Thus, individual memories and emotional reactions that would normally cluster together become "dissociated" and were experienced by hysterics in isolation from one another.

As Charcot became increasingly committed to this view of hysteria, he was struck by the fact that hypnotized subjects seemed to have much in common with hysterical patients. Highly responsive hypnotic subjects could experience paralyses, anesthesias, and amnesias, and they often performed consciously inexplicable acts (posthypnotic suggestions) just as hysterical patients did. Hypnosis and hysteria both produced physical and mental anomalies that made little sense anatomically and that seemed beyond the conscious control of the subject or patient. Moreover, some of Charcot's prize patients with *grande hystérie* turned out to be highly hypnotizable, and in fact demonstrated their cycles of symptoms even more perfectly when hypnotized.

From this coincidence, Charcot concluded that hypnotic effects and hysterical symptoms had the same cause and that hypnotic susceptibility in fact represented a *symptom* of hysteria: Only people with pathological nervous systems should experience such dissociated effects. Now deciding that hypnosis deserved further study as an aspect of hysteria, Charcot reasoned that the best cases to examine closely would be his major hysterics. One of his most important subjects was **Blanche Wittmann** (1859–1913), an attractive young woman whose spectacular performance of the stages of *grande hystérie* and haughty attitude toward other patients had earned her the nickname "Queen of the Hysterics" (see Figure 10.3).

When hypnotized, "Wit" (as she was called in the published reports) and the other compliant Salpêtrière subjects characteristically passed through three stages: *catalepsy,* in which they became muscularly relaxed, motionless, and generally insensitive to external stimulation; *lethargy,* in which the body muscles were generally flaccid, but sporadically activated into strong contractions and movements; and *somnambulism,* in which complex automatic movements and actions occurred upon suggestion. The final stage strongly resembled the deep somnambulistic trances of earlier magnetic and hypnotic subjects. Charcot recognized that many hypnotic subjects did not follow the three-stage progression, but he wrote them off according to his well-worn diagnostic formula. The three-stage subjects, he argued, represented a *type* he called **grand hypnotisme,** while the other more common subjects represented only incomplete, *formes frustes* of the hypnotized state.

F G 10.3 Charcot lecturing on Blanche Wittmann

In 1882, Charcot presented his theory of *grand hypnotisme* to the French Academy of Sciences. The subject of hypnotism had been in official disgrace in France ever since the Franklin Commission, and the Academy had twice since then rejected reports on it. But Charcot's immense prestige ensured he would be carefully heard, and his neurologically oriented theory appealed to the conservative, mechanistic biases of the scientific establishment. Thus, his presentation received official approval; Charcot finally reversed the legacy of Mesmer and succeeded in getting hypnotism accepted as a legitimate subject of study by an official French scientific organization.

The Triumph of the Nancy School

Just as Charcot made his triumphant presentation to the Academy in Paris, the seeds for dispute were being sown in Nancy by Bernheim, who was undertaking his own serious study of hypnotism. Bernheim had hypnotized hundreds of subjects as opposed to the select handful at the Salpêtrière, and we have seen he concluded that hypnotic susceptibility was a variable but *normal* characteristic related to suggestibility. In his patients, states of catalepsy and lethargy had *not* inevitably preceded somnambulism. He therefore attacked Charcot's theory, charging that *grand hypnotisme* was an artifact of the highly peculiar Salpêtrière setting. Charcot and his followers reacted angrily, and dispute filled the French scientific literature throughout the 1880s.

In this disagreement between an obscure doctor from the provinces against a grand figure from the capital, most scientific observers naturally leaned at first toward the Salpêtrière side. But gradually, weaknesses in the Salpêtrière position became clear to objective observers. Charcot himself did not hypnotize his subjects but left that task to younger assistants. Two of these, **Alfred Binet** (1857–1911) and **Charles Féré** (1852–1907) reported some particularly suspicious experiments with Blanche Wittmann. Harkening back to Mesmer, they reintroduced the magnet into hypnotic sessions. With Wit in the somnambulistic stage, they induced paralyses or other effects on one side of her body and then reversed the polarity of a large magnet they held in front of her. Wit's effects immediately transferred to the other side. The hypnotists similarly reversed emotional states: After telling

the hypnotized Wit that she felt very sad, for example, they transformed her piteous sobs into gay laughter with a simple flick of their
magnet. In all seriousness, they suggested that this was an experimental technique for discovering pairs of "complementary emotions"
analogous to the "complementary colors" already discovered by
researchers of color vision. While admitting that some of their results
seemed implausible, they assured their readers that the effects had
been "entirely unexpected" and had "issued from nature herself, . . .
showing an inflexible logic."[14]

But the logic of these experiments seemed questionable to **Joseph
Delboeuf** (1831–1896), a respected Belgian physiologist who previously had publicly rebuked the young Binet for rushing into print
with an ill-researched article on psychophysics. Delboeuf had a side
interest in hypnosis, and in the early stages of the Nancy-Salpêtrière
controversy he had accepted Charcot's theory of *grand hypnotisme.*
But when he saw the impetuous Binet's name on this Salpêtrière
study with improbable results, he began to doubt. "One fine morning
I could contain myself no longer," he wrote,[15] and he went to Paris to
observe the Salpêtrière scene for himself. He later offered a vivid portrait of what he found:[16]

> I will never forget those delicious hours. M. Féré and Binet are
> both young, both tall; M. Féré more reflective, it seems to me,
> and more accessible to objections raised; M. Binet more adven-
> turous and more affirmative; the former with serious physi-
> ognomy, and a clear and profound gaze, the latter with fine
> features and a mischievous expression. Between them sat . . .
> the placid and "appetizing" Alsacienne Wit . . . not only wear-
> ing a complacent look, but finding visible pleasure in getting
> ready to do anything that should be asked of her; then myself,
> the old scholar, head full of reflections and questions, but never
> having had at hand this kind of experimental offering, a veri-
> table human guinea pig.

When the young hypnotists began their demonstration for Delboeuf,
he observed that Wit was extraordinarily responsive to the slightest hints. Féré dealt with her "as if playing upon a piano. . . . A light
touch on any muscle—or even pointing to it without touching—made
Wit . . . contract any muscle, even in her ear." The celebrated magnet

was large and wielded openly before Wit; Binet and Féré also spoke openly about her expected responses as if she were not there. When Delboeuf asked why they did not use an electromagnet whose polarity could be reversed surreptitiously and take other measures to disguise their expectations from Wit, the hypnotists blithely responded that this was unnecessary because Wit was oblivious to such cues while in the somnambulistic stage of *grand hypnotisme.*

Delboeuf suspected otherwise and returned to Belgium to replicate the Salpêtrière experiments on his own—only with adequate precautions against transmitting prior expectations to his subjects. He concluded that not only magnetic effects but also the entire enactments of *grand hypnotisme* were artifacts: the results of patients with great investment in their roles as prize subjects responding to implicit or explicit suggestions from their examiners. Delboeuf became a strong and influential supporter of the Nancy school, and the tide began to turn in its direction.

By 1891 even the Salpêtrière protagonists admitted they had been wrong. Binet—whom we shall meet again both in this chapter and in Chapter 13—learned a particularly bitter but valuable lesson from the experience. As he went on to become the most proficient experimental psychologist in France, he would take great pains not only to guard against unintentional suggestion in his research but also to make *intentional* suggestion the explicit topic of some of his experiments, thereby helping to launch the discipline of experimental social psychology. Charcot, too, admitted his errors on hypnotism and privately predicted that his theories of hysteria would not long survive him. Soon after, in 1893, the warnings of his anonymous tormentor came true and he succumbed to a heart attack. Charcot's prediction was also correct, for people with different theories took over the Salpêtrière, and by 1899 all that remained of *grande hystérie* were a few former patients who would reenact its four stages for the payment of a fee.

Yet for all his mistakes, Charcot was among the first to explore interactions between emotional and physical factors, and he raised the important subjects of hysteria and hypnosis out of scientific obscurity. He trained many important students, including Freud and Binet, both of whom remembered him with respect as a master clinician who had identified important problems for them. Problem *finders* can be just as important as problem *solvers*, and Charcot filled that role admirably.

The Psychology of Crowds

Another subject of great public interest in late-nineteenth-century France was the behavior of crowds. Since the Revolution, France had experienced many social upheavals marked by "crazes" and examples of "mob hysteria." Inevitably, with the wide publicity given the Nancy-Salpêtrière controversy, some began to note similarities between the irrational behavior of hypnotized or hysterical subjects and that of people in crowds. Among the most influential of these was the energetic and controversial **Gustave Le Bon** (1841–1931; see Figure 10.4). Born into a wealthy family, Le Bon had the income and the leisure to indulge a wide variety of interests over the course of his long life. Adhering to a highly conservative political ideology, and holding views on ethnic differences that are offensively racist by today's standards, Le Bon produced two books on group behavior. Neither *The Psychology of Peoples* (1894) nor *The Crowd* (1895) treated its subject with subtlety or scholarly depth, but both explicitly raised several issues that have continued to engage social psychologists ever since.[17]

FIG 10.4
Gustave Le Bon
(1841–1931)

Le Bon asserted that the most fundamental social responses of any person derive from *unconscious* ideas and motives. Posthypnotic suggestions and amnesias dramatically highlighted such unconscious processes, but Le Bon believed they pervaded many nonhypnotic situations as well. He noted that when people are learning a new task they focus a great deal of conscious attention on their behavior, but once it has been fully and well learned they perform it unconsciously and automatically. Thus, the best-learned (and therefore most effective) motivating ideas always operate at such an unconscious level.

In his *Psychology of Peoples*, Le Bon argued that the most fundamental differences among nations or cultures derive from their different unconscious ideas and predispositions. Certain characteristic ideas within each group get so deeply assimilated in the course of development as to become ingrained, unconscious, and beyond the reach of normal rational deliberation. Le Bon pessimistically added that these unconscious national predispositions make genuine international harmony impossible. Although national leaders might be able to understand and rationally discuss each other's conscious ideas and motives, the more important unconscious ones must remain inaccessible. Thus, he saw international strife and warfare as inevitable.

In *The Crowd*, Le Bon argued that individuals' already modest degree of conscious control over their behavior becomes even further diminished when they congregate in groups. He asserted that people in crowds tend to abandon both individuality and rationality, assuming a kind of collective mind that can impel them to do things they would never dream of while alone. Unconscious racial ideas common to all members of the crowd presumably become especially dominant: "General qualities of character, governed by forces of which we are unconscious, and possessed by the majority of the normal individuals of a race in much the same degree. . . . in crowds become common property. . . . The heterogeneous is swamped by the homogeneous, and the unconscious qualities gain the upper hand."[18]

Because of its domination by unconscious ideas, the crowd, according to Le Bon, is intellectually inferior to an isolated individual and marked by characteristics such as "impulsiveness, irritability, incapacity to reason, the absence of judgment and of the critical spirit, the exaggeration of the sentiments, and others besides—which are almost always observed in beings belonging to inferior forms of evolution."[19]

Le Bon conceded that individuals in crowds sometimes perform heroic or noble acts, especially in warfare, that isolated individuals would be too timid to attempt. This behavior too presumably happens because of the greater impulsiveness and thoughtlessness of crowds. "Were peoples only to be credited with the great actions performed in cold blood," he wrote, "the annals of the world would register but few of them."[20] Le Bon also felt, however, that these occasional positive and heroic products of the group mind are more than counterbalanced by responses of a destructive nature.

In trying to explain why crowds behave as they do, Le Bon posited three factors. First, he argued that people in a crowd sense both the power of their numbers and the anonymity of their individual selves. Their power enables them to do things that would be impossible for individuals, and their presumed anonymity helps them disregard conventional assumptions of personal responsibility for their actions. Le Bon's second and third factors—the effect of *social contagion* and the presumably enhanced *suggestibility* of people in groups—had both been previously observed in mesmeric and hypnotic situations. In discussing them, Le Bon made the connection between crowd responses and hypnosis explicit:

> The most careful observations seem to prove that an individual immerged for some length of time in a crowd in action soon finds himself . . . in a special state, which much resembles the state of fascination in which the hypnotised individual finds himself in the hands of the hypnotiser. . . . [T]he individual forming part of a psychological crowd . . . is no longer conscious of his acts. In his case, as in the case of the hypnotised subject, at the same time that certain faculties are destroyed, others may be brought to a high degree of exaltation. Under the influence of suggestion, he will undertake the accomplishment of certain acts with irresistible impetuosity. This impetuosity is the more irresistible in crowds than in that of the single hypnotic subject, from the fact that, the suggestion being the same for all the individuals of the crowd, it gains in strength by reciprocity.[21]

Le Bon made further explicit connections between hypnosis and crowd phenomena in his analyses of the qualities of effective *leaders* of crowds. The most effective (and dangerous) crowd leader, he

believed, is unreflective, single-minded, irrational, and fanatical—
someone who

> has himself been hypnotized by an idea, whose apostle he has
> since become. It has taken possession of him to such a degree
> that everything outside it vanishes, and that every contrary
> opinion appears to him an error or a superstition. . . . The inten-
> sity of [his] faith gives great power of suggestion to [his] words.
> The multitude is always ready to listen to the strong-willed
> man, who knows how to impose himself upon it. Men gathered
> in a crowd lose all force of will, and turn instinctively to the per-
> son who possesses the quality they lack.[22]

Further, Le Bon noted that effective leaders routinely apply three
simple techniques in communicating with their followers that had
also been used by hypnotists. First is simple *affirmation*: The effective leader always concisely accentuates the positive about his cause,
denying opportunity for doubt and avoiding complicated reasoning.
Simple slogans and credos that may be shouted in unison, are easy to
remember, and are direct in their appeals to action and belief are the
stock in trade of a crowd leader. Second is constant *repetition* of the
affirmations: As the slogans get repeated over and over, they finally
become part of the followers' supremely powerful unconscious ideas.
Third, Le Bon noted that effective leaders always make sure that
at least a few enthusiastic supporters of their causes are planted in
audiences beforehand. These people can start a favorable "current of
opinion" that spreads through the crowd by social contagion. Needless to say, the principles of affirmation and repetition had long been
familiar to hypnotists, who typically repeated positive statements
such as "Sleep!" or "Your eyelids are getting heavier and heavier"
while inducing hypnosis. And ever since Mesmer's baquet, they had
been aware of the power of social contagion in enhancing the magnetic response.

  The Crowd was politically biased, unscholarly, and often sensationalistic in tone, but still it addressed under one cover a large number of
fundamental social psychological issues that had arisen in the previous century. These issues included the basic phenomena of social influence and suggestion, the qualities and techniques of leaders who exert

such influence, the complementary characteristics of the persons influenced, the characteristics of crowds, and the behavior of individuals who are members of groups or crowds. The book marked the culmination of what we may characterize as the "preexperimental" phase of the study of social psychology. Many important social phenomena were discovered and studied during this period, but usually in the context of clinical or medical settings, which sometimes partook of the mystical, the exotic, or the "abnormal." Around the turn of the century, however, Alfred Binet decided that many of these same social phenomena could be investigated systematically and experimentally, in laboratory settings. He went on to conduct a series of such experiments, thus creating a historical bridge to the establishment of a new discipline of experimental social psychology.

Binet's Experiments on Suggestion

Embarrassed by Delboeuf's exposure of the flaws in his Salpêtrière investigations of hypnosis, Binet ruefully came to characterize unintentional suggestion as "the cholera of psychology."[23] He also concluded, however, that although unintended suggestion posed great dangers, carefully controlled and *intentional* suggestion might be investigated systematically in a laboratory setting. From his new position as the unpaid director of a new psychology laboratory at the Sorbonne, Binet in 1894 collaborated with his student **Victor Henri** (1872–1940) on the first published study of that kind.[24] They devised a simple and easy test of visual memory for schoolchildren, in which subjects were briefly shown a single straight line and were soon after asked to choose the one of its same length from a pair of unequal lines. After determining that normal children could perform this task with nearly perfect accuracy, the experimenters tried to manipulate the responses with differing kinds of suggestion. Sometimes they established "preconceived ideas" by making the top (or bottom) line of the test pair correct for several consecutive trials and then switching. Other times they asked leading questions, such as "Are you sure? Mightn't it be the *other* line?" And sometimes the subjects were tested in groups, in which previously identified "leaders" had been instructed to give deliberately incorrect

responses to see whether the others would follow suit. All these manip-
ulations had measurable effects, somewhat greater on younger children than older ones, and with individual differences in the children's
suggestibility at all age levels.

In a later study, Binet showed children a poster with various stimulus items attached to it, including an uncanceled stamp, a coin, a
photograph, and a drawing. Afterward he asked his subjects to
recall details of what they had seen, with varying types of questions.
Directly misleading questions, such as "Wasn't the stamp canceled?"
produced a large number of incorrect responses, but even indirect or
neutral wording such as "Was the stamp canceled?" also led to several
mistakes. Children responded most accurately when simply asked to
provide open-ended descriptions of what they had seen. Binet concluded that if you want to derive the maximum accuracy in children's
testimony, "do not pose questions to them, even questions devoid of
precise suggestions, but simply ask them to describe everything they
recall and leave them with paper and pencil."[25]

Binet's studies showed clearly and elegantly how social phenomena such as conformity, suggestibility, and children's eyewitness testimony could be usefully studied in a laboratory setting, and they
strikingly resembled some later, more famous research. They did
not, however, arouse an immediate groundswell of interest among
his contemporary psychologists. This was partly because Binet soon
turned his attention to the problem of intelligence testing (as we shall
see in Chapter 13) and then died at a relatively young age. Also, however, the intellectual climate in early twentieth-century France was
not fully receptive to the nonclinical, experimental approach. Binet
is better regarded as an "anticipator" than as a "founder" of modern
experimental social psychology—that is, someone whose research
preceded and closely resembled later developments but did not provide the *immediate* stimulus for them.[26]

A similar designation is appropriate for **Norman Triplett** (1861–
1931), a psychologist at Indiana University in the United States who
was both an avid bicyclist and an investigator of motor development
in children. Noticing that bike racers went faster when in head-to-
head competition than when by themselves in individual time trials,
he conducted systematic studies of children given the task of wind-
ing fishing reels both by themselves and in pairs. Some children

significantly increased their reel-winding speed in the presence of a partner while others slowed down, thus demonstrating apparent effects of either social enhancement or inhibition of their performance. Triplett's 1898 account of his research in G. Stanley Hall's *American Journal of Psychology* was the first published, English-language study in experimental social psychology.[27] Like the earlier Binet studies, however, Triplett's experiment failed to inspire immediate follow-up work by himself or by others. A true *discipline* of experimental social psychology would have to await more favorable institutional conditions, as eventually occurred in the United States.

The Institutionalization of Social Psychology

Allport's Dissertation and Textbook

A young, Harvard-educated psychologist named **Floyd H. Allport** (1890–1978; see Figure 10.5) made three key contributions to the establishment of social psychology as an academic discipline. In 1919 he completed the first American doctoral dissertation devoted explicitly to a topic in experimental social psychology: "The Social Influence: An Experimental Study of the Effect of the Group upon Individual Mental Processes." Following a suggestion from his teacher Hugo Münsterberg, he studied and compared the performances of individuals acting alone versus being members of groups, on a series of simple timed tasks. The subjects in the group situation—like Triplett's fishing reel winders—performed a greater *quantity* of work, although the *quality* was no better (and in a few situations somewhat worse). Allport referred to this increase in energy or intensity of work when in the presence of others as *social facilitation*. Allport also discovered that when the tasks involved making *judgments* of qualities such as the pleasantness/unpleasantness of an odor or the heaviness of a weight, subjects in the group setting avoided the extremes of the judgment scales to a greater extent than when alone. He conceptualized this homogenization of responses as the result of a "conformity-producing tendency" in the group.

As an instructor at Harvard after receiving his degree, Allport met and impressed **Morton Prince** (1854–1929), a prominent Boston

FIG 10.5
Floyd Allport
(1890–1978)

neurologist who had become highly interested in the European work on hypnosis and its relation to psychopathology. In 1906 Prince had founded the *Journal of Abnormal Psychology*—the first American periodical specifically devoted to that subject—and in 1921 invited Allport to become his co-editor. Allport's influence immediately became evident in a decision to rename the periodical *The Journal of Abnormal Psychology and Social Psychology*. An editorial justifying the new title cited a recently increased interest in the study of social phenomena, and added, "It is doubtful whether this stage of interest and importance would have been attained but for the contemporary development of a sister science, abnormal psychology. Psychopathologists have in recent years delved deeply into the dynamics of human nature."[28] Thus, Allport was instrumental in providing a journal that explicitly solicited articles on experimental social psychology while openly acknowledging the historical connection between social and "abnormal" psychological phenomena. In 1925 the title was shortened to *The Journal of Abnormal and Social Psychology*, and for the next

40 years "*JASP*" remained the premier publishing outlet for American social psychologists.*

Allport soon left Harvard for a teaching position at the University of North Carolina, and while there he wrote the first successful textbook for the new field, simply titled *Social Psychology* (1924). Although longer on theory than on actual experimental results (which were largely confined to Allport's own dissertation studies), the book clearly laid out guidelines for a new discipline. Strongly influenced by John B. Watson's behaviorism, which was just then beginning to dominate American experimental psychology in general (see Chapter 9), Allport asserted that social psychology should focus exclusively on objectively observable responses made by individual subjects in objectively specifiable social situations. In doing so he strenuously rejected what he called the **group fallacy**—the notion that groups or crowds could constitute superorganisms or "group minds" going beyond the combined reactions of their individual members.

In summary, Floyd Allport promoted a new social psychology that would be experimental, objective, and focused on the reactions of individual subjects in controlled social situations. Slowly but surely this program became a reality and focused on increasingly "relevant" social and political issues. In 1937 Allport's North Carolina colleague **John Dashiell** (1888–1975) noted that the basic formats had been established for several kinds of experiments on social influence, but he lamented that none had yet been fully or systematically exploited. What was still lacking, he noted, was "not so much the need for discovering new concepts and points of view," as "a demand for more and ever more repetition and checking of the pioneer studies that have been made, and the introduction of experimental manipulation of the many variables involved in all such work."[29] Dashiell's call to experimental social psychologists resembled Pavlov's earlier

---

* In 1965, the journal reverted to its original title as just the *Journal of Abnormal Psychology* and confined its focus to clinical and psychopathological subjects. At the same time the APA created a new periodical, the *Journal of Personality and Social Psychology*, to focus on those two subject areas.

exhortation to researchers on conditioned reflexes: namely that they be *systematic* and *thorough* in their approach.

In the meantime, sociopolitical storm clouds were gathering in Europe, with the rise of Hitler and anti-Semitic policies that were making life unbearable there for Jewish scholars. Consequently, many eminent scientists emigrated to the United States, including Albert Einstein in physics and, in psychology, the founders of Gestalt Psychology Max Wertheimer, Kurt Koffka, and Wolfgang Köhler. A somewhat younger member of their school, the brilliant and versatile Kurt Lewin, also came to join them (see also Chapter 12). Besides enhancing the quality of American university faculties, these émigré psychologists naturally brought with them interests in the social and political issues that had come to the fore in Europe. Lewin, in particular, was struck by the contrasting effects on the general populace of the authoritarian Nazi leadership in his native Germany and the democratic government of his adoptive home. While at the University of Iowa in 1939, he and two colleagues conducted a study in which clubs of 11-year-old boys were led, on a randomly assigned basis, by adults who deliberately assumed an authoritarian leadership style (in which the leader made all decisions unilaterally, without discussion) or a democratic style (in which decisions were made by group consensus, after discussion). The groups were given a series of tasks to perform, such as to make masks, and their general behavior was observed. Although the two leadership styles produced similar levels of quantitatively measured output, the boys significantly preferred the democratic leaders, and they behaved more aggressively under the authoritarian leadership.[30] Lewin promoted further research on "group dynamics" and attracted several gifted graduate students to work with him on the subject, both at Iowa and at the Massachusetts Institute of Technology where he moved in 1944. We shall meet one of his most prominent students a little later in this chapter.

In the post–World War II era, experimental social psychology finally came of age in the United States with a series of studies that combined the programmatic rigor that had been prescribed by Dashiell with the social relevance of Lewin's leadership study. The leading investigator here was **Solomon Asch** (1907–1996), and his subject was **social conformity**.

Asch and Social Conformity

Born in Warsaw, Poland, Solomon Asch emigrated to New York as a teenager, studied at its City College and then Columbia University under Max Wertheimer, and finally joined the faculty of Swarthmore College, where he became a colleague of Wolfgang Köhler. He shared the Gestalt psychologists' social concerns and became particularly interested in a subject that had recently come to particular prominence. The atrocities of the Holocaust, in which ordinary people had seemingly obeyed orders to commit the most heinous acts, along with observations of German citizens' general acquiescence to government dictates during the Nazi regime, indicated that the tendency to conform and obey were not confined to atypical personality types but were perhaps universal tendencies affected by powerful *situational* factors. Social scientists and philosophers began to wonder about the *social* conditions affecting conformity and obedience.

At the same time, in the United States public concern had also arisen about the seemingly "conformist" nature of 1950s American society— a general and sometimes unsettling tendency to "go along with the crowd." This tendency was quite at odds with the pioneering, iconoclastic, self-reliant image of the American character so central to American national identity and so necessary for entrepreneurial success in a capitalist society. Thus, as the Cold War escalated, the concern about a tendency toward conformity was clearly embedded in a host of much larger social and political concerns. Asch decided to study this tendency with full scientific rigor in the laboratory.

In a popular summary of his research,[31] Asch traced the notion of "suggestibility" back to Bernheim and the Nancy School and added that all too often the term was taken to suggest a kind of passive and uncritical acquiescence to social pressure. Asch wondered, however, whether the subjects actually *believed* everything the suggestor told them or were merely "going along" with the suggestions while knowing that they were literally untrue. Did they experience conflict? And what about those subjects who remained resistant to the suggestions and did not go along? Asch sought to investigate these questions systematically.

In his original study Asch brought together small groups of male undergraduates for what was described as an experiment in "visual judgment." The visual task involved harkened back to Binet (although

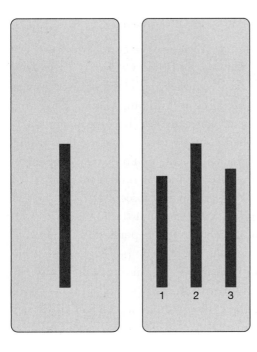

FIG 10.6
The stimulus cards in Asch's social conformity experiments

Asch for some reason failed to cite him), as subjects were asked to look first at a card with a single "standard" line on it and then at another card with three lines, only one of which was the same length as the standard, as shown in Figure 10.6. Subjects were asked to announce aloud their judgments as to which lines were the same length. Prior testing had shown this to be an extremely easy task for subjects when alone, who responded with nearly 100 percent accuracy.

In the experiment, however, only one person in each group was the true "subject," and he was positioned to always announce his decision last. The others were all confederates of the experimenter who gave their responses according to a prearranged script. In a typical session, all of the confederates gave correct responses on the first two trials and the subject naturally agreed; thus, it seemed as if everyone was in for a boring and very easy visual test. On the third trial, however, all of the confederates deliberately gave the same *incorrect* answer, and they continued to do so on many of the subsequent trials (occasionally giving correct responses to reduce the possibility that the true subject would suspect collusion). Asch described the typical subject this way:

> [H]e finds himself unexpectedly in a minority of one, opposed to a unanimous and arbitrary majority with respect to a clear

and simple fact. Upon him we have brought to bear two opposed forces: the evidence of his senses and the unanimous opinion of a group of his peers. Also, he must declare his judgments in public, before a majority which has also stated its opinion publicly.[32]

So how did subjects respond to this conflict? There were wide individual differences, but all subjects showed at least some overt signs of surprise and discomfort. On the first critical trial, nearly 20 percent of the subjects gave incorrect responses that conformed to the majority, and on subsequent trials that percentage nearly doubled. Only a quarter of the subjects remained completely independent and never agreed with the false majority, and a slightly smaller percentage went along with the majority all of the time; the largest group showed intermediate degrees of conformity.

In postexperiment interviews, some of the independent subjects said that they simply retained faith in their own judgments, while others said they believed the majority might have been correct but that it had been their duty to call them as they saw them. Some of the conforming subjects believed privately that the majority was incorrect but said they went along so as not to spoil the experiment; others of them attributed the discrepancy to some perceptual deficiency in themselves. In short, there were a wide range of individual reactions to the experimental situation, although all subjects found it at least mildly disturbing.

In follow-up experiments, Asch systematically varied the size of the group of confederates. When confronted with just a single "opponent" in a group of two, subjects agreed with false judgments less than 4 percent of the time; with two opponents the rate rose to 14 percent, and with three to nearly 32 percent. The effect peaked with seven opponents at 37 percent conformity, and it actually decreased slightly to 31 percent—perhaps a small "overkill" effect—with large groups of 15 opponents. In another experimental variation, one of the confederates was instructed to respond truthfully, so that the subject was confronted not just with a majority who disagreed with him but also with a supporter. In this situation, subjects gave incorrect, conforming responses less than 10 percent of the time. Surprisingly, an almost equal effect was produced when one of the confederates differed from the majority but chose the second of the two *incorrect* lines. Thus, the mere presence of a fellow dissenter—even if his dissent was obviously incorrect—was sufficient to "free" many subjects from the power of the group pressure.

Through these and other controlled variations on the experiment, Asch and his colleagues teased out many of the precise effects of group pressure on individual social responses. This work established a standard for much subsequent research, setting the stage for a wide variety of innovative programs. Among the most noteworthy of these was one promoted by a student of Kurt Lewin.

Festinger and Cognitive Dissonance

Leon Festinger (1919–1989) did his early graduate work with Lewin at Iowa and then followed his mentor to MIT, where he became an important member of Lewin's "group dynamics" research institute. After teaching at the Universities of Michigan and Minnesota, where he became an acknowledged authority on research methodology in social psychology, he moved to Stanford University in California. There he conducted his most famous research on what he called **cognitive dissonance**, a subject that merged experimental social psychology with the growing general interest among psychologists in cognitive processes such as thinking, reasoning and believing.[*] In general, the topic pertains to situations in which a person simultaneously holds two or more ideas or beliefs that actively conflict with each other. When the person becomes aware of these conflicts, he or she experiences an uncomfortable state of cognitive dissonance and becomes motivated to reduce it.[33]

Festinger's early interest in this state was aroused by an intriguing case study in group dynamics. A group of cult members from Chicago had become convinced that the world was going to be devastated by a vast flood on a particular midnight in 1954 but that they alone could be rescued and carried off in a flying saucer if they gathered at a certain place on that day. As "true believers," many of them had left jobs and families behind and sold their belongings in preparation for the cataclysmic event. Needless to say, Festinger and his research team (which included his younger colleagues Stanley Schachter and

---

[*] Chapter 3 noted the parallel events in the rise of cognitive neuroscience during the same period, and the fuller story of the "cognitive revolution" will be told in Chapter 14.

Henry Riecken) did not share this belief. But after reading about the group in the media, they thought it would be interesting to directly observe its members as the prophecy failed to materialize. Thus the psychologists managed to pass themselves off as fellow believers and infiltrated the group. They reported their firsthand observations of how the group behaved when the predicted disaster failed to materialize in their now-classic 1956 book, *When Prophecy Fails.*[34]

In brief summary, after midnight struck and nothing happened, the group seemed stunned, and after four hours its leader began to break down and cry. Soon, however, she received a "message from God" that the group had shown such faithfulness that the catastrophe had been called off. As word of this turn of events spread among the group, spirits rapidly improved. Instead of feeling humiliated or foolish, the group became exultant and in the following days actively sought publicity and began to proselytize for its cause.

According to Festinger's analysis of this situation, it had created a collection of conflicting ideas in the group's members: They had believed the world was going to end, they had made considerable personal sacrifices to prepare for that end, and yet the predicted catastrophe had not occurred. Their initial thoughts in reaction to the failed prediction—that they had been foolishly mistaken—added further dissonance to the mix. Festinger reasoned that the alternative idea—that they had actually saved the world by their beliefs and actions—resolved that dissonance. Festinger further reasoned that group dynamics played a role in this situation—that the dissonance-resolving idea gained increasing credibility as it was adopted by more and more members of the group. Here was a modern example of the contagion effect that had been observed and exploited by Mesmer a century and a half earlier.

In a later experimental study conducted jointly with James Carlsmith, Festinger clearly and ingeniously demonstrated the effects of dissonance in a more individualized, controlled setting. This time subjects were first required to spend an hour performing two extremely tedious tasks (repetitively placing spools in a tray and turning the pegs in a large pegboard by one quarter of a rotation). Following this task, each subject was asked to brief the "next subject"—actually a confederate of the experimenters—about the nature of the experience according to a script that described the work as extremely interesting and enjoyable. Some of the true subjects were paid one dollar for their participation, while others were offered twenty dollars (a substantial sum in the 1950s). Finally, all subjects were asked to fill out a rating form inquiring about how enjoyable, interesting and important they *actually* thought the task had been.

The main result was that subjects who had been paid only one dollar to tell the confederate the experience was enjoyable rated the experience significantly more positively than those who were paid twenty dollars to tell the same "fib." The reason, Festinger and Carlsmith argued, was that those in the one-dollar condition experienced more cognitive dissonance because they had given a falsely positive report about an experience that had actually been unpleasant, and for a nominally small fee. The twenty-dollar subjects, by comparison, had at least been well paid for perpetrating the falsehood, providing justification for their behavior. Meanwhile, the one-dollar subjects had reduced their dissonance by raising their actual opinion about the nature of their experience.[35]

There was an apparent practical lesson from this demonstration: To alter the opinions and attitudes of other people in a particular direction, convince them to engage in some overt act that is consistent with the desired opinion but that is minimally externally rewarded. They will then tend to actually change their opinion in that direction. Here was a potential technique for social influence and control that could be added to those emphasized by Le Bon and other group theorists.

Festinger and others continued to develop and refine the theory of cognitive dissonance throughout the 1960s, and as they did so other experimental approaches to social influence came to share center stage with them. In particular, a series of experiments on obedience by the young psychologist **Stanley Milgram** (1933–1984) came to be regarded as the most famous in the history of social psychology.

Stanley Milgram and Obedience

Solomon Asch spent the 1955–56 academic year as a visiting lecturer at Harvard, where the young graduate student Stanley Milgram (see Figure 10.7) was assigned to assist him. Milgram was immediately inspired to develop several refinements to Asch's experimental pro-

FIG 10 7 Stanley Milgram (1933–1984)

cedures, which became the basis of his Ph.D. dissertation research. First he automated the experimental conformity situation, using an auditory instead of a visual discrimination task, which was tape-recorded along with the scripted responses of the confederates. The subject was placed in the last in a row of closed booths after being told the others were already occupied by fellow subjects. Milgram added a new experimental condition, telling some subjects that the study results would be used in designing safety signals in airplanes—thereby placing a premium on the importance of providing accurate responses. Finally, interested in possible differences in "national character," Milgram conducted his studies on subjects in Norway and France. He found that the Norwegian subjects conformed slightly more frequently than the French, an apparent demonstration of the greater social cohesion of the former and individualism of the latter. And he found that the "aircraft condition" produced about a 10 per-cent reduction in incorrect conforming responses—statistically sig-nificant but not overly impressive.[56]

Milgram's adoption of the aircraft condition reflected his early con-cern with what he perceived to be the most significant limitation of the Asch experiments: the relative triviality of the experimental task. As a new assistant professor at Yale after receiving his degree, Milgram wondered how he might study behavior that was even more consequen-tial. Having grown up as a Jew in wartime New York, Milgram had been horrified by the compliant behavior of many German citizens who collaborated in the atrocities of the Hitler era. The subject was much in the news because of the capture, trial, and eventual execution in Israel of Adolf Eichmann. Charged with crimes against humanity for organizing the deportation and mass murder of Jews during the holocaust, Eichmann claimed in defense that he had been merely following orders. Eichmann's very public trial—it was televised all over the world—prompted grave concerns about what Jewish political theorist Hannah Arendt came to call "the banality of evil."[*] If Nazi war criminals were indistinguishable from "normal" people, could almost anyone be induced to commit such atrocities? Milgram now conceived of a conformity study in which the subject behavior would be obedience to an instruction to inflict punishment or pain.

Following the pattern of Binet and Asch, he wanted first to test individuals acting alone to establish the base rate for obedience and then determine how group pressure might increase the compliance levels. His new experiment featured a rectangular box labeled "Shock Generator, Type ZLB," with a row of thirty switches marked in 15-volt intervals from 15 volts on one end to 450 volts on the other. Beneath the switches were descriptive labels ranging from "slight shock" at the low end, through "strong shock" and "intense shock" in the middle, to "Danger, severe shock," and then just three red X's at the high end.

Subjects were recruited for a "study of memory," for which they would be paid $4.00. Upon arrival at the laboratory, they were met by the experimenter and by an accomplice posing as a second subject. Told that they would draw lots to determine who would be the "teacher" and who the "learner" in the experiment, each drew a slip of paper that said "teacher." The accomplice, however, always said that he had drawn the learner's role, and he was accordingly placed in a booth from which he could not be seen but where he could still communicate with the teacher. An electrode, said (falsely) to be connected to the Shock

---

[*] Hannah Arendt covered the Eichmann trial for *The New Yorker* magazine and subsequently wrote a book titled *Eichmann in Jerusalem: A Report on the Banality of Evil* (New York: Viking, 1963), in which she argued that the overwhelming majority of Nazi war crimes were committed by people who were "terrifyingly normal."

Generator, was attached to the learner's arm. In the ensuing experiment the teacher read through a list of pairs of words and then tested the learner by reading the first from each pair and asking the learner to recall the second. The teacher was instructed to administer a shock after each incorrect response, starting at the low end of the scale and increasing its intensity by one switch after each successive mistake.

Needless to say, the learner was preprogrammed to give many incorrect responses, and the experiment's only purpose was to see how far the teacher would go in inflicting punishment. At specified points on the scale, the learner's script called for him to grunt in pain, to bang on the wall, to complain about a heart condition, and at the end to cease responding at all. Whenever the teacher hesitated or questioned the experimenter about going on, the experimenter responded with one from a set of increasingly authoritative commands: "Please continue," "The experiment requires that you continue," "It is absolutely essential that you continue," and if none of those worked, "You have no other choice, you *must* go on."

Before the first experiment, Milgram described it to a group of colleagues and graduate students and asked them to predict how far a typical subject would go before breaking off. Overwhelmingly, they predicted that most subjects would stop after the first signs of obvious distress from the learner and that vanishingly few would carry on until the final, 450-volt shock. Not one of these presumed experts came close to predicting the results of the experiment, which seemed extraordinary in two ways.

First was the degree of obedience shown by the subjects. Virtually all continued to administer shocks after the learner's first cries of protest even as the descriptive labels on the shock box increased far into the "strong" and "intense" categories. And nearly two-thirds of the subjects continued all the way to the end of the scale—not unquestioningly, to be sure, but successfully prodded by the experimenter's flat-voiced commands that the experiment *must* be continued.

Proceeding systematically, Milgram conducted numerous variations on his original experiment, such as holding it in a streetcorner setting much less prestigious than Yale University, bringing the learner into closer proximity to the teacher, and, as in the original plan, introducing multiple teachers to see whether there was a conformity effect. Many of these conditions produced measurable reductions in the obedient responses, but none came close to matching the original low predictions of the experts. Conclusively and dramatically, Milgram's experiments indicated that normal subjects would obey instructions from a credible (or sometimes semi-credible) authority to inflict pain to a surprisingly and distressingly high degree.

Milgram's second extraordinary finding was that, in his own words: "The procedure created extreme levels of nervous tension. . . . Profuse sweating, trembling and stuttering were typical expressions of this emotional disturbance. One unexpected sign of tension—yet to be explained—was the regular occurrence of nervous laughter, which in some [subjects] developed into uncontrollable seizures."[37] In one "characteristic" case: "I observed a mature and initially poised businessman enter the laboratory smiling and confident. Within 20 minutes he was reduced to a twitching, stuttering wreck, who was rapidly approaching the point of a nervous collapse."[38] Although Milgram's colorful description may have slightly oversensationalized the general results of his experiment, there is no question but that most of his obedient subjects experienced great stress even as they were obeying.

Unsurprisingly, Milgram's published accounts and the film he made showing his experiment created a public as well as a professional sensation. The study had major ramifications both substantively, in terms of what it showed about human nature, and methodologically for social psychologists, in terms of what kinds of experiments they were subsequently allowed to perform.

Substantively, the Milgram experiments were the capstone of a long series of demonstrations of the power of certain *situations* to profoundly influence the social behavior of individuals, causing them to behave drastically differently from the way they would if left on their own. Mesmerism, hypnotism, crowds, and group membership had all been shown to affect behavior in some dramatic ways. Now here was evidence that most normal people would inflict severe punishment on others, merely on the instructions of a presumed authority such as a psychology professor, and despite some "internal" resistance to doing so. True, there were some defiant subjects who refused to administer extreme shocks and broke off the experiment, indicating that personality differences in the subjects were not completely irrelevant. But still, the fact that a strong majority of subjects did *not* break off suggested that the power of the situation, and its corresponding social expectations, could very often outweigh personal predispositions.

This general point was soon reinforced by the **Stanford Prison Experiment**, conducted by Milgram's friend **Philip Zimbardo** (b. 1933). In this study, 24 Stanford undergraduates, preselected for their psychological normality, were randomly assigned to play the roles of either prisoners or guards and then to live in a mock prison. Many of the subjects fell into their roles with such intensity—several of the "guards" manifested genuinely sadistic behavior and some of the "prisoners" became highly traumatized—that Zimbardo had to conclude the experiment prematurely after just six days. Here was a further demonstration of the ease with which ordinary people could be induced by situational factors to engage in extraordinary and even antisocial behavior. Zimbardo has recently established a website that simulates the prison study, and moreover draws implications from it for our understanding of much more recent real-life events, such as the mistreatment of Iraqi prisoners in the notorious Abu Ghraib jail.[39]

Ethical and Methodological Aftereffects

Milgram did his best to ensure that the emotional distress suffered by his subjects was temporary, assuaging it through postexperimental debriefings and assurance that their responses were normal as well as extremely valuable in providing data for the furtherance of knowledge. The majority of the subjects said that they were glad to have participated. But still, his graphic descriptions of his subjects' distress, and the fact that in the Stanford Prison Experiment Zimbardo had had to prematurely halt the study to prevent psychological damage, raised questions about whether adequate protections had been in place. Further questions arose regarding the ethics of using *deception* in experiments: either explicitly or implicitly misleading subjects about the true purposes of their studies. The debate extended beyond the boundaries of psychology per se, also focusing, for example, on a study by the military that recorded the responses of recruits aboard an airplane that they were falsely led to believe was about to crash.

The major result of this debate—and the concern over the ethics of human subject research more generally—was the eventual requirement across the sciences and medicine that all subjects in institutionally sponsored research must give their **informed consent** before participating; that is, they must be told about, and consent to undergo, the actual purposes and procedures of the experiment. To ensure conformity with this requirement, all research proposals involving human subjects must be subjected to strict scrutiny and approval from institutional review boards (IRBs) prior to any actual experimentation. Needless to say, experiments like Milgram's could no longer be performed in the same way today.

Milgram himself went on to conduct several extremely ingenious experiments that met the new ethical guidelines. In the "lost letter" study, for example, he left large samples of stamped and addressed letters on the windshields of cars, with a scrawled note saying "found near car." All letters had the same address—actually a post office box maintained by Milgram—but differed in the names of their addressees, which typically contrasted in their social or political implications: "Equal Rights for Negroes" vs. "Council for White Neighborhoods" in one study, for example, or "Friends of the Communist Party" vs. "The Medical Research Council" in another. Milgram wondered how many of each kind of envelope would actually be mailed back to him, how many would be opened or tampered with, and so on, and he found that the results provided quite sensitive measures of public opinion.

In another famous study, Milgram investigated the **small world phenomenon**, giving the name and address of a target person in Boston—a stockbroker there—to a random group of people in Nebraska and asking them to contact the target directly if they knew him personally (which never happened), and if not to pass along the same instruction to the person they knew who they felt would be *most likely* to know the target. Most of the subsequent chains wound up close to the stockbroker in Boston, and more than a quarter actually reached him, with an average of just six intermediaries; this provided the origin for the now common assertion that any two people in the world are interconnected by no more than "six degrees of separation" (if one knows how to identify them). During the 1970s and early 1980s, Milgram also conducted many innovative studies in urban psychology from his base at the City University of New York, before he died prematurely from a heart condition at the age of 51.[40]

Social Influence Today

In January 2009 the American Psychological Association's flagship journal, *American Psychologist*, devoted an entire Special Issue to the subject "Obedience—Then and Now." Reflecting on Milgram's obedience studies a half-century after their occurrence, the issue included a partial replication (which passed its IRB because it terminated at the point where the learner first complained about the painful shock) with results very similar to Milgram's.[41] It also included a thoughtful assessment by two prominent historians of psychology, Ludy Benjamin and Jeffry Simpson, who emphasized the previously made point that Milgram's obedience studies represented a sort of pinnacle in demonstrating the power of *situations* as determinants of human behavior, often overshadowing the influence of "internal" characteristics of individual people. The field of personality, as a consequence, began to shift its focus from a predominant emphasis on individual and presumably stable traits to one on the *interactions* between differing combinations of situations and traits.

Within social psychology, a significant change occurred regarding the types of situations that could be studied experimentally, because "high impact" situations such as those investigated by Milgram and Zimbardo could no longer be manufactured and manipulated in laboratory settings. Those situations that *could* be investigated experimentally now had to be much more mundane in their implications and impacts on their participants. High-impact situations had to be investigated via more "naturalistic" and nonexperimental methods, such as by interviewing and studying people who had already gone through traumatic experiences in the real world. The historians concluded: "The rise of research studying people in their natural lives and environments may be one of the most important legacies of the IRB changes informed by Milgram's obedience research."[42]

During the 1970s, some social psychologists feared that the new constraints had contributed to a "crisis" in their field. Despite the development of increasingly sophisticated research designs and statistical methods, the resulting studies too often appeared to have little social relevance. In describing this presumed crisis, the prominent social psychologist Muzafer Sherif looked back almost nostalgically on Milgram's obedience study with its "embeddedness in historical reality" and its "clean cut simple instrumentation that does not degenerate into the hollow front of technical embellishments and devious and cute cleverness in design."[43]

But still, creativity cannot be denied, and several more recent social psychologists have found ways to conduct "historically embedded" experiments on highly relevant topics, while still meeting the rigorous demands of IRBs. There is no better example, nor one more appropriately suited to conclude this chapter, than the "Lost in the Mall" study by **Elizabeth Loftus** (b. 1944) and her student Jacqueline Pickrell.

"Lost in the Mall"

The larger context for Loftus's research was a public debate that raged in the 1980s and early 1990s regarding the veracity of "recovered memories" of childhood abuse that were increasingly being reported by some psychotherapists' patients. At first these "memories" were uncritically accepted by some prosecutors and juries as true, resulting in the conviction and imprisonment of some of the alleged perpetrators of the abuse. Loftus, who was an expert on the "reconstructive" as opposed to "photographic" nature of memory, regarded these recollections more skeptically, as possible reconstructions or confabulations that had been directly or indirectly suggested by the therapeutic situation. As part of her research on the subject, she and Pickrell conducted an experiment in which **false memories** were deliberately created in their subjects. For ethical reasons and to satisfy IRB conditions, they could not try to induce truly horrific recollections; as an alternative, they devised a scenario for a hypothetical childhood event that would have been "mildly traumatic" and memorable, but without lasting negative consequences.

Their subjects were young adults whose families were interviewed to gather information about their childhoods. From this information the experimenters constructed four brief stories for each subject, three of which described real events that had actually occurred. The fourth was always a fictitious account of having been lost in a home town mall for an extended time before being rescued by a kindly elderly person and reunited tearfully with parents. All subjects were presented with the four stories, told that they had been constructed on the basis of interviews with their families, and asked to provide their own personal recollections of the events. Although most of the subjects "remembered" the false story with somewhat less clarity than the true ones, nonetheless they accepted it and provided further details and embellishments to it—for example, describing the clothes worn by the rescuer. And after being told that one of the stories was false and being asked to choose which one it was, nearly a quarter of the subjects chose one that was actually true and accepted the false mall experience as having been real.[44]

This result would not have surprised Alfred Binet, who a century earlier had already demonstrated that children's testimony and memories could be significantly influenced by the merest of *suggestions* that something might or might not have been true. But Loftus added several experimental refinements, and her study took on particular resonance because of its relevance to the "memory wars" that were raging at the time.[45] One positive consequence was that "recovered memories" of criminal abuse, no matter how sincerely related and recalled, now require much more extensive corroboration and validation before being accepted as legitimate evidence.

Thus, starting with Mesmer, proceeding through the early hypnotists and crowd leaders, and concluding with the work of social psychologists such as Asch, Milgram, Zimbardo, and Loftus, we have seen dramatic demonstrations of the power of social influence to affect behavior, belief, attitude, and even memory. The further study of these influences, and the particular conditions and situations in which they work, will undoubtedly continue to be a major goal of social psychology.

Summary

The modern history of the investigation of social influence processes begins with several figures who developed the techniques of mesmerism and **hypnotism**. From the eighteenth-century exploits of **Franz Anton Mesmer,** who promoted a theory of **animal magnetism**, through his student **Puységur**'s work on **artificial somnambulism**, to **José di Faria**'s concept of hypnotic susceptibility, the notion that people respond to social influence of various kinds has been exploited for a number of constructive and not-so-constructive purposes. Among the most useful was inducing hypnotic trance as a form of anesthesia during surgical procedures, pioneered in India by **James Esdaile** in the mid-nineteenth century. The Scottish physician **James Braid** lent the subject of hypnotism some scientific respectability by confirming its effects and publishing them in recognized periodicals.

Hypnotism in the medical context was further taken up by **Jean-Martin Charcot** in his studies of hysteric patients at the Salpêtrière Hospital in Paris, where he attributed hypnotic susceptibility to the presence of the same neuropathological condition that presumably underlay hysteria. This put him at odds with physicians of the Nancy school, who believed that hypnotic trances could be induced in normal subjects and were brought on by ordinary suggestibility. The debate was eventually decided in favor of the latter position, although Charcot's enormous prestige was essential in bringing the important subjects of hysteria and hypnosis out of scientific obscurity. The more general subjects of suggestibility and crowd behavior were given wide publicity by the flamboyant theorist **Gustave Le Bon**.

Alfred Binet studied suggestibility experimentally in the laboratory, and **Norman Triplett** did the same with social facilitation in the early 1900s. Both of these men can be considered "anticipators" of the field of experimental social psychology that began more formally in the United States with **Floyd Allport**'s Ph.D. dissertation on social facilitation and his 1924 textbook, *Social Psychology*. This text called for a social psychology focused on objectively observable responses made by individual subjects in objectively specifiable social situations. The more important lines of research that evolved as this approach took hold included **Solomon Asch**'s conformity studies, **Leon Festinger**'s research on cognitive dissonance, **Stanley Milgram**'s obedience studies, and **Philip Zimbardo**'s prison experiment. More recent research by **Elizabeth Loftus** and others has confirmed the profound influence that suggestibility can have on memory.

Key Pioneers

Allport, Floyd H., p. 431

Asch, Solomon, p. 434

Bernheim, Hippolyte, p. 415

Binet, Alfred, p. 422

Braid, James, p. 414

Charcot, Jean-Martin, p. 416

Dashiell, John, p. 433
de Chastenet, Amand Marie
    Jacques (Marquis de
    Puységur), p. 408
Delboeuf, Joseph, p. 423
Faria, José Custódio di, p. 410
Elliotson, John, p. 412
Esdaile, James, p. 413
Féré, Charles, p. 422
Festinger, Leon, p. 438
Gassner, Johann Joseph, p. 401

Henri, Victor, p. 429
Le Bon, Gustave, p. 425
Liébeault, Ambroise Auguste,
    p. 415
Loftus, Elizabeth, p. 448
Mesmer, Franz Anton, p. 402
Milgram, Stanley, p. 440
Prince, Morton, p. 431
Triplett, Norman, p. 430
Wittmann, Blanche, p. 421
Zimbardo, Philip, p. 445

Key Terms

animal magnetism, p. 405
artificial somnambulism, p. 409
baquet, p. 406
cognitive dissonance, p. 438
false memories, p. 448
forme fruste, p. 418
grand hypnotisme, p. 421
grande hystérie, p. 420
group fallacy, p. 433
hypnotism, p. 403
hysteria, p. 416
informed consent, p. 446
lucid sleep, p. 411
neurohypnology, p. 414

neurypnology, p. 414
perfect crisis, p. 409
petite hystérie, p. 420
post-hypnotic amnesia, p. 409
post-hypnotic suggestion, p. 409
small world phenomenon, p. 446
social conformity, p. 434
social contagion, p. 407
social facilitation, p. 407
social influence processes, p. 403
Stanford Prison Experiment, p. 445
suggestibility, p. 409
type, p. 418

Discussion Questions and Topics

1 The major focus of this chapter has been the history of human suggestibility and social influence as conceptualized by a number of major
figures, from the eighteenth century to today. Describe how the history
of suggestibility in the French pathological tradition came to be
connected to the history of social influence in the American context.

2 Milgram's obedience to authority studies are perhaps some of the
best known and most controversial in the history of psychology, in part
because of Milgram's use of deception. Discuss the conditions under

which the use of deception is justified in psychological research, and when it is not justified.

3 What has the history of social influence presented in this chapter taught you about the concept itself? What has modern research confirmed and disconfirmed about earlier theories and beliefs?

Suggested Readings

For Mesmer's biography, see Vincent Buranelli, *The Wizard from Vienna* (New York: Coward, McCann and Geoghegan, 1975), and for an excellent account of his movement's role in prerevolutionary France, see Robert Darnton, *Mesmerism and the End of the Enlightenment in France* (Cambridge, MA: Harvard University Press, 1968). Useful general histories of hypnosis are Alan Gauld's *A History of Hypnotism* (New York: Cambridge University Press, 1992); Chapter 2 of Henri F. Ellenberger, *The Discovery of the Unconscious* (New York: Basic Books, 1970); Frank Pattie's "A Brief History of Hypnotism," in *Handbook of Clinical and Experimental Hypnosis*, edited by Jesse E. Gordon (New York: Macmillan, 1967); Chapter 1 of Peter W. Sheehan and Campbell W. Perry, *Methodologies of Hypnosis: A Critical Appraisal of Contemporary Paradigms of Hypnosis* (Hillsdale, NJ: Erlbaum, 1976); and Chapter 9 of Gregory Zilboorg, *A History of Medical Psychology* (New York: Norton, 1967).

Biographical material on Charcot appears in Chapter 2 of Ellenberger, cited above, and in George F. Drinka, *The Birth of Neurosis: Myth, Malady and the Victorians* (New York: Simon & Schuster, 1984). Sigmund Freud's reminiscences of Charcot appear in his 1893 obituary, "Charcot," reprinted in *The Standard Edition of the Complete Psychological Works of Sigmund Freud*, vol. III (London: Hogarth, 1962). Mark S. Micale's "The Salpêtrière in the Age of Charcot: An Institutional Perspective on Medical History in the Late Nineteenth Century," in *Journal of Contemporary History* 20 (1985): 703–731, presents a vivid picture of the setting for Charcot's work. Gustave Le Bon's readable if sometimes outrageous *The Crowd* is available in paperback editions. For discussion of the context and importance of Le Bon's work, see Gordon W. Allport's "The Historical Background of Modern Social Psychology," in *The Handbook of Social Psychology*, vol. 1, edited by Gardner Lindzey and Elliott Aronson (New York: Addison-Wesley, 1968).

For details about Binet's work on hypnosis and suggestion, see Theta Wolf's *Alfred Binet* (Chicago: University of Chicago Press, 1973) and Raymond Fancher, "Alfred Binet: General Psychologist," in *Portraits of Pioneers in Psychology,* vol. III, edited by Gregory Kimble and Michael Wertheimer (Mahwah, NJ: Lawrence Elbaum Associates, 1998), 67–84. For a readable, although largely uncritical account of Stanley Milgram's background, life, and work, see Thomas Blass, *The Man Who Shocked the World: The Life and Legacy of Stanley Milgram* (New York: Basic Books, 2004).

Mind in Conflict

The Psychoanalytic Psychology of Sigmund Freud

11

Freud's Early Life
The Method of Free Association

The Interpretation of Dreams
The Primary and Secondary Processes
The Wish-Fulfillment Hypothesis

Self-Analysis and the Theory of Childhood Sexuality
Stages of Childhood Sexuality
Freudian Character Types

Psychoanalytic Psychotherapy
The Case of Dora

Metapsychology and the Ego's Defense Mechanisms

The Psychology of Women

Final Controversies and Freud's Legacy
Freud's Legacy

Freud and Psychology
Freud's Reception by Academic Psychology

Summary

Key Pioneers

Key Terms

Discussion Questions and Topics

Suggested Readings

'*But Doctor, I'm not asleep, you know; I can't be* hypnotized." Those words, half apologetic yet half taunting, rang in the ears of **Sigmund Freud (1856–1939)** one afternoon in 1892. The young Viennese doctor felt sure he could cure this patient of her troublesome symptoms if only he could hypnotize her. And yet, in spite of his repeated assertions—"You are feeling drowsy; your eyelids are heavier and heavier; soon you will be fast asleep!"—the patient remained disconcertingly awake.[1]

Freud's patient suffered from hysteria, a condition that irritated or baffled most of his colleagues, as its assorted symptoms had no discernible physical basis. Paralyses, tremors, losses of feeling and memory—these and many other problems usually associated with injury to the nervous system plagued hysterical patients, yet neurological examinations revealed no physical injuries. Perhaps understandably, most of Freud's fellow doctors dismissed hysterical patients as malingerers or fakers, simply trying to avoid their responsibilities through imaginary illnesses.

But Freud thought otherwise. He had studied with Jean Charcot, the great French neurologist who taught—as we saw in Chapter 10—that hysterical symptoms are real and worthy of serious attention. And Freud had visited the "Nancy school" in France, whose members had been partially successful in treating hysteria by hypnotizing patients and then simply and directly suggesting that the symptoms would disappear. Sometimes, though not always, they did. After returning home, Freud confirmed the partial success of direct hypnosis with some of his own hysterical patients.

More promising still, in Freud's view, was a technique using hypnosis indirectly, developed by his older friend **Josef Breuer** (1842–1925; see Figure 11.1) while treating just one remarkable hysterical patient named **Bertha Pappenheim** (1859–1936). While nursing her terminally ill father, the young woman had developed a series of debilitating hysterical symptoms. Breuer, a prominent physician who did not normally treat hysterics, made an exception for his family friends the Pappenheims. Gradually, and working together virtually as collaborators, doctor and patient devised a "**cathartic method**" that removed her symptoms.

In this treatment, Breuer hypnotized Pappenheim and then asked her to try to recall the first time she had experienced a physical sensation like one of her symptoms. Often, the hypnosis facilitated her recall of a previously "forgotten" but highly emotion-laden memory associated with the symptom. On remembering such an incident, she would give vent to its previously suppressed emotion. Following this emotional "catharsis," the symptom would disappear. For example, a

FIG 11.1
Josef Breuer
(1842–1925)

severe and involuntary squinting of the eyes was traced under hypnosis to an occasion when she had sat by her dying and comatose father's bed, much upset and with tears in her eyes. Her father had suddenly awakened and asked for the time. Trying to hide her distress, Bertha had had to squint to see her watch and reply. Afterward, memory for the incident disappeared but the squint remained as a permanent symptom. Remembering the scene under hypnosis, however, she finally expressed the long-suppressed emotion, and the symptom disappeared. Other symptoms were treated similarly.

As the treatment progressed, however, Pappenheim became increasingly and openly attached to Breuer emotionally—a development that disturbed the proper doctor greatly, and his wife even more so. At the earliest possible moment he terminated treatment and could never be persuaded to accept another hysterical patient. Over the next several years Pappenheim gradually recovered from both her infatuation with Breuer and her hysteria. She moved to Frankfurt and became one of Germany's first social workers and a feminist leader—accomplishments that led to her being commemorated on a German postage stamp in 1954 and recognized as an important historical figure in her own right.[2] As for Breuer, although he never treated another hysterical patient, he did tell his young colleague Freud about the case of Bertha Pappenheim. Years later, Freud remembered this when he began treating his own hysteric patients. He tried the cathartic method himself and found it worked far better than direct hypnosis, or any other technique he knew about. He treated several cases successfully and persuaded Breuer to collaborate in writing *Studies on Hysteria* (1895)—a book recognized today as the starting point for a new field that Freud came to call **psychoanalysis**.

In the book Freud and Breuer described several of their cases (including that of Bertha Pappenheim, disguised under the pseudonym "Anna O.") and offered the startling general hypothesis that "hysterics suffer mainly from reminiscences."[3] They did not mean ordinary reminiscences, but memories of emotionally charged experiences that have been somehow "forgotten" and placed beyond the reach of ordinary consciousness, to become disease-producing, **pathogenic ideas**. Without access to normal consciousness, the emotional energy accompanying pathogenic ideas could not be gradually expressed and dissipated in the normal way, but presumably remained bottled up or "strangulated." Stimuli that would normally arouse the memory now activated the strangulated emotional energy instead, which "discharged" into the musculature to produce a hysterical symptom. Thus, Freud and Breuer referred to many hysterical symptoms as **conversions** (of emotional into physical energy). With hypnotic assistance, however, patients could regain conscious access to their pathogenic ideas and therefore to the normal expression of their strangulated emotional energy. The causes of their symptoms could thus be removed.

Unfortunately, however, this promising cathartic method of treatment worked only with people who could be deeply hypnotized—and Freud had found to his chagrin that many patients could not be. Instead of falling into a sleeplike state in which their memories became exceptionally fluent, they remained puzzled, anxious, or even defiant: "But Doctor, I'm not asleep, you know; I can't be hypnotized."

Freud's efforts to solve this problem led to an expanded and ambitious theory, not just of hysteria, but of human nature in general. His remarkable solution did not emerge suddenly, however, nor was it simply the result of his own isolated genius. Developing over a period of several years, it integrated and synthesized a great many ideas Freud had been exposed to in a rich educational and personal background. We now turn to that background, as a preface to the theory that emerged.

Freud's Early Life

Sigmund Freud (see Figure 11.2) was born on May 6, 1856, in Freiberg, Moravia (now called Príbor, in the Czech Republic). In 1860 his family moved to Vienna, where Freud remained until the Nazi menace forced him to London in 1938, for the final year of his life. Freud's father, twenty years older than his mother, had had two sons by a previous wife, and one of them had a son of his own just before Sigmund was born. Sigmund himself was the first of eight children borne by

FIG 11.2
Sigmund Freud
(1856–1939)

his mother. Thus, he grew up as the oldest child in his immediate household but with half-brothers as old as his mother and a nephew older than himself. This unusual family constellation may have particularly sensitized Freud to the vagaries of family relationships, which he emphasized in his later theories.

As the oldest child in his immediate family, Sigmund became the unchallenged leader of his younger siblings. An outstanding student, he was granted a room of his own for study and ample book-buying funds—both considerable luxuries, given his father's modest income as a wool merchant. Freud justified these indulgences by developing independent talents—teaching himself Spanish so he could read *Don Quixote* in the original, for example—while remaining at the top of his class at his secondary school. His early interests in history and the humanities seemed to be drawing him toward a career in law, until a chance encounter with an inspiring essay on "Nature" aroused his scientific ambitions during his last year at the school. Almost on the spur of the moment, the 17-year-old Freud enrolled in the University of Vienna's medical school in 1873.

There, he encountered several outstanding teachers, beginning with the philosopher **Franz Brentano** (1838–1917). In 1874, the year of Wundt's *Principles of Physiological Psychology*, Brentano published an important book of his own, *Psychology from an Empirical Standpoint*. In it Brentano promoted what he called **act psychology**, in which he contrasted the essential nature of psychology's subject matter with that of the physical sciences. While the physical sciences study *objects*, for Brentano the fundamental units of psychological analysis were *acts* that always refer to or "contain" an object. For example, while a unit of physical analysis might be an atom, a psychological unit would be an act such as *thinking about* an atom, or *believing* that a particular kind of atom must exist, or *wanting* such a kind of atom to exist. Thus, all mental phenomena have an "aboutness," a quality of referring to or implicating some object in consciousness that Brentano called **intentionality**.

Brentano further taught that any adequate psychological theory must be "dynamic," or capable of accounting for the influence of ever-changing *motivational factors* on thought. He also distinguished sharply between the "objective reality" of physical objects and the "subjective reality" of private thought, and he skeptically but seriously examined the literature on unconscious thought. Brentano thus introduced the young Freud to several issues that would preoccupy him throughout his career.[4] Freud took five elective courses with Brentano in his first two years of medical school, and for a time he planned to take a philosophy degree with him after completing medical training. Soon, however, an even more influential teacher led him to change his mind.

Ernst Brücke, director of the university's Physiological Institute, became for Freud the figure "who carried more weight with me than anyone else in my whole life."[5] Together with Hermann Helmholtz, Emil Du Bois-Reymond, and other students of Johannes Müller, Brücke had been a founder of the enormously productive "new physiology" that rejected vitalism and sought mechanistic explanations for all organic phenomena (see Chapter 4). Tremendously impressed by Brücke and his mechanistic physiology, Freud began devoting all his spare time to volunteer research at the Institute—even delaying progress toward his medical degree so he could do so. He worked well and by 1880 had published four articles on neuroanatomy, looking forward to a career in that field.

Paying research positions were scarce, however, and Freud was a Jew in an anti-Semitic society that often discriminated in making university appointments. Still financially dependent on his father in 1882, Freud fell in love with Martha Bernays and suddenly realized he would have to have a paying job if he were ever to marry and support a family of his own. Somewhat reluctantly, he faced reality and began the practical training at Vienna's General Hospital that would qualify him for a private medical practice.

At the hospital, Freud naturally gravitated toward specialties connected with neurophysiology and concentrated his study under the famous brain anatomist **Theodor Meynert** (1833–1892). Freud became a prize pupil, particularly skilled in the diagnosis of localized brain injuries. In 1885, he won Meynert's support for a traveling grant to study in Paris with the celebrated Charcot. He impressed the French master as he had Meynert and won permission to translate some of Charcot's writings into German. Thus, when he returned to Vienna the following year, the 30-year-old Freud had impeccable credentials, and felt able at last to marry and to begin a private practice in the treatment of neurological diseases.

His return was marred, however, when he lectured to the Vienna Medical Society about his study with Charcot and reported favorably on the Frenchman's theory of hysteria—a subject that had been incidental to his interests when he went to Paris. Meynert objected to the theory, particularly Charcot's opinion that men as well as women could be hysterics. Freud felt that from this time forward he lost favor with the Viennese medical establishment and became an "outsider." He also soon found he could not make a living by treating just ordinary neurological cases, even though he bolstered his reputation by publishing well-received books on cerebral palsy and aphasia. He decided to augment his income by accepting patients with hysteria, and since he was among the very few Viennese doctors with the background and willingness to take their symptoms seriously, several patients came to him for help. Thus, almost by default, Freud arrived at his position at the beginning of this chapter, seeking a more widely applicable substitute for hypnosis in the cathartic treatment of hysteria.

The Method of Free Association

Freud took a first step toward solving his problem by recalling an incident from his visit to the Nancy clinic. A recently hypnotized subject had shown a typical posthypnotic amnesia until Bernheim, the hypnotist, placed a hand on the man's forehead and said, "Now you can remember." The subject immediately recalled his entire hypnotic experience in minute detail. Freud wondered if a similar technique might not help his patients overcome their *non*hypnotic amnesias for pathogenic ideas.

Accordingly, he devised a **pressure technique**, in which patients lay on a couch with their eyes closed as for hypnosis, but remained normally awake. Freud then asked them to recall their earliest experiences of their symptoms, until their memories inevitably failed before getting to the crucial pathogenic ideas. Freud then simply pressed their foreheads with his hand and confidently assured them that further memories would follow. Often the memories did return, and the chain of reminiscences could be continued. After repeated applications of pressure, some apparently genuine pathogenic ideas emerged, followed by emotional catharsis and symptom relief.

At first Freud applied pressure often, whenever it seemed to him that memories were flowing in an unpromising direction. But he soon learned how hard it was to distinguish unpromising from promising directions. Once, for example, a patient responded to pressure by reporting flickers and starlike flashes of light. Freud initially assumed these were merely phosphenes (the sensations of light that normally occur whenever the eyeball is pressed) and was about to try again when the patient suddenly said the images were assuming geometrical shapes—crosses, circles, triangles, and so on—that resembled Sanskrit writing. Now intrigued, Freud asked what the figures made the patient think about. The crosses symbolized "pain,' she reported, and a circle represented "perfection." Then she emotionally described and "catharted" her own feelings of pain and imperfection—feelings that had been recently intensified by reading an article in a spiritualist magazine, translated from the Sanskrit. Thus, she arrived at genuine pathogenic material, but through a roundabout train of interconnected associations. From experiences like this, Freud learned to heed *everything* his patients reported as potentially significant, even if it might seem unimportant at first.

Further, Freud gradually learned he did not have to apply physical pressure at all in order to stimulate the memory. He only had to encourage his patients to let their thoughts run free and to report fully and honestly whatever came to mind, even if it seemed irrelevant, stupid, embarrassing, obnoxious, or otherwise anxiety arousing. Though more difficult to follow than it sounds at first, this new practice of **free association** soon became Freud's standard method of treatment, used even with his hypnotizable patients. He believed it led reliably to pathogenic ideas and attuned him to several subtle but important psychological phenomena that had been masked by his previous reliance on hypnosis. When he used the old method, any peculiarity or failure in the treatment was too easily explained away as some deficiency of the hypnosis, such as the shallowness of the trance. But now, Freud focused more attention on the patient's associations per se, and on the relationship between the patient and himself. With this new focus, Freud discerned several new and interesting features of hysterical illness.

First, he found that the pathogenic ideas recalled under free association lacked the one-to-one relationship with particular symptoms that had seemed to be the rule in patients like Bertha Pappenheim. Instead, a whole *series* of pathogenic ideas were often revealed behind an individual hysterical symptom. A patient with hysterical hand tremors, for example, associated three different emotion-laden memories with her symptom: ones of being strapped on her hand as a childhood punishment, of once being badly frightened while playing the piano, and of being required to massage her father's back. The only common feature to these memories was that they all involved her hands; yet with the recall of each, and the expression of the emotion connected with it, her symptom's intensity decreased. In Freud's new terminology, her symptom had not been simply determined by a single pathogenic memory but instead was an example of **overdetermination**, having been caused by three of them acting in concert. He came to believe that most hysterical symptoms were similarly overdetermined.

Patients' attempts to recover memories through free association led Freud to another, even more important idea. He increasingly became convinced that unconscious pathogenic ideas had not been simply "forgotten" in the way unimportant details are. Instead, the memories seemed to have been subjected to a willful and active, although largely unconscious process of **repression** by his patients.

As evidence for this hypothesis, Freud observed that patients invariably "resisted" the free-association process somewhere along the line, and in many ways. Frustratingly often, they interrupted their associations suddenly and at crucial points, just as important and emotion-laden memories seemed about to be recalled. Occasionally in such instances, patients would show obvious signs of anxiety or embarrassment and directly admit that what had come to mind was too ridiculous or obnoxious to be expressed. More often, however, their resistance was indirect and unconscious. Their minds suddenly and mysteriously went blank, for example, or they subtly changed the subject or decided to question Freud's medical credentials and the justification for his unorthodox treatment methods. From the regularity of such direct and indirect resistances, Freud concluded his patients at some level did not *want* to recall some of their pathogenic ideas, although often they remained completely unaware of the fact.

This unconscious resistance suggested to Freud that his patients held very complex attitudes toward their illnesses. On the one hand, they genuinely suffered from their symptoms and wanted to cooperate with the doctor in getting rid of them. But on the other, their unconscious resistances undermined the progress of their therapy. Seemingly, a conscious part of each patient wanted to face the music and be cured, while another, unconscious part feared that the emotional pain of a successful treatment would be too much to bear and tried to sabotage the process. In short, Freud detected **intrapsychic conflict** in his patients, with different aspects of each personality clamoring for mutually exclusive goals. Later, he would come to see intrapsychic conflict as extending far beyond hysteria and pervading virtually all human activity.

A further hypothesis emerged because many of the most strongly resisted memories and ideas turned out to involve *sexual experiences* from childhood. Many patients reluctantly recalled scenes of early sexual mistreatment, often by parents or other close relatives. The patient with the hand tremor, for example, eventually recalled that her father had sexually assaulted her following the back massage. After several such reports, Freud speculated that repressed sexual experiences may have been *necessary* for hysteria to begin, constituting the most important pathogenic ideas that in some way began the entire repressive pattern.

In 1896, Freud boldly published this **seduction theory** of hysteria in a medical journal article. *All* hysterics, he asserted, must have undergone sexual abuse as children. Freud did not then believe children were capable of genuinely "sexual" experience, however, because he accepted the common view that the sexual impulse arises only after puberty. Thus, these children presumably did not immediately experience their seductions as sexual. But with puberty and the arousal of the sexual drive, the memories of those experiences presumably became sexualized "after the fact." This reversal of the normal process, with memories becoming *increasingly* emotionally charged over time, was perhaps what made them subject to repression. So now, instead of consciously remembering their seductions and experiencing new and uncomfortable emotions with the memories, the patients would unconsciously produce hysterical conversion symptoms as a substitute. Symptoms would thus function as **defenses** against psychologically dangerous pathogenic ideas, appearing in consciousness as the lesser of two evils—unpleasant perhaps, but still less anxiety arousing than the pathogenic ideas themselves.

Perhaps understandably, Freud's seduction theory was received poorly by many of his medical colleagues, who regarded him as something of a crank and stopped referring patients to him. Still worse, Freud himself soon began to believe that, in some cases at least, his patients' childhood seductions had often been imaginary rather than real. Despite the sincerity with which the scenes were recalled and reported, in several cases the stories did not stand up to other independent evidence. "I no longer believe in my neurotica [theory of the neuroses]," Freud ruefully confessed to a friend in 1897.[6]

But if these free associations were not real memories, what were they? Freud was haunted by this question for many months. He could not believe his entire approach to hysteria was wrong: His therapy often helped, and it still made sense to regard symptoms as defenses against pathogenic ideas of some kind, even if they were not actual memories. Sexuality must have been important in *some* way, or else why would so many patients report scenes of childhood seduction in their free associations? The seduction theory was obviously wrong in detail, yet promising in its general direction. Eventually, Freud corrected and reconstructed his theory of hysteria in a surprising new way. But to do so, he first had to investigate a new and superficially unrelated subject: the meaning and nature of **dreams**.

The Interpretation of Dreams

Freud became scientifically interested in dreams for several different reasons. For one, patients occasionally brought up dream material in the course of their free associations. For another, Meynert had taught that there were similarities between dreams and certain psychopathological conditions, a line of thought that Freud had elaborated on in some unpublished theoretical speculation of his own in

1895. And perhaps most important of all, Freud himself was a "good" dreamer, frequently remembering and being fascinated by his own dreams. In this combination of circumstances, Freud began subjecting dreams to analysis by free association—something he could do himself just as well as his patients. When he did so, he found that the free associations suggested a surprising new explanation for these common but often perplexing nighttime experiences. In 1900 Freud reported his findings in *The Interpretation of Dreams*, a long book commonly regarded as the most important of all his works.

Freud distinguished between the consciously experienced content of the dream, which he called its **manifest content**, and a hidden or **latent content**, which originally inspired the dream but which emerged in consciousness only after free association. The manifest content, typically marked by disjointed chronology and fantastic images, often seemed unintelligible to the dreamer and failed to "make sense" in terms of his or her normal waking experience. But the latent content—those ideas and memories called up after extensive free association to the manifest content—seemed to have the greatest personal significance for the dreamer. Moreover, dreamers often resisted the uncovering of this latent content, much as hysterical patients resisted the recollection of their pathogenic ideas.

Freud's associations to his own "Dream of Irma's Injection" exemplified his general findings. He had dreamed of a social gathering where "Irma," one of his real-life patients, had fallen ill and was given an injection of the chemical propyl by one of his medical colleagues. Then Freud vividly hallucinated the letters and numbers making up the formula for trimethylamin, yet another chemical substance. This strange manifest content made little immediate sense to Freud, for neither propyl nor trimethylamin was a real medicine, and a propyl injection would in fact have been dangerous.

But free association led to several ideas that did make sense. For one, Freud thought with relief that at least it was not he himself who had administered the ridiculous injection, so his colleague would have to bear responsibility for any unfavorable outcome. Further, he remembered that in real life Irma's nose had been operated on by his best friend, who had neglected to remove all the surgical packing. The patient, legally under Freud's care, had nearly died. Though Freud had made excuses for his friend and had been unwilling to blame him for negligence, he now had to admit to feelings of anger and reproach. Finally, he remembered a recent conversation with this same friend about the chemistry of sex, in which the substance trimethylamin had been mentioned. This led to the idea that Irma's illness must have been sexual in nature and, more dimly, to the thought that she was an attractive woman.

This fragmentary analysis illustrates several essential relations between latent and manifest content, which Freud came to believe held true generally. He argued that dreams often originate with a series of latent thoughts or ideas, which the sleeping mind *transforms* into manifest content by means of three processes he referred to collectively as the **dream work**.

First, the latent content seemed invariably to contain thoughts more anxiety or conflict arousing than those of the manifest content, so Freud concluded that the manifest content *symbolizes* the latent content, although in a relatively "safe" way with images less distressing than the unvarnished latent content. In his language, a process of **displacement** occurs, with the psychic energy of the highly charged latent content being deflected or displaced onto the related but emotionally more neutral ideas of the manifest content. Displacement thus serves a "defensive" function, enabling the dreamer to experience images less disturbing than the thoughts that originally inspired them.

In the second process of the dream work, several latent thoughts may be symbolized by a single image or element of the manifest content. In Freud's analysis discussed earlier, for example, trains of thought involving both sexuality and Freud's troublesome relationship with his friend were associated with the single image of "trimethylamin." Freud called this process **condensation**, on the logic that two or more latent thoughts sometimes "condense" onto a single manifest dream image.

Third, Freud observed that the manifest content typically represents latent *ideas* by means of concretely experienced *sensations*, or hallucinations. Dreams are not subjectively experienced as mere thoughts, but as real sights, sounds, feelings, and so on. Thus, Freud argued that the latent dream thoughts receive **concrete representation** in the subjectively real sensations of the manifest content.

The Primary and Secondary Processes

The sharp-eyed reader may have noted that the three aspects of the dream work closely resembled processes Freud had already postulated to underlie hysteria. In hysteria, several emotion-laden and resistance-arousing pathogenic ideas could presumably be indirectly and "defensively" symbolized by a single and highly concrete physical sensation—namely, the overdetermined symptom. The unconscious "meaning" of a symptom—that is, its originating pathogenic ideas—could only be determined by free association, just like the latent content that gave meaning to dreams. Thus, Freud saw both dreams and hysterical symptoms as resulting from similar unconscious symbolic processes.

Freud further reflected that these processes were directly opposite to the mental activities normally associated with "logical" or "scientific" thinking. In such thinking, we use terms that refer to concepts explicitly, rather than allusively and indirectly. We also use concepts with precisely limited rather than surplus meanings and that progress from concrete particulars to abstract generalizations in forming ideas, rather than the reverse. Moreover, in logical or scientific deliberation the various steps are available to consciousness and are subject to some degree of voluntary control. In dream or symptom creation, by contrast, all acts of displacement, overdetermination/condensation, and concrete representation occur unconsciously, and the dream or symptom finally appears involuntarily and "from out of the blue," as far as the dreamer or patient is concerned.

Accordingly, Freud hypothesized two ideal and diametrically opposed modes of mental activity—one unconscious and associated with dream and symptom formation, the other conscious and responsible for rational thought. Because he believed that infants are born with the capacity for dreams but have to learn how to think rationally, he labeled the unconscious mode of thought the **primary process** and the conscious mode the **secondary process**. Freud saw adults' dreams and hysterical symptoms as instances in which "mature," secondary-process thinking is abandoned in favor of the developmentally earlier primary process—that is, where a **regression** to earlier and more primitive ways of thinking has occurred.

Freud later came to believe that primary-process thought was not restricted to maladaptive or "abnormal" states such as dreaming and hysteria and could also play a *positive* role in creative and artistic thinking. He noted that artists and poets use symbols to make points indirectly by allusion (displacement); produce works that may be interpreted on several different levels of meaning (overdetermination/ condensation); and often symbolize abstract ideas by means of concrete scenes and images (concrete representation). Moreover, creative people often report that their inspirations occur to them involuntarily and from out of the blue—just the way dreams and hysterical symptoms intrude themselves into consciousness. In these cases, the "regression" to primary process modes of thinking serves a good and adaptive purpose.

With all these ideas, Freud did not "discover" the unconscious. He knew from his study with Brentano that many predecessors— going back at least to Leibniz with his "minute perceptions" (see Chapter 2)—had already postulated the existence of unconscious psychological activity. But Freud broke new ground by hypothesizing specific *rules* for the unconscious, describing it as a *lawful* phenomenon. Thus, his conceptualization of the primary process as an unconscious mode of thought characterized by displacement, overdetermination/condensation, and concrete representation was an important milestone in the history of dynamic psychology.

The Wish-Fulfillment Hypothesis

On a more immediately practical level, Freud's growing appreciation of the primary process in dreams helped him solve his dilemma regarding hysteria and the seduction theory. For a number of reasons— including some theoretical deductions as well as experiments with free association—Freud had concluded that *all* dreams represent some element of the **fulfillment of wishes**. As he and his patients analyzed their dreams by free association, it seemed in virtually every case that the latent content included significant though often conflict-laden *wishes*, even when the manifest content seemed the opposite of a wish fulfillment. In such cases, the disagreeable manifest content helped deflect attention from the embarrassing or anxiety-laden nature of the latent content, thus assisting the defensive process of displacement.

For example, one patient who prided herself on being a superb hostess dreamed that she had had to cancel an important dinner party because of lack of food in her house. In the manifest dream and upon awakening she felt great disappointment, and she challenged Freud to demonstrate how her dream could possibly represent the fulfillment of a wish. Free association, however, revealed that the newly married patient had been worried about her husband's attention to another woman, and he had reassured her by remarking that the potential rival was too thin for his taste. On the day before the dream, Freud's patient had met this woman, who had said in a complimentary way that she hoped to be invited soon for dinner, as the patient always served such excellent meals that she stuffed herself. Thus, the dream expressed the wish that the other woman would remain in a slender, unthreatening condition.

Another patient dreamed of the death of her favorite nephew—the very opposite of a wish fulfillment. But her free associations included recollections of an old boyfriend to whom she still felt strongly attracted and whom she had last seen at the real funeral of her nephew's older brother. Thus, her dream expressed a latent wish for a chance to see this desirable man again.

With this view of dreams, Freud found himself in an interesting logical position. Manifest dreams and hysterical symptoms seemed strikingly similar to each other structurally. Both symbolized unconscious and anxiety-arousing ideas indirectly by allusion (displacement); both could represent several unconscious ideas simultaneously with single images or symptoms (condensation or overdetermination); both gave concrete representation to ideas through subjectively real sensory or physical experiences; and both were created unconsciously and involuntarily. They only differed strikingly in their presumed causes, with dreams being stimulated by latent *wishes*, symptoms by apparent sexual *memories*.

But here, of course, was precisely where the seduction theory erred! Many of the sexual experiences so distinctly "remembered" by Freud's patients had never actually occurred. Freud now saw a possible explanation. Perhaps dreams and symptoms were similar in their origins as well as in their structure, and the sexual scenes reported by hysterical patients indirectly reflected *wishes* rather than actual experiences.* Such wishes would run counter to the civilized and consciously adopted values of his patients, who would deny and repress them. But perhaps the wishes were still real and demanded and achieved at least partial and symbolic expression through the unconscious primary process. This idea, shocking as it seemed at first, gained unexpected reinforcement when Freud seriously examined *his own* free associations during a personally difficult time in the late 1890s.

Self-Analysis and the Theory of Childhood Sexuality

After hypothesizing that hysterics' pathogenic ideas typically represented disguised sexual wishes, Freud had to do some hard thinking about the nature of human motivation. It now seemed that his patients, while outwardly completely proper and morally virtuous, secretly and unconsciously harbored sexual ideas and fantasies that respectable society would not tolerate. Furthermore, the ideas dated so far back into his patients' histories as to suggest they originated in childhood. As noted earlier, Freud at first shared the common belief that the normal human sexual instinct arises only after puberty. Thus, he may have been tempted to hypothesize that hysteria resulted from an abnormally precocious sexuality—that is, that

---

* Freud's sincerity in abandoning the seduction theory has been questioned by Jeffrey M. Masson in his provocatively titled book *The Assault on Truth: Freud's Suppression of the Seduction Theory* (New York: Farrar, Straus and Giroux, 1984). Masson charges that Freud merely caved in to the medical establishment by disavowing an unpopular point of view. Masson's charge of cowardice is weakened, however, by the fact that Freud seldom hesitated to stand up for other unpopular ideas throughout his life, and as the account in this chapter shows, he shortly developed an equally unpopular alternative to the seduction theory that seemed to him to better fit the facts.

hysterics were people with a pathological sexual instinct that arose prematurely and necessitated the extreme defensive reactions of conversion and dissociation.

Plausible as this idea might have seemed at first, Freud soon had to reject it for some intensely personal and painful reasons. In autumn of 1896 his father died at the age of 81, after a lingering illness. Though he had been expecting the death for some time, Freud was disconcertingly shaken by the event—"as if I had been torn up by the roots," he wrote to a friend.[7] For months he felt severely depressed, anxious, and unable to work—until finally he decided to regard himself as a patient and subject his own dreams and symptoms to systematic free association. He found some disturbing things in his "self-analysis," things that led him to regard his hysterical patients in a new and even more sympathetic light.

The interpretation of a vivid childhood dream, parts of which had recurred during his adult crisis, loomed large in Freud's self-analysis. In this dream, "I saw my beloved mother, with a peculiarly peaceful, sleeping expression on her features, being carried into the room by two (or three) people with birds' beaks and laid upon the bed."[8] Free association revealed a welter of significant but disturbing latent thoughts, associated with this highly condensed manifest content. First, Freud saw that the dream was about death. The beaked figures resembled pictures of Egyptian *funerary* gods Freud had seen in the family Bible, and the expression on his mother's face was exactly like the one he had actually seen on his *dying grandfather*, shortly before the original dream. This image combining his mother and dying grandfather led to the thought of a dying *father*, and Freud concluded with a shock that one of his dream's latent wishes must have been for the death of his father. In childhood, he apparently had harbored unconscious hostile wishes toward his consciously loved father.

Equally disturbing *sexual* associations soon followed. Freud recalled that the German slang term for sexual intercourse (*vögeln*) derived from the word for "bird" (*Vogel*). Further, he had first learned that slang term from an older boy named *Phillip*, and the family Bible with the beaked figures was an edition known as *Philippson's Bible*. Thus, notions of sexuality were strongly associated with the image of his sleeping mother, and Freud felt forced to conclude that even as a child he had had "sexual" wishes regarding her.

Freud thus interpreted his childhood dream as surreptitiously expressing two repugnant but still deeply felt wishes: for his father's death, and for his mother's sexual attentions. "Death" and "sexuality" had not meant exactly the same things to him as a boy that they did as an adult, with death implying simply the absence or removal, and sexuality meaning any kind of sensual, physical gratification. But Freud concluded that these were logical precursors to the adult concepts. And now he interpreted his peculiarly intense adult reaction to his father's death as the result of the fulfillment of his conflict-laden childhood wish. The "civilized" and conscious side of his personality had understandably rejected this wish, creating severe internal conflict and the eruption of his symptoms. Freud's admirers have observed that it took considerable courage to uncover and acknowledge such distressing truths about himself, and they include his self-analysis among the most important achievements of his life.

Soon, however, Freud came to believe he was not alone in having held repugnant childhood wishes. Indeed, he concluded that virtually *anyone* who honestly subjected himself or herself to analysis by free association would discover traces of similar wishes. Analyses of popular myths and legends as well as the dreams of "normal" people seemed to corroborate Freud's findings with hysterical patients and himself: The infantile desire to possess the opposite-sexed parent for one's exclusive sensual pleasure, and to be rid of the same-sex parent as the major rival for such attentions, seemed an almost inevitable consequence of growing up in a typical Western family. *Oedipus Rex*, the classic Greek tragedy by Sophocles, portrays a story in which these events occur: The hero, Oedipus, unwittingly kills his father and marries his mother. Thus, Freud named this apparently universal constellation of unconscious wishes the **Oedipus complex**.

Further observations convinced Freud that these "Oedipal" wishes and fantasies were accompanied by other disturbing residues from childhood. "Perverted" or "disgusting" free associations involving the mouth or anus also regularly emerged, and Freud concluded that these too represented childhood wishes—wishes regarded with horror and repressed by the conscious, adult side of the personality, but that continued to press unconsciously for expression via the primary process. By 1905, Freud had had sufficient experience with these kinds of ideas to propose a radically new theory of both childhood and sexuality, in a work entitled *Three Essays on the Theory of Sexuality.*

Stages of Childhood Sexuality

In the early 1900s, childhood was viewed by most as a period of innocence and purity, terminated and corrupted with the physiological developments of puberty. The normal sexual instinct was thought to be absent in children, arising only with puberty. And when the instinct finally did appear, it was assumed to be highly specific, impelling the individual toward the single goal of propagating the species through genital heterosexual intercourse.

Freud's new theory contradicted this popular view on all counts. From the apparent universality of Oedipal fantasies, he inferred that sexuality profoundly influences every child's mental life—although he saw the sexuality of childhood as much broader than the "normal" adult kind, involving many kinds of activities considered deviant or perverted from the adult perspective. Accordingly, Freud postulated a *generalized* form of human sexual drive, present from birth onward, and potentially capable of gratification in many ways. Its goal was physical or sensual pleasure of *any* kind, with "normal" genital stimulation being only one of its varieties.

According to this new theory, the human infant is born in a state Freud called **polymorphous perversity**, capable of taking sexual (that is, sensuous) pleasure from the gentle stimulation of any part of the body. In the course of normal development, however, certain parts of the body emerge as **erogenous zones**, or areas where the infant experiences satisfaction and sensual pleasure. In earliest infancy, the mouth or **oral zone** predominates as the location of this broadened form of sexual gratification. When toilet training begins and children start to find pleasure in the voluntary control of their bodily functions, the **anal zone** assumes particular importance. Only later, after children have developed fuller control over their bodies, does stimulation of the **genital zone** become a major source of sexual pleasure.

Freud argued that social factors within the family strongly interact with these developments, as many pleasurable activities arouse parental anxiety or disapproval and the child learns that only a relatively small number of gratifications are socially acceptable. Gradually, expressions of the originally undifferentiated sexual drive become channeled into socially acceptable forms, and by late adolescence they usually, but not always, assume a heterosexual-genital orientation. Thus, for Freud the "normal" expression of sexuality was not a preordained consequence of an inalterably fixed instinct, but one of the possible results of a long process of social and psychological development. Only after consciously abandoning most of their childhood forms of sexuality do individuals become "civilized" and sexually "normal." In sum, Freud argued that the traditional picture had things exactly backward: Children are not innocents who become corrupted sexually by the evils of the world; instead, they are born with primitive, undisciplined, and "perverted" tendencies that they must learn to curb as they mature and become civilized.

Freud further theorized that the conflict between unruly childhood sexuality and the forces of socialization typically becomes particularly acute at about the age of 5. By then, the three erogenous zones have usually been discovered, and the opposite-sex parent has been singled out as the most desirable source of sensual gratification, with the same-sex parent as the major rival. Thus, the Oedipus complex emerges. Oedipal wishes produce great inner conflict, however, because the child recognizes the same-sex parent as larger, stronger, and potentially dangerous. The child further believes that if that parent *knew* what he or she was thinking, a disastrous retaliation might occur. As a result, the Oedipal wishes themselves become dangerous, because they threaten to cast the child into a dangerous and hopeless battle. Here is the child's motive to repress the Oedipal wishes, to force them into unconsciousness so they no longer emerge to arouse anxiety. Most other aspects of childhood sexuality, associated as they are with Oedipal wishes, disappear from consciousness along with them.

Freud argued that the child at this point enters a **latency stage**, which lasts until the physical maturation of puberty reawakens the sexual drive with renewed force. During latency, the positive side of the child's feelings toward the same-sex parent dominates consciousness, facilitating a positive **identification** with that parent as a socially approved role model. Freud emphasized that these positive feelings had always existed alongside the negative ones, even during the height of the Oedipal complex. He believed that people's deepest feelings toward the important people in their lives are never completely positive or negative, but rather always combine both attitudes in a state he called **ambivalence**. During latency, however, the negative feelings toward the Oedipal rival have become repressed, along with childhood sexuality. Thus freed from the preoccupations and anxieties generated by the sexual drive, the child enters a psychologically tranquil period ideally suited for the kinds of learning tasks typically imposed by schools and other socializing institutions outside the immediate family.

Freud took pains to add, however, that the Oedipus complex and childhood sexuality are never *destroyed* but are merely *repressed*. They always persist beneath the surface of consciousness, seeking whatever indirect and disguised forms of expression they can find. Dreams provide one natural and usually benign outlet, hysterical symptoms a more extreme and maladaptive one. Further, Freud believed that differences in these childhood sexual experiences lead to some distinctive individual differences in a person's *character* as an adult.

Freudian Character Types

Although Freud believed that all people go through all of the stages of childhood sexuality, he also noted that in the course of their free associations patients differed in the emphasis on the three stages. Some of his early patients, for example, reported particularly intense images and experiences dating back to toilet training and the anal period of their development. He speculated that the parents of these individuals must have been relatively strict in their enforcement of toilet training, leading to a relative overemphasis or **fixation** of infantile sexuality at the anal stage. Further, Freud detected a particular pattern of *adult* personality characteristics in these patients. Namely, they tended to be relatively *orderly* in arranging their affairs, *parsimonious* in managing their money and resources, and *obstinate* in many of their interpersonal interactions. This triad of traits—which of course are relative rather than absolute in intensity—constitute what became known as the **anal character**. Freud and some of his followers soon deduced distinct character types resulting from fixations at the other stages. The **oral character**, which presumably results from relative overindulgence *or* under-indulgence in the earliest years, was likely to remain particularly interested throughout life in "oral" activities such as eating, drinking, smoking, or even talking. If overindulged as a child, the adult was likely to turn out cheerful and optimistic; if underindulged, as envious, acquisitive and pessimistic. The **phallic** or **genital** character, by contrast, seemed marked by adult traits of relative curiosity, competitiveness, or exhibitionism.

Psychoanalytic Psychotherapy

Even as Freud theorized about normal people's character, dreams, and the psychology of children, he continued to earn his living as a psychotherapist for disturbed adults. And like his general theories, his therapeutic technique changed and developed over the years.

At first, Freud saw his therapeutic task as simple and straightforward. All he had to do, it seemed, was encourage free association until the repressed pathogenic ideas became conscious and the symptoms became unnecessary. But Freud increasingly found that his patients' unconscious resistances to the treatment could be devilishly subtle and insidious and that he often had to be content with modest improvement rather than complete "cures" of his patients. Sometimes treatments that began promisingly ended disastrously, as in the instructive case of **Ida Bauer** (1882–1945), the gifted but troubled young woman referred to as "Dora" in Freud's published account.

The Case of Dora

Suffering from mild hysteria, 18-year-old Dora was brought to Freud by her father after threatening suicide. Intelligent and verbal, she took quickly to free association and seemed to understand Freud's early interpretations of her associations in terms of infantile sexuality. After just a few sessions, Freud wrote confidently to a friend that "the case has opened smoothly to my collection of picklocks."[9]

Dora's conflicts arose from her relationships with her parents and their close friends, a couple Freud called "Herr and Frau K." Dora's

father was often ill and in need of nursing, a service more often provided by Frau K. than by Dora's mother, whom she described as a
drab and unaffectionate woman obsessed by housecleaning. As Dora
entered adolescence, she recognized that Frau K. had become her
father's mistress as well as his nurse. Herr K. apparently made no fuss
about his wife's liaison with his friend but contented himself with
amorous adventures with his servants. As Dora grew into an attractive young woman, however, he also turned his attention toward her.
He presented her with an expensive jewel-case and once tried to kiss
her—an act Dora said disgusted her because of the strong smell of
cigar smoke on his breath.

This sordid situation reached a climax shortly before Dora saw
Freud, when her family and the K.'s shared a vacation house. Herr K.
openly complained to Dora that he got nothing from his wife and
propositioned her directly. Dora indignantly refused but said nothing
to her parents. Then every night for two weeks she had the same vivid
nightmare, after which she insisted on accompanying her father on
a business trip away from the vacation house. On the trip she told her
father about Herr K. and her nightmare ceased, although she began
to experience hysterical symptoms. After they worsened and she
threatened suicide, Dora's father brought her to Freud.

Once in analysis with Freud, Dora's dream recurred. Freud naturally asked her to describe it and free-associate to it. The manifest
content was the following:

> A house was on fire. My father was standing beside my bed
> and woke me up. I dressed myself quickly. Mother wanted to stop
> and save her jewel-case; but father said: "I refuse to let myself and
> my two children be burnt for the sake of your jewel-case." We
> hurried downstairs, and as soon as I was outside I woke up.[10]

Dora's fluent free associations to this dream lent Freud his initial
optimism about the case. Herr K. was obviously involved through
associations to the jewel-case and the fire, which recalled the smell
of tobacco smoke from his breath. Dora remembered that she had
always dressed quickly in the vacation house, as in the dream,
because her bed was in an exposed hall and she feared being seen
in partial undress by Herr K. The fire also seemed to symbolize the
sexual stirrings that Dora admitted she was beginning to feel. She

finally acknowledged a certain attraction to Herr K., along with her fear and repugnance.

Freud was not surprised when Dora also produced associations to childhood sexuality. The fire led to thoughts of water, which in turn recalled childhood memories of bedwetting and masturbation. After Dora remarked that her father used to wake her up at night and take her to the bathroom to prevent the bedwetting, Freud felt sure he understood the major latent wish expressed by the dream.

He believed the dream had substituted Dora's original Oedipal attraction to her father for her current, conflict-laden attraction for Herr K. He summarized: "She summoned up an infantile attraction for her father so that it might protect her against her present affection for a stranger."[11] The wish expressed by the dream was to run away with her father and to be protected by him from the disturbing impulses of her maturing sexuality, just as she had been protected by him from her bedwetting as a child. When Dora went with her father on the business trip, she fulfilled that wish in reality and the dream consequently ceased to recur.

Dora seemed to accept this interpretation, lending Freud added confidence that she would soon have full insight into her problems and be cured. Shortly afterward, however, she stunned him by announcing that she had had enough of his treatment and would return no more, even though many of her problems remained unresolved. She kept her word and never returned.

In retrospect, Freud realized that he had been totally insensitive to one whole dimension of the case and that he had failed to carry his interpretation of the dream as far as he should have. For while he had explained why the dream had originally occurred at the vacation house, he had not asked why it recurred in the course of the treatment. Its reappearance, he now believed, signified not only Dora's previous complicated feelings toward Herr K. but also her current ambivalence toward *Freud himself.* He too was a heavy cigar smoker, and he had frequently used the expression "There can be no smoke without fire" in the course of the treatment. And while he was not a philanderer like Herr K., he did openly discuss highly charged sexual topics with Dora. Thus, her dream was once again useful in expressing complex feelings about her emotional entanglement with a "stranger" and her wish to flee to the relative safety of her father—only this time the stranger was Freud and not Herr K. And just as Dora fulfilled the first wish by fleeing from Herr K., so she now fled from Freud.

This experience with Dora, reinforced by similar if less dramatic exchanges with other patients, convinced Freud that therapy sessions were inevitably complicated by what he called **transference** feelings. That is, patients tended to transfer onto him, as the therapist, attributes of the important people from their past lives who were implicated in their neurotic symptoms. Regardless of what Freud was "really" or "objectively" like, his patients often reacted to him *as if* he were like their mothers, fathers, or other emotion-charged figures such as Herr K. All too easily, as with Dora, transference feelings could become part of the resistance and hinder therapeutic progress. In short, Freud learned that for therapy to proceed optimally, he and his patients would have to pay just as much attention to the transference relationships between themselves as to the symptoms per se.

Individual symptoms now seemed less important to Freud, as he saw them as relatively superficial manifestations of underlying emotional conflicts, each one capable of expressing itself in many ways, including dreams, transference, and a variety of specific symptoms. Thus, symptoms were not independent entities. The disappearance of any particular symptom signified little, because the conflict that had caused it might promptly reexpress itself in another, equally maladaptive substitute. Any enduring "cure" thus required the uncovering and analysis of the entire complex of underlying conflicts—a process likely to take months or even years to complete.

To judge when an analysis approached successful completion, Freud now attended more to the transference relationship than to the symptoms. Both symptoms and transference reflected the same underlying conflicts, but the transference lay closer at hand for constant scrutiny. When Freud could feel that a patient was beginning to respond to him more as he really was and less as if he were a shadowy figure from the past, he judged that the long analytic process was finally nearing completion.

In the end, Freud did not provide the quick and specific cures for hysterical symptoms he had originally hoped for. Instead, he provided *psychoanalysis*—a long and often difficult process of self-examination that offered symptom relief almost as an incidental consequence of increased insight into one's unconscious mental life.

Metapsychology and the Ego's Defense Mechanisms

From the very beginning of his career, Freud sought to place his clinical discoveries within a broader theoretical context, to ask about the *general* features of the human mind that enabled it to produce individual symptoms, dreams, and transferences along with the great variety of everyday and "normal" mental phenomena. He referred to these attempts to develop a general model of the mind as his **metapsychology**.

Freud's earliest metapsychological theorizing relied heavily on his neurophysiological background. Consistent with Brücke's and Meynert's training, Freud attempted to hypothesize neurological structures and mechanisms capable of producing dreams and hysterical symptoms, as well as normal secondary-process thought. He wrote out his ideas in 1895 in a long draft manuscript never intended for publication but found by his editors after his death and published under the title *Project for a Scientific Psychology*. This uncompleted and sometimes obscure manuscript has proven extraordinarily interesting to Freud scholars for the light it sheds on Freud's developing but not yet mature theory. Among the subjects to receive their first treatment there were the opposition between primary and secondary processes, the wish-fulfillment theory of dreams, and the concept of an "ego" as the directive, executive agency in the mature human psyche.[12]

But while the *Project* was unquestionably a valuable undertaking for Freud, he soon came to feel that its neurophysiological framework imposed unnecessary constraints on his theorizing. The nervous system was too poorly understood to allow him to specify detailed neural mechanisms for all of the psychological phenomena that interested him. Thus, Freud decided to avoid neurological technicalities by expressing his metapsychology in completely psychological terms. He would try to keep his concepts *consistent with* available neurological knowledge, and he would hope that future neurological discoveries by others would suggest precise mechanisms to account for them. As he wrote in 1900:

> I shall entirely disregard the fact that the mental apparatus with which we are . . . concerned is also known to us in the

form of an anatomical preparation, and I shall carefully avoid the temptation to determine psychical locality in any anatomical fashion. I shall remain upon psychological ground.[13]

Freud's most famous descriptions of "psychical localities" appeared in a short 1923 book titled *The Ego and the Id*. In it he extrapolated from his clinical experience and argued that the human mind is constantly beset by three kinds of demands that inevitably conflict with one another and that the mind's major function is to resolve those conflicts as best it can.

The first class of demands arises from within the body itself, in biologically based urges for nourishment, warmth, sexual gratification (in the broadened Freudian sense of the term), and the like. Freud referred collectively to these internal, biologically based demands as the **instincts**. A second group of demands is imposed by external reality; in order to survive, a person must learn to manipulate the environment to avoid physical dangers and to obtain the objects necessary for gratifying the instincts. From his earliest metapsychological writings onward, Freud had emphasized situations in which instinctual and reality-based demands conflicted with each other, especially those in which instinctual gratifications had been delayed, modified, or abandoned because of the constraints of the real world.

By 1923, Freud had further come to believe that *moral* demands impinge on the mind independently of the instincts and external reality, because of the obvious fact that one's conscience often conflicts with both wishes and reality. People often refrain from gratifying their impulses because they think it would be *wrong*, even if there is nothing in physical reality to prevent them from doing so. People sometimes ignore the dangers of physical reality and risk their lives in the service of a moral ideal. Because moral demands could motivate people in directions contrary to both the instincts and the demands of physical reality, Freud believed that any complete model of the human psyche would have to make an important and separate place for them.

Accordingly, Freud's 1923 model posited separate systems to process and represent the three kinds of psychic demands. First, he postulated the **id** as the repository of unconscious but powerful impulses and energies from the instincts. Then he hypothesized a "perception-consciousness system"—habitually abbreviated simply as **pcpt.-cs.**—that conveys information about external reality to the mind. This system not only produces immediate consciousness of whatever is being perceived, it also leaves behind memories that remain open to future consciousness in a part of the psyche Freud described as "preconscious." Moral demands, arising independently of instincts and external reality alike, presumably originated from a separate agency completely within the psyche that Freud called the **superego**.

Thus the id, the external-perception system, and the superego all introduce their differing and inevitably conflicting demands into the psyche, which must sort them out and achieve some sort of compromise among them. Specific responses must be devised and executed that will permit some degree of instinctual gratification but that will not endanger the organism from physical reality or violate the dictates of conscience. Freud's hypothetical psychic agency for producing these compromises was the **ego.**[*]

While recognizing that graphical representations of abstract concepts may not appeal to everyone, Freud drew an "unassuming sketch" of his psychic structures, which is reproduced here as Figure 11.3.[14] The id lies open to the instincts from the body at the bottom of the diagram, while pcpt.-cs. is perched like an eye on the top, oriented to the external world. The superego is contained within the psyche to one side. Squarely in the middle, where it must mediate among all of the conflicting parties, is the ego.

Consistent with its central location in Freud's diagram, the ego attracted much of Freud's theoretical attention during the latter part of his career. He came to see virtually everything a person does as the result of some sort of *compromise* among conflicting demands, and hence a product of the ego. Some of the ego's compromises favor one kind of demand over the others, and some are more adaptive than others. Hysterical symptoms represent relatively maladaptive compromises in which considerations of external reality are largely

---

[*] In his original German publications Freud used the everyday words *Es* (literally, "it"), *Ich* ("I") and *Uber-Ich* ("over-I") for the id, ego, and superego, respectively. Freud's English translators substituted Latin words that mean the same thing. Some critics have complained that the Latinizations have made Freud's writings appear unnecessarily more technical and abstract in English than they actually are in German.

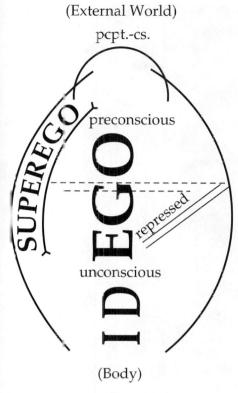

FIG 11.3 Freud's diagram of the psyche

ignored and the wishful pressures of the id are confronted mainly by the superego; thus, the id impulses receive disguised rather than overt expression. Dreams are similar, although not so maladaptive because they occur in a sleeping state in which the consequences of ignoring reality are not so severe. These relatively dramatic kinds of compromises, of course, had been the starting points for Freud's analysis of intrapsychic conflict.

Increasingly, however, Freud saw everyday life as dominated by other, less dramatic ego compromises he called **defense mechanisms**. Collaborating importantly in this theorizing was his daughter **Anna Freud** (1895–1982; see Figure 11.4), who had herself become a skillful theoretician as well as a pioneer in the psychoanalysis of children. Anna's 1936 book *The Ego and the Mechanisms of Defense* became the definitive delineation of the major defense mechanisms, of which we shall sample just a few here, for illustrative purposes.

FIG 11.4
Anna Freud (1895–1982)
with her father

The common defense mechanism of **displacement** is said to occur whenever someone redirects an impulse toward a substitute target that resembles the original in some way, but is "safer." A classic example is the man who suffers the taunts of his boss in silence, then "displaces" his anger at home by yelling at his wife and kicking his dog. Oedipal sexual impulses are presumably displaced when people fall in love with partners who resemble their opposite-sexed parents in some significant way—an extremely common occurrence, according to the Freuds.

The defense mechanism of **projection** occurs when a person does not directly acknowledge his or her own unacceptable impulses but reverses the onus by attributing them to someone else instead. If you become angry at someone but have a superego that interprets hostile feelings as morally wrong, you may project your anger and see your target as being angry and hostile toward *you* instead. You may then act aggressively toward your target but interpret your action as self-defense or retaliation rather than unprovoked hostility. A venerable psychologist's joke about the inkblot test illustrates the projection of sexuality: A patient repeatedly sees and reports sexual images in the ambiguous shapes of the inkblots, and the examiner says that the man is obsessed by sex. The patient replies indignantly, "What do you mean? *You're* the one who's showing the dirty pictures!"

In **intellectualization**, some impulse- and emotion-charged subject is directly approached, but in a strictly intellectual manner that avoids emotional involvement. An adolescent beset by sexual urges may read up in the technical literature on sexuality, for example, while avoiding any direct sexual entanglements. Academics and professors are said to intellectualize frequently, becoming technical experts in subjects associated with their personal emotional conflicts.

Some other defense mechanisms affect the *memory* of gratifications after they have been allowed to occur. In **denial**, for example, a person believes and behaves as if an instinct-driven event had never occurred. On hearing an adult approaching, two furiously fighting children may suddenly begin behaving quietly and sociably; after the adult departs they continue to be friends, successfully denying the aggression they had been openly expressing shortly before. More sophisticated than simple denial is **rationalization**, in which people act because of one motive but explain the behavior (to themselves as well as to others) on the basis of another, more acceptable one. For example, a father may get a certain amount of satisfaction from spanking his child but argue and believe afterward that the spanking had been completely "for the child's own good."

Another defense mechanism, **identification**, assumed particular importance when Freud attempted to find a psychological reason for the establishment of the superego. The id, of course, is part of one's innate biological nature, and the ego grows out of normal interaction with the realities and experiences of life. But how might a moral agency, making demands independent of both the body and its external reality, come into being? Freud's answer drew on his previous conception of the developmental stages and the assertion that a child's Oedipal conflict ends and latency begins when he or she "identifies" with the same-sex parent, thus "internalizing" that parent's prohibitions against childhood sexuality and Oedipal impulses. Following this identification and internalization, the "moral" demands for restraint come from within rather than without, and the part of the psyche that reflects the internalized parent is the superego.

The Psychology of Women

In 1923, the year Freud published *The Ego and the Id*, his life was darkened by the death of a favorite grandchild and his own diagnosis of cancer of the mouth (undoubtedly a result of his heavy cigar-smoking habit). Although he lived and was highly productive for another 16 years, his work perhaps inevitably took on a more somber, speculative, and often controversial tone.

One of his most controversial ideas, even among those who considered themselves his followers, concerned the psychology of women and arose in the context of his theorizing about the origins of the superego. As noted, Freud had theorized that the superego is the product of an internalization of the prohibitive aspects of the same-sex parent, in response to the intense conflicts of the Oedipal stage. Now, on the basis of differing free associations from some of his male and female patients, he concluded that an important difference exists between typical male and female Oedipal conflicts. During this stage, he believed, little boys and girls become acutely aware of the major obvious anatomical difference between them: the presence or absence of a penis. This presumably gives rise to a **castration complex**, which takes different forms for boys and girls.

For boys, Freud believed the predominant response was enhanced *anxiety*; having knowledge that there are people without penises, they irrationally but intensely fear that their fathers might castrate them too if they openly revealed their Oedipal wishes. Girls, who by contrast have already been "castrated," presumably respond not with anxiety but with *envy*, an unconscious wish to be like a boy and have a penis. A major consequence of this difference, Freud concluded, is that boys have a greater burden of Oedipal anxiety to deal with and hence require a stronger and more severe internalization of parental restraint to deal with it. In other words, boys develop stronger superegos than girls.

Freud published this idea in a short 1925 paper titled "Some Psychical Consequences of the Anatomical Distinction between the Sexes," candidly admitting that it was based on just "a handful of cases" and excusing its early publication because he believed "the time before me is limited." But still he declared, quite provocatively:

> I cannot evade the notion (though I hesitate to give it expression) that for women the level of what is ethically normal is different from what it is in men. Their superego is never so inexorable, so impersonal, so independent of its emotional origins as we require it to be in men. Character traits which critics of every epoch have brought up against women—that they show less sense of justice than men, that they are less ready to submit to the great exigencies of life, that they are more often influenced in their judgements by feelings of affection or hostility—all these would amply be accounted for by the modification in the formation of their superego which we have inferred. . . . We must not allow ourselves to be deflected from such conclusions by the denials of the feminists, who are anxious to force us to regard the two sexes as completely equal in position and worth.[15]

Predictably enough, Freud's outspoken statement aroused a great deal of surprise and controversy both within and without the psychoanalytic movement. There was surprise, because throughout his career Freud had been unusually (for his time) open to the full participation of women in the psychoanalytic movement he created. Both before and after his inflammatory article, he corresponded with and referred important patients to talented female analysts such as **Helene Deutsch** (1884–1982), Ruth Mack Brunswick (1897–1946), and Jeanne Lampl de Groot (1895–1987). And he took particular pride in the professional development of his daughter Anna, the only one of his six children to follow him into a psychoanalytic profession. The noted feminist scholar Juliet Mitchell has observed that "Psychoanalysis must be one of the very few scientific professions that, from its inception, exercised no discrimination against women."[16]

Despite the absence of institutional discrimination against them, several women analysts took issue with Freud's "phallocentric" view of female sexual development. Among the most prominent of these was **Karen Horney** (1885–1952; see Figure 11.5). One of the first

FIG 11.5
Karen Horney
(1885–1952)

women to have earned a medical degree in Germany, she joined the psychoanalytic movement in 1920 and soon became regarded as one of its most gifted practitioners and writers. Freud himself cited her "valuable and comprehensive studies" in the concluding paragraph of his controversial 1925 paper. Brushing aside the compliment, Horney argued that Freud's conception of female sexuality was excessively biased by his male point of view and misrepresented the actual physiological and psychological experience of being female. Regarding envy, she believed that the penis takes on particular *symbolic* importance only in societies dominated by male privilege and power. She also stressed the "blissful consciousness" and "ineffable joy" of bearing a child and giving birth and suggested that boys and men might feel envy for this feminine experience. Horney expressed these ideas, along with several technical arguments about the ways in which "penis envy" occurs in the female castration complex, in her 1926 paper "The Flight from Womanhood."[17]

The prominent American psychoanalyst **Clara Thompson** (1893–1958) later built on Horney's work and further disputed Freud's position that female inferiority was rooted in women's biological inadequacies, arguing extensively for a culturally and historically situated analysis of women's experiences, especially as they were affected by then-strongly held views about male superiority. Writing in the 1940s and early 1950s, she emphasized that the generally negative views of women's sexuality and sexual organs, rather than some innate inadequacy of the organs themselves, were responsible for feelings of inferiority in women.[8] She also pointed out that Freud's theories about the psychology of women were themselves a product of the type of female patients he saw and their particular cultural and historical position.[19]

Final Controversies and Freud's Legacy

During his final years, Freud wrote speculatively and often pessimistically about a number of other controversial issues. In *The Future of an Illusion* (1927) he addressed the nature of religious beliefs and concluded that they all are, at heart, "not precipitates of experience or end-results of thinking: they are *illusions*, fulfillments of the oldest, strongest, and most urgent *wishes* of mankind."[20] For Freud, the belief that there exists a benevolent God who watches over every individual and sees that he or she is rewarded in an afterlife for being good is nothing but the wishful residue of the young child seeking protection from a benevolent father. Such a belief cannot be *proven* false—but based as it is on a childhood wish, Freud felt the odds were very much against it.

In another somber work titled *Civilization and Its Discontents* (1930), Freud returned to reflections on the superego. Haunted by memories of the catastrophe of World War I and frightened by the incipient rise of Hitler in Germany, Freud had speculated that humans are often driven by an aggressive "death instinct" that he called **Thanatos**, which vies for control with the life-giving sexual instinct he now called **Eros**. He further theorized that a major vehicle for the expression of the death instinct's aggressive energy was the superego: sometimes by producing self-destructive feelings of excessive guilt, and other times by displacing the aggressive impulses outward. In the name of "moral" values such as patriotism, religion, and "justice," all sorts of acts of murder and carnage could be committed and approved by the superego. Indeed, with the rise of the technologies of war, even before the atom bomb, Freud feared that these tendencies threatened the very survival of the human species. In this new context, the hypothetically weak feminine superego—"never so inexorable, so impersonal, so independent of its emotional origins as we require it to be in men"—does not come across as so "inferior." Freud himself, however, never explicitly emphasized this rather obvious point.

Many of Freud's worst forebodings came all too true, as Hitler's rise made Vienna increasingly dangerous for Jews throughout the 1930s, and he and his immediate family finally fled to London in June 1938. His four elderly sisters were denied exit visas and stayed behind, later to perish in the Nazi gas chambers. Perhaps fortunately, Freud himself never learned of this, for he succumbed to his long illness on September 23, 1939, as Europe lay on the very brink of World War II.

Freud's Legacy

Few figures have ever left such an extraordinary intellectual legacy. Freud has remained almost constantly in the public eye ever since his death. Books defending or attacking him and his theories continue to pour from the presses, and new biographies continue to fascinate the public as his unpublished papers and correspondence become available to scholars. A major part of his legacy has naturally been in those fields of clinical practice and theory that provided Freud with his living. For psychotherapists and clinical theorists alike, Freudian theory has been a constant source of both inspiration and contention.

A significant group of therapists accepted *parts* of Freud's theory or acknowledged Freud as the starting point for their own somewhat different approaches. The **object relations** school, for example, originated in the close analysis of infants' earliest relationships with their mothers by **Melanie Klein** (1882–1960) and was further developed by the British psychoanalysts **W. R. D. Fairbairn** (1889–1964) and **D. W. Winnicott** (1896–1971). This school places less emphasis than Freud did on the role of the instincts and more on the details of *relationships* with love objects. **Erik Erikson** (1902–1994), working more intensively with children than Freud did, postulated a series of psycho*social* stages to parallel the child's typical development through the psycho*sexual* periods originally hypothesized by Freud, and he extended the developmental analysis to include later stages of the life cycle.

Several other clinicians started out as Freud's followers but later broke with him and his group for various reasons and went on to create their own "neo-Freudian" schools. For example, Alfred Adler, Carl Gustav Jung, and the previously mentioned Karen Horney (all of whom will be further discussed in the next chapter) all believed Freud had overemphasized sexuality in his theory and proposed their own alternative systems emphasizing various social or cultural factors. Still others who were originally trained in Freudian techniques subsequently reacted explicitly against them. As shall be elaborated in the next chapter, Carl Rogers came to feel that the classical Freudian psychoanalyst assumed an unwarranted air of omniscience in dealing with patients, and he developed a more nondirective **client-centered therapy** as an alternative. **Joseph Wolpe** (1915–1997) disagreed with the Freudian emphasis on underlying conflicts as opposed to individual symptoms and developed several techniques of **behavior therapy** to provide quicker, more symptom-specific relief. And **Aaron T. Beck** (b. 1921) began his career as a "classical" Freudian psychoanalyst but then developed an approach he called **cognitive therapy**, which attempts more directly to identify and correct "faulty" irrational thinking that presumably lies behind patients' symptoms.

Of course Freud's influence extended far beyond the strictly clinical fields. Indeed, following his death the poet W. H. Auden was moved to memorialize him in a poem containing these often-quoted lines:

> *If often he was wrong and at times absurd,*
> *To us he is no more a person now*
> *But a whole climate of opinion*
> *Under whom we conduct our differing lives.*[21]

Inevitably, that "whole climate of opinion" created by Freud had its effect on the field of academic psychology. The relationship between psychoanalysis and psychology during the first half of the twentieth century was complex and, as characterized by the historian Gail Hornstein, "problematic."[22] It is a fitting topic with which to conclude this chapter.

Freud and Psychology

Although Freud's work obviously dealt with psychological issues, his direct contact with *academic* psychologists was quite sparse. We have seen that he studied briefly with Franz Brentano as a young university student, and his early works made occasional and usually fleeting reference to the work of Fechner and Wundt. But his primary emphasis was practical and clinical, and his work was slow in coming to the attention of academic psychologists. Further, even though Freud had already written several of his most fundamental works by 1905, they remained untranslated from their original German and were not widely known outside his small but growing group of personal supporters.

This situation began to change after a few psychiatrists in Boston learned about and began experimenting with cathartic treatments for hysteria. In 1906 the first issue of Morton Prince's *Journal of Abnormal Psychology* carried an article by the neurologist J. J. Putnam titled "Recent Experiences in the Study and Treatment of Hysteria at the Massachusetts General Hospital, with Remarks on Freud's Method of Treatment by 'Psycho-Analysis.'" This was the first extended discussion of Freud and psychoanalysis in an English publication.[25] Although originally devoted to clinical subjects and somewhat off the beaten track of "mainstream" experimental psychology, this journal was still read by some academic psychologists (and, as noted in Chapter 10, played a role not long after in the emergence of social psychology as an important subdiscipline).

Among those who now took note of Freud's work was the formidable G. Stanley Hall—arguably the most important founder of psychological institutions in America. As described in Chapter 8, Hall had studied under both James and Wundt before creating *The American Journal of Psychology* in 1887 and becoming the founding president of the American Psychological Association in 1892. As President of Clark University in Worcester, Massachusetts, since its founding in 1889, he had built a graduate program that turned out more Ph.D.'s in psychology than any other American university of the time. Also a prolific researcher and writer, Hall brought the previously obscure term "adolescence" to public attention with his 1904 book *Adolescence: Its Psychology and Its Relation to Physiology,*

Anthropology, Sociology, Sex, Crime, Religion and Education. Newly alerted to Freud, Hall took particular interest in the just-published *Three Essays on the Theory of Sexuality* and noted their common interests in children's development and their sexuality. Seeing Freud as a potentially important ally, Hall invited him to participate in Clark University's twentieth-anniversary celebration as a lecturer, joining a group that included several distinguished experimental psychologists (see Figure 11.6).

At that event in the autumn of 1909, Freud delivered five lectures in German, each one extemporaneously planned on a walk just before its delivery. The lectures told the story of how he had arrived at the main points of his theory and technique. Although Freud was just one of several distinguished speakers at the celebration, Hall made sure that his lectures received press coverage and even ghost-wrote an appreciative account of them for *The Nation* magazine. Freud's name now appeared for the first time in the American popular press.[24] Even more consequentially, Hall persuaded Freud to re-create his lectures in writing, then promptly had them translated into English and published in the *American Journal of Psychology* under the title "The

FIG 11.6 Participants at the 1909 Clark University conference, the occasion of Freud's only visit to the United States

Origin and Development of Psychoanalysis" (1910). This vivid and lucid account presented Freud to the English-speaking world in his own everyday (if translated) language, and it remains today one of the best introductions to his thought.[25] The success of this publication opened the gates for English translations of Freud's longer works, as *The Interpretation of Dreams* appeared in 1913, followed by *The Psychopathology of Everyday Life* in 1914. Following a hiatus for the war, translations of his major works appeared almost immediately after their publication in German.

Freud's Reception by Academic Psychology

Despite its recognition by Hall, Freud's work was not enthusiastically greeted by most other academic psychologists. The "radical subjectivity" inherent in free association and Freud's emphasis on unconscious processes grossly violated the canons of scientific "objectivity" that many had so carefully cultivated. Even those who used introspective methods, such as Cornell University's Edward Bradford Titchener, insisted that introspectors must be rigorously trained to *strip* subjective meanings from their analyses and to reduce consciousness to its most elemental sensations (see Chapter 5 for more on Titchener's "structuralism"). Coincidentally, Titchener was a fellow lecturer at the Clark celebration, and when Freud met him at its opening reception he remarked, "Oh, you are the opponent!" The two then had a bantering conversation in which Titchener denied that he was a genuine opponent but instead someone who could "translate" Freud's theories "into modern psychological terms." Freud responded that if Titchener would only spend some time with *him*, he would see that all modern psychology needed to be "revolutionized" along psychoanalytic lines. Titchener thought but refrained from saying aloud: "Revolutionised, ye gods! That means, set back just about two generations."[26]

A frail William James, ailing with a severe heart condition that would take his life a year later, also came to Worcester for one day "to see what Freud was like," and the two had a cordial private conversation. In later private correspondence James confided that he suspected Freud of being a "regular *halluciné*" and "a man obsessed with fixed ideas" but added that he hoped the psychoanalysts "would push their ideas to their utmost limits."[27] Titchener too retained some respect for Freud as an individual even as he deplored his ideas. He wrote a friend that Freud's psychology "is antediluvian and his constructions largely precarious, but he . . . has worked and thought and suffered; and I have no stomach for controversy with him."[28]

Other mainstream psychologists showed less restraint and publicly treated his work with contemptuous dismissal. In 1917 Columbia's Robert Woodworth denigrated Freud's "rough and ready" methods and "one-sided and exaggerated" conclusions. Soon after that Knight Dunlap—who was John B. Watson's senior colleague at Johns Hopkins—described psychoanalysis as waging "an assault on the very life of the biological sciences," attempting to "creep in wearing the uniform of science, and to strangle it from the inside." As noted in Chapter 9, Watson himself along with Rosalie Rayner took a sarcastic swipe at Freud in their famous case report of "Little Albert." After describing how Albert's conditioned fear of a white rat had generalized to other furry objects and admitting that they had not deconditioned the response, they speculated: "The Freudians twenty years from now, . . . when they come to analyze Albert's fear of a seal skin coat . . . will probably tease from him a dream which upon their analysis will show that Albert at three years of age attempted to play with the pubic hair of the mother and was scolded violently for it." The powerful James McKeen Cattell publicly humiliated a younger psychologist at the 1923 APA convention for daring to mention Freud's name in a discussion and in one of his publications described Freud as someone "who lives in the fairyland of dreams among the ogres of perverted sex." Consistently with these attitudes, most psychology textbooks throughout the 1920s paid little or no attention to psychoanalysis.[29]

This willful blindness ran against the tide of popular opinion and culture, however; thanks in part to their lively accessibility and their relevance to everyday issues, Freud's works became widely known and his name became a veritable household word in America. By the early 1920s his face had appeared on the cover of *Time* magazine, and the lyrics of a popular song declaimed, "Don't tell me what you dream'd last night, For I've been reading Freud!"[30] Indeed, as Freud's popular fame increased the words *psychology* and *psychoanalysis* became increasingly confounded in the public mind.

By the early 1930s the tide could no longer be resisted, and a few younger psychologists began arguing that psychoanalytic ideas ought not be dismissed or derided but instead regarded as *hypotheses* to be investigated experimentally in laboratory situations. Among the most important of these was **Saul Rosenzweig** (1907–2004), whose doctoral research at Harvard investigated the memory for completed versus incompleted or interrupted tasks. His research was an elaboration of another classic doctoral study that had been conducted in the mid-1920s by **Bluma Zeigarnik** (1901–1988), under the supervision of Gestalt psychologist Kurt Lewin. Zeigarnik found that when subjects were asked to remember a series of tasks they had been asked to perform, some of which had been interrupted before their completion, their recall of the uncompleted tasks was significantly greater than for the completed tasks. This tendency to better remember uncompleted than completed tasks subsequently became known as the **Zeigarnik effect**. Rosenzweig's new twist to this research model was to deliberately lead his subjects to believe that some of their incompleted tasks were not just a simple matter of "unfinished business" but rather were the result of some sort of personal *failure*. It was suggested, for example, that the tasks were very easy to complete for most people and that only a few deficient individuals would not be able to finish them. Under these conditions the Zeigarnik effect was reversed, as the incompleted, "failed" tasks were more likely to be forgotten than the completed ones. Rosenzweig interpreted these results as an experimental demonstration of *repression*, the *motivated forgetting* of negative events.

Thinking that Freud himself would be interested by this experimental confirmation of part of his theory, Rosenzweig sent him his results but received a disappointingly laconic reply: "I cannot put much value on these confirmations because the wealth of reliable observations on which [psychoanalytic] assertions rest make them independent of experimental verification. Still, it can do no harm."[31] Indeed, from the beginning Freud had been quite indifferent to the results of laboratory investigations of his theory, believing that they inevitably lacked the "real life" background of actual clinical cases. But despite Freud's condescension, Rosenzweig's study showed other psychologists that at least some psychoanalytic concepts *could* be brought into in the laboratory, and it initiated a new strategy. Instead of ignoring or denigrating Freudian ideas, psychologists would now design controlled experiments to determine their validity and, in the words of historian Gail Hornstein, reinstate themselves "as arbiters of the mental world, able to make the final judgement about what would and would not count as psychological knowledge."[32]

The extent to which they actually achieved that goal may be debatable, but unquestionably, research by psychologists on psychoanalytic and related "psychodynamic" ideas quickly became a growth industry. Empirical studies of "Freudian" subjects such as dreams, childhood experience and character development, stages of sexual development, the role of conflict in learning, and the development of neurotic and psychotic responses proliferated in the psychological journals, with more than 400 such studies published in the 1940s and 1950s and at least a thousand more by the mid-1970s.[33] Accompanied by studies suggested by "neo-Freudian" and other competing clinical theories, these works became an essential component of the rise of "personality" as a major new subdiscipline of academic psychology. The fuller story of these developments will be told in the next chapter.

Summary

Although trained as a neurologist, **Sigmund Freud** became interested in Charcot's work on hypnosis and hysteria and, in collaboration with **Josef Breuer** developed a **cathartic method** that relied on hypnosis to recall repressed **pathogenic ideas** or memories that caused hysteria. Seeking a nonhypnotic method for recalling these memories, Freud developed the technique of **free association**. In this method, patients were encouraged to consciously identify and articulate the (often multiple) origins of their neurotic symptoms, whereupon they would often subside. In some cases, this process was actively resisted, and Freud hypothesized the presence of **intrapsychic conflict** and **repression**, whereby anxiety-laden memories are actively kept out of conscious awareness. Freud began to suspect that many of these anxiety-laden memories had to do with childhood sexual experiences, at first suggesting that these memories were of actual unwanted sexual advances from adult relatives, an idea he termed the seduction theory. Then, following a self-analysis of his own dreams, he changed his theory to suggest that these were actually memories of the *wish* for sexual gratification, rather than actual sexual seductions. Freud concluded that dreams and hysterical symptoms were both the results of unconscious psychological activity—a **primary process**—by which unacceptable and repressed wishes become transformed into conscious manifest dreams or symptoms. These and subsequent findings became the basis not only of a therapeutic approach but also a general theory of the mind that Freud called **psychoanalysis**.

Originally inspired by his "self-analysis" of his own dreams, Freud formulated the **Oedipus complex** and developed a theory of childhood sexuality in which children pass through three stages—oral, anal and phallic—on their way to their "mature" adult genitally oriented sexuality. Fixations occurring at any of these stages can result in particular character traits in the adult personality. Finally, as a further development of his therapeutic approach, Freud originated the concept of **transference**, in which patients may unconsciously transfer feelings about important figures in their lives onto the analyst in the therapeutic situation. Freud integrated his clinical discoveries within a broader theoretical context, formulating a **metapsychology** that outlined the *general* features of the human mind, including the **id**, **ego**, and **superego**. With this structure in place, he also outlined a number of **defense mechanisms** through which anxiety-provoking impulses are kept in check.

The last sections of this chapter dealt with Freud's intellectual legacy, the critique of his theories of female development by **Karen Horney** and **Clara Thompson**, and his reception by academic psychologists. Although the psychologists' reactions varied, most were initially quite dismissive. Eventually a few of them began to provide experimental evidence for or against some of Freud's theoretical concepts. Although Freud himself was unimpressed by these efforts, they turned into something of a cottage industry. Studies of Freudian concepts proliferated in the pages of academic psychology journals throughout the middle years of the twentieth century.

Key Pioneers

Bauer, Ida, p. 478
Beck, Aaron T., p. 493
Brentano, Franz, p. 460
Breuer, Josef, p. 456
Deutsch, Helene, p. 489
Erikson, Erik, p. 492

Fairbairn, W. R. D., p. 492
Freud, Anna, p. 485
Freud, Sigmund, p. 455
Horney, Karen, p. 489
Klein, Melanie, p. 492
Meynert, Theodor, p. 461

Pappenheim, Bertha, p. 456
Rosenzweig, Saul, p. 498
Thompson, Clara, p. 490

Winnicott, D. W., p. 492
Wolpe, Joseph, p. 493
Zeigarnik, Bluma, p. 498

Key Terms

act psychology, p. 460
ambivalence, p. 477
anal character, p. 477
anal zone, p. 475
behavior therapy, p. 493
castration complex, p. 488
cathartic method, p. 456
client-centered therapy, p. 493
cognitive therapy, p. 493
concrete representation, p. 468
condensation, p. 468
conversions, p. 458
defense mechanisms, p. 485
defenses, p. 466
denial, p. 487
displacement (in dreams), p. 468
displacement (Freudian defense
    mechanism), p. 485
dreams, p. 466
dream work, p. 468
ego, p. 484
erogenous zones, p. 475
Eros, p. 491
fixation, p. 477
free association, p. 463
fulfillment of wishes, p. 470
genital zone, p. 475
id, p. 483
identification, p. 476
instincts, p. 483

intellectualization, p. 487
intentionality, p. 460
intrapsychic conflict, p. 465
latent content, p. 467
latency stage, p. 476
manifest content, p. 467
metapsychology, p. 482
object relations, p. 492
Oedipus complex, p. 474
oral character, p. 478
oral zone, p. 475
overdetermination, p. 464
pathogenic ideas, p. 458
pcpt.-cs., p. 484
phallic/genital character, p. 478
polymorphous perversity,
    p. 475
pressure technique, p. 462
primary process, p. 469
projection, p. 486
psychoanalysis, p. 458
rationalization, p. 487
regression, p. 469
repression, p. 464
secondary process, p. 469
seduction theory, p. 465
superego, p. 484
Thanatos, p. 491
transference, p. 481
Zeigarnik effect, p. 498

Discussion Questions and Topics

1 One of the critiques of psychoanalysis by academic psychologists was that, as a theory, it had not been subject to rigorous experimental test. Rather, Freud derived his theory largely from observations of patients and their clinical case material. What are the strengths and limitations of each approach to theory development?

2 Although Freud's theories are not accepted by all, identify and describe a number of Freudian concepts or ideas that have seeped into everyday language and continue to shape our experience.

3 Karen Horney and Clara Thompson were introduced as two female analysts who disagreed with aspects of Freud's theory of female development. What were some of their criticisms? What were their alternative proposals?

Suggested Readings

The first major biography of Sigmund Freud was his follower Ernest Jones's *The Life and Work of Sigmund Freud*, 3 vols. (New York: Basic Books, 1953–1957); this work benefits from Jones's personal acquaintance with Freud and his own involvement in the development of psychoanalysis. A later and more objective work, benefiting from the extensive Freud scholarship published after Jones's biography, is Peter Gay's *Freud: A Life for Our Time* (New York: Norton, 1988).

Anyone interested in the ideas presented in this chapter deserves the pleasure of reading Freud's own words. There is no better starting point than *The Origin and Development of Psychoanalysis*, the series of five short lectures he delivered at Clark University, which are easily available online at http://psychclassics.yorku.ca/Freud/Origin/. Freud's complete psychological works have been translated, edited, and fully documented in twenty-four volumes by James Strachey in *The Standard Edition of the Complete Psychological Works of Sigmund Freud* (London: Hogarth, 1953–1974). Partly in response to criticism that the Strachey translations render Freud's everyday language overly technical, Adam Phillips has overseen the publication of a new series of translations intended to overcome that problem. Freud's most important individual works have been published separately, using one or the other of these translations, in paperback volumes. Freud's general introductions to his theory, written for nonspecialists, were *Introductory Lectures on Psychoanalysis* and *An Outline of Psychoanalysis*. Readers desiring a more detailed presentation of his theory are advised to examine his major works in the order in which they were written. One good sequence is *Studies on Hysteria* (1895), *The Interpretation of Dreams* (1900), *Three Essays on the Theory of Sexuality* (1905), *The Ego and the Id* (1923), and *Civilization and Its Discontents* (1930). Several secondary introductions to Freud are available in paperback. We will disavow modesty and particularly recommend Raymond Fancher's *Psychoanalytic Psychology: The Development of Freud's Thought* (New York: Norton, 1973).

For an excellent account of Freud's complex reception by academic experimental psychologists see Gail Hornstein, "The Return of the Repressed: Psychology's Problematic Relations with Psychoanalysis, 1909–1960," *American Psychologist* 47 (1992): 254–263.

Psychology Gets "Personality"

Gordon Allport, Abraham Maslow, and the Broadening of Academic Psychology

12

Allport's Early Life and Career
An Encounter with Freud
The Concept of "Personality"
Dissertation on Personality Traits
German Influences
Creating a Discipline

Allport's Personality Psychology
Nomothetic and Idiographic Methods
Psychoanalytic "Mechanisms" Versus "Functional Autonomy"

Personality Psychology Comes of Age
Nomothetic Approaches: Cattell, Eysenck, and the "Big Five"
Idiographic Approaches: Murray and 'Personology"

Allport as Social Activist and Teacher
Religion and Prejudice
Some Eminent Students

Abraham Maslow and Humanistic Psychology
A Paradoxical Early Life
Psychology at Wisconsin
Social Behavior in Monkeys

Maslow's New York Postgraduate Education
An Anthropological Mentor: Ruth Benedict
Neo-Freudian Mentors: Adler, Horney, and Fromm
Gestalt Mentors: Wertheimer and Goldstein

Maslow's Theory of Human Motivation
Self-actualization
The Hierarchy of Needs
A Positive Approach to Psychology

Establishing a Humanistic Psychology
Humanistic Allies: Rogers, May, and Allport
Maslow's Late Writings and the Legacy of Positive
Psychology

Summary

Key Pioneers

Key Terms

Discussion Questions and Topics

Suggested Readings

In April 1921, **Gordon W. Allport** *(1897–1967; see* Figure 12.1) was among the select group of advanced psychology graduate students invited to attend the annual meeting of Edward Bradford Titchener's "Society of Experimentalists." As noted in Chapter 5, Titchener had created this exclusively male organization to promote a resolutely "scientific" approach to psychology, as epitomized by his own *structuralism*, which sought to reduce all conscious experience to its most elemental sensations and feelings. It was the custom at these meetings for the invited students to deliver three-minute summaries of their dissertation research after which—it was hoped—the powerful Titchener would express his approval. For many budding male experimental psychologists this had been considered a major rite of passage into professional respectability.

Titchener, of course, had also been the main "opponent" to Freud at the 1909 Clark conference (see Chapter 11) and had set the tone for most academic psychologists in their subsequent antagonism toward psychoanalysis. Allport's invitation to the meeting may have been a mistake, because his dissertation research focused on the new psychological topic of "personality." Although not explicitly psychoanalytic, this was still a "soft" topic to which psychoanalysis bore some relevance. It contrasted markedly with the "hard" subjects of the other students' research, mainly on sensory topics such as the perceived brightness of different metals. Titchener's reaction was predictably negative, and Allport recalled that his report was "punished by the rebuke of total silence from the group, punctuated by a glare of disapproval from Titchener," who subsequently asked his supervisor

FIG 12.1
Gordon Allport
(1897–1967)

Herbert Langfeld why he had permitted a student to work on such an unscientific problem.[1]

Any disappointment Allport felt was only temporary, however, as the kindly Langfeld consoled him by saying, "You don't care what Titchener thinks," and soon after that, Allport recalled, "I found that I did not."[2] In fact, the episode marked a turning point at which the narrow experimentalism represented by Titchener was about to decline in influence and academic psychology was about to undergo a significant broadening of its scope. Allport would be at the forefront of this movement: Within three years he began teaching the first university courses explicitly devoted to the *psychology of personality*, and tirelessly promoting that field as an important new area of specialization.

One more small but significant sign of the new intellectual climate occurred six years later when a bright young Cornell undergraduate named **Abraham H. Maslow** (1908–1970) enrolled in what would be Titchener's final offering of his introductory psychology course before his death in August of that year. Although enthusiastic about the idea of psychology, Maslow found that Titchener's course, still resolutely focused on his old structuralist model, was "awful and bloodless and had nothing to do with people, so I shuddered and turned away from it."[3] Fortunately, Maslow soon transferred to the University of Wisconsin, where he encountered several more full-blooded and socially relevant approaches to psychology. As the first Ph.D. student of the soon-to-be famous primate researcher **Harry Harlow** (1905–1981), he wound up writing a pioneering dissertation investigating the social behavior of monkeys.

Allport and Maslow were thus alike in writing groundbreaking doctoral dissertations that stretched the boundaries of acceptable topics for psychological research. They shared a further similarity in their immediate postgraduate years, as both of them significantly expanded their outlooks after being exposed to important European psychologists. Allport traveled to Germany where he encountered and embraced Gestalt psychology in several of its forms. And Maslow, located in New York City in the late 1930s, met and befriended several of the eminent emigrés who had collected there after fleeing Hitler's regime. Among them were the principal Gestalt psychologists and several important neo-Freudian psychoanalysts.

With their enriched backgrounds, both of the young men went on to "found" important new domains within academic psychology. For Allport it was the extremely diverse field of **personality psychology**, which encompasses methodologies ranging from individual case studies through the large-scale statistical analysis of the interrelationships among innumerable personality traits. Maslow, after writing one of the earliest textbooks on abnormal psychology, became increasingly more interested in the topic of what enables people to be "normal" or "healthy." He formulated a highly influential theory of human motives as arranged in a hierarchy and took the lead in promoting a new "third force" (after behaviorism and psychoanalysis) in psychology that came to be known as **humanistic psychology**. Needless to say, neither Allport nor Maslow operated in a vacuum as they developed their ideas, being joined and supported by many others within a receptive intellectual climate. Their individual stories, however, illustrate an important stage in the development and evolution of modern academic psychology into the inclusive discipline that it remains today.

Allport's Early Life and Career

The youngest of four accomplished brothers, Gordon Allport grew up in suburban Cleveland, Ohio, where his father was an entrepreneurial doctor and his mother a retired schoolteacher with strong religious sensibilities. The two parents provided a home life "marked by plain Protestant piety and hard work."[4] An excellent high school student, Gordon was accepted in 1915 at Harvard, where his older brother Floyd had already received his bachelor's degree and was currently working on his pioneering Ph.D. in experimental social psychology (see Chapter 10). Gordon soon became an honor student in the Departments of Social Ethics and Psychology. Via Social Ethics he became heavily involved in many volunteer activities and "got a tremendous kick out of doing good."[5] He remained a committed social activist for his entire life.

His classroom introduction to psychology came from the German Hugo Münsterberg, William James's anointed successor at Harvard whose contributions to applied psychology will be discussed more fully in Chapter 15. Although Allport found aspects of Münsterberg's German-accented lectures to be mystifyingly impenetrable, he was fascinated by his teacher's argument that there are two legitimate but fundamentally different kinds of psychology: one *causal and objective*, emphasizing the deterministic and mechanistic linkages between specific stimuli and the responses they produce; and the other *purposive and subjective*, requiring psychologists to enter into and share their subjects' particular thought processes and points of view. Allport recalled that "the blank page dividing the two corresponding sections of [Münsterberg's] textbook intrigued me," and although he could not fully grasp the differences between them at the time, he wondered, "Could they not be reconciled and fused?"[6]

Münsterberg's dual conception of psychology exemplified a general attitude more common among continental European than English-speaking theorists. We have seen how continental thinkers such as Descartes, Leibniz, Kant and Wundt—each in their own distinctive ways—stressed the inadequacy of mechanistic explanation to account *completely* for the highest mental functions and the subjective qualities of consciousness and will. While acknowledging a major role for mechanistic explanation, each felt that there were limits to that undertaking and that some sort of complementary, non-mechanistic mode of understanding was also required. Intrigued by Münsterberg's version of this idea, Allport would later visit Germany and explore it more thoroughly.

In the meantime, however, once past Münsterberg's class, Allport was exposed to a more typically American vision of psychology. Having been initiated not too long before by William James (see Chapter 8), Harvard psychology tended to be broadminded, pluralistic, and oriented toward pragmatic goals. There was no better exemplar of this than Gordon's older brother Floyd, who just then was conducting his groundbreaking dissertation research on social facilitation. Although "socially relevant" in its subject matter, this research also reflected the behavioristic requirement of John Watson and others that it should be framed in terms of strictly observable and "objective" stimuli and responses. Gordon served as one of the subjects in Floyd's study and, more significantly, engaged in long discussions with him about the importance of proper methods and aims for psychology. After graduating in 1919 as an A student in both psychology and social ethics, Allport taught English and sociology for a year at a small American-operated school in Turkey before accepting a fellowship offer from Harvard to return for a Ph.D. in psychology.

An Encounter with Freud

On his way home, Allport stopped in Vienna to visit another older brother who was working there. Coincidentally, Sigmund Freud—who was just then becoming famous in the English-speaking world—lived and practiced there too. Allport later recalled: "With a callow forwardness characteristic of age twenty-two, I wrote to Freud that I was in Vienna and implied that no doubt he would be glad to make my acquaintance." Surprisingly enough, Freud invited him to his office. Once there, Allport found himself in the uncomfortable position of having wrangled an interview without planning in advance what to talk about. Desperately seeking "a suitable conversational gambit," he impulsively told Freud about a small boy he had just observed who had loudly and publicly expressed great anxiety about getting dirty. Thinking that Freud might be interested by this account of a juvenile dirt phobia, Allport was "flabbergasted" when

Freud "fixed his kindly therapeutic eyes upon me and said, 'And was that little boy you?'"

Some who knew Allport personally have noted that he was in fact fastidious about his own appearance and cleanliness, displaying at least some of the traits of a well adjusted Freudian "anal character." Further, as the youngest of four brothers he may have been especially sensitive to being characterized as a "little boy."[7] Allport himself acknowledged that in a *therapeutic* setting Freud's comment might have been on the mark. He also felt, however, that in this more casual context "therapeutic progress was not. . . . an issue." Freud had seemingly failed to appreciate his "manifest motivation, . . . a sort of rude curiosity and youthful ambition." Accordingly, the experience suggested to him that "depth psychology, for all its merits, may plunge too deep, and that psychologists would do well to give full recognition to manifest motives before probing the unconscious."[8] Allport retained this attitude for the rest of his life. He always acknowledged the importance of psychoanalysis and other depth psychologies and did much to promote their acceptance by academic psychologists. But he also insisted that when dealing with *normal* people, such approaches should always be preceded and complemented by an understanding of their more conscious assessments of themselves.

The Concept of "Personality"

Back at Harvard, Allport sought a dissertation topic that would be socially relevant like psychoanalysis, but more attuned to everyday life and social normality. He was helped here by Floyd, who had recently accepted a junior faculty position at Harvard while also becoming co-editor of the renamed *Journal of Abnormal and Social Psychology* (see Chapter 10 for details). Floyd made Gordon his editorial assistant, so the young graduate student was in a privileged position to learn about new developments in a broad range of psychological areas. Among the emerging new topics was "personality," a word that was gradually assuming a new meaning for psychologists. Derived from the Greek word *persona*, designating the mask worn by an actor in early drama that defined a particular role or character, the term had taken on some scientific and medical connotations during the 1800s as psychiatrists began writing about "alterations of personality" or "personality disorders." In the early 1900s the *Journal*'s founding editor Morton Prince had brought special attention to the dissociative condition called *multiple personality*. Soon thereafter, the term *personality* gained further meaning as a rough substitute for the traditional psychological word "character," designating that set of qualities or traits that make a person distinctive (i.e., that are *characteristic* of her or him). "Character" also carried evaluative or moral connotations, however, in the sense that a person's character is often thought of as being either good or bad. As psychologists strove to make their field more "objective," a more neutral term seemed desirable. Individual variations in character were increasingly relabeled and seen in a broader and less moralistic context, as differences in *personality.*[9]

This trend coincided with other important psychological currents, including the development of *tests* to measure individual variations in psychological qualities. The most prominent were *intelligence tests*, the full story of which will be recounted in Chapter 13. At the same time, a few psychologists became interested in measuring some non-intellective traits with instruments that soon became known as "personality tests." The University of Wyoming psychologist **June Etta Downey** (1875–1932), for example, used features of handwriting analysis in 1919 to obtain scores on personal traits such as impulsivity, carefulness, and forcefulness in her **Individual Will Temperament Test**. That same year Columbia University's Robert Woodworth (see Chapter 8) published the **Personal Data Sheet**—a series of questions to be answered yes or no, intended to screen out soldiers who were psychologically unfit for active duty in World War I. Although completed too late to be used in the war, it was one of the first attempts to develop an objective, self-report personality test.

Significantly, these developments occurred just as Freudian and other psychodynamic clinical theories were coming to wide notice, providing new categories of character or personality differences for description and analysis. Freud's anal and oral characters, described in Chapter 11, provided one obvious example. More directly relevant to academic experimental psychology was the work of Freud's erstwhile follower **Carl G. Jung** (1875–1961). Jung had accompanied Freud to the 1909 Clark conference as a self-identified disciple and while there delivered two lectures on what he called "The Association Method"—essentially what today we call the **word association test**. He had developed a substantial list of stimulus words, presented to subjects with instructions to provide for each "as quickly as possible the first word that occurs to your mind."[10] The examiner would record each response verbatim, as well as the amount of time the subject took before producing it. Representing a more formally standardized approach to obtaining the data of Freudian free association—looking for hesitancies, blockings, bizarre responses, and other indicators of psychic "complexes"—the procedure stands as another early example of a personality test.

In the years following the Clark conference, Jung increasingly dissented from Freudian psychoanalysis while promoting a rival **analytical psychology**. He continued to emphasize the importance of an unconscious mind and of dream analysis as a means of exploring it. But the Jungian unconscious was determined much less than Freud's by repressed sexuality and more by a broad range of biological, religious, cultural and even inherited "collective" factors. Analytical psychology also posited an influential theory of "psychological types," an essential component of which was a dimension of "temperament" that he labeled **extroversion-introversion** (sometimes alternatively spelled as extraversion-intraversion). Extroversion denotes a tendency to be oriented toward the external world, introversion toward the inner, subjective one. Thus, extreme extroverts are people who seek gratifications from outside themselves, showing tendencies to be gregarious, talkative, socially assertive, and much more comfortable in groups of people than when left on their own. Extreme introverts, by contrast, are oriented toward their own inner life: introspective, reflective, attracted to solitary activities such as reading and writing, and often uncomfortable in large groups. Jung saw this as a *dimensional* concept, with relatively few people occupying the extremes of extro- or introversion and most at various points in between the two. Conceived this way as a dimension, and with specific behaviors associated with its two poles, it became a natural category for early psychological testers to use as they attempted to measure differences in personality.

Dissertation on Personality Traits

Although Langfeld was Gordon Allport's nominal supervisor, his brother Floyd was a more important influence. The brothers contemplated this new area of "personality" together and then collaborated in writing an article titled "Personality Traits: Their Classification and Measurement," which they conveniently published in the journal they just happened to co-edit.[11] In contrast to earlier authors who had dealt with just selected aspects of the subject, the Allports provided a more systematic analysis and overview of the "elusive term" personality, with their central concept being the **trait**. They proposed a general model for the "composition of personality," consisting of four groups of traits under the general headings of Intelligence, Temperament, Self-Expression, and Sociality. Temperamental traits included "Emotional Breadth and Strength"; Self-expressive ones featured "extroversion-introversion" and "ascendance-submission"; and sociality highlighted "social participation" and "susceptibility to social stimuli."

Gordon's dissertation research was essentially a pilot study to empirically assess the promise of the new system. For fifty-five Harvard undergraduate subjects, he obtained ratings from close friends on ten nonintellective personality traits from the model. The fifty-five subjects also rated themselves on the same traits. The results, based on a small sample of subjects from a relatively restricted population and using new and unvalidated measures, were suggestive rather than conclusive. Sometimes the friends' ratings disagreed with each other, or conflicted with the self-ratings. The various trait measures did not intercorrelate with one another in consistent patterns. The most suggestive findings occurred when the subjects' results were represented on a graph, making it easy to distinguish individualized "profiles" (such as introverted or extroverted, with high or low social interests and high or low emotionality). This seemed a promising but as yet unvalidated avenue for summarizing individual personalities. Thus, in general Allport's dissertation demonstrated the *potential* for a systematic approach to research on personality—potential that he and others would expend much effort to fulfill in the ensuing years.

German Influences

In 1922 Allport won a fellowship for postgraduate study in Germany where he experienced "a new intellectual dawn," and some of the mystery he had earlier perceived in Münsterberg's division of psychology began to dissipate. First in Berlin, where Max Wertheimer and Wolfgang Köhler were young professors, he learned about "a new concept I had not heard of"—namely, Gestalt psychology. Unlike the behavioristic and atomistic psychology that prevailed in America, in which the whole organism was conceived of as simply the aggregate of all of its separate response tendencies, here was a "top down" approach in which a unifying whole could be much more than the sum of its parts (see Chapter 4 for more on Gestalt psychology). Allport later described this as a "kind of psychology I had been longing for but did not know existed."[12]

Moving from Berlin to Hamburg, Allport found a mentor who had adopted a Gestalt-like approach to the study of personality. The versatile and prolific **William Stern** (1871–1938) promoted a **personalistic psychology** in which the central concept was "the person" and the overriding goal was the understanding of each person's *individuality*. Stern argued that there are two ways to approach this goal. One was to investigate what he called **relational individuality**, defined by the subject person's relative or statistical positions on a large variety of separately measured traits. When the number of traits is large, no two people are likely to have exactly the same *pattern* of scores, even though they may be the same on a small number of the traits. Allport's dissertation research results illustrated this kind of individuality, as no two of his subjects wound up with exactly the same graphic profile across all of the ten traits he measured. More important to Stern than relational individuality, however, was what he called **real individuality**, a Gestalt-like conception of each person's unique and unified self that is more than the sum of its individual characteristics. Real individuality must be approached not by statistical comparisons with other persons but by examining the relationships of qualities *within* each person, primarily through the close analysis of individual life histories or case studies.[13]

Creating a Discipline

Allport returned from Germany to assume an untenured position in Harvard's Department of Social Ethics in 1924. There he offered what were almost certainly the first university courses explicitly devoted to personality psychology, called "Personality and Social Ameliorization" the first year and "Personality: Its Psychological and Social Aspects" the second, when it was offered jointly with the Psychology Department.[14] He then moved to the Psychology Department of Dartmouth College, where he offered personality courses for four years before returning to Harvard with a tenure-track position in psychology. At Dartmouth he nurtured the idea of writing a general book on personality, but once at Harvard he felt he had to establish quick credentials in a prestigious department that was notoriously volatile in its treatment of junior faculty. Intent on bolstering his publication record, he put his synthesizing textbook on the backburner while collaborating with colleagues and students on more immediately publishable projects. Several of these, however, related to the study of personality and helped establish its legitimacy.

With **Philip Vernon** (1905–1987), an English psychologist visiting at Harvard, Allport published both a study of expressive movement and, more consequentially, a paper and pencil test they called "A Study of Values." This test, which measured subjects' relative preferences for statements reflecting six kinds of values (theoretical, economic, aesthetic, social, political, and religious), quickly became one of the most widely used instruments in personality research. With Henry Odbert, a Dartmouth student who followed Allport to Harvard to obtain his Ph.D., he published the 1936 monograph "Trait names: A Psycho-Lexical Study." The authors scoured English dictionaries and identified some 18,000 different words used to describe personal characteristics or traits. Only a small proportion of these terms, they argued, describe dimensions or dispositions that are applicable to nearly everyone and that are potentially measurable. Intelligence was an obvious example of this type of trait. Another was the generalized tendency to be either dominant or acquiescent in relations with other people, suggesting an "ascendance-submission" dimension on which people may be ranked or scored. The vast majority of trait names, however, were not universally applicable but rather applied to some but not all people, or to people in certain highly specific situations.

Through these and other efforts, Allport secured his tenure at Harvard and became department chairman in 1937. In that banner year he also became editor-in-chief of the *Journal of Abnormal and Social Psychology* and finally completed the big book that had been cooking in his head since his Dartmouth years. *Personality: A Psychological Interpretation* became the first integrative textbook for the new field, a wide-ranging survey of the theories, methods and approaches in an important new discipline. Coincidentally, another textbook, *Psychology of Personality*, also appeared in 1937, by the younger psychologist **Ross Stagner** (1909–1997) from the University of Akron. Stagner had studied family influences on personality traits, in the course of which he corresponded with and received advice from Allport. His textbook was written independently of Allport's, however, and presented a more behavioristically oriented survey of the field. Both of these "first" textbooks on personality were successful, but Allport's was the more influential because it reflected his longer involvement in the field and covered it more comprehensively, incorporating continental as well as American and British viewpoints.

Allport's Personality Psychology

Allport's book opened by declaring that "the outstanding characteristic" of human beings is their *individuality* and that the major goal of personality psychology is the understanding and appreciation of that individuality. Pursuit of this goal poses an apparent problem for "scientific" psychology, however, because, as a Latin expression put it, *Scientia non est individuorum* ("Science is not about individuals").[15] Science, as normally practiced, seeks to establish *generalizations*—regularities and uniformities characteristic of whole classes of objects. In 566 dense pages of text, charts, and diagrams, Allport grappled with this apparent contradiction—first by exhaustively tracing the history of the concept of personality and summarizing the earliest approaches to its study, and then by defining the new field as a preeminently "big tent" discipline that should use the widest possible variety of methods and orientations. Along the way Allport presented his suggested resolution of two troublesome issues he had encountered earlier in his career: the "blank page" dilemma he had perceived separating Münsterberg's two kinds of psychology, and the problematic role of psychoanalysis and other depth psychologies in studying "normal personalities."

Nomothetic and Idiographic Methods

In his broad conceptualization of personality psychology, Allport identified two contrasting research styles, which he designated as **nomothetic** and **idiographic**. The first term derives from the Greek word *nomos* for "law," and nomothetic personality research studies people in terms of general laws or characteristics on which they vary to quantitatively specifiable degrees. The contrasting term derives from *idios*, the Greek for "one's own" and the root for English words such as *idiosyncrasy*. Idiographic research attempts to investigate and describe what it is that makes a given person unique, and its methods are much more likely to be qualitative than quantitative. Nomothetic approaches were those used in pursuing Münsterberg's causal, objective type of psychology and Stern's relational individuality; idiographic methods were more appropriate for Münsterbergian purposive psychology and Stern's search for real individuality.

Allport approved of both kinds of research. He himself had conducted nomothetic studies in his Ph.D. dissertation, in his development with Vernon of the Study of Values, and in his work with Odbert identifying dimensional traits, such as intelligence and ascendance-submission, on which every person can be comparatively rated. He noted that the vast majority of personality studies conducted up to 1937—most of which involved one or another type of "test"—had been nomothetic in nature. There was obviously nothing wrong with this kind of approach.

At the same time, however—and consistently with his German mentors—Allport insisted that nomothetics were not sufficient to produce a *complete* psychology of personality. He noted that the majority of dictionary trait names did *not* lend themselves to nomothetic scale building but rather applied to some but not all people, or to people in certain specific situations. He further argued that the peculiar qualities of individuality that set each person apart from everyone else must inevitably elude nomothetic analysis. For a complete, idiographic understanding of a personality it was necessary to closely examine the subject person's unique life history and the particular *interrelationships* among his or her major traits.

In a central chapter of his book, titled "A Survey of Methods," Allport designated the preparation of a life history or "case study" as potentially "the most revealing method of all," providing "a framework within which the psychologist can place all his observations gathered by other methods; it is his final affirmation of the individuality and uniqueness of every personality."[16] Within a case study, one may provide the specific scores and results obtained by the subject on various nomothetic measures, integrated within a narrative that includes the individual details and subjective reports provided by the subject himself or herself. Allport further noted that the value of a case study "does not cease with its synthetic treatment of a single personality. By comparing and analyzing many such studies it is possible to pass to the construction of psychological laws and to new hypotheses."[17] One powerful illustration of this was Freud's use of individual case studies such as Anna O., Dora, and other of his early patients in deriving his more general psychoanalytic ideas. But the Freudian example also illustrated—at least for Allport—some of the cautions required in the *interpretation* of such derived generalizations.

Psychoanalytic "Mechanisms" Versus "Functional Autonomy"

Allport acknowledged the great popularity of psychoanalysis and noted that "before Freud there was in general a fatal neglect of impulsive emotion and its subterranean workings." He credited psychoanalysis with providing a needed corrective to "the shortcomings of traditional intellectualistic psychology."[18] Its most significant concepts, he thought, were the "specific mechanisms" it postulated to account for the relationships between unconscious emotional factors and overt thought and behavior. He further allowed that "*some* of those mechanisms, provided they are kept in perspective . . . have value for the study of normal lives." He cautioned, however, that Freud's concepts were primarily derived "from the inductive study of unbalanced (anxious) personalities [so] they are not able, taken collectively, to provide a well-proportioned account of the *normal* course of development."[19] Although Freud's generalizations from his case studies might be valid, their validity was restricted to the abnormal population from which they were drawn.

Thus, Allport proposed two fundamental lessons for personality psychology—both also derived from his own personal encounter with Freud. First, he assumed that when dealing with "normal" personalities one should always take seriously and at face value their own *conscious* self-reports. If you want to know something about people, *ask them first* and do not immediately assume that their responses have been distorted by unconscious factors. And relatedly, do not rush to "pathologize" normal adult behavior by attributing it to motives and fixations dating from childhood. Freud made both of these mistakes, Allport believed, when he asked, "Was that little boy you?" in response to his report of a dirt-phobic child.

Allport did not deny that many traits such as cleanliness or orderliness may well *originate* in childhood experiences such as toilet training, as suggested by the Freudians, but he argued that these traits are maintained or even strengthened in the mature personality because they have become reinforcing or rewarding *in their own right*. In Allport's terminology, such traits come to manifest a **functional auton-omy** from their childhood origins, and for a full understanding of the mature, normal person, he insisted that this ongoing functionality was more important than those distant origins. It is interesting to note that at the same time Allport was introducing this concept, a group of young psychoanalysts were adopting some similar ideas. **Heinz Hartmann** (1894–1970) and **David Rapaport** (1911–1960), for example, promoted an **ego psychology** that asserted that with normal develop-ment many of the functions of the Freudian ego become independent of their distant origins in impulses of the id. They spoke explicitly of an "autonomous" ego and cited Allport among their many sources.[20]

In the years following the publication of his book, Allport contin-ued to encourage psychologists to study seriously—but not to over-emphasize—psychoanalysis and other depth psychologies. As editor of the *Journal of Abnormal and Social Psychology* in 1940 he declared that "it is of the utmost importance to encourage open discussion con-cerning the principles and practices of psycho-analysis among well informed psychologists."[21] He organized and published a symposium of nine articles written by psychologists who had themselves under-gone psychoanalytic treatment, and further oversaw the publication of myriad other articles on topics that had been directly or indirectly brought to prominence by Freudian psychology.

Personality Psychology Comes of Age

In sum, Gordon Allport promoted a new field of personality psychol-ogy that embraced the widest possible variety of methods and theo-retical approaches. In the years following the publication of his 1937 textbook he saw many of his prescriptions come to fruition, often fol-lowing directly upon his own work.

Nomothetic Approaches: Cattell, Eysenck, and the "Big Five"

In 1941 Allport was instrumental in bringing to Harvard the Eng-lish-born psychologist **Raymond B. Cattell** (1905–1998, no relation to the American James McKeen Cattell; see Figure 12.2). Cattell had

FIG 12.2
Raymond B. Cattell
(1905–1998)

been trained at the University of London in the emerging techniques of factor analysis, a set of statistical procedures in which the intercorrelations among large numbers of individual variables can be reduced to smaller "factors," "clusters," or "principal components." Prior to coming to Harvard, Cattell had done important work applying these techniques to varying types of intelligence test items. Upon interacting with Allport and other colleagues interested in personality at Harvard, he had the idea of subjecting measures of the myriad individual traits identified in the Allport-Odbert lexical study to such analysis, to see whether they might resolve themselves into a smaller group of comprehensible factors. This presented an enormous computational challenge, involving the calculation of thousands of individual correlation coefficients.

After developing this idea Cattell was lured to the University of Illinois in 1945 by the promise of one of the first major electronic computers, the "Illiac I," to assist in carrying out the project. His results, published in 1949, suggested that all of the thousands of individual trait names could be reduced to just sixteen "personality factors," each one defined as a set of strongly intercorrelated traits. Each factor represented a *dimension* on which individuals vary from one extreme to another. On the "warmth" factor, for example, highly rated individuals would be described by such terms as warm, outgoing, attentive to others, and affectionate; low scorers by cold, cool, distant, aloof, detached, and the like. Others of the sixteen factors included such general dimensions as social boldness/timidity, concreteness/abstractness in thinking, emotional stability/changeability, and trustingness/suspiciousness. Cattell and his colleagues developed the **Sixteen Personality Factor Questionnaire (16PF** for short), an easily administered multiple-choice test for measuring these factors, which has undergone several successful revisions.

The possibility that the collection of sixteen personality factors might themselves be factor analyzed was not lost on Cattell, and he conducted further studies showing that they had a statistical tendency to cluster together into just five even broader categories. For example, the primary factors of warmth, social boldness, liveliness, and affiliative tendencies intercorrelated in a cluster the group called extroversion/introversion. Cattell further noted, however, that the correlations among these components, although statistically significant, were less than perfect. Therefore, the same *global* score could be achieved with differing contributions from the four components. Thus, Cattell and his followers believed that although the broader factors held theoretical interest, the richer picture provided by scores on the sixteen primary factors was more powerful for predicting actual behavior.

A somewhat different view was promoted by another influential, London-trained psychologist, the prolific and disputatious **Hans J. Eysenck** (1916–1997).[*] Eysenck acknowledged Allport as the "patron saint" of personality psychology but vigorously rejected all idiographic methods and insisted that the field should be exclusively

---

[*] Cattell and Eysenck were both versatile and prolific authors whose writings extended into several areas, including the nature of intelligence. Both strongly argued in favor of the hereditary determination of intelligence and personality, and both aroused strong reactions both pro and con. Cattell's views were strongly attacked in William Tucker's book *The Cattell Controversy: Race, Science and Ideology* (Urbana: University of Illinois Press, 2009). A more appreciative overview of his life and career is presented on the Web page devoted to him at http://www.stthomasu.ca/%7Ejgillis/cattell.htm. Eysenck's professional life is fully and fairly described in Roderick Buchanan's *Playing with Fire: The Controversial Career of Hans Eysenck* (New York and Oxford, UK: Oxford University Press, 2010).

and resolutely nomothetic. "To the scientist," he argued in 1952, "the unique individual is simply the point of intersection of a number of quantitative variables."[22] Eysenck and his colleagues sought to reduce the number of those variables to a minimum and so conducted extensive factor analytic studies which suggested that the hundreds of individual trait measures could ultimately be categorized into just *three* primary clusters or factors. One of these he called *extroversion/introversion*, defined similarly to the Cattell group's factor. Another they labeled **neuroticism**, because its component traits all related to a general tendency to experience or to be free from anxiety. The third was **psychoticism**, which connoted a tendency, either voluntary or involuntary, to overlook the boundaries of everyday or common sense "reality." Eysenck argued that by far the most powerful information one can have about an individual personality is his or her relative standing on these three general dimensions—often said to constitute the **PEN model** of personality (based on the initial letters of the three dimensions).

Some more recent theorists have returned to Cattell's conception of five major dimensions.[23] Accepting Eysenck's general factors of neuroticism and extraversion, they have replaced the somewhat vague psychoticism with three new broad dimensions they have labeled **openness** (involving imagination, sensitivity and attentiveness to inner feelings), **conscientiousness** (the tendency to be careful and self disciplined), and **agreeableness** (the tendency to be cooperative and empathetic in dealing with others). These dimensions are are often dubbed the **Big Five**, summarized by their first letters as *OCEAN*.

One limiting factor that should be noted about these factorial models is that they are purely descriptive and contain no explicit information about how the traits develop or the motivational factors that may influence them. That said, they remain highly useful and efficient tools for summarizing much of the information about an individual's personality

Idiographic Approaches: Murray and "Personology"

Allport himself did not conduct a great deal of idiographic research, his most significant project being the analysis and publication of a series of evocative letters written by a woman he called Jenny.[24] In his teaching, however, he regularly addressed the question of how individual life histories might best be written, and he strongly supported the idiographic research of others—most notably that of his Harvard colleague and friend **Henry A. Murray** (1893–1988). Born into a wealthy family and formally trained in medicine and biochemistry, Murray and his companion **Christiana Morgan** (1897–1967) became patients and friends of Carl Jung in the early 1920s.* This association led to a strong fascination with Jungian as well as Freudian and other psychodynamic psychologies, and in 1927 Morton Prince named Murray his assistant director at the newly created Harvard Psychological Clinic. Murray eventually became director, although his lack of formal credentials in psychology and his enthusiastic endorsement of psychodynamic theories made him suspect in the eyes of many at the university, and his official status there was often tenuous. The increasingly influential Allport supported him strongly, however, enabling Murray to hold on and make the clinic a world famous center for personality research. He expressed his appreciation to Allport in a certificate reproduced here as Figure 12.3.

Together with numerous talented students and colleagues whom he attracted to the Clinic, Murray promoted the intensive study of relatively small numbers of individual cases and in particular sought techniques for demonstrating and illustrating their individuality. Among these was the **Thematic Apperception Test**, or **TAT** (developed by Murray in collaboration with Christiana Morgan), in which subjects are presented with a series of standardized pictures and asked to construct stories about them. The widely varying stories told to the same stimuli reflect individual particularities in the personalities of their subjects. Murray's group used the TAT and other innovative techniques, including interviews and detailed auto-

---

* Although married to others, Murray and Morgan carried on an extraordinary love affair that lasted until Morgan's death by suicide in 1967. Their story from Murray's side is told in Forrest Robinson, *Love's Story Told: A Life of Henry A. Murray* (Cambridge, MA: Harvard University Press, 1992) and from Morgan's in Claire Douglas, *Translate This Darkness: A Life of Christiana Morgan, the Veiled Woman in Jung's Circle* (Princeton, NJ: Princeton University Press, 1993).

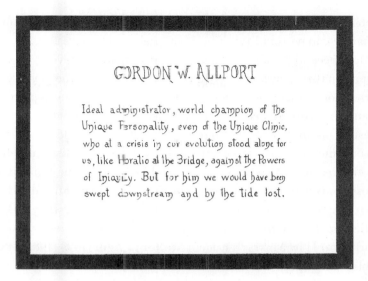

FIG 12.3 Certificate given to Allport to recognize his support of the Harvard Psychological Clinic

biographical statements, to gather extensive personality-relevant data from fifty-one individual Harvard undergraduates over several years. Partly guided by a conceptual scheme in which individuals were seen as motivated, often unconsciously, by some twenty-seven **psychogenic needs**, which become aroused in multifarious ways by environmental **presses**, the group composed detailed case reports on each of their subjects. The needs in their system included ones for *affiliation* with others, for *achievement* in overcoming obstacles, for *power*, or domination over others, and for *autonomy*, or independence from others. They presented their general findings, and the full description of a single case in the groundbreaking 1938 book *Explorations in Personality*.[25]

The Murray group's concept of needs was pursued in a more nomothetic direction by **David McClelland** (1917–1998) and his students in the 1950s and 1960s. Focusing particularly on the need for achievement (which they called n-Ach) and to a lesser extent the needs for affiliation (n-Aff) and power (n-Pow), they devised scoring systems measuring the extents to which achievement-, affiliation-, and power-related fantasies were related in subjects' TAT stories. They then showed that these fantasy-based scores correlated with overt behavior and personality traits in comprehensible ways.[26]

More recently and in a more directly idiographic vein, a group of personality psychologists have united to form the Society for Personology, an organization explicitly devoted to developing and promoting Murray's case study method and to answering Allport's question as to how psychological life histories should be written. Several members of the society have worked to establish guidelines for the responsible writing of **psychobiography**—the explicit use of psychodynamic personality theories to illuminate an individual's biography. One of the first examples of this genre was a study of Adolf Hitler, predicting his eventual suicide and prepared secretly during World War II by Murray's student **Walter Langer** (1899–1981). It was published long after the war, in 1972.[27] Several personologists have contributed to a recent *Handbook of Psychobiography*, which marks the increasing maturation of this approach.[28]

In that handbook personologist Dan McAdams argues that individual lives can be most profitably approached and conceptualized at three separate but complementary levels. The first emphasizes relatively stable dispositional traits, including the psychometrically validated "Big Five." The second level considers more particularized personal qualities, such as goals, motives, needs, and values contextualized in the life experiences of the individual and assessed by various techniques including the TAT and personal interviews. The third explores the individual's "life stories," focusing on narratives of the self that integrate and give meaning to the other material in terms of identity, unity, thematic consistencies, and so on.[29] This proposed integration of the nomothetic and idiographic surely would have pleased Allport.

Allport as Social Activist and Teacher

No account of Gordon Allport's career would be complete without mentioning several contributions—scientific, institutional and personal—that extended beyond personality psychology per se but reflected his lifelong commitment to social ethics and "doing good."

Religion and Prejudice

Raised in a socially conscious and pious household, Allport maintained a broad religious commitment and sensibility throughout his life. As a Harvard professor he gave occasional talks in the Memorial Chapel and maintained membership in the Episcopal Church. He believed that some kind of religious sensibility is an important, even essential aspect of the normal, healthy personality. At the same time, however, he was acutely aware of the social damage that was often perpetrated in the name of religious beliefs. The enormities of the Nazi genocide were the most extreme example, but Allport was also fully aware of the casual anti-Semitism that pervaded his own academic culture. During the 1930s, he had worked hard to find American refuges for imperiled Jewish psychologists from Europe. He was successful in some cases, including that of his former teacher William Stern, but too many other times he was thwarted. Religious arrogance and intolerance manifested itself in many other ways, as well, leading Allport to write *The Individual and His Religion*, published in 1950.[30] In that book he posited a sharp distinction between **immature** and **mature religion**. The former is a religious attachment adopted largely for self-aggrandizing reasons and is unreflective, literal minded, bigoted, and intolerant of other beliefs or even ambiguity. Mature religion, by contrast, maintains belief in a spiritual reality while simultaneously accepting an inevitable unknowableness and mystery regarding ultimate questions. It encourages humility, self-questioning, and tolerance for the viewpoints of others.

One frequent characteristic Allport noted in holders of immature religion aroused his particular interest: namely, prejudice against holders of different views. This general topic became the subject of one of his most influential books, *The Nature of Prejudice*, published in 1954. In it he defined prejudice as "an antipathy based upon a faulty and inflexible generalization,"[31] and he went on to describe an ascending "scale" of the degrees of its manifestation within a person or society. The lowest stage is one in which the members of a majority, or *in group*, make *derogatory jokes* about a minority, or *out group*. Although often seen by its perpetrators as harmless, this behavior all too often presages the ascending stages of *avoidance* of the out group, followed by active *discrimination* against them, and finally rising to *active aggression* and, in extreme cases like Nazi Germany, attempts to *exterminate* the out group.

As a means of reducing the noxious effects of prejudice, Allport put forth the **contact hypothesis**: the proposal that prejudice between groups can be reduced if in-group and out-group members are placed in situations where they must interact with each other collaboratively and with equal status in pursuing a common goal. Some overriding governmental or institutional authority may also be necessary to overcome the initial avoidance tendencies and support integration. The gradual but successful desegregation of the armed forces provides one example of the successful application of the contact hypothesis. In 1958 Allport prepared a shorter version of his book intended for a nonacademic audience, and to his great pleasure it went on to be one of the best selling social psychological books ever published.[32]

Allport's social activism extended into the realm of institution building. In 1936 he was a leader in the creation of the Society for the Psychological Study of Social Issues (SPSSI) and was one of its earliest presidents. Originally inspired by the social and economic calamities of the Great Depression and the rising threat of Hitlerian Germany, this group remains today an important independent organization for socially concerned psychologists and other social scientists. It also maintains a connection as Division 9 of the American Psychological Association and promotes the goal of applying psychological knowledge to "the critical problems of today's world." A decade later Allport collaborated with colleagues from the Psychology, Sociology, and Anthropology Departments at Harvard to create a new Department of Social Relations, in which students would be encouraged to pursue interdisciplinary and socially relevant approaches to their research.

Some Eminent Students

During his long teaching career in the Departments of Psychology and Social Relations, Allport supervised and influenced many students who went on to highly distinguished careers of their own. Stanley Milgram, whose monumental studies of conformity and obedience are detailed in Chapter 10, was one, and he repeatedly expressed his indebtedness to Allport for his early support and encouragement. **Thomas Pettigrew** (b. 1931) came to study prejudice with Allport in the mid-1950s, accompanying him on a field trip to South Africa before becoming a full colleague and one of the leading experts on black-white relations in the United States and elsewhere. Among his many publications are extensive empirical studies of Allport's intergroup contact theory, as well as a moving tribute to his mentor that appeared in the *Journal of Social Issues* (the flagship journal of the SPSSI) in 1999.[33]

Gardner Lindzey (1920–2008) came to Harvard in 1946 as one of Allport's first graduate students in the new Department of Social Relations. In 1951, after completing his Ph.D. and becoming an assistant professor in the department, he proposed to his mentor the idea of producing a *Handbook of Social Psychology*, which would comprehensively describe the field. Allport declined Lindzey's request to serve as co-editor but strongly supported the project by helping to solicit eminent contributors from across the field, with Allport himself writing the opening chapter on the historical background of modern social psychology. The *Handbook* quickly became the definitive reference in the field and is currently available in an expanded fifth edition. Lindzey also contributed greatly to the status of personality psychology when he co-authored, with his former teacher Calvin Hall, the seminal textbook *Theories of Personality* (1957).[34] Allport again strongly supported this project, reading and commenting on the draft chapters and using them in his undergraduate personality class. This text presented a *theory-oriented* approach to personality, beginning with chapters on Freud and Jung and proceeding to describe the approaches of some dozen others, including Lewin, Cattell, Eysenck, the learning theorists, Murray, and Allport himself. An enormous success, this text sold over a million copies in several editions and became the standard introduction to the field for countless undergraduates.

During the final decade of his life, Gordon Allport (see Figure 12.4) found that his stress on the importance of studying psychological normality and health, as well as his endorsement of broad and eclectic research methodologies, meshed very well with the ideas of several other psychologists who were just then promoting a "third force" or humanistic psychology. Although he did not officially "join" this new

FIG 12.4
Gordon Allport
in his later years

movement his work had helped lay the groundwork for it, and, as he had done with Gardner Lindzey and other of his students, he strongly supported its efforts. We turn next to the fuller development of this third force, via the life story of Abraham Maslow.

Abraham Maslow and Humanistic Psychology

A Paradoxical Early Life

The story of Maslow's early life presents an apparent paradox, for this future founder of a "positive psychology," known for his genial and kindly personality, always recalled his childhood with considerable bitterness. The firstborn child in 1908 of Jewish immigrants to New York City from Russia, Maslow wrote "My childhood and boyhood were miserably unhappy." His father, who provided an adequate but hardly lavish income as a barrel maker, "misunderstood me, thought me an idiot and a fool." His mother was "a horrible creature" whom he disliked "not only [for] her physical appearance, but also her values and world view, her stinginess, her total selfishness." His parents often made fun of his large nose and "skinny" physique, leading him to believe as an adolescent that there was never "anyone yet who is so ugly or unhandsome" as he was.[35] He himself asked the question: "I've always wondered where my utopianism, ethical stress, humanism . . . and all the rest came from."[36]

Maslow's younger siblings recalled their parents more fondly than he did, so that it is possible he exaggerated their actual faults. Whatever else they may have done, they recognized his strong intellectual interests and, although they could not fully understand them, still supported them to a certain degree. Young Maslow also encountered some other, more positive influences outside his immediate household. It also remained true, however, that there was often a certain "edge" to Maslow's writings, especially his private ones, where his positivity was tinged with some darker overtones. In general, Maslow's story provides a good demonstration of the fact that psychological theories linking childhood unhappiness to future negativity are valid only in a statistical sense and that there will always be individual variations. It also confirms Allport's argument that every personality has its individual quirks which require idiographic analysis.

Among the most important unquestionably positive influences in Maslow's early life was a close friendship with his cousin Will Maslow. More outgoing than "Abe" but equally curious, intelligent, and socially concerned, Will became an inseparable companion as they jointly pursued broad interests in literature, music, politics, and athletics—becoming known by their classmates at the demanding Boys High School of Brooklyn as the "Gold Dust twins."[37] They graduated with similar records: mainly excellent grades mixed with a few mediocre ones, and strong achievements in extracurricular activities.

At that time Cornell University was the only Ivy League school willing to accept more than token numbers of Jewish students and moreover offered a special scholarship examination for those with limited financial means. Abe felt certain that his less than perfect academic record would automatically disqualify him and chose not to compete. The more adventurous Will did try, and to his surprise won one of the scholarships. Thus, the "twins" separated as Will went to Cornell* and Abe embarked on a diverse and at first erratic undergraduate career. He started with a year of assorted liberal arts courses at the publicly funded City College of New York. The next year at his father's urging, he started courses at the Brooklyn Law School while remaining a part-time liberal arts student at City College. At law school the idealistic Maslow quickly became offended by the absence of moral concerns in legal arguments, and he quit in disgust following a discussion of the subject of "spite fences" (fences built deliberately to block off or annoy neighbors).

Learning that he could transfer to Cornell at a reasonable expense, Abe (see Figure 12.5) joined Will in Ithaca, New York, in the winter of 1927 and took Titchener's Introductory Psychology course. Despite his dislike of the course, he managed to earn a respectable B grade and did comparably well in several other classes. He was not comfortable at Cornell, however, mainly because of the disdain and casual anti-Semitism demonstrated by wealthier students toward those who, like him, had to wait tables to earn their tuition. After one term Maslow returned home to resume classes at City College. The idea of getting away for college still appealed to him, however, and in the spring of 1928 he learned that the University of Wisconsin in Madison was both liberal in its educational philosophy and affordable as a publicly funded institution. Impressed by its catalog, he applied and was accepted for the following September.

During the ensuing summer, he happened to read *The Psychologies of 1925*, a book that had been recommended to him by one of his City College teachers.[38] This collection of essays by the leading psychologists of the day, describing their personal approaches to the field, included one by John B. Watson advocating his behaviorist vision. This, Maslow recalled, "really turned me on . . . In the highest excitement I suddenly saw unrolling before me into the future the possibility of *a science of psychology*, a program of work which

---

* Will too would go on to a distinguished later career, eventually becoming a leader of the American Jewish Congress and marrying into the family of Israel's first prime minister, David Ben-Gurion.

FIG 12.5
Abraham Maslow
(1908–1970)

promised real progress, real advance, real solutions of real problems."
So excited by reading th s, Maslow immediately "danced down Fifth
Avenue, jumping and shouting and gesturing."[39]

If it seems strange that the future father of humanistic psychology
should have been originally attracted to the psychology of a staunch
behaviorist, it should be recalled that Watson was an enormously effective communicator who exuded optimism about the promise and
potentialities of behaviorist psychology. "Give me a dozen healthy
infants . . . and my own specified world to bring them up in," he famously intoned, he would guarantee to train each one "to become
any type of specialist I might select."* Watson further argued that
behaviorist techniques could be effective tools for promoting social
improvement and reducing bigotry and racial prejudice. Here was

---

See Chapter 9 for details about Watson's ambitious program for behaviorist psychology.

promise of a psychology far different from the "bloodless" and so-cially irrelevant doctrines that had been promoted by Titchener. As a result, Maslow arrived at Wisconsin filled with enthusiasm.

Psychology at Wisconsin

Maslow could not have found a more congenial setting, as his new university fostered progressive values and its small psychology department treated its students cordially and with individual attention. Maslow married his cousin Bertha Goodman during his first year, and the young couple socialized regularly with their fellow students and faculty alike. Among his student cronies was Ross Stagner, who would later become a personality researcher, author of the pioneering text-book mentioned earlier, and a founding member of the SPSSI. The psychology faculty were friendly and approachable and to Maslow's pleasure included several who were "almost evangelistic in their excitement about the behaviorist promise."[40] Best known and most senior among them was Clark L. Hull, who had earned his Ph.D. at Wisconsin in 1918 and remained as a faculty member. In 1928 he was in the early stages of developing his mathematically based "mechanistic behaviorism" (described in Chapter 9), which he would more famously promote soon after moving to Yale. Maslow arrived at Wisconsin just in time to take and enjoy Hull's course on behavioristic experimental psychology.

More directly important for Maslow were two younger psychologists just beginning their careers. **William Sheldon** (1898–1977) was just starting to develop an approach in which he combined behaviorist methodology with a theory about predisposing body types, or "somatotypes." Sheldon classified bodies as being predominantly *ectomorphic* (thin and lightly muscled), *endomorphic* (relatively high on body fat), or *mesomorphic* (muscular) and then investigated the relationships between each body type and differing personality characteristics. Sheldon became Maslow's supportive advisor as he completed his bachelor's degree, teaching him not only psychology but also how to buy a suit that would fit his ectomorphic frame.[41] Then in 1930, just as Maslow was accepted into the Wisconsin's graduate program, a fresh-faced and brand new Ph.D. from Stanford arrived by the name of Harry Harlow. Having studied learning in rats for his dissertation research, Harlow was charged with developing the department's animal laboratory. Wishing it to include animals more humanlike than rats, he joined forces with the local zoo and established the department's soon-to-be-famous Primate Laboratory. Maslow was appointed Harlow's assistant on his first monkey studies and then chose to become his first doctoral student.

Social Behavior in Monkeys

Maslow wanted to study monkeys for several reasons. As a committed behaviorist he knew that his research should be "objective" and free of contamination by subjective or introspective reports. Watson had justified his own early research partly on the grounds that animals could not provide such reports and in that sense were ideal behavioristic subjects. Primates, being close to humans on the phylogenetic scale, held an intrinsic interest all their own and further shared some important *social* characteristics with humans. In particular, Maslow noted that in their colonies they engaged frequently in behavior that could be classified as either sexual, or as related to status on a dominance hierarchy.

Coincidentally, Maslow had been reading with interest some of Freud's works, just coming to wide popular notice in the 1920s, along with the contrasting writings of Freud's one-time disciple **Alfred Adler** (1870–1937) promoting what he called **individual psychology**. Arguing that Freud had overemphasized sexuality, Adler asserted that the deepest source of human motivation lies in the helplessness and weakness of the human infant, which gives rise to an **inferiority complex**. The exact forms of these complexes vary widely, depending on circumstances such as constitutional weaknesses ("organ inferiorities," in Adler's language) and the varying environmental demands placed on the child. A gifted child from whom much is expected, for example, may develop a stronger sense of intellectual inferiority than a subnormal child who is not pressed to succeed. But in all cases, Adler argued, children develop strong motives to cope with and overcome their own perceived inferiorities—in other words, to achieve mastery, power and *dominance* over their environments.

Noting that Freud stressed sexuality while Adler emphasized dominance, Maslow wondered whether systematic observation of monkey behavior might help sort out the relative importance of the two factors. Would their sexual behavior be strongly determined by a monkey's position in the dominance hierarchy, or would social dominance be largely a function of sexual dominance? In the first phase of his dissertation research he spent countless hours unobtrusively observing and recording the spontaneous social behavior of the primates in the local zoo. He identified specific behaviors that reflected dominance, such as preempting food from others, bullying, and staring down competitors. Cringing, running away, or remaining passive under aggression reflected its opposite, submission. Sexual behavior, Maslow noted, "went on all the time,"[42] occurring between both heterosexual and homosexual pairs and from a variety of physical positions. In a second, more experimental phase of the research, twenty pairs of similarly-sized monkeys were food-deprived for a day while isolated in their individual cages and then placed together in a single small chamber where food treats were tossed in. The subsequent behavior could then be classified as sexual, dominant/submissive, or both.

From these extensive observations Maslow concluded that although the sexual and dominance motives had some independent causes (for example, sexual behavior was partly determined by hormonal cycles), in practice they usually interacted with each other. And when they did, he thought that dominance predominated over pure sexuality. Sexual behavior was frequently used as a means of establishing dominance, and in groups where a female was highly dominant the males avoided approaching her sexually at all. Maslow saw his results as giving the edge to Adler over Freud, and it was no coincidence that his first publication summarizing his results appeared in an explicitly Adlerian periodical, the *International Journal of Individual Psychology*, in 1935.[43] A year later he published a much more extensive account of his research in the mainstream *Journal of Genetic Psychology*, thus establishing strong credentials as a pioneering primate researcher. Harlow, who would soon become internationally famous as an investigator of the effects of social isolation and maternal deprivation in monkeys, said of Maslow's research: "To say that [it] was ahead of its time is an understatement of magnificent magnitude."[44] One of the most significant ways in which it was ahead of its time was in its attempt to assess the relative importance of differing motive systems—a theme that Maslow himself would develop to great consequence in his later career.

Maslow's New York Postgraduate Education

Having completed his dissertation, Maslow had to find a job, a difficult enough task for anyone during the depression years and especially so for Jewish candidates. A clear anti-Semitism pervaded most psychology departments and in fact had induced Maslow's supervisor to change his legal surname from its original "Israel" to Harlow despite the fact that he was not a Jew. Some of Maslow's teachers urged him to consider changing his own first name to something less Jewish sounding than Abraham—a suggestion that he vigorously rejected. Thus, despite his outstanding qualifications, all of Maslow's applications for teaching appointments were unsuccessful.[*] Finally, Maslow presented his research in a symposium chaired by the eminent Edward L. Thorndike at the 1935 meeting of the American Psychological Association in Michigan. A deeply impressed Thorndike offered Maslow a postdoctoral fellowship to work as his assistant at Columbia Teachers College on a large project he called Human Nature and the Social Order. Himself a pioneering animal behavior researcher (see Chapter 3), Thorndike had now become more interested in human than in animal research, and a major goal of this project was to determine the relative contributions of heredity versus environment in producing a variety of social behaviors.

Overjoyed to have employment back in his home city of New York, Maslow nonetheless soon began to chafe in the new position. Used to being his own boss while conducting research, he began stealing time from his assigned duties to carry out his own projects. He

---

[*] For more detail on the extraordinary special difficulties encountered by Jewish applicants for academic jobs during this period see Andrew Winston, "'The Defects of His Face': E. G. Boring and Anti-Semitism in American Psychology, 1923–1953," *History of Psychology* 1 (1998): 27–51.

conducted intimate interviews with women subjects regarding their sexual behavior and their tendencies toward dominant personalities. Although the topic derived directly from his previous research on monkeys, his extension of it into the realm of human sexuality was unusual for its time, to say the least. Further, Maslow developed some doubts about Thorndike's basic conceptualization of the nature-nurture question. Thus at the same time that he was conducting unauthorized and potentially scandalous private research within Thorndike's facility, he wrote an extended memorandum to his superior describing his objections to his theory.

Summoned to meet with Thorndike about the memo, Maslow belatedly realized he had been cheeky and feared that he might get fired. Instead, Thorndike's response was "practically angelic."[45] After saying that he did not particularly like the dominance research or agree with the memo, Thorndike added that Maslow had achieved some of the highest scores ever recorded on the aptitude tests he took at the beginning of his fellowship. Asserting confidence in his tests Thorndike went on, "I'll assume that if I give you your head, it'll be the best for you and for me—and for the world."[46] Maslow would be free to work completely on his own for the two years he remained at Teachers' College, and moreover Thorndike would support his applications for full-time teaching jobs.

Even Thorndike's endorsement was minimal help against the pervasive anti-Semitism of the time until finally, in 1937, Maslow obtained a poorly paying and not very prestigious position at Brooklyn College. The job did carry a crucial fringe benefit, however, in that in enabled Maslow to remain in New York. He later recalled: "It's fair to say that I have had the best teachers, both formal and informal, of any person who ever lived, just because of the fortunate accident of being in New York City when the very cream of European intellect was migrating away from Hitler . . . There has been nothing like it since Athens."[47] Indeed, Maslow's experience in the "new Athens" served him much as Allport's German sojourn had done for him, fifteen years earlier—broadening and leavening his original behavioristic viewpoints with a variety of alternatives. On his own initiative he established personal friendships with several neo-Freudian psychoanalysts and Gestalt psychologists who had arrived from Europe, along with some important anthropologists.

An Anthropological Mentor: Ruth Benedict

Maslow's wife Bertha had studied anthropology at Wisconsin, and when her teacher Ralph Linton (1893–1953) moved to New York to become chair of Columbia University's Anthropology Department, the couple renewed acquaintance with him. Through Linton, Maslow got to know several other anthropologists, including **Ruth Benedict** (1887–1948) who especially impressed him with her personal as well as her professional qualities. Benedict had overcome the twin handicaps of being partially deaf and being a woman in a male-dominated field. In 1934 she published the groundbreaking book *Patterns of Culture*, in which she promoted the idea that "culture"—a term that had previously had a rather restricted and technical use within anthropology—could be thought of as analogous to that of "personality" within psychology. Culture was "personality writ large" as one commentator put it.[48] Her book described three ethnic groups whose institutions and customs promoted distinctively different styles of culture. Two of these groups she designated with terms borrowed from the philosopher Friedrich Nietzsche: "Appolonian" culture promoted behavior that was generally rational and restrained, while "Dionysian" societies were exuberant, emotional, and relatively unrestrained. Members of her third type of society, the "Paranoid," tended to be distrustful and antagonistic. Here was a clear connection between anthropology and psychology that fascinated Maslow. Coincidentally, at just the time he was absorbing these ideas, his old Wisconsin friend Ross Stagner was writing his pioneering textbook on personality. Stagner invited Maslow to write a concluding chapter for the book on the relationship between psychology and anthropology, and Maslow obliged with "Personality and Patterns of Culture."

In 1938 Benedict convinced Maslow to spend several weeks living within a Blackfoot Indian community in western Canada. There he gained a firsthand appreciation of the interrelated notions that (a) cultural factors do set conditions within which specific personality traits are more or less likely to occur but that also (b) all human beings share a basic humanity and basic needs that override their cultural differences. He expressed his conclusion in words that echoed Leibniz's contention two centuries before (see Chapter 2) that experience shapes but does not create the mind, which has a preexisting structure: "It would seem that every human being comes at birth into a society not as a lump of clay to be molded by society, but rather as a structure which society may warp or suppress or build upon."[49]

Neo-Freudian Mentors: Adler, Horney, and Fromm

Among the eminent European emigrés Maslow got to know and learn from in New York were three prominent neo-Freudian psycho-analysts. Alfred Adler (see Figure 12.6), whose writing had helped inspire Maslow's dissertation research, now lived in New York and held informal evening seminars at his home. Maslow attended these evenings regularly and soon became a friend and dining companion. From this firsthand contact he learned much more about Adler's theory—perhaps most significantly the notion that a person's original sense of inferiority can often have a *positive* outcome by establishing a powerful motive to overcome it. Adler emphasized cases like that of the ancient Greek Demosthenes who overcame a childhood speech impediment and went on to become the greatest orator of his age; or of the American President Theodore Roosevelt who overcame

FIG 12.6
Alfred Adler
(1870–1937)

a frail and sickly childhood to become the embodiment of vigorous physical activity and accomplishment. Adler further impressed Maslow with his contention that all human beings possess an innate sense of "social interest," an impulse to cooperate productively and even altruistically with their fellows. Although this tendency may be thwarted or distorted by unfortunate early experiences, Adler argued that it was something "primary" that had to be *blocked* by negative factors to inhibit its expression. He contrasted this view to Freud's, which posited a "selfish" search for personal gratification and pleasure as primary, having to be diverted by education and experience into socialized behaviors and interests. The two theories were diametrically opposed on this score.

Maslow also became friendly with the erstwhile Freudians Karen Horney and her younger colleague and friend, **Erich Fromm** (1900–1980). Horney, as noted in Chapter 11, originally clashed with Freud on his theory of female psychology. After emigrating to New York in 1934, she deviated from him even further by deemphasizing infantile sexuality in favor of the view that the child's needs for *security* are more important. Feelings of insecurity often go hand in hand with those of inferiority, so her theory complemented Adler's in many ways. Also deeply impressed by Ruth Benedict and the other New York anthropologists, Horney strongly emphasized the role of culture in determining normal and abnormal behavioral patterns. In a course titled "Culture and Neurosis" she extended her critique of Freud's theory by arguing that it is male-dominated culture rather than anatomy that primarily determines the typical differences between masculine and feminine personalities.

Although trained as a Freudian analyst, Erich Fromm's orthodoxy had been tempered by exposure to the neo-Marxist social theories prevalent at the University of Frankfurt's Institute for Social Research, where he worked prior to emigrating to New York. Once in New York he became a teaching colleague of Ralph Linton's and adopted many of the same anthropological ideas as Maslow. During the early years of their friendship Fromm was working on his first book, the hugely successful *Escape from Freedom* (1941). Among the ideas he was developing was the conviction that human beings are unique among animal life by their relative freedom from domination by their instincts. Born helpless and then dependent on others during a protracted childhood, they eventually *learn* how to manipulate their environment and make conscious decisions among innumerable possible alternatives.

Expanded freedom and consciousness come at a price, however, in the awareness of what Fromm later called "existential dichotomies"— intractable problems that are an inevitable part of the human condition. Choosing freely to do or to be one particular thing, for example, inevitably rules out the alternatives: the "road not taken" situation memorialized by the poet Robert Frost. Accordingly, one person can achieve only a small fraction of possibilities that open up to him or her. Further, human intelligence brings with it a conscious knowledge of mortality and of the fact that one lives and dies as an isolated individual, albeit in a society populated with fellow humans. The struggle to retain one's individuality within a society can pose difficulties, particularly in societies whose institutions and customs promote maladaptive ways of "escaping from freedom." Writing as a European emigrant in the late 1930s, Fromm was particularly concerned about those totalitarian and fascistic societies in which individuality was suppressed by rigid authoritarian controls. He also saw potential dangers in democratic societies, however, particularly in their pressures toward consumerism, conformity, and "going along with the crowd." In his later writings Fromm (see Figure 12.7) increasingly emphasized these dangers in his adoptive homeland.

Through his friendly interaction with these diverse theorists, Maslow came away not with a confirmed or unified theoretical view of human nature but rather with a sense of the diversity and complexity of human motivation. He came to view humans as motivated not by a single, "sovereign" motive (such as Freudian sexuality) but instead by a complex network of biological, personal, social and cultural factors.

Gestalt Mentors: Wertheimer and Goldstein

Like Gordon Allport, young Maslow had his psychological views transformed by personal experience with the German Gestalt psychologists. After attending lectures by Max Wertheimer at the New School for Social Research, Maslow made a point of getting to know

FIG 12.7
Erich Fromm
(1900–1980)

him personally. Particularly impressive to Maslow was Wertheimer's extension of the Gestalt point of view from its original focus on perception to the general subjects of learning and creativity. Wertheimer argued that the most important kind of learning does not occur by the gradual and laborious trial-and-error process emphasized by many American behaviorists; rather he saw it as occurring in sudden flashes of insight, in those "Aha!" moments that are often reported by creative people. The experience is somewhat akin to the sudden perception of a Gestalt in the classic demonstrations, as when the figure and ground suddenly shift and a pair of black profiles become replaced in consciousness by the perception of a white vase, or vice versa (see Chapter 4). Wertheimer argued that something similar occurs in complex problem situations when suddenly, in a flash as it were, the components of a puzzling situation are put together in a novel way.

Informal and congenial in manner, Wertheimer struck Maslow as impressive as a person as he was as a psychologist. An almost father-son-like relationship developed between the two, as Wertheimer took

FIG 12.8 Max Wertheimer and Abraham Maslow sharing the lecture stage at Brooklyn College in New York City in the 1930s

an active interest in the younger man and encouraged him in ways that his real father never could (see Figure 12.8). In doing so he imparted two related ideas or "lessons" that would prove crucial to Maslow's later career. First, he emphasized the strong feelings of joy and other positive emotions that often accompany those Aha moments when suddenly the world is perceived in a new and appreciative way. Maslow would later refer to these as **peak experiences** and attempt to study them systematically. And in a related but more general sense, Wertheimer argued that traditional psychology placed too much emphasis on illness and maladjustment and not enough on these and other *positive* aspects of human experience. Maslow would later take this lesson particularly to heart, and become famous for doing so.

Through Wertheimer Maslow met and also became friendly with the neurologist Kurt Goldstein (see Figure 12.9). As noted in Chapter 4, Goldstein had applied Gestalt concepts in his analysis of brain-injured soldiers, noting that the brain as a whole seemed to try to take over the functions affected by damage to its specific smaller parts. He referred to the overarching tendency of the human "organism" to maintain its integrity and wholeness in the face of injury to its parts

FIG 12.9
Kurt Goldstein
(1878–1965)

as a motive toward "self-actualization." Maslow would later adopt that term in his own motivational theory—although in a somewhat different sense from Goldstein's, and of which the older neurologist did not fully approve.

In sum, while still a young psychologist in New York Maslow underwent an informal but remarkable postgraduate education that expanded his outlook in many ways. From the anthropologists he learned that "human nature" is considerably broader than most psychologists assumed; from his neo-Freudian friends he learned that a multiplicity of motives may be posited to explain human behavior, many of them social and impelling people toward positive goals (and not just the avoidance of negative states or circumstances); and from the Gestaltists he learned to emphasize creativity and positivity in the thought processes.

Maslow's Theory of Human Motivation

All of these ideas intermingled as Maslow began his teaching career at Brooklyn College. Assigned to teach abnormal psychology, he became popular with students, who frequently came to him for informal counseling in which he was able to put many of the ideas of his clinical mentors to the test. At the same time—influenced by Wertheimer's emphasis on positivity and probably also by Allport's recently published textbook contending that depth psychologies are not always appropriate for explaining well-adjusted individuals— he saw the need for a new course dedicated to the normal, healthy personality. He began offering such a course in 1940, even as he was collaborating with the psychiatrist Bela Mittleman in writing *Principles of Abnormal Psychology: The Dynamics of Psychic Illness* (1941). One of the very first abnormal psychology texts, this book tellingly opened with an extended chapter by Maslow on psychological normality and health, as a counterpoint to the material about maladjustment and illness that followed it.

Self-actualization

Maslow's interest in psychological health had been stimulated by interactions with his New York mentors, who had impressed him as much by their personal as by their intellectual qualities. Ruth Benedict and Max Wertheimer particularly stood out, and Maslow later recalled that his investigations

> did not start out as research [but] as the effort of a young intellectual to understand two of his teachers whom he loved, adored and admired and who were very, very wonderful people. I . . . sought to understand why these two people were so different from the run-of-the-mill people in the world . . . They were puzzling. They didn't fit. It was as if they came from a different planet.[50]

Even granting that Maslow may have overidealized his mentors to some degree, they were unquestionably productive and creative, sociable and altruistic, and they seemed *not* to be driven by any of the deprivation-based motivational systems posited by most clinical theories. Further, their most prominent needs and urges seemed to come from within themselves and to be minimally derived from the environmentally based rewards and punishments emphasized by the behaviorists. In trying to put a summarizing descriptive label on these extremely healthy individuals, Maslow seized on a term he had heard used by Kurt Goldstein in a different context: "self-actualized." For Goldstein self-actualization had referred to efforts of brain-damaged people to regain or retain their sense of organic integrity and wholeness. For Maslow, the term suggested the tendency of intact and extremely psychologically healthy people to fulfill the potential within themselves.* As he put it, **self-actualization** occurs when "the individual is doing what he is fitted for. A musician must make music, an artist must paint, a poet must write, if he is to be ultimately happy. What a man *can* be, he *must* be . . . This tendency might be phrased as the desire to become more and more what one is, to become everything that one is capable of being."[51]

The Hierarchy of Needs

Having developed an idea of the type of motives that most strongly influence the healthiest of people, Maslow next considered the question of how strivings for self-actualization needs interact with, or are influenced by, the more primal and "base" urges that dominate behavior in less highly functional people. His solution—brilliant in its simplicity and constituting his most famous theoretical contribution to psychology—was the concept of motives as arranged in a *hierarchy*. His explosive original statement of this appeared in the 1943 *Psychological Review* article "A Theory of Human Motivation."

Maslow began his argument by noting that under conditions of extreme deprivation the motives of hunger and thirst are unquestionably paramount:

> It is quite true that man lives by bread alone—where there is no bread . . . But what happens to man's desires when there is plenty of bread and his belly is chronically filled? . . . *At once other (and "higher") needs emerge* and these, rather than physiological

---

* Although Goldstein may have been miffed at Maslow for expropriating "his" term, in fact "self-actualization" had been used even before him, by nineteenth-century philosophers such as Kierkegaard, Nietzsche, and Marx, and in senses closer to Maslow's than to Goldstein's. Maslow himself seems to have been unaware that he was actually returning to an older use of the term.

hungers, dominate the organism. And when these in turn are satisfied, again new (and still "higher") needs emerge and so on. This is what we mean by saying that the basic human needs are organized into a hierarchy of relative prepotency.[52]

Borrowing the term from Henry Murray, Maslow went on to propose five general categories of "needs" arranged hierarchically. The most elemental ones, whose lack of satisfaction is physically catastrophic for the individual and which dominate every other concern if unmet, are the **physiological needs**. When these needs are met (as they almost always are within modern civilized society), the next ones to arise are the **safety needs**: the requirement to be protected from threats by predators, criminals, extremes of climate and temperature, or other hazardous environmental circumstances. Maslow noted that these needs, too, are routinely satisfied in civilized societies, apart from episodic and "accidental" crisis situations. They do, however, manifest themselves quite clearly in children, who frequently and overtly express their fears about real or imagined dangers, and also strikingly in the symptoms of many neurotic patients—for example, irrational phobias and other expressions of unjustified anxiety.

Once physiological and safety concerns have been satisfied, the **love needs** become prominent—strong desires for affection, friendship, and a sense of belongingness within a social group. These needs can interact with but are essentially independent of the more physiologically based sexual urge. Maslow believed that frustrations in the satisfaction of love needs are quite common in modern society, noting that "practically all theorists of psychopathology have stressed the thwarting of love needs as basic in the picture of maladjustment."[53] If these needs have been satisfied, however, what Maslow called **esteem needs** rise to the surface. These needs include

desire for a stable, firmly based, (usually) high evaluation of themselves, for self-respect, or self-esteem, and for the esteem of others. By firmly based self-esteem, we mean that which is soundly based upon real capacity, achievement and respect from others . . . Satisfaction of the self-esteem need leads to feelings of self-confidence, worth, strength, capability and adequacy of being useful and necessary in the world. But thwarting of these needs produces feelings of inferiority, of weakness and of helplessness.[54]

Only when these first four levels of needs have been adequately satisfied do the highest needs for self-actualization come strongly into play. The entire hierarchy is frequently represented as a pyramid such as the one in Figure 12.10, with each higher level resting on a broader foundation of the lower satisfactions. Maslow's paragons of psychological health, then, were people sufficiently satisfied in their "lower" needs that they were freed up to pursue the full creative potential within themselves. In later writings Maslow would characterize the four lower levels as **deprivation needs** because they are created by *deficiencies* in a person's life. These contrast with the **being needs** for self-actualization, which urge the individual toward the positive fulfillment of *potentialities* within the self.

A Positive Approach to Psychology

In the years immediately following the publication of this theory, Maslow became increasingly upset by what he saw as mainstream psychology's overemphasis on the lower, deprivation needs, the abnormal,

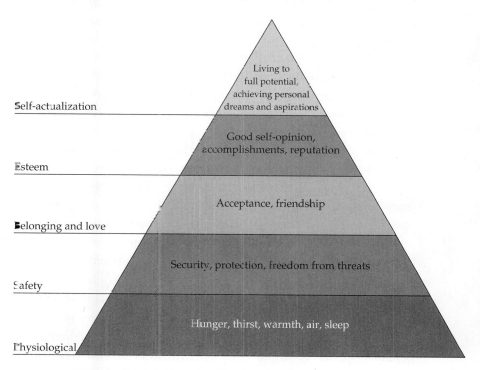

FIG 12.10 Maslow's Hierarchy of Needs pyramid

and the deficient. "The psychology of 1949 is largely a psychology of cripples and sick people, . . . based upon the study of men at their worst," he declaimed. Behavioristic research on animal learning was no help because "even the greatest human genius could not show his intelligence" on even the most difficult of mazes or other standard learning problems.[55]

Accordingly, Maslow began to examine the life histories of people whom he considered to be self-actualized, starting with Benedict and Wertheimer whom he knew personally but then extending to the biographies of famous figures such as Thomas Jefferson, Albert Einstein, Eleanor Roosevelt, and the African American scientist George Washington Carver. He also tried to identify a group of college students who could be described as self-actualized. He presented his main results, preceded by an exposition of his hierarchical theory of motivation, in his 1954 book, *Motivation and Personality.*

Maslow identified several characteristics that distinguished his self-actualized subjects in their maturity. They tended to be unusually *objective* and *"efficient"* in their perceptions of reality, arriving at accurate judgments about people or situations quickly and with minimal distortion from their emotions. They also showed unusually high *acceptance*, both of themselves and of others as inevitably imperfect human beings. They were *spontaneous* and *natural* rather than artificial or pretentious, were *problem centered* and not easily distracted from their tasks at hand, and showed a vibrant but nonhostile *sense of humor.* Virtually by definition they were *creative*, and *independent* in their judgments.

Borrowing a term from Fromm, Maslow noted that self-actualizers tended to be very good at the "resolution of dichotomies"—at finding and performing behaviors that satisfy two apparently opposing motives at the same time. For example, they could manage to be at once unselfish in fostering the welfare of others but selfish in finding great personal gratification and meaning in the act of doing so. Maslow also found that many if not all his self-actualized subjects experienced various forms of the *peak experiences* originally called to his attention by Wertheimer. Sometimes these were moments of overwhelming joy upon arriving at a specific new discovery or insight; Maslow's own ecstatic response on reading Watson and realizing that psychology could be his own "calling" might be one example. Other peak experiences were described by their subjects as more "mystical" in nature: sudden, overwhelming sensations or beauty, harmony, and oneness with the world. Maslow concluded his description of self-actualizers by saying that in these ways,

> Healthy people are so different from average ones, not only in degree but in kind as well, that they generate two very different kinds of psychology. It becomes more and more clear that the study of crippled, stunted, immature and unhealthy specimens can yield only a cripple psychology and a cripple philosophy. The study of self-actualizing people must be the basis for a more universal science of psychology.[56]

In 1954 Maslow referred to the new and more universal science as "Positive Psychology," and his book concluded with a brief Appendix titled "Problems Generated by a Positive Approach to Psychology."[57] Here he briefly discussed the major traditional content areas (e.g., learning, perception, motivation, intelligence, social psychology and personality) and offered brief suggestions as to how each might be pursued, with greater emphasis on the positive efforts of the best and most creative individuals rather than on the stumbling blocks. In learning, for example, behaviors and skills acquired via curiosity or internally driven desires to know should be emphasized, as opposed to trial-and-error learning motivated by hunger or other deprivation-driven motives. In social psychology, traditional topics such as suggestibility, prejudice, obedience and power should be at least supplemented by studies of altruism, individualism, freedom, and democratic tolerance.

Establishing a Humanistic Psychology

Motivation and Personality consolidated Maslow's reputation as an important and innovative voice in psychology. Even before its publication he was attracting favorable notice, and the virulent anti-Semitism that had limited his employment opportunities in the late 1930s was beginning to wane. In 1951 he received an offer he could not refuse when he was approached by the brand new Brandeis University in Waltham, MA, to see whether he would be interested in becoming the founding chair of its Psychology Department. Although Jewish-sponsored and named after the eminent Jewish Supreme Court Justice Louis Brandeis, the school was intended from the beginning to be nonsectarian in its hiring and admissions policies. Albert Einstein and the composer/conductor Leonard Bernstein were among the new school's famous sponsors and fundraisers, so here was a potentially prestigious institution that promised to practice the kind of tolerance and nondiscrimination Maslow believed in. Moreover, he would be given a free hand in selecting the key personnel in a brand new psychology department.

Although he could have opted to hire exclusively or primarily those who shared his personal views, he chose instead to bring together a diverse faculty with widely differing orientations. These included staunch behaviorists and experimentalists, as well as clinicians from varying schools and his old mentor Kurt Goldstein. Among the most notable of his later appointments was a young Ulric Neisser, whom we shall meet in Chapter 14 as a major founding influence on the hugely successful new field of cognitive psychology.

Even as he was establishing a diverse department at Brandeis, however, Maslow continued in his writings and involvements in the larger outside world to promote his vision of a positive psychology. Noting the relative dominance of behaviorism and psychoanalysis (broadly conceived) as movements in mainstream psychology, he called for the establishment of a new and different "third force." He found several important allies in this venture, who joined with him in creating the institutions for a *humanistic psychology*.

Humanistic Allies: Rogers, May, and Allport

Among the most important of Maslow's new allies was the "client-centered" psychotherapist **Carl Rogers** (1902–1987; see Figure 12.11). Six years older than Maslow, Rogers coincidentally had preceded him at both Wisconsin and Columbia Teachers College. At Wisconsin Rogers started as an agricultural student before switching to religion to prepare for the ministry. Then as a student at the Union Theological Seminary in New York he attended a seminar on the subject of "Why Am I Entering the Ministry?"—which convinced him that his true vocation lay elsewhere. He wound up in the clinical psychology program at neighboring Columbia Teachers College. After gaining his degree he worked first as a child therapist and then as a counselor for university students. From 1945 through 1957—the period when

FIG 12.11
Carl Rogers
(1902–1987)

Maslow got to know him well—Rogers was a professor and director of the counseling center at the University of Chicago.

From his experience in dealing with bright but troubled young adults, Rogers gradually abandoned the Freudian and neo-Freudian techniques in which he had been trained while developing his own unique approach. This he described most fully in his 1951 book, *Client-Centered Therapy*—the title of which accurately epitomized its approach and philosophy. In the traditional psychotherapies in which Rogers had been trained, the therapist would periodically interrupt the patient's free associations or other accounts to interject *interpretations* of the material based on the therapist's own theoretical system; for example, a Freudian would interpret in terms of repressed childhood sexuality, an Adlerian in terms of perceived inferiorities, and so on. Rogers, by contrast, came to believe that the validity of any particular "insights" should be determined not by their conformity with some preexisting theory held by the therapist but by his "clients" themselves. Rogers's deliberately chose the term "client" instead of the traditional "patient" to designate the recipients of his therapy because it implied a greater sense of equality between him and them in mutual partnerships.

Consistently with this orientation, Rogers developed a "nondirective" counseling approach that was epitomized by a technique he called **reflection**—essentially, the mirroring back to the client the substance of what he or she just said but in different words. The reflection is intended to demonstrate that the therapist is genuinely listening and trying to understand what is being said, while encouraging further exploration of the issue under discussion. Additionally, the therapist must consistently try to react to the client with an unthreatening respect or *unconditional positive regard*. Within this highly accepting, empathic, and facilitative setting the client may come to an increasing sense of self-awareness, which may help relieve or mitigate the problem. On a higher theoretical level, Rogers believed that everyone is born with a healthy growth-oriented inclination called an "actualizing tendency" and that problems arise when feelings of low self-worth derail people from this natural tendency. Thus, in his language, as well as his conviction that human beings should be approached by emphasizing the positive, Rogers was very much in tune with Maslow.

Maslow and Rogers came together with other psychologists of similar persuasion at numerous conferences and professional society meetings. Among the most important was the "Symposium on Existential Psychology" held at the 1959 meeting of the American Psychological Association and organized by the American psychologist and therapist **Rollo May** (1909–1994; see Figure 12.12). Trained like Rogers at Union Theological Seminary, where he earned a bachelor of divinity degree, May subsequently spent three years confined to a sanatorium with a dangerous case of tuberculosis. Confronting the very real possibility of an early death, May read deeply in the writings of existentialist philosophers, and their interpretations by his theology professor and friend Paul Tillich. After recovery he obtained a clinical psychology degree from Columbia, and went on to develop an **existential psychotherapy** that emphasized the *quest for meaning* in life as the paramount issue for modern humanity. Although somewhat more somber in its implications than the theories of Maslow and Rogers, this quest for meaning bore significant similarity to their drives for "actualization." Thus, the three were natural allies in their promotion of a nonreductionistic third force in psychology that would emphasize the attainment of positive goals and self-fulfillment.

The group found a natural "elder statesman" for their movement in the person of Gordon Allport, who also participated in the

FIG 12.12
Rollo May
(1909–1994)

symposium. Although never a therapist, Allport had famously and for many years emphasized the importance of studying "normality" and of taking people's own accounts of themselves seriously. Together with his promotion of nonreductive idiographic methods, these ideas resonated strongly with the younger third-forcers' basic inclinations. Allport's contribution to May's symposium noted that what traditional psychologies regard as "symptoms" become transformed into an understandable grappling with existential problems under the newer theoretical viewpoints.

In 1960 May published all of the papers delivered at the symposium in a short volume that is considered by many to have launched the third force as a recognizable *movement* in psychology. The movement gained momentum the following year when Maslow joined with a growing number of like-minded scholars to establish a new *Journal of Humanistic Psychology*, with himself as co-editor and May, Erich Fromm, and Kurt Goldstein among the members of a distinguished editorial board. The journal attracted enough subscribers that its founders were encouraged to establish a new formal organization, the Association for Humanistic Psychology. Thanks in part to a grant obtained by Allport, the group held its inaugural meeting in Philadelphia in 1963.

The following year a special invitational conference was held in Old Saybrook, Connecticut, where the philosophy, aims, and themes for the new association were discussed. It attracted a distinguished cast of participants from America and abroad and may fairly be said to have put humanistic psychology "on the map" of public consciousness.[58]

Maslow's Late Writings and the Legacy of Positive Psychology

Maslow contributed several articles to the new journal he co-edited. Among the most influential was one presenting the results of a "thought experiment" in which he imagined the kind of community that would be produced by a thousand self-actualizing people and their families stranded together on a desert island. Calling this utopian society **eupsychia**, he tried to imagine institutions that would foster maximum freedom for people to realize their full potential. In an interesting aside, he noted that all of the previous depictions of utopian societies had been written by men and that his eupsychia would differ from them by including the interests and values of self-actualized women.[59]

As the 1960s progressed Maslow found himself becoming internationally famous, cited often in the popular media as a representative of a new and "liberated" psychology. His notion of eupsychia was adopted by some influential organizational psychologists in attempts to develop management strategies that promote self-actualization. And to his surprise and pleasure, he was formally recognized by mainstream psychologists when elected president of the American Psychological Association in 1968.

Also throughout the late 1960s, however, his health was gradually failing. Perhaps more than coincidentally, his work on a revised edition of *Motivation and Personality* showed a subtle but significant darkening of his mood. Parts of the new edition, including the Appendix outlining his program for a positive psychology, remained unchanged from the first. But whereas the first edition had expressed optimism about identifying and fostering future self-actualizers among the college population, the second declared this situation to be virtually impossible. The full criteria for self-actualization required time and maturation to be fully met, and many of the most promising of the college students Maslow studied in the early years had failed abjectly to realize their promise. He had come to appreciate that "growth is often a painful process" in which many things can go wrong. Consistently with this revised thinking, he now asserted that a thorough knowledge of psychopathology and depth psychology is "a necessary prophylactic" against overly optimistic illusions and that "Freud is still required reading for the humanistic psychologist."[60] In the same vein he insisted in a 1969 article that the third force of humanistic psychology must *not* be thought of as antagonistic to psychoanalysis but rather as *including* and *building upon* it. He coined the term "epi-Freudian" to describe his attitude—*epi*, the Greek word for "upon"—to avoid the "sophomoric, two-valued, dichotomized orientation . . . of being either pro-Freudian or anti-Freudian."[61]

In a further cautionary note Maslow's second edition emphasized that the state of self-actualization, while highly desirable, does not bring with it constant happiness and bliss. Perhaps drawing from his personal experience he now proposed a "grumble theory": the notion that the gratification of any need, even of the very highest, self-actualizing sort, produces a happiness that is only transient. Quickly enough something else inevitably comes up and demands satisfaction. "The human hope for eternal happiness can never be fulfilled," he declared. Although genuine happiness "does come and is obtainable and is real," it also has an "intrinsic transience . . . [and] is episodic, not continuous."[62]

In June 1970, shortly after these words had been written but before they were published, Maslow died of a sudden heart attack—at just 62 and at the peak of his reputation and mental powers. Like Gordon Allport, he had significantly broadened the field of psychology and left an enduring legacy. The institutions Maslow created never quite achieved the "mainstream" status within psychology that he originally hoped for, but they still exist under slightly different names as the *Society* for Humanistic Psychology (Division 32 of the American Psychological Association) and its affiliated journal *The Humanistic Psychologist*. But on the conceptual level, his hierarchical motivational theory is still widely taught, and the term *self-actualization* has entered the popular psychological lexicon.

Further, some distinctly Maslovian ideas have moved very much into the mainstream with the recent movement called **positive psychology**, promoted by the former APA President **Martin Seligman** (b. 1942) and his associates. Early in his career Seligman introduced the influential concept of "learned helplessness" as a major factor in depressive conditions—a factor that could often be overcome through cognitive behavioral therapy. Sometime in the late 1980s, he experienced a sort of epiphany whose nature is captured in the title of the article about him, "Martin Seligman's Journey from Learned Helplessness to Learned Happiness," as well as that of his own 1991 book *Learned Optimism: How to Change Your Mind and Your Life*.[63] In an explicit echo of Maslow, Seligman now argued that mainstream psychology has tended to overfocus on understanding and overcoming pathological and abnormal conditions, at the expense of studying psychological positivity, health, and the conditions that promote happiness. Elected president of the American Psychological Association in 1998, Seligman designated positive psychology as the organization's official theme for his presidential year. At his base at the University of Pennsylvania, Seligman and his colleagues established a Positive Psychology Center designed to promote "the scientific study of the strengths and virtues that enable individuals and communities to thrive." Besides sponsoring an extensive research program, the center also offers a master's level training program in Applied Positive Psychology. The movement attracted worldwide attention, culminating in 2007 with the establishment of the International Positive Psychology Association (IPPA)—an organization that currently has some 3000 members from 70 countries.[64]

Summary

As a graduate student, **Gordon W. Allport** became interested in the emerging concept of "personality" that was just beginning to be studied by psychologists. Influenced by his Harvard mentors, his older brother Floyd, and his exposure to psychoanalytic ideas and early personality tests, Allport focused his dissertation on developing a general model of the composition of personality. In this work he proposed the concept of the **trait** as an important unit of personality and assessed Harvard undergraduates on four sets of traits, thus demonstrating the promise of a *systematic* study of personality that would be further developed in the years to come.

After his dissertation work, Allport traveled to Germany and was heavily influenced by the holistic, top-down approach of the Gestalt psychologists and the Gestalt-like personality theory of **William Stern**. He returned to

Harvard as an instructor and delivered the first course in personality psychology. He then published the first textbook in the field in 1937. In this book, he emphasized the limitations of psychoanalytic theory for understanding *normal* personality development, insisting that in most cases, conscious self-reports could be taken at face value and normal adult behavior need not be pathologized with reference to childhood experiences. He also made the important distinction between **nomothetic** and **idiographic** research methods, arguing that both methods were needed to produce a complete psychology of personality.

The nomothetic research tradition was subsequently developed by **Raymond B. Cattell** and **Hans J. Eysenck**, both of whom developed personality models based on factor analyses of self-ratings on large numbers of trait terms. The idiographic research tradition was carried on by **Henry A. Murray** and his colleagues at the Harvard Psychological Clinic, and is today represented by the many personological psychologists who conduct in-depth studies of individual lives.

Like Allport, **Abraham H. Maslow** also made important contributions to understanding the normal healthy personality. Although originally trained in the systematic observation of animal behavior in the laboratory, Maslow was subsequently exposed to a much wider scope of psychological thinking. Through the influences of several post-graduate intellectual mentors, including **Ruth Benedict, Alfred Adler, Max Wertheimer,** and **Erich Fromm,** Maslow developed an expansive outlook on human motivation that proved foundational for his theoretical innovations. He became interested in uncovering and describing the conditions under which people achieve their highest levels of potential, a state he called **self-actualization**. His most famous contribution to psychology, the *hierarchy* of needs, describes the motivational stages through which individuals move on their path toward self-actualization.

Concerned that psychology was becoming excessively oriented around a deficiency model of human functioning, Maslow then turned his attention to the qualities inherent to a self-actualized personality. He did this by studying the lives of people who he considered to have achieved self-actualization, many of whom described having **peak experiences**. He then proposed an approach to psychology that would focus on the growth-enhancing, positive aspects of human motivation, as distinguished from the more pessimistic and deterministic views of behaviorism and psychoanalysis. This approach became known as the "third force" of **humanistic psychology**. Maslow was joined by several allies in his endeavor to establish this new area, including **Carl Rogers, Rollo May,** and Gordon Allport. The field of humanistic psychology continues to this day and has been joined by a related contemporary movement called **positive psychology**.

Key Pioneers

Adler, Alfred, p. 535

Allport, Gordon W., p. 506

Benedict, Ruth, p. 539

Cattell, Raymond B., p. 520

Downey, June Etta, p. 512

Eysenck, Hans J., p. 522

Fromm, Erich, p. 511

Harlow, Harry, p. 508

Hartmann, Heinz, p. 520

Jung, Carl G., p. 512

Langer, Walter, p. 526

Lindzey, Gardner, p. 529

Maslow, Abraham H., p. 507

May, Rollo, p. 554

McClelland, David, p. 525

Morgan, Christiana, p. 524

Murray, Henry A., p. 524

Pettigrew, Thomas, p. 529

Rapaport, David, p. 520

Rogers, Carl, p. 552

Seligman, Martin, p. 557

Sheldon, William, p. 534

Stagner, Ross, p. 516

Stern, William, p. 515

Vernon, Phillip, p. 516

Key Terms

agreeableness, p. 523

analytical psychology, p. 513

being needs, p. 549

Big Five, p. 523

conscientiousness, p. 523

contact hypothesis, p. 528

deprivation needs, p. 549

ego psychology, p. 520

esteem needs, p. 548

eupsychia, p. 556

existential psychotherapy, p. 554

extroversion, p. 513

functional autonomy, p. 520

humanistic psychology, p. 508

idiographic methods, p. 517

immature religion, p. 527

individual psychology (Adler), p. 535

Individual Will Temperament
   Test, p. 512

inferiority complex, p. 535

introversion, p. 513

love needs, p. 548

mature religion, p. 527

neuroticism, p. 523

nomothetic methods, p. 517

openness, p. 523

peak experiences, p. 544

PEN model, p. 523

Personal Data Sheet, p. 512

personalistic psychology, p. 515

personality psychology, p. 560

physiological needs, p. 548

positive psychology, p. 557

presses (environmental), p. 525

psychobiography, p. 526

psychogenic needs, p. 525

psychoticism, p. 523

real individuality, p. 515

reflection, p. 554

relational individuality, p. 515

safety needs, p. 548

self-actualization, p. 547

Sixteen Personality Factor
   Questionnaire (16 PF), p. 522

Thematic Apperception Test (TAT),
   p. 524

trait (personality), p. 514

word association test, p. 512

Discussion Questions and Topics

1 Gordon Allport asserted that a complete understanding of personality requires both idiographic and nomothetic research strategies. Define these two strategies and give an example of work undertaken in each of these traditions, as discussed in the chapter.

2 As Abraham Maslow developed his ideas about human motivation, he distinguished his approach from that of Freud in several ways. Explain how Maslow differed from Freud, especially via the influence of his neo-Freudian mentors.

3 Both Allport and Maslow made important institutional as well as theoretical contributions to the fields of personality psychology and humanistic psychology respectively. Describe some of these institutional contributions and what role they might play in establishing the legitimacy of a new field.

Suggested Readings

Gordon Allport's short autobiography, along with several other of his very readable later articles, appears in his book *The Person in Psychology: Selected Essays* (Boston: Beacon Press, 1968). His early life and career are described in much more detail in Ian Nicholson's *Inventing Personality: Gordon Allport and the Science of Selfhood* (Washington, DC: American Psychological Association, 2003), a work that also captures the more general intellectual and cultural climate that gave rise to personality psychology. Several interesting essays about Allport and other personality psychology pioneers may be found in Kenneth H. Craik, Robert Hogan, and Raymond N. Wolfe (eds.), *Fifty Years of Personality Psychology* (New York: Plenum Press, 1993). Allport's first textbook, *Personality: A Psychological Interpretation* (New York: Henry Holt and Company), may seem overly dense to the casual reader, but he provides a more accessible account of most of his central ideas in the later *Pattern and Growth in Personality* (New York: Holt, Rinehart and Winston, 1961).

Edward Hoffman's revised edition of *The Right to Be Human: A Biography of Abraham Maslow* (New York: McGraw-Hill, 1999) presents a full and sympathetic account of Maslow's life and work. Maslow's posthumously published *Motivation and Personality*, 2nd edition (New York: Harper & Row, 1970), is interesting for its presentation of his basic ideas, as well of the changes his thinking underwent in the latter part of his career.

Maslow's classic paper "A Theory of Human Motivation," as well as several important articles by Gordon Allport, are easily accessible online via the Web site *Classics in the History of Psychology* (http://psychclassics.yorku.ca/).

The Developing Mind

Alfred Binet, Jean Piaget, and the
Study of Human Intelligence

13

Binet's Early Life and Career
Individual Psychology

The Binet Intelligence Scales
The 1905 Tests
The 1908 and 1911 Scales

The Rise of Intelligence Testing

Piaget's Early Life and Career

Genetic Epistemology

Piagetian Influences

Summary

Key Pioneers

Key Terms

Discussion Questions and Topics

Suggested Readings

In the late 1880s, the beleaguered young psychologist **Alfred Binet** (1857–1911; see Figure 13.1) found instruction as well as welcome diversion by observing the behavior of his two young daughters, Madeleine and Alice. As the outspoken disciple of Jean Charcot and supporter of the fanciful theory of *grand hypnotisme* (described in Chapter 10), Binet found himself under increasing professional attack at work. But at home he was enchanted by the growing abilities of his girls, and as an inveterate experimenter he could not resist trying out several new psychological tests he had read about. These home experiments yielded data for three scientific publications and produced some important new attitudes in Binet about the nature and measurement of intelligence.[1]

FIG 13.1
Alfred Binet
(1857–1911)

Some of the tests measured reaction time and sensory acuity, following the recent model of Francis Galton's Anthropometric Laboratory. As shown in Chapter 7, Galton hypothesized that innate and hereditary intelligence would be associated with powerful and efficient nervous systems. His tests were intended primarily for young adults, but Binet tried them on his much younger daughters and was surprised at what he found. When they paid attention to the task of reaction time, the girls responded just as quickly as normal adults. They did not always pay attention, however, and so had slower *average* reaction times than adults. But Binet thought this finding signified a difference between children and adults in *attention*, not in underlying neurological reactivity or sensitivity. Further, on tests of sensory acuity requiring the discrimination of variously sized angles or the matching of colors, 3-year-old Alice did almost as well as normal adults, and 5-year-old Madeleine scored slightly *better.*

Tests that did show major differences between children and adults required skills largely untapped by Galton's measures. Binet's daughters could not *name* the colors printed on strips of paper as quickly as adults, for example, even though they could discriminate and match the same colors by sight just as well. And when asked to define simple everyday objects, the children did not offer formal "definitions" as adults would but responded by describing immediate actions or purposes. For example, a knife "is to cut meat," a box "is to put candies in," and a snail was, simply and emphatically, "Squash it!"[2]

At this point in his career, Binet was not concerned with measuring different levels of intelligence as Galton and some others had been. But the experiments left him with a permanent distrust of Galton's whole general approach to testing. When young children with manifestly undeveloped intellects could approach or match the performance of adults, such measures hardly seemed promising discriminators of intelligence *between* adults or anyone else. Much more promising, it seemed, would be tests involving "higher" and more complex functions such as language and abstract reasoning. A decade and a half later, when Binet finally did turn his attention to the specific problems of developing an intelligence test, these attitudes would bear fruit and enable him to succeed where Galton and many others had failed.

Binet was not the only pioneer investigator of intelligence to learn from his children. Some thirty years after Binet's first experiments with Madeleine and Alice, the Swiss psychologist **Jean Piaget** (1896–1980) systematically observed the behavior of his daughter Jacqueline and her cousin Gérard in looking for lost objects. A chance observation of 13-month-old Gérard at play with a ball started things off. First the ball rolled under an armchair where Gérard could still see it; he crawled after it and retrieved it. Later the ball disappeared from his sight under a fringed sofa on the other side of the room. After just a cursory glance at the sofa, Gérard crossed the room to the *armchair* and searched for the lost ball in the place he had found it the time before.

From this "irrational" reaction, Piaget inferred that the baby Gérard lacked an adult's sense of the ball as a distinct "object," independent and separate from himself and his perception of it. Subsequently, as Piaget's daughter Jacqueline passed through infancy he carefully studied her developing grasp of what he called the **object concept**. During her earliest months, she acted as if objects ceased to exist as soon as they left her immediate sensory awareness. For example, when Piaget placed a toy in front of her she reached to get it, but she immediately stopped when he blocked her view of it with his hand or a screen. When he placed a cloth over the toy, in full view, she made no attempt to remove the cloth and recover the toy. By 11 months she would search actively and successfully for such hidden objects, while still showing a limitation reminiscent of Gérard: When Piaget placed a toy parrot under bedcovers to Jacqueline's immediate left, she promptly retrieved it; but when he next ostentatiously hid it under covers on her right, she looked for it where she had been successful before, on the left. At 21 months, however, she was fully proficient at locating hidden objects, as Piaget documented in the following report:

> I put a coin in my hand, then put my hand under a coverlet. I withdraw my hand closed; Jacqueline opens it and finds nothing, then searches under the coverlet until she finds the object. I take back the coin at once, put it in my hand and then slip my closed hand under a cushion situated on the other side (on her left and no longer on her right); Jacqueline immediately searches for the object under the cushion.[3]

Jacqueline could now conceive of objects as entities in their own right, having an existence apart from her own immediate experience of them. And only now, Piaget reasoned, could she logically be expected to attach *names* to stable and meaningful object concepts and to begin the sort of verbal discourse and thought that characterizes mature intelligence. This reinforced his hypothesis, already established on other grounds, that the mind or "intelligence" of a child is *not* simply a miniature replica of the adult's but something that grows and develops through a series of stages that originally bear little obvious similarity to the finished result.

Binet's and Piaget's observations of their children constituted small but important parts of their overall investigations, which established the fact that a full understanding of the adult mind requires prior understanding of the child's. In moving now to the fuller stories of these two psychologist/fathers, we shall see the foundations of two different but equally influential approaches to the study of human intelligence.

Binet's Early Life and Career

Alfred Binet's wealthy parents separated soon after his birth on July 11, 1857, in Nice, France. He was raised in Nice and Paris mainly by his amateur artist mother, although his physician father figured in at least one crucial childhood experience. To cure Alfred's timidity, Dr. Binet forced him to touch a cadaver. The "treatment" served only to increase the boy's anxieties, and its memory haunted him thereafter.

After a creditable if unspectacular secondary-school career, Binet took a degree in law but decided against practice. Then he tried medical school, where the horrors of the operating theater evidently brought flashbacks to his childhood trauma. He suffered a severe breakdown and withdrew without a degree. At age 22, dispirited, emotionally exhausted, and vocationless, he began passing time by reading extensively in Paris's great library, the Bibliothèque Nationale. Apparently by accident, he discovered books on the new experimental psychology, became fascinated, and realized that he had at last found his vocation.

Binet plunged untutored into this new field, with more enthusiasm than discretion. He read a few studies of the "two-point threshold," showing that when two points are simultaneously pressed against the skin, they must be separated by some minimum distance that varies both with individuals and with the parts of the body stimulated if they are to be correctly perceived as two rather than one. After experimenting briefly on himself and some friends, he wrote an article proposing a "new" theory of this phenomenon, which appeared in 1880 as Binet's first scientific publication. His pleasure at seeing his work in print quickly changed to embarrassment, as the Belgian physiologist Joseph Delboeuf (see Chapter 10) published a critical reply: Binet's experiments had flaws, and the "new" theory had already been published years before by Delboeuf himself.

Undaunted, Binet next became enthusiastic about the associationistic psychology of John Stuart Mill, one of Locke's most important successors in stressing the importance of experience and education in shaping human character. In a second published article, Binet made the extreme claim that "the operations of the intelligence are nothing but diverse forms of the laws of association: all psychological phenomena revert to these forms, be they apparently simple, or recognized as complex."[4] Although associationism clearly had merits (and Binet's appreciation of them would eventually help him succeed where the arch-hereditarian Galton had failed in devising a workable intelligence test), this statement went much too far. Work in "dynamic psychology" had already clearly demonstrated that ideas can become *dis*associated or *dis*connected from each other and that a given stimulus can lead to totally different trains of association under different motivational conditions. Laws of association could not easily account for these phenomena, and Binet was fortunate to escape a second public rebuke.

Evidently finding this out on his own, Binet next sought training in the new dynamic psychology from one of its most famous proponents. The eminent Jean Charcot, just then developing his theories of *grand hystérie* and *grand hypnotisme* at Paris's Salpêtrière Hospital, accepted the enthusiastic and independently wealthy young Binet as an unpaid assistant and trainee. Binet remained with Charcot for nearly eight years, becoming one of the most prolific researchers of the "Salpêtrière school." He published three books and more than twenty papers on topics ranging from mental imagery to sexual "fetishism" (a term he originated, to denote cases in which patients invest inappropriate objects or body parts with sexual significance).

Binet's most publicized work at the Salpêtrière involved the hypnotic reactions of Charcot's prized "major hysterics." He and his colleague Charles Feré produced astonishing results in deeply hypnotized subjects merely by reversing the polarity of a horseshoe magnet in their presence: Symptoms moved from one side of the body to the other, for example, and emotions turned into their opposites. As recounted in Chapter 10, these implausible results aroused the skepticism of Binet's old nemesis Delboeuf, who visited the Salpêtrière and saw the young experimenters' carelessness in openly expressing their expectations to the hypnotized subject. Delboeuf's consequent exposé helped turn the tide of informed opinion against Charcot's entire theory of *grand hypnotisme* in favor of the less flamboyant Nancy school.

At first, Binet tried to defend himself and Charcot by arguing that Delboeuf and the Nancy school could not reproduce the Salpêtrière findings only because they lacked access to the crucial cases of "major hysteria"—found more easily in the big city than in the provinces. Delboeuf responded sarcastically:

What has the school of the Salpêtrière replied to my deductions, so strongly upheld by facts? That my subjects and those of Nancy were only "commonplace *somnambules*," that Paris alone had access to "profound hypnotism," while we—we had only "*le petit hypnotisme*," a hypnotism of the provinces! It would be difficult to find in the history of the sciences another such example of an aberration perpetuating itself . . . by pure overweening pride.[5]

Finally, in 1891 Binet himself recognized the terrible truth that he had placed too much faith in Charcot's name and prestige and had accepted the master's theories too uncritically. Humbled, he admitted publicly that his earlier hypnotic studies "present a great many loopholes for error. . . . One of the chief and constant causes of mistakes, we know, is found in suggestion—that is to say, in the influence the operator exerts by his words, gestures, attitudes, even by his silences, on the subtle and alert intelligence of the person he has put in the somnambulistic state."[6] From this school of hard knocks, Binet learned an invaluable lesson about how psychological experiments ought *not* be conducted. Never again would he trust unauthenticated authority or go out on a limb for a position he had not tested thoroughly himself.

Further, just as the hypnosis debacle was coming to a climax, Binet began his series of experiments at home with his daughters (see Figure 13.2). Besides suggesting to him the weakness of the Galtonian approach to mental testing, his observations of Madeleine and Alice reinforced one *positive* lesson from Charcot and the Salpêtrière. In conducting intensive studies of relatively few cases, Charcot had inevitably emphasized the essential *individuality* of all subjects in psychological study. Binet found ample further evidence of individuality in his two daughters.

A proud and doting father, he saw both his girls as bright and able. But from earliest childhood onward they *demonstrated* their intelligence in characteristically different ways—the elder Madeleine always proceeded cautiously and deliberately, while the younger Alice behaved with greater enthusiasm and imagination. For example, in learning to walk, Madeleine held onto a chair or table for support and ' risked abandoning that support only when she had visually selected

FIG 13.2
Alfred Binet's daughters,
Madeleine (left) and Alice

another object a short distance away which would offer new support; she directed herself very slowly towards the second object, . . . with great seriousness and in perfect silence." Alice, by contrast, was "a laughing and turbulent child" who "never anticipated which object could furnish support, because she advanced without the slightest hesitation to the middle of an empty part of the room. She cried out, she gestured, she was very amusing to watch; she advanced staggering like a drunken man, and could not take four or five steps without falling."[7]

Such stylistic differences recurred in countless other situations, leading Binet to characterize the sensible and down-to-earth Madeleine as "the observer" (*"l'observateur"*) and the more impulsive and fanciful Alice as "the imaginer" (*"l'imaginitif"*). And for the rest of his career Binet would also respect the great individuality of every person's intelligence, lending his mature psychology a particular sensibleness and power.

Individual Psychology

By 1891, the 34-year-old Binet had learned enough positive and negative lessons at the Salpêtrière and at home to become a first-rate experimental psychologist. He lacked only a position, for he under-

standably did not wish to remain at the Salpêtrière after his humiliation, and other institutions—just as understandably—did not beat
down his door with offers. Finally in late 1891 Binet had a chance
meeting in a railroad station with Henri Beaunis, a physiologist and
the director of the newly created Laboratory for Physiological Psychology at the Sorbonne in Paris. Beaunis had favored the Nancy
school against Binet and Charcot in the hypnosis controversy and
must have seemed an unlikely ally. Nevertheless, Binet summoned
his courage and offered to work without pay in the new laboratory.
With a meager budget, Beaunis perhaps felt he had little to lose. In
any case, he appointed Binet as his unpaid assistant and got a wonderful bargain. Binet soon gained recognition as France's leading
experimental psychologist and succeeded Beaunis as director of
the laboratory in 1894. The following year he founded *L'Annee Psychologique*, the first French journal explicitly devoted to experimental psychology. He remained at the Sorbonne, always without pay,
until the end of his life.

Among the first topics Binet studied from his new Sorbonne base
was *suggestibility*—that "cholera of psychology" that had ruined
his hypnotic experiments. His controlled experiments on suggestibility in children, as described in Chapter 10, helped set the stage
for modern experimental social psychology. Binet summarized these
experimental results statistically, giving average numbers of correct
and incorrect responses for groups of subjects under the various conditions. But as he did so, he also recalled the positive lesson of individuality he had learned from Charcot and from his own daughters.
"Mere numbers cannot bring out . . . the intimate essence of the
experiment," he warned. He felt uneasy about expressing "all the
oscillations of thought in a simple, *brutal* number, which can have
only a deceptive precision. . . . It is necessary to complete this number
by a description of all the little facts that complete the physiognomy
of the experiment."[8]

Binet now also looked zealously for signs of suggestibility in *himself*
whenever he conducted an experiment. When he found it he reported
it, as in a study from the late 1890s involving head measurements
from several hundred subjects. Following Galton, he had hypothesized a positive relationship between head circumference and mental ability. To his chagrin, however, he found that when he *expected*

heads to be small, his measurements averaged some 3 millimeters less than when he reexamined the same heads under more neutral expectations. This discrepancy exceeded the disappointingly small *real* difference he found between the average head circumferences of schoolchildren classified by their teachers as either very bright or very dull. Besides illustrating the experimental dangers of suggestibility, these findings further convinced Binet of the inadequacy of the Galtonian theory of mental testing.

In other work during the 1890s, Binet conducted in-depth case studies of unusually talented people, including several of France's most famous authors and two "lightning calculators"—men who could quickly and accurately perform complicated mathematical operations entirely in their heads. He learned from these studies that sharers of the same special ability often go about exercising it in entirely different ways. One calculator always *saw* the numbers in his imagination as he worked, for example, while the other always *heard* them instead. Some authors worked best during intense, intermittent periods of "spontaneous inspiration," while others—with equally good results—wrote methodically and systematically for shorter periods every day. Thus different people used different intellectual strategies to arrive at similar extraordinary results.

So impressed was Binet by this fact of individuality that in 1895, he and his younger colleague Victor Henri launched a program they called **individual psychology** (not to be confused with the approach of the same name promoted by Alfred Adler, described in Chapter 12). They sought a series of short tests, administerable to one person in less than two hours, that could provide information comparable in richness, complexity, and comprehensiveness to that obtained from the many hours of observations and interviews traditionally devoted to individual case studies. Ideally, a short summary of these test results would serve as an adequate substitute for the sort of extended case reports Binet had written of his extraordinary subjects.

In trying to develop such tests, Binet continued to experiment with his daughters Madeleine and Alice. Throughout their adolescence they served as subjects on scores of tasks designed to test their memory, judgment, imagination, and general personality. Some of these tasks required word associations, the interpretation of inkblots, or the telling of stories about "neutral" stimuli; thus, Binet anticipated several **projective tests** that would later come into vogue with clinical and personality psychologists, including Murray and Morgan's TAT as described in Chapter 12. Binet summarized the results of twenty such tests in his 1903 book *L'Étude Experimentale de l'Intelligence* (*The Experimental Study of Intelligence*)—regarded by some psychologists as Binet's most creative work. This book repeatedly showed how the two girls had continued to manifest their "intelligence" in characteristically different ways—Madeleine as the down-to-earth "observer" and Alice as the "imaginer." Consider, for example, the two teenage girls' contrasting responses when their father asked them to write something about a chestnut tree leaf:

> Madeleine: "The leaf was gathered in the autumn, because the folioles are all almost yellow except for two, and one is half green and yellow. . . . The folioles are not of the same size: out of the seven, four are much smaller than the three others. The chestnut tree is a dicotyledon, as one can tell by looking at the leaf, which has ramified nervures."

> Alice: "This . . . has just fallen languidly in the autumn wind. . . . Poor leaf destined now to fly along the streets, then to rot, heaped up with the others. It is dead today, and it was alive yesterday! Yesterday, hanging from the branch it awaited the fatal flow of wind that would carry it off, like a dying person who awaits his final agony. But the leaf did not sense its danger, and it fell softly in the sun."[9]

Although Binet's attempts to realize the goals of individual psychology produced some interesting isolated results, he was forced to conclude in 1904 that the program as a whole had failed. No short combination of tests had emerged that could satisfactorily substitute for an extended case study. Binet ruefully concluded: "It is premature to look for tests permitting a diagnosis during a very limited time (one or two hours), and . . . much to the contrary, it is necessary to study individual psychology without limiting the time—especially by studying outstanding personalities."[10] The most significant concrete results of individual psychology remained his extended case studies of his daughters and of a few prominent literary figures.

But while technically unsuccessful, Binet's testing experiments in individual psychology helped pave the way for his most famous achievement. He had gained valuable experience by trying out innumerable tests of varied functions such as memory, imagination, comprehension, attention, suggestibility, and the aesthetic and moral senses. He had confirmed his belief that only relatively *direct* tests of the higher, complex mental functions measured significant intellectual differences. When he began in 1905 to seek a test of "intelligence" in a narrower and more specific context than he had been concerned with before, these experiences helped him to succeed where Galton and his other predecessors had failed.

The Binet Intelligence Scales

During the first years of the twentieth century, Binet and many others became increasingly interested in the problem of mental *subnormality*. The recent passage of universal education laws in France and elsewhere had brought a new public visibility to mentally handicapped children. Previously, most such children had either dropped out of school at an early age or never attended at all. Now they were required by law to attend school—and since they usually could not keep up with an ordinary curriculum, they required special attention and special schools.

   In 1904, Binet joined a government commission charged with investigating the state of the mentally subnormal in France and soon concluded that accurate *diagnosis* of subnormality posed the most pressing problems. "It will never be a mark of distinction to have passed through a special school," he remarked, "and those who do not merit it must be spared the record."[11] Thus with **Théodore Simon** (1873–1961), a young physician who had come to study psychology with him in 1899, Binet set out to develop a test to identify children whose mental handicap rendered them permanently unable to benefit from an ordinary education.

The 1905 Tests

Binet and Simon started out with few theoretical predispositions regarding the "intelligence" whose deficiency they hoped to measure. They proceeded empirically, identifying groups of children who had been unequivocally diagnosed as subnormal or normal by their teachers or doctors, and then testing them on many specific measures. They avoided tests that relied heavily on reading, writing, and other clearly school-related skills, not wanting to confuse lack of intelligence with mere lack of schooling. But they did not hesitate to try items that assumed a basic familiarity with everyday French life and culture—many of which Binet had already used in his earlier studies of his daughters and other children.

At first Binet and Simon were frustrated because, while the normal and subnormal groups showed differences in average performance on most items, no item came close to being a perfect discriminator. At least a few of the normal children failed on every test while some subnormal children passed. But soon a key insight dawned—one that seemed obvious once recognized but that had eluded previous workers in the field. *Age* had to be considered: Normal and subnormal children might both learn to pass the same tests, but normal children invariably did so at a younger age. Binet and Simon summarized: "It was almost always possible to equate subnormal children with normal children very much younger."[12] Following this insight, it became common to describe the subnormal population as mentally "retarded."

This idea enabled Binet and Simon in 1905 to construct the first test of intelligence that actually worked, comprising thirty separate items of increasing difficulty. The first item simply tested whether subjects could follow a lighted match with their eyes, demonstrating the elementary capacity for *attention* that is prerequisite for all intelligent behavior. Next, subjects had to grasp a small object placed in their hand, to unwrap and eat a piece of candy, to shake hands with the examiner, and to comply with a few simple spoken or gestured requests. Normal children could do all of these things by the age of 2, but the most profoundly retarded of any age could *never* do some of them. Intermediate problems, passable by normal 5- or 6-year-olds but by none of the moderately retarded, required them to state the differences between pairs of objects such as "paper and cardboard" and "a fly and a butterfly" and to memorize and repeat sentences such as "I get up in the morning, dine at noon, and go to bed at night." The more difficult items which in effect defined the upper borderline of subnormality, required subjects to find rhymes for the French word *obéissance*; to construct a sentence containing the three given words "Paris," "river," and "fortune"; and to figure in their heads what time it would be if the hands of a clock were reversed (for example, twenty past six would become half past four). Most normal children of 11 or 12 could pass these items, but few genuinely subnormal individuals of any age could.

The 1908 and 1911 Scales

The Binet-Simon test of 1905 marked a turning point in the history of psychology, for it truly made useful discriminations among lower degrees of intelligence. But it focused primarily on the very retarded and the very young, while many of the most difficult educational decisions involved older children close to the borderline of "normality." Accordingly, Binet and Simon extended and refined their pool of items, producing revised intelligence tests in 1908 and 1911. On these, each item was specifically designated according to the age at which a sample of normal children had first been able to pass it. Thus, each item at the 6-year level had been passed by a minority of normal 5-year-olds, about half of the 6-year-olds, and a majority of older children. The 1908 revision contained fifty-eight items located at age levels between 3 and 13; its 1911 counterpart had five questions for each age between 5 and 15, and five more in an "adult" category. The following are a few examples.

At the *3-year level*, children had to name common objects in a picture, correctly repeat a six-syllable sentence, and point to their eyes, noses, or mouths upon request. At *6*, they were expected to state the difference between morning and evening and count thirteen coins. At *10*, they normally could reproduce several line drawings from memory, answer questions involving social judgment such as why people should be judged by their acts rather than their words, and detect and describe the logical absurdities in statements such as "The body of an unfortunate girl was found cut into 18 pieces; it is thought that she killed herself." Items at the *15-year level* asked subjects to correctly recall seven digits and to deal with problems such as "My neighbor has been receiving strange visitors. He has received in turn a doctor, a lawyer, and then a priest. What is taking place?"

With age-standardized items such as these, Binet had a genuine "scale" of intelligence, capable of providing a single score or

intellectual level for each child who took it. Questions were always asked in ascending order of difficulty, until five in a row were missed. Then the examiner took the highest year for which all five items had been successfully passed as the base, then added one-fifth of a year for each subsequent correct answer to compute the child's intellectual level. For example, a child who answered all of the questions at the age-7 level, four at age 8, and two at age 9 would be assigned an overall intellectual level of 8.2 years.

In diagnosing mental subnormality, Binet compared each child's tested intellectual level with his or her actual age. He collected statistics suggesting that children whose intellectual levels trailed their ages by less than two years could usually manage in the regular school system, while those who showed greater discrepancies (about 7 percent of the population) usually had trouble. Accordingly, he proposed a rule of thumb that children with intellectual levels more than two years behind their actual ages be seriously considered for special education.

Even as he suggested this rule, however, Binet also counseled caution. He still denied the ability of "brutal" numbers to adequately summarize any complex quality and emphasized that different children could achieve identical intellectual levels by correctly answering widely varying patterns of specific questions. He also recognized that no score could be valid for a child who was poorly motivated to take the test or who had been reared in a culture other than that of the sample of children he had used to standardize his questions. And the early proponent of Mill's associationism still emphatically believed that the "intelligence" measured by his test was not a fixed quantity but something that grows naturally with time and that— at least for retarded children and within limits—may be increased by training. He developed a program he called **mental orthopedics**, with exercises such as the games of "Statue," in which children had to freeze in position upon hearing a signal, and "Concentration," in which they had to remember several objects that were briefly removed from a box and then rehidden. Children whose deficits stemmed from an inability to sit still and to concentrate often benefited from these exercises, increasing not only their "intellectual levels" as measured by Binet's tests but also their intelligent behavior in real life.

The Rise of Intelligence Testing

At the height of his powers when he developed mental orthopedics and his revised intelligence scales, Binet had little time to enjoy his accomplishments. His wife suffered from an ill-defined malady that inhibited social life, and Binet himself seemed susceptible to gloomy thoughts, reflected in a series of plays he co-authored with André de Lorde, a popular dramatist known as the "Prince of Terror." Protagonists in these plays included a released psychiatric patient who murders his brother, a deranged father who kills his infant son after being denied admission to an asylum, and another father who performs ghoulish experiments trying to restore his dead daughter to life.[13] All too soon the ultimate tragedy occurred in real life, as Binet himself suffered a stroke and died in 1911, at the early age of 54.

As his most enduring legacy, Binet left behind the basic technology that still underlies modern intelligence tests. Although some psychologists still hope to find measures of innate intelligence that are "culture free" and closely tied to direct neurophysiological functions, all of the most practically useful tests developed to date still rely on items basically like Binet's—questions directly entailing a variety of higher and complex functions such as memory, reasoning, verbal facility, and practical judgment. But while Binet might feel comfortable about the item content of most modern intelligence tests, he probably would have reservations about some *other* developments in their interpretation and use—developments that began to occur almost immediately after his death.

One concerned the general conception of "intelligence" assumed to be measured by the items. Binet himself had adopted a flexible and pragmatic definition of intelligence, seeing it as a rather loose collection of separate capacities for memory, attention, reasoning, and the like, all tied together by a faculty he simply called "judgment" or "good sense." A rival view, the theory of **general intelligence**, or *g*, was effectively promoted by the English psychologist **Charles Spearman** (1863–1945) soon after Binet's death.

Spearman first observed and emphasized a fact that has been repeatedly confirmed ever since—namely, that when correlation coefficients (see Chapter 7) are computed between them, all of the various items and submeasures used on intelligence tests tend to be positively and hierarchically intercorrelated with each other. People who do well on vocabulary tests, for example, tend to score high on arithmetic problems, the detection of similarities, the assembling of painted blocks into specified patterns, the memory for digits, or any of the other items. Further, while all the subtests tend to intercorrelate positively, some of them achieve generally higher levels of correlation than others. Subtests involving abstract reasoning (such as similarities), for example, intercorrelate more strongly than do measures of rote memory with other items across the board.

To explain these findings, Spearman theorized that all intellectual tasks must entail the exercise of a single common "factor" he called "general intelligence" and abbreviated as g. He further proposed that each individual type of item required an ability specific to itself, an s factor; his theory is accordingly called the **two-factor theory of intelligence**. Writing metaphorically, Spearman went on to liken each person's g capacity to an overall supply of mental energy or power, capable of driving any number of specific neurological "engines" required for performing different specific tasks (and thus constituting the material basis for the individual s factors). Thus a person's performance on any task is theoretically a joint function of the overall energy or g available, as well as the efficiency of the particular s engine involved. The hierarchical nature of the correlations suggested that some tasks, such as abstract reasoning, depended relatively much on g and relatively little on s; for rote learning the proportions were reversed. But even tasks relatively "unsaturated" with g—such as rote learning—required *some* degree of mental energy. Thus, for Spearman the single most important fact to know about any person's intelligence was his or her general intelligence level, or overall mental power.

Although not the only possible explanation for the observed hierarchies of positive intercorrelations, Spearman's theory attracted support from its inception. Suggesting that "intelligence" is not so much a loose collection of varying functions and aptitudes as a network of engines all driven by a common energy source, it fostered attitudes toward testing quite different from Binet's. While Binet believed that different intelligence levels could be represented only approximately and inadequately by numbers, Spearman's theory suggested that a single figure representing each person's g level, or overall "mental horsepower," would be the most important thing to know about that person's intelligence.

A means of calculating such single numbers from Binet's intelligence tests was proposed in 1912 by the German psychologist William Stern (introduced in Chapter 12 as a pioneer in the development of personality psychology), with his concept of the **intelligence quotient**. Stern had worried over experimental findings showing that the discrepancy between a child's real or "chronological age" and the tested intellectual level or "mental age" (as Binet's term was usually translated) often increased over time. When retested after exactly one year, children whose scores were below par the first time usually gained less than one year in mental age, while those who had been above average gained more than a year. Thus, Binet's suggestion to adopt a two-year discrepancy between chronological and mental age as diagnostic of subnormality seemed suspect, because it implied different standards for different age groups. Many children's discrepancies inevitably grew from less than two at an early age to more than two later on, making diagnoses of subnormality relatively more frequent at later ages.

To remedy this inequality, Stern suggested taking not the absolute discrepancy between mental and chronological age as the measure of retardation but rather the *ratio* of mental age to chronological age—a fraction Stern called the "intelligence quotient." Thus a 5-year-old with a mental age of 4 would have an intelligence quotient of 4 divided by 5, or 0.80; to achieve the same quotient, a 10-year-old would have to get a mental age of 8, two years rather than one behind the chronological age.

While perhaps simplifying the problem of diagnosis, Stern's innovation had one effect that Binet would certainly have deplored. As a final, summary score of test results, the intelligence quotient was much further removed from the actual "physiognomy of the experiment" than the simple mental age or intellectual level. Binet had complained because the same mental age could be produced by different patterns of specific answers; now the problem was compounded because the same intelligence quotients could be produced by different combinations of mental and chronological ages.

For some psychologists, however, this simplification of results carried a major benefit. The intelligence quotient was potentially interpretable as an index of a unitary, quantifiable intellectual power like Spearman's *g*. All that remained was to demonstrate that *high* quotients were indicative of superior intellectual power. In 1920 this was not a foregone conclusion. Binet himself had experimented briefly on children with advanced mental ages, been disappointed with the results, and had concluded that "the most valuable applications of our scale will not be for the normal subject, but instead for the inferior degrees of intelligence."[14] That is, he saw his tests as primarily useful in detecting the *lack* of intelligence in subnormal children, and doubted their usefulness in measuring higher degrees intelligence.

The first major attempt to demonstrate otherwise occurred during World War I, when tests adapted for group administration were given to nearly two million U.S. Army recruits. The results were used not only to screen out "mental defectives" but also to select high-scoring individuals for advanced training. But while this program represented a spectacular organizational accomplishment for psychologists and helped place intelligence testing "on the map" of public consciousness, the war ended before the tests' validity in predicting positive performance could be accurately or fully evaluated. In fact, there were many glaring deficiencies and inequalities in the way the testing program was run.[15]

First to argue persuasively for the usefulness of Binet tests in diagnosing superior intelligence was **Lewis M. Terman** (1877–1956; see Figure 13.3), a Stanford University psychologist who had worked on the army program. Terman in 1916 had introduced "The Stanford Revision of the Binet-Simon Scale," an extensive reworking of Binet's test adapted for American subjects and standardized on a considerably larger sample of children. The "Stanford-Binet" quickly became the most widely used individual intelligence test in North America. When introducing this test, Terman had endorsed Stern's intelligence quotient concept and further suggested that the fraction be multiplied by 100 to eliminate decimals, with the result being abbreviated as the IQ. Ever since, an exactly average level of intelligence has been denoted by an IQ of 100.

Terman's major interest, however, lay in children with IQs *higher* than average. Perhaps partly because he had himself been a precocious student who passed through school much faster than most, he suspected that "advanced" children in general tended to grow up to

FIG 13.3
Lewis Terman
(1877–1956)

be unusually capable adults. To test his hypothesis, he followed two complementary strategies. First, he and his graduate student **Catharine Cox** (1890–1984; see Figure 13.4) examined the childhood biographies of more than 300 eminent historical "geniuses."[16] Although data were often scanty, virtually every case showed considerable evidence of childhood accomplishment in advance of one's years—often quite spectacular accomplishment. (Included in Terman-Cox's list of documented child prodigies were several pioneers from earlier chapters of the present book, including Descartes, Leibniz, Kant, Darwin, and Galton.) Terman and Cox argued accordingly that *if* Binet-type intelligence tests had been available in the past, most people who turned out to be intellectually eminent in adulthood would also have achieved high IQs as children.

Terman's second attempt to relate childhood precocity to adult achievement followed a complementary strategy and led to his most extensive and famous research program. In the early 1920s his students tested more than 250,000 California schoolchildren to

FIG 13.4
Catharine Cox
(1890–1984)

dentify a group of 1,528 "gifted children" with IQs above 140. He then proceeded to investigate all aspects of these children's lives at regular intervals as they grew up. Terman's successors continued to study the survivors of this group into old age, in perhaps the most extensive longitudinal study of a single group ever conducted by psychologists.[17]

And how did these gifted individuals fare? Statistically speaking, the answer is that they did very well indeed. Compared to a random sample, a high proportion entered the professions, with many earning national or international reputations. More than 30 became eminent enough to be listed in *Who's Who*. Taken as a whole, the group attained more education, earned more money, and in general led healthier and apparently happier lives than the national average.

At the same time, however, the study showed that high IQ alone did not guarantee success. A significant minority failed to lead objectively successful lives, and further, the group contained surprisingly few individuals successful in the creative arts (as opposed to the professions). None won the Nobel Prize or became highly celebrated "geniuses." In countless other studies since Terman's, IQ scores in the general population have been found to correlate moderately but far from perfectly with variables such as academic grades, years of education finally completed, and salary levels in adulthood. Thus, in general, high IQs have turned out to be good but far from infallible predictors of intellectual success. Despite the widespread tendency to equate high IQs with "genius," the evidence suggests that the tests still work relatively better for their original purpose—the diagnosis of lower levels of intelligence.

Still, Terman and other advocates made IQ scores into common intellectual currency, and a vast testing industry developed. New tests were subsequently designed for adults, calculating IQ scores not by the traditional mental age to chronological age ratio, but according to the distributions of results within each age group. Thus a 25-year-old and a 60-year-old, each with an IQ of 100, stand at the exact average of people in their age groups. IQs of 80, 110, and 135 always stand respectively at about the 9th, 74th, and 99th percentiles for the age group in question.

In sum, modifications of Binet's testing procedures became applied to all segments of the population, with results often summarized by a single score for each subject. Inevitably, these scores were also interpreted by some—particularly those sympathetic to Spearman's conception of intelligence as dominated by a biologically given general factor—as Galton's long-sought measure of *hereditary* natural ability. Others have disputed this contention, seeing IQ as a variable primarily determined by environment and education, rather than heredity. Indeed, there remains great disagreement today over the exact meaning of intelligence test scores, reflected, for example, in the perennial debate over the the "IQ controversy." Were he alive today, Binet himself would undoubtedly regret all of the fuss about these issues but be pleased to see that his testing techniques have retained their usefulness for individual educational and clinical diagnoses.

One further development would probably please him as well. In 1920, the young Swiss psychologist Jean Piaget came to work for Binet's old colleague Simon, in one of Binet's old laboratories. Using a clinical interview method much like that endorsed by Binet, Piaget arrived at a new conception of the stages by which children's intelligence normally develops with age. Concerned with qualitative rather than quantitative intellectual developments, Piaget revolutionized the field of child psychology.

Piaget's Early Life and Career

Jean Piaget (see Figure 13.5) was born on August 9, 1896, in Neuchâtel, Switzerland, the son of a scholar who wrote prolifically about medieval literature and the local history. Piaget recalled his mother as being intelligent and kindly, but also prone to emotional disorders that often made the domestic atmosphere uncomfortably tumultuous. To cope with the tumult, he said he identified with his father and buried himself in serious intellectual work. Even as a child he wrote prodigiously, and he continued throughout his life to publish at a rate not far short of Wundt's. When asked as an adult how he could write so much, Piaget frankly replied, "Fundamentally I am a worrier whom only work can relieve."[18]

As a young boy Piaget produced a pamphlet describing his "invention" of a combination wagon/locomotive and a handwritten booklet titled *Our Birds.* Then at 10 he was "launched" (his own term) as a published writer when a local amateur naturalists' magazine accepted his hundred-word note describing an albino sparrow he had observed. Soon thereafter he became a voluntary helper to the director of Neuchâtel's natural history museum, a man who specialized in malacology, the study of mollusks. Piaget learned this field too, and between the ages of 15 and 19 he published twenty-one malacological papers in assorted international journals. Few readers knew

FIG 13.5 Jean Piaget (1896–1980) in maturity, interacting with children

his age, and one offered him a curator's job in Geneva that Piaget had to decline because he still had two years of high school remaining.

This background in scientific observation and methodology helped Piaget get through an emotionally difficult late adolescence, plagued by religious preoccupations and what he called "the demon of philosophy." His godfather helped him resolve his crisis by suggesting that philosophical and even theological concerns could be brought into connection with biology:

> I recall one evening of profound revelation. The identification of God with life itself was an idea that stirred me almost to ecstasy because it now enabled me to see in biology the explanation of all things and of the mind itself. . . . The problem of knowing (properly called the epistemological problem) suddenly appeared to me in an entirely new perspective and as an absorbing topic of study. It made me decide to consecrate my life to the biological explanation of knowledge.[19]

Piaget now immersed himself in philosophical works that tried to integrate biology and epistemology, especially the writings on "creative evolution" by **Henri Bergson** (1859–1941). Bergson saw the universe as divided into two fundamental substances: living and inert matter, with the living matter evolving constantly so as to better apprehend and operate freely within the inert matter with which it must contend. But while impressed by Bergson's general notion of mind as progressively adapting to and "understanding" external reality, Piaget felt dissatisfied by the lack of solid experimental support provided for the argument. "At that moment," he recalled, "I discovered a need that could be satisfied only by psychology."[20] He had little notion of what formal psychology was, but his interests had conspired to create his life's ambition: the construction of an empirically and experimentally based theory explaining how people come increasingly to know about their world. His goal here resembled John Locke's in the *Essay Concerning Human Understanding*, but in conceptualizing the human mind as a biologically given, organic, and evolving entity, Piaget would also follow in the tradition of Locke's great rival, Leibniz.

Before pursuing his great goal, however, Piaget was forced by ill health to spend his twentieth year recuperating in the mountains.

During this time he read a little psychology, but concentrated mainly on writing a philosophical novel entitled *Recherche* (literally, *Search* or *Quest*). Although far from a masterpiece, the novel was published in 1917. Returning from the mountains, he enrolled in the doctoral program at his home University of Neuchâtel, where psychology was not offered. Instead, Piaget took courses in biology, geology, chemistry, and mathematics, while writing a thesis on local mollusks. He received his Ph.D. in natural history at age 22. Only at this point did the internationally known malacologist, published novelist, and amateur philosopher seek training in psychology.

At first he went to Zurich, where he studied briefly with Freud's erstwhile follower Carl Jung and learned something about abnormal psychology. Then, seeking something more experimental, he went to Paris and the Sorbonne, where he had a chance meeting with Binet's collaborator, Théodore Simon. Simon had moved to Rouen following Binet's death but remained the nominal director of Binet's old pedagogical laboratory in Paris. He wanted to use the laboratory to standardize the French translations of a series of reasoning tests recently developed by Cyril Burt, the most enthusiastic English proponent of the Binet-Simon approach to testing.* Impressed by Piaget, Simon offered him the job of supervising this project. Piaget held reservations about the project and the entire ' psychometric" approach to studying intelligence, but the opportunity to be his own master in a good-sized laboratory seemed too good to refuse. He soon found that the seemingly pedestrian task of standardizing children's intelligence tests could lead to unexpected and exciting findings. He summarized his early discoveries as follows:

> I noticed that though Burt's tests certainly had their diagnostic merits based on the number of successes and failures, it was much more interesting to try to find the *reasons* for the failures. Thus I engaged my subjects in conversations patterned after psychiatric questioning, with the aim of discovering something about the reasoning processes underlying their right, but especially their wrong answers. I noticed with amazement that

---

* Many years later Burt would publish the apparently fraudulent set of separated-twin studies described in Chapter 7, purporting to demonstrate the great heritability of intelligence.

the simplest reasoning task involving the inclusion of a part in the whole . . . presented for normal children up to the age of eleven or twelve difficulties unsuspected by the adult.[21]

By careful questioning of individual children, Piaget attempted to cut through the simple, "brutal" numbers that normally stood as intelligence test scores, in order to reveal the children's actual underlying thought processes. Had he been alive, Binet certainly would have applauded, even though Piaget's findings pointed to a view of intelligence different from his own.

Binet's testing approach assumed that intelligence grows with age in primarily a *quantitative* sense. Using similar types of items for many age levels, it showed that older children could perform more tasks more quickly than younger children of comparable intellectual rank—suggesting that intelligence increases with age in much the same way that height and weight do. Piaget, by focusing on the reasoning processes underlying incorrect answers, concluded that this represents only one aspect of intellectual development. He found evidence that older children do not just think "faster" or "more" than younger ones; they also think in entirely different ways, using cognitive abilities and structures that enable them to understand some problems and concepts completely beyond the grasp of younger children. In short, intelligence develops *qualitatively* with age, as well as quantitatively.

Piaget saw that the systematic study and description of qualitative developments in maturing children's intelligence could provide an approach to the epistemological problem that interested him so much. By learning how children understand the world, and how their thought processes gradually mature and become more like adults', he could come to grips with the nature of human knowledge itself. Moreover, his new view of intelligence showed promising analogies to the biology he thought fundamental to any worldview. Just as a physically growing embryo gradually develops new organs and structures out of rudimentary predecessors, and these new structures make possible the performance of totally new functions, so the intellect presumably develops in gradual stages that allow the emergence of new ways of thought. To emphasize this presumed link between the biological and the intellectual, Piaget coined the name **genetic epistemology** for his program to study the development of children's

FIG 13.6
Jean Piaget and
Bärbel Inhelder
(1913–1997)

intelligence. (He used the term *genetic* to denote "developmental," not to suggest that intelligence is necessarily hereditary or determined by the genes.)

Piaget spent the rest of his life tirelessly pursuing this project, moving to Geneva to become director of research at the Jean Jacques Rousseau Institute in 1921. He remained affiliated with the Institute until his death in 1980. Although at first he worked in relative obscurity, he gradually attracted students from around the world, developing intense collaborations that resulted in hundreds of studies in genetic epistemology that reshaped the way psychologists think about both childhood and intelligence. One of his chief collaborators would be **Bärbel Inhelder** (1913–1997; see Figure 13.6), a young Swiss psychologist who, first as his student and then as his lifelong colleague, co-authored nine books with Piaget and succeeded him as chair of genetic and experimental psychology at the University of Geneva in 1971. We return to their joint work on construction of quantities and the stage of formal operations in the next section.

Genetic Epistemology

Piaget's voluminous publications describe children of different ages working at simple but ingeniously devised tasks in widely diverse areas, including rattle play, language use, moral judgment, the conception of numbers, space perception, algebra, the description of dreams and fantasies, and cognition in general. Within each area, he and his collaborators found evidence of sequential **stages of development**—systematic and qualitative differences between the ways younger and older children conceptualized and attacked the tasks. This vast corpus of work cannot be summarized briefly, but its general nature may be illustrated by some of the specific findings regarding stages of general cognitive development.

Piaget's studies suggested the existence of four major sequential stages between infancy and late adolescence: the *sensory-motor stage*, the *preoperational stage*, the *stage of concrete operations*, and the *stage of formal operations*. Each successive stage introduces new cognitive structures and strategies permitting the solution of previously insoluble problems; thus the stages may be defined in terms of tasks that children in them can and cannot do.

Piaget's conception of the first, **sensory-motor stage**—which he saw as extending from birth to approximately 2 years of age—derived from observations of his own nephews and children such as those described in the introduction to this chapter. "I learned in the most direct way," he recalled, "how intellectual operations are prepared by sensory-motor action, even before the appearance of language."[22] As the term implies, a child's "intelligence" during this stage presumably involves elementary sensory and motor activities and has nothing to do with abstract thought in the adult sense. Before one can think about objects in any abstract way, one must first learn how they strike the senses and how they can be manipulated—the general goal of the sensory-motor period.

More specifically, the sensory-motor child must achieve the sense of what Piaget called **object constancy**—the knowledge that objects continue to exist even when outside immediate sensory awareness. His observations of Gérard and Jacqueline, described in this chapter's introduction, illustrate various stages in the development of object constancy. Piaget noted that it arises gradually, as infants gain increasing mastery over their bodies and learn to manipulate objects and their appearances. As they do so, they take great delight in games such as peekaboo, where the repetitive disappearance and reappearance of familiar faces and objects hold particular fascination. And only after children learn to make many objects disappear and reappear through their own efforts—by reversing or alternating the behaviors that produce appearance or disappearance—do they acquire the sense of a stable universe containing continually existing objects independent of themselves. Only after objects are recognized as permanent does it become possible to *name* them, signifying their continuing independent existence by using words to represent them.

Once these rudiments of language have been acquired, enabling children to express and symbolize the continuing existence of specific objects in the world, they are equipped for the second, **preoperational stage**, which lasts approximately from ages 2 through 7. Although preoperational children can recognize that objects continue to exist even when they cannot immediately see or act upon them, they strikingly fail to understand that certain *properties* of objects—such as their quantity or volume—remain the same regardless of transformations of their specific appearance.

The first publication on the question of **conservation of quantity** appeared in 1936 in a paper by Bärbel Inhelder, in which she reported a simple experiment suggested to her by Piaget on her twentieth birthday. Drop a cube of sugar into a glass of water, he suggested, and ask children what happens as the cube dissolves and disappears.[23] Inhelder found that children between the ages of 5 and 11 changed their interpretations of the fate of the sugar cube. While the youngest children reported their belief that the sugar had completely disappeared (although noting that the water may have become sweeter), the oldest children believed that the weight and volume of the sugar had been conserved but that the sugar had broken up into bits so small that they were impossible to see. The older children reasoned that if those bits were reassembled, they would yield the same quantity of sugar as before. This was the first time, Inhelder noted, that she and Piaget had heard explicit expressions of *reversibility*, and she intended to make this the topic of her dissertation research. Piaget, however, had other plans. During one of their frequent walks in the Genevan mountains, Piaget suggested instead that they collaborate on a book-length project on the construction of quantity. As Inhelder later recalled:

> I remember the exact place and date of this proposal: it was on a sunny winter day as we were walking in the early afternoon along the Salève, the Genevan's favorite hiking mountain.

> I felt some regret at abandoning my project for a thesis, but was excited by the idea of taking part in a major scientific enterprise. At the time, I certainly did not think this would lead to a long-lasting, fascinating collaboration.[24]

Piaget's proposal marked the beginning of the research project that resulted in their co-authored book *The Child's Construction of Quantities: Conservation and Atomism*.[25] In this work, Piaget and Inhelder showed that the idea of conservation of matter, or the child's ability to understand what happens when matter takes different forms, proceeds in a regular sequence. Children first develop the ability to understand the conservation of quantity, then the conservation of weight, and finally volume.

Children in the preoperational stage of development are not yet able to understand the conservation of quantity when the same amount of matter is simply transformed into various shapes. Consider the following example. A child receives two lumps of clay and is instructed to remove small bits from the larger one to create a second lump of the same size. Then the experimenter breaks up one of the equal lumps into many pieces and places them in a pile, asking the child which now has more clay, the remaining large lump or the new pile? Virtually all preoperational children will be deceived by the different appearances of the two choices, and see one as having more clay than the other. Most will note that the pile takes up more space and looks bigger, and so choose it; a minority will emphasize the smallness of the pieces in the pile and choose the single large lump.

Similarly, a preoperational child may be misled by the appearances of equal quantities of liquids. Shown two identical glasses of orange juice, most preoperational children will judge that one of the contents miraculously becomes "more" than the other when poured into a taller and thinner glass, because the liquid rises higher in the new container. A few children say it becomes less because the column is thinner, but in either case a misjudgment is made because of the differences in appearance. In Piaget and Inhelder's terms, preoperational children fail to appreciate the conservation of quantity— that the overall amounts of substances remain the same even as they assume different shapes and configurations.

Besides showing that young children may be tricked into thinking they have more or less of particular foods or beverages just by altering their presentation, these simple experiments beautifully illustrate a central insight of Piaget's research program. Older children and adults think about abstract properties such as quantity or amount in altogether different ways from young children. Not just "better" with numbers, or capable of handling larger quantities, they make judgments of quantity on an altogether different basis. Younger children judge according to the way things immediately look. Older children have learned that by reversing behaviors in these new contexts they can re-form a pile of clay pieces into its originally sized lump, or repour the tall, thin column of juice into its original shape in the original glass. They mentally transcend the immediate appearance of things and recognize that the same quantity may manifest itself in many different guises.

In an extension of this work to a new population (and to satisfy her dissertation requirements!), Inhelder used some of the same previously described tasks to investigate the intelligence of mentally retarded (what we would now call developmentally delayed) children while she worked as a school psychologist in her home canton of St. Gall, Switzerland. She found that, in general, retarded children followed the same developmental sequence as normally-developing children, but did so much more slowly. In addition, however, there were qualitative differences. Retarded children tended to oscillate between distinctly different levels of performance, a phenomenon unique to them and uncharacteristic of normal development.

At age 7 or so most normal children begin to enter Piaget's **concrete operations stage**, in which they successfully solve most conservation problems but remain tied to the immediately given situation in still other ways. They cannot completely solve some kinds of conceptual and reasoning problems until entering the **formal operations stage**, which typically begins to emerge around the age of 11 or 12. This stage, Inhelder and Piaget showed, is characterized by the emergence of experimental or inductive reasoning.[26] One of the experimental tasks they developed to investigate this development required the systematic manipulation of chemicals and nicely illustrated the differences between these last two stages. In this task subjects received four flasks numbered 1 through 4 and a smaller container labeled "g" (not to be confused with Spearman's *g* for general intelligence), each filled with an identical-looking transparent liquid. The experimenter explained that by adding a few drops of *g* to the correct combination of liquids from Flasks 1 through 4, a chemical reaction could be produced turning the entire mixture yellow. Subjects were then invited to experiment with the liquids and discover the correct combination.

In actuality, g was potassium iodide, a chemical colorless by itself but that produces a yellow precipitate when mixed with oxygenated water in an acid solution. Flasks 1 and 3 held dilute sulfuric acid and oxygenated water, respectively, so the combination of g+1+3 yielded the desired result. Flask 2 contained plain water, which had no effect on the reaction; but Flask 4 held thiosulfate, a chemical base that neutralizes sulfuric acid. Thus g+1+2+3 also produced the color, but g+1+2+3+4 did not.

Although both concretely and formally operational children could solve this problem, they typically went about doing so in very different ways, and with vastly different consequences. The younger, concretely operational children usually proceeded by trial and error, trying random mixtures until finally hitting on one that worked. As far as they were concerned, the task was then finished. Formally operational children, by contrast, could see at once that there were only a limited number of possible combinations and that these could be investigated systematically and completely—yielding the maximum possible amount of information from their experiments. Thus, some started out by adding g to each of the four liquids by itself, discovering that no single chemical produced yellow with g. Then they tried each of the six possible combinations of two chemicals with g (1+2, 1+3, 1+4, 2+3, 2+4, and 3+4), until discovering the one that worked.

Even after finding an answer, however, formally operational children often continued to experiment with the five remaining untested combinations: the four possible combinations of three (1+2+3, 1+2+4, 1+3+4, and 2+3+4), and all four mixed together. Following this complete set of trials, they could generalize about the nature of the chemicals—recognizing that the contents of Flask 4 could counteract the crucial 1+3 combination, while adding Flask 2 made no difference. In being able to conceptualize all the possible combinations at the outset, and then to test them systematically, the formally operational children were able to extract the maximum amount of information from their experiments.

From innumerable observations like these, Piaget, Inhelder and their collaborators demonstrated that rational, adult, "scientific" thinking and the knowledge that proceeds from it represent the end points of extensive developmental processes. At the beginning of life, human thinking remains tied to the sensory and bodily experiences of the immediate present. Only gradually does it come to deal with imagined rather than immediately experienced concepts: first the memories of objects when they are no longer physically present, then abstract properties such as quantity that may remain constant throughout a variety of transformations of specific form, and finally the matrices of combinatorial possibilities in problems like the chemistry experiment.

In summarizing the implications of his work in 1970, Piaget emphasized the *active* nature of these developmental processes:

> I find myself opposed to the view of knowledge as a passive copy of reality. . . . I believe that knowing an object means acting upon it, constructing systems of transformations that can be carried out on or with this object. Knowing reality means constructing systems of transformations that correspond, more or less adequately, to reality. The transformational structures of which knowledge consists are not copies of the transformations in reality; they are simply possible isomorphic models among which experience can enable us to choose. Knowledge, then, is a system of transformations that become progressively more adequate.[25]

Piaget's work thus represented and integrated several venerable strands in the history of mental philosophy. Like Locke, he sought to understand the nature and limits of human knowledge. But like Descartes he saw the rational mind as an active rather than passive participant in the creation of that knowledge, and like Leibniz he stressed the organic and biological nature of that active mind. And in seeing knowledge as a series of "transformations" of external reality produced by the mind, involving developing conceptions of space, number, causality, and the like, Piaget partook strongly of the tradition of Kant.

Piagetian Influences

The Piagetian research program has stimulated countless contemporary developmental psychologists, who continue to study various aspects of the child's mind as it develops from infancy through maturity. Besides having considerable theoretical interest, this work has inevitably been of great practical interest to educators. Piaget himself, while admitting that he was no pedagogue, argued that schools could improve their teaching by always providing pupils with problems and challenges appropriate to their stages of intellectual development. For instance, it is foolish to try to instruct preoperational children in the formal, hypothetico-deductive reasoning processes of mature scientists, but it is possible and desirable to help such children develop conservation of quantity by giving them many opportunities to manipulate and transform the shapes and appearances of varying substances. Piaget advised: "It is a matter of presenting to children situations which offer new problems, problems that follow developmentally on one another. You need a mixture of direction and freedom."[28]

Educators have naturally been interested in the question of how far children's development and learning can be *accelerated* by such practices. Piaget himself saw intellectual development as tied to biological and social development as well. Therefore, while intellectual growth in a child may presumably be nurtured and facilitated like physical growth, it cannot be accelerated beyond certain natural and biologically given limits. The exact nature of those limits, the extent to which children may be speeded through the developmental stages, and the desirability of doing so, all became important issues.

One of the first to pursue those issues was the American psychologist **Jerome Bruner** (b. 1915), who was instrumental along with his colleague George A. Miller in establishing a new Center for Cognitive Studies at Harvard in 1960. As shall be detailed in the next chapter, this was a major step in the so-called "cognitive revolution," which challenged the behavioristic orthodoxy in American psychology. Bruner invited Bärbel Inhelder to be one of the first sabbatical visitors at the center for four months in 1961, where she served as an ambassador for the Piagetian program. More than coincidentally,

Bruner and his colleagues were just then developing a new "theory of instruction" based in part upon it.

According to this theory, an ideal technique for teaching new material is to move the student smoothly through three **modes of representation** of that material, paralleling the Piagetian stages of cognitive development. The student begins by *doing something* with the material under study, representing it in the **enactive mode**. Next he or she focuses on its *perceptual* qualities, employing the **iconic mode** of representation, before finally appreciating its *abstract* qualities in the **symbolic mode**. Developmentally, children learn to use enactive representation during the sensory-motor stage, iconic during the preoperational stage, and symbolic during the operational stage. But even mature individuals typically progress through all three of these modes when encountering new objects. First they want to know what to do with the new object, then they explore its perceptual features, and only finally can they represent it symbolically.

Bruner and his colleagues devised an ingenious system that exploited this sequence in teaching young children mathematics. To begin, the children were given a set of cut-out pieces of three shapes labeled "X²" for a large square; "X" for a rod equal in length to the large square's side; and "1" for a small square whose sides were equal to the width of X (see Figure 13.7). The children were encouraged to play with these forms, putting them together to create different shapes. As they did so, patterns such as those in represented by Figures b and c emerged. Thus the children came to "know" the pieces enactively and iconically, in terms of what to do with them and of their appearance in different patterns.

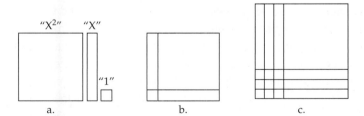

FIG 13.7 Materials used in Bruner's system for teaching young children mathematics

As they did this task, while also incorporating the *names* of the different pieces, the children began to represent the relationships symbolically. From Figure b, for example, they learned that a new square whose sides are $X + 1$ long contains one X^2, two X's and one 1. Thus:

$$(X + 1)^2 = X^2 + 2X + 1$$

From constructions like Figure c they learned that $(X + 3)^2 = X^2 + 6X + 9$; and from the totality of their experience with several constructed squares, many of the students as young as 8 were able to learn the formula for quadratic equations:

$$(X + a)^2 = X^2 + 2aX + a^2$$

Thus, like many of his predecessors among psychology's pioneers, Jean Piaget produced knowledge that at once held both important theoretical *and* practical implications. He and his colleagues raised issues about human experience and conduct that had widespread influence, from developmental, to cognitive, to educational psychology. Further, the profound epistemological aspect of his system—how we come to know what we know—continues to fascinate contemporary scientists and philosophers.

Summary

Alfred Binet and **Jean Piaget** were both concerned with how the intellectual capacities and qualities of the mind develop. Binet's interest in this topic was piqued, in part, by his observations of his two daughters, who expressed remarkably different *kinds* of intelligences, and by his in-depth case studies of unusually talented people. He became so impressed by the individuality of these cases that he launched a program called **individual psychology**. Although ultimately unsuccessful, Binet's attempts to derive a series of short tests that could provide information comparable in richness to that obtained from many hours of observations helped pave the way for his most famous achievement: the Binet-Simon intelligence test. This test, a notable improvement over previous efforts, reflected Binet's conviction that only relatively *direct* tests of the higher, complex mental functions measured significant intellectual differences. It was also based on his insight, gleaned from studying children already identified as "normal" and "subnormal" in intellectual capability, that the chronological *age* at which a child could respond correctly to an item on a test was crucial for understanding the child's intellectual level. Normal and subnormal children might both learn to pass the same tests, but normal children invariably did so at a younger age.

These insights led to the development of a set of age-standardized items providing a genuine "scale" of intelligence, capable of providing a single score or **intellectual level** for each child who took it. Binet, however, acknowledged that his scale was better at identifying subnormality than at making discriminations at higher levels of ability. He also remained firm in his beliefs that the single score on an intelligence test could never completely sum up a subject's intellectual ability and that this score could not represent a fixed capacity. In fact, convinced that intelligence is malleable, he even developed a set of **mental orthopedics** to help children perform better on his tests. In developments after Binet's death, of which he would not have approved, **William Stern** and **Lewis Terman** proposed the **intelligence quotient (IQ)** as a single numerical result of the test, which was interpretable by some as an index of **Charles Spearman**'s controversial notion of the subject's **general intelligence**, or *g*.

Jean Piaget was concerned more with *qualitative* than quantitative intellectual developments. In his work on the development of reasoning in children, he found evidence that older children do not just think "faster" or "more" than younger ones, they also think in entirely different ways. He used the term **genetic epistemology** to describe his system of understanding how the developing mind comes to know. Working with many collaborators, including closely with his student and then colleague **Bärbel Inhelder**, Piaget posited a number of stages characterizing the ways children figure out different tasks and make sense of the world around them. These include the **sensory-motor stage**, the **preoperational stage**, the **concrete operational stage**, and the **formal operational stage**. Piaget's work showed that the acquisition of knowledge involves an active process of interacting with the world, or, as he put it, "knowing an object means acting upon it." Jerome Bruner and his colleagues built on this insight in developing a "theory of instruction" based on three **modes of representation**: **enactive**, **iconic**, and **symbolic**. The Piagetian research program has continued to stimulate countless contemporary developmental psychologists in both theoretical and applied endeavors.

Key Pioneers

Bergson, Henri, p. 586

Binet, Alfred, p. 563

Bruner, Jerome, p. 596

Cox, Catharine, p. 582

Inhelder, Bärbel, p. 589

Piaget, Jean, p. 565

Simon, Théodore, p. 574

Spearman, Charles, p. 578

Terman, Lewis M., p. 581

Key Terms

concrete operations stage,
p. 593

conservation of quantity, p. 591

formal operations stage, p. 593

general intelligence (*g*), p. 578

genetic epistemology, p. 588

individual psychology (Binet and
Henri), p. 572

intellectual level, p. 576

intelligence quotient
(IQ), p. 580

mental orthopedics, p. 577

modes of representation, p. 597

   enactive, p. 597

   iconic, p. 597

   symbolic, p. 597

object concept, p. 565

object constancy, p. 590

preoperational stage, p. 591

projective tests, p. 572

sensory-motor stage, p. 590

stages of development, p. 590

two-factor theory of
intelligence, p. 579

Discussion Questions and Topics

1 Discuss the ways in which Binet's ideas about the nature of intelligence and how to measure it changed as subsequent psychologists further developed his methods. Which developments would he have approved of? Of which would he have been more skeptical?

2 Piaget was concerned with qualitative rather than quantitative intellectual developments. Explain what is meant by "qualitative intellectual developments," and give several examples from his research program.

3 Both Binet's and Piaget's research programs emphasized the importance of different *kinds* of intelligence or ways of coming to know the world. Other psychologists, such as Spearman, have promoted a much more unitary view of intelligence. Describe the evidence for and against each view. What are the practical implications of each?

Suggested Readings

The best English-language study of Binet's life and work remains Theta H. Wolf, *Alfred Binet* (Chicago University of Chicago Press, 1973). An abbreviated account is provided in Raymond E. Fancher, "Alfred Binet, General Psychologist," in Gregory Kimble and Michael Wertheimer (eds.), *Portraits of Pioneers in Psychology*, vol. III (Washington, DC: American Psychological Association, 1998), 67–84. Binet and Simon's articles introducing their intelligence tests of 1905, 1908, and 1911 appear in English translation in A. Binet and T. Simon, *The Development of Intelligence in Children* (*The Binet-Simon Scale*), reprint edition (New York: Arno Press, 1973). For a fuller story of Binet and his successors in the intelligence-testing field, see Raymond E. Fancher, *The Intelligence Men: Makers of the IQ Controversy* (New York: Norton, 1985). An interesting account of the various social and political meanings of intelligence testing in France and the United States through World War II is provided in John Carson, *The Measure of Merit* (Princeton, NJ, and Oxford, UK: Princeton University Press, 2007). For a detailed account of Lewis Terman's career, see Henry Minton, *Lewis M. Terman: Pioneer in Psychological Testing* (New York: New York University Press, 1988).

Piaget's autobiography appears in Richard I. Evans, *Jean Piaget: The Man and His Ideas* (New York: Dutton, 1973), along with transcripts of an informative interview and Piaget's general article titled "Genetic Epistemology." An informative and detailed study of his early life is Fernando Vidal's *Piaget Before Piaget* (Cambridge, MA Harvard University Press, 1994). John Flavell's *The Developmental Psychology of Jean Piaget* (New York: Van Nostrand, 1963), which brought Piaget's theories to an English-speaking readership, and Herbert Ginsburg and Sylvia Opper's *Piaget's Theory of Intellectual Development*, 3rd edition (Englewood Cliffs, NJ: Prentice-Hall, 1988) provide good overviews of his work. Piaget's observations of object constancy in his nephew and daughter are included in his book *The Construction of Reality in the Child* (New York: Basic Books, 1954). Bärbel Inhelder's autobiography appears in *A History of Psychology in Autobiography*, vol. 8, edited by Gardner Lindzey (Stanford, CA: Stanford University Press, 1989), 209–243. Many of the most important observations of later intellectual development appear in Bärbel Inhelder and Jean Piaget, *The Growth of Logical Thinking from Childhood to Adolescence* (New York: Basic Books, 1958; originally published 1955). Bruner's method for teaching quadratic equations is fully described in Chapter 24 of his *Beyond the Information Given* (New York: Norton, 1973).

Machines, Minds, and Cognitive Psychology

Leibniz and the Mechanization of Logic

Charles Babbage and the Analytical Engine

Alan Turing's Machine and Test
Electronic Computers, von Neumann Architecture, and the Turing Test

Intelligent Machines

Minds Versus Machines
Strong Versus Weak Artificial Intelligence

Ulric Neisser and Cognitive Psychology
Artificial Intelligence and Cognitive Psychology
Cognitive Psychology
"Ecological" Influences on Cognitive Psychology
Conclusion

Summary

Key Pioneers

Key Terms

Discussion Questions and Topics

Suggested Readings

14

As a child **Blaise Pascal** *(1623–1662) often watched* his tax-collector father spend laborious hours on hand calculation of complicated accounts, and as a youth he himself was sometimes recruited to help out. This work was not only disagreeable but also subject to frequent errors when the human calculators were fatigued. A mathematical prodigy who at age 12 had worked out many principles of Euclidean geometry without formal instruction, Pascal now had a more practical inspiration—namely, for the design of a calculating *machine* that would be both easy to use and immune to fatigue. Perhaps surprisingly, however—at least from a modern perspective—his

603

idea for a practical and labor-saving device was also seen in its time as having some serious philosophical implications.

Based partly on the developing seventeenth-century technology for making clocks, Pascal's invention consisted of a series of adjacent ten-toothed cogwheels, so arranged that each complete revolution of a wheel on the right produced a rotation of one tooth (one-tenth of a revolution) in the wheel to its left. Thus the "addition" of ten units of movement in any wheel resulted in a "carry" of one unit on the wheel to its left. Numerals attached to the wheels could allow for the reading and recording of the results. This is the same basic mechanism used in recent times in such devices as automobile odometers and gas, electricity, and water meters.

Pascal spent the years between 1639 and 1645—while just in his late teens and early twenties—building various models of his calculator. This task severely tested the available technology for manufacturing precision parts, and even his best machines remained subject to jamming and frequent breakdowns. Nevertheless these "Pascalines" (as they were called by their inventor; see Figure 14.1) sometimes really worked, and when they did they aroused reactions of wonder and astonishment in all who saw them. One observer remarked that its inventor "knew how to animate copper and give wit to brass"; another wrote that Pascal had "reduced to mechanism

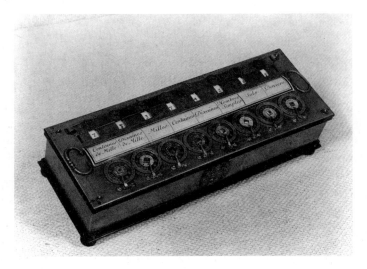

FIG 14.1 One of the Pascalines built by Blaise Pascal

a science which is wholly in the human brain."[1] Pascal himself was struck by his machine's *philosophical* implications, particularly with respect to Descartes' assertion that animals are essentially mechanical automatons, devoid of the exclusively human and nonmechanistic capacity for rational thought. Yet Pascal had now constructed a new kind of machine that, in his own words, "produces effects which approach nearer to thought than all the actions of animals."[2] And if machines could be constructed with the ability to reason, then reason obviously could not logically be seen as the uniquely defining and nonmechanistic human factor.

More disturbed by the suggestion that humans might be completely machinelike than that they might resemble animals, Pascal finally reassured himself with the thought that a mechanical calculator "does nothing which can allow us to say that it has will, like the animals [and humans]."[3] Accordingly, he went on to declare, in one of his most famous statements: "The heart has its reasons which reason knows nothing of. . . . We know the truth not only by the reason, but by the heart."[4] For Pascal, matters of emotion and the will, operating independently of and sometimes antagonistically to the cold voice of reason, became the main differentiators between minds and machines.

These reactions to a mechanical device that could do no more than add and subtract may seem exaggerated from our present perspective. But in fact they did make sense in the context of their times, and indeed they presaged some not-too-different attitudes that persist today in many modern reactions to computers as "thinking machines." To appreciate their seventeenth-century context, we must first understand that what we regard today as "simple" arithmetic was then a relatively recent cultural acquisition. Problems in addition and subtraction that are now easily mastered by young schoolchildren had lain beyond the capacity of even the greatest minds in medieval Europe. Medieval writings on technical subjects seldom even mentioned specific numbers greater than ten but rather referred to quantities in vague terms such as "a bit more" or "a medium-sized piece."[5] Actual numerical calculations were virtually unheard of.

The reason for this lay in the helter-skelter system of Roman numerals used in medieval times to represent numbers. Imagine the task of adding four hundred and twenty-seven to three hundred and forty-nine when those numbers are represented not by their familiar

427 and 349 but by CDXXVII and CCCXLIX, and you can grasp the essence of the difficulty. Extensive and precise calculations became possible only following the adoption of Arabic numerals, a brilliant convention that had arisen in India and been nurtured by the Arabs before being introduced into Europe. With its zero symbol and ingenious system of representing successive groups of powers of ten in successive columns to the left (i.e., units, tens, hundreds, thousands, etc.), Arabic numeration made possible a clearly describable and internally consistent *system* for manually solving problems in arithmetic. The new facility for calculation that followed the introduction of Arabic numerals proved to be an essential factor in the great advances generally associated with the European "scientific revolution." The observation and precise measurement of variables could now have an important practical purpose, because calculations could show their relationships to each other as mathematically specifiable laws. Galileo, one of the great initiators of this new approach, declared in 1623 that the "grand book" of the universe "is written in the language of mathematics."[6] We have already seen in earlier chapters how Descartes, Leibniz, and Newton extended the reach of mathematical explanation into increasingly farther domains of the physical world.

Galileo's hypothesis that mathematics constitutes the basic "language" of science was carried a step further by the English philosopher Thomas Hobbes[*] in his *Leviathan* of 1651, where he argued that *human reason itself* is essentially a form of mathematical calculation:

> In what manner so ever there is place for addition and subtraction, there also is place for reason, and where these have no place, there reason has nothing at all to do; for reason is nothing but reckoning (that is the adding and subtracting of consequences). . . . When a man reasoneth, he does nothing else but conceive a sum total from addition of the partials; or conceive a remainder, from subtraction of one sum from another.[7]

By the middle of the seventeenth century three important developments had occurred that would later coalesce to create a major current

---

[*] As noted in Chapter 2, Hobbes was also a predecessor of Locke in proposing the notion of the "social contract."

in modern cognitive psychology. First was the ever-increasing ability to perform mathematical calculations according to prescribed and systematic rules, calculations that yielded scientific laws that greatly enhanced the comprehensibility of the physical world. Second was the notion, partially realized by Pascal, that since the principles of calculation were perfectly regular and precisely specifiable, they could potentially be performed by machines. And third was the intuition of Hobbes that these specifiable and systematic calculational processes resembled the essence of human rational thought in general.

Over the past three and a half centuries these three ideas have been continuously broadened and deepened. Increasingly powerful calculating machines and computers have been invented, vastly surpassing the capacity of the Pascaline. And concurrently, the very definitions of mathematics and "calculation" themselves have broadened increasingly. First arithmetic, then traditional algebra, and finally mathematics in general have come to be seen only as specific examples of more general schemes for systematic symbol manipulation. Thus, in modern translation Hobbes's hypothesis asserts that rational thought consists essentially in the manipulation of symbols of some kind, according to certain precisely specifiable rules. The idea that these "thought processes" might also be performed by our increasingly sophisticated computing machinery lies at the heart of the modern discipline known as **artificial intelligence**, typically abbreviated simply as **AI**. And just as Pascal had mixed feelings about the implications of his Pascaline, so have more recent scientists expressed a variety of attitudes regarding the power, potentialities, and philosophical implications of the new machines. Our first principal character in this progression, Gottfried Leibniz, makes a return visit from Chapter 2.

Leibniz and the Mechanization of Logic

Wonderful as Pascal's machine seemed in its time, it had a serious limitation in that it could only add and subtract. Multiplication or division could be accomplished only through successive acts of addition or subtraction; for example, to multiply five times seven the operator would have to enter (add) the number seven five successive times. Here was an obvious source of both tedium and error. A young

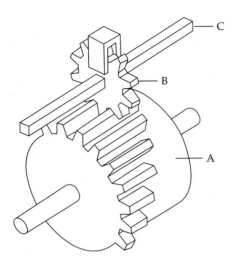

FIG 14.2
Leibniz's stepped cylinder

Leibniz solved this problem during his prodigiously productive stay in Paris in the early 1670s by inventing a new mechanism he called a "stepped cylinder" and incorporating it into a calculator that could multiply and divide in single operations (see Figure 14.2). As noted in Chapter 2, he took the device to London in 1673 and so impressed the members of Britain's Royal Society that he was named one of its first non-British Fellows. A few years later he arranged with Peter the Great of Russia to have a machine sent to the Emperor of China as an example of the overwhelming superiority of Western technology. Somewhat immodestly, Leibniz thought his calculator should be commemorated by the motto "Superior to Man."[8]

In contrast to Pascal, Leibniz was philosophically untroubled by the thought of a machine that could calculate numbers better than a human being. In fact, he allowed his imagination to roam even farther by conceiving a general way in which calculating machines might one day surpass human beings not only in arithmetic but in the solving of problems in *logic*. Here, potentially, was penetration by a machine into a process traditionally held to lie at the very heart of human rational thought.

Leibniz conceived, first of all, of constructing a new *universal language* for philosophy, whose terms and characters would transcend national differences in the same way that mathematical symbols do. He imagined that the different words or concepts in this language would "contain" one another in various logical hierarchies, similarly to the way in which the concept of "human" is logically contained in that of "animal," which in turn is contained in "living thing." Thus, the statements "a human is an animal," "an animal is a living thing," and "a human is a living thing" are all assertions of the "embeddedness" of the first concept in the second. Leibniz believed that a concept such as "living thing" might itself be embedded in still-higher-order concepts, which might in turn be embedded in others. But eventually, he argued, a limit should be reached and one could arrive at a level of "first terms" that are not further analyzable.

If this language were completed, Leibniz believed that a great many traditional logical arguments could be precisely translated into statements of *inclusion*, such as when the syllogism

> Every animal is a living thing,
> and every human being is an animal,
> therefore every human being is a living thing.

becomes rendered as:

> *Living thing* includes *animal*,
> and *animal* includes *human being*,
> therefore *living thing* includes *human being*.

Other sorts of translations could involve statements of "not including" or "excluding." For example, the hypothetical proposition "No just person can be unhappy" could be expressed as "The concept of *the just person* excludes the concept of *the unhappy person*."[9] Note that these operations of including and excluding are similar to those of addition and subtraction. Further, with the completion of the new universal language of first terms and all intermediate relations of embeddedness, all concepts could essentially be assigned *numbers* representing their precise degrees of inclusiveness relative to each other.

With the new language, people of all differing persuasions and national backgrounds would be able not only to converse with each other in common terms but also to *calculate* the solutions to many of the problems that divide them. And because machines like Leibniz's own could perform calculations more reliably than humans, people confronting complicated logical or even ethical dilemmas could simply say, "Let us calculate" and proceed to do so by setting the dials and turning the handle of a machine. Here was a visionary yet quite specific proposal for a potential *application* of Hobbes's hypothesis that "when a man reasoneth, he does nothing else but conceive a sum total from addition of the partials; or conceive of a remainder, from subtraction of one sum from another."

Of course Leibniz's dream of a universal language never came true, and after his death the subject of logic followed a different course from the one he envisaged. Logical statements did not become essentially reduced to arithmetic; instead, both classical logic and traditional mathematics came to be seen as examples of a still more general **symbolic logic**. Before turning to this issue, however, we must mention one further invention of Leibniz that would also play a major role in future computer developments.

At the same time he was inventing his calculator and developing the infinitesimal calculus, Leibniz also came up with the idea for **binary arithmetic**—the representation of all numbers by just ones and zeroes. In this system, successive digits to the left represent increasing powers of *two* instead of the ten in our standard Arabic decimal notation. Thus, in binary the numbers from zero through ten are written 0, 1, 10, 11, 100, 101, 110, 111, 1000, 1001, and 1010. Arithmetic in binary, as in decimal, is perfectly straightforward and follows easily specifiable rules—but it also entails much longer rows of numerals than the decimal system, and more carrying or borrowing. For these reasons binary arithmetic did not lend itself to easy mechanical simulation by the gear-and-cogwheel technology used in the early calculators. So even though Leibniz developed binary arithmetic and his mechanical calculator at the same point in his life, the possibility of combining the two ideas into a binary-based calculator—or indeed of finding any practical application at all for binary arithmetic—never occurred to him. We shall see, however, that such a possibility was finally taken seriously in the twentieth century, and with momentous consequences.

But before that could happen, both calculator technology and theoretical mathematics had to undergo considerable intermediate development during the nineteenth century. A central figure in both of these areas was an English mathematician and mechanical visionary named **Charles Babbage** (1792–1871), who began his career by following explicitly in the footsteps of his great predecessor Leibniz.

Charles Babbage and the Analytical Engine

The precocious son of a wealthy English banker, Charles Babbage studied mathematics independently as a teenager and found upon entering Cambridge University that he knew more than his teachers. In his independent study he had ventured to obtain and read work by continental mathematicians who had pursued the calculus using the notation system originally devised by Leibniz. At Cambridge as in the rest of Britain, mathematicians had patriotically but obstinately continued to use the notation devised by Leibniz's bitter rival, Newton. Although logically equivalent, the Leibnizian system proved both easier to use and more conducive to progress than the Newtonian, and as a consequence mathematics had flourished on the continent but languished in Britain throughout the eighteenth century.

Babbage found a small group of other internationally minded mathematics students at Cambridge, and together they formed the Analytical Society—a student group devoted to nothing less than the reform of English mathematics. Their first goal was to replace the Newtonian notation, in which the infinitesimal units of the calculus were represented by dots, with Leibniz's convention of using the letter d, as in the expressions dx, dy, etc. In a witty parody of the theological tracts then common at the university, Babbage wrote that the society would promote "the principles of pure D-ism as opposed to the Dot-age of the university."[10] The group succeeded, and under their leadership Leibnizian notation soon became standard in Britain as in the rest of the world.

Babbage's attention at Cambridge was also drawn to a mathematical problem of a more practical kind. Complicated calculations were often performed with the help of tables of logarithms, and Babbage recognized that these lengthy tables contained a sprinkling of many small but troublesome errors. He related in his autobiography that a friend once encountered him "in a kind of dreamy mood" and asked what he was dreaming about. Babbage's reply: "I am thinking that all these Tables pointing to the logarithms might be calculated by machinery."[11] A few years later, after Babbage had joined the Royal Astronomical Society, his attention was again drawn to the insidious effects of numerous small errors in the tables used for astronomical calculations. Resolving to make his undergraduate dream come true, he devised a new type of mechanical calculator that would not just do simple arithmetic but would generate accurate mathematical tables as complete as desired for any kind of polynomial function.

Babbage called his brainchild the **difference engine** because it would use what he called the "method of differences." The basic idea may be illustrated with the example of a simple polynomial function, the sequence of squared numbers. The squares of the numbers zero through six are 0, 1, 4, 9, 16, 25, and 36. From these numbers one can calculate the "first differences" by subtracting each square from the one immediately above it: 1 minus 0 equals 1; 4 minus 1 equals 3; 9 minus 4 equals 5; etc. Note that these first differences increase regularly by two: 1, 3, 5, 7, and so on. Thus, when "second differences" are calculated by subtracting each first difference from the one above it, all are equal to 2 (3 minus 1, 5 minus 3, 7 minus 5, etc.). With this knowledge, it follows that one can reverse these subtractive processes and generate as complete a table of squares as one wants simply by using addition. That is, first differences may be produced by adding 2 to 1 to get 3, then 2 to 3 to get 5, 2 to 5 to get 7, and so on. Then (starting with the number 2) one can add each number's first difference to the preceding number's square to obtain its own square: 3 plus 1 equals 4; 5 plus 4 equals 9; 7 plus 9 equals 16; and so on.

Babbage demonstrated that tables for many of the most important mathematical and physical functions—including logarithms, actuarial probabilities, and even astronomical configurations—could be generated in a similar way, although in more complicated cases one had to extract third, fourth, or even higher-order differences before arriving at a column that was all the same. And if addition could be mechanized, so could the generation of these tables by a difference engine—much more complex than previous calculating machines, but following the same principles. Babbage designed and built a small-scale prototype of such a device and demonstrated it for the Astronomical Society in 1821. His model interested the government because of its many possible practical uses, and he was granted £1,500 to construct a full-scale version. Unfortunately, however, technical difficulties intervened, and after eleven years and substantial further investment by both the government and Babbage personally, one exasperated official sarcastically declared that the only use of such a machine would now be to calculate the vast sums that had been squandered on it.[12] Support was discontinued and Babbage was left a bitter man. His only solace was knowing that his *idea* was right—as would be confirmed in 1854 when a Swedish printer named George Scheutz actually built a working difference engine.

But while bitter and disappointed, Babbage continued to dream and design. Indeed, even as his difference engine project ground to a halt, he conceived an even more visionary device that he called the **analytical engine**. The difference engine, while more powerful than any of its predecessors, had still been confined to the single task of solving polynomial equations; in current terminology, it was a fixed-function or single-purpose computer. Babbage's new dream—another inspired one that turned out to be prophetically correct—was of a single machine capable of performing virtually *any* type of calculation. It would be fed not only the basic data to be processed but also a set of instructions as to what kinds of processing it should undergo, and in what order. The instructions, like the data, could be changed from one operation to another. Thus, Babbage conceived of his analytical engine as a "universal machine," or what we call today a **programmable computer**.

Babbage's analytical engine required five main components. First would be an input system for the data and instructions, modeled after an earlier invention by the French weaver **Joseph Jacquard** (1752–1834). Jacquard had used a set of stiff cards, each one with a different pattern of punched holes, to regulate his looms as they wove many different intricate patterns. The holes selectively permitted rods to pass through and activate different threads in the loom, and for each successive throw of the loom a new card would enter the control position. Thus the "program" for any desired complex pattern would be written in a properly sequenced deck of cards. Variations on this idea of input via punched cards would remain at the heart of computer technology well into modern times.

The second component of Babbage's analytical engine, the "mill," would perform the actual calculations and resembled the difference engine (see Figure 14.3). Closely connected was the third component, a "control" mechanism to receive instructions from the input and ensure that the mill would perform the prescribed calculations in the proper sequence. Fourth, a "memory" store was required, to retain not

FIG 14.3 The "mill" from a model of Babbage's analytical engine

only the original data fed to the machine but also, crucially, the *results* of calculations performed by the machine, for possible use in still further computations. And fifth, Babbage proposed an output device for presenting the final results of the engine's series of calculations. These five principal components still define the modern computer.

If the practical problems involved in building a difference engine had been daunting, for the analytical engine they were overwhelming. The smallest of imprecisions in a part could hinder smooth functioning, an effect that increased geometrically with the number of parts. Babbage's difference engine prototypes were small enough to be cranked by hand, but a completed analytical engine, by comparison, would have been the size of a small locomotive, and like a locomotive it would require the power of a steam engine to drive it! Unsurprisingly enough after the difference engine debacle, Babbage received no government or other official support for his analytical engine.

Babbage did gain an important ally, however, when his plan attracted the fascinated interest of **Ada, the Countess of Lovelace** (1815–1852). The only daughter of the famous poet Lord Byron and a gifted mathematician in her own right, Lady Lovelace studied Babbage's plan carefully, engaged him in conversation about its more obscure points, and wrote a series of "notes" that remain the best sources of information about it.[13] Those notes reveal that she appreciated—perhaps better than Babbage himself did—both the machine's potential and some of its more philosophical implications.

Lovelace described the analytical engine as a potential "executive right-hand of abstract algebra," and as a sort of mathematical loom that "weaves algebraical patterns just as the Jacquard-loom weaves flowers and leaves." And as an up-to-date mathematician she knew that the boundaries of algebraic analysis were expanding rapidly, rendering the engine potentially applicable to a surprisingly wide variety of problems: "Supposing, for instance, that the fundamental relations of pitched sounds in the science of harmony and musical composition were susceptible of mathematical expression, the engine might compose elaborate and scientific pieces of music of any degree of complexity or extent."[14] This possibility may not have impressed Babbage, who had little ear for music and carried on a lifelong battle against public organ grinders. But still, Lovelace correctly prophesied that the applications of a universal calculating machine would some-day go well beyond the traditional domains of mathematics.

Even as she appreciated the analytical engine's potentially great versatility, however, Lovelace also foresaw a clear limitation of its capabilities:

> It is desirable to guard against the possibility of exaggerated ideas that might arise as to the powers of the Analytical engine. . . . It has no pretensions whatever to *originate* anything. It can do whatever *we know how to order it* to perform. It can follow analysis; but it has no power of *anticipating* any relations or truths. Its province is to assist us in making *available* what we are already acquainted with [emphasis in original].[15]

Thus, while she thought an analytical engine might one day produce a musical composition, it could only be one that follows predetermined and precisely defined rules. Anything that breaks or modifies the previously established rules—as happens in cases of genuine human creativity—would require a human as opposed to a purely mechanical touch. Known as the **Lovelace objection**, this constraint is commonly expressed today as: "Computers can only do what they have been programmed to do."

When Ada Lovelace died prematurely in 1852, only in her thirties, Babbage lost his most important moral support. His bitterness and irascibility increased, leading his friend Charles Darwin to describe him as "a disappointed and discontented man whose expression was often or generally morose. . . . One day he told me he had invented a plan by which all fires could be effectively stopped, but added—'I shan't publish it—damn them all, let all their houses be burnt.'"[16] Of course, Babbage had some real reasons to feel disillusioned, having produced mechanical designs that were truly valid but too far ahead of their time to win anything except neglect and scorn during his lifetime.

Babbage did live long enough, however, to see a major culmination of the generalizing movement in mathematics that he and his Analytical Society fellows had initiated at Cambridge. In 1847 a brilliant and largely self-taught young Englishman named **George Boole** (1815–1864) published a revolutionary book entitled *Mathematical Analysis of Logic*, which argued that all of traditional mathematics should be thought of as just one of many possible forms of systematic symbol manipulation. In the new and broader definition Boole was proposing, mathematics would no longer be just the science of number and magnitude, but "a method resting upon the employment of Symbols, whose laws of combination are known and general, and whose results admit of a consistent interpretation."[17] Among the fields that should be thought of under this expanded definition as "mathematical" was logic. Just as symbols could denote specific numerals and arithmetical operations, so could they be used to represent specific logical operations or properties such as *and, or, if*, etc.

Seven years later in *Investigation of the Laws of Thought*, Boole actually translated much of the content of traditional logic into this formal, mathematics-like terminology—now appropriately referred to as **Boolean algebra**. In creating this new discipline of symbolic logic, Boole actualized Leibniz's dream of formally uniting the fields of logic and computational mathematics. In the early twentieth century Boole's project was carried still further by the philosophers Alfred North Whitehead (1861–1947) and Bertrand Russell (1872–1970), whose monumental *Principia Mathematica* (1910–1913) provided a seemingly definitive resolution of all mathematics into the terms of symbolic logic.

From the perspective of our present story, this work raised the possibility that a universal machine capable of performing all kinds of mathematical or algebraical calculations in the traditional sense might also be turned to the solution of any appropriately symbolized problem in logic and reasoning. The serious pursuit of this idea awaited the contributions of yet another brilliant Cambridge-educated English mathematician named **Alan Mathison Turing** (1912–1954).

Alan Turing's Machine and Test

The second son of an English member of the Indian Civil Service, Alan Turing (see Figure 14.4) showed an early bent for mathematics and science and at the age of 14 was sent by his ambitious parents to the prestigious Sherborne School in southwest England. So anxious was he to arrive at the school on time, in the face of a national railway strike, young Alan reportedly rode his bicycle unaccompanied—a trip of more than 60 miles. Once in school, in a pattern reminiscent of

FIG 14.4
Alan Turing
(1912–1954)

Darwin and Galton many years earlier, he found that his scientific gifts were devalued, and he chafed under an overwhelming emphasis on classical studies. His headmaster was soon writing to his parents: "He must aim at becoming *educated*. If he is to be solely a *scientific specialist*, he is wasting his time at [Sherborne] school."[18] Still, he persisted and finally gained admission in 1931 to his second choice of Cambridge University Colleges, King's College.

At Cambridge his mathematical abilities and originality of mind were finally recognized, and for his thesis research he grappled with a complex question in formal number theory known as the *Entscheidungsproblem* or "decision problem." This problem in and of itself bore no direct relation to mechanical calculating devices, but Turing found that he could solve it partly by imagining a kind of device that has come to be called a **Turing machine**, for the manipulation of what he called "computable numbers." By computable numbers he meant any set of numbers *or symbols* capable of being manipulated in the Boolean sense, according to some set of formally specifiable and self-consistent rules.

The mathematical details of Turing's solution need not concern us, but his imaginary machine has played a major role in the modern development of AI. As shown in Figure 14.5, its only two essential components are a *tape* and a *head*. The tape is divided into squares, each of which may be blank or may contain a single symbol from

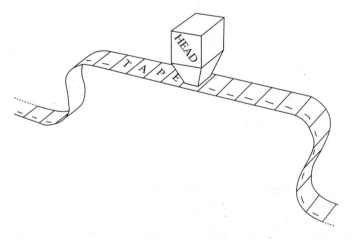

FIG 14.5 Diagram of a Turing machine
[Adapted from John Haugeland, *Artificial Intelligence: The Very Idea* (Cambridge, MA: MIT Press, 1985), 134]

some finite set of computable numbers. The head, which is capable of assuming some finite number of internal states, rides above the tape and "reads" the squares one at a time. After reading each square, the head performs a specific operation depending on which particular symbol (or blank) it has read, and its own particular internal state. Each operation has just three components: (1) the head may "overwrite" the symbol with a new one or a blank, or it may keep it the same; (2) it may move the tape one square to the right or to the left, bringing another symbol to be read and operated on, or it may halt; and (3) it may alter its own internal state or keep it the same.

In a 1937 paper describing his thesis research,[19] Turing formally proved not only that such a simple-seeming machine could be "programmed" to perform any specifiable kind of calculation, but also more important, that it would be possible to create instructions for a "universal" Turing machine, capable of copying, move for move, the operations of all other simpler and more specific machines. With a completely different and simpler "architecture" than Babbage's analytical engine, here was another machine with potentially universal calculating power. In the 1930s all of this was purely theoretical, because even for a simple calculation such as addition the programming steps required were tedious and, from a human perspective, unacceptably inefficient. And a universal machine's program must necessarily be enormously more complex than those they can mimic, because their operations must be flexible enough to cover all possibilities.

Still, the concept of the Turing machine conclusively proved the *possibility* of building a universal computing machine of some kind, and in the years following 1937 a new type of computer architecture came to be developed, just as "simple" as the Turing machine in its essential components but vastly more efficient in its capacity for processing symbols. Turing himself played a role in these developments, along with many other scientists mainly in Britain and the United States.

Electronic Computers, von Neumann Architecture, and the Turing Test

After introducing his imaginary machine, Turing gained hands-on experience with some very real calculating devices of quite a different type, as he led the top-secret British effort to break German codes during World War II. Those codes, generated and changed at frequent intervals by a complex machine called "Enigma" and believed by the Germans to be indecipherable, were in fact often deciphered by specific-purpose computing machines designed by Turing and his team. After receiving coded messages via punched paper tape, these machines substituted letters and numbers for one another in various patterns on a trial-and-error basis until finding one that produced comprehensible messages. There were always many hundreds of thousands of possible codes to be tested, and often the machines failed to find the correct ones. But by using first electric telephone-type relays and later electronic tubes as their basic processing mechanism, these machines were almost unimaginably faster than anything previously developed. The most powerful machine, nicknamed "Colossus," contained 2,000 tubes able to process input from punched tape at the then-amazing rate of 5,000 characters per second. Often enough these machines churned out the correct decoding, giving the Allies invaluable advance knowledge of strategic German fleet and troop movements. Indeed, they played a major role in shortening the war. Furthermore, the machines' electronic circuitry and speed of operation presaged future developments in the design and manufacture of what we know today as computers.

The potential special relevance of electronic circuitry to universal computation had already been pointed out in 1938 by a young engineering graduate student at MIT named **Claude Shannon** (1916–2001). His study, "A Symbolic Analysis of Relay and Switching Circuits,"[20] certainly ranks among the most important master's theses ever written. Shannon demonstrated, first, that notations in binary code (that is, entirely in combinations of ones and zeroes) could be used to represent not only ordinary arithmetic but also the much more generalized problems characteristic of Boolean algebra and symbolic logic. Indeed, the binary code proved to be ideal for representing dichotomous logical conditions such as true/false and either/or. Further, Shannon pointed out that these binary codes could all be represented mechanically by sequences of relay circuits capable only of being open or closed. That is, patterns of switches in an "on" or "off" state could be used to represent the patterns of ones and zeroes constituting the binary code. If Leibniz could have looked over Shannon's shoulder as he wrote this thesis, he would surely have smiled to see his ideas for binary arithmetic and the mechanical calculation of logical problems brought together in such a powerful new way.

These ideas were developed further by the Americans **Warren McCulloch** (1898–1969) and **Walter Pitts** (1923–1969) in a 1943 paper titled "A Logical Calculus of the Ideas Immanent in Nervous Activity," which conceptualized the brain and nervous system as a vast "nervous network" of interconnected neurons, each one capable of being either activated or not ("on" or "off") and of transmitting its excitation or not to its neighbors in a manner directly analogous to a network of binary switches. This raised the possibility that an electronic computer using binary digital mechanisms might serve as a more or less exact model of what actually goes on in the brain and nervous system during logical thought.

In the meantime, the war spurred great progress in calculating technology in the United States, just as in Turing's Britain. Scientists at Harvard University and IBM Corporation cooperated to build a gigantic, all-purpose calculator called the Harvard Mark I, 55 feet long and 8 feet high when completed in 1943. Capable of being programmed to perform any kind of numerical calculation, it was a true, modern-day electrical realization of Babbage's analytical engine. But although marvelously engineered and impressive to see, the Mark I used electromagnetic relays instead of the much faster electronic tubes. Almost immediately, a tube-based universal calculator called the Electronic Numerical Integrator and Calculator (ENIAC) was conceived by scientists at the University of Pennsylvania's Moore School of Engineering. And when a member of the ENIAC team had a chance conversation with the Princeton mathematician **John von Neumann** (1903–1957), a collaboration was established that changed the nature of computing forever.

Assigned during the war to work on top-secret government projects including the atom bomb, von Neumann, like Turing, became acutely aware of the need for increasingly fast and powerful calculating machines. More than coincidentally, he had secret wartime meetings with Turing when the Englishman visited the United States for consultations regarding his own top-secret code-breaking work. When von Neumann learned of the Moore School's ENIAC project, he was immediately interested and actively involved himself in one of the most important problems of computer design. Although the operating speed of the new-breed electronic calculators had increased exponentially with new technology, a bottleneck remained in the relative slowness of the process of instructing the machines which calculations to perform. In all universal machines from Babbage's analytical engine through the proposed new ENIAC, each new calculating task required a new set of instructions to be fed into the machine. Here was an obvious inefficiency, that would have to be corrected if the enormous calculating potential of the new computers was to be realized fully.

Von Neumann's great contribution was to show how a computer could avoid this inefficiency by making use of **stored programs**—that is, by internally storing many of its operating instructions in its own memory, along with the data and the results of its calculations. He recognized that different complex calculations invariably entail the use of the same component processes, or "subroutines," only in different combinations, at different points in the operations, and applied to different data. In a remarkable feat of engineering design, he showed how these component subroutines could be stored in the computer's memory as preset sequences of binary-coded instructions and then accessed at just the appropriate points in widely varying computational sequences. It was now possible to construct higher-order **assembly languages** for computer instructions, in which complex hierarchies of subroutines could be arranged and electronically executed following simple commands. Commonly used computer programming languages such as BASIC, COBOL, FORTRAN, C, and Pascal all followed from this basic idea.

Following von Neumann's contribution, computer developments rapidly occurred on both the mechanical and the conceptual fronts. On the "hardware" side of things, the invention first of transistors and then of silicon "chips" provided ever smaller, faster, and more reliable substitutes for electronic tubes as the basic binary switching mechanism in computers. And on the conceptual side, von Neumann's inspiration led to a great concentration by computer scientists on the general issues of *programming*—on the sophisticated and maximally efficient use of these powerful new machines. Even today, however, computers and many of their programs follow the same basic design as proposed by von Neumann and are said to be based on a "von Neumann architecture."

By the early 1950s a new intellectual context had been created for mechanical calculators. It was now certain that "universal machines" of several types were possible, and while those based on Babbage's or Turing's early models entailed major practical difficulties, those using electronic circuitry to represent binary-coded and modularly stored instructions in a von Neumann architecture were both feasible and possible. Further, Shannon and others had shown how problems in logic as well as traditional calculation could be mechanically represented by networks of binary switches, and McCulloch and Pitts had conceptually linked exactly this kind of architecture with the structure of the human nervous system. For the first time, it became plausible to regard machines as performing acts that not only resembled but that to some degree might be *the same as* thought processes in human beings. The issue of machine as mind (and conversely of mind as machine) assumed a new prominence.

Unsurprisingly, Alan Turing was among the first to seriously explore this question. In a 1950 paper titled "Computing Machinery and Intelligence," Turing raised the question "Can machines think?" and proposed to answer by means of what he called "the imitation game." As one example of this game, he suggested a situation in which a man and a woman are in a room separate from an interrogator, who communicates with them exclusively through typewritten messages. The interrogator's task is to determine, through asking questions and receiving answers, which is the man and which the woman. To complicate matters, however, one of the respondents is instructed to respond deceptively, and the other is told to assist the interrogator in arriving at the correct solution. Neither respondent is compelled to tell the truth, so direct questions such as "Are you the man or woman?" are not of any help. Turing proposed that experiments be conducted to determine how often, on the average, an interrogator would be taken in by the deceptive participant and led to make an incorrect final decision. Then he continued with the key question:

> What will happen when a machine takes the part of [the man or the woman] in this game? Will the interrogator decide wrongly as often when the game is played like this as he does when the game is played between a man and a woman? These questions replace our original, "Can machines think?"[21]

In essence, this **Turing test** assesses the "intelligence" of a machine according to its ability to interact with a human being in some complex task requiring genuinely intelligent behavior, in a manner indistinguishable from that of a real person. The only constraint is that some impersonal communication medium such as a typewriter (or nowadays a computer terminal) be used in order to eliminate nonverbal cues such as physical appearance, tone of voice, and so on. Although Turing himself was intensely interested in the "internal states" of the machines involved, he proposed that his test focus primarily on their directly observable inputs and outputs. During a period of behavioristic dominance (particularly in America), many were tempted to deemphasize the role of inner states, and as we shall see the Turing test aroused some controversy on that score. Nevertheless, for several decades a primary goal for researchers in artificial intelligence has been development of machines and programs capable of at least imitating—and sometimes surpassing—skilled human beings in the performance of various complex intellectual tasks.

Unfortunately, Turing himself could not participate fully in the postwar development of intelligent machines. Ever open and outspoken in his views, he was openly gay in an era when homosexuality was still a crime in Britain. Arrested and convicted in 1952 and given a choice of going to prison versus a year of probation with hormonal castration, he opted for the latter. As a consequence of his overt homosexuality, however, he lost his security clearance, and Britain and the world were denied the services of a brilliant scientist who had helped win the war and who as much as anyone was responsible for initiating the computer age. Turing became increasingly depressed by these developments, and on June 8, 1954, he was found dead of cyanide poisoning with a half-eaten apple by his side. Almost certainly he committed suicide, while contriving the circumstances to lead his mother to believe it had been an accidental poisoning.[22]

Intelligent Machines

Among the first to seriously attempt the computer simulation of complex human reasoning were **Allen Newell** (1927–1992) and **Herbert Simon** (1916–2001) at California's Rand Corporation. Working on one of the new breed of computers nicknamed the "Johnniac" (after John von Neumann), they looked long and hard for a feasible and interesting symbol-manipulation task to start with. After considering and rejecting several possibilities, including chess playing and Euclidean geometry, they finally selected a project with almost poetic appropriateness: a program to reproduce formal proofs for some of the basic theorems in Whitehead and Russell's *Principia Mathematica*. Those theorems, of course, lay at the heart of symbolic logic itself and represented the culmination of the movement to integrate mathematics into general logic, which has been noted throughout this chapter.

Their program, called **Logic Theorist** (**LT**) and introduced in 1956, contained representations in its memory of five basic logical axioms and three permissible operations for transforming (translating) the terms of a newly introduced statement into other terms that were logically consistent. The program followed a strategy of "backward reasoning" in constructing its proofs. That is, instead of starting with the axioms and proceeding in a "forward" direction to construct a proof, LT began with the proposed theorem itself and attempted to work backward and "decompose" it into axioms.

Compared to human logicians, LT had a limited store of permissible operations. Nevertheless, it successfully generated valid proofs for a substantial number of theorems from *Principia Mathematica*, one of which Bertrand Russell himself described as more elegant and efficient than his own. (But when Newell and Simon submitted the proof to the *Journal of Symbolic Logic*, with "Logic Theorist" named as a co-author, it was rejected for publication because of its nonhuman origins.) LT's creators, since moved to the Carnegie Institute of Technology in Pittsburgh, believed they had achieved something revolutionary. Noting that backward reasoning is characteristic of many creative problem-solving activities by humans, Simon announced to one of his classes in 1956, "Over Christmas Allen Newell and I invented a thinking machine."[23]

Yet Newell and Simon recognized that LT, for all its virtues and successes, had some glaring shortcomings and limitations when compared to a human thinker. In particular, it worked by applying all possible transformations to all possible terms in a predetermined order without preselection. Such an exhaustive and systematic search through all possibilities, referred to as an **algorithm**, is appropriate and useful only when the possibilities are relatively few. It worked well for LT with its limited number of transforming operations to try, just as it worked for Piaget's formally operational children (described in Chapter 13) as they systematically tested all the possible chemical combinations in their attempts to produce colored and colorless liquids. But in many other real-life intellectual problems, the numbers of possibilities to be considered are emphatically not few in number. In playing chess, for example, an average game consists of about forty pairs of moves and countermoves by the two players. Assuming that each individual move represents one out of some thirty to thirty-five legal possibilities, to which the opponent has a comparable number of options for a countermove, an algorithmic analysis of all possibilities for just one pair of moves would entail approximately a thousand combinations. Extending the analysis to two pairs would entail a thousand times a thousand, and the number increases a thousandfold for each successive level. The number of possible combinations in a typical game of forty moves is 10 to the 120th power—the number 1 followed by 120 zeroes—a figure far exceeding the total number of atoms in the known universe.

Chess is just one of a number of intellectual tasks routinely performed by human beings in which such a "combinatorial explosion" occurs if one tries to systematically consider all possible moves and outcomes. Conversational language—the activity proposed by Turing for his original "Turing Test"—is another. Assuming that any genuinely conversational machine would have to have a vocabulary of several thousand words at its disposal, the number of possible grammatical sentences it could construct is more than astronomical. In conversation as in chess, an algorithmic strategy like that of LT is neither appropriate nor possible. Instead, some principles of *preselection* must guide the search for solutions, suggesting hunches or possibilities that seem particularly likely to lead to success. In the language of Newell and Simon, **heuristic** as opposed to algorithmic strategies would sometimes have to be adopted by a genuinely intelligent computer program, strategies to limit the "search space" to be explored for solutions. Thus, the Carnegie scientists began work on a new and more ambitious artificial intelligence program, which they called the **General Problem Solver**, or **GPS**.

As its name implied, GPS was designed to be a *general* program capable of solving several kinds of problems. Newell and Simon began by observing a group of human subjects, asking them to think out loud as they worked on a variety of different tasks such as planning chess moves, proving theorems, or solving problems in cryptarithmetic (where letters are substituted for numbers according to a code that has to be figured out). Following these human models, they designed GPS to use a **means-ends analysis**, in which the *desired* solution-state for a problem is regularly compared to its actual current state and the difference or "distance" between the two is assessed. As its heuristic, GPS was equipped to recognize some twelve kinds of differences between the two states (for example, differences in position or grouping of chess pieces, or differences in signs or connectives in logical statements) and was programmed with a set of specific operations that experience had shown to be particularly useful for reducing each specific kind of difference.

For example, if GPS detected three kinds of difference between its current and desired states, it would attempt to apply just the three sets of operators that had proven useful for reducing those particular differences. If one or more of the operators proved inapplicable in the current situation, these would still be held "in reserve" or "in memory" by the program to be tried after the other operations have been performed. GPS would measure the new distance between current state and desired goal after each operation, and if the distance was being reduced, the selected "path" of operations would continue until the distance became zero and the problem was therefore solved. Sometimes, however, the continued use of the initially selected operators would begin to *increase* the distance, thus representing a false solution or "blind alley"—a situation that also often confronts human problem solvers. In these cases, GPS was programmed to try alternative paths. Thus, GPS had an ability to test various possible paths to a solution and to pursue the most promising while abandoning false leads—a flexibility that mimicked actual human reasoning much more closely than LT ever could. GPS indeed succeeded in solving a number of problems in chess strategy, cryptarithmetic, and some other logical puzzles, with at least a semblance of human efficiency. While acknowledging its imperfections, the program's creators saw it as an important step, offering "a series of lessons that give a more perfect view of the nature of problem solving and what is required to construct processes that accomplish it."[24] In other words, they saw GPS as a simplified but possibly valid *model* of real human intellectual functioning, one that demonstrated some genuine attributes of "intelligence" while "thinking" in the same general way human beings do.

In arguing for this important similarity between machine and mind, Newell and Simon did *not* claim that their computer exactly mimicked the human brain in terms of its physical-mechanical operations. McCulloch and Pitts, of course, had suggested that a binary-coded, digital computer could potentially provide a virtually exact model of the human brain and nervous system, thus raising the possibility that one day an actual computerized "brain" might be constructed, structurally similar to a human brain in all details except for the materials it was constructed from. The GPS group, however, adopted a point of view known as **computational functionalism** and claimed only to have demonstrated a "functional equivalence" between computer and brain: "Our theory is a theory of the information *processes* involved in problem solving and not a theory of neural or electronic *mechanisms* for information processing [emphasis added]."[25]

The hypothesis of computational functionalism highlights a point already implicitly made in our historical survey of "universal machines": namely, that architectures as diverse as Babbage's, Turing's, and von Neumann's are all capable of performing the whole range of specifiable computational tasks—albeit with very different kinds of mechanisms. The brain, perhaps, will turn out to be a universal machine with yet another kind of architecture. This does not undermine the possibility of a valid program of artificial intelligence, however, because all universal machines retain a *functional* similarity in their capacity to perform the same computations in the same sequences. Thus, the essential problem for AI is to show not that brain and computer are identical in their mechanical detail but rather that they use the same sequences of computational steps or calculations in solving their problems—that is, that they approach their problem-solving and other "thinking" tasks in the same functional manner. In the language of modern computer technology, computational functionalism suggests that the essential similarity between artificial and natural intelligence lies in the software rather than the hardware involved.

Minds Versus Machines

The development of LT GPS, and some other early AI programs in the 1950s and early 1950s stirred great excitement and optimism for the future. Even as GPS was still on the drawing board, Herbert Simon boldly predicted that before 1970 computer programs would be capable of defeating the world's chess champion; would derive important new mathematical theorems and compose music accepted by experts as having genuine aesthetic value; and would transform major psychological theories into computer language.[26] Another half-joking prediction made the rounds among AI scientists, to the effect that people would be fortunate if, within the foreseeable future, computers still kept them around as pets.

Simon's predictions turned out to be overly optimistic in that it took much longer to fulfill them than he thought it would, and the exact nature of their fulfillment requires some qualifying discussion. For all the hopes with which he and his colleagues had launched GPS, by 1970 the whole project had in fact been canceled. There were two major reasons for the project's loss of momentum, and both raised issues that continue to be relevant today. First, while GPS was intended to be an authentically general program capable of solving many different types of problems, its generality turned out to be very limited—restricted basically to "closed" logical problems expressible in formal symbols and susceptible to clear-cut "correct" solutions. Other important kinds of problems, such as learning to navigate in a new territory or to acquire a new skill, were beyond the program's capacity. The second reason lay in the recognition that GPS could only detect those differences and use those operators that had been incorporated into it by its human creators. Thus the hard part—the essential formulation of the problems, specification of the search spaces to be explored, and plotting of specific strategies to be followed—had to be done by human beings. Just as Ada Lovelace had remarked about Babbage's analytical engine, GPS could have "no pretensions whatever to *originate* anything." Its creative intelligence lay much more in its human originators than in the program itself.

Partly in reaction to GPS's failure to achieve real generality, many subsequent AI projects have aimed at solving relatively specific kinds of problems, within domains sometimes referred to as "microworlds." In pursuing their more specialized problems, some AI scientists have employed a **connectionist computing model**, sometimes also referred to *parallel distributed processing (PDP)*, that differs in several ways from the earliest programs. LT, GPS, and the other early programs worked by performing a specified sequence of operations on a specified set of symbols, with both the operations and the symbols being stored in specific memory locations. These programs have been described as **serialist** and **symbolic** in their processing strategy. In connectionist models, by contrast, many operations go on simultaneously, and their "objects" are *patterns of activity* throughout the whole system, rather than symbols in prespecified locations.

Some of these connectionist programs have shown the capacity to simulate important aspects of logical problem solving that seemed beyond the capacity of serialist models. In particular, they can show a more humanlike response to problems they cannot completely solve. Whereas serialist programs typically stop or "crash" when they run out of options or are given defective data to process, PDP programs can continue indefinitely in making responses that arrive ever closer to a complete solution, even though they may never actually get there. AI scientists refer to this more humanlike response to unsuccessful or incomplete learning as *graceful degradation.*

Using both connectionist and serialist models on ever faster and more powerful computers, AI scientists have by now created an impressive array of special-purpose programs. A few of these have performed so impressively that some have called into question the Lovelace objection regarding computers' supposed lack of originality. This issue has been extensively discussed by the British psychologist Margaret Boden, who poses not one but a whole series of "Lovelace Questions."[27] Besides the ultimate "Can a computer ever really be creative?" Boden also asks, "Can a computer *appear to be* creative?" and "Can computational concepts help one to *understand* creativity?" In answering these questions she makes a distinction between **improbabilist** and **impossibilist creativity**. The first entails putting already familiar ideas or components together in novel but useful or interesting combinations, but according to preset rules. We demonstrate a form of this creativity each time we construct a previously unuttered sentence out of the words in our vocabulary, according to the rules of English grammar. Impossibilist creativity, by contrast, entails changing the rules themselves—in Boden's terms, effecting a "transformation of conceptual space." Einstein produced one such transformation in physics when he rejected the classical Newtonian assumptions of absolute and uniform dimensions of space and time and substituted the assumptions of relativity.

Boden suggests that AI programs have demonstrated elements of improbabilist creativity showing a capacity not only to create novel combinations but also to "map" and "explore" conceptual spaces according to preestablished rules. Some even have the capacity to change their rules—although they must do so according to some "higher-order" rules or instructions with which they have been programmed. Thus, the answer to the "ultimate" Lovelace question depends on whether one is requiring impossibilist creativity. To the other Lovelace questions, however, regarding the appearance of creativity by computers and the usefulness of computational concepts for an understanding of creativity, Boden answers a resounding yes.

Strong Versus Weak Artificial Intelligence

Thanks in part to nanotechnology and the exponential growth in their sheer computing power and speed—which in some cases exceed those of the human brain—properly programmed machines can now defeat world chess champions and perform "intelligently" on such diverse tasks as Euclidean geometry, recognizing and describing tonal harmony and "expressiveness" in music, diagnosing medical conditions, assembling haiku poems and short stories out of preprogrammed elements, drawing line figures, and analyzing chemical compounds.

Some of these programs are convincing enough in generating conversational responses that they can fool human judges into believing that they are actual, interacting human beings. Thus, they may be said to pass the requirements of the Turing test.

As noted earlier, however, the Turing test focused exclusively on the observable stimuli and responses that define the machine-human interactions. But even as they succeed in producing coherent and convincing responses, are these new machines really demonstrating a truly humanlike "intelligence"? The philosopher **John Searle** (b. 1932) addressed this issue by means of a provocative "thought experiment" known as the **Chinese room**.[28] In this exercise Searle imagined that he himself, who does not speak or understand Chinese, might be isolated in a room into which Chinese speakers could pass slips of paper with questions or comments written on them in Chinese. He further imagined that while he would understand not a whit of the meaning of these messages, he would have at his disposal an immensely detailed rulebook with precise directions about how to respond to any query. That is, he would look in the book for a pattern of "squiggles" (as they would subjectively seem to him) corresponding to the input questions and find an appropriate pattern of squiggles to send out in response. Assuming that the rulebook was complete[*] and composed by people who really understood Chinese, that response would be completely intelligible and logical to any Chinese interrogator, even though Searle himself would know nothing about what it meant.

Searle argues that in this situation he would be responding exactly like a computer programmed to read and respond to a formal system of symbols. Indeed, if the rules could be codified in a book for Searle, they could also be easily incorporated into a computer program that would pass the Turing test. And yet, as Searle emphasizes, there is a vast difference between his own or a computer program's responses in the Chinese room and those of a genuine speaker of Chinese. Searle and the computer program would be responding completely in terms of *syntactic* operations—that is, operations involving the formal manipulation of symbols according to specified rules. A genuine Chinese speaker—or Searle himself when conversing in his native English rather than Chinese—would have a further *semantic* comprehension of the actual *meaning* of the symbols.

Searle's distinction between these two kinds of responding recalls the one made by Freud's teacher Franz Brentano in 1874 between physical and psychological phenomena (see Chapter 11). For Brentano, physical phenomena entailed *objects* in lawful interaction with one another, while mental phenomena were *acts* that "contained"

---

[*] Of course, such a rulebook in real life would be impossibly long, as its creators would have to use a virtually algorithmic consideration of the Chinese language and would thus encounter a combinatorial explosion of possible conversational possibilities. Thus, Searle's exercise seems destined to remain a thought experiment rather than the real thing.

objects and lent *meaning* to them in the form of beliefs about them or desires regarding them This "aboutness" or *intentionality* of genuinely mental acts is what Searle saw as missing from his own or a computer's purely mechanical responses in the Chinese room but as characterizing the responses of a genuine Chinese speaker.

Searle's argument provoked considerable and complex discussion, as some critics argued that the intentionality and understanding would lie in the *system* of Searle as responder combined with the makers of the rulebook. It can be counterargued, however, that this is akin to asserting that intentionality resides in the system of computer *combined with* its programmer—a far cry from demonstrating that the computer or the program by themselves possess intentionality. Other critics have suggested that when and if sufficiently complex programs are ever written to pass a stringent form of the Turing test, intentionality will somehow arise as a sort of "emergent" property. But this possibility has been doubted by still others, who argue that intentionality and the very capacity for consciousness itself are qualities that have developed out of the long evolutionary history of the human species and that cannot be jerry-built into any computer program, however complex it might be. The debate is far from resolved and shows no sign of being resolved in the foreseeable future.

On one important point, however, Searle and his critics agree: namely, that computer modeling can be a useful *tool* for studying and understanding aspects of the cognitive process even if it cannot exactly reproduce that process. Boden made essentially this point in arguing that computer models can manifest *aspects* of the creative process and be helpful in *understanding* creativity, even if they are not themselves fully creative in the impossibilist sense. Searle himself differentiated between what he called **weak AI** versus **strong AI**. Weak AI holds that computer processes might be useful *models* for significant aspects of human cognitive processes, and the computer thus can be a useful tool for testing certain concrete hypotheses about how the mind *might* work in some of its functioning; Searle has no quarrel with this position. He objects only to strong AI: the assumption that a computer program can ever actually *be* a mind, indistinguishable from the real thing in all functional respects.

Note that Searle's objections to strong AI rest on a thought experiment—that is, an introspective consideration of his own conscious, subjective states. He imagined that there would be a distinctive difference between his own subjective states when conversing in an English whose meaning that he truly understands and in a meaningless system of Chinese "squiggles" produced "mechanically" according to hard-and-fast rules. He further imagined that any machine could function only in the latter way. But how can we be sure? Even if a computer could tell us, in Chinese, English, or any other language, that it was consciously experiencing intentionality, and if it could describe the experience in apparently realistic detail, by Searle's argument it could still be seen as responding "mechanically" through purely syntactic rules.

Many behaviorists, of course, responded to issues such as this one by declaring all consideration of subjectivity and consciousness—that is, anything not obviously susceptible to "objective" and potentially mechanistic analysis—simply out of bounds from their conception of psychology. Such was the essential position of AI scientists who would evaluate their products strictly by means of the Turing test—that is, in terms of their completely observable, "behavioral" output. There is no question that this point of view can be useful, both in establishing clear-cut experimental goals to be aimed for and in suggesting rules for the elimination of incorrect models. Machines that cannot pass the Turing test can never be taken as having a completely humanlike intelligence. And as we have seen, the possibility remains that more and more aspects of human rational thought will become interpretable as the systematic manipulation of formal symbol systems, potentially performable by a computer. Nevertheless, voices such as Searle's, questioning the ability of mechanism ever to account for intentionality and consciousness, and thus to provide a *complete* explanation of human thinking, show that psychology's essential nature and scope remain wide open to debate centuries after Descartes.

Regardless of where one stands on this "ultimate" question of the extent to which machines can be minds, there is no doubt but that computer technology played a major role in shaping current psychology. During the behavioristic 1940s and 1950s, many psychologists tended to emphasize the relationships between objectively observable stimuli and their resultant responses while paying little or no attention to the processes *within* the behaving organism that mediated these relationships. In the meantime, however, computer scientists were demonstrating the importance not just of their machines' physical qualities but especially of the internal programs that processed the data put into them. Intelligent machines could not be constructed or understood without strict attention to those central processes. Perhaps inevitably, increasing numbers of psychologists (there had always been a few) became convinced that human beings, like intelligent machines, cannot be understood without a similar emphasis on *their* internal processes. The new computer technologies provided some powerful models and hypotheses as to how these processes might be approached. This set the stage for a new *cognitive psychology* that quickly challenged the dominance of behaviorism. Many individuals from many institutions participated in this "cognitive revolution." For illustrative purposes, we shall focus on the psychologist who wrote the first textbook for the new discipline, who interacted with a large number of its other important figures, and who is sometimes regarded as its "father."

Ulric Neisser and Cognitive Psychology

Enthusiasm for baseball played an indirect but important role in determining the psychological interests of **Ulric Neisser** (1928–2012; see Figure 14.6). Born in Germany, he was the son of a distinguished Jewish economist who foresaw the oncoming Hitlerian disaster and emigrated to the United States in 1933. Neisser recalls that while growing up his supreme goal was to fit in and succeed in the American environment, and nothing being more "American" than baseball, he became an avid fan. He opens his autobiography with a childhood memory that reflected that interest and also illustrated a theoretical psychological issue that would interest him in later life.[29] His memory was of listening to a baseball game on the radio when the broadcast was interrupted by a news flash that the Japanese had just attacked Pearl Harbor. This was what Neisser would later call a "**flashbulb memory**," a vividly recalled image of exactly where one was and what one was doing when some particularly momentous event occurred. Despite the vividness of his recollection, however, Neisser later realized that it could not be accurate because the attack occurred in December when no baseball was being played or broadcast. Still

FIG 14.6
Ulric Neisser
(1928–2012)

later he learned that a professional *football* game had been played on that day between the New York Giants and the Brooklyn Dodgers, names identical to those of two baseball teams. So he had been listening to football but remembered it as baseball, which lay much closer to his heart. Here was a homely but compelling demonstration of the fact that memory is not a photo-perfect replica of past experience but rather a *construction* built on that experience as modified and *processed* by myriad emotional and other mental factors.[*]

Neisser further wrote that his enthusiasm exceeded his skill in playing baseball, so he was "the kid who was always chosen last" to be on a team. This experience helped to produce a "lifelong sympathy with the underdog," and he became a committed "infracaninophile" (a latinized term meaning "underdog-lover").[30] This tendency extended into his later academic life, when he became a psychology

---

[*] As noted in Chapter 10, psychologists such as Alfred Binet and Elizabeth Loftus have demonstrated and studied this phenomenon in the laboratory.

major at Harvard in the late 1940s. As he learned about the contrasting approaches of behaviorism and Gestalt psychology, he immediately preferred the latter:

> My antipathy to behaviorism stemmed not only from its dreary mechanical view of human nature but from the sheer fact of its dominance. I was already a committed infracaninophile, and Gestalt psychology was clearly the underdog in a department that included B. F. Skinner. I was particularly impressed by the way that Max Wertheimer and the other Gestalt psychologists viewed human nature "from above" rather than "from below."[31]

Although there were no self-identified Gestaltists at Harvard, several young faculty members were then extending the range of their research into broadly "cognitive" areas that went beyond the strict behavioristic guidelines. Jerome Bruner (see Chapter 13) and Leo Postman (1918–2004) were studying the influence of expectancy and other motivational variables on perception—an approach soon called the "New Look" in perception. **George A. Miller** (b. 1920) was developing interests in language and in a new area that was soon called "information theory." In work that echoed back 50 years to James Mckeen Cattell's study of apperception in Wundt's laboratory, Miller showed that the maximum number of items or "chunks" of information that may be held in mind at any one time was "the magical number seven, plus or minus two."[32]

Miller supervised Neisser's undergraduate thesis research, a perception study that produced limited results but helped him gain admission to the master's program at Swarthmore College where the Gestalt psychologist Wolfgang Köhler was on the faculty. Neisser also met and was befriended by the new assistant professor Henry Gleitman (b. 1925). Later a renowned teacher and textbook author, Gleitman was fresh off a Ph.D. with the "purposive behaviorist" E. C. Tolman at California. Although calling himself a behaviorist, Tolman was in the minority camp of psychologists who emphasized those "intervening variables" such as motives, purposes, and learned Gestalt-like patterns that come between a stimulus and its response.*

---

* See Chapter 9, pp. 378–379, for more on Tolman and his relationship to other prominent behaviorists.

Gleitman enlisted Neisser as an enthusiastic collaborator in "the life and death struggle between the mechanistic behaviorists, led by Clark Hull . . . , and the Gestalt-oriented expectancy theorists, led by Tolman."[33] Neisser returned to Harvard to complete his Ph.D. with a dissertation in psychophysics and in 1960 accepted a teaching position at Brandeis University in nearby Waltham.

At Brandeis his psychological horizons expanded farther. His department chair Abraham Maslow (who himself had been profoundly influenced by Gestalt psychology) advocated strenuously for a "third force" in psychology, to counter what he thought were the two overly dominant schools of behaviorism and psychoanalysis (see Chapter 12). Maslow personally hoped the third force would turn out to be his own brand of humanistic psychology, emphasizing the goal of "self-actualization," but he also tolerated alternative challenges to the psychological orthodoxy of the time. Neisser began to conceive of just such a challenge as he forged a crucial friendship with Oliver Selfridge (1926–2008), a brilliant young computer scientist at MIT's Lincoln Laboratory.

Artificial Intelligence and Cognitive Psychology

Selfridge had been a prominent early advocate of machine intelligence and had helped to organize the 1956 conference at which the term *artificial intelligence* was introduced into common use. Working on the problem of *machine pattern recognition*—an AI project to develop computer programs capable of responding differentially to different written letters or Morse Code symbols—Selfridge had created the playfully named *Pandemonium*. In this general program, several subroutines or miniprograms he called "demons" worked independently on separate aspects of the problem, *but all at the same time*—one of the first successful examples of parallel processing by a computer. Selfridge showed that when provided appropriate feedback about the accuracy of its final judgments (based on the combined input from the demons), this system could improve its performance over time, or *learn*.[34]

Neisser became a part-time consultant in Selfridge's lab, and the two collaborated in writing an accessible account of the Pandemonium program in an article for *Scientific American*.[35] More consequentially, Neisser became interested in the question of how *human* subjects tackle these same kinds of recognition problems and began his own research on the subject. As he did so, he gradually concluded that "although machine pattern recognition was intriguing, human pattern recognition was even more so." Eventually he found himself "profoundly ambivalent" about the mind as machine metaphor. "Computation and programming were obviously a rich source of ideas about mental processes—a source that I was using freely myself," he conceded. But "on the other hand my most basic intuitions, stemming from Gestalt psychology, humanistic thinking, and everywhere else, were offended by the suggestion that minds and brains were nothing but computers."[36] In a 1963 paper titled "The Imitation of Man by Machine," Neisser argued that computerized "thinking" is much less faceted than the human variety, does not undergo a normal course of development, and is not driven in the same way by multiple and interacting motives and feelings.[37]

Gradually during the early 1960s, all of Neisser's interests, predispositions, and influences began to coalesce around a central idea: "Perception, the span of attention, visual search, computer pattern recognition, problem solving, and remembering were all interrelated aspects of *information processing*. Perception and pattern recognition were input, remembering was output, and everything in between was one or another kind of processing" [emphasis added].[38] He further reflected that although he was not the only or first person to have expressed this idea, no one had written a book about it. Thus arose the inspiration for *Cognitive Psychology*, a textbook that would effectively launch a new academic specialty area.[39]

Cognitive Psychology

Neisser was certainly correct in acknowledging that he was not the first or only one to have had the idea for new "cognitive" subdiscipline. In 1960 his former mentors Miller and Bruner had established a new Center for Cognitive Studies at Harvard, using the term *cognitive* "defiantly" to mark their deviation from the old behavioristic orthodoxy.[40] In touting the new cognitive approach, Miller and his colleagues Eugene Galanter and Karl Pribram published *Plans and the Structure of Behavior* in 1960. This influential book proposed the typical computer sequence of test, operate, test (again), and exit (popularly abbreviated as the TOTE unit) as a model for human thinking. Among the many other topics to assume new prominence at the center were language and cognitive development in children. As noted in Chapter 9, the psycholinguist Noam Chomsky had strongly criticized Skinner's behavioristic analysis of language and proposed an innately given "transformational grammar" that shapes all human linguistic activity. The Harvard and MIT psychologist **Roger Brown** (1925–1997) was conducting seminal research on the acquisition and development of grammatical skills in children. And for the first time in America, sustained attention was being paid to Piaget and Inhelder's work on cognitive development in children, which had just been translated into English in 1958. As noted in Chapter 13, Bärbel Inhelder was one of the first sabbatical fellows at the Center, and her work with Piaget provided the stimulus for Bruner's adaptation of it into a new educational theory.

Neisser's particular approach to cognitive psychology, emphasizing the mind's *processing* of its sensory inputs, was essentially a modern updating of the earlier conception of the human mind as an active, transformative agency. Despite his unwillingness to fully equate human mental processes with those of machines, Neisser nonetheless used concepts and language from the emerging computer technology. His very conception of information processing as a sequence starting with input, followed by central processing that results in a final processed output, echoed Babbage's model for the functions of a universal engine. The word *processing* was itself borrowed from computer terminology, which designated the crucial component of a computer the *central processing unit*, or CPU. In general then, Neisser's "revolutionary" book on cognitive psychology consolidated many intellectual currents already in the psychological atmosphere during the 1960s while reconnecting them with some of psychology's most foundational ideas.

Neisser's book defined its subject, *cognition*, as "all the processes by which the sensory input is transformed, reduced, elaborated, stored, recovered, and used."[41] He comprehensively summarized work done over the previous two decades on the general subjects of visual cognition, audition and language, memory, and thought. Little of this content represented new or original research by Neisser himself, but by being brought together between two covers it achieved an effect similar to that of Wundt's *Principles of Physiological Psychology* nearly a century earlier: It defined a new discipline. In Neisser's words:

> *Cognitive Psychology* legitimized and interconnected a wide range of research programs, bringing them together by giving them a name. Many psychologists found themselves in a position like Molière's Monsieur Jourdan, who suddenly discovered that he had been speaking prose all his life! Most were pleased by the discovery, and "cognitive psychology" soon became an indispensible rubric. In the blink of an eye, there were cognitive journals, courses on cognition, training programs in cognitive psychology, and conferences of every kind.[42]

"Ecological" Influences on Cognitive Psychology

As the new cognitive psychology exploded into a growth industry, extending into virtually all academic psychology departments, it dealt with an ever-expanding range of topics, old and new. Neisser personally participated in several of these developments, including a notable debate on the venerable issue of human visual perception. Neisser's text had declared that the "proximal stimuli" for visual perception—the patterns of light waves that actually impinge on the visual system—are vastly different from both the original physical sources of the light and the conscious sensations that result after processing by the nervous system. In short, he emphasized the large amount of mental "construction" presumably involved in arriving at a conscious visual perception. Neisser was quickly challenged on this point by the Cornell University psychologist **James J. Gibson** (1904–1979), who promoted an **ecological psychology** which stressed that mind can only be understood as a partner in relation to its environment and that the properties of that environment are presented to the mind quite *directly*. Thus, Gibson argued that the essential structural information about visual stimulation already exists "in the light" and can be directly picked up by the mind without further construction or information processing. Gibson's wife, Eleanor Jack Gibson, has already been noted in Chapter 4 for her famous "visual cliff" experiments that challenged the Helmholtzian, inferential explanation of depth perception. This ability in extremely young and inexperienced infants to detect a "falling off" place was a good example of the direct pickup of information.

Neisser, who became a colleague and friend of the Gibsons at Cornell, found himself persuaded by many of their arguments. Ultimately, he concluded that he had overemphasized the degree of perceptual construction that goes on and agreed with Gibson that *some* important elements of sensory information can be "picked up" directly from the environment. He still found ample room for processing, however, especially when that information is thought about or remembered. Indeed, some of his most influential cognitive research involved the constructed nature of *memory*. Still influenced by the Gibsons, however, he believed that most laboratory studies of memory used artificial situations that trivialized the subject, so he argued for an "ecological" approach that would investigate memory in its natural, real-life settings.

One opportunity for such research arose when the transcripts of President Richard Nixon's tape-recorded conversations were published and could be compared against his counsel John Dean's testimony about them during the Watergate hearings. Despite Dean's reputation as a "human tape recorder," the actual recordings showed that he was incorrect on many details and had several contexts mixed up. But he had been correct in the more *general* sense that a real cover-up had taken place with the president's explicit approval. This example was similar in many respects to Neisser's own memory of learning about the Pearl Harbor attack: Memory sometimes could be "wrong on the surface but right in a deeper sense."[43]

Later, Neisser directly investigated the "flashbulb memories" of student subjects to two disasters: the explosion and crashing of the spacecraft *Challenger* in 1986, and the 1989 earthquake near San Francisco. Immediately after both events, he had freshmen college students write descriptions of exactly what they had been doing when they heard the news. Two or three years later he asked them to recall the events once again and compared the two accounts. In many cases the second accounts differed dramatically from the presumably more accurate, immediate recollections. He also found, however, that students who had actually *experienced* the California quake—as opposed to merely hearing about it—were more accurate in their secondary recollections.[44] All these findings dovetailed nicely with the contemporaneous work being conducted by other memory researchers such as Elizabeth Loftus (see Chapter 10) demonstrating the reconstructed nature of memory.

Neisser became involved in several other cognitive projects in the 1980s and 1990s, including a study of the forms of self-knowledge and chairing an American Psychological Association Task Force on the status of intelligence testing. By then, the new cognitive approach had extended its reach into innumerable areas of investigation signified by terms such as cognitive neuroscience, cognitive behavioral therapy, cognitive developmental psychology, and many more. Several of these have been highlighted in the course of this book. In assessing his personal role in promoting these developments, Neisser was modest: "I was not really the father of cognitive psychology, only the godfather who gave it a name. The name itself was not even very original, given that the Harvard Center for Cognitive Studies was already functioning. . . . The main thing about developments such as these is not what part I played in them but that psychology has moved ahead because of them."[45]

Conclusion

Neisser was surely justified in touting the genuine advances in knowledge produced by cognitive psychology. We certainly know a great deal more about how people sense, perceive, remember, and think than we did before the "cognitive revolution." Advances in neuroimaging technology now allow us to see inside the head, and the brain, in ways that were probably unimaginable to philosophers and scientists even half a century ago. In a history text such as this one, however, it is only appropriate to conclude the chapter by noting that these advances represent the latest stage in a tradition dating back to Descartes—namely, of applying the best available mechanistic models to the explanation of psychological phenomena while wrestling with the issue of the *limits* of such explanation. Descartes himself drew the line at consciousness, will, and rationality. Pascal and Hobbes anticipated modern AI by bringing aspects of rationality under the mechanistic purview, but Pascal emphatically denied that a machine could ever manifest will. Leibniz and Wundt excluded apperception from any mechanistic or deterministic analysis, and Lovelace denied that even a universal machine could ever be original. The issue has been highly charged emotionally for many people, as the nineteenth-century "new physiologists" actually swore an oath to embrace mechanism and reject vitalism. Fechner and James, while appreciating the explanatory power of the new mechanistic physiology, both suffered breakdowns precipitated by the philosophical implications they drew from it.

Following the behavioristic hiatus, the new breed of cognitive psychologists adopted language and concepts from computer technology and AI research in restoring attention to the internal states and processes that underlie our psychological reactions. Even as they make great progress, however, they continue to debate whether phenomena such as consciousness, will, or intentionality will ever be explicable in purely mechanistic terms, reproducible in machines, or visible on an fMRI scan. The only certainty is that they will never know if they do not try, and the results of their efforts will be valuable, and certainly controversial, whether or not they succeed.

Summary

Blaise Pascal's simple computing machine, the Pascaline, was the first in a series of theoretical and technological innovations in the quest to construct mechanical analogues of the human mind, a field eventually known as **artificial intelligence (AI)**. After the Pascaline, Leibniz's invention of the stepped cylinder, his description of a *universal language* for philosophy whose terms and characters would operate in the same way that mathematical symbols do, and his invention of **binary arithmetic** all moved this endeavor forward. Charles Babbage later designed a **difference engine** that could calculate polynomial functions mechanically and—with technological inspiration from the weaving industry—conceptualized an **analytical engine** that was in basic respects an early form of the modern **programmable computer**. George Boole's invention of **symbolic logic** provided universal language, making possible the translation of traditional logic problems into formal, mathematics-like terminology.

In the mid-1900s **Alan Turing** conceptualized the **Turing machine**, a hypothetical computer capable of manipulating any set of numbers or symbols according to some set of specifiable and self-consistent rules. Turing also proposed the **Turing test**, which was essentially an elaborate game to determine whether a computer program could successfully fool human interrogators into thinking they were conversing with a human being. **Claude Shannon** demonstrated that notations in binary code could be used to represent problems characteristic of Boolean algebra and symbolic logic and that binary codes could be represented mechanically by sequences of open and closed relay circuits. Building on this idea, **Warren McCulloch** and **Walter Pitts** then conceptualized the brain and nervous system as a vast network of interconnected neurons, each one capable of being either activated or not in a manner directly analogous to a network of binary switches. **John von Neumann**'s innovation of stored programs spurred the development of increasingly sophisticated computer hardware, enabling **Allen Newell** and **Herbert Simon**'s invention of a "thinking machine" called the **Logic Theorist (LT)**, which they subsequently replaced with the **General Problem Solver (GPS)**, a machine theoretically capable of solving any number of different problems. For the first time, it became plausible to regard machines as performing acts that not only resembled but might be identical to human reasoning. The limits and implications of the "mind as machine" metaphor are addressed in the **weak** and **strong AI** positions.

Alongside developments in AI and computing was the explosive growth of a new discipline of cognitive psychology. A seminal contributor here was **Ulric Neisser**, who despite personal ambivalence about the "mind as machine" metaphor, drew on many of the concepts and language developed by computer and AI researchers. He emphasized the mind's *processing* of its sensory inputs and used the term *information processing* to describe how the mind receives, manipulates, and then responds to stimuli. He also coined the term **flashbulb memory** and investigated the constructed aspects of memory.

Key Pioneers

Babbage, Charles, p. 610
Boole, George, p. 616
Brown, Roger, p. 640
Gibson, James J., p. 641
Jacquard, Joseph, p. 613
Lovelace, Ada, the
   Countess of, p. 614

McCulloch, Warren, p. 621
Miller, George A., p. 637
Neisser, Ulric, p. 635
Newell, Allen, p. 624
Pascal, Blaise, p. 603
Pitts, Walter, p. 621
Searle, John, p. 631

Shannon, Claude, p. 620

Simon, Herbert, p. 624

Turing, Alan Mathison, p. 617

von Neumann, John, p. 621

Key Terms

algorithm, p. 626

analytical engine, p. 613

artificial intelligence (AI), p. 607

assembly languages, p. 622

binary arithmetic, p. 610

Boolean algebra, p. 616

Chinese room, p. 631

computational functionalism, p. 628

connectionist computing
   model, p. 630

difference engine, p. 612

ecological psychology, p. 641

flashbulb memory, p. 635

General Problem Solver
   (GPS), p. 626

heuristic, p. 626

impossibilist creativity, p. 630

improbabilist creativity, p. 630

Logic Theorist (LT), p. 625

Lovelace objection, p. 615

means-ends analysis, p. 627

programmable computer, p. 613

serialist processing, p. 630

stored programs, p. 622

strong AI, p. 633

symbolic logic, p. 610

symbolic processing, p. 630

Turing machine, p. 618

Turing test, p. 624

weak AI, p. 633

Discussion Questions and Topics

1 Outline the weak and strong AI positions. Which position do you hold and why?

2 Throughout this chapter, the importance of *technological* innovations in the efforts to build "thinking machines" has been emphasized. Describe some of the technologies that facilitated the construction of mechanical analogues of human reasoning.

3 If the processes underlying human reasoning were ever completely described and explained, what philosophical implications would this have? That is, what impact would it have on our beliefs about ourselves as human beings?

Suggested Readings

Four readable general histories of computing devices and artificial intelligence are Christopher Evans's *The Mighty Micro: The Impact of the Computer Revolution* (London: Gollancz, 1979), Howard Gardner's *The Mind's New Science: A History of the Cognitive Revolution* (New York: Basic Books,

1985), John Haugeland's *Artificial Intelligence: The Very Idea* (Cambridge, MA: MIT Press, 1985), and Verron Pratt's *Thinking Machines: The Evolution of Artificial Intelligence* (New York and Oxford, UK: Basil Blackwell Ltd., 1987). Many key papers in modern AI history, including those by McCulloch and Pitts, Turing, Searle, and Newell and Simon, are reprinted in *The Philosophy of Artificial Intelligence*, edited by Margaret A. Boden (Oxford, UK: Oxford University Press, 1990). For an interesting analysis of many ingenious AI programs, also see Boden's *The Creative Mind: Myths and Mechanisms*. (London: Weidenfeld and Nicholson, 1990).

Ulric Neisser's "founding" textbook, *Cognitive Psychology*, was published in 1967 by Appleton-Century-Crofts (New York). His short but engaging "Autobiography" appears in Gardner Lindzey and William M. Runyan's *A History of Psychology in Autobiography*, vol. IX (Washington, DC: American Psychological Association, 2007), 268–301. And for an overview of the more general developments behind modern cognitive psychology, see Robert Hoffman's "American Cognitive Psychology" in *A Pictorial History of Psychology*, edited by W. G. Bringmann, H. E. Luck, R. Miller, and C. Early (Chicago: Quintessence Publishing, 1997), 594–598. The personal lives and careers of the Gibsons as a couple in science are recounted by Eleanor Jack Gibson in *Perceiving the Affordances: A Portrait of Two Psychologists* (Mahwah, NJ: Lawrence Erlbaum, 2002).

Origins of Applied Psychology

From the Courtroom to the Clinic

15

Hugo Münsterberg and Psychology in the Courtroom
Münsterberg's Early Life
Moving to America
Applied Psychology
German Nationalism

Lillian Gilbreth and the Psychology of Management
California Origins
Efficiency and the Worker
Gilbreth, Inc.

Lightner Witmer and the Clinical Method
Early Training and Career
The Psychological Clinic
Applied Psychology Meets Resistance

Leta Stetter Hollingworth: Clinician, Feminist, Professionalizer
Early Years
Becoming a Psychologist
Pioneer of the Psychology of Women
Professionalizer of Clinical Psychology

Applied Psychology Today

Summary

Key Pioneers

Key Terms

Discussion Questions and Topics

Suggested Readings

On a warm day in late June 1907, **Hugo Münsterberg** (1863–1916; see Figure 15.1), arguably one of the most famous psychologists in America,[1] left the leafy enclave of Harvard Yard in Cambridge, Massachusetts, and boarded a train for Boise, Idaho,

FIG 15.1
Hugo Münsterberg
(1863–1916)

where a spectacular murder trial was unfolding. The accused, Harry Orchard, was a one-time organizer for the powerful labor union Industrial Workers of the World. He had been arrested for the assassination of the former governor of Idaho, Frank Steunenberg, a longtime opponent of organized labor. Orchard initially denied his guilt, but under the influence of Steunenberg's widow he later confessed to having committed the murder, in collusion with at least sixteen others, purportedly at the behest of a small group of insiders in the Western Federation of Miners. Foremost among those Orchard implicated was well-known labor leader Big Bill Haywood. Haywood's lawyers declared that Orchard's confession was a lie brokered in return for a reduced sentence and that Haywood was innocent. The trial quickly mobilized pro- and anti-union sentiments across the United States. If Haywood were found guilty of Orchard's accusations, no less than the future of organized labor in the West would be at stake.[2]

After a four-day journey, Münsterberg arrived in the Boise courtroom armed with a suitcase full of psychological apparatus in time to see Orchard deliver his final testimony. What could a Harvard professor, arrived from Germany fifteen years earlier to replace William James as director of the Harvard Psychological Laboratory, contribute to these courtroom proceedings?

Hugo Münsterberg and Psychology in the Courtroom

Münsterberg's trip to Boise was catalyzed by two factors. First, Münsterberg was a prominent popularizer of the new psychology and had been commissioned by *McClure's* magazine to write an article about the trial. Although initially skeptical about the value of applied psychology, Münsterberg had become well known for his popular articles about the ways in which psychological knowledge could be applied to many areas of life.[5] He was especially adamant that scientific psychology was superior to common sense and that its methods should be used in many situations to improve the judgments of laypeople. Second, in his own work Münsterberg had become intrigued by the impact of emotion, suggestion, and dissociation on perception. He felt that these processes had implications for the psychology of testimony and the detection of deceit. Psychological expertise, Münsterberg was convinced, could be applied in the courtroom.

It was in this context that Münsterberg arrived in Boise to gather material for his article and try out some of his psychological tests and hypotheses. After Orchard's final testimony was delivered, the governor of Idaho himself drove the ambitious psychologist from the courtroom to the penitentiary in which Orchard was being held. There, over the course of 7 hours, Münsterberg administered almost 100 tests to try to discern the veracity of Orchard's claims. Foremost among the tests was a version of a word-association test, a procedure pioneered by Swiss psychiatrist Carl Jung (and described in Chapter 12). By presenting Orchard with loaded words like *revolver, blood,* and *pardon* and recording both the content of his responses and the time it took to produce an association, Münsterberg believed he could root out whether Orchard was lying or telling the truth.

In fact, Orchard's performance on the tests satisfied Münsterberg that he *was* telling the truth and that it was Haywood and his cronies who had been the masterminds behind the murders. Convinced that his tests were not only useful but indeed infallible, Münsterberg packed his bags and boarded the train back to Boston to write up his article, which he anticipated would appear after the trial ended.

However, when Münsterberg arrived in Boston exhausted after the long trip in the hot, crowded train, he was caught off-guard by a particularly persistent newspaper reporter and prematurely divulged that he was convinced of Orchard's truthfulness. The news hit the wire the next morning, and newspapers across the country reported Münsterberg's verdict. To defend his remarks, Münsterberg granted an interview explaining how he had come to his conclusion based on the results of his psychological tests. He refrained, however, from actually publishing these results. Meanwhile, a young colleague did write an extensive article for the *New York Herald Tribune* in which he described a number of the instruments that were used in the laboratory to measure the physiological responses that might indicate lying, such as the pneumograph, which recorded breathing rate, and the sphygmograph, which recorded heart rate. Although Münsterberg had not actually used these instruments with Orchard, further distortions of fact led one newspaper to report that Münsterberg had invented a "lying machine." In fact, an undergraduate student of Münsterberg's—William Moulton Marston—subsequently did go on to develop the polygraphic device that became known as the "lie detector." Marston also created the comic book character Wonder Woman, who, as readers may recall, used her Golden Lasso of Truth to force unsuspecting villains to divulge their lies![4]

Despite Münsterberg's ill-timed pronouncement of Orchard's innocence and corresponding indictment of Haywood, Haywood was actually acquitted. Without corroborating evidence to support Orchard's claims that he was acting at the behest of Haywood, Orchard was charged with the assassination and sentenced to hang. His sentence was later commuted to life imprisonment, and he died in prison in 1954.

Undeterred by his apparent "mistake" in pronouncing Orchard innocent, Münsterberg collected a number of the articles he had written on the psychology of testimony, confessions, and the influence of suggestion and published them in a popular book, *On the Witness Stand: Essays in Psychology and Crime*, in 1908. It was a bestseller and established Münsterberg's reputation as an applied psychologist and a popular, if somewhat sensationalistic, writer. In the introduction to the book, Münsterberg wrote proudly of his own scientific laboratory at Harvard, describing its twenty-seven rooms "overspun with electric wires and filled with chronoscopes and kymographs and tachistoscopes and ergographs."[5] But he quickly drew his readers' attention to the necessity of a rigorous applied psychology. Applied psychology, he noted, stood in relation to experimental psychology as engineering stood to physics. The time for the application of psychology to education, medicine, art, economics, and law, wrote Münsterberg, "is surely near."[6]

Although the new psychologists who founded the discipline of experimental psychology in the late 1800s initially focused on establishing the scientific credentials of their discipline by opening laboratories, developing apparatus, and running experiments, the idea of *applying* the procedures and findings from the psychological laboratory to everyday life—that is, giving it a *practical* function—had been broached at least as early as 1890. In that year, American psychologist James McKeen Cattell (see Chapter 5), who had studied with both Wundt in Germany and Galton in England, wrote that mental tests, of the sort that had been used in the laboratory to measure basic mental processes, could be of both scientific *and* practical value:

> Psychology cannot attain the certainty and exactness of the physical sciences unless it rests on a foundation of experiment and measurement. A step in this direction could be made by applying a series of mental tests and measurements to a large number of individuals. The results would be of considerable scientific value. . . . Individuals, besides, would find their tests interesting, and, perhaps, useful in regard to training, mode of life or indication of disease.[7]

In 1893, at the Chicago World's Fair, Cattell, University of Wisconsin psychologist Joseph Jastrow, Münsterberg, and others participated in designing and promoting the Psychology Exhibit, where fairgoers could have their mental capacities and characteristics measured by the new "scientists of the mind." In this public venue, other professionals were also introduced to the new field. Teachers were particularly interested in how these mental tests could be used in education. In fact, the interface between psychology and education would become extremely important in the development of applied psychology, as we will see later. Ironically, Münsterberg, who would eventually come as close as any psychologist to earning the title "founder of applied psychology,"[8] was originally disdainful of applying psychology to education. As his involvement in applied psychology deepened, however, he would dramatically change his views. How did the young German, trained in Wundt's Leipzig laboratory, become one of America's most famous applied psychologists?

Münsterberg's Early Life

Hugo Münsterberg was born on June 1, 1863, in Danzig, Germany (now called Gdansk, part of Poland). His father, Moritz, was a Jewish businessman who married into a prosperous family of lumber merchants. Hugo was Moritz's third son, but the first by his second wife Minna Anna Bernhardi, or Anna as she was known. Anna gave birth to Hugo and then one more son in 1865, before dying tragically in 1875, when Hugo was about to turn 12 years old. Moritz and his four sons were bereft but became more devoted to each other in the wake of their loss, and Hugo went out of his way to emulate and please his father. He became a diligent student, took up physical activities of which his father approved, and educated himself through travel and public lectures. In 1880, Moritz died suddenly at the age of 55. Now it was just the four brothers.

In 1881, Hugo completed his rigorous course of studies at the Danzig gymnasium with distinction. His oldest brother, Otto, had taken over their father's business and was in charge of administering Hugo's inheritance. At first Hugo traveled to Switzerland to study French at the University of Geneva. He fully immersed himself in Genevan society, often writing home not only about the satisfaction of his studies but of the fashionable company in which he found himself and the kaleidoscope of social events he encountered. Evidently somewhat alarmed by the frivolity he perceived in some of Hugo's reports, Otto was skeptical about his younger brother's proposal to extend his travels the following year to Paris, where he would supposedly write a "major history of culture."[9] After some negotiations, it was decided that Hugo would go to Leipzig to continue his studies in medicine.

As the child of an entrepreneur, Münsterberg was in the distinct minority of Leipzig students who did not come from long lineages of the highly educated elite. In addition, because of anti-Semitic rules, Jewish students were barred from pursuing government-related careers. Thus, there were large numbers of Jewish students in the professions of medicine, law, journalism, and the arts. Hugo's choice of medicine accorded both with his personal interests and these practical constraints. However, in the summer of 1883 he enrolled in a lecture course taught by the eminent Professor Wilhelm Wundt (see Chapter 5), who had recently established the first laboratory in experimental psychology. Excited by the prospect of an academic career and by the subject matter of the new psychology, Münsterberg completed a doctorate in psychology under Wundt in 1885 before completing his education with an M.D. from Heidelberg two years later. He then procured an unpaid position as an instructor, or *Privatdozent*, at the University of Freiburg, where his research and publishing career in the new psychology began.

Moving to America

One of Münsterberg's first publications was a report in which he challenged his teacher Wundt's conception of the will, arguing that the will was actually the experience of internal motor processes engendered in response to stimuli, rather than a feeling experienced directly. This article attracted the favorable attention of Wundt's American rival William James who, as we saw in Chapter 8, had proposed a somewhat similar theory. In addition to publishing, Münsterberg also established a laboratory at his home in Freiburg, which began to attract students from the United States. In 1891 he wrote a paper espousing the scientific character of the new psychology and the need for rigorous laboratory research. Thus, when he received an invitation from James to come to Harvard for a three-year appointment as director of the Psychological Laboratory there, Münsterberg leapt at the chance. Despite his love of his native Germany, a Harvard invitation was too tempting to turn down. Münsterberg and his family set sail for New York in the fall of 1892.

Münsterberg's three years at Harvard were a success. He quickly became fluent in English and was a popular lecturer. James and others found him interpersonally agreeable, and he attracted many students to the laboratory. Favorites among these early students were Mary Whiton Calkins and writer Gertrude Stein (see Chapter 8).[10] When, in the spring of 1895, Münsterberg returned to Freiburg, where his leave of absence was running out, he held an offer from Harvard that allowed him to take two years to decide whether he would return on a permanent basis. Münsterberg was ambivalent, but ultimately Harvard won out. He cut his ties to Germany and returned to the United States at age 34 to become professor of experimental psychology at Harvard. Little did he know that he would end up spending the rest of his illustrious, but relatively short, career so far from his homeland.

Applied Psychology

After his return to Cambridge, Münsterberg spent only a few more years actively directing and conducting research in the laboratory. Increasingly, his interests were turning to the incipient area of applied psychology. Although he had been previously disdainful of applied efforts, especially those of his Clark University colleague G. Stanley Hall who was using psychology in education,[11] Münsterberg eventually did an about-face, ultimately writing dozens of books and articles on the applications of psychology, even an article titled "Psychology and the Teacher" in 1909. By 1906 he had abandoned the laboratory entirely. Over the remaining ten years of his life, between 1906 and 1916, he published twenty books, most of which were on applied topics.

As this chapter's opening vignette indicates, one of Münsterberg's first forays into both applied psychology and the popular press was his work on legal testimony. A second foray was individual psychotherapy, which he practiced at Harvard over several years. In fact, the interest in dissociation and suggestibility that had motivated some of his forensic work in part led him to his interest in psychotherapy.

In a period when "psychotherapeutics" in American culture meant faith healing, mind cure, Christian Science, and the Emmanuel Movement, which preached that faith and science were reconcilable and that the powerful forces of the mind could cure the body,

Münsterberg generally positioned himself as an objective, scientific outsider. His approach was that any therapies, including Freudian ones, that assumed the existence of an unconscious were unscientific. When Freud made his only visit to America in 1909 at the invitation of G. Stanley Hall (see Chapter 11), Münsterberg was conveniently out of the country on a tour of Canada. Münsterberg was a vocal opponent of psychoanalytic theory. His own therapeutic assumptions, if not his techniques, stood in stark contrast to those of psychoanalysis and were more functional in nature. In Münsterberg's approach, clients were trained to try to forget their troubles and to suppress maladaptive behaviors, rather than bring repressed conflicts to light.[12] In 1909 Münsterberg published the book *Psychotherapy*, possibly the first book on the topic by a psychologist.[13]

Among Münsterberg's many and varied interests, a dominant one was the application of psychology to business and industry, an approach beginning to become known in Germany and elsewhere as **psychotechnics**. Münsterberg's America was marked by rapid urbanization and industrial expansion, including mechanization and other technological advances. To help deal with these changes, the American engineer **Frederick Winslow Taylor** (1865–1915) had developed a system called **scientific management**, the goal of which was to increase efficiency and productivity in the factory. This increased efficiency would be brought about by the careful application of *scientific* rather than "rule-of thumb" methods to the world of work. One of the changes that Taylor promoted was the breakdown of skilled labor into standardized tasks through a careful analysis of industrial work using time and motion studies. The emphasis was on increasing rates of production through increased efficiency; in practice, this meant figuring out how to enable workers to do more in less time by giving them quick, repetitive, menial tasks, often on an assembly line. It was Taylor's intention that scientific management would bring business owners higher profits, and the most productive workers higher wages.

Although initially quite successful, Taylor's system eventually encountered resistance from workers and their unions for a number of reasons. Taylor's own naïveté about how workers might respond to his system and his disdain for organized labor no doubt fueled some of this resistance. Many workers reacted unfavorably to what they perceived as Taylor's overly mechanistic methods. As a result, a number of strikes occurred in factories where the Taylor method was used, and the U.S. Congress actually passed legislation banning some of its key elements, such as using stopwatches to time workers' performance.[14]

Münsterberg admired Taylorism and embraced its main principles of expert analysis, increased efficiency, and rationalization of the workplace. This rationalization, Münsterberg argued, should include not only an analysis of the tasks but an analysis of the workers themselves. Münsterberg thus devoted much of his time and energy to devising tests that would match workers' aptitudes to appropriate jobs. He believed, apparently genuinely, that menial laborers, because of their special traits, would be as happy and fulfilled in their positions as any other worker. Ultimately, for the success of any personnel selection procedure, tests that could reproduce the mental and physical skills necessary for the job needed to be devised. Those who scored best on the tests could be placed in the jobs that corresponded to their skills.

To better understand the nature of work, Münsterberg sent out questionnaires to industrial manufacturers and personally visited a number of factories. In 1911 he was approached by a regional director for the Hamburg-American shipping line to devise a test that could be used to screen out incompetent ship captains. After extensive experimental fiddling, Münsterberg settled on a card-sorting task he felt would reveal the ability to make complex decisions quickly and accurately. It is not clear whether the company used the test or whether it successfully made these discriminations.

Demand for Münsterberg's expertise, however, increased unabated— as did his popular reputation. The next spring he was contracted by the American Association of Labor Legislation to research the mental traits that would predispose potential trolley car drivers to accidents. This time, Münsterberg developed a task that was significantly more complex than the card-sorting task he had previously devised for the ship captains. He constructed miniaturized approximations of the actual dilemmas that trolley car drivers would encounter in their work. Using scores on these tests, Münsterberg rank-ordered job applicants. He also used the tests to rank-order successful and unsuccessful drivers and compared the applicants' scores with those of the successful operators to weed out those not suited to the job.

In 1913 Münsterberg's book *Psychology and Industrial Efficiency*, first written in German, was published in English. For a brief period it was on the nonfiction bestseller lists. In it, he described these and many other tests he had devised to help fit workers to industrial, technical, and even sales positions. In 1915 he published *Business Psychology*. With these two books, Münsterberg firmly established his professional and popular reputation as a pioneer of industrial psychology.

German Nationalism

Münsterberg had traveled a long way from his laboratory beginnings and the commitment to scientific psychology that had originally secured his position at Harvard. He had also traveled a long way from his native Germany to advance his reputation and realize his professional ambitions. In many respects, however, Münsterberg's heart had always remained in his homeland. As an ardent German nationalist, he had positioned himself as an ambassador of German culture in his adopted home since the beginning of his tenure at Harvard. As the first World War began and the United States considered entering the war against Germany, Münsterberg's nationalism became increasingly problematic, both professionally and personally, and he was shunned by many of his American colleagues and friends. Ultimately, the stress that this ostracism engendered may have contributed to his premature death. In 1916, at the beginning of a lecture to a class of his Radcliffe students, Münsterberg collapsed at the lecture podium. His almost instant death, at the age of 53, was caused by a cerebral hemorrhage.

Although with Münsterberg's sudden and dramatic demise the field had lost a colorful, and at times controversial, pioneer, it was about to acquire another. In 1914, between the publication of Münsterberg's volumes on industrial efficiency and business psychology, another soon-to-be classic in the developing area of industrial psychology appeared: *The Psychology of Management*. Its author, a 36-year-old mother of six, was Lillian Moller Gilbreth.

Lillian Gilbreth and the Psychology of Management

When **Lillian Moller Gilbreth** (1878–1972; see Figure 15.2) published *The Psychology of Management* using only her initials—L. M.—because of the publisher's request that publicity for the book not reveal that she was a woman (a request, she later reported, that offended her husband Frank's feminist sensibility more than it did hers), she had completed all of the requirements for her Ph.D. in psychology at the University of California, Berkeley—except one. Although her dissertation, which became the book, was accepted, her degree was denied at the last minute by the Academic Senate because she hadn't met the requirement that she spend her last year of study in residence. Gilbreth, a partner in her husband's engineering business, had not stayed behind in her native California when the company, and her large family, moved east to accommodate a new

FIG 15.2
Lillian Moller Gilbreth
(1878–1972)

contract. Denied her degree, she promptly enrolled in nearby Rhode Island's Brown University, which had one of the earliest programs in applied psychology. She earned her Ph.D. there in 1915. Her second dissertation titled *The Elimination of Waste*, applied the principles of scientific management to the work of classroom teachers. According to some historians of psychology, hers was the first Ph.D. awarded in the field of industrial psychology.[15] Three days after she was awarded her doctorate, she gave birth to her seventh child.

Lillian and her husband, engineer **Frank Bunker Gilbreth** (1868–1924), were to have a total of twelve children, six boys and six girls, hence the title of the bestselling first account of the Gilbreth family exploits, *Cheaper by the Dozen* (1948), written by two of her children. It was followed by a second book, *Belles on Their Toes* (1950), which chronicled the family's life after the death of Frank Gilbreth in 1924. Although she was mythologized as a wife and mother in *Cheaper by the Dozen* (and the movie it spawned), Lillian Gilbreth's *professional* career and her contributions to applied psychology rank among the most impressive in psychology's history.

California Origins

Lillian Moller was born in Oakland, California, the eldest of nine children. Her parents, William Moller and Annie Degler Moller, were of German descent, and the family was quite affluent. They were also close-knit and traditional. Daughters were expected to learn domestic tasks and stay close to home. Thus, when Lillian, a serious, straight-A student, graduated from high school and decided she would like to attend the University of California to study literature, her father was strongly opposed. He felt that she should devote herself to her interests in music, reading, and travel and that college was suitable only for women who had to earn a living, usually by teaching; he was adamant that none of his daughters should have to work. Interestingly, Lillian had a rather unconventional aunt who, after a divorce (also uncommon at the time), pursued a medical education and became a practicing psychiatrist, moving to Vienna where she studied with Freud. Thus, there were examples of highly educated women in Lillian's family, and several of her cousins were already students at the university. She was determined to join them.

Reluctantly, her father finally relented and Lillian enrolled at the University of California to study English literature. She graduated in 1900 and was the university's first female commencement speaker. Prior to her speech, she was advised by the university president to be "womanly" in her presentation, to wear a dress with ruffles, and not try to imitate a man.[16] Lillian took his advice to heart and gave a successful speech, evidently impressing her father so much that he agreed to her plan to pursue a master's degree. One of her undergraduate professors recommended that she study at Columbia University in New York City, so she headed to the East Coast and enrolled at Columbia's Barnard College. Luckily, the family had plenty of relatives there, and Lillian was soon caught up in her studies and in making social contacts. When winter descended on the city, however, the native Californian was unprepared and quickly fell ill. Relatives alerted Lillian's father to her plight, and he arrived unannounced, whisking her back to the safety and warmth of California. When she recovered, she continued her courses at her alma mater, completing a thesis on Ben Jonson's *Bartholomew's Fair*, for which she steeped herself in Elizabethan history and literature.

On the completion of her M. Litt. at the University of California in 1902, Lillian embarked on a tour of Europe with three other young women and a chaperone, stopping first in New York to visit relatives and then continuing to Boston to board the ship for Europe. The trip was an eventful and exciting one for a number of reasons. Foremost among them was Lillian's introduction, in Boston, to her chaperone's cousin, Frank Bunker Gilbreth. An extroverted, energetic man several years Lillian's senior, Frank Gilbreth owned a construction company and made no secret of the fact that work consumed his interest and his time. His interest in Lillian, however, soon became quite apparent as well. The feeling was mutual, and in 1904, they were married.

Frank Gilbreth immediately began relaying knowledge of his chosen trade to his young bride, even as they began their soon-to-be large family together. Without a college education himself, Frank Gilbreth heartily supported his wife's continued education, but he encouraged her to pursue something practical. Becoming more and more interested in engineering and management, and coming under the influence of Taylor's system, Frank was moving away from construction and began to apply scientific management principles to tasks such as bricklaying. Lillian was his partner in life and work, and as she was helping him develop his ideas she went back to school and worked on her Ph.D. in an appropriately practical field: applied psychology. By 1915 Lillian had earned her degree and was a full partner in Frank's firm, bringing her psychological training to bear on problems of work.

Efficiency and the Worker

Both Lillian and Frank were proponents of Taylor's system of scientific management. Frank, with Lillian's collaboration, published *Motion Study* in 1911, the same year that Taylor published his *Principles of Scientific Management.* The Gilbreths developed and used complex **motion studies** to identify the most efficient way to get a task done. Using a movie camera to record in detail the movements required to perform tasks, the Gilbreths analyzed many different kinds of work and activities, from manufacturing, to surgery, to athletics. As a result of their studies, they identified 18 basic motions of the hand, calling these units **"therbligs,"** an anagram of Gilbreths. Part of their philosophy was that efficiency should reduce fatigue, and motion studies should reveal how to design machinery and methods to make workers' movements both more efficient and easier. They characterized their method as the "quest for the one best way" to get a task done. As a result of their analyses of surgical operations, for example, they noticed that surgeons often spent an inordinate amount of time searching for instruments. Their recommendations resulted in the now-ubiquitous practice of having a surgical nurse place the instrument in the surgeon's hand as requested. The emphasis on efficiency, shared by both Taylor's and the Gilbreths' systems, was parodied in the popular press, as seen in this cartoon of a "Taylorized kiss" that appeared in *Life* magazine in 1913 (see Figure 15.3).

Unlike Taylor, the Gilbreths were interested in investigating how the most efficient motions affected the individual worker. They hoped to use this information to design work that was maximally efficient *and* rewarding. The Gilbreth's philosophy was captured in Lillian's 1914 monograph: "The outline here given as to how men must, ultimately, under Scientific Management, be selected, serves

From "Life," 1913.

Efficiency Crank: Young man, are you aware that you employed fifteen unnecessary motions in delivering that kiss?

FIG 15.3 Cartoon parodying the efficiency movement, in *Life* magazine, 1913

to show that, far from being "made machines of," men are selected to
reach that special place where their individuality can be recognized
and rewarded to the greatest extent."[17]

This combination of *psychology* and management represented
a departure from strict Taylorism and reflected Lillian Gilbreth's
humanistic outlook. Her training in psychology, rather than engineering, predisposed her to see the human being as the most important
element in industry, and the well-being of the worker as central in the
design of the workplace. She emphasized the need to fit the job to the
worker, not vice versa. She also believed in the need to improve communication among workers, foremen, and managers and advocated
for the role of workers in critiquing methods of operation. As those
most directly involved in and affected by the work itself, workers, she
believed, should be consulted and receive recognition and rewards for
the ideas they generated. She even suggested that workers should share
in any profits that might accrue from their increased efficiency.

This participatory attitude carried over into all areas of her life,
including the running of her large and boisterous household.
Although, like her husband, she saw the benefit (and even necessity!) of using their management principles to organize family life,
this didn't mean that children were reduced to interchangeable cogs
in the domestic machine. Two of her children, Frank and Ernestine,

contrasted their mother and their father this way: "Mother saw her children as a dozen individuals, a dozen different personalities, who eventually would have to make their ways separately in the world. Dad saw them as an all-inclusive group, to be brought up under one master plan that would be best for everybody. What was good for Anne, he believed, would be good for Ernestine, for Bill, for Jack."[18]

Together with Frank, and continuing after his death, Lillian Gilbreth spread their method to determine the "one best way"[19] beyond the realm of industrial production to figure out how to improve many other kinds of problems and tasks, including vocational rehabilitation for the physically handicapped, and homemaking. After World War I, she and Frank became concerned with the plight of the thousands of soldiers who had become physically disabled as a result of their war injuries. They used motion studies to identify the kinds of work these men could do and the accommodations they would need to help them become productive workers and citizens. They also began to train managers and professors in their techniques, running summer institutes out of their home near Montclair, New Jersey, for many years.

Gilbreth, Inc.

These institutes were especially important to Lillian after Frank's untimely death of a heart attack in 1924. Faced with the challenge of being the sole breadwinner for 11 children on the cusp of their college educations (one of the 12 children, Mary, had died of diphtheria in 1912), Gilbreth undertook to continue the consulting business on her own. In fact, only three days after her husband collapsed on a commuter train platform while talking to her on the phone, she called a meeting of her large family and laid out their options. They could move to California where her own mother had offered to take them in; they could stay on the East Coast, where friends had offered to adopt some of the children; or they could try to stay together in their own home. This last option would require Gilbreth taking over the business full-time and was surely a gamble. The decision was unanimous to take that gamble. The next day, Gilbreth boarded a steamship with the tickets her husband had purchased for himself. She traveled to London and Prague, to the First International Management

Congress, where she delivered the talks she and her husband had jointly authored. The work of Gilbreth, Inc., and the unity of the Gilbreth family, would continue.

Initially unsure whether her clients would renew their contracts with the company operating under the sole direction of a woman, Gilbreth reinstituted the summer workshops she and Frank had developed, offering them as 16-week study courses in which she trained students in time and motion methods at her home laboratory. Students came from as far away as Germany, Belgium, England, and Japan to be trained in her Institute for Motion Study. As her reputation grew, she received new requests for her consulting services. She was hired by Macy's department store in New York City to study and improve the work of saleswomen. In order to fully understand the nature of the job, Gilbreth worked in the store herself. Her recommendations for how to increase job satisfaction and reduce fatigue included employee suggestion boxes, newsletters, a three-point promotion plan, hourly rest periods, and aptitude surveys. Her expertise was also used by Sears, Roebuck, & Company and Johnson & Johnson. In some cases, her services included not only management consulting but market research as well. For example, she carried out studies for Johnson & Johnson on the psychological effects of various kinds of sanitary napkin packaging.

In the late 1920s, Gilbreth turned her attention to the work of the homemaker. Ultimately, she was hired by most of the major appliance manufacturing companies to engineer kitchen design and individual appliances to the needs of the users. Her innovations included the shelves inside refrigerator doors and the foot-pedal trash can. Her studies resulted in the design principle of the kitchen triangle, which minimizes the motions needed to move between the kitchen's three major work areas. In 1927 she published *The Homemaker and Her Job* and in 1928, *Living with Our Children*, in which she stressed the need for domestic responsibilities to be shared and efficiently managed in order to create a happy and fulfilled household. Every housewife and mother, she wrote, needs to be an effective, efficient manager.

By 1929, with the future of Gilbreth, Inc., assured and the family on firmer financial footing, Gilbreth quit teaching at home and became a full-time consultant, committed to figuring out the one best way and convinced that the best way had to include both an analysis of the job and the way the worker felt about it. As the Depression worsened in 1930, President Herbert Hoover struck an emergency presidential committee to study the problem of unemployment. He asked Gilbreth to be a member of the committee, and she devised a federal program called "Share the Work" to stimulate the creation of new jobs. In 1935, she became a part-time professor of management at Purdue University in Indiana. During World War II, in which five of her six sons served (fortunately, all survived the war), Gilbreth, by then in her mid-sixties, served as a consultant at war plants and military bases. Over the course of her career, she would serve on committees under Presidents Roosevelt, Eisenhower, Kennedy, and Johnson on issues ranging from civil defense, to aging, to the rehabilitation of the physically handicapped.

Lillian Gilbreth remained professionally active until her death in 1972, at the age of 94. In 1966, she became the first woman awarded the Hoover Medal for distinguished public service by an engineer. During the period 1928–1964, she received 23 honorary degrees. In 1984, as a result of a campaign by the women's division of the American Society of Mechanical Engineers, she was featured on a commemorative United States postage stamp. To date, she is the only psychologist to receive this honor.

As an applied psychologist, Gilbreth has only recently come to the attention of historians of psychology and the social sciences, perhaps because so much of her work and professional affiliations were subsumed under the fields of management and engineering. However, her absence in many historical accounts can also be attributed to the more general neglect of women's contributions by those surveying the field. One historian of psychology has noted that despite her impressive accomplishments, neither Gilbreth nor three other women who made important contributions to industrial psychology were listed in a study of 538 important contributors to psychology that was published in 1974.[20] Even in histories of applied psychology, a field where women have traditionally been well represented in proportion to their numbers in psychology as a whole (although not necessarily in industrial/organizational psychology itself), Gilbreth has received little mention by historians surveying the field.

While Münsterberg has been called the father of applied psychology and spent much of his time applying psychology to industry, and

Gilbreth has been called the mother of industrial psychology,[21] we noted earlier that the interface between psychology and education was an especially important one for the history of applied psychology. In fact, it was an educational problem that captured the attention of the man who would later be called the father of clinical psychology.

Lightner Witmer and the Clinical Method

In the fall of 1892, as Hugo Münsterberg was setting sail to the United States from Germany to take up his first post at Harvard, an American schoolteacher, **Lightner Witmer** (1867–1956; see Figure 15.4), was preparing to leave Germany as well. Witmer had just completed his doctoral studies in Wundt's Leipzig laboratory and was returning to his native Philadelphia to take up a prearranged post as director of the psychological laboratory at the University of Pennsylvania. If they had not met already, the two men would soon cross paths at the inaugural meeting of the American Psychological Association at the University of Pennsylvania in December 1892. Their relationship would turn out to be a tumultuous one.

Although initially on friendly terms, Witmer and Münsterberg would eventually exchange sharp words over a number of issues, revealing not only their strong personalities but the professional tensions that beset the field at this time. When, in 1907, Witmer belittled the Harvard laboratory on the basis of Münsterberg's critique of the use of experimental psychology in education (a cause championed by Witmer), Münsterberg responded in his usual thin-skinned manner, and the formerly collegial relationship between the two men began to deteriorate. About a year later, Witmer published a brash indictment of William James, whose interests in psychic phenomena and spiritualism and general philosophical outlook offended Witmer's sense of the scientific nature of the new psychology. Even though Münsterberg and James held increasingly different views themselves, Münsterberg took Witmer's attack on James quite personally and demanded that Witmer's membership in the American Psychological Association be revoked. He also attacked Witmer's Psychological Clinic because its director, Witmer himself, did not hold an M.D. degree, which Münsterberg, of course, did. Witmer and Münsterberg

FIG 15.4
Lightner Witmer
(1867–1956)

shared a headstrong ambition and dogmatism that no doubt contributed to their antagonism. These qualities also fueled their important contributions to the development and professionalization of applied psychology in the first two decades of the twentieth century.

Early Training and Career

Born June 28, 1867, in Philadelphia, Lightner Witmer was the eldest son of a prosperous pharmacist of Pennsylvania Dutch stock. Witmer's ancestors were Mennonite, but his great-great-grandfather, David Sr., left the Mennonite church and converted to Episcopalianism. Witmer's father established a successful retail pharmacy business, and each of his four children went on to develop professional careers.

After college preparatory studies at the prestigious Episcopal Academy of Philadelphia, the 17-year-old Witmer enrolled at the University of Pennsylvania as an undergraduate in 1884, receiving his degree four years later. For the next two years he taught history and English at a local secondary school, Rugby Academy, and took graduate classes at the university. At this point his career path was unclear to him, and he considered both law and political science before settling on psychology. In 1889, while still a secondary-school teacher, Witmer had an experience that would prove important to his later work. It was, as he described it years later, an episode in which his "attention was first drawn to the phenomena of retardation."[22] By retardation, Witmer literally meant a case where a child's development had become retarded, or slowed, in comparison with his or her peers, and he or she had been held back in school.

In his role as Rugby Academy's English teacher, Witmer was presented with an upper-level-aged student who had extreme difficulties with both written and spoken language. The student could not articulate well and was unable to either speak or write proper sentences. Witmer soon discovered that traditional instruction was not helpful. He described the boy as having "verbal deafness," such that he could not distinguish accurately among phonetically similar words. Witmer realized that to help the boy, he needed to change his tutoring strategy. Instead of grammar lessons, he led him through elementary drill training in articulation, in the hopes of remediating his very early language deficiencies. He supplemented this drill with very basic grammar lessons.

With Witmer's assistance, the student's verbal skills improved to the point where he was admitted to university. But when Witmer later encountered him again as a pupil in one of his university classes, he was having difficulty passing. Witmer believed that if the child had received intervention early enough, he might have been able to completely overcome his deficiencies: "I was confident at the time, and this confidence has been justified by subsequent experience with similar cases, that if he had been given adequate instruction in articulation in the early years of childhood, he could have overcome his defect."[23] Witmer was to retain this belief in the importance of early intervention and the potential of remediation throughout his career.

In 1890 Witmer became a full-time graduate student and assistant to James McKeen Cattell in the psychological laboratory at the University of Pennsylvania. The laboratory was newly established, and Cattell equipped it in true Leipzig style. Cattell's tenure would be short, however. By June 1891 he was gone, leaving Philadelphia for a higher-paying position—at the then-staggering salary of $2500 dollars a year—at Columbia University in New York City. Cattell, himself a student of Wundt, recommended that the newly admitted Witmer travel to Leipzig and complete his doctoral research there, then return to the University of Pennsylvania to take up Cattell's vacated position as director of the laboratory.

Witmer took Cattell's advice and earned his doctorate with Wundt in Leipzig with a study of the aesthetic preference for geometrical figures of varying proportions. His research drew heavily on Gustav Fechner's work in experimental aesthetics (see Chapter 4), specifically testing the observation, made from the time of the Ancient Greeks, that an ideal ratio called the golden section characterized the proportions of the most aesthetically pleasing forms. Although not a groundbreaking piece of research, it was certainly enough to earn Witmer his scientific credentials and his Ph.D. He successfully completed his oral examination in 1892 and was officially awarded his degree in 1893, after he had returned to the United States.

When Witmer returned to Philadelphia, he assumed his position as successor to Cattell in the psychological laboratory at the University of Pennsylvania and continued to conduct experimental research. In 1894 he began to teach a graduate course in child psychology. In March 1896, one of his students—a teacher named Margaret Maguire, who was convinced that psychologists, if they were worth their practical salt, should be able to remedy educational problems—brought in a 14-year-old boy who could not spell. Witmer described "Charles Gilman" (as he was called in the published report) as of "somewhat more than average intellectual ability," but in addition to his poor spelling, he had problems with reading and language use. On careful examination, it was discovered that Charles had very poor eyesight; part of the cure for his bad spelling turned out to be a pair of glasses! Once his visual impairment was corrected, Witmer was able to work with him on his language difficulties, and Charles' academic performance improved considerably.

The Psychological Clinic

Witmer later claimed Gilman as the first case in the work of the psychological clinic. In 1896 he established a clinic at the University of Pennsylvania where children with educational problems, including both moral (behavioral) and mental deficiencies, could be brought for assessment and remediation. In December of that year, Witmer gave an address at the meeting of the American Psychological Association in which he outlined a program of practical work in psychology. His scheme included a number of components, including the investigation of mental development in schoolchildren using statistical and clinical methods, a clinic supplemented by a training school for the treatment of children suffering from retardation or physical defects that interfered with school progress, and the opportunity for psychology students to train for careers in the school system as psychological experts on mental and moral retardation.

Although formally established in 1896, the Psychological Clinic took only a slow trickle of cases in its first decade. Witmer later reported that he had neither the means nor the personnel to handle large numbers of cases in those early years. Also, he wanted to accrue more in-depth experience with individuals before expanding his work. Examination of the clinic's case records of this period reveals that a wide range of referrals were made and that Witmer himself did most of the examinations. He saw children (and a few adults) with problems ranging from stammering to aggressive behavior, sleep disturbances, overexcitability, refusal to eat, physical and developmental disabilities, brain injury, and melancholia, among other conditions.[24] Learning as he went, he consulted such well-known physicians as **S. Weir Mitchell** (1829–1914), also based in Philadelphia, who was known for his use of the "rest cure" to help treat neurasthenia, especially in women.[25]

Central to what Witmer came to call the **clinical method** was consultation with other professionals, including physicians, teachers, and social workers. As he developed it, the method involved a medical exam and psychological testing. Testing encompassed various cognitive and academic tasks. Witmer would also take a number of physical measurements and often referred children to specialists for specific examinations, especially those whom he suspected of having enlarged adenoids. Part of the accepted medical lore of the day was that enlarged adenoids could cause a variety of negative mental and developmental effects in children.

By about 1907, Witmer felt he had accrued sufficient experience to expand the work of the clinic, and the number of cases increased dramatically. He also started consulting at the Pennsylvania Training School for Feeble-Minded Children in Elwyn, just a few miles southwest of Philadelphia, and retained this position for 50 years. In 1908 he opened up a separate, private residential school in Wallingford, Pennsylvania, which came to be called the Rose Valley School. This facility was entirely independent from the university, although some of Witmer's students trained there. Witmer was to direct it well past his retirement from the university, and was committed to delivering professional care in a 24-hour therapeutic environment as well as overseeing the facility and its administration. Revenue was generated on what we would now call a fee-for-service basis, paid by parents who had children in residence. A small number of pro bono cases were also accepted.[26]

In 1907 Witmer also started a journal called *The Psychological Clinic: A Journal for the Study and Treatment of Mental Retardation and Deviation.* The journal was made possible through the very generous gift of a private donor, Mary L. Crozer, whom Witmer had approached with a request for $10,000 (about $150,000 in today's terms) to support the further development of the clinic and the journal. After some initial hesitation, Crozer granted Witmer's full request and the journal was launched. The primary articles were case reports from the clinic. Clearly, Witmer had now turned his thoughts to professionalizing the new field.

In the inaugural issue, Witmer published an article titled simply, "Clinical Psychology."[27] In it, he defined clinical psychology as a method and indicated that the clinical method could, theoretically, be used not only with children with developmental delays but with normal, precocious, and advanced children as well. He clearly articulated the close relationship, as he saw it, between the psychological *laboratory* and the *clinic* Indeed, he felt that the distinction between experimentation and application was artificial. He also noted the relationship of the new profession to medicine, education, and social work, but warned that training in these professions was not sufficient to practice clinical psychology. A new profession, with its foundations in psychology but supplemented by specific training in the clinical method, would be required.

Over the next several years, Witmer would train numerous students in clinical psychology who would then become important practitioners in their own right. During this time, more clinics were established and increasing numbers of psychologists began working in applied settings. **Grace Fernald** (1879–1950) and **Augusta Fox Bronner** (1881–1966) both worked at the Juvenile Psychopathic Institute in Chicago, where they undertook detailed assessments of delinquent youth in order to formulate individualized treatment plans. Both used the title "clinical psychologist" and were also involved in research and in test development. By 1914 there were psychology clinics at 19 American universities.[28] In 1906 one of G. Stanley Hall's students, **Henry Herbert Goddard** (1866–1957), became director of psychological research at the New Jersey Training School for Feeble-Minded Boys and Girls at Vineland. Soon after, Goddard traveled to Europe and was introduced to the recently developed Binet-Simon scales of intelligence (see Chapter 13), which he brought back to the United States and translated for English use. Witmer used Binet's intelligence test in his assessments, but he (like Binet) did not view intelligence as a reified entity easily captured in a single score. He was committed to using a large battery of tests and actually devised two of his own, the Witmer Formboard Test and the Witmer Cylinders Test.

Applied Psychology Meets Resistance

Although Witmer himself saw a close relationship between experimental and applied psychology and was unambivalent about his status as an applied psychologist, not all of his academic colleagues felt so confident about this aspect of their field. As the number of psychologists doing applied work increased in the first two decades of the twentieth century, they began to experience resistance from within their own discipline, from academic psychologists, and from other fields, such as psychiatry. This resistance seemed to increase as the popularity of applied psychology itself grew.

Some academic psychologists looked down on their colleagues' attempts to apply their science, arguing that their theories were undeveloped and their techniques were not supported with empirical evidence. Applied work was seen as messy and impure, and threatened the scientific credentials of the relatively new field. Psychiatrists, sensing impending competition from these nonmedically trained practitioners, also began to turn a critical eye on clinical psychology. In a 1916 report by the New York Psychiatrical Society the following

udgment was handed down by a committee investigating the activities of psychologists:

> We recommend that the Society express its disapproval of psy-
> chologists (or those who claim to be psychologists as a result of
> their ability to apply any set of psychological tests) undertaking
> to pass judgment upon the mental conditions of the sick, defec-
> tive, or otherwise abnormal persons when such findings involve
> questions of diagnosis, or affect the future care and career of
> such persons.[29]

Under such attack, applied psychologists responded by forming
their own association, separate from the American Psychological
Association (APA), called the American Association of Clinical Psychologists (AACP), in 1917. At least three factors underlay psychologists' motivation to establish a professional organization. The first
had to do with the upsurge of testing jobs in the public school system during the second decade of the 1900s. Immigration, urbanization, and mandatory schooling legislation in the United States
had led to a public school system in which large numbers of children of highly varying ability levels were being thrown into classrooms together. The services of testers were in high demand to help
identify, categorize, and sort students into appropriate programs.
Additionally, the profile of testing was heightened in the period
leading up to and following World War I, during which thousands
of recruits in the U.S. Army were administered psychological tests.
Thus, test development and administration became a burgeoning
industry.

In this rush toward testing, unqualified individuals without
appropriate academic backgrounds had been found to be in charge
of assessing and diagnosing mentally and educationally exceptional
children throughout the country. Psychologists began to worry about
asserting some control over the appropriate qualifications and standards for professional work. **J. E. Wallace Wallin** (1876–1969), one
of the psychologists concerned about this trend, wrote an article in
Science in 1913 in which he attempted to delineate the exact nature of
clinical psychology, the aims of clinical work, the kinds of cases clinical psychologists could handle, and how clinical psychology was different from other closely related professions. He concluded his article

with an admonition that reflected his colleagues' concerns about appropriate credentialing:

> Clinical work, both in psychology and medicine, requires clinical training. The assumption that any psychologist or educationist is qualified to do successful psycho-clinical work after learning how to administer a few mental tests, is preposterous and fraught with the gravest consequences.[30]

The second factor motivating clinical psychologists to create their own organization had to do with their low professional status, both within their own profession and vis-à-vis physicians and psychiatrists. By establishing a professional organization and formal credentialing procedures, clinical psychologists sought to elevate their status above mere technicians and emulate more established professions, such as medicine and engineering.

Finally, the AACP was founded because clinical psychologists did not feel their needs were being met by the major scientific organization of psychologists, the American Psychological Association, whose bylaws clearly indicated the exclusive goal of the association: to advance psychology as a science.

Thus, at the 1917 APA meeting in Pittsburgh, a roundtable discussion on a new organization was held, and those present decided to form the AACP to define and establish standards in the field of clinical psychology. Evidently, word got out among the APA membership that this meeting had taken place, and it became the consuming topic of conversation in the corridors and the cloakrooms. Present at the roundtable discussion that led to the formation of AACP were the aforementioned J. E. Wallace Wallin, a psychologist who worked in the public school system with developmentally delayed children, and a newly minted Ph.D. clinical psychologist, Leta Stetter Hollingworth. It is to Hollingworth's contributions that we now turn.

Leta Stetter Hollingworth: Clinician, Feminist, Professionalizer

To many contemporary students of psychology, the field of clinical psychology seems both familiar and well-established. When one thinks of a psychologist, the image that most often comes to mind is a mental health practitioner—often a therapist. We have already shown the important role that Lightner Witmer played in establishing a clinical role for psychologists early in the twentieth century and how that role differed in many respects from what we now consider clinical psychology. It was not until after World War II that the profession of clinical psychology became formally organized along the lines that seem so familiar today. Only during and after World War II did it become more common for clinical psychologists to engage in psychotherapy, for example (despite Münsterberg's early foray into this area). As we have seen, the original clinical psychologists were mental testers, and testing preoccupied the field through the first half of the twentieth century. At this time, enough psychologists were undertaking work in applied settings such as schools, hospitals and courts that it began to seem necessary to explore a formal definition for the field and decide on appropriate training and credentialing. **Leta Stetter Hollingworth** (1886–1939; see Figure 15.5), who had recently earned her doctorate at Columbia University with eminent psychologist E. L. Thorndike (see Chapter 8), was asked to contribute her thoughts to a symposium on this issue in 1918. Many

FIG 15.5
Leta Stetter
Hollingworth
(1886–1939)

of her ideas and recommendations, although not adopted at the time, foreshadowed the issues that would resurface later in the century.

Hollingworth, an early clinical psychologist, earned her master's degree at Columbia University Teachers College in 1913. She continued her graduate studies while working at the New York City Clearing House for Mental Defectives, where, like most of her clinical colleagues—many of them women—she administered mental tests. In this period, and accelerating after the first world war as testing grew in popularity, there arose in psychology a separate sphere of women's work in the field—namely, applied psychology and, specifically, testing. Although psychology, at its inception, was a scientific field and women entered the field *as scientists*, as application and testing spread, women students were often advised to become testers, especially with children. This role was seen as congruent with their innate aptitudes and interests. It also gave them an occupation at a time when academic positions were few in number and were largely given to men.

During her time at the Clearing House, Hollingworth was employed to administer the recently translated Binet tests of intelligence to "mentally inferior" individuals for the purposes of commitment by the courts. She then worked at New York's Bellevue Hospital and was offered a position as director of a laboratory to be established there, just as she was awarded her Ph.D. She declined this offer and instead took up a position in educational psychology at her alma mater, Columbia Teachers College, while continuing to do direct clinical work until 1920. Thus, unlike many of her female clinical colleagues, Hollingworth did successfully enter the academy and stayed there for the rest of her career, often using her clinical experiences to generate research questions. Her career trajectory, however, was not a smooth one. Were it not for a determined disposition, a keen intellect, a supportive spouse, and the Coca-Cola Company, Hollingworth might never have realized her professional ambitions.

Early Years

Born in a dugout house on the Nebraska frontier in 1886, Hollingworth was truly of pioneering stock. Her father was a migrant farmer and preacher with an outgoing, even boisterous personality

(Leta's husband, Harry Hollingworth, later described his father-in-law as a "rollicking young cowboy minstrel"). Her father's absenteeism was a prominent aspect of Leta's young life. Her mother, Margaret Danley Stetter, gave birth to three daughters, Leta being the eldest. Interestingly, upon Leta's birth, her mother, although no doubt heavily preoccupied with household and childrearing duties in the relatively primitive conditions in which she lived, bought a small, red, leather-bound notebook in which she kept a diary of her firstborn's experiences and development over her first year of life. The account is written in the first person—that is, from the point of view of the infant herself. Given that Margaret Danley Stetter died soon after her third child was born, when Leta was only about 3, the red, leather-bound notebook eventually became one of Leta's prized possessions.

On their mother's death, the three Stetter daughters moved to their grandparents' farm and attended a one-room log schoolhouse. This relatively happy period came to an end with the remarriage of their vagabond father, who, with his new wife, reclaimed his daughters and moved the newly reunited family into his house in Valentine, Nebraska. By all accounts, their stepmother was not a kind person, and she forbade the girls beloved grandparents from visiting. When a family servant left, their stepmother often made Leta and her sisters do hours of chores before they left for school in the morning. At this time, Leta began to refer to her home life as the "fiery furnace," and later remarked in a letter, "There's no place like home—thank God."[51]

Despite the unhappiness of her home life in this period, Leta did well in high school and quickly developed a reputation as a creative writer and poet. She graduated at the age of 16 in 1902 and was enabled by her family to attend the University of Nebraska in Lincoln. There, in addition to studying English literature (among other subjects), she met her future husband, Harry Hollingworth. When Leta graduated in June 1906, she had completed 71 credits in Languages and Literature and 11 credits in psychology. She had also completed the University Teaching Course and was qualified to teach in any of the public schools in the state of Nebraska, specializing in English and English literature. She had aspirations to become a professional writer. And she was engaged to Harry.

Becoming a Psychologist

In September of her graduating year, Leta Stetter moved to DeWitt, Nebraska, her fiancé Harry's hometown, and took a position as assistant principal of the high school. After a year of teaching, she moved to a better position in a larger town and spent a year and a half there before she was able to join Harry in New York City, where he had begun his doctoral studies in psychology at Columbia University. The couple were able to reunite in the city with the expectation that Leta would procure a job as a teacher while Harry finished his degree. They were married on New Year's Eve, 1908.

Unfortunately, Leta soon ran into a rather large roadblock. In 1908 married women were barred from teaching in New York public schools. With this professional outlet closed to her, and her husband's modest salary barely enough to support them, Hollingworth found herself confined for several years to the domestic realm—namely, the couple's tiny Manhattan apartment. During these years, she described her main activity as "staying at home eating a lone pork chop."[32] She tried her hand at writing short stories in the hopes of selling them to magazines and took a few graduate classes in literature, but by and large these were profoundly unsatisfying intellectual years.

In 1911 the fortunes of the young couple dramatically improved thanks to an unlikely source: the Coca-Cola Company. **Harry Hollingworth** (1880–1956) had received his Ph.D. in 1909 and was working as an instructor at Barnard College, but finances were still tight and living in New York City was expensive. The Coca-Cola Company had recently been charged with violating the Pure Food and Drug Act because the elevated levels of caffeine in their product were considered an additive harmful to human health. In order to prepare the case to defend their product, lawyers for the company were looking for a psychologist who would study the behavioral effects of caffeine on human beings. When James McKeen Cattell turned the job down, the company approached Harry. Confident that he could conduct an objective, unbiased investigation despite being paid by the company with a vested interest in the study's results, Harry accepted the contract and asked Leta to direct the studies, since he was working full-time at Barnard.

Over the course of two months, in February and March 1911, Harry and Leta designed and conducted an intensive and elaborate series of experiments with ten male and six female subjects chosen to be representative of the cola-drinking market. The experiments took place in a six-room Manhattan apartment rented specifically for the study. During the day, three experimental groups and one placebo-control group undertook multiple series of tests under varying conditions to evaluate the effects of caffeine on mental and motor abilities, including sleep. During the evenings, after the subjects had gone home, the data were analyzed with the help of several graduate students from Columbia. By the end of the study, over 64,000 individual measurements had been taken.[35]

The Hollingworths travelled to Chattanooga, Tennessee for the trial in March, and there Harry testified, based on the results of their experiments, that the levels of caffeine in Coca-Cola did not impair human mental or motor performance. Although a mild stimulant, the only negative effects that the subjects reported were minor problems sleeping on the days following administration of the higher doses. Although Harry's testimony did not put the case to rest (eventually, after several more rounds of legal strategy and appeals, the company decided to reduce the amount of caffeine in their formula by 50 percent and the case was effectively dropped), the study itself was important for a number of reasons. First, it was a pioneering study applying scientific psychology to an industrial or business problem. Second, it was much more methodologically sophisticated than most psychological studies at the time. Finally, and perhaps most important for the Hollingworths, it paid extremely well. As Leta remarked in a letter to her cousin at the conclusion of the studies, "We did a big experiment for the Coca-Cola company and made quite a 'wad' of money."[36] This "wad" of money was Leta's ticket to a graduate education.

Pioneer of the Psychology of Women

Leta Hollingworth enrolled in Columbia Teachers College in 1911, and began her studies with Edward Thorndike. Although Thorndike would later be associated with an environmentalist stance on intellectual ability and male-female differences, at the time Hollingworth encountered him he was still heavily under the influence of his more traditional mentor, James McKeen Cattell. Cattell, like many other scientists of the time, held the view that men and women had inherently different intellectual capacities and that men were exclusively capable of the highest levels of achievement in any field. Both Thorndike and Cattell were proponents of the **variability hypothesis**, a widely held belief that men were more variable than women on both physical and psychological characteristics and thus were more likely to occupy positions at the lowermost and uppermost ends of the distribution of any trait (see Chapter 6). According to this belief, women were confined to mediocrity, whereas men drove the engines of natural selection and evolutionary progress. Thorndike, although a proponent of this view, was also open to empirical data bearing on the issue. Hollingworth was soon to supply it.

When Leta Hollingworth earned her master's degree in 1913 and began her position as a clinical psychologist at the Clearing House for Mental Defectives in New York City, she quickly seized the opportunity to test the contentious variability hypothesis. She examined 1,000 cases of "mental defect" diagnosed during 1912 and 1913 and concluded that, in absolute terms, men *did* outnumber women. Ostensibly, this fact supported one aspect of the hypothesis: that men were more likely to occupy the lower end of the distribution of mental ability as evidenced by their higher institutionalization rates. However, she discerned an interesting bias in the data. As age at time of admission increased, the proportion of women to men admitted increased as well. She interpreted this as evidence that while mentally defective men might be detected early because of their inability to meet social expectations for male achievement, mentally defective women were more likely to escape institutionalization until later in life because their social roles allowed them to remain in the home where they could take care of small children and do menial tasks. She conducted another study of institutional admissions a few years later that supported this interpretation. Further, with physician Helen Montague, she conducted a separate study examining variability in anatomical traits in a sample of 2,000 infants—1,000 males and 1,000 females—at the New York Infirmary for Women and Children. Although male babies were, on average, slightly larger than female babies on all anatomical traits, there were no differences *in variability* between the sexes.

In a 1914 article in which she reviewed and critiqued the available evidence for the variability hypothesis, Hollingworth concluded forcefully that one reason that male achievement and eminence had historically outranked womens was that women's lives were consumed with the bearing and rearing of children and the performance of domestic tasks. As she wrote:

> Surely we should consider *first* the established, obvious, inescapable, physical fact that women bear and rear the children, and that this has always meant and still means that *nearly 100 per cent of their energy is expended in the performance and supervision of domestic and allied tasks, a field where eminence is impossible* [italics in original]. . . . Men of science who discuss at all the matter of woman's failure should thus seek the cause of failure in the most obvious facts. . . . Otherwise their discussion is futile scientifically.[35]

For her dissertation research, Hollingworth decided to investigate yet another unfounded assumption about women: that they became functionally impaired during menstruation, a belief known as "**functional periodicity.**" This belief, although untested, was often invoked to claim women's unsuitability for certain types of work and responsibilities, such as voting, and to reinforce prevailing stereotypes of women as physically and emotionally fragile. Scientists were no less likely than nonscientists to hold this belief. As Hollingworth wrote in a 1914 report:

> [T]he tradition emanating from the mystic and romantic novelists, that woman is a mysterious being, half hysteric, half angel, has found its way into scientific writing. Through the centuries gone those who wrote were men, and since the phenomenon of periodicity was foreign to them, they not unnaturally seized upon it as a probable source of the alleged "mystery" and "caprice" of womankind.[36]

Borrowing methodologically from her experience on the Coca-Cola project, Hollingworth designed two separate studies. In her first study, she compared the performances of six women and two men on a series of mental and motor tasks presented daily over a period of four months. In the second study, she monitored a group of seventeen women every 3 days over a period of 30 days to see if their performance on these tasks varied as a function of their menstrual cycles. Her data led her to an unambiguous conclusion: "Careful and exact measurement does not reveal a periodic mental or motor inefficiency in normal women."[37]

Hollingworth was awarded her Ph.D. in 1916. That year, she published a co-authored article in *Scientific Monthly* titled "Science and Feminism," in which she and **Robert Lowie** (1883–1957), a cultural anthropologist, clearly articulated the relationship between their scientific and feminist commitments. Empirical data, they pointed out, were needed to justify feminist objectives. They wrote, "Feminism demands the removal of restrictions placed on woman's activity," noting that opponents of feminism justified these restrictions because of "the alleged unfitness of women to undertake certain forms of activity."[38] Lowie and Hollingworth then reviewed anthropological, anthropometric, and psychological research for any evidence supporting the unsuitability of women for work on the basis of innate differences in ability or intellect. Hollingworth also reviewed her own and others' work showing absolutely no demonstrable differences in variability between the sexes, writing of the variability hypothesis, "The theory exists, but the evidence does not." She then took on the superstitions surrounding the functional periodicity of women, writing, "A long and patient search through this literature brings to light a veritable mass of conflicting statements by men of science, misogynists, practitioners, and general writers, as to the dire effects of periodicity on the mental and physical life of women; but the search reveals scarcely a single fact."[39]

Hollingworth was an active suffragist and member of the New York Woman Suffrage Party. In 1912 she and twenty-four other women founded the Heterodoxy Club, whose only criterion for membership was the holding of unorthodox opinions. Although Hollingworth herself was not a political radical, the membership of the club included some of the era's most radical intellectuals. Rose Pastor Stokes, the founder of the American Communist Party; Charlotte Perkins Gilman, noted feminist and writer; and Mary Ware Dennett, the co-founder with Margaret Sanger of the National Birth Control League, are just a few examples. All were highly educated and many were involved in labor and socialist movements. Hollingworth, although in many ways an outlier in the group given her relative social conservatism, was a devoted member of Heterodoxy for twenty-five years.[40]

Professionalizer of Clinical Psychology

On the basis of her clinical skills and research training, Hollingworth was offered the directorship of a newly established psychological laboratory at Bellevue Hospital on the completion of her Ph.D. She chose instead an academic position in educational psychology at Columbia Teachers College, a post left vacant on the death of **Naomi Norsworthy** (1877–1916), the first female Ph.D. at Columbia, who had eventually secured a faculty position there. In 1918 Hollingworth published her recommendations for a course of training for clinical psychologists. She began by recommending that the question of legal certification be set aside until training and accreditation issues were addressed. She suggested that the American Psychological Association compile a list of departments of psychology where appropriate clinical training was being offered and that these universities should be recognized as official training sites. She argued forcefully that the minimum requirement for clinical practice should be a doctoral level degree, noting that the creation of an MA-level "assistant psychologist" position would not only represent inadequate training, but would confuse the public and serve to undercut Ph.D.-level practitioners. Finally, she also recommended the formation of a professional degree that would emphasize practical training, called a Doctor of Psychology. Although not adopted at the time, these recommendations indicated that even in this early period, many of the same professional issues that would come to face architects of clinical psychology in the post–World War II period were already emerging. In 1919 the AACP returned to APA as the Section on Clinical Psychology and asked the organization to consider issuing certificates to clinical psychologists as an early form of credentialing. A few certificates (about twenty-five by some estimates) were issued, but the enterprise was not a success and the program was dropped. Formal licensing procedures, as Hollingworth had already suggested, had not yet come of age.

In addition to her professionalization efforts, Hollingworth continued to conduct clinical work, becoming more and more interested not in diagnosing subnormal children but in identifying and helping highly gifted children who were having educational and emotional difficulties. She published two books on subnormal children in the early 1920s but then devoted much of the rest of her career to two major projects studying the abilities and experiences of gifted children, one at New York Public School 165, and the other at a special school for gifted children, Public School 500, also known as the Speyer School. In this latter project she helped design a curriculum to optimize learning and development that was geared to the individual strengths and weaknesses of the student. She published a book in 1926, called *Gifted Children*, that became a standard reference work in schools of education for many years. She also developed her interest in the exceptionally gifted child, defined as the child who scores above 180 on IQ tests. She conducted a longitudinal study of twelve exceptionally gifted children, reporting her results in a book published in 1942 called *Children Above 180 IQ*.

The book, which is still widely read by educators, was published posthumously by Harry Hollingworth. Three years earlier, in November 1939, after a long struggle with cancer that she managed to conceal even from her beloved husband, Leta Hollingworth died at the age of 53. Months earlier, the couple had traveled back to their native state to receive honorary degrees from the University of Nebraska. At that otherwise happy time, Leta had urged Harry, who was still unaware of her illness, to help her pick out their final resting place.

Applied Psychology Today

In the early years of the twentieth century, the pioneers of applied psychology often had to contend with the attitude that their efforts would sully the scientific respectability of their home discipline. Today's industrial, school, consulting, and clinical psychologists are fully integrated into the profession and have in fact come to dominate it. One major turning point was World War II. The war provided increased demand for the expertise of applied psychologists in a wide range of tasks, including personnel selection for both the army and the navy, the design of instrumentation for military air-craft and vehicles,[41] and the testing of thousands of soldiers for place-ment as well as capacity for specialized jobs such as intelligence work. But most significantly perhaps, World War II pushed psychologists in greater numbers into providing *new* clinical services. Without enough psychiatrists to meet the demand for the diagnosis and ther-apy of psychiatric casualties during the war, psychologists were called in to help. At the war's end, with thousands of war veterans in need of psychological services, the Veteran's Administration and the U.S. Public Health Service began working with the American Psychologi-cal Association and several universities to develop a formal program in clinical psychology and to accredit programs that already existed. In 1949, with funds from the newly established National Institute of Mental Health, a conference was held in Boulder, Colorado, to reach consensus on a national training model.

The outcome of that meeting, which subsequently became known as the Boulder Conference, was a statement of seventy resolutions concerning the training of clinical psychologists. Foremost among these resolutions was the conviction that clinical psychologists be trained in research as well as practice, generating what was called the **scientist/practitioner model of clinical training** that is still in place today in North American Ph.D. programs. The dual research/practice focus has proven to be a difficult one to sustain, however, with many critics of the model arguing that professional training suffers at the expense of research training and urging exploration of alternative models. In 1973 a conference in Vail, Colorado, was dedicated to just such exploration, and the Psy.D., or Doctor of Psychology degree, was formalized. According much less weight to research training and much more to practical and professional training, Psy.D. programs, many of which are administered through free-standing professional schools, now graduate more professional psychologists than their scientist/practitioner counterparts.

Applied psychology encompasses much more than clinical psy-chology, of course, as our discussions of Münsterberg and Gilbreth have shown. Today, psychologists can be found from the courtroom to the clinic and almost everywhere in between. Just as early applied psychologists responded to the need for the new psychology to prove its practical worth, today's applied psychologists continue to expand their purview in response to the needs of an ever-changing population. As the behavioral aspects of physical health and illness (including obesity, hypertension, and heart disease, for example) become increasingly better understood, clinical health psychologists will no doubt experience ongoing and increasing demand for their services. And as the population ages, providing clinical services and support for the elderly will no doubt be taken up by increasing numbers of geropsychologists. If the history of applied psychology reveals anything, it is that psychologists are highly effective in devising services that meet the demands and needs of the market.

Summary

Quite soon after the new psychology was established as an experimental discipline, psychologists turned their attention to the discipline's practical or applied potential. **Hugo Münsterberg**, although initially known for his strong experimental, laboratory background, eventually became one of the first prominent advocates of applying psychology to practical problems. He published widely read texts on the psychology of legal testimony, psychotherapy, education, personnel selection, and the psychology of business. He also devised tests of vocational skills to help companies select workers for various jobs.

Lillian Moller Gilbreth, who received one of the earliest Ph.D.'s in applied psychology, began her career collaborating with her husband Frank, a self-trained engineer. Initially influenced by the principles of **scientific management** devised and promoted by **Frederick Winslow Taylor**, the Gilbreths soon developed their own distinctive approach to efficiency in the workplace. They conducted elaborate motion studies of individual tasks to figure out the "one best way" to do a job most efficiently and with the least strain on the worker. After her husband's death, Gilbreth expanded her expertise to designing appliances and kitchens that would minimize strain on the homemaker, and she made recommendations to employers to help them create more enjoyable and productive workplaces for their employees. Both Münsterberg and Gilbreth were early pioneers of industrial psychology, among their many other accomplishments.

Lightner Witmer established what is considered the first psychological clinic, where he provided assessment and remedial services to schoolchildren who were having difficulty learning. He called his approach the **clinical method**. Although in many ways Witmer's work was different from what we now think of as clinical psychology, he was nonetheless important in establishing a clinical role for psychologists very early in the discipline's history.

This clinical role, which came to consist largely of mental testing until after World War II, was taken up by **Leta Stetter Hollingworth**. Her involvement with exceptional children at both ends of the ability spectrum was representative of the work of many applied psychologists in this period, the majority of whom were women employed in testing roles in hospitals, clinics, schools, and courts. Hollingworth was also an early contributor to the debates around the appropriate training and credentialing of applied psychologists. Her recommendations, although not taken up at the time, foreshadowed many of the issues around the professionalization of clinical psychology that would resurface after World War II. Hollingworth's empirical research on the psychology of women also anticipated the formal establishment of this important field, which did not occur until the 1970s.

Key Pioneers

Bronner, Augusta Fox, p. 674

Fernald, Grace, p. 674

Gilbreth, Frank Bunker, p. 661

Gilbreth, Lillian Moller, p. 660

Goddard, Henry Herbert, p. 674

Hollingworth, Harry, p. 680

Hollingworth, Leta Setter, p. 677

Lowie, Robert, p. 684

Mitchell, S. Weir, p. 672

Münsterberg, Hugo, p. 649

Norsworthy, Naomi, p. 685

Taylor, Frederick Winslow, p. 657

Wallin, J. E. Wallace, p. 675

Witmer, Lightner, p. 668

Key Terms

clinical method, p. 672

functional periodicity, p. 683

motion studies, p. 663

psychotechnics, p. 657

scientific management, p. 657

scientist/practitioner model of
  clinical training, p. 687

therbligs, p. 663

variability hypothesis, p. 682

Discussion Questions and Topics

1 In what ways does Lightner Witmer's practice of clinical psychology both resemble and differ from the kinds of clinical psychology that are practiced today?

2 Applied psychology takes many forms. Discuss the ways in which each pioneer in this chapter practiced his/her own form of applied psychology. What assumptions about human nature informed their practices?

3 Although women now outnumber men in most areas of applied psychology, Lillian Gilbreth and Leta Hollingworth both experienced certain professional disadvantages because of their gender. Describe some of these disadvantages and the ways in which these two women overcame them.

Suggested Readings

For an overview of the development of applied psychology, from school to counseling, to clinical, to industrial/organizational, see Ludy T. Benjamin and David B. Baker's *From Séance to Science: A History of the Profession of Psychology in America* (Belmont, CA: Thomson/Wadworth, 2004). For a history of the use of social science in industry, written with a clear social management bent, see Loren Baritz's *The Servants of Power* (Middletown, CT: Wesleyan University Press, 1960), and for a history of the profession of psychology in America that focuses on mid-century and immediate post–World War II developments, see Donald Napoli's *Architects of Adjustment* (Port Washington, NY: Kennikat Press, 1981). For the important role of government funding and the National Institute of Mental Health in the development of post–World War II clinical psychology and its training programs, a topic to which we allude in our conclusion, see *Psychology and the National Institute of Mental Health: A Historical Analysis of Science, Practice, and Policy*, edited by Wade E. Pickren and Stanley F. Schneider (Washington, DC: APA, 2005).

Matthew Hale's biography of Hugo Münsterberg, *Human Science and the Social Order* (Philadelphia: Temple University Press, 1980) places his work within the wider developments in applied psychology that characterized the early twentieth century. Lillian Gilbreth's life and work are captured in a number of biographical and autobiographical sources. Her autobiography, written in 1941, is titled *As I Remember* (Norcross, GA: Engineering and Management Press, 1998). She is also the subject of a full-length biography, Jane Lancaster's *Making Time: Lillian Moller Gilbreth—A Life Beyond "Cheaper by the Dozen"* (Boston: Northeastern University Press, 2004). For further information about early women pioneers of industrial/organizational psychology, see Laura Koppes, "American Female Pioneers of Industrial and Organizational Psychology During the Early Years," *Journal of Applied Psychology* 82 (1997): 500–515.

Lightner Witmer is the subject of a biography by Paul McReynolds, *Lightner Witmer: His Life and Times* (Washington, DC: APA, 1997). For his role in the development of clinical psychology, see also J. M. O'Donnell, "The Clinical Psychology of Lightner Witmer: A Case Study of Institutional Innovation and Intellectual Change" *Journal of the History of the Behavioral Sciences* 15 (1979): 3–17. Leta Stetter Hollingworth's life is recounted by her husband Harry Hollingworth in *Leta Stetter Hollingworth: A Biography* (Bolton, MA: Anker Publishing Company, 1990, original edition published by University of Nebraska Press in 1943). Hollingworth's distinguished contributions to the psychology of gifted children are featured in another biography, Ann G. Klein's *A Forgotten Voice: A Biography of Leta Stetter Hollingworth* (Scottsdale, AZ: Great Potential Press, Inc., 2002). Her contributions to the psychology of women are analyzed by Stephanie Shields in her article "Ms. Pilgrim's Progress: The Contributions of Leta Stetter Hollingworth to the Psychology of Women," *American Psychologist* 30 (1975): 852–857.

Notes

Chapter 1. René Descartes and the Foundations of Modern Psychology

1. Richard Watson, *The Life of René Descartes* (Boston: Godine, 2002).
2. William R. Shea, *The Magic of Numbers and Motion: The Scientific Career of René Descartes* (Canton, MA: Watson Publishing International, 1991), 127.
3. René Descartes, *Discourse on Method*, in *Discourse on Method and Meditations*, ed. and trans. L. J. Lafleur (New York: Library of Liberal Arts, 1960), 7–8.
4. Ibid., 5.
5. Julian Jaynes, "The Problem of Animate Motion in the Seventeenth Century," in *Historical Conceptions of Psychology*, ed. M. Henle, J. Jaynes, and J. J Sullivan (New York: Springer, 1973), 166–179.
6. Descartes, *Discourse*, 9.
7. Quoted in Jack Vrooman, *René Descartes: A Biography* (New York: Puntam's, 1970), 23.
8. Ibid., 49–50.
9. Charles Singer, *A Short History of Scientific Ideas to 1900* (London: Oxford University Press, 1970), 226.
10. Descartes, *Discourse*, 10.
11. Ibid., 15.
12. René Descartes, *Treatise of Man*, trans. Thomas Steele Hall (Cambridge, MA: Harvard University Press, 1972), 113.
13. Ibid., 21.
14. Jaynes, "Problem of Animate Motion," 171.
15. Descartes, *Treatise of Man*, 106.
16. Quoted in John Morris, *Descartes Dictionary* (New York: Philosophical Library, 1971), 15.
17. Descartes, *Discourse*, 24.
18. Ibid., 25.
19. Beatrice H. Zedler, "The Three Princesses," *Hypatia*, 4 (1989): 30.

20. See Andrea Nye, *The Princess and the Philosopher* (Lanham, MD: Rowman and Littlefield, 1999), and Deborah Tollefson, "Princess Elizabeth and the Problem of Mind-Body Interaction," *Hypatia*, 14 (1999): 59–77.

21. These quotations from the correspondence are taken from *Women Philosophers of the Early Modern Period*, ed. Margaret Atherton (Indianapolis: Hackett, 1994), 9–21.

22. René Descartes, *Passions of the Soul*, excerpted in *Descartes: Philosophical Writings*, ed. and trans. Norman Smith (New York: Modern Library, 1958), 265–296; see pp. 275–276.

23. Ibid., 283–284.

Chapter 2.   **Philosophers of Mind: John Locke and Gottfried Leibniz**

1. Quotations reported in Maurice Cranston, *John Locke: A Biography* (London: Longmans, 1957), 417.

2. Ibid., 76.

3. Ibid., 90.

4. Ibid., 100.

5. Walter Edgar, *South Carolina: A History* (Columbia: University of South Carolina Press, 1998), 42–43.

6. John Locke, *An Essay Concerning Human Understanding*, vol. I, 5th ed. (London: Dent, 1965/1706), xxxii.

7. Maurice Cranston, *Locke* (London: Longmans, Green & Co., 1961), 17.

8. Ibid., 482.

9. Locke, *Essay*, I, xxxv.

10. Ibid., 81.

11. Ibid., 77.

12. Ibid., 114.

13. Maurice von Senden, *Space and Sight: The Perception of Space and Shape in the Congenitally Blind before and after Operation* (New York: Free Press, 1960); Richard Gregory, *Eye and Brain* (New York: McGraw-Hill, 1973), 193–198.

14. Locke, *Essay*, II, 133.

15. Locke, *Essay*, I, 108.

16. Ibid., 336.

17. Quoted in D. B. Klein, *A History of Scientific Psychology: Its Origins and Philosophical Backgrounds* (New York: Basic Books, 1970), 456.

18. G. W. Leibniz, *Writings on China*, trans. and ed. D. J. Cook and H. Rosemount, Jr. (Chicago: Open Court, 1994), 70.

19. For more on Leibniz's Chinese research, see R. Fancher and H. Schmidt, "Gottfried Wilhelm Leibniz: Underappreciated Pioneer of Psychology," in *Portraits of Pioneers in Psychology*, vol. 5., ed. G. Kimble and M. Wertheimer (Washington, DC: APA Press, 2003).

20. For a series of accounts of indigenous psychologies, see U. Kim and J. W. Berry, *Indigenous Psychologies: Research and Experience in Cultural Context* (London: Sage, 1993), and even more recently *Indigenous and Cultural Psychology: Understanding People in Context*, ed. U. Kim, K. Yang, and K. Hwang (New York: Springer, 2006).

21. G. MacDonald Ross, *Leibniz* (New York: Oxford University Press, 1984), 26.
22. Ibid.
23. Quotations in Mary W. Calkins, *The Persistent Problems of Philosophy* (New York: Macmillan, 1907), 76.
24. For a discussion of Leibniz's changing attitudes on the question of differences and similarities between animals and human beings, see Mark Kulstad, *Leibniz on Apperception, Consciousness, and Reflection* (München: Philosophia Verlag, 1991).
25. G. W. Leibniz, *New Essays on Human Understanding*, trans. and ed. Peter Remnant and Jonathan Bennett (Cambridge, UK: Cambridge University Press, 1982), 48.
26. Ibid., 50.
27. Ibid., 52.
28. Ibid., 51.
29. Ibid., 53.
30. Ibid., 54.
31. Ibid., 54–55.
32. Ibid., 56.
33. Ibid., 166.

Chapter 3.   Physiologists of Mind: Brain Scientists from Gall to Penfield

1. Quoted in Robert M. Young, *Mind, Brain and Adaptation in the Nineteenth Century* (Oxford, UK: Clarendon Press, 1970), 10.
2. Quoted in *A Source Book in the History of Psychology*, ed. Richard J. Herrnstein and Edwin G. Boring (Cambridge, MA: Harvard University Press), 212.
3. Quoted in Stanley Finger, *Origins of Neuroscience: A History of Explorations into Brain Function* (New York: Oxford University Press, 1994), 33.
4. Diagram adapted from John D. Davies, *Phrenology: Fad and Science* (New Haven, CT: Yale University Press, 1955), 6.
5. Quoted in J. M. D. Olmsted, "Pierre Flourens," in *Science, Medicine, and History*, vol. 2, ed. E. A. Underwood (New York: Oxford University Press, 1953), 296.
6. Ibid., 293.
7. Quoted in Young, *Mind, Brain and Adaptation*, 61.
8. Walther Riese, "Auto-observation of Aphasia Reported by an Eminent Nineteenth Century Medical Scientist," *Bulletin of the Institute of the History of Medicine* 28 (1954): 241.
9. Quoted in Finger, *Origins of Neuroscience*, 379.
10. Quoted in Byron Stookey, "A Note on the Early History of Cerebral Localization," *Bulletin of the New York Academy of Medicine* 30 (1954): 571.
11. Quoted in Howard Gardner, *The Shattered Mind* (New York: Knopf, 1975), 68.
12. S. I. Franz, "On the Functions of the Cerebrum II: The Frontal Lobes in Relation to the Production and Retention of Simple Sensory-motor Habits," *American Journal of Physiology* 8 (1902): 1–22,.
13. Quoted in Finger, *Origins of Neuroscience*, 343.
14. Adapted from Karl S. Lashley, *Brain Mechanisms and Intelligence* (Chicago: University of Chicago Press, 1929), 74.

15. Ibid., 24–25.

16. Quoted in Keith Oatley, *Brain Mechanisms and Mind* (London: Thames and Hudson, 1972), 145.

17. Roberts Bartholow, "Experimental Investigations into the Functions of the Human Brain," *The American Journal of the Medical Sciences* 67 (1874):30–313, quotations from pp. 309, 311, 312.

18. Quoted in Peter Nathan, *The Nervous System* (Harmondsworth, UK: Penguin Books, 1969), 241.

19. Ibid., 239.

20. Wilder Penfield and Lamar Roberts, *Speech and Brain-Mechanisms* (Princeton, NJ: Princeton University Press, 1959), 45–47.

21. William Beecher Scoville and Brenda Milner, "Loss of Recent Memory after Bilateral Hippocampal Regions," *The Journal of Neurology, Neurosurgery, and Psychiatry* 20 (1957): 12.

22. Ibid.

23. Wilder Penfield, *The Mystery of the Mind* (Princeton, NJ: Princeton University Press, 1975), 80.

24. M. S. Gazzaniga, R. B. Ivry, and G. R. Mangun, *Cognitive Neuroscience: The Biology of the Mind*, 3rd ed. (New York: Norton, 2009).

25. From the journal's website: http://www.informaworld.com/smpp/title~db=all~content=g909176135~tab=summary.

Chapter 4.   The Sensing and Perceiving Mind: Theories of Perception from Kant through the Gestalt Psychologists

1. Quoted in J. Bronowski and Bruce Mazlish, *The Western Intellectual Tradition* (New York: Harper & Row, 1960), 474.

2. Other major critical works by Kant included *Prolegomena to Any Future Metaphysics* (1783), *Critique of Practical Reason* (1788), *Groundwork of the Metaphysics of Morals* (1790), and *Critique of Judgement* (1790).

3. Quoted in Siegfried Bernfeld, "Freud's Scientific Beginnings," *American Imago* 6 (1949): 171.

4. Quoted in Leo Koenigsberger, *Hermann von Helmholtz*, trans. Frances A. Welby (New York: Dover, 1965), 64, 73.

5. Ibid., 90.

6. Hermann von Helmholtz, "Recent Progress in the Theory of Vision," in *Selected Writings of Hermann von Helmholtz*, ed. Russell Kahl (Middletown, CT: Wesleyan University Press, 1971), 192.

7. Quoted in Nicolas Pastore, "Re-evaluation of Boring on Kantian Influence, Nineteenth Century Nativism, Gestalt Psychology and Helmholtz," *Journal of the History of the Behavioral Sciences* 10 (1975): 387.

8. Hermann von Helmholtz, "The Facts of Perception," in *Selected Writings of Helmholtz*, 381.

9. See William R. Woodward, "Fechner's Panpsychism: A Scientific Solution to the Mind-Body Problem," *Journal of the History of the Behavioral Sciences* 8 (1972): 367.

10. Ernst Heinrich Weber (1795–1878) on Weber's Law, 1834, in *A Source Book in the History of Psychology* ed. Richard J. Herrnstein and Edwin G. Boring (Cambridge, MA: Harvard University Press, 1965), 64 (emphasis added).

11. Quoted in Thomas H. Leahey, *A History of Psychology: Main Currents in Psychological Thought*, 2nd ed. (Englewood Cliffs, NJ: Prentice-Hall, 1987), 197.

12. Wolfgang Köhler, *The Task of Gestalt Psychology* (Princeton, NJ: Princeton University Press, 1969), 60.

13. Ibid., 66.

Chapter 5. Wilhelm Wundt and the Establishment of Experimental Psychology

1. Wilhelm Wundt, "Die Geschwindigkeit des Gedankens," *Gartenlaube* (1892): 263–265.

2. Erwin A. Esper, *A History of Psychology* (Philadelphia: Saunders, 1964), vi.

3. Wilhelm Wundt, "Neuere Leistungen auf dem Gebeite der physiologischen Psychologie," *Vierteljahrsschrift fur Psychiatrie in ihren Beziehungen zur Morphologie und Pathologie des Central-Nerven-Systems, der physiologischen Psychologie, Statistik und gerichtlichen Medicin* 1 (1867), 23–56.

4. Letter from William James to Thomas W. Ward, November 1867, in *The Letters of William James*, vol. 1, ed. Henry James (Boston: Atlantic Monthly Press, 1920), 118–119.

5. Quoted from "Selected Texts from the Writings of Wilhelm Wundt," trans. and ed. Solomon Diamond in *Wilhelm Wundt and the Making of a Scientific Psychology*, ed. R. W. Rieber (New York: Plenum Press, 1980), 5, 157, 158.

6. Quoted in S. Diamond, "Wundt before Leipzig," in *Wilhelm Wundt*, ed. R. W. Rieber, 59.

7. William James, "Review of Wundt's Principles of Physiological Psychology," reprinted in *Wundt Studies: A Centennial Collection*, ed. W. G. Bringmann and Ryan D. Tweney (Toronto: C. J. Hogrefe, 1980), 116, 120. The review originally appeared unsigned in *North American Review* 121 (1875): 195–201.

8. The article appeared in English translation as Wilhelm Wundt, "Spiritualism as a Scientific Question," *Popular Science Monthly* 15 (1879): 577–593.

9. Quotes taken from Marilyn E. Marshall and Russell A. Wendt, "Wilhelm Wundt, Spiritism, and the Assumptions of Science," in *Wundt Studies*, 169–171.

10. James McKeen Cattell, "The Psychological Laboratory at Leipsic," *Mind* 13 (1888): 37–51.

11. James McKeen Cattell, "The Time Taken Up by Cerebral Operations," *Mind* 11 (1886): 220–242, 377–392, 524–538.

12. Ibid., 387.

13. Ibid., 534.

14. Quoted in Arthur L. Blumenthal, *Language and Psychology: Historical Aspects of Linguistics* (New York: Academic Press, 1975), 21.

15. Quoted from E. B. Titchener, "The Province of Structural Psychology" in *The Great Psychologists: A History of Psychological Thought*, 5th ed., ed. R. I. Watson and R. B. Evans (New York: Harper Collins, 1991), 398.

16. Quoted in Thomas H. Leahey, *A History of Psychology: Main Currents in Psychological Thought*, 2nd ed. (Englewood Cliffs, NJ: Prentice-Hall, 1987), 189–190.
17. See the list of Titchener's doctoral students appended to the end of E. G. Boring's obituary of Titchener: Edwin G. Boring, "Edward Bradford Titchener: 1867–1927," *American Journal of Psychology* 38 (1927): 489–506.
18. See C. J. Goodwin, "On the Origins of Titchener's Experimentalists," *Journal of the History of the Behavioral Sciences* 21 (1985): 383–389.
19. See L. Furumoto, "Shared Knowledge: The Experimentalists, 1904–1929," in *The Rise of Experimentation in American Psychology*, ed. J. G. Morawski (New Haven, CT: Yale University Press, 1988), 104–105.
20. Ibid., 108–109.

Chapter 6.   Charles Darwin and the Theory of Evolution

1. Charles Darwin, *The Autobiography of Charles Darwin*, ed. Nora Barlow (New York: Norton, 1969), 27, 28.
2. Ibid., 47, 48.
3. Ibid., 60.
4. Charles Darwin, *The Correspondence of Charles Darwin*, vol. 1, ed. Frederick Burkhardt and Sydney Smith (Cambridge, MA: Cambridge University Press, 1985), 160, Note 1; 181, Note 4.
5. Darwin, *Autobiography*, 62.
6. Henslow to Darwin, August 24, 1831, in Darwin, *Correspondence*, vol. 1, 128–129.
7. Darwin, *Autobiography*, 72.
8. Frederick Watkins to Darwin, September 18, 1831, in Darwin, *Correspondence*, vol. 1, 159.
9. Darwin to R. W. Darwin, February 7, 1831, ibid., 201.
10. Quoted in Alan Moorehead, *Darwin and the* Beagle (Harmondsworth, UK: Penguin Books, 1971), 47.
11. Ibid., 86.
12. Charles Darwin, *The Voyage of the* Beagle (New York: Bantam Books, 1972), 335.
13. Quoted in Moorehead, *Darwin and the* Beagle, 247.
14. These notebooks still exist and have now been published, offering an extraordinary inside look into the thought processes of one of the world's greatest scientists. See *Charles Darwin's Notebooks, 1836–1844: Geology, Transmutation of Species, Metaphysical Enquiries*, ed. Paul H. Barrett et al. (Ithaca, NY: Cornell University Press, 1987).
15. Quoted from P. H. Gosse in Lynn Barber, *The Heyday of Natural History* (London: Jonathan Cape, 1960), 247.
16. Quoted in Howard E. Gruber, *Darwin on Man* (London: Wildwood House, 1974), 234–235.
17. Quoted in Ronald W. Clark, *The Survival of Charles Darwin: A Biography of a Man and an Idea* (New York: Random House, 1984), 76.
18. Darwin, *Autobiography*, 123.
19. Quoted in Clark, *The Survival of Charles Darwin*, 84.
20. Ibid., 109.

21. T. H. Huxley to Charles Darwin, November 23, 1859, in *The Life and Letters of Charles Darwin*, vol. II, ed. Francis Darwin, (New York: Appleton, 1887), 27.

22. Quoted in Clark, *The Survival of Charles Darwin*, 142–143. Clark also gives some slightly differing versions of the Oxford confrontation.

23. Charles Darwin, *On the Origin of Species by Means of Natural Selection, or the Preservation of Favoured Races in the Struggle for Life* (London: Murray, 1859), 488.

24. Charles Darwin, *The Descent of Man, and Selection in Relation to Sex*, 2nd ed. (London: Murray, 1879), 6.

25. Ibid., 56 (emphasis added).

26. Ibid., 126.

27. Ibid., 608.

28. Janet Brown, *Charles Darwin: Voyaging* (Princeton, NJ: Princeton University Press, 1995), 66.

29. Ibid., 198.

30. Darwin, *Descent*, 608.

31. Stephanie Shields and Sunil Bhatia, "Darwin on Race, Gender, and Culture," *American Psychologist* 64 (2009): 113.

32. Darwin, *Descent*, 563.

33. Ibid., 564.

34. See Stephanie Shields, "Passionate Men, Emotional Women: Psychology Constructs Gender Difference in the Late 19th Century," *History of Psychology* 10 (2007): 92–110.

35. Charles Darwin, *The Expression of the Emotions in Man and Animals* (Chicago: University of Chicago Press, 1965; originally published 1872), 360.

36. Charles Darwin, "A Biographical Sketch of an Infant," *Mind: Quarterly Review of Psychology and Philosophy* 2 (1877): 285.

37. Ibid., 292.

38. Ibid., 294.

39. Darwin, *Autobiography*, 108–109.

40. Jerome Barkow, Leda Cosmides, and John Tooby, eds., *The Adapted Mind: Evolutionary Psychology and the Generation of Culture* (New York: Oxford University Press, 1992); Stephen Pinker, *How the Mind Works* (New York: Norton, 1997).

Chapter 7.   **The Measurement of Mind: Francis Galton and the Psychology of Individual Differences**

1. Francis Galton, *Inquiries into Human Faculty and Its Development* (New York: Dutton, 1907), 19–20.

2. Francis Galton, *Memories of My Life* (London: Methuen, 1908), 35.

3. Ibid., 27, 37.

4. Quoted in Karl Pearson, *The Life, Letters and Labours of Francis Galton*, vol. 1, (Cambridge, UK: Cambridge University Press, 1914–1930), 164.

5. Galton, *Memories*, 79.

6. The complete phrenologis's report is preserved in File 81 of the Galton Papers, housed in the Archives of the Library at University College London. Portions of

it have been published in D. W. Forrest, *Francis Galton: The Life and Work of a Victorian Genius* (London: Elek, 1974), 37, and in Raymond E. Fancher, *The Intelligence Men: Makers of the IQ Controversy* (New York: Norton, 1985), 24.

7. Galton to Darwin, February 23, 1851, quoted in Pearson, *Life of Galton*, vol. 1, 232.

8. For details, see Raymond Fancher, "The Concept of Race in the Life and Thought of Francis Galton," in *Defining Difference: Race and Racism in the History of Psychology*, ed. Andrew S. Winston (Washington, DC: American Psychological Association, 2004), 49–75.

9. Pearson, *Life of Galton*, vol. 1, 240.

10. Ibid., vol. 2, Plate XVIII.

11. For details about his breakdown and its eventual resolution, see Raymond E. Fancher, "Eugenics and Other Victorian 'Secular Religions,' " in *The Transformation of Psychology: Influences of 19th Century Philosophy, Technology, and Natural Science*, ed. C. D. Green, M. Shore, and T. Teo (Washington, DC: American Psychological Association, 2001), 3–20.

12. Francis Galton, *Hereditary Genius* (Gloucester, MA: Peter Smith, 1972; originally published 1869), 45.

13. Ibid., 80.

14. Ibid., 81–82.

15. Darwin to Galton, December 3, 1869, quoted in Galton, *Memories*, 290; Charles Darwin, *The Descent of Man, and Selection in Relation to Sex*, 2nd ed. (London: Murray, 1879), 28.

16. Translated from Alphonse de Candolle, *Histoire des Sciences et des Savants depuis Deux Siècles* (Geneva: Georg, 1873), 93–94.

17. De Candolle to Galton, January 2, 1873, in Pearson, *Life of Galton*, vol. 2, 137. For a full account of Galton's interaction with de Candolle, see Raymond E. Fancher, "Alphonse de Candolle, Francis Galton, and the Early History of the Nature-Nurture Controversy," *Journal of the History of the Behavioral Sciences* 19 (1983): 341–352.

18. Francis Galton, *English Men of Science: Their Nature and Nurture* (London: Frank Cass, 1970; originally published 1874), 148–150.

19. Ibid., 12.

20. Francis Galton, *Inquiries into Human Faculty and its Development* (New York: Dutton, 1907), 172. This volume reprints Galton's original 1875 article on twins, along with several of his other shorter writings.

21. Galton, *Hereditary Genius*, 45.

22. Francis Galton, "Hereditary Talent and Character," *Macmillan's Magazine* 12 (1865): 165.

23. Adapted from data in Pearson, *Life of Galton*, vol. 3a, 14.

24. Francis Galton, "Co-relations and Their Measurement, Chiefly from Anthropometric Data," *Proceedings of the Royal Society* 45 (1888): 135–145.

25. Clark Wissler, "The Correlation of Mental and Physical Tasks," *The Psychological Review*, Monographic Supplements (3:6, 1901).

26. Galton, *Inquiries*, 138, 145.

27. Quoted in Forrest, *Francis Galton*, 281.

28. See Fancher, "The Concept of Race in the Life and Thought of Francis Galton," 49–75.

29. Horatio Newman, Frank Freeman, and Karl Holzinger, *Twins: A Study of Heredity and Environment* (Chicago: University of Chicago Press, 1937).
30. Ibid., 362.
31. See Susan Farber, *Identical Twins Reared Apart* (New York: Basic Books, 1981).
32. For details about the Burt "scandal," see Raymond Fancher, *The Intelligence Men: Makers of the IQ Controversy* (New York: Norton, 1985), Chapter 5.
33. T. Bouchard, D. Lykken, M. McGue, N. Segal, and A. Tellegren, "Sources of Human Psychological Differences: The Minnesota Study of Twins Reared Apart," *Science* 250 (1990): 227.
34. Richard Herrnstein and Charles Murray, *The Bell Curve: Intelligence and Class Structure in American Life* (New York: Free Press, 1994); Arthur Jensen, *The g Factor: The Science of Mental Ability* (Westport, CT: Praeger, 1998).

Chapter 8. **William James and Psychology in America**

1. Kurt Danziger, "On the Threshold of the New Psychology: Situating Wundt and James," in *Wundt Studies: A Centennial Collection*, ed. Wolfgang G. Bringmann and Ryan D. Tweney (Toronto: Hogrefe, 1980), 363–379.
2. Quoted in Arthur L. Blumenthal, *Language and Psychology: Historical Aspects of Psycholinguistics* (New York: Wiley, 1970), 238.
3. William James, *The Principles of Psychology*, vol. 1 (New York: Dover, 1950; originally published 1890), 192–193.
4. William James to Carl Stumpf, February 6, 1887, in *The Letters of William James*, vol. 1, ed. Henry James (Boston: Atlantic Monthly Press, 1920), 263.
5. Quoted in F. O. Mattheissen, ed., *The James Family: Including Selections from the Writings of Henry James Senior, William, Henry & Alice James* (New York: Knopf, 1961), 161.
6. Gay Wilson Allen, *William James: A Biography* (New York: Collier Books, 1967), 67.
7. Quoted in Jean Strouse, *Alice James: A Biography* (New York: Bantam Books, 1980), 128.
8. James, *Letters*, vol, 1, 58.
9. William James to Thomas W. Ward, c. November 1867, ibid., 118–119.
10. William James, *The Varieties of Religious Experience: A Study in Human Nature* (New York: Penguin, 1982; originally published 1902), 160. James here attributed the passage to an anonymous French correspondent, but it has since been identified as autobiographical. See Mattheissen, *The James Family*, 216–217.
11. James, *Letters*, vol. 1, 147–148.
12. Quoted in Howard M. Feinstein, "The 'Crisis' of William James: A Revisionist View," *The Psychohistory Review* 10 (1981): 74.
13. James, *Letters*, vol 2, 16.
14. Allen, *William James*, 305.
15. James to Henry Holt, May 9, 1890, in James, *Letters*, vol. 1, 293–294.
16. James, *Principles of Psychology*, vol. 1, 237–238.
17. Ibid., 244.

18. Ibid., 121.

19. Ibid., 127.

20. Ibid., 123–127.

21. Ibid., vol. 2, 449–450.

22. Ibid., 463.

23. Ibid., 561–562.

24. Ibid., 576.

25. James, *Letters*, II, 2–3.

26. James to Theodore Flournoy, September 28, 1909, ibid., 327–328.

27. Poem by Josiah Royce, quoted in Allen, *William James*, 471.

28. Quoted in Ruth Brandon, *The Spiritualists* (Buffalo, NY: Prometheus Books, 1984), 245–246.

29. Quoted in Howard M. Feinstein, *Becoming William James* (Ithaca, NY: Cornell University Press, 1984), 301.

30. Quoted in Allen, *William James*, 494.

31. Sigmund Freud, "The Origin and Development of Psychoanalysis," *American Journal of Psychology* 21 (1910): 181–218.

32. Quoted in Norma J. Bringmann and Wolfgang G. Bringmann, "Wilhelm Wundt and His First American Student," in *Wundt Studies*, ed. Wolfgang Bringmann and Ryan Tweney (Toronto: Hogrefe, 1980), 178.

33. Edwin G. Boring, *A History of Experimental Psychology*, 2nd ed. (New York: Appleton-Century-Crofts, 1957), 519.

34. Robert Val Guthrie, *Even the Rat Was White: A Historical View of Psychology*, 2nd ed. (Needham Heights, MA: Allyn & Bacon, 1998). Chapter 8 is devoted to the life and career of Francis Cecil Sumner.

35. Elizabeth Scarborough and Laurel Furumoto, *Untold Lives: The First Generation of American Women Psychologists* (New York: Columbia University Press, 1987), 29–35.

36. Mary Whiton Calkins, Autobiography, in *A History of Psychology in Autobiography*, vol. 1, ed. Carl Murchison (Worcester, MA: Clark University Press, 1930), 31.

37. Scarborough and Furumoto, *Untold Lives*, 42.

38. Ibid., 44–46.

39. There have been periodic attempts to persuade the Harvard Corporation to reconsider its position and retrospectively grant Calkins her degree. In 1927, Christian Ruckmick, a psychologist at the University of Iowa, had a group of 13 Harvard graduates signed a petition to this effect. Signatories included such eminent psychologists as R. S. Woodworth, R. M. Yerkes, and E. L. Thorndike. More recently, e-mail petitions and websites have been attempted, but it seems unlikely that Harvard will reverse its decision.

40. Edward Lee Thorndike, Autobiography, in *A History of Psychology in Autobiography*, vol. 3, 264.

41. Geraldine Joncich, *The Sane Positivist: A Biography of Edward L. Thorndike* (Middletown, CT: Wesleyan University Press, 1968), 105–106.

42. E. L. Thorndike and R. S. Woodworth, "The Influence of Improvement in One Mental Function upon the Efficiency of Other Functions," *Psychological Review* 8 (1901): 247–261.

Chapter 9. **Psychology as the Science of Behavior: Ivan Pavlov, John B. Watson, and B. F. Skinner**

1. Ivan Pavlov, *Conditioned Reflexes: An Investigation of the Physiological Activity of the Cerebral Cortex* (New York: Dover, 1960), 3.
2. B. Babkin, *Pavlov: A Biography* (Chicago: University of Chicago Press, 1949), 214.
3. Ibid., 37.
4. Ibid., 110.
5. George A. Miller, *Psychology: The Science of Mental Life* (New York: Harper & Row, 1962), 189.
6. Quoted by W. Horsley Gantt, *Introduction to I. Pavlov, Conditioned Reflexes and Psychiatry* (New York: International Publishers, 1941), 35.
7. John Broadus Watson, "Autobiography," in *A History of Psychology in Autobiography*, vol. 3, ed. Carl Murchison (Worcester, MA: Clark University Press, 1936), 271; also see Kerry W. Buckley, *Behaviorism and the Professionalization of American Psychology: A Study of John Broadus Watson*, 1878–1958 (Ann Arbor, MI: University Microfilms International, 1982), 1–3.
8. Watson, "Autobiography," 272.
9. Ibid., 274, 276.
10. Walter Van Dyke Bingham, "Autobiography," in *A History of Psychology in Autobiography*, vol. 4, ed. E. G. Boring, H. S. Langfeld, H. Werner, and R. M. Yerkes (Worcester, MA: Clark University Press, 1952), 7.
11. Watson, "Autobiography," 274.
12. Ibid.
13. Buckley, *A Study of Watson*, 67ff.
14. John B. Watson, "Psychology as the Behaviorist Views It," *Psychological Review* 20 (1913): 159.
15. Ibid., 158.
16. John B. Watson, "The Place of the Conditioned Reflex in Psychology," *Psychological Review* 23 (1916): 89.
17. Watson, "Autobiography," 278.
18. John B. Watson, *Psychology from the Standpoint of a Behaviorist* (Philadelphia: Lippincott, 1919), 200.
19. Ibid.
20. Ibid., 201.
21. Ibid., 214.
22. John B. Watson and Rosalie Rayner, "Conditioned Emotional Reactions," *Journal of Experimental Psychology* 3 (1920): 4.
23. Ibid., 5.
24. Ibid., 7.
25. Ibid., 12–13.
26. Ibid., 12, 14.
27. Hall Beck, Sharman Levinson, and Gary Irons, "Finding Little Albert: A Journey to John B. Watson's Infant Laboratory," *American Psychologist* 64 (2009): 605–614.
28. Buckley, *A Study of Watson*, 178ff.
29. Ibid., Chapter 9.

30. Watson, "Autobiography," 280.

31. Quoted in Richard J. Herrnstein, *Introduction to John B. Watson, Behavior: An Introduction to Comparative Psychology* (New York: Holt, Rinehart and Winston, 1967), xxii.

32. John B. Watson, *Behaviorism* (New York: Norton, 1970), 94, 104.

33. Mary Cover Jones, "Albert, Peter, and John B. Watson," *American Psychologist* 29 (1974): 581–583.

34. Mary Cover Jones, "A Laboratory Study of Fear: The Case of Peter," *Pedagogical Seminary* 31 (1924): 309.

35. Mary Cover Jones, "The Elimination of Children's Fears," *Journal of Experimental Psychology* 7 (1924): 390.

36. Jones, "Albert, Peter, and John B. Watson," 582.

37. John B. Watson, *Psychological Care of Infant and Child* (New York: Norton, 1928), 40–41.

38. Ibid., 81–82.

39. Quoted in Mufid James Hannush, "John B. Watson Remembered: An Interview with James B. Watson," *Journal of the History of the Behavioral Sciences* 23 (1987): 137.

40. Watson, "Autobiography," 281.

41. See Jill G. Morawski, "Organizing Knowledge and Behavior at Yale's Institute of Human Relations," *Isis* 77 (1986): 219–242.

42. B. F. Skinner, "Autobiography," in *A History of Psychology in Autobiography*, vol. 5, ed. G. E. Boring and Gardner Lindzey (New York: Appleton-Century-Crofts, 1967), 407.

43. Ibid., 396.

44. B. F. Skinner, *Particulars of My Life* (New York: Knopf, 1976), 237.

45. Ibid., 249.

46. Ibid., 264.

47. Ibid., 298.

48. B. F. Skinner, "A Case History in Scientific Method," in *Psychology: A Study of a Science*, vol. II, ed. Sigmund Koch (New York: McGraw-Hill, 1959).

49. Ibid., 362.

50. Adapted from F. S. Keller and W. N. Schoenfeld, *Principles of Psychology* (New York: Appleton-Century-Crofts, 1950), 45.

51. B. F. Skinner, *Walden Two* (New York: Macmillan, 1962), 264.

52. For more information on the evolution of one of these communities, as recounted by one of its founders, see Kat Kinkade's *Is It Utopia Yet?* (Louisa, VA: Twin Oaks Publishing, 1994). Also see Hilke Kuhlmann's *Living Walden Two: B. F. Skinner's Behaviorist Utopia and Experimental Communities* (Urbana and Chicago: University of Illinois Press, 2005).

53. B. F. Skinner, *A Matter of Consequences* (New York: Alfred A. Knopf, 1983), 395.

54. Gerald E. Zuriff, *Behaviorism: A Conceptual Reconstruction* (New York: Columbia University Press, 1985), 255.

55. B. F. Skinner, *Verbal Behavior* (New York: Appleton-Century-Crofts, 1957), 449.

56. Noam Chomsky, "A Review of B. F. Skinner's *Verbal Behavior*," *Language* 35 (1959): 26–58.

57. B. F. Skinner, *Beyond Freedom and Dignity* (New York: Bantam/Vintage, 1971), 76.

58. Skinner, "Autobiography," 412.

Chapter 10. Social Influence and Social Psychology: From Mesmer to Milgram

1. Frank Pattie, "A Brief History of Hypnotism," in *Handbook of Clinical and Experimental Hypnosis*, ed. Jesse E. Gordon (New York: Macmillan, 1967), 13.
2. Quoted in Vincent Buranelli, *The Wizard from Vienna* (New York: Coward, McCann and Geoghegan, 1975), 59.
3. Ibid., 67.
4. Pattie, "Brief History," 21.
5. For details on Faria, see Peter W. Sheehan and Campbell W. Perry, *Methodologies of Hypnosis: A Critical Appraisal of Contemporary Paradigms of Hypnosis* (New York: Erlbaum, 1976), 21ff.
6. Gregory Zilboorg, *A History of Medical Psychology* (New York: Norton, 1967), 352.
7. Edwin G. Boring, *A History of Experimental Psychology*, 2nd ed. (New York: Appleton-Century-Crofts, 1950), 121.
8. Zilboorg, *History of Medical Psychology*, 352–353.
9. Boring, *History of Experimental Psychology*, 123–124.
10. Melvin A. Gravitz and Manuel I. Gerton, "Origins of the Term Hypnotism Prior to Braid," *American Journal of Clinical Hypnosis* 27 (1984): 107–110.
11. Henri F. Ellenberger, *The Discovery of the Unconscious* (New York: Basic Books, 1970), 87.
12. Mark S. Micale, "The Salpêtrière in the Age of Charcot: An Institutional Perspective on Medical History in the Late Nineteenth Century," *Journal of Contemporary History* 20 (1985): 703.
13. Sigmund Freud, "Charcot," in *The Standard Edition of the Complete Psychological Works of Sigmund Freud*, Vol. 3, ed. James Strachey (London: Hogarth, 1953–1974), 12.
14. Alfred Binet and Charles Féré, "La Polarisation Psychique," *Revue Philosophique* 19 (1885): 375.
15. Quoted in Theta Wolf, "Alfred Binet: A Time of Crisis," *American Psychologist* 19 (1964): 764.
16. Quotations from Theta Wolf, *Alfred Binet* (Chicago: University of Chicago Press, 1973), 50.
17. The original French titles for these works were, respectively, *Lois psychologiques de l'évolution des peuples*, and *La psychologie des foules*.
18. Gustave Le Bon, *The Crowd* (New York: Viking, 1960), 29.
19. Ibid., 35–36.
20. Ibid., 34.
21. Ibid., 31–32.
22. Ibid., 118–119.
23. Wolf, *Alfred Binet*, 158.
24. A. Binet and V. Henri, "De la suggestibilité naturelle chez les enfants," *Revue Philisophique*, 38 (1894): 337–347.
25. Translated from A. Binet, *La Suggestibilité* (Paris: Schleicher, 1900), 294.
26. The differentiation between anticipators and founders was suggested in G. Sarup, "Historical Antecedents of Psychology: The Recurrent Issue of Old Wine in New Bottles," *American Psychologist*, 33 (1978): 478–485.
27. Norman Triplett, "The Dynamogenic Factors in Pacemaking and Competition," *American Journal of Psychology* 9 (1898): 507–533.

28. Morton Prince and Floyd H. Allport, "Editorial Announcement," *Journal of Abnormal Psychology and Social Psychology* 16 (1921): 1–2.

29. John Frederick Dashiell, "The Need and Opportunity for Experimental Social Psychology," *Social Forces* 15 (1937): 492.

30. Lewin, K., Lippitt, R. and White, R. K. "Patterns of Aggressive Behavior in Experimentally Created 'Social Climates,' " *Journal of Social Psychology* 10 (1939): 271–299.

31. Solomon E. Asch, "Opinions and Social Pressure," *Scientific American* 193 (1955): 31–35.

32. Ibid., 31.

33. The general theory is presented in Leon Festinger, *A Theory of Cognitive Dissonance* (Evanston, IL: Row Peterson, 1957).

34. Leon Festinger, Henry Riecken, and Stanley Schachter, *When Prophecy Fails: A Social and Psychological Study of a Modern Group That Predicted the Destruction of the World* (Minneapolis: University of Minnesota Press, 1956).

35. Leon Festinger and James M. Carlsmith, "Cognitive Consequences of Forced Compliance," *Journal of Abnormal and Social Psychology* 58 (1959): 203–210.

36. Stanley Milgram, "Nationality and Conformity," *Scientific American* 205 (1961): 45–52. Also see Thomas Blass, *The Man Who Shocked the World: The Life and Legacy of Stanley Milgram* (New York: Basic Books, 2004), 51–53.

37. Stanley Milgram, "Behavioral Study of Obedience," *Journal of Abnormal and Social Psychology* 67 (1963): 371.

38. Ibid., 377.

39. The Web address is http://www.prisonex.org.

40. For details on Milgram's life and work, see Blass, *The Man Who Shocked the World.*

41. Jerry M. Burger, "Replicating Milgram: Would People Still Obey Today?" *American Psychologist* 64 (2009): 1–11.

42. Ludy T. Benjamin, Jr., and Jeffry A. Simpson, "The Power of the Situation: The Impact of Milgram's Obedience Studies on Personality and Social Psychology," *American Psychologist* 64 (2009): 17.

43. Muzafer Sherif, "Crisis in Social Psychology: Some Remarks Towards Breaking Through the Crisis," *Personality and Social Psychology Bulletin* 3 (1977): 371.

44. E. Loftus and J. Pickrell, "The Formation of False Memories," *Psychiatric Annals* 25 (1995): 720–725.

45. For a first-person account of Loftus's entire research program and of her role in the "memory wars," see her autobiography: "Elizabeth F. Loftus," in Gardner Lindzey and William McK. Runyan, *A History of Psychology in Autobiography*, vol. IX (Washington, DC: American Psychological Association, 2007), 198–227.

Chapter 11.   **Mind in Conflict: The Psychoanalytic Psychology of Sigmund Freud**

1. Sigmund Freud and Joseph Breuer, *Studies on Hysteria*, in *The Standard Edition of the Complete Psychological Works of Sigmund Freud*, vol. 2, ed. James Strachey (London: Hogarth, 1953–1974), 108.

2. For example, see Meredith M. Kimball, "From 'Anna O.' to Bertha Pappenheim: Transforming Private Pain into Public Action," *History of Psychology* 3 (2000): 20–43.

3. Ibid., 7.

4. For more detail on Brentano's likely influence on Freud, see Raymond Fancher, "Brentano's *Psychology from an Empirical Standpoint* and Freud's Early Metapsychology," *Journal of the History of the Behavioral Sciences* 13 (1977): 207–227.

5. Sigmund Freud, "The Question of Lay Analysis," in *Standard Edition*, vol. 20, 253.

6. Letter from Sigmund Freud to Wilhelm Fliess dated September 21, 1897, published in Freud, "Extracts from the Fliess Papers," *Standard Edition*, vol. 1, 259.

7. Sigmund Freud, *The Origins of Psycho-Analysis* (New York: Basic Books, 1954), 170.

8. Sigmund Freud, *The Interpretation of Dreams*, in *Standard Edition*, vol. 4, 583.

9. Freud, *Origins of Psycho-Analysis*, 325.

10. Sigmund Freud, "Fragment of an Analysis of a Case of Hysteria," in *Standard Edition*, vol. 7, 64.

11. Ibid., 86.

12. For more on the *Project for a Scientific Psychology* and its role in the development of Freud's theory, see Raymond E. Fancher, *Psychoanalytic Psychology: The Development of Freud's Thought* (New York: Norton, 1973), especially Chapter 3.

13. Sigmund Freud, *Interpretation of Dreams*, in *Standard Edition*, vol. 5, 536.

14. Adapted from Sigmund Freud, *New Introductory Lectures on Psycho-Analysis*, in *Standard Edition*, vol. 22, 78.

15. Sigmund Freud, "Some Psychical Consequences of the Anatomical Distinction between the Sexes," in *Standard Edition*, vol. 19, 248–258, quotations from 258, 249, 257–258.

16. Juliet Mitchell, *Psychoanalysis and Feminism* (New York: Pantheon, 1974), 322.

17. Karen Horney, "The Flight from Womanhood: The Masculinity Complex in Women as Viewed by Men and by Women," *International Journal of Psychoanalysis* 3 (1926): 324–339.

18. Clara Thompson, "Some Effects of the Derogatory Attitude Toward Female Sexuality," *Psychiatry* 13 (1950): 349–354.

19. Clara Thompson, "Cultural Pressures in the Psychology of Women," *Psychiatry* 5 (1942): 331–339.

20. Sigmund Freud, *The Future of an Illusion*, in *Standard Edition*, vol. 21, 30 (emphasis added).

21. W. H. Auden, "In Memory of Sigmund Freud," in *Collected Poems* (New York: Random House, 1976), 215–216.

22. Gail Hornstein, "The Return of the Repressed: Psychology's Problematic Relations with Psychoanalysis, 1909–1960," *American Psychologist* 47 (1992): 254–263.

23. J. J. Putnam, "Recent Experiences in the Study and Treatment of Hysteria at the Massachusetts General Hospital, with Remarks on Freud's Method of Treatment by 'Psycho-Analysis,'" *Journal of Abnormal Psychology* 1 (1906): 26–41.

24. R. B. Evans and W. A. Koelsch, "Psychoanalysis Arrives in America: The 1909 Psychology Conference at Clark University," *American Psychologist* 40 (1985): 946.

25. Sigmund Freud, "The Origin and Development of Psychoanalysis," *American Journal of Psychology* 21 (1910): 181–218.

26. Evans and Koelsch, "Psychoanalysis Arrives in America," 944–945.

27. Quoted in Saul Rosenzweig, *The Historic Expedition to America (1909): Freud, Jung and Hall the King-maker* (St. Louis: Rana House, 1994), 174.

28. Evans and Koelsch, "Psychoanalysis Arrives in America," 947.

29. Robert S. Woodworth, "Some Criticisms of the Freudian Psychology," *Journal of Abnormal Psychology,* 12 (1917): 174; Knight Dunlap, *Mysticism, Freudianism and Scientific Psychology* (St. Louis: Mosby, 1920), 8; John B. Watson and Rosalie Rayner, "Conditioned Emotional Reactions," *Journal of Experimental Psychology* 3 (1920): 14; James M. Cattell, "Some Psychological Experiments," *Science* 63 (1926): 5. See Hornstein, "Return of the Repressed," for further details.

30. John C. Burnham, "From Avant-garde to Specialism: Psychoanalysis in America," *Journal of the History of the Behavioral Sciences* 15 (1979): 129.

31. For details on this exchange, see David Shakow and David Rapaport, *The Influence of Freud on American Psychology* (Cleveland, OH: World Publishing Company, 1968), 129–131.

32. Hornstein, "Return of the Repressed," 258.

33. Ibid.

Chapter 12. **Psychology Gets "Personality": Gordon Allport, Abraham Maslow, and the Broadening of Academic Psychology**

1. Gordon W. Allport, "An Autobiography," in *The Person in Psychology: Selected Essays* (Boston: Beacon Press, 1968), 385.

2. Ibid.

3. Quoted in Edward Hoffman, *The Right to Be Human: A Biography of Abraham Maslow*, rev. ed. (New York: McGraw-Hill, 1999), 23.

4. Allport, "Autobiography," 379.

5. Quoted in Ian Nicholson, *Inventing Personality: Gordon Allport and the Science of Selfhood* (Washington, DC: American Psychological Association, 2003), 34.

6. Allport, "Autobiography," 380.

7. See Alan Elms, "Allport's *Personality* and Allport's Personality," in *Fifty Years of Personality Psychology*, ed. Kenneth H. Craik, Robert Hogan, and Raymond N. Wolfe (New York: Plenum Press, 1993), 39–55.

8. Allport, "Autobiography," 383–384.

9. For details, see Nicholson, *Inventing Personality*.

10. Carl G. Jung, "The Association Method," *American Journal of Psychology* 31 (1910): 220.

11. F. H. Allport and Gordon W. Allport, "Personality Traits: Their Classification and Measurement," *Journal of Abnormal and Social Psychology* 16 (1921): 6–40.

12. Allport, "Autobiography," 386–387.

13. Nicholson, *Inventing Personality*, 112–113.

14. Ibid., 139–141.

15. Gordon W. Allport, *Personality: A Psychological Interpretation* (New York: Henry Holt and Company, 1937), 3.

16. Ibid., 389.

17. Ibid., 395.

18. Ibid., 181.

19. Ibid., 183.

20. For example, see David Rapaport, *Organization and Pathology of Thought: Selected Sources* (New York: Columbia University Press, 1951).

21. Quoted in David Shakow and David Rapaport, *The Influence of Freud on American Psychology* (Cleveland, OH: World Publishing Co., 1968), 77.

22. H. J. Eysenck, *The Scientific Study of Personality* (New York: Macmillan, 1952), 18.

23. Several research groups contributed importantly to the emergence of the five factor consensus. See J. M. Digman, "Emergence of the Five-Factor Model," *Annual Review of Psychology* 41 (1990): 417–440.

24. Gordon W. Allport, *Letters from Jenny* (New York: Harcourt Brace, 1965).

25. Henry A. Murray, *Explorations in Personality* (New York: Oxford University Press, 1938). A recent reissue, with a new Foreword by Dan McAdams, was published in 2007 by Oxford University Press.

26. See, for example, David McClelland, *The Achieving Society* (Princeton, NJ: Van Nostrand, 1961), and David McClelland, *The Roots of Consciousness* (Princeton, NJ: Van Nostrand, 1964).

27. Walter Langer, *The Mind of Adolf Hitler: The Secret Wartime Report* (New York: Basic Books, 1972).

28. Irving Alexander, *Personology: Method and Content in Personality Assessment and Psychobiography* (Durham, NC: Duke University Press, 1990); Alan Elms, *Uncovering Lives: The Uneasy Alliance of Biography and Psychology* (New York: Oxford University Press, 1994); William M. Runyan, *Life Histories and Psychobiography: Explorations in Theory and Method* (New York: Oxford University Press, 1982); and William T. Schultz, ed., *Handbook of Psychobiography* (New York: Oxford University Press, 2005).

29. Dan McAdams, "What Psychobiographers Might Learn from Personality Psychology," in Schultz, *Handbook of Psychobiography*, 64–83.

30. Gordon W. Allport, *The Individual and His Religion* (New York: Macmillan, 1950).

31. Gordon W. Allport, *The Nature of Prejudice* (Reading, MA: Addison Wesley, 1954), 9.

32. Gordon W. Allport, *The Nature of Prejudice* (Garden City, NY: Anchor Doubleday, 1958).

33. Thomas Pettigrew, "Gordon Willard Allport: A Tribute," *Journal of Social Issues* 55 (1999): 415–428.

34. Calvin S. Hall and Gardner Lindzey, *Theories of Personality* (New York: Wiley, 1957).

35. Quotation from Ian Nicholson, "Giving Up Maleness: Abraham Maslow, Masculinity and the Boundaries of Psychology," *History of Psychology* 4 (2001): 81.

36. Quotations from Maslow's unpublished writings taken from Hoffman, *The Right to Be Human*, 1–9.

37. Ibid., 11.

38. Carl Murchison, ed., *Psychologies of 1925* (Worcester, MA: Clark University Press, 1926).

39. Hoffman, *The Right to Be Human*, 30.

40. Ibid., 37.

41. Ibid., 36.

42. Ibid., 55.

43. Abraham H. Maslow, "Individual Psychology and the Social Behavior of Monkeys and Apes," *International Journal of Individual Psychology* 1 (1935): 47–59.

44. Hoffmann, *The Right to Be Human*, 57.

45. Ibid., 78.

46. Ibid., 66.

47. Ibid., 80.

48. Margaret Mead, Preface to New Edition of Ruth Benedict, *Patterns of Culture*, (New York: Mentor Books, 1959), v.

49. Quoted in Hoffman, *The Right to Be Human*, 117.

50. Quoted in ibid., 139, 141.

51. H. Maslow, "A Theory of Human Motivation," *Psychological Review* 50 (1943): 382.

52. Ibid., 375.

53. Ibid., 381.

54. Ibid., 382.

55. Quoted in Hoffman, *The Right to Be Human*, 172.

56. Abraham H. Maslow, *Motivation and Personality*, 2nd ed. (New York: Harper & Row, 1970; originally published 1954), 179–180.

57. Ibid., 281–293.

58. C. Aanstoos, I. Serlin, and T. Greening, "History of Division 32 (Humanistic Psychology) of the American Psychological Association," in *Unification Through Division: Histories of the Divisions of the American Psychological Association*, vol. V., ed. Donald Dewsbury (Washington, DC: American Psychological Association, 2000).

59. Hoffman, *The Right to Be Human*, 240.

60. Maslow, *Motivation and Personality*, xiii.

61. Abraham M. Maslow, "Toward a Humanistic Biology," *American Psychologist* 24 (1969): 724.

62. Maslow, *Motivation and Personality*, xv.

63. Rob Hirtz, "Martin Seligman's Journey from Learned Helplessness to Learned Happiness," *The Pennsylvania Gazette*, 1999, available online at http://www .upenn.edu/gazette/0199/hirtz.html; Martin Seligman, *Learned Optimism: How to Change Your Mind and Your Life* (New York: Knopf, 1991).

64. Figures from the IPPA website: www.ippanetwork.org.

Chapter 13. **The Developing Mind: Alfred Binet, Jean Piaget, and the Study of Human Intelligence**

1. The papers appeared in French in 1890 and may be found in English translation in *The Experimental Psychology of Alfred Binet: Selected Papers*, ed. R. H. Pollack and M. W. Brenner (New York: Springer, 1969), under the titles "The Perception of Lengths and Numbers in Some Small Children" (79–92), "Children's Perceptions" (93–126), and "Studies of Movements of Some Young Children" (156–167).

2. Binet, "Children's Perceptions," 120.

3. Jean Piaget, *The Construction of Reality in the Child* (New York: Basic Books, 1954), 79.

4. Translated from Alfred Binet, "Le Raissonnement dans les Perceptions," *Revue Philosophique* 15 (1883), 4_2.

5. Quoted in Theta H. Wolf, *Alfred Binet* (Chicago: University of Chicago Press, 1973), 61.

6. Alfred Binet, "Alterations of Personality," in *Significant Contributions to the History of Psychology*, Series C, vol. 5, ed. D. W. Robinson (Washington, DC: University Publications of America, 1977; originally published 1891), 76.

7. Binet, "Studies of Movements of Children," 157.

8. Translated from Alfred Binet, *La Suggestibilité* (Paris: Schleicher, 1900), 119–120 (emphasis added).

9. Translated from Alfred Binet, *L'Etude Experimentale de l'Intelligence* (Paris: Schleicher, 1903), 218–219.

10. Quoted in Wolf, *Alfred Binet*, 140.

11. Translated from Alfred Binet and Théodore Simon, "Sur la Necessite d'Etablir un Diagnostic Scientifique des Etats Inferieurs de l'Intelligence," *L'Annee Psychologique* 11 (1905): 164.

12. Translated from Alfred Binet and Théodore Simon, "Applications des Methodes Nouvelles au Diagnostic du Niveau Intellectuel chez les Enfants Normaux et Anormaux d'Hospice et d'Ecole Primaire," *L'Annee Psychologique* 11 (1905): 320–321.

13. See Theta H. Wolf, "A New Perspective on Alfred Binet: Dramatist of Le Théatre de l'Horreur," *The Psychological Record* 32 (1982): 397–407.

14. Alfred Binet and Théodore Simon, "Le Developpement de l'Intelligence chez les Enfants," *L'Annee Psychologique* 14 (1908): 85.

15. For accounts of the army testing, see Daniel J. Kevles, "Testing the Army's Intelligence: Psychologists and the Military in World War I," *Journal of American History* 55 (1968): 565–581, and Franz Samelson, "World War I Intelligence Testing and the Development of Psychology," *Journal of the History of the Behavioral Sciences* 13 (1977): 274–282. Stephen Jay Gould's *The Mismeasure of Man* (New York: Norton, 1981) presents a scathing description of many of the deficiencies and inefficiencies in the actual conduct of the army testing.

16. Lewis M. Terman, "The Intelligence Quotient of Francis Galton in Childhood," *American Journal of Psychology* 28 (1917): 209–215, and Catharine Cox, *The Early Mental Traits of Three Hundred Geniuses* (Stanford, CA: Stanford University Press, 1926). Details about the subsequent career of Catharine Cox (Miles) can be found in her obituary, written by Robert R. Sears, "Catharine Cox Miles: 1890–1984," *American Journal of Psychology* 99 (1986): 431–433.

17. See Daniel Goleman, "1,528 Little Geniuses and How They Grew," *Psychology Today* (February 1980): 28–43.

18. Jean Piaget, "An Autobiography," in Richard I. Evans, *Jean Piaget: The Man and His Ideas* (New York: Dutton, 1973), 105–143, see 138n.

19. Ibid., 111.

20. Ibid.

21. Ibid., 118–119 (emphasis added).

22. Ibid., 128.

23. Bärbel Inhelder, "Observations sur le principe de conservation dans la physique de l'enfant," *Cahiers de Pédagogie Expérimentale et de Psychologie de l'Enfant* 9 (1936): 1–16.

24. "Bärbel Inhelder," in Gardner Lindzey, *A History of Psychology in Autobiography*, vol. 8 (Stanford, CA: Stanford University Press, 1989), 209–243, see 214.

25. Jean Piaget and Bärbel Inhelder, *The Child's Construction of Quantities* (London: Routledge, 1974; translated from the French edition of 1941).

26. Bärbel Inhelder and Jean Piaget, *The Growth of Logical Thinking from Childhood to Adolescence: An Essay on the Construction of Formal Operational Structures* (New York: Basic Books, 1958; originally published 1955).

27. Jean Piaget, *Genetic Epistemology* (New York: Norton, 1970), 15.

28. Quoted in Evans, *Jean Piaget*, 53.

Chapter 14.　**Machines, Minds, and Cognitive Psychology**

1. Quotations in Morris Bishop, *Pascal: The Life of Genius* (New York: Greenwood Press, 1968), 31, and Ernest Mortimer, *Blaise Pascal: The Life and Work of a Realist* (London: Methuen, 1959), 66.

2. Quoted in J. Bronowski and Bruce Mazlish, *The Western Intellectual Tradition from Leonardo to Hegel* (New York: Harper Torchbooks, 1960), 240.

3. Ibid.

4. Blaise Pascal, *Pensées*, ed. Louis Lafuma (London: Dent, 1973), 57, 59 (nos. 277, 282).

5. Vernon Pratt, *Thinking Machines: The Evolution of Artificial Intelligence* (New York and Oxford, UK: Basil Blackwell Ltd., 1987), 20.

6. Quoted from Galileo's *Il Saggiatore* in *Bartlett's Familiar Quotations*, 14th ed., ed. Emily Morrison Beck (Boston: Little, Brown, 1968), 211.

7. Quoted in Stanley L. Jaki, *Brain, Mind and Computers* (Washington, DC: Regnery Gateway, 1989), 24. From Thomas Hobbes, *Leviathan*, Part I, Chapter 5.

8. G. MacDonald Ross, *Leibniz* (Oxford, UK: Oxford University Press, 1984), 12.

9. For more extensive discussion of Leibniz's approach to logic see Pratt, *Thinking Machines*, Chapter 5.

10. Charles Babbage, "Passages from the Life of a Philosopher," abridged version in *Charles Babbage and His Calculating Engines*, ed. Philip Morrison and Emily Morrison (New York: Dover, 1961), 25.

11. Ibid., 33.

12. Christopher Evans, *The Mighty Micro: The Impact of the Computer Revolution* (London: Gollancz, 1979), 28.

13. "Sketch of the Analytical Engine Invented by Charles Babbage by L. F. Menabrea, with Notes upon the Memoir by the Translator, Ada Augusta, Countess of Lovelace," in *Babbage and His Calculating Engines*, 225–295.

14. Ibid., 251–252, 249.

15. Ibid., 284.

16. Nora Barlow, ed., *The Autobiography of Charles Darwin 1809–1882* (New York: Norton, 1952), 108.

17. Quoted in Carl B. Boyer, *A History of Mathematics*, 2nd ed., rev. Uta C. Merzbach (New York: Wiley, 1989), 578.

18. Andrew Hodges, *Alan Turing: The Enigma of Intelligence* (London: Burnett Books, 1983), 26.

19. A. M. Turing, "On Computable Numbers, with an Application to the *Entscheidungsproblem*," *Proceedings of the London Mathematical Society* 42 (1937): 230–265.

20. Claude E. Shannon, "A Symbolic Analysis of Relay and Switching Circuits," *Transactions of the American Institute of Electrical Engineers* 57 (1938): 1–11.

21. A. M. Turing, "Computing Machinery and Intelligence," *Mind* 49 (1950): 434.

22. See Hodges, *Alan Turing*, for full details.

23. Quoted in Howard Gardner, *The Mind's New Science: A History of the Cognitive Revolution* (New York: Basic Books, 1985), 146.

24. G. Ernst and A. Newell, *GPS: A Case Study in Generality and Problem Solving* (New York: Academic Press, 1969), 2.

25. Quoted in Gardner, *Mind's New Science*, 148.

26. John Haugeland, *Artificial Intelligence: The Very Idea* (Boston: MIT Press, 1985), 250–251.

27. Margaret Boden, *The Creative Mind: Myths and Mechanisms* (London: Weidenfeld and Nicholson, 1990).

28. John Searle, "Minds, Brains and Programs," *Behavioral and Brain Sciences* 3 (1980): 417–424.

29. Ulric Neisser, "Autobiography," in *A History of Psychology in Autobiography*, vol. IX, ed. Gardner Lindzey and William M. Runyan (Washington, DC: American Psychological Association, 2007), 269–270.

30. Ibid., 271.

31. Ibid.

32. His results were later published in a classic article, G. A. Miller, "The Magical Number Seven, Plus or Minus Two: Some Limits on Our Capacity for Processing Information," *Psychological Review* 63 (1956): 81–97.

33. Neisser, "Autobiography," 278.

34. His first published description of this was Oliver Selfridge, "Pandemonium: A Paradigm for Learning," in *Proceedings of the Symposium on Mechanisation of Thought Processes*, ed. D. V. Blake and A. M. Utley (London: 1959), 511–529.

35. O. G. Selfridge and U. Neisser, "Pattern Recognition by Machine," *Scientific American* 203 (1960): 60–68.

36. Neisser "Autobiography," 281–282.

37. Ulric Neisser, "The Imitation of Man by Machine," *Science* 193 (1963): 193–197.

38. Neisser "Autobiography," 282.

39. The first book to be titled *Cognitive Psychology* was published in 1939 by T. V. Moore, a Benedictine monk who had studied with Wundt and Külpe. Moore directed the psychology laboratory at Catholic University in Washington, DC. For a description of Moore's work and some conjectures about why his book did *not* launch a new field, see Aimée M. Surprenant and Ian Neath, "T. V. Moore's (1939) Cognitive Psychology," *Psychonomic Bulletin and Review* 4 (1997): 342–349.

40. Quoted in Robert Hoffman, "American Cognitive Psychology," in *A Pictorial History of Psychology*, ed. W. G. Bringmann, H. E. Luck, R. Miller, and C. Early (Chicago: Quintessence Publishing, 1997), 596.

41. Ulric Neisser, *Cognitive Psychology* (New York: Appleton-Century-Crofts, 1967), 4.

42. Neisser, "Autobiography," 284.

43. Ibid., 290.

44. E. Winograd and U. Neisser, eds., *Affect and Accuracy in Recall: Studies of "Flashbulb" Memories* (New York: Cambridge University Press, 1992).

45. Neisser, "Autobiography," 297.

Chapter 15. **Origins of Applied Psychology: From the Courtroom to the Clinic**

1. Matthew Hale in *Human Science and Social Order: Hugo Münsterberg and the Origins of Applied Psychology* (Philadelphia: Temple University Press, 1980), 3.
2. Details of Münsterberg's involvement in the Orchard case are drawn principally from Hale, *Human Science and Social Order*, and Margaret Münsterberg's *Hugo Münsterberg: His Life and Work* (New York: D. Appleton and Company, 1922).
3. Münsterberg was well known for his inconsistent views and rapid ability to change positions. Another example was his opinion on the existence of the unconscious, a construct that he at times denied and at other times invoked—see Frank J. Landy, "Hugo Münsterberg: Victim or Visionary?" *Journal of Applied Psychology* 77 (1992): 787–802.
4. For a lively account of Marston's colorful career, see Geoffrey Bunn, "The Lie Detector, Wonder Woman, and Liberty: The Life and Work of William Moulton Marston," *History of the Human Sciences* 10 (1997): 91–119.
5. Hugo Münsterberg, *On the Witness Stand* (New York: Doubleday, 1908), 3.
6. Ibid., 9.
7. James McKeen Cattell, "Mental Tests and Measurements," *Mind* 15 (1890): 373.
8. Anne Anastasi, a noted expert on testing and psychometrics, in her book *Fields of Applied Psychology* (New York: McGraw-Hill, 1964), 4, called Münsterberg "the first all-round applied psychologist in America."
9. As noted in Phyllis Keller, *States of Belonging: German-American Intellectuals and the First World War* (Cambridge, MA: Harvard University Press, 1979), 13.
10. Ibid., 27.
11. As described in Ludy T. Benjamin, "Hugo Münsterberg: Portrait of an Applied Psychologist," in *Portraits of Pioneers in Psychology*, vol. IV, ed. G. A. Kimble and M. Wertheimer (Washington, DC: APA, 2000), 113–129.
12. For a discussion of the contrasts between Münsterberg's and Freud's outlooks, see Hale, *Human Science and Social Order*, Chapter 9.
13. Benjamin, "Hugo Münsterberg: Portrait of an Applied Psychologist," 120.
14. Rita Mae Kelly and Vincent Kelly, "Lillian Moller Gilbreth (1878–1972)," in *Women in Psychology: A Bio-bibliographic Sourcebook*, ed. A. N. O'Connell and N. F. Russo (New York: Greenwood Press, 1990), 117–124.
15. Robert Perloff and John L. Naman, "Lillian Gilbreth: Tireless Advocate for a General Psychology," in *Portraits of Pioneers in Psychology*, vol. II, ed. G. A. Kimble, C. A. Boneau, and M. Wertheimer (Washington, DC: APA, 1996), 107–116.
16. Lillian M. Gilbreth, *As I Remember: An Autobiography* (Norcross, GA: Engineering & Management Press, 1998), 73.
17. L. M. Gilbreth, *The Psychology of Management* (New York: Sturgis & Walton, 1914), 32.
18. Frank B. Gilbreth Jr. and Ernestine Gilbreth Carey, *Cheaper by the Dozen* (New York: T. Y. Crowell Co., 1948), 52. Quotation is from the First Perennial Classics Edition published by HarperCollins in 2002.
19. Shortly after her husband's death in 1924, Lillian Gilbreth wrote his biography, which she titled *The Quest of the One Best Way*.
20. This observation was made by Laura Koppes in "American Female Pioneers of Industrial and Organizational Psychology During the Early Years," *Journal of*

Applied Psychology 82 (1997): 500–515, of Robert I. Watson's 1974 volume *Eminent Contributors to Psychology.*

21. Gwendolyn Stevens and Sheldon Gardner, *The Women of Psychology, Volume I: Pioneers and Innovators* (Cambridge, MA: Schenkman Publishing Company, 1982).

22. Lightner Witmer, "Clinical Psychology," *Psychological Clinic* 1 (1907): 1.

23. Ibid., 2.

24. Paul McReynolds, *Lightner Witmer: His Life and Times* (Washington, DC: APA, 1997), 118–119.

25. S. Weir Mitchell was feminist writer Charlotte Perkins Gilman's physician. His prescription of the rest cure for Gilman inspired her to write the famous short story "The Yellow Wallpaper," in which the protagonist, instead of finding mental and physical respite, is actually driven insane by the supposed cure.

26. One of Witmer's students, David Mitchell, is regarded as the first psychologist to have worked in private practice.

27. It should be noted that although Witmer has been touted as father of clinical psychology, the use of the phrase *clinical psychology* was not an original contribution. A prominent clinical tradition marked the development of psychology in France at the end of the nineteenth century, exemplified in the work of Binet, Charcot, and others. A journal called the *Journal of Clinical and Therapeutic Psychology* was published in Paris between 1897 and 1901. See McReynolds, *Lightner Witmer*, 132.

28. Ludy T. Benjamin and David B. Baker, *From Séance to Science: A History of the Profession of Psychology in America* (Belmont, CA: Thomson/Wadworth, 2004), 44.

29. As cited in L. S. Hollingworth, "Activities of Clinical Psychologists," *Psychological Bulletin* 14 (1917): 225

30. J. E. Wallace Wallin, "Clinical Psychology: What It Is and What It Is Not," *Science* 37 (1913): 902.

31. Harry L. Hollingworth, *Leta Stetter Hollingworth: A Biography* (Lincoln: University of Nebraska Press, 1943), 33.

32. Ibid., 73.

33. For a description of the study and subsequent trial and its significance in the history of applied psychology, see Ludy T. Benjamin, Anne M. Rogers, and Angela Rosenbaum, "Coca-Cola, Caffeine, and Mental Deficiency: Harry Hollingworth and the Chattanooga Trial of 1911," *Journal of the History of the Behavioral Sciences* 27 (1991): 42–55.

34. Ann G. Klein, *A Forgotten Voice: A Biography of Leta Stetter Hollingworth* (Scottsdale, AZ: Great Potential Press, 2002), 72.

35. L. S. Hollingworth, "Variability as Related to Sex Differences in Achievement: A Critique," *American Journal of Sociology* 19 (1914): 528.

36. L. S. Hollingworth, "Functional Periodicity: An Experimental Study of the Mental and Motor Abilities of Women During Menstruation," *Teachers College, Columbia University, Contributions to Education* 69 (1914), 94.

37. Ibid., 95.

38. Robert H. Lowie and Leta Stetter Hollingworth, "Science and Feminism," *The Scientific Monthly* 3 (1916): 277.

39. Ibid., 283.

40. Ann G. Klein, *Leta Stetter Hollingworth: A Biography*.

41. This work was another aspect of applied psychology, human factors psychology, that had started before WWI throughout Europe and North America and has continued in various forms, including ergonomics and task analysis. See Chapters 2 and 3 of Robert R. Hoffman and Laura G. Militello, *Perspectives on Cognitive Task Analysis: Historical Origins and Modern Communities of Practice* (Boca Raton, FL: CRC Press/Taylor and Francis, 2009).

Glossary

Key Pioneers

Ach, Narziss (1871–1946) A Würzburg psychologist who performed directed-association studies that revealed the importance of determining tendencies or mental sets.

Adler, Alfred (1870–1937) A one-time disciple of Sigmund Freud who promoted a school he called individual psychology and the concept of the inferiority complex.

Agassiz, Louis (1807–1873) An eminent Harvard biologist and America's most outspoken critic of Charles Darwin's *Origin of Species*.

Allport, Floyd H. (1890–1978) A founder of experimental social psychology who wrote the first American doctoral dissertation in the field (on social facilitation), co-edited the first journal devoted to it, and wrote its first major textbook

Allport, Gordon W. (1897–1967) An American psychologist who was instrumental in establishing the field of personality psychology; he also made important contributions as a social psychologist with studies of religion and prejudice.

Angell, James Rowland (1869–1949) An American functionalist who, along with Carr and Dewey, was a leader in this field at the University of Chicago.

Aristotle (384–322 B.C.E.) Ancient Greek philosopher whose empiricist theory of the mind and writings on the functions of the *psyche* (soul) profoundly influenced Western mental philosophy.

Asch, Solomon (1907–1996) An American social psychologist who became famous for his experimental studies of social conformity and suggestibility in groups.

Aubertin, Ernest (1825–1893) A physician, and the son-in-law of Bouillaud, whose theory of localization precipitated one of the critical incidents in the history of brain science.

Babbage, Charles (1792–1871) An English mathematician and inventor who helped reform English mathematics by introducing Leibnizean calculus and who designed the difference engine and the analytical engine.

Bain, Alexander (1818–1903) A Scottish philosopher/psychologist who was among the first to write psychology textbooks that integrated neural physiology and psychology in the mid-1800s. He influenced James with his writings on habit.

Bartholow, Roberts (1831–1904) A physician who was one of the first to conduct brain stimulation experiments on conscious human subjects.

Bauer, Ida (1882–1945) The real name of Sigmund Freud's patient "Dora."

Bechterev, Vladimir M. (1857–1927) A Russian physiologist who studied conditioned responses in animals and humans.

Beck, Aaron T. (b. 1921) An American psychiatrist and psychoanalyst who created cognitive therapy, which focuses on correcting the distorted thinking and irrational thoughts that are presumed to underlie psychological distress, such as depression.

Beeckman, Isaac (1588–1637) A physician and mathematician who became a mentor to Descartes and revitalized his intellectual interests.

Bell, Charles (1774–1842) The Scottish scientist who first developed and published on the law of specific nerve energies.

Benedict, Ruth (1887–1948) An anthropologist whose book *Patterns of Culture* suggested the idea that "culture" within anthropology was analogous to that of "personality" within psychology. She was an important influence on Maslow.

Bergson, Henri (1859–1941) A French philosopher whose theory of "creative evolution" influenced Piaget.

Berkeley, George (1685–1753) An Irish bishop who applied Locke's associationistic principles to the systematic analysis of visual depth perception.

Bernheim, Hippolyte (1840–1919) A French physician who was influenced by Liébeault's work with hypnotism and became founder of the Nancy School, which argued that susceptibility to hypnosis is a normal human characteristic akin to general suggestibility.

Bessel, Friedrich Wilhelm (1784–1846) A German astronomer who showed that the recorded telescopic measurements of astronomical observers differed in consistent ways and that the difference could be accounted for if each astronomer's "personal equation" were kept in mind.

Binet, Alfred (1857–1911) A French psychologist who promoted a faulty theory of hypnosis while working for Charcot, before going on to conduct pioneering experimental studies of suggestibility in children. Late in his career, with Théodore Simon, he developed the first successful tests of intelligence in children.

Boole, George (1815–1864) An English mathematician who expanded the definition of mathematics in creating Boolean algebra, a new form of symbolic logic.

Boring, E. G. (1886–1968) An experimental psychologist who became America's first important historian of psychology.

Bouillaud, Jean Baptiste (1796–1881) A French physician who rejected much of phrenology but who felt there was some truth to the notion of an area that controlled language in the frontal region of the cortex.

Boyle, Robert (1627–1691) A proponent of the new experimental science who strongly influenced Locke, established the Royal Society of London, and conducted a famous experiment demonstrating what came to be known as *Boyle's law*, which holds that the volume of a gas varies inversely with the pressure upon it.

Braid, James (1795–1860) A Scottish physician who confirmed Puységur's and Faria's previous research on mesmeric techniques and who also coined the term *hypnotism*; he helped the subject achieve scientific respectability.

Brentano, Franz (1838–1917) A German philosopher who influenced Freud and is known primarily for his theory of "act psychology" and intentionality.

Breuer, Josef (1842–1925) An Austrian physician who treated Bertha Pappenheim ("Anna O.") then collaborated with Sigmund Freud and published *Studies on Hysteria* (1895) with him.

Broca, Paul (1824–1880) The first establishment figure seriously and effectively to challenge Flourens's conception of the undifferentiated cerebral cortex. His findings from investigations of sensory aphasia ushered in a new period of interest in the localized functions of the brain.

Bronner, Augusta Fox (1881–1966) An early clinical psychologist who worked at the Juvenile Psychopathic Institute in Chicago, where she undertook detailed assessments of delinquent youth in order to formulate individualized treatment plans.

Brown, Roger (1925–1997) An American psychologist who conducted seminal research on the acquisition and development of grammatical skills in children.

Brücke, Ernst (1819–1892) An early mechanistic physiologist who became one of Freud's favorite teachers during his medical school years.

Bruner, Jerome (b. 1915) An American psychologist who, along with Miller, established a new Center for Cognitive Studies at Harvard in 1960 and created new theories of teaching and learning based on modes of representation.

Burt, Sir Cyril (1883–1971) A British psychologist who represented himself as Galton's intellectual successor and who published a now-discredited twin study that suggested an extremely high heritability for intelligence.

Calkins, Mary Whiton (1863–1930) One of the first women to overcome gender discrimination and establish a career in psychology. A student of James, she developed the paired-associates technique for studying memory as well as an influential system of self psychology. She went on to become a president of the American Psychological Association and the American Philosophical Association.

Carr, Harvey (1873–1954) An American functionalist who, along with Angell and Dewey, was a leader in this field at the University of Chicago.

Cattell, James McKeen (1860–1944) An American experimental psychologist who studied under Wundt and created instruments to measure reaction times to make inferences about apperception. Later he became an important figure at Columbia University.

Cattell, Raymond B. (1905–1998) An English-born psychologist best known for his development of the Sixteen Personality Factor Questionnaire (16 PF).

Charcot, Jean-Martin (1825–1893) An eminent French neurologist whose theories of hysteria and hypnosis were proven false but brought those subjects into the scientific mainstream. He mentored Sigmund Freud and founded the Salpêtrière School.

Chomsky, Noam (b. 1928) An American psycholinguist whose conception of the innate grammatical sense in human beings contradicted Skinner's behaviorist theory of verbal behavior and helped lay the foundation for cognitive psychology.

Clark, Kenneth B. (1914–2005) A well-known African American psychologist who, along with his wife Mamie Phipps Clark, conducted psychological studies of the effects of race and racial prejudice on personality development. Their studies contributed to the Supreme Court's 1954 decision in *Brown v. Board of Education* to make the segregation of public schools by race illegal in the United States.

Clark, Mamie Phipps (1917–1983) See entry for **Clark, Kenneth B**.

Cooper, Sir Anthony Ashley (1621–1683) The first Earl of Shaftesbury, the patron, friend, and chief supporter of Locke.

Copernicus, Nicolaus (1473–1543) A Polish astronomer who posited the idea of a heliocentric solar system—that the sun rather than the earth is the center of the system.

Cox, Catharine (1890–1984) An American psychologist who was a student and then colleague of Terman's and studied giftedness in children.

Cuvier, Georges (1769–1832) The most celebrated scientist in France, known appropriately as the "Dictator of Biology," who supported the ablation studies of Flourens.

Darwin, Charles Robert (1809–1882) An English naturalist whose travels to the Galápagos Islands in the 1830s guided him toward developing the theory of evolution by natural selection, which profoundly influenced all of the life sciences including psychology.

Darwin, Erasmus (1731–1802) One of the most famous intellectual figures of his day: a doctor, inventor, poet, and general man of science who had theorized about evolution; the grandfather of Charles Darwin and Francis Galton.

Dashiell, John (1888–1975) An early American proponent of a social psychology that was experimental, objective, and focused on the reactions of individual subjects in controlled social situations.

de Candolle, Alphonse (1806–1893) A Swiss botanist who collected biographical information on more than 300 eminent European scientists, which pointed to the strong importance of environment relative to heredity, in contrast to Galton's position.

de Chastenet, Amand Marie Jacques (Marquis de Puységur) (1751–1825) A student of Mesmer's who discovered the "perfect crisis" and "artificial somnambulism."

Delboeuf, Joseph (1831–1896) A Belgian physiologist who became a strong supporter of the Nancy School of hypnotism after disconfirming the "magnetic" theories of Binet and Féré.

Descartes, René (1596–1650) French philosopher and mathematician who promoted an interactive dualism between a material body and immaterial mind or soul; he went further than his predecessors in positing mechanistic explanations for the body's functions, but insisted that the highest functions of consciousness, will and reasoning, were non-mechanistic attributes of the rational soul; he also laid the foundations for the modern distinction between body and mind and the question of how far mechanistic analysis can go in accounting for psychological processes.

Deutsch, Helene (1884–1982) A successful female analyst, supported by Sigmund Freud, who wrote about the psychology of women.

Dewey, John (1859–1952) An American functionalist who, along with Carr and Angell, was a leader in this field at the University of Chicago.

Donaldson, Henry H. (1857–1938) A neurologist who studied the nervous system of white rats and supervised the early work of Watson.

Donders, F. C. (1818–1889) A Dutch physiologist who devised the subtractive method and used this mathematical formula to measure reaction times and make inferences about the speed of mental processes.

Downey, June Etta (1875–1932) A psychologist from the University of Wyoming who created one of the first personality tests, the Individual Will Temperament Test, based on handwriting analysis.

Du Bois-Reymond, Emil (1818–1896) An early mechanistic physiologist and colleague of Helmholtz's who established the electrochemical nature of the nerve impulse.

Ebbinghaus, Hermann (1850–1909) A German physiologist who devised an experimental approach to studying memory using nonsense syllables.

Ehrenfels, Christian von (1859–1932) An Austrian who prefigured Gestalt psychology with his writings about our inability to introspectively break down whole objects or ideas into separate sensory elements.

Elliotson, John (1791–1868) A British physician who faced ridicule for becoming an early supporter of research on mesmerism and hypnosis.

Erikson, Erik (1902–1994) A children's psychoanalyst who expanded Sigmund Freud's concept of psychosexual stages of personality development to include psychosocial factors.

Esdaile, James (1808–1859) A Scottish physician who practiced in India and demonstrated that mesmeric techniques could induce anesthesia during surgery.

Eysenck, Hans J. (1916–1997) A London-trained psychologist who created a three-factor, PEN model of personality that assesses a person's standing on the dimensions of psychoticism, extroversion/introversion, and neuroticism.

Fairbairn, W. R. D. (1889–1964) A British physician and psychoanalyst who helped develop the object relations school of psychoanalysis.

Faria, José Custodio di (1746–1819) A Portuguese priest who showed that hypnotic phenomena are more dependent on the susceptibility of the subjects than on the powers of the hypnotist.

Fechner, Gustav Theodor (1801–1887) A German scientist whose work on the measurement of the relationship between subjective and physical stimulus intensities showed the possibility of a mathematically based experimental psychology, in a field now known as psychophysics.

Féré, Charles (1852–1907) An assistant of Charcot's who experimented with hypnosis and who with Binet promoted an incorrect "magnetic theory" about it.

Fernald, Grace (1879–1950) An early clinical psychologist who worked at the Juvenile Psychopathic Institute in Chicago where she undertook detailed assessments of delinquent youth in order to formulate individualized treatment plans.

Ferrier, David (1843–1928) A Scottish neurologist who, throughout the 1870s, demonstrated several other functionally distinct "centers" in the cortex, to accompany Broca's area and the motor strip.

Festinger, Leon (1919–1989) An American social psychologist who studied with Kurt Lewin and later developed the theory of cognitive dissonance.

Flourens, Pierre (1794–1867) A French scientist who opposed Gall's phrenology and conducted ablation studies in animals suggesting that the brain's cortex functions as a unified whole.

Franz, Shepherd Ivory (1874–1933) An American psychologist who trained Lashley and studied the effects of cortical ablations on cats and whose innovation was to combine the method of ablation with that of animal training.

Freeman, Frank N. (1880–1961) A psychologist who, along with Newman and Holzinger, did the first major study of separated twins in 1937.

Freud, Anna (1895–1982) Sigmund Freud's daughter and an early child analyst, who further developed the theories of defense and defense mechanisms.

Freud, Sigmund (1856–1939) A Viennese physician who created the therapy and general psychological theory that became known as psychoanalysis.

Fritsch, Gustav (1837–1927) A German physiologist who, along with Hitzig, discovered the motor strip through electrical stimulation experiments.

Fromm, Erich (1900–1980) A neo-Freudian analyst whose 1941 book *Escape from Freedom* and later works emphasized the importance of social and cultural factors in shaping human personality.

Galen (ca. 130–200 C.E.) A Greek physician and philosopher who adopted the four-humor theory of health.

Galilei, Galileo (1564–1642) An Italian astronomer, natural philosopher, and physicist who created a theory of primary and secondary qualities similar to Descartes' theory of simple natures at around the same time.

Gall, Franz Josef (1758–1828) A German physician who demonstrated the general importance of the brain for all of the higher human functions, while also originating the popular nineteenth-century movement known as phrenology.

Galton, Francis (1822–1911) A versatile English scientist and cousin of Charles Darwin, who promoted the notions of hereditary intelligence and eugenics. In doing so Galton laid the foundations for modern intelligence testing and the broad field of behavior genetics.

Gassner, Johann Joseph (1727–1779) A priest who claimed to cure many illnesses through the use of exorcism in the eighteenth century; his cures were explained by Mesmer as actually the result of animal magnetism.

Gibson, Eleanor Jack (1910–2002) A psychologist at Cornell University in New York who devised the "visual cliff" studies that resulted in the idea that depth perception occurs innately or extremely early in development, without prior learning.

Gibson, James J. (1904–1979) An American psychologist known for his ecological psychology, stressing that mind must be understood in relation to its environment, and that many aspects of the environment present themselves to the mind directly, without mediation.

Gilbreth, Frank Bunker (1868–1924) A self-taught engineer who was influenced by Taylor's system of scientific management. He collaborated with his wife, Lillian Moller Gilbreth, to create motion studies to examine the movements involved in a variety of work tasks, ultimately seeking the "one best way" to get a job done.

Gilbreth, Lillian Moller (1878–1972) An early industrial/organizational psychologist who wrote *The Psychology of Management*. She worked with her husband, Frank Bunker Gilbreth, to create motion studies to research the efficiency of factory workers, and she consulted with businesses on a range of employee and workplace issues using their motion study approach.

Goddard, Henry Herbert (1866–1957) An American psychologist and eugenicist who studied under Hall and became director of psychological research at the New Jersey Training School for Feeble-Minded Boys and Girls at Vineland.

Goldstein, Kurt (1878–1965) A German neurologist who was impressed by Gestalt principles and argued that brain injuries should be assessed holistically; he was also an early promoter of the term *self-actualization*.

Hall, G. Stanley (1844–1924) The first American to earn a Ph.D. in experimental psychology under James. He went on to found many important institutions, including the American Psychological Association and numerous journals. He also became a leader in child study and developmental psychology, popularizing the term *adolescence*.

Harlow, Harry (1905–1981) An American primate researcher best known for his work on the social behavior of monkeys and the biological "need" for love; he was Maslow's dissertation supervisor.

Hartley, David (1705–1757) A contemporary of Hume's and a physician who attempted to integrate associationism with neurophysiology by arguing that specific "ideas" are occasioned by minute vibrations in specific locations of the brain and nerves.

Hartmann, Heinz (1894–1970) A psychoanalyst who pioneered the area of ego psychology and who, along with Rapaport, promoted the notion of autonomous ego functions.

Harvey, William (1578–1657) A British physician who was the first to demonstrate that the heart is a pumping mechanism that circulates blood, rather than an organ that continuously creates new blood.

Hebb, Donald O. (1904–1985) A neuropsychologist from McGill University who published *The Organization of Behavior* in 1949. This book related learning and other behavior to the hypothetical functioning of "neurological networks" in the brain that he called cell assemblies.

Helmholtz, Hermann (1821–1894) A German student of Müller who expanded on the doctrine of specific nerve energies, promoted the law of conservation of energy, and established many of the foundations of experimental psychology with his studies of sensation and perception.

Henri, Victor (1872–1940) A student and collaborator of Binet's who worked with him on studies of suggestibility in children and on developing the program of Individual Psychology.

Henslow, John Stevens (1796–1861) An English clergyman and professor at Cambridge University who lectured on botany, influenced Charles Darwin, and recommended that Darwin become Captain FitzRoy's naturalist on the voyage of the *Beagle*.

Hering, Ewald (1834–1918) A contemporary of Helmholtz who theorized about color afterimages and promoted the opponent theory of color vision.

Hitzig, Eduard (1838–1907) A German physiologist who, along with Fritsch, discovered the motor strip through electrical stimulation experiments.

Hobbes, Thomas (1588–1679) An English philosopher who promoted the notion of the social contract and the idea that human reasoning is a form of mathematical-like calculation.

Hollingworth, Harry (1880–1956) A psychologist (and husband of Leta Stetter Hollingworth) who was hired by the Coca-Cola Company in 1911 to study the behavioral effects of caffeine on human beings.

Hollingworth, Leta Stetter (1886–1939) An early clinical psychologist who conducted pioneering studies of the psychology of women, developed and oversaw programs for gifted children, and advocated for higher degree training for clinical psychologists, thus professionalizing the field.

Holzinger, Karl (1893–1954) A statistician who, along with Freeman and Newman, conducted the first major study of separated twins in 1937.

Hooker, Joseph (1817–1911) A British botanist who was a trusted friend to Charles Darwin and supported his theory of evolution by natural selection.

Horney, Karen (1885–1952) A feminist psychoanalyst who argued that Sigmund Freud's conception of female sexuality was biased by his male point of view. She emphasized the role of culture in determining normal and abnormal behavioral patterns, arguing that it is male-dominated culture rather than anatomy that primarily determines the typical differences between masculine and feminine personalities.

Hull, Clark (1884–1952) An American psychologist best known for his development of a mathematically based "mechanistic behaviorism."

Hume, David (1711–1776) A Scotsman who followed Aristotle in proposing two specific laws of association that determine how and when ideas get linked together by experience. Also stimulated Kant by his skeptical analysis of the notion of causality.

Huxley, Thomas Henry (1825–1895) An expert on primate anatomy who supported Charles Darwin's theory of evolution by natural selection and defended the theory publicly; he became known as "Darwin's bulldog."

Inhelder, Bärbel (1913–1997) A Swiss psychologist who co-authored nine books with Piaget and worked especially on the stages of cognitive development.

Jacquard, Joseph (1752–1834) A French weaver who invented punch cards to "program" mechanical looms and whose work influenced Babbage.

James, William (1842–1910) A Harvard professor who established the first psychology laboratory in America and created an intellectual climate receptive to the new field with his 1890 textbook *The Principles of Psychology*. His work stressed the usefulness of psychological ideas, consistently with a philosophical view he called pragmatism.

Jones, Mary Cover (1896–1987) An American psychologist who, under the supervision of Watson, conducted the first study using systematic desensitization as a fear removal procedure.

Jung, Carl Gustav (1875–1961) A Swiss psychiatrist and psychoanalyst who amended Sigmund Freud's theory of the unconscious by including spirituality, the influences of culture, and the importance of symbols in personality development. He invented the word association test and introduced the dimension of extroversion-introversion in his analysis of psychological types.

Kant, Immanuel (1724–1804) A German philosopher who embarked on a program of "critical philosophy" that emphasized the role of an active mind in creating the phenomenal world, and thus created a foundation for the establishment of experimental psychology.

Klein, Melanie (1882–1960) A psychoanalyst who emphasized the importance of the earliest mother-infant relationship and helped found object relations theory.

Koffka, Kurt (1886–1941) One of the founders of the school of Gestalt psychology.

Köhler, Wolfgang (1887–1967) One of the founders of the school of Gestalt psychology, who later studied insight learning in chimpanzees and introduced the idea of psychophysical isomorphism.

Külpe, Oswald (1862–1915) A student of Wundt's and founder of the "Würzburg School," who promoted introspective experiments on several of the higher processes, thus contradicting Wundt's view that this was not possible.

Ladd-Franklin, Christine (1847–1930) An American mathematician and vision researcher who promoted an evolutionary theory of color receptors and who unsuccessfully challenged Titchener's policy of banning women from his invitation-only group, the Society of Experimentalists.

Lamarck, Jean-Baptiste (1744–1829) A French zoologist who proposed that species evolve and change owing to the inheritance of bodily changes produced by the voluntary exercise or disuse of particular organs.

Lange, Carl (1834–1900) A Danish physiologist who, like James, theorized about the relationship between emotions and bodily reactions, creating the James-Lange theory of emotion.

Lange, Ludwig (1863–1936) A German physicist who studied under Wundt and whose research focused on differing stimulus-response reaction times for perception versus apperception.

Langer, Walter (1899–1981) An American psychoanalyst and student of Murray who wrote one of the first psychobiographies: a study of Adolf Hitler during World War II.

Lashley, Karl Spencer (1890–1958) An American psychologist known for his study of learning and memory and his research that suggested memories are not localized to one part of the brain but rather are distributed throughout.

Lavater, Johann Kaspar (1741–1801) A Swiss mystic and theologian who promoted the art of physiognomy, or reading character from the physical signs of the body, usually the face.

Le Bon, Gustave (1841–1931) A French theorist who wrote about the behavior of crowds, likening it to the effects of hypnosis.

Leeuwenhoek, Anton van (1632–1723) A lens grinder who developed the modern microscope and influenced Leibniz's theory of the cosmos.

Leibniz, Gottfried Wilhelm (1646–1716) A German philosopher and contemporary of Locke. He proposed a system for understanding the world as composed of dynamic units called monads. He differed from Locke in assuming that rather than a blank slate at birth, the mind has innate propensities or natural inclinations that are uncovered in interaction with the environment.

Lewin, Kurt (1890–1947) A Gestalt-trained psychologist who created a "field theory," arguing that every individual person resides in a unique *psychological* field or life space, which is the totality of his or her psychological situation at any given moment. He also became a pioneering experimental social psychologist, promoter of action research, and investigator of group dynamics.

Liébeault, Ambroise Auguste (1823–1904) A French doctor who successfully treated his patients with direct hypnotic suggestion, becoming a founder of the Nancy School of hypnosis.

Lindzey, Gardner (1920–2008) A student and then colleague of Gordon Allport's who edited the first *Handbook of Social Psychology* in 1951 and co-authored the seminal textbook *Theories of Personality* in 1957.

Locke, John (1632–1704) An English philosopher and contemporary of Leibniz, who theorized that the human mind was a *tabula rasa* at birth and that all human knowledge comes through experience, a position known as *empiricism*.

Loeb, Jacques (1859–1924) A mechanistic biologist who influenced the work of Watson and who had introduced the concept of tropism to account for plant and animal movement.

Loftus, Elizabeth (b. 1944) An American social psychologist whose "Lost in the Mall" research focused on false memories and the fallibility of eyewitness accounts.

Lovelace, Ada, the Countess of (1815–1852) Daughter of the poet Byron and a gifted mathematician who promoted Babbage's analytical engine and foresaw many of its potential uses; she also introduced the Lovelace Objection: that computers could never become genuinely creative.

Lowie, Robert (1883–1957) A cultural anthropologist who co-authored the article "Science and Feminism" with Leta Stetter Hollingworth, published in *Scientific Monthly* in 1916.

Lyell, Charles (1797–1875) An English geologist whose book *The Principles of Geology* promoted the theory of uniformitarianism, which strongly influenced Charles Darwin.

Malthus, Thomas (1766–1834) A British political economist and demographer whose writings on population growth influenced Charles Darwin's development of the theory of adaptation by natural selection.

Masham, Lady Damaris Cudworth (1659–1708) An accomplished philosophical and theological scholar who corresponded with Locke. During the final phase of his life, she hosted him as a paying guest on her Essex estate.

Maslow, Abraham H. (1908–1970) An American psychologist and promoter of the "hierarchy of needs" theory of human motivation and the concept of self-actualization; a major founder of humanistic psychology.

Maxwell, James Clerk (1831–1879) A Scottish scientist who studied color vision and who provided the most complete analysis of color mixing in 1855.

May, Rollo (1909–1994) An American psychologist who developed existential psychotherapy, which focused on the quest for meaning in human life; he was also instrumental in the founding of humanistic psychology.

McClelland, David (1917–1998) An American psychologist noted for his work on achievement motivation, or the need for achievement.

McCulloch, Warren (1898–1969) An American neuropsychologist and cyberneticist who, along with Pitts, conceptualized the brain as a network of interconnected neurons that work analogously to a network of binary switches.

Mersenne, Marin (1588–1648) A French priest who compiled works on philosophy, mathematics, music, and natural science and who mentored Descartes, providing intellectual and personal support.

Mesmer, Franz Anton (1734–1815) A Viennese physician who developed the theory of animal magnetism to explain phenomena now called hypnosis.

Meynert, Theodor (1833–1892) An Austrian psychiatrist and neuroanatomist who mentored Sigmund Freud during his residency at the Vienna General Hospital from 1882 to 1885.

Milgram, Stanley (1933–1984) An experimental social psychologist best known for his studies on conformity and obedience in the 1960s in which subjects were told to deliver shocks to a confederate to test their willingness to obey the orders of an authority.

Mill, James (1773–1836) A nineteenth-century philosopher who was a proponent of empiricism and associationism.

Mill, John Stuart (1806–1873) The son of James Mill who, like his father, claimed that individual differences among people arise from associationistic and empiricist principles.

Miller, George A. (b. 1920) An American psychologist who founded the Center for Cognitive Studies at Harvard University with Bruner and who conducted research showing the capacity of short-term memory is approximately seven items.

Milner, Brenda (b. 1918) A neuropsychologist from McGill University known for her work on memory and her case study of the patient H.M.

Mitchell, S. Weir (1829–1914) A physician whom Witmer consulted, well known for his use of the "rest cure" to help treat neurasthenia, especially in women.

Molyneux, William (1656–1696) An Irish scientist whose question whether a congenitally blind person, suddenly granted sight, would be able to visually distinguish a cube from a sphere, stimulated Locke.

Morgan, Christiana (1897–1967) A lay psychoanalyst who, with Murray, created the projective personality test called the Thematic Apperception Test, or TAT.

Müller, Johannes (1801–1858) A German physiologist who promoted the law of specific nerve energies.

Münsterberg, Hugo (1863–1916) A German industrial psychologist, and former student of Wundt, brought to Harvard by James in 1892 to direct the Harvard psychological laboratory. Münsterberg became well known in the United States for his development and promotion of applied psychology.

Murray, Henry A. (1893–1988) A Harvard psychologist who promoted a personological approach to psychology, involving the intensive study of relatively small numbers of individual cases; he created the projective Thematic Apperception Test, or TAT, along with Morgan.

Neisser, Ulric (1928–2012) A psychologist whose integrative textbook, *Cognitive Psychology*, is regarded as the launching event for that new subdiscipline; he conducted research focusing on information processing, cognition, intelligence, and memory.

Newell, Allen (1927–1992) A computer scientist and developer, with Herbert Simon, of the early AI programs Logic Theorist and General Problem Solver.

Newman, Horatio (1875–1957) A biologist who, along with Freeman and Holzinger, did the first major study of separated twins in 1937.

Norsworthy, Naomi (1877–1916) The first female awarded a Ph.D. in psychology from Columbia University; she later took an academic position in educational psychology at Columbia Teachers College.

Paley, William (1743–1805) An English philosopher/theologian who promoted the "argument from design" as an objection to theories of gradual evolution.

Pappenheim, Bertha (1859–1936) A patient treated for hysteria by Breuer and referred to by the pseudonym Anna O. in publications. Pappenheim collaborated with Breuer in creating the cathartic method of treatment.

Pascal, Blaise (1623–1662) A French mathematician, inventor, and philosopher who developed the Pascaline, one of the first mechanical calculators. He believed machines could reproduce rational but not emotional human processes.

Pavlov, Ivan Petrovich (1849–1936) A Nobel Prize–winning Russian physiologist who, after studying digestion and reflexive salivary responses, established the tenets of classical conditioning. He influenced both Watson and Skinner.

Pearson, Karl (1857–1936) A British mathematician who refined Galton's statistical techniques using measurements from his anthropometric data and devised the modern method of calculating the correlation coefficient.

Peirce, Charles Sanders (1839–1914) An American philosopher and mathematician who was a colleague of William James and who wrote on semiotics, pragmatism, and symbolic logic. He supervised the doctoral work of Ladd-Franklin at Johns Hopkins University.

Penfield, Wilder (1891–1976) A Montreal-based neurosurgeon who used brain stimulation on conscious human patients to seek new surgical treatments for intractable cases of epilepsy. Discovered the interpretive cortex.

Pettigrew, Thomas (b. 1931) A student and later colleague of Gordon Allport's who studied prejudice in the mid-1950s and became a leading expert on the social psychology of race relations.

Piaget, Jean (1896–1980) A Swiss developmental psychologist who created genetic epistemology, a stage theory of intellectual development emphasizing the qualitative differences in reasoning that characterize each stage.

Pitts, Walter (1923–1969) An American mathematician who, along with McCulloch, conceptualized the brain as a network of interconnected neurons that work analogously to a network of binary switches.

Plateau, Joseph (1801–1883) A Belgian physicist who initially suggested that Fechner's law might more accurately be described as a *power function* rather than the logarithmic one proposed by Fechner.

Plato (429–347 B.C.E) Ancient Greek philosopher who was a proponent of the nativist view that the mind contains within itself certain forms, concepts, and truths that are innate but that require concrete experiences after birth to bring them out or instantiate them.

Postman, Leo (1918–2004) An American cognitive psychologist who, along with Bruner, studied the influence of expectancy and other motivational variables on perception.

Prince, Morton (1854–1929) An American neurologist who founded the *Journal of Abnormal Psychology*—the first American periodical specifically devoted to that subject. He published early articles on Sigmund Freud and hired Floyd Allport as co-editor when the journal expanded to cover social psychology.

Princess Elizabeth of Bohemia (1618–1680) The granddaughter of England's King James I (1566–1625), she had an important intellectual friendship and correspondence with Descartes.

Puységur, Marquis de *See* de Chastenet, Amand Marie Jacques.

Quetelet, Adolphe (1796–1874) A Belgian statistician who collected measurements such as height and weight from large populations and found they formed a bell-shaped curve, or normal distribution.

Rapaport, David (1911–1960) A psychoanalyst who pioneered the area of ego psychology and, along with Hartmann, promoted the notion of autonomous ego functions.

Rayner, Rosalie (1899–1935) A research assistant with Watson on the "Little Albert" experiment. She later married Watson and collaborated on *Psychological Care of Infant and Child*.

Renouvier, Charles (1815–1903) A French philosopher whose writings about free will influenced William James.

Rogers, Carl (1902–1987) An American psychologist who developed client-centered therapy and joined with Maslow and others in the creation of humanistic psychology.

Romanes, George J. (1848–1894) A British naturalist and friend of Charles Darwin who was granted full access to Darwin's research on animal behavior and whose work played a role in founding the field of comparative psychology.

Rosenzweig, Saul (1907–2004) An American psychologist who conducted one of the first experimental investigations of psychoanalytic theory in the laboratory.

Sanford, Edmund C. (1859–1924) A psychologist at Clark University and expert on experimental apparatus who advised Calkins on how to equip her psychology laboratory at Wellesley College.

Searle, John (b. 1932) An American philosopher who created the Chinese room thought experiment to challenge the existence of strong AI, the idea that computers can have humanlike intelligence.

Sechenov, Ivan M. (1829–1905) A Russian physiologist who argued that all behavior, including such higher functions as thinking, willing, and judging, could be explained in terms of an expanded reflex concept.

Sedgwick, Adam (1785–1873) A British professor at Cambridge who lectured on geology and influenced Charles Darwin.

Seligman, Martin (b. 1942) An American psychologist and APA president who strongly promoted the development of the positive psychology movement.

Shannon, Claude (1916–2001) An American electrical engineer who theorized that patterns of relay circuits in "off" or "on" position could be used to represent information in binary code.

Sheldon, William (1898–1977) A teacher of Maslow's who combined behaviorist methodology with a theory about predisposing body types or "somatotypes."

Simon, Herbert (1916–2001) Computer scientist and developer, with Newell, of the early AI programs Logic Theorist and General Problem Solver.

Simon, Théodore (1873–1961) A physician who collaborated with Binet in developing the first practically useful test of children's intelligence.

Skinner, B. F. (1904–1990) A Harvard psychologist well known for the development of operant conditioning and for his application of the principles of reinforcement to the design of cultures.

Sophie the Countess Palatine (1630–1714) The youngest sister of Descartes' intellectual confidante Elizabeth of Bohemia and friend and supporter of Leibniz.

Sophie Charlotte (1668–1705) The daughter of Sophie the Countess Palatine and an intellectually sophisticated friend and self-described disciple of Leibniz.

Spearman, Charles (1863–1945) An English psychologist who proposed the notion of general intelligence, or g, and the two-factor theory of intelligence.

Spencer, Herbert (1820–1903) A philosopher who, after Charles Darwin's publication of *Origin of Species*, coined the term *survival of the fittest* and promoted social Darwinism.

Spinoza, Benedict (1632–1677) A philosopher who promoted a view that has come to be known as *pantheism*—the notion that God is not an independent being that controls the universe, but rather that God *is* the entire universe.

Stagner, Ross (1909–1997) A University of Akron psychologist who published an early, behavioristically oriented textbook on the psychology of personality in 1937.

Stern, William (1871–1938) A German psychologist whose "personalistic psychology," emphasizing the concept of the person as a central Gestalt-like concept, strongly influenced Gordon Allport; as an investigator of children's intelligence, Stern also introduced the idea of the intelligence quotient.

Stevens, S. Smith (1906–1973) A Harvard psychologist who agreed with Plateau's idea that a power function might better describe some of the subjective stimuli measurements not covered by Fechner's logarithmic law.

Sumner, Francis Cecil (1895–1954) Hall's last Ph.D. student and the first African American to receive a doctorate in psychology, at Clark University, in 1920.

Taylor, Frederick Winslow (1865–1915) An American engineer who developed the theory of scientific management, also known as Taylorism.

Terman, Lewis M. (1877–1956) An American psychologist who researched "giftedness," worked on the World War I army intelligence testing program, and introduced the Stanford revision of the Binet-Simon scale of intelligence.

Thompson, Clara (1893–1958) An American physician and psychoanalyst who focused on the psychology of women in the cultural context.

Thorndike, Edward Lee (1874–1949) An American comparative psychologist who studied with James and went on to become the country's best-known psychologist after James's death. Thorndike became famous for his studies of trial-and-error learning and formulation of the law of effect, and his studies with Woodworth on the transfer of training.

Titchener, Edward Bradford (1867–1927) One of Wundt's most influential students and leader of the structuralist school; he believed that experimental psychology's major goal was the atomistic analysis of the elements of consciousness.

Tolman, Edward Chace (1886–1959) An American psychologist best known for his experimental work with rats in mazes that led to the formulation of the concept of latent learning and a position known as purposive behaviorism.

Triplett, Norman (1861–1931) A psychologist from Indiana University who conducted one of the first controlled studies of social facilitation.

Turing, Alan Mathison (1912–1954) An English mathematician whose invention of the Turing machine, and conceptualization of the Turing Test, profoundly influenced the development of the fields of computer science and artificial intelligence.

Ussher, James (1581–1656) An Irish archbishop who, after adding up the ages of the Old Testament patriarchs after Adam and Eve as given in the Bible, estimated the earth's age as only about 6,000 years, which accorded well with catastrophism theory.

Vernon, Phillip (1905–1987) An English psychologist who collaborated with Gordon Allport in studies of expressive movement and the measurement of values.

Virchow, Rudolf (1821–1902) An early mechanistic physiologist who later pioneered the field of cell pathology.

von Neumann, John (1903–1957) A Princeton mathematician who conceptualized an "architecture" of stored computer programs that became the standard in the development of early artificial intelligence projects.

Wallace, Alfred Russel (1823–1913) A British naturalist who independently conceived a theory of evolution by natural selection, which prompted Charles Darwin to publish his similar work on the theory.

Wallin, J. E. Wallace (1876–1969) A psychologist who was concerned about the lack of qualifications and professional standards in the area of clinical psychology. He wrote an article in *Science* in 1913 in which he voiced these concerns.

Washburn, Margaret Floy (1871–1939) The first American woman to be officially awarded a doctorate in psychology, under the supervision of Titchener at Cornell

University. Washburn studied learning and mental processes in animals and wrote an influential comparative psychology text called *The Animal Mind*.

Watson, John Broadus (1878–1958) An American psychologist and prime promoter of behaviorism, who asserted that psychology's proper subject matter is observable behavior and that the goal of psychology is the prediction and control of behavior.

Watt, Henry J. (1879–1925) A Scottish student of Külpe who developed the method of directed association, in which subjects were asked to associate words in a highly "specific" rather than "free" manner.

Weber, Ernst Heinrich (1795–1878) A German physiologist and colleague of Fechner who established the just noticeable difference (jnd) as the unit of subjective weight discrimination.

Wernicke, Carl (1848–1905) A German neurologist who used localization theory as the basis of an influential theory of aphasia.

Wertheimer, Max (1880–1943) A former student of Ehrenfels whose studies on optical illusions, apparent movement, and the phi phenomenon helped found the field of Gestalt psychology. Also promoted a theory of productive thinking and became a mentor to Maslow.

Willis, Thomas (1621–1675) A British scientist who studied brain anatomy in unprecedented detail and made several fundamental discoveries, such as the presence of gray matter and white matter. He published the first accurate and detailed *Anatomy of the Brain* in 1664, illustrated with plates by the celebrated architect Christopher Wren.

Winnicott, D. W. (1896–1971) A British pediatrician and psychiatrist who helped found the object relations school of psychoanalysis.

Witmer, Lightner (1867–1956) An American schoolteacher and psychologist who studied under James McKeen Cattell and Wilhelm Wundt and is best known for developing the clinical method and establishing the first psychological clinic at the University of Pennsylvania.

Wittmann, Blanche (1859–1913) A hysteric patient of Charcot's whose spectacular performances of the stages of *grande hysterie* earned her the nickname "Queen of the Hysterics."

Wolpe, Joseph (1915–1997) A South African physician who developed several techniques of behavior therapy, believing they provided quicker, more symptom-specific relief than psychoanalysis.

Woodworth, Robert Sessions (1869–1962) An American student of both William James and James McKeen Cattell who investigated the transfer of training theory with Edward Thorndike and who created an early personality test called the Personal Data Sheet.

Wundt, Wilhelm (1832–1920) A German physiologist who established the first psychology lab at the University of Leipzig in 1879 and whose work and textbooks established the foundations for the development of experimental psychology as a discipline.

Young, Thomas (1773–1829) An English scientist who, like Helmholtz, suggested that the retina contains three types of receptor cells necessary for color vision.

Zeigarnik, Bluma (1901–1988) A Russian psychologist and student of Lewin's who discovered the tendency to better remember uncompleted than completed tasks, since known as the Zeigarnik effect.

Zimbardo, Philip (b. 1933) An American social psychologist well known for his research on obedience and his creation of the Stanford Prison Experiment.

Zöllner, Johann (1834–1882) A German astrophysicist and Leipzig colleague of Wundt's who strongly differed with him over the genuineness of "psychic" phenomena.

Key Terms

agreeableness One of the Big Five personality traits; a tendency to be cooperative and empathic in dealing with others.

ablation Surgically removing specific small parts of an animal subject's brain and observing any consequent changes in the behavior or function of the animal after recovery from the surgery.

absolute threshold Fechner's term for the smallest intensity of a stimulus that could be perceived, classified as the zero point on a scale of psychological intensities.

act psychology A psychological theory posited by Brentano, who suggested that the units of psychological analysis were "acts" that "contain" an object.

algorithm A strategy that systematically tests all of the possible solutions to a problem.

ambivalence Sigmund Freud's idea that both positive and negative feelings could occur simultaneously toward the same object (e.g., one could both love and hate one's mother at the same time).

anal character The result of fixation during the toilet training period of a child's life, producing adults who may be orderly in arranging their affairs, obstinate in their relationships, and parsimonious in managing their money.

anal zone In psychoanalytic theory, the erogenous zone that becomes a focus of fascination for children as they learn to find pleasure in being able to voluntarily control their bodily functions during toilet training.

analytic geometry The branch of geometry pioneered by Descartes in which the numerical relationships of algebraic equations are expressed visually through the use of a coordinate graphing system.

analytical engine Babbage's planned but never-finished "universal machine," capable of performing virtually *any* type of calculation; prototype for what today we call a programmable computer.

analytical psychology The name given by Jung to his psychological system, which focused less than Freudian psychology on sexuality and more on the roles of culture, religion, dream analysis, the collective unconscious, and psychological types or temperaments.

animal magnetism A theory posited by Mesmer suggesting that the human body was filled with and surrounded by a magnetic force field that could become disaligned and weakened, creating the symptoms of illness.

animal spirits Descartes' term for the clear yellowish liquid that resided in the brain's ventricles. Today we call this cerebrospinal fluid.

Anthropometric Laboratory An exhibit mounted by Galton at London's International Health Exhibition of 1884, where visitors were administered neurophysiologically based tests conceived as prototypes for modern intelligence tests.

aphasia A group of speech disorders resulting from damage to specific areas of the brain.

apparent movement *See* **phi phenomenon**.

apperception Process that occurs when ideas are "registered" in consciousness, accompanied by self-awareness, and also become subject to focused attention and rational analysis in terms of underlying principles and laws.

argument from design A contention put forth by the philosopher/theologian Paley suggesting that because humans and the various species of animals were so complicated and so perfectly constructed and adapted, they must have been *designed* as finished products by God.

artificial intelligence (AI) The capacities of computers and other mechanical devices to mimic human thought processes and intelligence.

artificial somnambulism A term used by Puységur to describe a peaceful state that could be induced in magnetic therapy, similar to sleepwalking and unlike Mesmer's "crisis" states. Also called **perfect crisis**.

assembly languages Higher-order computer instructions, or computer languages, in which complex hierarchies of subroutines may be arranged and electronically executed following simple commands.

association of ideas The linkage of ideas or memories such that the thought of one tends automatically to bring the other to mind.

astigmatism An imperfect alignment of the refractive surfaces in the eye lens that distorts the images one sees.

auditory area A functionally distinct area of the temporal lobe responsible for the processing of auditory stimuli.

baquet The French word for *tub*, a part of the apparatus in Mesmer's magnetic therapies that would be filled with water and magnetized iron filings.

behavior analysis The contemporary discipline that developed out of B. F. Skinner's contributions. It comprises experimental, applied, and philosophical branches.

behavior therapy Therapeutic techniques designed to change behavior using classical conditioning approaches; behavior therapy was pioneered by Wolpe among others.

behaviorism A school of psychology that rules out subjective reports in favor of objectively verifiable observation, and that suggests learning is based on the acquisition and interconnection of associations through various forms of conditioning.

being needs Maslow's alternate term for self-actualization, which urges the individual toward the positive fulfillment of *potentialities* within the self. Contrast with **deprivation needs**.

Big Five A contemporary factor-analytic approach to personality theory that considers the traits of openness, conscientiousness, extroversion, agreeableness, and neuroticism (OCEAN) to be the major building blocks of personality.

binary arithmetic The representation of all numbers with just ones and zeroes.

blind spot A defect in the small part of the retina where the optic nerve leaves the eye; it contains no light-sensitive receptor cells.

Boolean algebra A form of mathematics created by George Boole, making possible the discipline of symbolic logic.

British associationism A form of mental philosophy, largely initiated by Locke, that focused on associationism.

Broca's aphasia *See* **motor aphasia**.

Broca's area The area of the frontal lobe, identified by Paul Broca, where ablation causes impairments in expressive speech, a condition known as Broca's aphasia, or motor aphasia.

castration complex In Freudian theory, a complex that occurs during childhood in which boys irrationally fear that their father might castrate them while girls have an unconscious wish to be like a boy and have a penis.

catastrophism A predominant nineteenth-century theory holding that the geological features of the natural world could be attributed to sudden and massive cataclysms such as Noah's flood.

categories Kant's term for the characteristics automatically imposed by the mind on phenomenal experience, defining their *quality*, *quantity*, *relationships*, and *mode*.

cathartic method A psychoanalytic technique originated by Breuer and his patient Anna O., and further developed by early Freud, in which the venting of emotions is thought to eliminate hysterical symptoms.

cell assemblies The term used by Hebb to explain the hypothetical functioning of "neurological networks."

cerebellum The structure situated at the base of the brain that is responsible for balance, motor control, and some cognitive functions such as language and attention.

cerebrospinal fluid (CSF) A clear bodily fluid that occupies the ventricular system around and inside the brain and spinal cord.

Chinese room A thought experiment proposed by philosopher Searle, comparing a native speaker of Chinese with one who responds perfectly but "mechanically" with the aid of a complete book of rules. The latter, like a computer, would not demonstrate "strong" artificial intelligence.

client-centered therapy A form of psychotherapy developed by Rogers in which the psychotherapist focuses on creating a comfortable and nonjudgmental environment for the client.

clinical method Witmer's multidimensional method of assessing children for behavioral and learning difficulties; the method involved testing both physical and mental abilities and consulting with a range of other professionals, including social workers and physicians.

coefficients of correlation Numerical values that represent the strength of the relationship between two variables that range from -1 to $+1$.

cognitive dissonance According to Festinger, the experience of holding two or more incompatible or contradictory beliefs, which produces such an uncomfortable state of dissonance that one becomes motivated to reduce it.

cognitive neuroscience An interdisciplinary field that coalesced in the 1970s around the study of the mind-brain relationship. It is composed of psychologists, biologists, neurologists, philosophers, and others who research various aspects of the question "How are the functions of the brain and nervous system related to awareness, perception, and reasoning?"

cognitive therapy A form of psychotherapy pioneered by Beck that focuses on correcting distorted thinking and irrational thoughts.

color afterimages Phenomenon described by Hering, in which an afterimage in the complementary color remains after staring at a colored object.

color mixing Phenomenon studied by Maxwell and others, showing that varying mixtures of spectral light can produce the same color sensations as pure spectral colors.

commissures Bundles of nerve tissue (white matter) that connect the two cerebral hemispheres.

comparative psychology A subdiscipline of psychology that studies the similarities and differences among various animals' psychological functions to shed light on these processes in human beings.

complementarity hypothesis A widely held view during the Victorian era that men and women have evolved to have different but complementary psychological characteristics. This belief accorded intellectual superiority to men but emphasized the virtuousness and moral superiority of women.

complementary colors Pairs of spectral colors (e.g., red-green and blue-violet) that, when mixed together, create a sensation of *white* light indistinguishable from sunlight.

complex ideas Ideas produced when simple ideas are combined by the mind.

computational functionalism The notion that AI programs may mimic the "functional" processes that humans go through in solving problems, but using a different kind of physical "architecture."

concrete operations stage Piaget's third stage of development, in which children around the age of 7 can successfully solve most conservation problems.

concrete representation According to Sigmund Freud, the idea that latent dream thoughts receive "concrete representation" in the subjectively real sensations of the manifest content; part of the dream work.

condensation Aspect of Sigmund Freud's dream work in which two or more latent thoughts "condense" onto a single manifest dream image; similar to overdetermination.

conditioned (conditional) reflexes Pavlov's notion of physiological reflexes that have been learned.

conditioned response (CR) The learned response in a Pavlovian conditioned reflex.

conditioned stimulus (CS) An originally neutral stimulus that, after being paired with an unconditioned stimulus, triggers a conditioned response in a Pavlovian conditioned reflex.

conduction aphasia A type of speech disorder that occurs when the association fibers between Broca's area and Wernicke's area are damaged, resulting in a loss of self-monitoring, but with comprehension and general fluency unimpaired.

connectionist computing model A model in which many operations go on simultaneously and their objects are patterns of activity throughout the whole system, rather than symbols in prespecified locations.

conscientiousness One of the Big Five personality traits; a tendency to be careful and self-disciplined.

conservation of energy The idea that energy can be transformed from one state to another but can never be created or destroyed by any physical process.

conservation of quantity A Piagetian term referring to the ability to perceive that overall amounts of substances remain the same even as they assume different shapes and configurations.

contact hypothesis Gordon Allport's notion that prejudice between groups can be reduced if in- and out-group members are placed in situations where they must interact with each other collaboratively and with equal status in pursuing a common goal.

contingencies of reinforcement The specific conditions under which responses are reinforced or not.

conversions Hysterical symptoms, interpreted by Freud as the result of emotional energy becoming strangulated and then converted to physical symptoms.

cortex The outermost and largest layer of the cerebrum. It plays a key role in memory, attention, perception, thought, language, and consciousness.

creative synthesis Wundt's theory that apperceived ideas may be combined and organized in many ways, including some that have never been experienced before.

cumulative record The graphical representation of rates of response under different reinforcement schedules generated by an automated recorder in operant conditioning experiments.

defense mechanisms In psychoanalytic theory, unconscious psychological strategies used by the ego to effect compromise resolutions to conflicting demands from the id, superego, and external reality.

defenses General psychoanalytic term for responses that serve to protect a person against consciously entertaining psychologically dangerous pathogenic ideas.

demonstrative knowledge Locke's term for knowledge attained by stepwise logical deduction.

denial A psychoanalytic defense mechanism that comes into play when one is unable to face reality or admit the truth.

deprivation needs According to Maslow, the four lower levels of his hierarchy of needs, created by deficiencies in a person's life. Contrast with **self-actualization** or **being needs**.

determining tendencies The idea put forth by Ach that introspective instructions did not consciously enter into the subjects' associational processes but rather predetermined them in particular directions before the experiments began. Similar to **mental sets**.

difference engine A mechanical device created by Babbage in the early nineteenth century to calculate polynomials and other mathematical functions.

differentiation A phenomenon that occurs in Pavlovian conditioning when dissimilar stimuli are presented repeatedly but never reinforced by a succeeding unconditioned stimulus.

directed association Studies conducted Watt, a student of Külpe, in which subjects were asked to associate to stimulus words that were highly "specific" rather than freely associating to them.

displacement (Freudian defense mechanism) Redirection of an impulse toward a substitute target that resembles the original in some way but that is "safer."

displacement (in dreams) Deflection of the psychic energy of highly charged latent content onto the related but emotionally more neutral ideas of the manifest content; one aspect of the dream work in Freudian theory.

dizygotic twins *See* **fraternal twins**.

dream work In Freudian theory, processes by which latent content becomes transformed into manifest content, primarily through displacement, condensation, and concrete representation.

dreams Hallucinations that occur during sleep.

dualism A philosophical viewpoint suggesting that there is a sharp distinction between the mind and the body.

ecological psychology Gibson's approach to psychology, which stressed that the mind can only be understood as a partner in relation to its environment and that the properties of that environment are presented to the mind quite *directly*.

ego In Freudian theory, the psychic structure that mediates conflicts that arise between the instinctual demands of the id, the demands of external reality, and the moral demands of the superego.

ego psychology A development within psychoanalysis, holding that with normal development many of the functions of the Freudian ego become independent of their distant origins in impulses of the id.

empiricism The philosophy that knowledge is gained through experience and that innate ideas do not exist.

enactive *See* **modes of representation**.

equipotentiality A form of neural plasticity, first identified by Flourens and revisited by Lashley, in which healthy areas of the brain have the ability to take over the functions of damaged areas.

erogenous zones In Freudian theory, areas of the human body that have heightened sensitivity and that stimulate the production of erotic sensations and sexual excitement.

Eros The term Sigmund Freud used, late in his career, to denote the life-giving sexual instinct in human beings.

esteem needs According to Maslow, the needs for self-respect and personal achievement that become salient once physiological, safety, and love needs have been adequately met.

eugenics A term coined by Galton to describe his project for improving the human race through selective breeding.

eupsychia Maslow's term for a utopian society in which every human being has the ability to become self-actualized and reach his or her full potential.

evolutionary psychology A broad subdiscipline of psychology that draws upon all aspects of modern evolutionary theory to devise empirically testable hypotheses about human behavior.

existential psychotherapy A form of psychotherapy, promoted by May, that emphasizes the *quest for meaning* in life as the paramount issue for modern humanity.

experiential responses Hallucinatory "dreams" or "flashbacks" of real events from the past, usually with unremarkable content, reported by Penfield's patients during his cortical stimulation studies.

experimental neuroses A dramatic behavioral change that occurred in some of Pavlov's animal subjects when they were forced to confront an ambiguous differentiation task. This behavior appeared to be similar to stress-induced breakdowns in human beings.

extension For Descartes, the spatial dimensions occupied by the body. Extension was one aspect of his theory of simple natures, the other being motion.

extinction curve A mathematical curve that represents a reduction in response rate in the absence of reinforcers, in operant conditioning.

extroversion A personality dimension introduced by Jung, defined as a tendency to be oriented toward the external world, showing traits such as gregariousness, talkativeness, and social assertiveness; it contrasts with introversion, and is sometimes spelled *extraversion*. The term was later adopted to designate one of the Big Five and PEN personality factors.

false memories Fictitious recollections of events that can be created in suggestible subjects.

fear response According to Watson, one of the three innate emotional reactions in infants, elicited by sudden and unexpected loud sounds or the sudden loss of support.

Fechner's law The assertion that the observed relationship between physical and subjective stimulus intensities for many different senses can be expressed by the single general mathematical formula $S = k \log P$.

fixation Sigmund Freud's term for the arrest of a child's developmental progress at the oral, anal, or phallic stage of psychosexual development.

fixed-interval reinforcement schedule An operant conditioning schedule in which responses are reinforced only after the passage of some specified period of time.

fixed-ratio reinforcement schedule An operant conditioning schedule in which responses are reinforced only after a preset number of responses have been made.

flashbulb memory Neisser's term for a vividly recalled (although not necessarily accurate) image of exactly where one was and what one was doing when some particularly momentous event occurred.

forgetting curve Ebbinghaus's term to describe the rapid decline, and later leveling off, of memory loss that occurs between memory retest sessions.

formal operations stage Piaget's fourth stage of development, typically beginning around age 11 or 12 and characterized by the emergence of experimental or inductive reasoning.

forme fruste A term used by Charcot to describe neurological diseases that occur in an incomplete form.

fraternal twins Twin pairs whose genetics are as similar to each other as ordinary brothers and sisters.

free association A technique used by Sigmund Freud in which one is asked to say, openly and honestly, the first thoughts and ideas that come to mind, without edit.

fulfillment of wishes According to Freudian theory, the primary goal of dreams, albeit often in disguised form.

functional autonomy A term proposed by Gordon Allport to describe the state achieved by motives that may have originated in childhood but that are maintained because they have become reinforcing or rewarding in their own right and are thus autonomous of their earliest origins.

functional periodicity A commonly held social and scientific belief that women become functionally impaired during menstruation. This belief was empirically tested by Leta Stetter Hollingworth (and others) and found to be without validity.

functionalism A position prominent among many early American psychologists that focused attention on the utility and purpose of behavior, in contrast to Titchenerian "structuralism," which sought only to define and describe the contents of conscious experience.

general intelligence (g) Spearman's concept of a single common factor of generalized mental "power," applicable in some degree to all intellectual tasks.

General Problem Solver (GPS) An artificial intelligence program designed by Allen Newell and Herbert Simon, intended to be capable of solving a broad range of types of problems.

generalization A phenomenon that occurs when conditioned reflexes can be elicited by stimuli similar but not identical to the original conditioned stimulus.

genetic epistemology Piaget's term for the study of the biologically based stages of development in children's thought.

genital zone The primary erogenous zone posited by Sigmund Freud in the final stage of human psychosexual development, beginning at puberty, when adolescents begin to direct their sexual urges outwardly toward an opposite-sex peer.

Gestalt psychologists A group of psychologists who in the early 1900s uncovered ways in which an active and creative mind molds important aspects of conscious perceptual experience, emphasizing the ways in which the mind perceives wholes or Gestalts as opposed to separate, individual elements.

grammatical structure A set of rules that govern the composition of sentences and phrases in any given language; seen as innate by Chomsky.

grand hypnotisme Charcot's now discredited concept of the major form or type of hypnotism, characterized by the three stages of catalepsy, lethargy, and somnambulism.

grande hystérie Charcot's now discredited concept of the major form or type of hysteria, characterized by a progression from the epileptoid stage, to the large movement stage, to a hallucinatory stage, and finally to a delirious stage.

gray matter A pulpy gray tissue occupying the outer surface of the brain, the inner part of the spinal cord, and several discrete centers within the brain; composed primarily of neuronal nuclei, and contrasts with **white matter**.

group fallacy Floyd Allport's term for the notion, which he believed to be mistaken, that groups or crowds can constitute superorganisms or "group minds" going beyond the combined reactions of their individual members.

heuristic A technique for problem solving that limits the search space by relying on best guesses and shortcuts based on the probability of finding a solution; it contrasts with algorithms, which exhaustively examine all possible solutions.

higher-order conditioning Type of conditioning that occurs when a conditioned reflex is first established to one stimulus, which then goes on to serve as the unconditioned stimulus in a further series of pairings.

hippocampus A brain structure lying beneath the temporal lobe that is important for memory.

humanistic psychology A "third force" in psychology, after behaviorism and psychoanalysis, that was established in the 1950s by Maslow, Rogers, May, and others who focused on positive motivation, the potential for growth, the need for self-actualization, and the creation of meaning.

hypnotism The process of inducing a mental state of concentration and relaxation, resulting in a state of high suggestibility in a subject.

hysteria A psychogenic disorder in which patients experience physiological symptoms, such as fits of violent emotion, paralysis, anesthesia, amnesias, and other neurological like symptoms, without obvious organic causes.

iconic *See* **modes of representation**.

id In Freud's structural model of the psyche, the source and reservoir of biologically given, instinctual drives.

identical twins Twin pairs who are genetically identical to each other. Also called **monozygotic twins**.

identification In Freudian theory, a process that occurs when a child assimilates aspects of the same-sex parent into his or her own personality; one result is the superego.

idiographic methods Research methods that focus on the study of individual cases and typically involve qualitative rather than quantitative analyses, with the aim of describing what makes people distinct from one another and unique.

imageless thoughts Transitory states, discovered by Würzburg introspectors, that were not definable in terms of sensations and feelings.

immature religion Gordon Allport's concept of a religious attachment that is adopted largely for self-aggrandizing reasons and is unreflective, literal minded, bigoted, and intolerant of other beliefs or ambiguity.

impossibilist creativity Margaret Boden's concept of the capacity to assemble already familiar ideas or components in novel but useful or interesting combinations that violate or are different from preset rules.

individual differences The measurable differences found between individuals in terms of personality and character.

individual psychology (Adler) A theoretical approach based on the idea that the deepest source of human motivation lies in the ability to overcome feelings of inferiority.

individual psychology (Binet and Henri) The name given by Binet and Henri to their program to develop a series of short tests that would produce information about a person comparable in richness and complexity to an in-depth case study.

Individual Will Temperament Test One of the first personality tests; created by Downey to measure traits such as impulsivity, carefulness, and forcefulness by means of handwriting analysis.

inferiority complex A construct proposed by Alder to denote the pattern of inferiority feelings, and motives to overcome those feelings, that arises in all children.

infinitesimal calculus A form of mathematics created by Gottfried Leibniz and Isaac Newton that works by conceptualizing any continuously varying quantity as an infinite series of imperceptibly changing "instants" or "infinitesimals."

information processing The complex sequence of activities by which stimuli are received, recognized, categorized, and recorded in memory.

informed consent The process of explaining a research study to participants before they agree to join, thus informing them of the effects the study may have on them.

innate ideas The concept that ideas exist *a priori*, or prior to our concrete experiences.

instincts In Freudian theory, demands placed on the human organism that arise from within the body itself—that is, biologically based urges for nourishment, warmth, and broadly defined sexual gratification.

intellectual level Binet's term for the result of his intelligence tests, later somewhat misleadingly translated by his successors as *mental age*.

Intellectualization Freudian defense mechanism in which a conflict-laden subject is approached rationally and abstractly but without emotional involvement.

intelligence quotient (IQ) A mathematical formula developed by Stern and Terman to summarize the results of a Binet-type intelligence test, calculated by dividing mental age by chronological age and multiplying by 100.

intelligence tests Methods originally conceived by Galton to measure people's hereditary abilities by means of a series of simple tests of head size, reaction time, and sensory acuity. The failure of his approach led to development of an alternative age-based scale by Binet in France which became the prototype for modern "IQ tests."

intentionality Brentano's term referring to the attitude taken in a mental act toward the object being thought about.

interpretive cortex The area of the brain that, when stimulated during Penfield's studies, produced two types of psychical responses: interpretive and experiential.

interpretive responses In Penfield's cortical stimulation studies, responses given by some patients in which they inexplicably saw their immediate situations in new lights.

intrapsychic conflict Freudian notion that the mind is constantly confronted with irreconcilable demands from innate biology, the external world, and the moral sense or conscience.

introspection The observation and reporting of one's own subjective "inner experience" in psychological experiments.

introversion A personality dimension introduced by Jung, defined as a tendency to be oriented toward one's inner life and showing traits such as introspectiveness, reflectiveness, attraction to solitary activities, and discomfort in large groups. It contrasts with extroversion and is sometimes spelled *intraversion*.

intuitions Kant's term for the human mind's automatic ordering of all phenomenal experience in terms of space and time.

intuitive knowledge Locke's term for the awareness of such immediately obvious things as the difference between black and white.

James-Lange theory of emotion A theory proposed independently by William James and Carl Lange hypothesizing that emotion is a consequence rather than a cause of the bodily changes associated with it.

just noticeable difference (jnd) The minimum amount of difference between two stimulus intensities necessary for an observer to tell them apart. This concept was introduced by Weber and later used by Fechner as basis of his scale of psychophysical intensities.

latency stage In Freudian theory, a quiescent stage of childhood during which earlier oral, anal, and phallic urges have been repressed.

latent content In Freudian theory, the hidden meaning of dreams that lies beneath the manifest content.

latent learning Tolman's term for learning that can occur "incidentally" and without immediate reinforcement, becoming obvious only at a later time.

law of contiguity The law that ideas experienced either simultaneously or in rapid succession—that is, contiguously in time—will tend to be linked together in the future.

law of effect Thorndike's assertion that when certain stimulus-response sequences are followed by pleasure, they are strengthened, while responses followed by annoyance or pain tended to be "stamped out."

law of mass action Lashley's notion that the efficiency of performance of a learned reaction will be reduced in proportion to the degree of cortical injury or ablation suffered by an organism.

law of specific nerve energies The idea that each sensory nerve in the body conveys one and only one kind of sensation.

laws of association by contiguity or similarity The notion that ideas that have been experienced closely together in time (contiguously) or that are similar to one another will become closely associated.

life space A concept suggested by Lewin in which every individual person resides in a unique *psychological* field, or life space, which is the totality of his or her psychological situation at any given moment.

Logic Theorist (LT) A computer program designed by Allen Newell and Herbert Simon in 1956 that reproduced formal proofs for some of the basic theorems in Albert North Whitehead and Bertrand Russell's book *Principia Mathematica.*

logical positivism A philosophy of science stating that all scientific constructs must be linked to a series of statements tied to observable events that can be empirically verified.

love Along with fear and rage, one of three emotions that Watson believed to be innate.

love needs The motives to obtain affection, friendship, and a sense of belongingness; conceptualized as coming after the physiological and safety needs in Maslow's hierarchy.

Lovelace objection The notion put forward by Ada Lovelace that the analytical engine could follow only predetermined and precisely defined rules and that it was not capable of genuine creativity; commonly expressed today as "Computers can only do what they have been programmed to do."

lucid sleep Faria's term for a form of artificial somnambulism in which one goes into a deep trance state.

manifest content In Freudian theory, the actual images, thoughts, and content of a dream as experienced by the dreamer; it is actually a transformation of the precipitating but more psychologically dangerous latent content.

mature religion Gordon Allport's concept of a religious sensibility that entails belief in a spiritual reality with simultaneous acceptance of an inevitable unknowableness and mystery regarding ultimate questions. Mature religion encourages humility, self questioning, and tolerance for the viewpoints of others.

means-ends analysis A heuristic General Problem Solver program in which the desired solution-state for a problem is regularly compared to its actual current state and the difference or "distance" between the two is assessed.

mechanism A doctrine suggesting that *all* natural processes are potentially understandable in terms of physical and chemical principles.

mechanistic behaviorism A variant of behaviorism put forth by Hull, whose theoretical position involved establishing complex mathematical laws in which learning was accounted for in terms of the specifiable relationships among a host of operationally defined variables.

mental chronometry The use of response times in psychophysical studies to measure the speed of information processing and to make inferences about the components of consciousness and other central processes; one of the major research strategies in Wundt's experimental psychology laboratory.

mental imagery Phenomenon originally studied by Galton, when he asked subjects to imagine various scenes and describe them in detail as to brightness and color, distinctness, apparent location, and the like.

mental orthopedics A program of mental exercises developed by Binet to increase intellectual levels in children.

mental sets *See* **determining tendencies**.

metapsychology Sigmund Freud's general model of the mind that integrates his clinical discoveries within a broader theoretical context, to ask about the *general* features of the human mind.

minute perceptions The smallest unit in Leibniz's continuum of consciousness, which ranged from the clear, distinct, and rational *apperceptions* through the more mechanical and indistinct *perceptions*, and terminating in what he called minute perceptions; provided theoretical basis for postulating unconscious psychological processes.

modes of representation Bruner's term for three ways of knowing about things, parallelling the Piagetian stages of cognitive development and characterized as:

enactive The first mode of representation in Bruner's theory, in which things are "known" by the actions that are appropriate for them.

iconic Bruner's second mode of representation, in which things are "known" primarily in terms of their perceptual qualities.

symbolic Bruner's third and final mode of representation, in which the student appreciates the abstract qualities of the object of study.

monads The ultimate, dynamic units of reality that Leibniz described as containing energies and forces that had the ability to perceive and register impressions of the rest of the world, arranged hierarchically in terms of their qualities and functions. He identified three types:

rational monads Units first and closest to God in the hierarchy of finite monads, corresponding to the conscious souls or minds of human beings.

sentient monads Units lying beneath the rational monads, comprising the souls of living but nonhuman organisms.

simple monads Units that make up the "bodies" of all matter, whether organic or inorganic.

monogenesis A Victorian-era theory suggesting that all human races shared a common ancestry.

monozygotic twins *See* **identical twins**.

motion studies A method developed by the Gilbreths in which movie cameras were used to record the detailed physical movements required to perform certain tasks, thus revealing how to design machinery and methods to make work more efficient and easier for the worker.

motor aphasia a speech disorder that occurs when there is damage to the left frontal lobe, resulting in the inability to vocalize comprehensible speech. Also known as **Broca's aphasia**.

motor strip A functionally distinct area of the cortex, mapped by Fritsch and Hitzig, where stimulation produced specific movements on the opposite side of the body.

nativism Notion that the mind contains within itself certain innate properties and/or ideas that are prior to and independent of concrete experience; contrasts with **empiricism**.

natural selection The theoretical mechanism postulated by Charles Darwin and Alfred Russel Wallace suggesting that those organisms best adapted for a particular environment will survive and propagate, thus passing on their characteristics through the generations.

necessary truths Leibniz's term for organizing principles that are innate in the human mind, including the axioms of mathematics and logic, and the capacity for self-reflection and apperception.

negative afterimages The tendency to see stationary objects as moving in the direction opposite to that of a moving object that has been observed immediately before.

negative reinforcement A response contingency in which the probability of a response is increased when it is followed by the removal or reduction of an aversive stimulus.

neurons Nerve cells that are the core units of the nervous system and are found in the brain, spinal cord, and peripheral ganglia; composed of cell nuclei, axons and dendrites.

neuropsychology A branch of psychology that studies the structure and function of the brain as it relates to psychological processes and behavior.

neuroticism A personality factor in Eysenck's PEN model that indicates one's tendency to experience and be preoccupied by anxiety.

neurohypnology *See* **neurypnology.**

neurypnology One of Braid's initial terms for the technique of "mesmerism," later altered to *hypnosis*.

nomothetic methods Personality research methods that study people in terms of general dimensions or characteristics on which they vary to quantitatively specifiable degrees. They typically entail statistical surveys of large numbers of subjects and description of individuals in terms of their standing in relation to the larger group.

nonsense syllables Consonant-vowel-consonant combinations, such as *taz*, *bok*, and *lef*, created by Ebbinghaus to study memory; he believed they could serve as neutral or meaningless stimuli to be memorized in his experiments.

normal distribution A bell-shaped distribution that occurs when more statistical data fall in the middle ranges than at the extremes and when successive scores tend to be more widely separated from one another at the extremes.

noumenal world Kant's concept of the external world as made up of "things-in-themselves," existing in a "pure" state independent of human experience.

object concept In Piaget's theory, the recognition that something has a permanent existence apart from one's immediate experience of it.

object constancy A Piagetian concept indicating a child's recognition that objects continue to exist even when they are out of sight.

object relations A later psychoanalytic school of thought that places major importance on the mother-infant bond in human development.

Oedipus complex Freudian term for a group of largely unconscious ideas and feelings that focus on one's desire to possess the parent of the opposite sex and destroy or eliminate the parent of the same sex.

openness One of the Big Five personality traits; one's tendency to be imaginative and sensitive to one's inner feelings.

operant conditioning Skinner's term for the conditioning that occurs when organisms learn to actively manipulate, control, and "operate upon" their environments by encountering consequences. It contrasts with the more passive Pavlovian or respondent conditioning.

optical illusions A conscious impression of a visual stimulus that differs demonstrably in some respect from its "objective" properties.

oral character In Freudian theory, a tendency to be talkative, overeat, smoke, or drink too much resulting from a fixation at the oral stage during the first two years of development.

oral zone The first erogenous zone posited in Freudian theory; essentially the mouth, which is the earliest locus of pleasurable stimulation for an infant, via breastfeeding.

overdetermination In Freudian theory, the causation of a single symptom by two or more pathogenic ideas acting in concert.

paired-associates technique A technique developed by Calkins to study associative learning and memory.

pantheism The notion, promoted by Spinoza and others, that God is not an independent being that controls the universe but rather that God *is* the entire universe.

paraphasias A term coined by Wernicke to explain a group of speech disorders marked by the use of numerous peculiar words and the mispronunciation of words due to brain damage.

passions Descartes' term for the conscious experience of emotions.

pathogenic ideas In Freudian theory, emotion-laden memories or thoughts that are out of conscious awareness and thus cause hysterical symptoms.

pcpt.-cs. The "perception-consciousness system"—the part of Sigmund Freud's structural model of the psyche that conveys information about external reality to the ego.

peak experiences According to Maslow and Wertheimer, the strong feelings of joy and other positive emotions that often accompany "Aha" moments when the world is suddenly perceived or appreciated in a new way.

Pearson's *r* A correlation coefficient developed by Karl Pearson to denote the strength of a linear relationship between two variables.

PEN model A personality model promoted by Eysenck that describes personality in terms of the three primary dimensions: psychoticism, extroversion/introversion, and neuroticism.

perceptions The meaningful interpretations given to sensations.

perceptual adaptation The idea that when one's visual field is altered (e.g., when images are shifted to the left or right from their normal locations while wearing special glasses) one's brain adapts to these new perceptions automatically and unconsciously.

perceptual field The overall environment in which figure-ground and other Gestalt effects occur.

perfect crisis *See* **artificial somnambulism**.

Personal Data Sheet An early objective personality test devised by Robert Woodworth, designed to screen out recruits who were psychologically unfit for active duty in World War I.

personal equations Consistent individual differences in the reaction times for taking measurements by astronomical observers.

personalistic psychology An approach to psychology promoted by William Stern in which the central concept is the person as an individual.

personality psychology An important psychological subdiscipline pioneered by Gordon Allport and others that studies the nature of human individuality and uses methodologies ranging from idiographic individual case studies through nomothetic studies of the statistical relationships among numerous measurable personality traits.

petite hystérie A *forme fruste* of hysteria conceptualized by Charcot in which patients exhibited minor forms of hysteria.

phallic/genital character In Freudian theory, the constellation of curiosity, competitiveness, or exhibitionist traits that may emerge if a fixation occurred during the phallic/genital psychosexual stage of development.

phenomenal world Kant's concept of the world as subjectively experienced, after being processed and transformed via the intuitions and categories of the mind.

phi phenomenon A perceptual illusion and form of apparent movement described by Wertheimer in which certain combinations of spacing and timing of still images can cause the sensation of motion.

phrenology Doctrine originated by Gall, localizing specific psychological faculties in specific regions of the brain, which are reflected in specific bumps and indentations of the skull.

physiognomy The art of associating particular facial characteristics with specific psychological qualities, effectively promoted by Lavater.

physiological needs The needs for food, shelter, and physical satisfaction that constitute the most elemental needs in Maslow's hierarchical model.

polygenesis A Victorian-era theory suggesting that non-European "savage" peoples represented a distinctly different species of being.

polymorphous perversity According to Freudian theory, the state of a newborn infant in which literally any part of the body is a potential source of broadly conceived, "sexual" gratification.

positive psychology An area of modern psychology promoted by Seligman in response to the tendency of mainstream psychology to overfocus on pathology and abnormal conditions; it comprises the scientific study of psychological positivity, health, and the conditions that promote happiness.

positive reinforcement A response contingency in which the probability of a response is increased when it is followed by a desired consequence.

post-hypnotic amnesia The forgetting of events from a hypnotic state after awakening from it.

post-hypnotic suggestion Completion of a suggested hypnotic effect after the subject has "awakened" from the hypnosis.

power law A relationship proposed by S. Smith Stevens asserting that S (the subjective intensity of a stimulus) is a function of P (the physical intensity of a stimulus) raised to a particular power times a constant $S = kP^n$. Also known as **Stevens' law**.

pragmatism A term originated by Peirce but adopted by James to denote the evaluation of ideas relativistically, according to their usefulness in varying situations—an approach that eventually became a hallmark of James's general philosophy.

preoperational stage Piaget's second stage of development, in which children have developed an appreciation of object constancy but are still unable to understand concepts such as the of conservation of quantity.

presses (environmental) External cues or forces that trigger unconscious motivations and various psychogenic needs, in Murray's model for personality analysis.

pressure technique A transitional technique between hypnosis and free association, in which Sigmund Freud placed his hand on a patient's forehead while assuring him or her that relevant memories would occur.

primary colors The colors red, green, and blue, which are the building blocks for all the kinds of color sensation.

primary process Sigmund Freud's conception of the basic "rules" by which unconscious thought processes typically occur: displacement, condensation/overdetermination, and concrete representations of abstract thought. Generally the opposite of the conscious, secondary process.

primary qualities (Galileo) According to Galileo, the three primary qualities that resided inherently in matter: shape quantity, and motion.

primary qualities (Locke) According to Locke, the qualities of solidity, extension, figure, and mobility; material objects in the world truly "have" these qualities, which accordingly constitute the fundamental units for constructing a true picture of the world.

primary reinforcers Sometimes called *unconditioned* or *natural reinforcers*, reinforcers that do not require pairing with another stimulus to function as a reinforcer, such as food, water, sleep, and sex.

programmable computer A device that performs any number of tasks based on a specified set of instructions.

programmed instruction An educational technique devised by Skinner in which complicated subjects such as mathematics are broken down into simple, stepwise components that are presented to students in order of increasing difficulty, such that students are positively reinforced for every incremental response.

projection Freudian defense mechanism in which one's own unacceptable feelings are repressed and then attributed to someone else instead.

projective tests Tests that use responses to unstructured or ambiguous stimuli to assess underlying and often unconscious processes and motivations.

psychic causality Wundt's notion that there are different rules in place for apperceptive processes that do not follow the same mechanistic causality that distinguishes perceptive processes.

psychoanalysis A form of psychotherapy and a general psychological theory developed by Sigmund Freud.

psychobiography A genre of life writing that uses psychodynamic personality theory to interpret and illuminate an individual's biography.

psychogenic needs Murray's system of twenty-seven needs based on unconscious motivations, including needs for affiliation, achievement, autonomy, and power.

psychophysical isomorphism Köhler's idea that perceptual and brain processes are not identical but share the same structural and relational properties and should be studied as an organized, whole system, not just as a conglomeration of separate individual components.

psychophysical parallelism Leibniz's conception of the mind-body relationship suggesting that monads do not mutually influence one another but rather pursue independent but parallel and harmonious courses.

psychophysics Term introduced by Fechner to denote the search for lawful relationships between measurable psychological and physiological variables.

psychotechnics The application of psychology to business and industry, an approach that was the focus of Münsterberg's work.

psychoticism One of the personality factors in Eysenck's PEN model denoting generally one's relative ability to remain in touch with reality.

purposive behaviorism A form of behaviorism formulated by Tolman suggesting that behavior is goal directed and often mediated by unobservable "intervening variables."

radical environmentalism A view put forth by Watson suggesting that environmental factors had an overwhelmingly greater importance than heredity in determining behavior.

rage Along with fear and love, one of three emotions Watson believed to be innate.

rational monads *See* **monads**.

rational soul *See* **soul**.

rationalism A philosophical position arguing that questions about nature, knowledge, and the truth can only be answered by reason.

rationalization Freudian defense mechanism in which a person's true motivations are denied and a false excuse or explanation is substituted for them.

reaction times The measurable times between the introduction of stimuli and the completion of various kinds of responses to them.

real individuality Stern's term to denote a Gestalt-like conception of each person's unique and unified self that is greater than the sum of its individual characteristics.

redundancy hypothesis The idea that each individual memory gets stored in several different locations throughout the cortex, with the number increasing as the memory becomes better established and more widely associated with other memories.

reflection A psychotherapeutic technique devised by Rogers that entails a mirroring back to the client the substance of what he or she says, but in different words that encourage deeper exploration of the issues expressed.

reflex An involuntary neurophysiological response to a stimulus from the external world.

regression In Freudian theory, the reversion to an earlier, more primitive way of thinking or behaving.

regression line A line created when the means of each of the columns in a scatter plot are represented by X's across a graph; they tend to array themselves into an approximately straight line.

regression toward the mean A statistical term referring to the phenomenon in which extreme scores on one correlated variable tend to be associated with scores closer to the mean on the other.

reinforcement schedules The rewarding of behaviors based on a specified time interval or number of responses, resulting in characteristic patterns of response.

reinforcer A consequence that results in an increase in a desired behavior.

relational individuality A term used by Stern to define a person's relative or statistical positions on a large variety of separately measured personality traits.

repression In Freudian theory, the prevention or expulsion from consciousness of anxiety-arousing thoughts or memories.

respondent conditioning A term used by Skinner to define Pavlov's classical conditioning in contrast to operant conditioning.

safety needs The need to be safe from threats by predators, criminals, extremes of climate and temperature, or other hazardous environmental circumstances; it is the second level of needs, following physiological ones, in Maslow's hierarchy.

scatter plots A mathematical diagram that displays the values for two intercorrelated variables for a set of data.

scholastic philosophers A group of medieval philosophers who supported the doctrine that the components of a "thing" corresponded to the perceptible properties of that "thing" (e.g., a thing's shape, color, and temperature).

scientific management A system developed by Taylor to increase efficiency and productivity in the factory, generally accomplished by having workers to do more in less time by giving them quick, repetitive, menial tasks, often on an assembly line.

scientist/practitioner model of clinical training A model of training that emerged from the 1949 Boulder Conference stipulating that clinical psychologists be trained in research as well as practice.

secondary process Sigmund Freud's conception of the modes of thinking associated with conscious rationality; generally the opposite of the unconscious primary process.

secondary qualities (Galileo) According to Galileo, qualities that do not reside inherently in matter but arise only after the primary qualities impinge on the human senses.

secondary qualities (Locke) According to Locke, the qualities the mind perceives in objects, such as sounds, colors, temperatures, tastes, and odors—characteristics that derive as much from the perceiving sense organs as from the objects themselves.

secondary reinforcers Reinforcers that acquire their power only after having been paired with other, primary reinforcers.

seduction theory An early theory proposed by Freud and then abandoned, suggesting that all hysterics must have undergone sexual abuse as children.

self psychology The position developed and promoted by Calkins that the conscious self should be the subject matter of psychology. In her system, and in contrast to behaviorism, the self was an active, guiding, and purposive agency present in all acts of consciousness and essential to any complete introspective report.

self-actualization The striving toward the positive fulfillment of potentialities within the self; in Maslow's theory it occurs only after the first four levels of his hierarchy of needs have been adequately satisfied.

self-questionnaire method A research method pioneered by Galton that collected biographical, demographic, and personal information in order to confirm the influence of heredity on the development of intelligence.

sensations The "raw elements" of conscious experience, requiring no learning or prior experience. In vision, for example, they include the spatially organized patches of light with varying hues and brightnesses that fill one's visual field, quite independently of any "meaning."

sensitive knowledge According to Locke, aspects of knowledge that depend on the particular patterns of sensory experiences one happens to have with objects in the world.

sensitive soul *See* **soul**.

sensory aphasia A condition in which patients can speak perfectly fluently with correct syntax, but their understanding of spoken language is severely impaired and their speech is marked by numerous peculiar words and mispronunciations called *paraphasias*. Also known as **Wernicke's aphasia**.

sensory strip A functionally distinct area of the brain, bordering the motor strip, responsible for mediating sensory functions from various parts of the body.

sensory-motor stage Piaget's earliest stage of development, from birth to 2 years of age, in which a child's intelligence involves sensory and motor activities and has nothing to do with abstract thought in the adult sense.

sentient monads *See* **monads**.

separated identical twins Monozygotic twins who have been reared in separate, independent environments. Their study is potentially useful in determining the relative influences of heredity and environment.

serialist processing A type of sequential computer processing used by LT, GPS, and other early computer programs that worked by performing a specified sequence of operations on a specified set of symbols, with both the operations and the symbols being stored in specific memory locations.

sexual selection A specific variant of natural selection theorized by Charles Darwin suggesting that the quality of mate selection plays a role in the passing down of characteristics favorable for survival.

simple ideas Locke's term for the most basic ideas established in early life, recording the most basic sensations and reflections.

simple monads *See* **monads**.

simple natures According to Descartes, the only two properties of physical phenomena that could not be further analyzed or doubted: extension (the space occupied by a body) and motion.

Sixteen Personality Factor Questionnaire (16 PF) A personality scale developed by Raymond B. Cattell, based on the factor analysis of the intercorrelations among many trait measures, that assesses sixteen basic dimensions of personality.

Skinner box An experimental chamber created by B. F. Skinner to study schedules of reinforcement in animals.

small world phenomenon A social phenomenon researched by Milgram, indicating that most people can be interconnected through a small chain of mutual acquaintances—the "six degrees of separation" effect.

social conformity A concept studied by Asch, Milgram, and other social psychologists to explain how individuals feel pressured to conform to the ideas and opinions of other group members.

social contagion The increased likelihood of people responding in a particular way when they are part of a group and see others as doing so.

social contract A theory, initiated by Hobbes and elaborated on by Locke and others, that individuals come together in groups and submit to a centralized authority for purposes of mutual protection.

social Darwinism A view promoted by Spencer, who suggested that political systems and societies, like all human and animal species, evolve because of natural selection and that therefore the current systems represent the "survival of the fittest."

social facilitation The enhancement in the performance of a task as a result of being in a social or group setting.

social influence processes A broad term to indicate a set of processes studied by social psychologists involving how people's behaviors, attitudes, and beliefs are shaped by other people and social situations.

social neuroscience A newly emerging interdisciplinary field that studies the neurological underpinnings of social thought and behavior using a variety of imaging techniques (also called *social cognitive neuroscience*).

sociobiology A recently developed theoretical approach that hypothesizes that the unit of evolution is the individual gene, rather than the group or entire organism.

soul English translation of the Greek *psyche*, denoting the essential ingredient differentiating the living from the nonliving; the animating force within all living things. Aristotle proposed the existence of a hierarchy of souls of varying degrees of complexity:

vegetative soul The ability all organisms, including plants, have to nourish themselves and reproduce.

sensitive soul In animals, the ability to engage in the more complex functions of locomotion, sensation, memory, and imagination.

rational soul Only in human beings, the ability to reason and take on the highest moral values; this soul was viewed as immortal and capable of existing without the body.

stages of development Piaget's notion of developmental periods marked by qualitative differences in the ways younger and older children conceptualize and solve problems and tasks.

Stanford Prison Experiment A study by Zimbardo in which male students at Stanford University lived in a mock prison and took on the roles of "prisoners" or "guards" to examine the role of social influence.

Statistical correlation A mathematical procedure used to explain the strength of a relationship between variables.

Stevens' law *See* **power law.**

stimulus error The inappropriate imposition of "meaning" or "interpretation" onto introspections conducted under Titchener's structuralist rules.

stored programs A concept put forth by von Neumann in which a computer's operating instructions are stored in its own memory, along with the data and the results of its calculations.

stream of thought James's term for the streamlike, fluid, and continuous quality of thought that makes it impervious to atomistic or reductionistic analysis.

strong AI The theory that computers have the ability to equal or exceed the ability of human beings in performing intellectual tasks, going about them in the same ways and experiencing similar states of consciousness.

structuralism A term coined by Titchener to define his approach to experimental psychology, which emphasized first the discovery of the "structure" of mental phenomena before looking at their "function."

subtractive method A method created by Donders to measure reaction times, in which the average reaction time for a simple task was subtracted from the average time for a more complex task, with the conclusion that the difference had been the time required for a "higher" mental function such as "discrimination."

suggestibility A psychological process in which one person is able to influence and guide the thoughts and behaviors of another.

superego The element in Sigmund Freud's structural model of the psyche that deals with moral demands, arising independently of instincts and external reality alike, typically originating from an identification with the same-sex parent.

symbolic *See* **modes of representation.**

symbolic logic A subfield of mathematics originated by Boole that includes both classical logic and traditional mathematics.

symbolic processing Performing a specified sequence of operations on a specified set of symbols, with both the operations and the symbols being stored in specific memory locations.

systematic desensitization A deconditioning technique in which a pleasant stimulus is presented at the same time as a fear-evoking stimulus, with the latter presented at a level that does not evoke a full-blown fear response, with the hope that over repeated exposures, the fearful response will be eliminated.

Thanatos Sigmund Freud's late conception of an aggressive "death instinct," in conflict with the "life instinct," Eros.

Thematic Apperception Test (TAT) A projective personality test created by Henry Murray and Christiana Morgan in which respondents are presented with a series of standardized pictures and are asked to construct stories about them. This test was designed to assess unconscious motivations.

theory of evolution by natural selection *See* **natural selection**.

therbligs A term coined by the Gilbreths to define the eighteen independent motions of the hand they discovered with their motion study research; an anagram of their name.

tomography A general term referring to the imaging of the body as collections of sections or "slices" created by various kinds of penetrating waves. Among the more common types of tomograms are CT (computed tomography) or CAT scans and MRI (magnetic resonance imaging) scans.

trait (personality) The term used to describe habitual patterns of behavior, temperament, intelligence, sociality, and emotion.

transfer of training The notion that the positive effect of instruction and exercise in one discipline of study can be transferred to other areas of mental function, disconfirmed by the experiments of Thorndike and Woodworth.

transference Freud's term for unconscious feelings toward important figures from childhood that are redirected toward the therapist in an analytic situation.

Turing machine A hypothetical "universal" computer proposed by Alan Turing that was capable of manipulating any set of numbers or symbols according to some set of formally specifiable and selfconsistent rules.

Turing test A test suggested by Alan Turing to assess the intelligence of a machine according to its ability to interact with a human being in a manner indistinguishable from that of a real person.

twin study method A research technique introduced in 1875 by Galton, and still used today, in which fraternal and identical twins are compared to assess the impact of genetics or environmental factors on their development.

two-factor theory of intelligence Spearman's theory that the performance of all intellectual tasks require both a single common factor, which he called general intelligence or g, and a second, specific factor (s) which is unique to it.

type A term used by Charcot to describe the major or complete form of certain neurological diseases.

unconditioned reflexes Pavlov's term for innate and automatic reactions that must exist prior to any conditioning or learning, such as salivating when food is presented.

unconditioned response (UR) The response component of a Pavlovian unconditioned reflex.

unconditioned stimulus (US) The stimulus component of a Pavlovian unconditioned reflex.

unconscious inference According to Helmholtz, the idea that perceptual adaptation and other perceptual phenomena might result from a process in which there is an unconscious adoption of certain rules.

uniformitarianism A theory strongly promoted by Lyell holding that the earth's major features resulted from gradual processes occurring over vast stretches of time, rather than according to the then-predominant alternative theory of catastrophism.

variability hypothesis A widely held social and scientific belief inspired by evolutionary theory, and closely related to Charles Darwin's "variation hypothesis," that men are more variable than women on both physical and psychological characteristics and thus more likely to occupy positions at the lowermost and uppermost ends of the distribution of any trait.

variable-interval reinforcement schedule An operant conditioning schedule in which responses are reinforced only periodically after randomly varying intervals of time.

variable-ratio reinforcement schedule An operant conditioning schedule in which reinforcement occurs after a number of responses that varies randomly but has a constant average value. It typically produces a high rate of response.

variation hypothesis The idea advanced by Charles Darwin that across all species, including human beings, males have been more modified by evolution than females and accordingly they tend to show more variability among themselves.

vegetative soul *See* **soul**.

ventricles A system of four communicating cavities (ventricles) within the brain that is continuous with the central canal of the spinal cord.

visual area A functionally distinct area of the brain's anterior occipital lobe responsible for processing visual stimuli.

vitalism A school of thought suggesting that all living organisms are imbued with an ineffable "life force" that gives them their vitality and that is not analyzable by scientific methods.

Völkerpsychologie A nonexperimental branch of psychology proposed by Wundt that dealt with the *communal* and *cultural* products of human nature, such as religions, mythologies, customs, and languages, using historical and comparative analysis.

voluntaristic psychology General term describing Wundt's psychology, which emphasized events such as apperception, creative synthesis, and psychic causality, which were associated with the will or voluntary effort.

Weak AI Searle's notion that computer processes might be useful *models* for significant aspects of human cognitive processes but without actually duplicating the processes of a human mind.

Wernicke's aphasia *See* **sensory aphasia**.

Wernicke's area The area in the temporal lobe discovered by Wernicke that, if damaged, can cause sensory aphasia.

white matter The fibrous white tissue that occupies the interior layers of the brain; composed primarily of neuronal axons.

word association test A test created by Jung, in which a list of stimulus words is presented to the respondent with instructions to provide for each the first word or thought that comes to mind, in a process akin to Freudian free association.

word-association experiment Technique pioneered by Galton in which he responded to randomly presented written words with the first few thoughts that come to mind; may have partially inspired Freud's free association test.

Young-Helmholtz trichromatic theory Idea proposed by Thomas Young and Hermann von Helmholtz suggesting that there are three types of receptor cells in the eyes, each one responding to a different spectral hue, and making color vision possible.

Zeigarnik effect The tendency to better remember uncompleted than completed tasks.

Credits

Chapter 1

Page 16: René Descartes by Jan Baptiste Weenix, 1643, Centraal Museum, Utrecht http://commons.wikimedia.org/wiki/Commons:GNU_Free_Documentation_License; p. 21: Engraving by A. Bosse, 1624, after Thomas Francini http://commons.wikimedia.org/wiki/Commons:GNU_Free_Documentation_License; p. 33: From Descartes. R. (1662), *Trait de L'homme*, Cambridge University Press; p. 39: akg-images.

Chapter 2

Page 54: Bettmann/Corbis; p. 56: © Devonshire Collection, Chatsworth Reproduced by permission of Chatsworth Settlement Trustees/Bridgeman Art Library; p. 57: National Portrait Gallery London, www.npg.org.uk; p. 70: Scottish National Portrait Gallery, Edinburgh, Scotland/The Bridgeman Art Library; p. 72: Alamy; p. 77: Maerkisches Museum, Berlin/The Bridgeman Art Library; p. 78: National Trust Photo Library/Art Resource, NY.

Chapter 3

Page 98: Mary Evans Picture Library/Alamy; p. 104: The National Library of Medicine, Bethesda; p. 110: Alamy; p. 115: Carl Wernicke, 1900, author: Max Glauer http://commons.wikimedia.org/wiki/Commons:GNU_Free_Documentation_License; p. 119: Archives of the History of American Psychology, The Center for the History of Psychology, The University of Akron; p. 124: Notman, McGill University Archives, PR010146 p. 128: Neuro Media Services, Montreal Neurological Institute, McGill University.

Chapter 4

Page 140: Alamy; p. 146: National Library of Medicine, NIH; p. 147: Johannes Müller, Naturforscher; 1856; 154:103

from "Die großen Deutschen im Bilde" (1936) by Michael Schönitzer, http://commons.wikimedia.org/wiki/Commons:GNU_Free_Documentation_License; p. 163: Smithsonian Institution Libraries; p. 175 (all): Granger Collection; p. 178: © Topham Picturepoint/The Image Works.

Chapter 5

Page 193: Alamy; p. 206: Granger Collection; p. 216: Granger Collection; p. 220: Columbia University Rare Book and Manuscript Library; p. 221: Archives of the History of American Psychology, The Center for the History of Psychology, The University of Akron; p. 224: Archives of the History of American Psychology, The Center for the History of Psychology, The University of Akron.

Chapter 6

Page 232: Lebrecht Music and Arts Photo Library/ Alamy; p. 236: © National Portrait Gallery, London; p. 248: Alamy; p. 260: Library of Congress.

Chapter 7

Page 270: SSPL/Getty Images; p. 272: Images from History of Medicine, National Library of Medicine, Bethesda; p. 283: © The Natural History Museum/The Image Works; p. 298: from *Twins: A study of heredity and environment* by Horatio H. Newman, Frank N. Freeman, and Karl J. Holzinger, 1937, The University of Chicago Press, p. 308.

Chapter 8

Page 306: Alamy; p. 326: Images from History of Medicine, National Library of Medicine, Bethesda; p. 331: Wellesley College Archives; p. 337: New York Public Library.

Chapter 9

Page 350: RIA Novosti /Alamy; p. 360: Archives of the History of Psychology, University of Akron; p. 369: Archives of the History of Psychology, University of Akron; p. 383: Nina Leen/Time & Life Pictures/Getty Images; p. 394: Ladies Home Journal, October 1945.

Chapter 10

Page 402: Lebrecht Music and Arts Photo Library/Alamy; p. 407: Bibliotheque Nationale, Paris/The Bridgeman Art Library; p. 421: The National Library of Medicine, Bethesda; p. 425: akg-images; p. 432: Syracuse University Archives; p. 441: © Alexandra Milgram.

Chapter 11

Page 457: Mary Evans Picture Library/ Alamy; p. 459: Max Halberstadt/Images from the History of Medicine (NLM); p. 486: Library of Congress p. 490: Bettmann/Corbis; p. 495: Clark University Archives.

Chapter 12

Page 507: Courtesy Robert Allport; p. 521: Image 0000950 courtesy of the University of Illinois Archives; p. 525: Courtesy Robert Allport; p. 530: Harvard University Archives; p. 533: Brandeis University Archives; p. 540: Granger Collection; p. 543: Bettmann/Corbis; p. 544: Brooklyn College Archives; p. 545: Images from History of Medicine, National Library of Medicine, Bethesda; p. 553: Carl Rogers Collection at the Davidson Library, UC Santa Barbara; p. 555: Hulton Archive/ Getty Images.

Chapter 13

Page 564: Images from History of Medicine, National Library of Medicine, Bethesda; p. 570: Collection of author; p. 582: Images from History of Medicine, National Library of Medicine, Bethesda; p. 583: Archives of the History of American Psychology, The Center for the History of Psychology, The University of Akron; p. 585: Bill Anderson/Photo Researchers, Inc; p. 589: Reproduced from the book by J. J. Ducret (1990) *Jean Piaget, Biographie et parcours intellectuel*. Neuchatel: Delachaux et Niestle.

Chapter 14

Page 604: Granger Collection; p. 614: Alamy; p. 617: Granger Collection; p. 636: Photo by Sandra Condry.

Chapter 15

Page 650: Collection of Helmut E. Luck and are reproduced in "A Pictorial History of Psychology" edited by Wolfgang. G. Bringmann, Helmut E. Luck, Rudolf Miller, and Charles E. Early. Carol Stream, IL: Quintessence Publishing Co. 1997; p. 660: Courtesy of the Sophia Smith Collection, Smith College Archives; p. 664: Collection of Raymond Fancher; p. 669: Archives of the University of Pennsylvania; p. 677: Archives of the History of American Psychology, The Center for the History of Psychology, The University of Akron.

Index

Page numbers in *italics* refer to illustrations.

A

AACP (American Association of Clinical
  Psychologists), 675, 676
absolute threshold, 169, 171
Abu Ghraib, 445
Ach, Narziss, 222
act psychology, 460–461
adaptation, perceptual, 160–161, 178–179
Adapted Mind, The (Barkow, Cosmides,
  and Tooby), 264
Adler, Alfred, 493, 535–536, *540*,
  540–541, 559
Adolescence (Hall), 328, 494–495
adoptive relatives, biological *vs.,* 281–282
advertising, Watson's career in, 371–372
Africa, exploration of, 276, 277
Agassiz, Louis, 310
agreeableness, 523
AI, *see* Artificial Intelligence (AI)
Alexander II, 350
algorithms, 626
Allport, Floyd H., *431*, 431–434, 450, 509,
  511, 513–514
Allport, Gordon, 11, 335, *507*, *508*, *530*,
  542, 557, 558–559
  dissertation on personality traits,
    513–514
  early life and career of, 509–517
  Freud and, 510–511
  humanistic psychology and 554–555
  nomothetic and idiographic methods
    of, 517–519
  *Personality: A Psychological
    Interpretation,* 516, 517
  personality concept of, 511–513
  personality psychology and 507, 508,
    515–520
  on prejudice, 527–528
  on religion, 527
  as a social activist, 526–528
  as a teacher, 528–530
  Titchener and, 506–507
altruistic behavior, 263
American Association of Clinical
  Psychologists (AACP), 675, 676
American Communist Party, 684
American Jewish Congress, 532n
American Journal of Psychology, 327, 329,
  333, 343, 431, 494, 495–496
American Men of Science, 335, 342
American Philosophical Association, 335
American Psychological Association
  (APA), 134, 328, 675
  divisions of, 388, 528
  presidents of, 322, 343, 365, 494,
    556, 558
American Psychologist, 447
American Society for Psychical
  Research, 322–323
amnesia, post-hypnotic, 409
anal character, 477
Analytical Engine, 613–617, *614*, 619, 621,
  622, 629, 640, 644
analytical geometry, 23, 24
analytical psychology, 513
Analytical Society, 611
anal zone, 475
Anatomy of the Brain (Willis), 96
anesthesia, chemical and hypnotic,
  413–414
Angell, James Rowland, 341, 362
anima, 8
Animal Education (Watson), 362
animal experiments
  of Thorndike, 337–340
  of Watson, 361–362
Animal Intelligence (Romanes), 261
animal magnetism, 405–406, 450
Animal Mind, The (Washburn), 218, 336
animal souls, 18, 30–31

animal spirits (cerebrospinal fluid), 31, 34, 35, 43, 44, 96
L'Annee Psychologique, 571
Anthropological Society, Paris, 110, 111
Anthropology from a Pragmatic Point of View (Kant), 142
Anthropometric Laboratory, 269–271, *270,* 272, 289, 290, 300–301, 564
anthropometric tests, 269–271, *270,* 272, 289, 290, 300–301, 564
anti-Semitism, 537, 538, 655
APA, *see* American Psychological Association (APA)
aphasia, 112
    Broca's, 117
    conduction, 117
    motor, 116, 117
    Penfield and, 125
    sensory, 116–117
    Wernicke's, 117
    Wernicke's theory of, 115–118
apoplexy, 97
apparent movement, 173
apperception
    creative synthesis in, 210–211
    definition of, 83–84
    language and, 212–213
    in Leibniz's philosophy, 83–84, 88, 91
    psychic causality and, 212
    in Wundt's psychology, 209–210, 217
applied psychology
    contemporary, 686–688
    development of, 653–654
    Gilbreth and, 659, 660–668, 687, 688
    Münsterberg and, 653–654, 656–659, 667, 687
    resistance to, 674–676
    Taylor and, 657–658, 663, 664–666, 688
    see also clinical psychology; courtroom psychology
Arabic numerals, 605–606
archaeopteryx, 250
Arendt, Hannah, 442n
argument from design, 243

Aristotle, 7, 8, 28
    on brain, 95–96, 113
    soul concept of, 18–19, 52, 86
    world view of, 18
Arnold Philipp Friedrich, 192, 194, 195
Artificial Intelligence (AI), 91, 132, 607, 643–644
    backward reasoning and, 625–626
    chess problems and, 626, 629
    cognitive psychology and, 638–639
    computational functionalism and, 628
    General Problem Solver and, 626–628, 629, 630
    graceful degradation and, 630
    heuristic strategies for, 626
    Hobbes and, 606–607, 643
    intentionality and, 633
    Lovelace Objection to, 615–616, 629
    means-ends analysis and, 627–628
    philosophical implications of, 604–606, 607, 608
    problem solving and, 624–631
    Searle on, 631–635
    strong *vs.* weak, 633–634, 645
    Turing Test and, 624, 626, 631–635
    von Neumann architecture and, 621, 622, 623
    World War II and, 618–620
    see also computers
artificial somnambulism, 409–410, 450
Art of Travel, The (Galton), 277
Asch, Solomon, 11, 183, 434–438, 440, 442, 449, 450
Assault on Truth, The (Masson), 472n
Assayer, The (Galileo), 26
assembly languages, 622
association
    directed, 222, 227
    free, 218, 294, 462–466, 473, 479–480, 499
    verbal, 208
association areas, 115
associationism, British, 69
astigmatism, 155
atomism of Titchener, 214
Aubertin, Ernest, 109–111, 112

Auden, W. H., 493
August, Ernst, 76, 79
auras in epilepsy, 124–125
axons, 97n

B

Babbage, Charles, 610–617, 619, 621, 622,
    623, 628, 629, 640, 644
backward reasoning, 625–626
Bain, Alexander, 313
Baldwin, James Mark, 363
Barkow, Jerome, 264
Bartholow, Roberts, 123
Bastien and Bastienne (Mozart), 404
Bauer, Ida, 478–81
Beagle, H.M.S., 237, *238,* 239–242, 252,
    265, 285
Beaumont, William, 352–353
Beaunis, Henri, 571
Bechterev, Vladimir M., 365
Beck, Aaron T., 493
Beeckman, Isaac, 22–23
behavior analysis, 394
behaviorism, 10, 119, 133, 342, 347–396
    child care and, 375–377
    creation of, 349, 363–364
    Descartes' influence on, 368
    Locke's influence on, 70
    mechanistic, 379
    purposive, 379
    radical environmentalism and,
        373, 375
    see also operant conditioning;
        Pavlov, Ivan Petrovich; reflexes;
        reinforcement; Skinner, B. F.;
        Watson, John Broadus
Behaviorism (Watson), 372, 373, 376, 381
Behavior of Organisms, The (Skinner),
    387
behavior therapy, 493
Behavior (Watson), 364–365
Bell, Charles, 143
Bell Curve, The (Herrnstein and Mur-
    ray), 300
Benedict, Ruth, 539–540, 541, 546, 550,
    559
Ben-Gurion, David, 532n

Benjamin, Ludy, 447
Bergson, Henri, 586
Berkeley, George, 69, 89
Bernays, Martha, 461
Bernhardi, Minna Anna, 654
Bernheim, Hippolyte, 415–416, 422,
    435, 462
Bernstein, Leonard, 552
Bessel, Friedrich Wilhelm, 196
Beyond Freedom and Dignity
    (Skinner), 392
Bible, literal interpretation of, 239
Big Five, 523, 526
binary arithmetic, 73–74, 79, 610, 644
Binet, Alfred, 11, 435, 442, 449, 450,
    563, *564,* 567–578, 598
    Charcot and, 563, 568–569
    death of, 578
    early life and career of, 567–574
    The Experimental Study of
        Intelligence, 573
    hypnosis studies of, 422–424
    individual psychology and, 570–574
    intelligence tests of, 289, 563–65,
        569–570, 572–578, 579, 580, 581,
        598–599, 674
    legacy of, 578
    suggestion experiments of, 429–431,
        571–572
Binet, Alice, 563, 564–565, 569, 570,
    570, 572–573
Binet, Madeleine, 563, 564–565,
    569–570, *570,* 572–573
Binet-Simon intelligence test, 574–577,
    598–599
Binet-Simon scales of intelligence, 674
"Biographical Sketch of an Infant, A"
    (Darwin), 257–258
biological relatives, adoptive *vs.,*
    281–282
blind spot, 155–156
blushing, 256
Boden, Margaret, 630–631
body-soul interaction, Descartes on,
    37–45, 46, 48
Boineburg, Johann Christian von, 72, 75
Boole, George, 616, 644

Boolean algebra, 616, 620, 645

Boring, E. G., 329

Bouillaud, Jean Baptiste, 109

Boulder Conference, 687

Boyle, Robert, 55, *56*, 59, 62

Boyle's law, 55

Braid, James, 414–415, 416, 450

brain, 95–135
    ablation of, 105–108, 112, 114, 118–120, 125, 135
    Aristotle's view of, 95–96, 113
    Broca's area of, 112, 114, 115–116, 117, 119
    Descartes' physiology of, 31–34, 41–43, 46, 96
    equipotentiality of, 120–121
    Franz's work on, 118–120
    frontal lobes of, 115
    Gall's work on, 97–104, 120
    halves of, 97–98
    hologram theory of, 122
    law of mass action of, 121
    lost functions recovered by, 118–119
    mind and, 131–132
    motor strip of, 113–114, 115–116, 125, 135
    Pavlov's theory of, 357–359
    redundancy hypothesis of, 122
    sensory strip of, 114, 125, 135
    size of, intelligence and, 99–101
    stimulation of, 122–127, 135
    verbal memory and, 108–109
    Wernicke's area of, 117, 119
    Willis's research on, 96–97
    see also cortex; localization of brain function

Brain Mechanisms and Intelligence (Lashley), 120

Brentano, Franz, 460–461, 632

Breuer, Josef, 456–458, *457*, 499

British Association for the Advancement of Science, 249

British associationism, 69

Broca, Paul, *110*, 110–113, 120, 130, 135

Broca's aphasia, 117

Broca's area, 112, 114, 115–116, 117, 119

Bronner, Augusta Fox, 674

Brown, Roger, 640

Brown v. Board of Education of Topeka, 330

Brücke, Ernst, 146, 461, 482

Bruner, Jerome, 596–598, 599, 637, 639, 640

Brunswick, Ruth Mack, 489

Buchanan, Roderick, 522n

Bunsen, Robert, 194

Bunsen burner, invention of, 194

Burt, Cyril, 299, 587, 587n

Busby, Richard, 54

C

calculus, 74–75, 81, 81n, 611

Calkins, Mary Whiton, 325, 330–336, *331*, 343, 656

Candide (Voltaire), 80

Carlsmith, James, 439–440

Carr, Harvey, 341

Cartesian coordinates, 23

castration complex, 488–489

catalepsy, 421

catastrophism, 239

cathartic method, 456, 458, 499

Catholic Church, 28, 45

Cattell, James McKeen, *206*, 227, 335, 338, 637, 653, 670, 671, 680
    on Freud, 497
    reaction-time experiments of, 205–208
    women and, 681–682

Cattell, Raymond B., 520–522, *521*, 522n, 523, 559

Cattell Controversy, The (Tucker), 522n

causality
    Hume and, 140–141
    Kant's concept of, 141–142
    psychic, 211, 227

cell assemblies, 128

cerebellum, 100, 105–106, 107–108

cerebrospinal fluid (CSF), 31, 34, 35, 43, 44, 96

Chandoux (chemist), 27n

Charcot, Jean-Martin, 416–422, *421*, 450
    Binet and, 563, 568–569, 571
    Freud and, 424, 456, 461, 462
    hysteria studies of, 418–422
    medical career of, 417–418

Charles I, 54
Charles II, 55, 57, 60, 61, 232
Chicago's World Fair (1893), 653
child care, behaviorism and, 375–377
child psychology, 256–258
children
    Bruner's study of, 596–598
    Erikson's psychosocial stages of,
        492–493
    Hall's work on, 328–329
    Piaget's studies of, 91, 565–566,
        584, 587–595, 626
    sexuality of, 472–475, 499
        Dora and, case of, 480
        stages of, 475–477
Children Above 180 IQ (Hollingworth), 686
*Child's Construction of Quantities,
    The* (Piaget and Inhelder), 592
Chinese room thought experiment,
    631–634
Chomsky, Noam, 216, 226, 391, 540
Christina, Queen, 45
Church of England, 58, 244
Civilization and Its Discontents (Freud),
    491
Clark, Kenneth B., 330
Clark, Mamie Phipps, 330
client-centered therapy, 493
Client-Centered Therapy (Rogers), 553
clinical psychology, 672, 673–674, 689
    Hollingworth and, 677–686
    Witmer and, 668–676, 688–689
Coca-Cola Company, 680–681
coefficients of correlation, 292, 301
cognitive dissonance, 438–440
cognitive neuroscience, 133
cognitive psychology, 183, 635
    Artificial Intelligence and, 638–639
    "ecological" influences on, 641–643
    Neisser and, 638–643
Cognitive Psychology (Neisser), 639,
    640–641
cognitive revolution, 133
cognitive therapy, 493
color afterimages, 177–178
color mixing, 157–159
color vision, *156*, 156–159, 177–178, 219
"Colossus" machine, 620

commissures, 98
"Comparative Anatomy of Angels, The"
    (Fechner), 165
comparative psychology, 261–262
complementarity hypothesis, 254
complementary colors, 157
composite portraiture system, 295
computational functionalism, 628
computed tomography (CT), 132
computers
    assembly languages for, 622
    Babbage's Analytical Engine,
        613–617, *614*, 619, 621, 622, 644
    connectionist, 630–631
    creativity and, 630–631
    development of electronic, 619–624
    hardware developments in, 621–622
    Leibniz's calculating machine,
        73, 74, 607–610
    Pascal's calculating machine, *604*,
        604–605, 607
    Turing machine, *618*, 618–619, 626
    see also Artificial Intelligence (AI)
"Computing Machinery and
    Intelligence" (Turing), 623
concrete operations stage, 593–594, 599
concrete representation in dreams, 468
condensation in dreams, 468
conditioned response, 354
conditioned stimulus, 354
conditioning, *see* reflexes
conduction aphasia, 117
cones in retina, 177
conformity, social, 434–438
conic sections, 74
connectionist programs, 630–631
conscientiousness, 523
"Conservation of Force, The"
    (Helmholtz), 149–150
conservation of quantity, 591
contact hypothesis, 528
*Contents of Children's Minds on Entering
    School, The* (Hall), 328
*Contributions to the Theory of Sensory
    Perception* (Wundt), 191, 197
conversions, 458
Cooper, Anthony Ashley, *57*, 57–59, 60, 72
Copernicus, Nicolaus, 18

"Co-relations and Their Measurement,
    Chiefly from Anthropometric Data"
    (Galton), 292–93
cornea, 154
cortex
    auditory area of, 114, 125
    description of, 96
    Flourens's ablation experiments on,
        106–107, 112, 113
    Franz's ablation experiments on,
        118–120
    interpretive, 126
    language center in, 109–110
    reflexes and, 357
    secondary auditory region of, 126
    secondary visual region of, 125–126
    temporal lobe of, 126
    visual area of, 114, 125
Cosmides, Leda, 264
courtroom psychology, 649–652
Cox, Catherine, 582, 583
creative synthesis, 210, 227
creativity, computers and, 630–631
Critique of Pure Reason (Kant), 142
Cromwell, Oliver, 55, 57
Crowd, The (Le Bon), 425, 426
crowds, psychology of, 425–429
Crozer, Mary L., 673
CSF, see cerebrospinal fluid (CSF)
CT (computed tomography), 132
Cudworth, Ralph, 62
culture, 539–540
Cuvier, Georges, 104–105

D

Darwin, Charles Robert, 231–265, 232,
    260, 265, 582
    Babbage and, 616
    Beagle voyage of, 237, 238, 239–242,
        252, 265, 285
    "A Biographical Sketch of an Infant,"
        257–258
    character and physical appearance of,
        99n, 232–233, 234, 235
    child psychology and, 256–258, 329
    death of, 259
    The Descent of Man and Selection in
        Relation to Sex, 250–255, 265, 283

early life of, 233–237, 273, 274
evolution theory of, 10, 233, 241,
    242–250, 265
The Expression of the Emotions, 251,
    255–256, 262–263, 265
on function of animal characteristics,
    240–242
Galton and, 272, 276–278, 282–283,
    288, 301
geological uniformitarianism and,
    239–240
influence of, 259–265
On the Origin of Species, 249, 250,
    260, 277, 278, 301, 310
professional career of, 242
psychology and, 250–258
on social Darwinism, 260
Darwin, Erasmus, 233, 243, 243n, 244,
    265, 278
Darwin, Robert, 233, 234, 236–237,
    242, 273
Darwin, William "Daddy," 257–258
Dashiell, John, 433–434
Dean, John, 642
de Candolle, Alphonse, 283, 283–286
declarative memory, 130–131
defense mechanisms, 466, 483–488, 500
Delboeuf, Joseph, 423–424, 429, 567, 568
demonstrative knowledge, 65–66
dendrites, 97n
denial, 487
Dennett, Mary Ware, 684
deprivation needs, 548
Descartes, René, 8, 12, 15–48, 16, 103,
    509, 582, 595, 605, 606, 634, 643
    analytic geometry invented by,
        6, 23, 24, 74
    Beeckman and, 22–23
    death of, 45
    Discourse on Method, 36–37, 45
    early life of, 17–27
    early writings of, 22, 25
    education of, 17–19
    existence postulate of, 36–38, 47
    family background of, 17
    in Holland, 45
    influence of, 45–47, 91
    intellectual crisis period, 20–22

intellectual method of, 24–27

Le Monde, 27–35

life-transforming dreams of, 15–17, 25

meditation practiced by, 15, 19, 21,
23, 45

Mersenne and, 19, 22, 36

military experience of, 22, 23

mind-body dualism concept of, 37–39,
46, 48, 132, 211

physics and physiology theories of,
27–35, 46, 52–53, 82–83, 85

possible schizophrenic breakdown
of, 22

relations with Church, 28, 45

in Sweden, 45

"Treatise of Light," 28

"Treatise of Man," 30, *33*, 348

universal science sought by, 28

*Descent of Man and Selection in Relation
to Sex, The* (Darwin), 250–255,
265, 283

desensitization, systematic, 374

design, argument from, 243

determining tendencies, 222

Deutsch, Helene, 489

Dewey, John, 341, 361, 375

Difference Engine, 612–613, 644

differential calculus, 75

differentiation, conditioned reflexes and,
356, 358

digestion, physiology of, 350, 352–353

directed association, 222, 227

Discourse on Method (Descartes),
36–37, 45

discrimination, 527–528

displacement, 486

dizygotic twins, 286

Donaldson, Henry H., 361–362

Donders, F. C., 205

Dora, case of, 478–481

Dostoyevsky, Fyodor, 124, 126

Douglas, Claire, 524n

Downey, June Etta, 220, 512

dreams, 466–472

concrete representation in, 468

condensation in, 468

displacement in, 468

latent *vs.* manifest content of, 467–468

primary and secondary processes in,
469–470

regression in, 469

as wish-fulfillment, 470–472

work process of, 468

dualism, Descartes' conception of,
37–45, 46, 48, 132

Du Bois-Reymond, Emil, 146, 150, 152,
195, 310, 311, 326, 461

Dunlap, Knight, 497

dynamic psychology, 46

E

Ebbinghaus, Hermann, 3, 215, 223–225,
224, 227

ecological psychology, 641–642

Edmondstone, John, 252

effect, law of, 339–340, 343

efficiency of workers, 657–658, 663–664,
666

ego, 484, 484n, 500

Ego and the Id, The (Freud), 483, 488

*Ego and the Mechanisms of Defense,
The* (Freud), 485

ego psychology, 520

Egypt, 73

Ehrenfels, Christian von, 172, 175

Eichmann, Adolf, 442, 442n

Eichmann in Jerusalem (Arendt), 442n

Einstein, Albert, 552

Ekman, Paul, 262

Electronic Numerical Integrator and
Calculator (ENIAC), 621–622

Elements of Psychophysics (Fechner), 117,
179, 191, 223

Elimination of Waste, The (Gilbreth), 661

Eliot, Charles, 314, 322, 332

Elizabeth of Bohemia, 12, *39*, 39–40, 43,
44, 45, 76, 77

Elliotson, John, 412–413, 414

emotions

conditioned reactions, 366–371, 372

Darwin's theory of, 255–256,
262–263

Descartes' theory of, 43

James-Lange theory of, 319, 342

James on, 319–320

Emotions and the Will, The (Bain), 313

empiricism
  Descartes and, 38, 47
  of Hume, 140–141
  of Locke, 51, 60, 61, 62–67, 71, 91, 140
enactive mode, 597, 599
energy, conservation of, 149–150
English Men of Science (Galton), 286
ENIAC (Electronic Numerical Integrator
  and Calculator), 621–622
Enigma machine, 620
environmentalism, radical, 373, 375
epilepsy, 418
  H.M. and, case of, 129–130
  Penfield's research on, 123–127, 135
equipotentiality, 120–121
Erikson, Erik, 492–493
erogenous zones, 475–476
Eros, 491
Escape from Freedom (Fromm), 541
Esdaile, James, 413, 450
*Essay Concerning Human Understand-
  ing, An* (Locke), 51, 60, 61, 62–67, 68,
  73, 85–86, 586
esteem needs, 548, *549*
ethics of human subject research, 445–447
eugenics
  definition of, 288
  Galton and, 287–295, 301
eupsychia, 556
evolution
  Darwin's theory of, 10, 233, 242–250,
    265
  geographical distribution of species
    and, 240–242
  natural selection and, 233, 246–250
evolutionary psychology, 264
excitation, conditioned reflexes and,
  357–359
existential dichotomies, 542
existential psychology, 554
exorcism, 401–402
experiential responses, 126–127
experimental neuroses, 258–259,
  356, 396
experimental psychology, 218–220, 653
  Cattell and, 205–208
  establishment of, 191–192, 197–199,
    200, 201, 203–204

first U.S. doctorate in, 203
growth of, 204
limits of, 215–216
women's participation in, 219–220
Experimental Study of Intelligence, The
  (Binet), 573
*Expression of the Emotions in Man and
  Animals, The* (Darwin), 251, 255–256,
  262–263, 265
extension, Descartes' theory of, 25, 47
extinction curve in operant conditioning,
  385, *385*
extroversion, 513
eye, physical properties of, 154–156, *156*
Eysenck, Hans J., 522–523, 522n, 559

F
Fairbairn, W. R. D., 492
Faria, José Custódio di, 410–412, 414,
  416, 450
fear response, 367, 370, 374
Fechner, Gustav Theodor, 6, 9, 145,
  162–172, *163*, 191, 201, 202, 223,
  644, 671
  early years of, 163–164
  invalid period of, 166
  Naturphilosophie and, 164–165
  pen name of, 164
  on perception and sensation, 163
  philosophy of, 165–167
  psychophysics work of, 167–172,
    184, 197, 271
  satirical articles of, 164, 165
Fechner's law, 171, 180, 184, 225
Féré, Charles, 422–424
Fernald, Grace, 674
Ferrier, David, 114, 120, 135
Festinger, Leon, 438–440, 450
figure and ground, 175, *176*
fistulas, 353
FitzRoy, Robert, 232, 234, 237, 240
fixed-interval reinforcement schedule,
  385–386, *386*
fixed-ratio reinforcement schedule, 386
flashbulb memories, 635, 642–643, 645
Flourens, Pierre, *104*, 104–108, 118, 120, 135
fMRI (functional magnetic resonance
  imaging) scans, 133, 644

Foolish Wisdom and Wise Folly, 77
force fields, 181
forgetting curve, 225
formal operations stage, 593–595, 599
forme fruste, 418
fovea, 154
Franklin, Benjamin, 408
Franz, Shepherd Ivory, 118–120, 135
fraternal twins, 286
Frederick I, 80
Frederick V, 39
free association, 218, 294, 462–466,
    473, 479–480, 499
Freeman, Frank N., 297
French Revolution, 407, 408
Freud, Anna, 485, *486*, 489
Freud, Sigmund, 17, 146, 455–456, *457,
    486*, 499–500, 536, 661
    academic psychology's reception of,
      494–499
    Allport and, 510–511
    on character types, 477–473
    Charcot and, 424, 456, 461, 462
    childhood sexuality theory of,
      472–477, 499
    Civilization and Its Discontents, 491
    controversies and, 491–492
    on defense mechanisms, 466,
      483–488
    Dora, case of, 478–481
    dreams and, 466–472, 473
    early life of, 459–462
    The Ego and the Id, 483, 488
    free association and, 218, 294,
      462–466, 473, 479–480, 499
    Hall and, 329, 494, 495–496, 657
    hysteria studies of, 455–456,
      464–466, 472–473, 484–485
    The Interpretation of Dreams,
      467–472, 496
    James and, 322, 496–497
    legacy of, 492–493
    metapsychology theory of, 482–488
    moral demands and, 483
    Oedipus complex and, 474–475,
      476–477, 487, 488, 500
    psychoanalysis and, 46, 217–218, 458,
      478–481, 494, 500, 519
    on the psychology of women, 488–491
    *Three Essays on the Theory of
      Sexuality*, 475, 495
    Titchener and, 496, 497, 506
    on transference, 481
    unconscious motivated behavior
      and, 89, 91, 256
Friedrich, Johann, 76
Friedrich, Max, 203, 205
Friedrich Nietzsche, 539
Fritsch, Gustav, 113, 122, 135
Fromm, Erich, 541–542, *543*, 550, 559
frontal lobes of brain, 115
Frost, Robert, 381, 542
functional autonomy, 519–520
functionalism, 341, 343
functional magnetic resonance imaging
    (fMRI) scans, 133, 644
functional periodicity, 683
Future of an Illusion, The (Freud), 491

G
Galanter, Eugene, 639–640
Galápagos Islands, 240, 241–242
Galen, 31, 419
Galilei, Galileo, 26, 27–28, 30, 36n, 53, 606
Gall, Franz Joseph, 9, 97–104, *98*, 109,
    120, 134
Galton, Francis, 6, 10, 250, 262, *272*,
    272–301, 582, 653
    The Art of Travel, 277
    controversies and, 295
    Darwin and, 272, 276–278, 282–283,
      288, 301
    early life and career of, 273–277
    English Men of Science, 286
    eugenics and, 287–295, 301
    Hereditary Genius, 278–283, 288
    influence of, 295–300
    intelligence testing and, 270–271,
      273, 564, 565, 568, 571–572
    on nature-nurture question, 279–287,
      299, 301
    phrenology and, 275–276
    statistical correlation concept of,
      289–293
    Tropical South Africa, 276
    women and, 271, 272, 276

Gassner, Johann Joseph, 401–402, 403, 405
Gazzaniga, Michael, 133, 134
gender, Darwin on, 252–255
general intelligence, 578, 599
generalizations, 355–356, 396, 517
General Problem Solver (GPS), 626–628, 629, 630, 645
genetic epistemology of Piaget, 588–595, 599
genital character, 478
genital zone, 475
geological uniformitarianism, 239–240
George I, 79, 81
Gestalt psychology, 145, 172–177, 180–183, 184, 434, 508
Gibson, Eleanor Jack, 178, 220, 641–642
Gibson, James J., 641, 642
Gifted Children (Hollingworth), 686
Gilbreth, Frank Bunker, 660, 661, 662–663, 665, 666, 688
Gilbreth, Lillian Moller, 659, *660,* 660–668, 687, 688
Gilman, Charles, 671
Gilman, Charlotte Perkins, 684
Gleitman, Henry, 637, 638
"Glorious Revolution," 61, 69
Goddard, Henry Herbert, 674
Goldstein, Kurt, 182, 544–445, *545,* 547, 547n, 552
Goodman, Bertha, 534
GPS (General Problem Solver), 626–628, 629, 630, 645
graceful degradation, 630
grand hypnotisme, 421–422, 423, 424, 563, 568
grand mal seizures, 418
gray matter, 96
group fallacy, 433
Guillotin, Joseph, 408
Gulliver's Travels (Swift), 108

H
habit, 318–319
Haeckel, Ernst, 258n, 329
Hall, Calvin, 529
Hall, G. Stanley, 203, 325–330, *326,* 343, 431, 656, 674
    child studies of, 328–329, 494–495
    early life and career of, 325–326
    Freud and, 329, 494, 495–496, 657
    James and, 325, 327, 328, 329, 330, 494
    recapitulationist theory of, 258n, 328
    Wundt and, 326, 327, 328, 329, 330, 494
Handbook of Physiological Optics (Helmholtz), 153
handwriting analysis, 512
Hanover, House of, 75, 76–81
Harlow, Harry, 508, 535, 536
Hartley, David, 69–70
Hartmann, Heinz, 520
Harvard Mark I, 621
Harvey, William, 30
Haywood, Bill, 650, 652
Hebb, Donald O., 128
Heckscher House, 374
Hell, Maximillian, 404, 405
Helmholtz, Hermann, 9, *145,* 145–162, 184, 190–191, 195–196, 198, 199, 219, 461
    early life of, 145–146
    education of, 146–148
    mechanism of, 148–152, 172
    military service of, 149, 150
    nerve impulse experiments of, 150–152, 191, 196
    ophthalmoscope invented by, 150
    other achievements of, 162
    on perception and sensation, 153–154, 159–162, 163, 166, 167, 177–179
    place in psychology, 150, 162
    vision studies of, 153–156, *156,* 158, 159, 247
Henri, Victor, 429, 572
Henslow, John Stevens, 235, *236,* 237, 239, 240
Heraclitus, 317
Hereditary Genius (Galton), 278–283, 288
Hering, Ewald, 177
Herrnstein, Richard, 300
heuristic strategies, 626
hierarchy of needs, Maslow's, 547–549, *549,* 559
higher-order conditioning, 355
hippocampus, 129, 129n

historiography, 4
History of the Sciences and Scientists over Two Centuries (de Candolle), 283–284
Hitler, Adolf, 434, 491, 492, 526
Hitzig, Eduard, 113, 122, 135
H.M., case of, 129–31, 131n, 135
Hobbes, Thomas, 68, 606–607, 610, 643
Hollingworth, Harry, 679, 680–681, 686
Hollingworth, Leta Stetter, *677*, 677–686, 689
holograms, 122
Holt, Henry, 315, 316
Holzinger, Karl, 297
Homemaker and Her Job, The (Gilbreth), 666
Hooker, Joseph, 247, 248
Hoover, Herbert, 667
Horney, Karen, 489–490, *490*, 493, 500, 541
Hornstein, Gail, 493, 499
How the Mind Works (Pinker), 264
Hull, Clark, 378, 379, 534, 638
humanistic psychology, 508, 533–534, 551–558, 559
human motivation, Maslow's theory of, 545–551
human subject research, ethics of, 445–447
Hume, David, 69, *70*, 140–141
Huxley, Thomas Henry, 249–50, 285
Huygens, Christian, 62, 73
hypnotism, 6, 403, 449
    founding of, 412–415
    hysteria and, 416, 420–421, 456–457
    limits of, 410
    Nancy-Salpêtrière controversy of, 415–429, 568–569
    post-hypnotic amnesia and, 339
    post-hypnotic suggestion and, 409
    receptivity of subject and, 409–410, 410–412
    see also Faria, José Custódio di; Mesmer, Franz Anton
hysteria
    Charcot's studies of, 418–422
    Freud's studies of, 455–456, 464–466, 484–485

childhood sexuality theory, 472–475
    Dora and, case of, 478–481
    hypnosis and, 416, 420–421, 568–569
    mob, 425
    overdetermination in, 464
    seduction theory of, 465–466, 499–500
    term, origins of, 419

I

IBM Corporation, 621
Ickes, Harold, 362, 371
Ickes, Mary, 362, 371
iconic mode, 597, 599
id, 483–484, 500
ideas
    complex, 64–65, 91
    innate, 38
    Locke on, 63–65, 91
    pathogenic, 458
    simple, 64, 91
identical twins, 286, 296–298
identification, 487–488
idiographic methods, 517–519, 523–526, 559
illusions, optical, 143, 173, 196
imageless thoughts, 221–222, 227
immature religion, 527
impossibilist creativity, 630–631
improbabilist creativity, 630
Individual and His Religion, The (Allport), 527
individual differences, 261–262, 272, 278
individuality
    Allport on, 517
    Binet and, 569–570
    Stern on, 515
individual psychology, 535, 570–574, 598
Individual Will Temperament Test, 512
inference, unconscious, 161–162, 196–197
inferiority complex, 535
infinitesimal calculus, 74, 82
information processing, 183, 645
information theory, 637
informed consent, 446
Inhelder, Bärbel, 589, *589*, 591–592, 593, 595, 596, 599, 640

inhibition, conditioned reflexes and, 357–359

innate ideas, 38, 41

innate reflexes, 34, 367–368

instincts, 483

institutional review boards (IRBs), 446, 447, 448

integral calculus, 75

intellectualization, 487

intelligence
brain size and, 99–101
Galton and, 270–271, 273, 564, 565, 568, 571–572
general, 578
sensory acuity and, 271
Thorndike and, 341
two-factor theory of, 579

intelligence quotient (IQ), 580, 599

intelligence tests, 512
of Binet, 289, 563–565, 569–570, 572–578, 579, 580, 581, 598–599, 674
Galton and, 288–289, 301
rise of, 578–584

intentionality, 460

International Positive Psychology Association (IPPA), 558

Interpretation of Dreams, The (Freud), 467–472, 496

interpretive cortex, 126

interpretive responses, 126

intrapsychic conflict, 364, 499

Introduction to Psychology (Calkins), 334

introspection, 214, 217

introspective psychology, 214–215, 217–218

introversion, 513

intuitions, 142

intuitive knowledge, 65

Investigation of the Laws of Thought (Boole), 616

IPPA (International Positive Psychology Association), 558

IQ (intelligence quotient), 580, 599

IRBs (institutional review boards), 446, 447, 448

isomorphism, psychophysical, 181–182

J

Jacquard, Joseph, 613, 614

James, Alice, 309

James, Henry, Jr., 309

James, Henry, Sr., 308–309, 308n, 310, 312

James, William, 10, 199, 201n, 226, 305–324, *306*, 342–343, 509, 510, 644, 655, 668
Calkins and, 325, 330, 332, 333, 334, 343
early life of, 307–314
on emotions, 319–320
Freud and, 322, 496–497
on habit, 318–319
Hall and, 325, 327, 328, 329, 330, 494
influence of, 305–306, 324–325, 343
later career of, 321–324
pragmatism and, 313
The Principles of Psychology, 306, 307, 315–316, 324, 325, 329, 333, 337, 342
Psychology, 322
stream of consciousness and, 317, 342
Talks to Teachers, 322
as a teacher, 314–321
Thorndike and, 325, 337–338, 341, 343
Varieties of Religious Experience, 322
on will, 313, 320–321
Wundt and, 306–307, 311

James I, 39, 79

James II, 61

James-Lange theory of emotion, 319, 342

Jameson, Dorothea, 220

Jastrow, Joseph, 653

jnd (just noticeable difference), 170–172, 184

Jones, Mary Cover, 374, 396

Journal of Abnormal and Social Psychology, 432–433, 511, 512, 516, 520

Journal of Genetic Psychology, 328

Journal of Humanistic Psychology, 555

Jung, Carl Gustav, 524, 587, 651
Freud and, 493, 513
word association test of, 512–513

just noticeable difference (jnd), 170–172, 184

K

Kant, Immanuel, 9, 90, 139–140, *140*, 150, 184, 509, 582, 595
  Anthropology from a Pragmatic Point of View, 142
  Anthropology from of Pure Reason, 142
  on causality, 141
  Critique of Pure Reason, 142
  Helmholtz and, 159–160
  on psychology, 168, 191
Klein, Melanie, 492
knowledge
  demonstrative, 65–66
  intuitive, 65
  Locke on, 59–60, 63, 65–67
  sensitive, 66, 67
Koffka, Kurt, 172, *173*, 174–176, 180, 184, 434
Köhler, Wolfgang, 172, *173*, 174–176, 180, 181–182, 183, 184, 434, 435, 514, 637
Kosslyn, Stephen, 133
Külpe, Oswald, 215, *221*, 221–223, 227

L

Ladd-Franklin, Christine, 219–220, *220*, 262, 335, 336
Lamarck, Jean-Baptiste, 244, 260, 265
Lampl de Groot, Jeanne, 489
Lange, Carl, 319
Lange, Ludwig, 208, 209
Langer, Walter, 526
Langfeld, Herbert, 507
language
  apperception and, 212–213
  assembly, 622
  cortex and, 109–110
  infant acquisition of, 258
  Leibniz's universal, 608–610, 616, 644
  sentences as fundamental unit of, 212–213
  thought and, 212–213
  Völkerpsychologie and, 197
Lashley, Karl Spencer, *119*, 119–122, 135, 365, 365n
latency stage of sexuality, 476–477
latent content of dreams, 467–468
latent learning, 378–379
Lavater, Johann Kaspar, 99, 252n

Lavoisier, Antoine, 408
law of association by contiguity, 69
law of association by similarity, 69
law of effect, 339–340, 343
law of mass action, 121, 135
law of specific nerve energies, 143
Learned Optimism (Seligman), 558
learned reflexes, 34
learning
  latent, 378–379
  Thorndike's theory of, 341
  see also operant conditioning
Le Bon, Gustav, *425*, 425–429, 440, 450
Lectures on the Human and Animal Mind (Wundt), 198
Leeuwenhoek, Anton van, 76, 84
Leibniz, Gottfried Wilhelm, 9, 12, 39, 71–91, *72*, 509, 582, 595, 643–644
  alchemy and, 72
  Artificial Intelligence and, 91
  calculating machine of, 73, 74, 607–610, 644
  career as a courtier, 72–73, 75–81
  death of, 81
  Descartes and, 47, 53, 73, 74, 82–83, 85, 91
  education of, 71
  influence of, 90–91, 92
  inventions of, 73, 607–610
  Locke and, 51–52, 63n, 81, 82, 85–91
  Masham and, 62
  mathematical work of, 73–75, 79–80, 81, 606, 607–610, 611
  and the mechanization of logic, 607–610
  nativism and, 141
  New Essays on Human Understanding, 85–91
  other activities of, 75–72
  philosophy of mind of, 75, 76, 79–80, 82–91, 197
  posthumous recognition of, 80
  Theodicy, 81
  universal language desired by, 608–610, 616, 620–621, 644
lens, 154
lethargy, 421
Leviathan (Hobbes), 606

Lévi-Strauss, Claude, 216
Lewin, Kurt, 182–183, 434, 498
Leyden jar, 406
Liébeault, Auguste Ambroise, 415–416
lie detector machine, 652
life space, 182
light, Descartes on, 29–30, 32
Lindzey, Gardner, 529
Linnean Society, 248
Linton, Ralph, 539
"Little Albert," Watson-Rayner study
    of, 368–371, *371*, 372, 373–375, 396,
    497
"Little Peter" study, 374–375
Living with Our Children (Gilbreth), 666
localization of brain function
    Broca's work on, 111–113, 135
    hologram theory and, 122
    Lashley's work on, 119–122
    motor strip and, 113–114, 115–116
    Penfield's work on, 125–127
    in phrenology theory, 97–104
    Wernicke's work on, 115–118, 135
Locke, John, 9, 53–71, *54*, 91, 567, 595
    *An Essay Concerning Human Un-
        derstanding,* 51, 60, 61, 62–67, 68,
        73, 586
    character of, 55, 61
    Cooper and, 57–59, 72
    death of, 52, 62
    Descartes and, 47, 52–53, 56, 63–64, 91
    early years of, 53–54
    education of, 54–55
    empiricism of, 51, 60, 61, 62–67, 71, 140
    Holland self-exile of, 60–61, 62
    on ideas, 63–65
    influence of, 68–71, 92
    on knowledge, 59–60, 63, 65–67
    Leibniz and, 51–52, 63n, 73, 82, 85–91
    Mashams and, 62
    on mind, 62–67, 197
    political involvement of, 58–59, 60
    Two Treatises of Government, 60, 61, 68
Loeb, Jacques, 361
Loftus, Elizabeth, 448–449, 450, 643
logarithms, 170, 170n, 611
logic, symbolic, 219, 610, 616, 625, 644
logical positivism, 378

Logic Theorist (LT), 625–626, 627, 629,
    630, 645
Lombroso, Cesare, 99n
Lorde, André de, 578
"Lost in the Mall" study, 448–449
Louis XIV, 73
love as innate response, 367–368
Lovelace, Ada, 614–616, 629
Lovelace objection, 615–616, 629
love needs, 548, *549*
Love's Story Told (Robinson), 524n
Lowie, Robert, 684
LT (Logic Theorist), 625–626, 627, 629,
    630, 645
lucid sleep, 411
Lyell, Charles, 239, 240, 247, 248, 265

M

magnetic resonance imaging (MRI)
    scans, 132
magnetism, 7, 404, 405–406
Maguire, Margaret, 671
Malebranche, Nicolas de, 73
Malthus, Thomas, 245, 265
manifest content of dreams, 467–468, 471
maps, weather, 277
Marie, Queen, 372
Marston, William Moulton, 652
Mary II, 61
Masham, Damaris Cudworth, 62, 81
Masham, Francis, 62
Maskelyne, Nevil, 196
Maslow, Abraham H., 11, 181, 507–508,
    533, 544, 559, 638
    death of, 557
    early life of, 530–534
    education of, 531–535
    hierarchy of needs, 547–549, *549,* 559
    humanistic psychology and, 508,
        533–534, 551–558
    human motivation theory of, 545–551
    late writings of, 556–558
    legacy of, 557
    mentors of, 539–545
    Motivation and Personality, 550, 551,
        556
    positive approach to psychology,
        549–551, 556–558

self-actualization and, 546–547, *549*, 550–551, 557, 559

study of social behavior in monkeys, 535–537

Thorndike and, 537–538

Maslow, Will, 531–532, 532n

mass action, law of, 121, 135

Masson, Jeffrey M., 472n

materialism, 165

Mathematical Analysis of Logic (Boole), 616

mature religion, 527

Maxwell, James Clerk, 157

May, Rollo, 554, 555, *555*, 559

McAdams, Dan, 526

McClelland, David, 525–526

McCulloch, Warren, 621, 625, 628, 645

Meaning of Truth, The (James), 324

means-ends analysis, 627–628

mechanism

  Fechner and, 165

  Helmholtz and, 148–152, 172

mechanistic behaviorism, 379

mechanistic physiology, 30–35

Meditations on First Philosophy (Descartes), 45

memory

  declarative, 130–131

  Ebbinghaus's studies of, 223–225, *224*

  flashbulb, 635, 642–643, 645

  Lashley's research on, 119–122

  Milner's research on, 127–131, 133, 135

  Penfield's research on, 126–127

  procedural, 131

  verbal, 108–109, 114

  visual, 429–430

mental chronometry, 197, 205, 223, 227

Mental Evolution in Animals (Romanes), 261

mental imagery, 294

mental orthopedics, 577, 599

mental sets, 222

Merritte, Arvilla, 371

Merritte, Douglas, 371

Mersenne, Marin, 19, 26n, 35

Mesmer, Franz Anton, 6, *402*, 402–408, 410, 449–450

mesmerism, 412–414, 444, 449

metapsychology, 482–488, 500

Meynert, Theodor, 461, 462, 466, 482

Milgram, Stanley, 11, 440–447, *441*, 449, 528–529

  dissertation research of, 440–441

  obedience studies of, 442–447, 450

Mill, James, 70

Mill, John Stuart, 70, 567

Miller, George A., 133, 596, 637, 639

Milner, Brenda, 127–131, *128*, 132, 133, 135

mind

  Descartes on mind-body dualism, 37–45, 46, 48, 132

  Kant on categories of, 141–142

  Leibniz's philosophy of, 82–91, 197

  Locke on, 62–67, 197

  Penfield's research on brain and, 131–132

minute perceptions, 88–89

Mises, Dr., *see* Fechner, Gustav Theodor

Mitchell, Juliet, 489

Mitchell, S. Weir, 672

Mittleman, Bela, 546

mob hysteria, 425

modes of representation, 597, 599

Molaison, Henry Gustav (H.M.), 129–131, 131n, 135

Moller, Annie Degler, 661

Moller, William, 661, 662

Molyneux, William, 65

monads, in Leibniz's philosophy, 82–85, 86–87, 88, 91

Monde, Le (The World) (Descartes), 27–35

monkeys, social behavior in, 535–537

monogenists, 252

monozygotic twins, 286

Montague, Helen, 682

Moore, Gordon, 360–361

moral demands in Freud's theories, 483, 488

Morgan, C. Lloyd, 337

Morgan, Christiana, 524, 524n

Motion Study (Gilbreth), 663

motivation, Maslow's theory of, 545–551

Motivation and Personality (Maslow), 550, 551, 556

motor aphasia, 116, 117

Mozart, Leopold, 404–405
Mozart, Wolfgang Amadeus, 404
MRI (magnetic resonance imaging)
    scans, 132
Müller, Johannes, 143, 145, 146–48, *147*,
    150, 158, 194, 195, 310, 461
multiple personality, 512
Münsterberg, Hugo, 322, 333–334, 338,
    509–510, 514, 518, *650*, 688
    applied psychology and, 653–654,
        656–659, 667, 687
    courtroom psychology and, 649–652
    death of, 659
    early life of, 654–655
    move to America, 655–656
    Witmer and, 668–669
Münsterberg, Moritz, 654
Münsterberg, Otto, 654
Murray, Charles, 300
Murray, Henry A., 524–526, 524n,
    548, 559

N

Nancy school of hypnosis, 415–416,
    422–424, 435, 456, 568
Nanna (Fechner), 166
Napoleon I, 73, 103
National Academy of Sciences, 341
National Birth Control League, 684
nativism
    Descartes and, 38, 46, 47
    Kant and, 141
    Leibniz and, 141
natural selection as mechanism for
    evolution, 233, 246–250, 265
nature-nurture question
    Galton on, 279–287, 299, 301
    Thorndike on, 538
Nature of Prejudice, The (Allport), 527
Naturphilosophie, 164–165
Nazi war crimes, 441–442, 442n, 492
"necessary truths," 86
needs, hierarchy of, 547–549, *549*
negative afterimages, 174
negative reinforcements, 389
Neisser, Ulric, 635–644, *636*, 645
    Artificial Intelligence and, 638–639
    cognitive psychology and, 638–643
    Maslow and, 552, 638

neobehaviorism, 378
nerves
    impulse speed of, 150–152, 191, 196
    specific energies of, 143–144, 158
neurohypnology, 414
neurons, 97n
neurophysiology, 143–144
neuropsychology, 31
neuroscience
    cognitive, 133
    social, 134
neuroticism, 523
neurypnology, 414
Newell, Allen, 624–628, 645
New Essays on Human Understanding
    (Leibniz), 85–91
Newman, Horatio, 297
Newton, Sir Isaac, 53, 61, 62, 72,
    404, 611
    invention of calculus and, 74, 81, 81n,
        606, 611
    solar spectrum discovered by,
        156–157
New York Academy of Sciences, 340
New York Times, 372
Nixon, Richard, 642
Nobel Prize, 583
nomothetic methods, 517–519,
    520–523, 559
nonsense syllables, 224, 227
normal distributions, 279–280, 301
Norsworthy, Naomi, 685
noumenal world, 141, 142, 145, 184
*Nouveaux Essais sur l'Entendement
    Humain (New Essays on Human
    Understanding)* (Leibniz), 52
Novissima Sinica (News from China)
    (Leibniz), 79

O

obedience
    Benjamin and Simpson on, 447
    Milgram's study of, 442–447
object concept, 565–566
object constancy, 590–591
object relations, 492
occultism, 202
OCEAN, 523
Odbert, Henry, 516

Oedipus complex, 474–475, 475–477, 487, 488, 500
Oedipus Rex (Sophocles), 474
On the Origin of Species (Darwin), 249, 250, 260, 277, 278, 301, 310
"ontogeny recapitulates phylogeny," 258n
openness, 523
operant conditioning
    development of, 382–383, 396
    extinction curve in, 385, 385
    philosophical implications of, 389–394
    reinforcement in, 384–387, 386
ophthalmoscope, 150
optical illusions, 143, 173, 196
optic nerve, 144
oral character, 478
oral zone, 475
Orchard, Harry, 650, 651–652
Organization of Behavior, The (Hebb), 128
Our Birds (Piaget), 585
overdetermination, 464

P
paired-associates technique, 334, 343
Paladino, Eusapia, 323
Paley, William, 243
Palmer, G., 158n
pantheism, 76
Pappenheim, Bertha, 456–458, 464
Paradis, Maria-Theresia, 405–406
parallel distributed processing (PDP), 630–631
paraphasias, 116, 117
Paris Anthropological Society, 110, 111
Pascal, Blaise, 603–606, 607, 608, 644
Pascalines, 604, 604–605, 607, 644
passions, Descartes' theory of, 43
Passions of the Soul (Descartes), 45
pathogenic ideas, 458, 499
Patterns of Culture (Benedict), 539
Pavlov, Ivan Petrovich, 10, 347–360, 350, 395–396
    brain theory of, 357–359
    character of, 351
    conditioned reflex studies of, 348, 349, 353–360

death of, 359
digestive studies of, 352–353
early life and career of, 349–353
influence of, 359–360, 381–382, 383
laboratory of, 351
Nobel Prize of, 348, 353
as physiologist, 348, 349, 350–353, 357
pcpt.-cs. 484
PDP (parallel distributed processing), 630–631
peak experiences, 544, 550, 559
Pearson, Karl, 292–293, 301
Pearson's r, 293, 301
Pedagogical Seminary, 328
Peirce, Charles Sanders, 219, 323–324
Penfield, Wilder, 124
    on brain-mind relationship, 131–132
    epilepsy research of, 123–127, 135
    Milner's work with, 128–129
PEN model of personality, 523
Penn, William, 61
perception, 183–185
    adaptation and, 160–161, 178–179
    Fechner on, 163
    Helmholtz on, 153–154, 159–162, 163, 166, 177–179
    Leibniz on, 88–89
    Locke on, 63
    syllogistic reasoning and, 161–162
    unconscious inference and, 161–162
    see also apperception; mental chronometry; optical illusions; psychophysics
perceptual field, 181
perfect crisis, *see* artificial somnambulism
Personal Data Sheet, 512
personal equations, 196
personality
    Allport's concept of, 511–513
    Allport's dissertation on, 513–514
    PEN model of, 523
    Stagner's studies of, 516–517
    theory-oriented approach to, 529
Personality: A Psychological Interpretation (Allport), 516, 517
personality psychology
    Allport and, 507, 508, 515–520, 529
    Big Five and, 523, 526

personality psychology (*continued*)
  Cattell and, 520–522
  Eysenck and, 522–523
  Lindzey and, 529
  Murray and, 524–526
  personology and, 526
  Stern and, 515
Peter the Great, 608
petit mal seizures, 418
PET (positron emission tomography)
  scans, 132, 133
Pettigrew, Thomas, 529
phallic character, 478
phenomenal world, 141–142, 184
*Philosophische Studien (Philosophical
  Studies)*, 203, 203n, 336
phi phenomenon, 174, 184, 205
phrenology, 9, 97–104, *102*
  criticisms of, 101–104
  definition of, 99
  Flourens's discrediting of, 104–108,
    135
  Gall and, 97–104, 134
  Galton and, 275–276
physics, Descartes and, 27–35, 46,
  52–53, 82–83
physiognomy, 99, 232
physiological needs, 548, *549*
Physiological Psychology (Wundt), 223
physiology
  mechanistic, 30–35
  psychology and, 200–201, 348
Piaget, Jacqueline, 565
Piaget, Jean, 11, 216, *585*, 585–589, *589*,
  598, 640
  child studies of, 91, 565–566, 584,
    587–595, 626
  early life and career of, 585–589
  genetic epistemology of, 588–595, 599
  influence of, 596–598
pineal glands, Descartes' theory of,
  41–43, 96
Pinker, Stephen, 264
Pitts, Walter, 621, 623, 628, 645
Plans and the Structure of Behavior
  (Miller, Galanter, and Pribram),
  639–640
Plateau, Joseph, 179

Plato, 7, 86, 112
Playing with Fire (Buchanan), 522n
Pluralistic Universe, A (James), 324
polygenists, 252
polymorphous perversity, 475
Popham, Alexander, 53–54
positive psychology, 551, 556–558, 559
positive reinforcement, 390
positivism, logical, 378
positron emission tomography (PET)
  scans, 132, 133
Posner, Michael, 133
post-hypnotic amnesia, 409
post-hypnotic suggestion, 409
Postman, Leo, 637
power law (Stevens), 179–180
pragmatism, 313, 323–324
Pragmatism (James), 324
prejudice, 527–528
preoperational stage, 591–593, 599
pressure technique, 462–463
Pribram, Karl, 639–640
primary and secondary qualities,
  Galileo's theory of, 26
primary colors, 158, 158n
primary process in dreams, 468–469, 500
Prince, Morton, 431–432, 494, 524
Principia Mathematica (Whitehead and
  Russell), 616–617, 625
Principles of Abnormal Psychology
  (Maslow and Mittleman), 546
Principles of Geology (Lyell), 239
Principles of Gestalt Psychology (Koffka),
  180
Principles of Philosophy (Descartes), 45
Principles of Physiological Psychology
  (Wundt), 200–201, 326, 460, 641
Principles of Psychology, The (James),
  306, 307, 315–316, 324, 325, 329, 333,
  337, 342
Principles of Psychology (Spencer), 260
Principles of Scientific Management
  (Taylor), 563
procedural memory, 131
Productive Thinking (Wertheimer),
  180–181
programmed instruction, Skinner and,
  388–389

Project for a Scientific Psychology
(Freud), 482
projection, 486–487
projective tests, 572–573
"Proof That the Moon Is Made of Iodine"
(Fechner), 164
psyche, 8, 18, 484–485, *485*
psychic causality, 211, 227
psychic secretions, Pavlov's study of,
348–349
psychoanalysis, 458, 489, 497
Allport on, 519–520
Dunlap on, 497
Freud and, 46, 217–218, 458,
478–481, 494, 500, 519
functional autonomy *vs.* mechanisms
of, 519–520
Psychoanalysis of Freud and Adler
(Sumner), 330
psychobiography, 526
psychogenic needs, 525
Psychological Care of Infant and Child
(Watson), 375–376
Psychological Clinic, The, 673
Psychological Review, 334, 340, 363, 364
psychology
act, 460–461
analytical, 513
anti-Semitism and, 537, 538
applied, 653–654
behaviorist, *see* behaviorism
child, 256–58
clinical, *see* clinical psychology
cognitive, *see* cognitive psychology
comparative, 261–262
in the courtroom, *see* courtroom
psychology
of crowds, 425–429
Darwin and, 250–258
dynamic, 46
Ebbinghaus on, 3
ecological, 641–642
ego, 520
evolutionary, 264
existential, 554
experimental, *see* experimental
psychology
Fechner's place in, 166

Gestalt, 145, 172–177, 180–183
Helmholtz's place in, 150, 162
humanistic, 508, 533–534, 551–558,
559
individual, 535, 570–574, 598
individual differences in, 261–262,
272, 278
introspective, 214–215, 217–218
Leibniz's influence on, 90–91, 92
Locke's influence on, 68–71, 92
Personality, *see* personality
psychology
physiology and, 200–201
positive, 549–51, 556–558, 559
as science, 145, 532
self, 335, 343
social, *see* social psychology
voluntaristic, 210–211, 222, 227
women in, 12–13, 332–336
Psychology and Industrial Efficiency
(Münsterberg), 659
"Psychology as the Behaviorist Views It"
(Watson), 363–365
Psychology from an Empirical Standpoint
(Brentano), 460
*Psychology from the Standpoint of a
Behaviorist* (Watson), 366
Psychology (James), 322
Psychology of Management, The
(Gilbreth), 659, 660
Psychology of Peoples, The (Le Bon),
425, 426
Psychology of Personality (Stagner),
516–517
*Psychopathology of Everyday Life,
The* (Freud), 496
psychophysical isomorphism, 181–182
psychophysical parallelism, 85
psychophysics
absolute threshold in, 169
Fechner's work on, 167–172, 184,
197, 271
just noticeable difference (jnd) and,
170–172
Steven's power law of, 179–180
Weber's work on, 168–169
Wundt's work on, 204–205
psychosomatic illness, 44

psychotechnics, 657
Psychotherapy (Münsterberg), 657
psychoticism, 523
purposive behaviorism, 379
Putnam, J. J., 494
Puységur, Marquis de, 408–410, 414, 450

Q
Quetelet, Adolphe, 279

R
race
    Darwin on, 252–255
    Galton and, 296
radical environmentalism, 373, 375
rage as innate response, 367
Raichle, Marcus, 133
Ramachandran, V. S., 132
Rapaport, David, 520
rationalism, 38, 46, 47
rationalization, 487
rational monads, 83, 88, 91
rational soul, 18, 31, 36, 48, 96
Rayner, Rosalie, 368–371, *371*, 372, 374, 497
reaction-time experiments of Cattell, 205–208
real individuality, 515
"Recent Advances in the Field of Physiological Psychology" (Wundt), 199, 311
Recherche (Piaget), 587
redundancy hypothesis, 122
reflection, 554
reflexes
    conditioned, 348, 353–360, 366
    Descartes' theories of, 32–34, *33*, 48
    differentiation and, 356, 358
    excitation and, 357–359
    experimental neuroses and, 258–259, 356
    generalization and, 355–356
    higher-order conditioning and, 355
    inhibition and, 357–359
    innate, 34, 367–368
    learned, 34
    unconditioned, 349, 354, 357
Reflexes of the Brain (Sechenov), 348

regression in dreams, 469
regression line, 291–292, 301
regression toward the mean, 291, 301
reinforcement
    contingencies of, 384–387, 396
    in operant conditioning, 384–387
    positive and negative, 389–390
    primary and secondary, 388
    schedules of, 385–387, *386*
relational individuality, 515
religion, immature *vs.* mature, 527
Renouvier, Charles, 312, 313
repression, 364, 498, 499
respondent conditioning, 387
retina, 177
Riecken, Henry, 438–439
Robinson, Forrest, 524n
Rogers, Carl, 493, 552–54, *553*, 559
Romanes, George J., 261
Roman numerals, 605–606
Roosevelt, Franklin, 362
Roosevelt, Theodore, 540–541
Rosenzweig, Saul, 498
Royal Astronomical Society, 611, 612
Royal Geographic Society, 276, 277
Royal Medical Society, 413
Royal Society, 12, 68, 73, 75, 242, 608
Royce, Josiah, 219, 332–333
Russell, Bertrand, 324, 381, 616–617, 625

S
safety needs, 548, *549*
salivation, 353
Salpêtrière school of hypnosis, 416–422, 568–569, 570–571
Sanford, Edmund C., 333
Sanger, Margaret, 684
scatter plots, 290–291, 301
Schachter, Stanley, 438–439
Scheutz, George, 613
scholastic philosophy, 18
scientific management system, 657–658, 663–665, 666, 688
scientist/practitioner model of training, 687
Scoville, William, 129, 130
Searle, John, 631–635
Sechenov, Ivan M., 348

secondary process in dreams, 468–469
Secret of Swedenborg, The (James), 308n
Sedgwick, Adam, 235–236, 239
seduction theory of hysteria, 465–466,
    472n, 499–500
self-actualization
    Goldstein on, 545, 547, 547n
    Maslow on, 546–547, 549, 550–551,
        557, 559
self psychology, 335, 343
self-questionnaire method, 284–285
Selfridge, Oliver, 638
Seligman, Martin, 557–558
sensation, 174–175, 183–185
    Fechner on, 163, 167
    Helmholtz on, 153–154, 163, 177–179
    Locke on, 63
    Wundt's categories of, 214
sensitive knowledge, 66, 67
sensitive souls, 18
sensory aphasia, 116–117
sensory-motor stage, 590–591, 599
sentient monads, 84, 88
separated identical twins study, 296–298
sexism, 219–220
sexuality
    Freud's theory on, 472–477, 480, 499
    Maslow and Thorndike's study of, 538
    monkeys and, 536–537
sexual selection, 253–254
Shaftesbury, Earl of, *see* Cooper, Anthony
    Ashley
Shannon, Claude, 620–621, 623, 645
Shaw, George Bernard, 381–382
Sheldon, William, 534
Sherif, Muzafer, 448
Simon, Herbert, 624–628, 629, 645
Simon, Théodore, 574–577, 584
simple monads, 84
simple natures, Descartes' theory of,
    25, 47
Simpson, Jeffry, 447
Sixteen Personality Factor Question-
    naire, 522
Skinner, B. F., 10, 379–395, *383*, 396
    Beyond Freedom and Dignity, 392
    children of, 393–394
    crib designed by, 393–394, *394*
"Dark Year" of, 381
    early life and education of, 379–381
    influence of, 394–395, 396
    operant conditioning and, *see* operant
        conditioning
    Pavlov and, 381–382, 383
    programmed instruction and, 388–89
    reputation of, 393–394
    Verbal Behavior, 391
    Watson and, 381, 383
Skinner box, 382–384, *384*
Slade, Henry, 201–202
sleep
    Descartes' theory of, 34–35
    lucid, 411
small world phenomenon study by
    Milgram, 446–447
social conformity, 434–438
social contagion, 407, 427, 431
social contract, 68–69
social Darwinism, 259–261
social facilitation, *see* social contagion
"Social Influence, The" (Allport), 431
social influence processes, 403
social neuroscience, 134
social psychology, 449–450
    Allport and, 431–434
    Asch and, 434–438
    changes in experiments, 447–449
    cognitive dissonance and, 438–440
    "Lost in the Mall" study, 448–449
    Milgram and, 440–447
Social Psychology, 432–433, 450
Societies of Harmony, 408
Society for Personology, 526
Society for the Psychological Study of
    Social Issues (SPSSI), 528, 534
Society of Experimentalists, 219–220,
    336, 506
sociobiology, 263–265
Sociobiology (Wilson), 263
solar spectrum, 156–157
"Some Psychical Consequences of the
    Anatomical Distinction Between the
    Sexes" (Freud), 488–489
Some Thoughts Concerning Education
    (Locke), 62
somnambulism, 409–410, 421, 450

Sophie Charlotte, 39, 76–77, *78*, 80, 81

Sophie of Hanover (Countess Palatine), 12, 39, 76, 77, *77*, 79, 81

Sophocles, 474

soul
    animal, 18, 30–31
    Aristotelian concept of, 18–19, 52, 86
    Descartes' concept of, 37–45
    innate ideas of, 38
    rational, 18, 31, 36, 48, 96
    sensitive, 18
    vegetative, 18, 30–31

Spearman, Charles, 578–580, 594, 599

speech, loss of, 108–109, 111–112
    see also aphasia

Spencer, Herbert, 259–261

Spinoza, Benedict, 75–76

"Spiritualism as a Scientific Question" (Wundt), 202–203

SPSSI (Society for the Psychological Study of Social Issues), 528, 534

St. Germain, mechanical statues of, 21, *21,* 31, 32

St. Martin, Alexis, 352–353

Stagner, Ross, 516–517, 534, 539

Stanford Prison Experiment, 445

statistical correlation, Galton's concept of, 288, 289–293

Stein, Gertrude, 315, 656

Stern, William, 514, 518, 527, 558, 580, 599

Stetter, Margaret Danley, 679

Steunenberg, Frank, 650

Stevens, S. Smith, 179–180

Steven's law, 179–180

stimulus, error, 217

stimulus intensities, *see* psychophysics

Stokes, Rose Pastor, 684

stored programs, 622

stream of consciousness, 317, 342

stream of thought, 317

stroke, speech loss following, 108–109

strong Artificial Intelligence, 633–634, 645

structuralism of Titchener, 215–218, 226, 227, 341, 506

Stuart, Elizabeth, 39

Studies on Hysteria (Freud and Breuer), 458

subtractive method in mental chronometry, 205

suggestibility
    Binet and, 429–431, 571–572
    Le Bon on, 427

Suggestive Therapeutics (Bernheim), 416

Sumner, Francis Cecil, 330

superego, 484, 488, 491, 500

Swedenborg, Emanuel, 308, 308n

Swift, Jonathan, 108, 109, 111, 116

Sydenham, Thomas, 58, 62

syllables, nonsense, 224, 227

syllogism, 219

syllogistic reasoning, 161–162

"Symbolic Analysis of Relay and Switching Circuits" (Shannon), 620–621

symbolic logic, 219, 610, 616, 625, 644

symbolic mode, 597, 599

Syntactic Structures (Chomsky), 391

systematic desensitization, 374

T

tachistoscope, 174

Talks to Teachers (James), 322

Tan, case of, 111–112, 116, 130

Task of Gestalt Psychology, The (Köhler), 181

TAT (Thematic Apperception Test), 524, 526, 573

Taylor, Frederick Winslow, 657–658, 663, 688

Taylorism, 657–658, 663, 664

Terman, Lewis M., 581–584, *582,* 599

Thackeray, William, 317

Thanatos, 491

"The Defects of His Race" (Winston), 537n

Thematic Apperception Test (TAT), 524, 526, 573

Theodicy (Leibniz), 81

Theories of Personality (Hall and Lindzey), 529

Theory of the Sensation of Tone as a Physiological Basis for the Theory of Music, The (Helmholtz), 153

therbligs, 663

Third International Congress of Psychology (1896), 305

Thirty Years War, 22

Thompson, Clara, 490–491, 500

Thompson, Helen Bradford, 552

Thorndike, Edward Lee, 336–342, *337*, 537, 677

    animal intelligence studies of, 337–340, 385

    early life and career of, 336–338

    James and, 325, 337–338, 341, 343

    learning theories of, 341

    on the nature-nurture question, 538

thought

    general ideas and, 212–213

    imageless, 221–222, 227

    James on, 317

thought meter of Wundt, 189–190, *190*, 196, 197

Three Essays on the Theory of Sexuality (Freud), 475, 495

Tischer, Ernst, 203

Titchener, Edward Bradford, 214, *216*, 227, 508

    atomism of, 214

    Freud and, 496, 497, 506

    Society of Experimentalists and, 219–220, 336, 506

    structuralism of, 215–218, 226, 227, 341, 506

    women and, 219–220, 336

Tolman, Edward Chace, 378–379, 637, 638

tomography, 132

Tooby, John, 264

Tories, 60n

traits, personality, 513–514, 558

transference, 481, 500

transfer of training, 340–341, 343

Translate This Darkness (Douglas), 524n

"Treatise of Light" (Descartes), 28

"Treatise of Man" (Descartes), 30, *33*, 548

Treatise on the Passions of the Soul (Descartes), 40

trichromatic theory, 177, 178

Triplett, Norman, 430–431, 430

Tropical South Africa (Galton), 276

tropism theory of Loeb, 361

Tucker, William, 522n

Turing, Alan Mathison, *617*, 617–619, 620, 621, 623–624, 628, 645

Turing Machine, *618*, 618–619, 645

Turing Test, 624, 626, 631–635, 645

twins, studies of, 286–287, 295, 296–298, 301, 587n

two-factor theory of intelligence, 579

Two Treatises of Government (Locke), 60, 61, 68

U

unconditional positive regard, 554

unconditioned reflexes, 349, 354, 357

unconditioned responses, 354, 396

unconditioned stimulus, 354

unconscious

    in Freud's theories, 89, 91, 256

    in Leibniz's philosophy, 88, 89

unconscious inference, 161–162, 196–197

uniformitarianism in geology, 239–240

universal language of Leibniz, 608–610, 616, 644

Ussher, James, 239

V

variability hypothesis, 682

variable-interval reinforcement schedules, 386–387

variable-ratio reinforcement schedules, 386–387

variation hypothesis, 254

Varieties of Religious Experience (James), 322

vegetative souls, 18, 30–31

ventricles, 31

Verbal Behavior (Skinner), 391

verbal memory, 108–109, 114

Vernon, Philip, 516

Virchow, Rudolf, 146

vision

    color, *156*, 156–159, 177–178, 219

    Helmholtz's study of, 153–156, *156*, 158–159

"visual cliff" experiments, 178

visual memory, 429–430

visual perception
  Descartes' conception of, 42, *42*
  Helmholtz and, 153–154, 159–162
vitalism, 147, 152
Völkerpsychologie, 197–198, 211–215, 225, 227
Voltaire, 80
voluntaristic psychology, 210–211, 222, 227
voluntary repetition, 313
von Neumann, John, 621, 622, 623, 625, 628, 645

W

Walden Two (Skinner), 390, 393, 396
Wallace, Alfred Russel, 247–248, *248*
Wallin, J. E. Wallace, 675–676
Walsh, Mary, 308
Ward, W. S., 413
Washburn, Margaret Floy, 218, 220, 335–336
Watergate hearings, 642
Watson, John Broadus, 10, 119, *360*, 360–379, 396, 433, 510
  advertising career of, 371–372
  Animal Education, 362
  Behavior, 364–365
  Behaviorism, 372, 373, 376, 381
  behaviorism and, 363–364
  behaviorist writings of, 364–379
  conditioned emotional reactions and, 366–371, 372
  early life and career of, 360–364
  on Freud, 497
  influence of, 376–379, 381, 532–534, 550
  "Little Albert" study of, 368–371, *371*, 372, 396, 497
  "Little Peter" study and, 373–375
  Psychological Care of Infant and Child, 375–376
  "Psychology as the Behaviorist Views It," 363–365
  Psychology from the Standpoint of a Behaviorist, 366
  radical environmentalism of, 373, 375
Watson, Mary, 362, 371
Watson, Rosalie, 374, 376–377

Watson-Rayner study of "Little Albert," 368–371, *371*, 372, 396, 497
Watt, Henry J., 222
weak Artificial Intelligence, 633–634, 645
weather maps, 277
Weber, Ernst Heinrich, 168, 171, 179, 201
Weber's law, *see* Fechner's law
Wedgwood, Emma, 242
Wedgwood, Josiah, 237
Wedgwood, Susannah, 233
Wells, H. G., 381–382
Wells, Horace, 413–414
Wernicke, Carl, *115*, 115–118, 120, 135
Wernicke's aphasia, 117
Wernicke's area of brain, 117, 119
Wertheimer, Max, 172, 173–176, 180–181, 183, 184, 434, 514, 542–544, 546, 550
Whigs, 60, 60n, 61, 61n
Whitehead, Alfred North, 616–617, 625
white matter, 96–98, 115
Wilkinson, Garth, 309
will, James on, 313, 320–321
William of Orange, 61
Willis, Thomas, 55, 96–97
Will to Believe and Other Essays (James), 324
Wilson, E. O., 263
Winnicott, D. W., 492
Winston, Andrew, 537n
wish-fulfillment hypothesis, 470–472
Witmer, Lightner, 668–676, *669*, 688–689
Wolpe, Joseph, 493
women
  Cattell's view on, 681–682
  Freud on the psychology of, 488–491
  Galton and, 271, 272, 276
  in psychology, 12–13, 332–336
  Titchener and, 219–220, 336
Woodworth, Robert Sessions, 512
  on Freud, 497
  transfer of training study and, 340–441, 343
word-association experiment, 294
word association test, 512–513
World, The (Monde, Le) (Descartes), 27–35, 36

Wren, Christopher, 96
Wundt, Wilhelm Maximilian 9, 90, 172,
    189–215, 201n, 227, 305, 322, 509,
    643–644, 653
    apperception in psychology of,
        209–210, 217
    categories of sensation, 214
    *Contributions to the Theory of Sensory
        Perception*, 191, 197
    death of, 226
    early life of, 192–194
    early research of, 194–196
    experimental psychology and,
        191–192, 197–198, 203–204
    Hall and, 326, 327, 328, 329,
        330, 494
    imageless thoughts and, 221–222
    James and, 306–307, 311
    at Leipzig, 201–215
    *Principles of Physiological Psychol-
        ogy*, 200–201, 326, 460, 541
    psychophysics and, 204–205
    "Recent Advances in the Field of
        Physiological Psychology," 199, 311
    reputation and influence of, 225–226,
        655, 671
    speech analysis by, 213
    thought meter of, 189–190, *190*, 196,
        197
    Zöllner's estrangement from,
        201–203

Y

Young, Thomas, 158
Young-Helmholtz trichromatic theory,
    158

Z

Zeigarnik, Bluma, 498
Zeigarnik effect, 498
Zend-Avesta (Fechner), 166
Zimbardo, Philip, 445, 449, 450
Zoist, 413
Zöllner, Johann, 201–203